Industrial and Urban Growth Policies at the Sub-National, National, and Global Levels

Umar G. Benna
Benna Associates, Nigeria

A volume in the Advances in Public Policy and Administration (APPA) Book Series

IGI Global
DISSEMINATOR OF KNOWLEDGE

Published in the United States of America by
IGI Global
Information Science Reference (an imprint of IGI Global)
701 E. Chocolate Avenue
Hershey PA, USA 17033
Tel: 717-533-8845
Fax: 717-533-8661
E-mail: cust@igi-global.com
Web site: http://www.igi-global.com

Library of Congress Cataloging-in-Publication Data

Names: Benna, Umar G., 1942- editor.
Title: Industrial and urban growth policies at the sub-national, national, and global levels / Umar G. Benna, editor.
Description: Hershey : Information Science Reference, [2019]
Identifiers: LCCN 2018031757| ISBN 9781522576259 (hardcover) | ISBN 9781522576266 (ebook)
Subjects: LCSH: Industrial policy--Environmental aspects--Case studies. | City planning--Environmental aspects--Case studies. | Urban policy--Case studies. | Information technology--Economic aspects.
Classification: LCC HD3611 .I3694 2019 | DDC 338.9--dc23 LC record available at https://lccn.loc.gov/2018031757

This book is published in the IGI Global book series Advances in Public Policy and Administration (APPA) (ISSN: 2475-6644; eISSN: 2475-6652)

British Cataloguing in Publication Data
A Cataloguing in Publication record for this book is available from the British Library.

For electronic access to this publication, please contact: eresources@igi-global.com.

Advances in Public Policy and Administration (APPA) Book Series

G. David Garson
North Carolina State University, USA

ISSN:2475-6644
EISSN:2475-6652

Mission

Proper management of the public sphere is necessary in order to maintain order in modern society. Research developments in the field of public policy and administration can assist in uncovering the latest tools, practices, and methodologies for governing societies around the world.

The **Advances in Public Policy and Administration (APPA) Book Series** aims to publish scholarly publications focused on topics pertaining to the governance of the public domain. APPA's focus on timely topics relating to government, public funding, politics, public safety, policy, and law enforcement is particularly relevant to academicians, government officials, and upper-level students seeking the most up-to-date research in their field.

Coverage

- Government
- Law Enforcement
- Political Economy
- Politics
- Public Administration
- Public Funding
- Public Policy
- Resource Allocation
- Urban Planning

IGI Global is currently accepting manuscripts for publication within this series. To submit a proposal for a volume in this series, please contact our Acquisition Editors at Acquisitions@igi-global.com or visit: http://www.igi-global.com/publish/.

The Advances in Public Policy and Administration (APPA) Book Series (ISSN 2475-6644) is published by IGI Global, 701 E. Chocolate Avenue, Hershey, PA 17033-1240, USA, www.igi-global.com. This series is composed of titles available for purchase individually; each title is edited to be contextually exclusive from any other title within the series. For pricing and ordering information please visit http://www.igi-global.com/book-series/advances-public-policy-administration/97862. Postmaster: Send all address changes to above address.

Titles in this Series

For a list of additional titles in this series, please visit: www.igi-global.com/book-series

Advanced Methodologies and Technologies in Government and Society
Mehdi Khosrow-Pour, D.B.A. (Information Resources Management Association, USA)
Information Science Reference • copyright 2019 • 726pp • H/C (ISBN: 9781522576617) • US $275.00 (our price)

Handbook of Research on Promoting Peace Through Practice, Academia, and the Arts
Mohamed Walid Lutfy (London School of Economics, UK) and Cris Toffolo (Northeastern Illinois University, USA)
Information Science Reference • copyright 2019 • 553pp • H/C (ISBN: 9781522530015) • US $275.00 (our price)

Handbook of Research on Military Expenditure on Economic and Political Resources
Ramesh Chandra Das (Katwa College, India)
Information Science Reference • copyright 2018 • 564pp • H/C (ISBN: 9781522547785) • US $325.00 (our price)

Technology and the New Generation of Active Citizens Emerging Research and Opportunities
Paolo Beneventi (Independent Researcher, Italy)
Information Science Reference • copyright 2018 • 173pp • H/C (ISBN: 9781522537700) • US $135.00 (our price)

Examining the Private Sector's Role in Wealth Creation and Poverty Reduction
Scott A. Hipsher (Webster University, Thailand)
Information Science Reference • copyright 2018 • 325pp • H/C (ISBN: 9781522531173) • US $185.00 (our price)

Handbook of Research on Examining Global Peacemaking in the Digital Age
Bruce L. Cook (Chicago ORT Technical Institute, USA)
Information Science Reference • copyright 2018 • 435pp • H/C (ISBN: 9781522530329) • US $295.00 (our price)

Positioning Markets and Governments in Public Management
Helisse Levine (Long Island University, USA) and Karina Moreno (Long Island University, USA)
Information Science Reference • copyright 2018 • 294pp • H/C (ISBN: 9781522541776) • US $215.00 (our price)

Establishing Food Security and Alternatives to International Trade in Emerging Economies
Vasily Erokhin (Harbin Engineering University, China)
Business Science Reference • copyright 2018 • 406pp • H/C (ISBN: 9781522527336) • US $195.00 (our price)

Smart Technologies for Emergency Response and Disaster Management
Zhi Liu (Waseda University, Japan) and Kaoru Ota (Muroran Institute of Technology, Japan)
Information Science Reference • copyright 2018 • 312pp • H/C (ISBN: 9781522525752) • US $225.00 (our price)

IGI Global
DISSEMINATOR OF KNOWLEDGE

701 East Chocolate Avenue, Hershey, PA 17033, USA
Tel: 717-533-8845 x100 • Fax: 717-533-8661
E-Mail: cust@igi-global.com • www.igi-global.com

Table of Contents

Section 2
Industrial and Urban Growth Policies at the Continental Level

Section 3
Industrial and Urban Growth Policies at the National Level

Detailed Table of Contents

This chapter discusses issues related to managing the avatar-based supply chains as expert knowledge for smart solutions in creating sustainable urban systems. Avatar-based supply chains as expert knowledge is a new term that describes the planning, search, production, distribution, and delivery of Mkrttchian's digital avatars from the place of origin to consumption. These supply chains are very different from traditional ones because they relate to a specific product-expert knowledge, which is created through electronic data distributed on the internet between business partners and value-added service providers operating in a general digital economy paradigm using blockchain technologies. This chapter focuses on the analysis of business relations and this integration into sustainable urban systems.

This chapter uses the term urban chaos as an alternative to words such as anarchy, randomness, and disorder. It expresses the visual and behavioral failure that describes a property that was not taken into consideration when dealing with the theme of hardship cities. The terms livability and quality of life focus on measuring functional, social, economic, and political indicators, ignoring visual and behavioral indicators as not essential for creating cities of hardship. This work presents two concepts, chaos city (CC) and order city (OC) based on the reviews of livability, quality of life, and the writings of Christopher Alexander, to demonstrate the lack of standards of livability to the visual and behavioral indicators. The addition of these indicators helps to classify cities of hardship from the perspective of the relationship between chaos and order and tries to provide guidelines and proposed action plan related to urban policies (UP) that enable the transformation of CC to OC.

The chapter deals with issues related to the construction and development of the digital economy in one particular region: Republic of Armenia. This country is considered the digital sector of which may become the largest in the country in the next five years. The digital revolution affects all areas of the Armenian economy. Prior to this, the Armenian economy was known as the mining industry, a food producer, and a food. Today, according to statistics, Armenia's leading mining and energy companies are already one step ahead of their colleagues in the economically successful implementation of digital technology. Naturally, in such successes of digital transformations, there are key components. The authors hope that the examples of development and thought about the driving springs of these transformations, chosen in consideration of the interests of the development of the Russian digital economy, can be interesting and useful for Russian enterprises that have started their digital transformations.

Section 2
Industrial and Urban Growth Policies at the Continental Level

On the issues of industrial and urban growth policies at the level of the continents, the contributing researchers focus on African smart cities, changing roles in the public and the private sectors, defining gaps strategies and strides of Fourth Industrial Revolution, and Sub-Saharan Africa and North Africa industrial and urban growth policies. The predominantly African researchers—but some working in the Middle East and other parts of the world—analyzed the challenges and opportunities of smart cities in Sub-Saharan Africa; the shift in the leading roles from public to private sector in African industrial urban growth; exploring the gaps, strategies, and strides of the Fourth Industrial Revolution in Africa; and a comparative analysis of industrial and urban growth policies in Sub-Saharan Africa and North Africa.

The aim of this chapter is to interrogate and diagnose the concept of smart cities as it has been applied to Sub-Saharan Africa (SSA) in a bid to decrypt the opportunities and challenges characterizing its manifestation in space and actuality. The chapter is a product of the critical engagement of scholarly work that compares the best practices in the development and promotion of the smart city concept against those practices that are antithetical and retrogressive in light of this good cause. To crystallize the realities, the chapter makes use of case studies that speak to these contrasting experiences. Case studies in SSA reveal differential practices with South Africa emerging as a country doing very well relative to others in the region. Some cities, especially the small and intermediate ones, fail to break even in terms of the revenue collections. This is partly because they have failed to attract investment in the form of industries or retain them because of politically induced instabilities.

Africa is the last of the major global regions to urbanize and to economically benefit therefrom largely due to centuries of the fragmented spatial system by geographic, trading zone, colonial experiences, and logistics barriers. Recently, however, the integration of African urban spatial structure was spearheaded by the private sector under the guidance of the public sector. This chapter analyzes the goals driving integration, the tools used by private and the public sectors in setting the stage for integrative urban growth through industrialization, and then identifies the future opportunities and challenges in sustaining the momentum. The chapter comprises of an introduction, a conceptual framework, the gluing elements, the review of the development guidance system, opportunities and challenges ahead, future research direction, and conclusion.

The chapter stresses that Africa requires a clear position of how "leapfrogging" into the FOIR should be informed by clear and unambiguous policy goals and strategies so that a sustainable development route is created. Political will, global connectivity, and straightforward pathways are fused in the menu. Africa is neither a monolithic nor a homogenous space where events and developments happen in a linear pattern. The traditional perspective about Africa perceives the region as motley of so many variations and controversies – spatial, temporal, gender, racial, and ideological. This is evident from the fact that Africa has portions of its economy that are pre-modern, modern, and post-modern. The "resource curse" phenomenon seems to hold water in both debate and practice in some circles. Countries and states should avoid falling into the proverbial trap of unequal exchange in form of transacting the natural endowments that Africa is known for.

The purpose of this chapter is to compare industrial and urban growth policies in Sub-Saharan Africa (SSA) and North Africa (NA) with the aim to draw lessons and inform policy and research in the subject. The chapter advances the argument that industrial and urban growth ought to be directly related. This follows the development trajectory and urbanization trend in the Global South which was birthed and sustained by the Industrial Revolution. The case study approach has been used to develop this chapter where Africa is first divided into two broad territories, SSA and NA. Subsequently, cases are selected from Lusophone, Anglophone, and Francophone countries. The analysis considers in detail Zimbabwe, South Africa, Guinea-Bissau, Algeria, and Egypt.

Section 3
Industrial and Urban Growth Policies at the National Level

Researchers from Mexico, Nigeria, and Russia presented chapters on national opportunities and challenges related to industrial and urban growth policies. From Mexico came three chapters dealing with the interplay of smart water, governance, and adaptive capacity to enhance the development of Mexico's green and blue city-regions; the exploration of the role of the economic and environmental factors in the dynamics of rural and urban shrinkage transformation processes in Mexico; and an institutional entrepreneurship analysis of biodiesel companies in Mexico. From Nigeria is a chapter on technology assessment of national renewable energy potentials by university academic research and development actors, and from Russia is a research making a comparative cross-cultural analysis of regions in Australia and Russia to overcome barriers across cultures and small businesses practices.

Nigeria, as the giant of Africa, is in a state of limbo because of its overreliance on oil money, which retarded its level of growth and development. The discovery of crude oil forced the Nigerian government to shift attention away from agriculture. This neglect of agriculture negatively affected Nigeria as both agriculture and manufacturing activities were halted. Ironically, the growth created by oil revenue was not sustained and directed to the other sectors of the economy for widespread multiplier effects. As declining oil prices reveal the economic weaknesses of the country, there is pressure for Nigeria to seek an alternative means of revenue. Nigeria is now transitioning from oil to industrial cities. It is against this background that this chapter is illustrating how the economy's overdependence on oil is transitioning to a more diversified alternative by transforming cities. This chapter focuses on Birnin Kebbi as a case study for a medium-size city that has huge growth potential.

The authors believe that the transition to Industry 4.0 will have a strong impact on the level of urbanization in Russia. The level of urbanization is influenced by many factors, which include the level of economic development of the country, migration of the population, natural and climatic conditions. The highest level of urbanization is typical for industrialized regions. This suggests that it is necessary to develop industry and move to Industry 4.0. The purpose of this chapter is to show the relationship between urbanization and Industry 4.0, as well as to increase the level of knowledge about digital production, the internet of things, the Industry 4.0, and urbanization. The chapter explains the role of Industry 4.0 in the current changing environment. The chapter deals with the most important problems and opportunities of the fourth industrial revolution.

Preface

INTRODUCTION

Urbanization is a mega-trend with deep impacts on growth and transformation worldwide especially the global South (UNDESA, 2014; ECA, 2017). In some continents, such as Africa and Asia, the rate and scale of urbanization is restructuring their demographic profiles and transforming their economic, environmental, and social systems which, in turn, is generating opportunities for urbanization-led growth. ECA (2017) suggests strategies for achieving desirable outcomes: energize local manufacturing, create highly productive companies, turn cities into engines for sustainable industrial production, and integrate industrialization into all aspects of urban and regional development.

The public sector is best in linking urban and regional development process, often through diversifying into new high technology, knowledge- intensives, or digital industries, while the private sector institutions follow and guide their members to start new business lines (Yigitcanlar & Bulu, 2016). They also help informal workers to use their smartphones and new skills to formalize their operations often in new more formal locations. The top-down and bottom-up approach appears to help nations face the global pressing challenges, such as poverty, illiteracy, income inequality, unemployment, regional disparity and unbalanced national development (ECA, 2017).

The relationship between urbanization and growth is not always linear. There are cases of urbanization with or without industrialization (Jedwab et al., 2014). For urbanization to create growth, however, it requires overcoming the following challenges: urban agglomeration and scale economies must benefit the growth of high-productivity activities and the effective management of the potential side effects of successful industrial cities.

EXPLORATION OF URBAN AND INDUSTRIAL GROWTH TRENDS

Global Trends

Growth Factors

Current and future urban and industrial growth policies need to respond to the evolving factors affecting global activities. These factors include the forces of digitization exerting influence on the global economy, the structural shifts they have triggered, and the most promising growth opportunities they have generated, the emerging industry 4.0, digital platforms, and digital services. Industry 4.0 is capable of boosting productivity by about 30%, enables labor costs reduction and has size and location flexibility to meet sudden customer demands worldwide. The digital platforms attract local and cross-border customers and enable companies achieve 100% growth rate in three years (Deloitte 2017). The digital services enable rapid growth of cross-border services such as online booking, entertainment sites, improve assets performance and generate new value-added services.

Evolving Global Events

Evolving events can affect global pattern of public policy decisions, private investments and household socio-economic behaviors. These trends are exemplified by the decentralization of decision-making centered from a unipolar to a multipolar world, the deliberate de-urbanizing and fragmenting the Middle East in the name of War on Terror, and rupture of financial system as triggered by the financial crisis of 2008 that triggered the rise of alternative financial systems (Oxford 2017). Part of this trend is the rise of populists' national politics and the retreat of global politics as evidenced by the election of President Trump and the Brexit. Another relevant trend is the shifting of power from US-EU axis to a global South BRICS axis. These trends converged to create new global industrial and urban development actors.

New Decision-Making Environment

The new decision-making environment presents the global public and private sector decision-makers with all-embracing imperatives (BCG, 2017). The new norm is that investor's attractiveness of nations now includes many indicators such as the potentials of local market, areas of growth, partnership opportunities. Others are cross-border connectivity of markets, speed of digital delivery of goods and services, and the ease of doing digital business with little physical interactions. In this age of rising protectionism and anti-globalization policies, investors should also consider their business model so that they can turn global challenges into opportunities (BCG, 2017; ECA, 2017, McKinsey, 2016).

Continental Trends

Growth Factors

Sustained growth began with the end of regional wars in the global South: in Africa after the Cold War and apartheid and a series of civil wars; in Asia it was after the World II, colonial arm struggles; and cultural revolution in China, and in South America it was after the revolutionary struggles. These conflicts were followed by periods of varying political, economic and regulatory reforms at various stages across many parts of these continents.

As the legal framework of the new global economy evolves, digital technology offers government and business leaders the opportunity to rapidly increasing connectivity, which is transforming every industry, sector, and society. As discussed in the previous section, the major forces at work in creating new opportunities at the continental level are the shift towards Industry 4.0, the development and use of digital platforms across borders, and the rise of digitally enabled services. These shifts create opportunities for the rapid and equitable development of most parts of the emerging continents. The evolving continental events are good indicators of the speed of development in respective regions.

In Africa, after the postcolonial period of "hopeless", it is now a "rising" continent of opportunities, where average labor productivity is growing by 2.7% a year. Trade between Africa and the rest of the world has increased by 200% since 2000. Inflation dropped from 22% in the 1990s to 8% in the past decade. Foreign debts declined by a quarter, budget deficits by two-thirds. Since 2000 Africa has sustained growth, despite 2008 global crisis, of over 5% in many countries and attracted FDI at 19.5% between 2007 and 2013 (EY, 2014; ECA, 2017).

Asia is reshaping the manufacturing and services sector, and a global leader in electronics, software and ICT services, with strong emphasis in m-payments using its vast mobile networks. New opportunities RE created by the pattern of mobiles-to-consumers, rise of social media, and digital banking opportunities, especially in nations with large unbanked and rural populations like India. For businesses, as barriers removed, more opportunities and choices are created to expand locally and become important players in the continent and beyond. Thus, even some of the SME have achieve astonishing results of some 80% revenue rise, 150% jobs rise, and opportunities for innovation has risen seven fold (PWC, 2017).

South America has average annual GDP growth of about 3% in the past 15 years, but the output per worker has gone up at only 0.6% per year since 2000, one of the weakest (OECD, 2017). Its urban economic growth rate is not helped by the falling fertility rates, nor has the end of the commodity-price boom. Unfortunately, the region's compound annual growth rate of 2.3% between 2000 and 2015 is projected to drop to 1.1% between 2015 and 2030 (OECD, 2017).

Decision-Making Environment

Africa

In Africa, the increase in the ease of doing business is due to a number of factors. Among them are sound macro-econ management, improved business environment, diversified economies, democratic political reforms in many countries, increased penetration and use of Information Technology that is contributing over 7% of the GDP in Sub-Saharan Africa, and the general upward trend in GDP and HDI ranking (EY, 2017). Not surprisingly, an inclusive and sustained growth is projected such that by 2030 SSA income be similar to the current emerging Asia.

Asia

The decision-making environment is helped by the accepted strategy that region's integration is through trade, the development of networked digital infrastructure and the policy of reshaping the manufacturing and services sectors to meeting current standards. In this process, the role of governments is usually limited to infrastructure provision and coordination, public services delivery, open government data for public use, and to provide guidance to long-term and broad-based gains, establishing smart cities system. Asia allocates to government high role in digital development, which helps some countries leap over development hurdles (OECD, 2018). This enabling policy environment ensures that Asian investors make the most of the advances technologies to fast-track the region's economic development.

South America

Probably social tensions, it is unclear if governments, businesses, and citizens accepted the need to play active parts in translating development concepts into reality (McKinsey, 2017). Clearly, there is need for broad concerted leadership from the society to shape a new agenda that will enable the region to overcome its demographic and urbanization challenges, boost productivity, and bolster growth for the long-term.

National Trends

The nations in the global North are more urbanized, backed by sound industrial policies that generate high personal income levels, which guarantee reasonably good urban quality of life. Table 1 shows continents, the number of nations and other characteristics. The global South nations, however, are facing many challenges to ensure sustained development to meet the demands for goods and services of their population growth and rapid urbanization to create jobs and income opportunities for their young population.

Naturally, in the processes of demographic, urbanization, and geopolitical transformations, there are winners and losers. The greatest winner is China, which has become the global factory and is increasing its sphere of influence across the world using soft power. The other gainer is India, which is specializing in the services sector especially Information technology, health and knowledge industries. Similarly, UAE is emerging as the hub of distributive trade and global real estate market. Some Island states, such as Singapore, Hong Kong, and Bahrain are emerging as global financial and business centers

Losses

USA squandered wealth and prestige in fighting unwinnable wars against non-state terrorists, and by fighting wars of aggression against states in the Middle East, thereby creating global refugee crisis and Islam phobia. Britain too has lost some of its geopolitical influence and its legacy of fair mindedness through its unquestioned backing of USA disastrous wars. The relative decline of national governments has influenced the rise of cities such New York and London as important global players.

The Role of Digital Technology

The key instrument in these transformations is the role played by digital technology in fundamentally changing the way citizens live, and their embrace of digital platforms through which all urban development actors can interact with each other, forming a web of digitally connected smart cities. These are making the urban decision-making environment much more effective and are enabling cities to operate more efficiently with greatly improved productivity and economic growth. Probably encouraged by these positive urban gains, there have also been a number of ambitious attempts to design the ultimate urban system by nations around the world including Dongtan in China, Masdar in Abu Dhabi, Migaa in Kenya and Songdo in South Korea. As a result, there arise global smart cities market concept and value that is expected to grow from USD 312.03 Billion in 2015 to USD 757.74 Billion by 2020, at a CAGR of 19.4% (PWC 2017).

Table 1. Continents, nations, population, area, density, and world population share

#	Continent	No. of Nations	Population (2018)	Area (Km²)	Density (P/Km²)	World Population Share
1	Asia	50	4,545,133,094	31,033,131	146	59.55%
2	Africa	54	1,287,920,518	29,648,481	43	16.87%
3	Europe	51	742,648,010	22,134,900	34	9.73%
4	North America	23	587,615,976	21,329,926	28	7.70%
5	South America	12	428,240,515	17,461,112	25	5.61%
6	Australia/Oceania	14	41,261,212	8,486,460	5	0.54%
7	Antarctica	0	0	13,720,000	0	0.00%
Source: Worldometer.info (2018)						

Subnational Trends

Subnational urban and industrial policy-making organizations are the essential building blocks for global growth that can respond to the increasing demands of demographic transformations and rapid population growth. Largely through these institutions, many societies worldwide have made huge progress in raising the quality of life for large groups of people in recent decades. In the last two decades, more than 1.2 billion people were lifted out of poverty especially in Asia (World Bank, 2015). The growth of these organizations was influenced by the factors of demographic changes, rapid urbanization, rise in personal income and growth of middle class. Naturally, the rising digital activities are also an important growth factor.

In some parts of the world, however, the continued weakness of sub-national institutions has enabled criminal elements to create mischiefs, weakening local governance and services delivery system and exasperating security problems. These issues, along with the slow growth, high unemployment and widening inequalities have positioned inclusive growth at the center of the policy debate in many global regions. An important issue in this debate is the ability of the subnational governments to develop policies that generate stronger economic growth as well as ensure better sharing of the benefits of enhanced affluence among social groups (Deaton, 2013).

The Global Subnational Government (SGN) Structure and Size

According to a study by the United Cities & Local Governments (2017), out of the sample of 522 629 SGNs, including 250 706 from India, there are categories consisting of single-tier, two-tier and three-tier nations. Table 2, shows the municipal-level, intermediate level, and the of state/regional-level institutions, which are decentralized agencies normally elected through universal suffrage and empowered with public services delivery functions and some with budget, staff and assets allocation autonomy. The growth of these SNGs has not only given rise to major cities(such as mega-cities and mega-regions), but also increased the profiles of some city-states (such as Singapore, Qatar, Bahrain, Hong Kong etc, as hubs of finance, learning, tech, global trade, and tourism). There is also the trend of emerging "regions of opportunities", as California, whose urban centers and industrial production make a geopolitically significant unit within a nation state.

Table 2. Number of subnational governments by level (2015-16)

	Number of Municipal-Level Governments	Number of Intermediate-Level Governments	Number of State/ Regional-Level Governments	Total Number of SNGs
Single-tiered SNG countries	5 718	0	7*	5 725
Two-tiered SNG countries	302 843	102	1 050	303 995
Three-tiered SNG countries	201 187	11 079	643	212 909
Total	509 748	11 181	1 700	522 629
Source: United Cities & Local Governments (2017).				

ORGANIZATION OF THE BOOK

Section 1: Industrial and Urban Growth Policies at Global Level

The worldwide deep penetration of digital technology and the widespread innovation in platform development have turned networked cities into powerful engines of growth for regions at the sub-national, national, continental and global levels. This section reviews the experiences of industrial and urban growth policies at these levels by the geographically and professionally diverse contributors to this book. In the first chapter, Benna explores the enhancement of quality of urban environment and of urban life through colorful and innovative industries based on natural resources, human capital and technology capital. The author highlights new policy and research areas with symbolic color-bases, emphasizes how digital technology is prime mover in all public and industrial activities, and stresses that the key to growth is not the mere concentration of population but of productive activities based on innovative use of natural resources, human and technological capitals.

The next chapter in this section by Mkrttchian et al., focuses on the creation of sustainable urban system by strengthening business relationships and their integration into the economy using supply chain management of avatar-based as the expert knowledge for smart solutions. The authors trace the avatar-based supply chains processes from production to consumption places using blockchain technology, explaining the application of specific product-expert knowledge using Internet based business partners and suppliers, and emphasizes the importance of quality business relationships and their integration into the urban systems for public good.

The third chapter by Abusaada and Elshater, is concerned with transforming chaos in urban environment into quality of urban life by converting what they call Chaos City (CC) into Order City (OC). They hold that urban chaos is a factor of hardship, reflecting low livability and quality of life but includes concepts of anarchy, randomness, and disorder; and then uses (CC) and (OC) to demonstrate the lack of standards of livability by using the visual and behavioral indicators. The authors suggest an approach to the transformation of CC to OC.

The fourth chapter, by Mkrttchian et al., analyzes innovative avatar-based management tool in achieving quality of urban environment, urban growth and urban life through digital revolution. As part of the spatial spread of digital revolution affects all areas of the economy of Armenia and a region in Russian Federation, the application of digital technology is penetrating all sectors including mining and energy generation, thus transforming not only the economy but also its active participants including the diverse enterprises and their supporting human capital.

Section 2: Industrial and Urban Growth Policies at Continental Level

Four research themes are reviewed on the topic that is related to the continental experiences. The first chapter by Chirisa et al., focuses on establishing the innovative industrial activities in Africa that are gaining strength despite obvious gaps, unclear strategies and how to muddle through. The authors stress that the key to success are establishing clear goals, workable strategies, and effective institutions with the political will, global connections and well-defined processes are vital. They are vital due to the enriching diversity in unity, not chaos, of the continent moving at different speeds and yet among the highest world's growth regions. Furthermore, the authors warn that the potentially rich natural, human and technological resources should not send Africa into a "fools paradise", as there are huge gaps to bridge.

The second chapter in this section, by Suleiman and Benna, focuses on the private sector taking the lead in the integration of urban growth and industrial policies in Africa. Despite long period of colonial neglect of industrial development and the fragmentation of Africa spatially, economically, and culturally, many African and non-African companies show evidence of industrial activities in urban centers. The success achieved maybe attributed to the organization for integration and its digital tools for integration coordination put in place by many development institutions. Future challenges and opportunities in sustaining the momentum are many but seem to be taken seriously by all the development actors.

In the third chapter in this section, Chirisa et al. suggest the leapfrogging of the most productive innovative machine from "failed" Africa into "rising" Africa and critique the practice of transplanting ideas from the West into Africa, based on a system nurtured in different soil, environments, and actors and possibly for different purposes. The authors suggest that the opportunities are tremendous and worth pursuing, with regular course-course correction overtime. The challenges, on the other hand, include the inability to attract FDI, which can be remedied through Local Direct Investments initiative, which more needs nurturing.

In another chapter, Chirisa et al. analyze African urbanization that has Western Industrial Revolution roots but grafted in diverse colonial systems in Africa's regions. The authors discuss ways of ensuring that urban and industrial policies converge to ensure that adequate public goods can be produced to meet the needs of the projected billions of African youthful in decades to come. Regionally, despite an early start by North Africa over Sub-Saharan Africa, it is not clear if this is being sustained or can be sustained in the long-run. Optimistically, the analysis implies that Africa's regions will collaborate with the continental institutions, businesses and citizens to use digital infrastructure in ways to establish a formidable global growth pole.

Section 3: Industrial and Urban Growth Policies at National Level

In the first chapter in this section, Professor Garcia draws our attention to the threats posed by population growth and rapid urbanization to water security in many nations. Based on Mexican example, the author develops a theoretical basis for the Smart Cities model that meets global challenges in water security adaptation strategies resilient enough to secure future water quotas. Hence, the chapter links to water resources and social resilience strategies to social learning and governance in cities, which mostly are featured as Green and Blue Cities in the Smart City paradigm.

The traditional role of public sector of investing in high-risk sectors with high national benefits potentials is the focus of the first chapter in this section. Vargas-Hernández and Kyari analyze institutional entrepreneurship of biodiesel companies in Mexico seeking to understand the relationship between public and private investment. After identifying the framework of the current situation covering aspects related to formal institutions, laws, rules, and regulatory bodies, the research concluded that the institutions in Mexico have increased their maturity and incentive to increase the number of producers and distributors of biodiesel thus taking advantage of the growing market.

The important role of Technological Innovations in driving national development is the focus of the next chapter by Akinwale, et al. They argued that oil-rich Nigeria can use its huge human capital resources in its universities to diversify its energy sources by promoting R&D to tap into its rich renewable energy potentials. Their survey of existing university research facilities shows that, like in most other areas, Nigeria is punching below its weight. However, given the required funding, sound university-government-industry collaboration, not only will huge demand-supply gap be narrowed but also energy source spatial specialization (fossil in coastal and renewable in the hinterland) can be created.

A wider analysis looks at the cross-cultural issues of small business activities in Russia and Australia seeking to demonstrate the power and global reach of agile micro businesses. A team of six researchers headed by Mkrttchian, et al., used blockchain technology cross-cultural growth activities to promote Russia and Australia. Even small firms are beginning to conduct cross-border activity as a first stage in global role playing in global business, signifying that micro and small businesses can use local knowledge to compete effectively with the globally integrated enterprises.

While the other chapters in this section are concerned with industrial and urban growth, the fourth chapter by Vargas-Hernández, Esparza-López and Kyari, draws our attention the de-urbanization challenges as neglected concerns, especially in global South. The authors argue that although rural and urban shrinkages are triggered by external factors, in Mexico the main issues are that of internal migration flows. The shrinkages there, unlike in developed countries, have internal causes and seem resistant to normal incentives to reverse the process, which implies that new research and new tools have to be found to achieve the reversal of the rural and urban migration flows.to avoid adverse socio-economic consequences.

Section 4: Industrial and Urban Growth Policies at Sub-National Level

Focusing on the convergence of innovative technologies to create many possibilities, one of which is leapfrogging for the lagging regions and nations, Gamidullaeva et al., analyze the emergence of Industry 4.0 Technologies and the leapfrogging opportunities this generates for the Russian. While the transformation to Industry 4.0 advances humanity, yet its blind pursuit cannot be the absolute objective, but more towards achieving sustained and increased competitive advantage over global competitors, the kind of competitive spirit that forces Russian into leading industrial power with a sizeable portion of global value chain.

In the process of industrial and urban growth, sometime contradictions between production and urban life emerge to create socio-political tensions, which digital technology can greatly reduce. Mkrttchian et al. in their chapter argue that in Russia the principles of integration, metabolism, and improved physical quality of the urban environment are used to reduce this tension. The emerging effective tools are digitally innovative production system, efficient transport, and logistic infrastructure and management systems. The others are the provision and maintenance of high quality, communal, residential and cultural facilities, all digitally connected.

Many nations are trying to turn their "resource-curse" economies into "resource-opportunities". The transformation from oil-based economy to cities-based economy requires many re-orientations for Nigerian urban actors, argues Rabiu Bena, the author of this section's second chapter. The tools to achieve re-orientation include agricultural investments- as import-substitution strategy to generate jobs and industrial raw-material -and the building refineries for local use and for export. Other strategies include developing vibrant region-serving knowledge-based economy, business parks, and international commercial facilities. As a regional agriculture center, Birnin Kebbi seeks to specialize in agro-based, knowledge-based, regional commercial and innovative hub.

The level of urbanization has a role to play attracting industrial development and in the Russian Federation important the nature of the economy, migration rate, natural and climatic conditions, argue Gamidullaeva et al.. They hold that the quality future industrial growth is more assure if built on the dynamic base of cities, and then upgrade them to Industry 4.0, and through this process lessons can be gain about urbanization-Industry 4.0 relationships, build knowledge on relationships of digital production, the Internet of things, the industry 4.0, and urbanization. The research also explains the role of Industry 4.0, and highlights its challenges and opportunities in the current social dynamics

REFERENCES

African Union. (2018). *Agenda 2063*. Retrieved from https://au.int/en/agenda2063

BCG. (2018). *Why Countries Need New Job Creation Strategies*. Retrieved from https://www.bcg.com/publications/2018/new-globalization-why-countries-need-new-job-creation-strategies.aspx

Boston Consulting Group (BCG). (2017). *New business models for a new global landscape*. Retrieved from https://www.bcg.com/publications/2017/globalization-new-business-models-global-landscape.aspx

Deaton, A. (2013). *The Great Escape Health, Wealth, and the Origins of Inequality*. Retrieved from https://press.princeton.edu/titles/10054.html

Deloitte. (2017). *Rewriting the rules for the digital age*. Retrieved from https://www2.deloitte.com/content/dam/Deloitte/global/Documents/About- Deloitte/central-europe/ce-global-human-capital-trends.pdf

ECA. (2017). *Urbanization And Industrialization For Africa's Transformation*. Retrieved from https://www.uneca.org/publications/economic-report-africa-2017

Ernest & Young (EY). (2017). *EY Global Information Security Survey 2017-18*. Retrieved from https://www.ey.com/gl/en/services/advisory/ey-global-information-security-survey-2017-18

Ernst & Young (EY). (2014). *Global View 2014*. Retrieved from https://www.ey.com/Publication/vwLUAssets/EY_Global_review_2014/$FILE/Global_review_2014.pdf

Jedwab, R., Gollin, D., & Vollrath, D. (2014). *Urbanization with and without Industrialization*. Working Papers. 2014-01. Retrieved from https://ideas.repec.org/p/gwi/wpaper/2014-01.html

McKinsey & Company. (2017). *Jobs lost, jobs gained*. Retrieved from https://www.mckinsey.com/featured-insights/future-of-organizations-and-work/jobs-lost-jobs-gained-what-the-future-of-work-will-mean-for-jobs-skills-and-wages

McKinsey& Company. (2016). *Urban world: Meeting the demographic challenge in cities*. Retrieved from https://www.mckinsey.com/featured-insights/urbanization/urban-world-meeting-the-demographic-challenge-in-cities

OECD. (2018). *Economic Outlook for Southeast Asia, China and India 2018*. Retrieved from http://www.oecd.org/dev/economic-outlook-for-southeast-asia-china-and-india-23101113.htm

Oxford Economics Research Team. (2017). *The World's Most Competitive Cities*. Retrieved from https://www.oxfordeconomics.com/recent-releases/the-worlds-most-competitive-cities

PWC-Global. (2017). *Reimagining the possible*. Retrieved from https://www.pwc.com/gx/en/about/global-annual-review-2017.html

UN-DESA. (2014). *World Urbanization Prospects –Revision*. Retrieved from https://esa.un.org/unpd/wup/publications/files/wup2014-report.pdf

United Cities & Local Governments. (2017). *Subnational governments around the world Structure and finance*. Retrieved from https://www.oecd.org/regional/regional-policy/Subnational-Governments-Around- the-World-%20Part-I.pdf

World Bank. (2015). *Ending Poverty and Sharing Prosperity*. Retrieved from http://www.worldbank.org/content/dam/Worldbank/gmr/gmr2014/GMR_2014_Full_Report.pdf

Worldometer.info. (2018). *Geography: Continents*. Retrieved from http://www.worldometers.info/geography/7-continents/

Yigitcanlar, T., & Bulu, M. (2016). *Urban Knowledge and Innovation Spaces*. Retrieved from https://www.tandfonline.com/doi/full/10.1080/10630732.2016.1164443

Acknowledgment

I would like to acknowledge my deep appreciation of the effort of everyone who contributed to the development of this book and wish to thank him or her for his or her instrumental contributions.

First, to the chapter authors, I owe deep gratitude for responding to our "call for chapter proposal" and for their quick responses to my repeated requests for more and more improvements in the process of chapter development.

Second, I would like to thank the Editorial Advisory Board members and/or reviewers for their constructive suggestions, and earnest reviews of the chapter assigned to them. Their efforts and hard work guarantee the production of this book of high quality.

Third, to Dr. Nuhu M. Dalhat of Dammam University, I extend my special thanks for taking the trouble to conduct similarity test of all the chapters in some cases multiple times.

Fourth, I would like to express my thanks many members of the IGI-Global management team, especially Erin Wesser (Assistant Managing Editor, Acquisitions), Kayla Wolfe (Managing Editor, Acquisitions) & Lindsay Johnston (Managing Director), and Jan Travers (Director of Intellectual Property and Contracts) from IGI Global publisher, for their untiring coordination and suggestions throughout the development of this book.

I am grateful to Ms. Marianne Caesar and Ms. Josephine Dadeboe, both Assistant Development Editors - Books from IGI Global publisher, for their valuable assistance throughout the whole editing process of this book.

Lastly, I also want to thank IGI Global, International Publisher of Progressive Academic Research, for its commitment to publish and stimulate innovative ideas and giving me the opportunity to publish this book so quickly.

Umar G. Benna
Benna Associates, Nigeria

Section 1
Industrial and Urban Growth Policies at the Global Level

The first section comprises studies with global concerns and covers diverse researches in Nigeria, Egypt, and the Russian Federation analyzing themes dealing with the urban economy, migration chaos, and roles of digital tools in entrepreneurship and urban growth. Specifically, the chapters explore the emerging colored economies' contributions to urban growth now and in the future, especially in the Global South; the increasing application of avatar-based expert solutions to achieve sustainable urban system; the analysis of tools for turning urban chaos to order cities in the increasingly global migratory environment; and the highlighting the rise of avatar-based management as help system to entrepreneurs as part of their emerging tools.

Chapter 1
A New Colorful Pathway Chosen:
The Emerging Trend of Colored Urban Economies

Umar Garba Benna
Benna Associates, Nigeria

ABSTRACT

In response to the rapid population growth and rapid urbanization, governments and entrepreneurs worldwide are spinning off many types of green, blue, and silver policies to generate urban growth or to reduce the effects of grey, brown, and black economies that have negative growth activities. Central to the emergence of these economies is digital technology that is contributing virtual and white economy to the list. This chapter explores the motives underpinning the emergence of these economies; the key policy actors and their main activities, policy tools, and strategies and growth outcomes at various levels. The chapter starts with a short introduction and develops a conceptual framework with which to analyze the trends policy-goals that shape the growth activities and the emerging growth patterns and consequences at the subnational, national, and supranational levels.

INTRODUCTION

Over the centuries, the processes of urbanization and natural resources (especially land) development have been engaged in an unbalanced conflict. Since the financial crises of 2008, however, it seems urbanization has the upper hand. That date is estimated to be the beginning of urban majority population worldwide and henceforth most urban growth will occur in Asia followed by Africa and Latin America (hereafter referred to as the global South) and China, India and Nigeria are expected to generate 90% of this growth (UNDESA, 2014). Within the global South, the urban population is expected to double between 2000 and 2030, but in this period, the urban footprint is projected to triple from 200,000 to 600,000 square kilometers (Angel et al., 2005). The size of this increase in land area is equal to the total built-up area worldwide in 2000, implying that the global South needs to build an entirely new urban world in just three decades (World Bank, 2010).

DOI: 10.4018/978-1-5225-7625-9.ch001

Cities are the engines of growth: Duranton (2008), for example, found strong evidence that cities globally bolster productive efficiency but it is inconclusive that they promote self-sustaining growth in developing countries. World Bank (2000) reports that goods and services are often produced most efficiently in cities of high population concentration, with access to a skilled labor pool, a network of firms as suppliers, and a large customer base. The role of globalization to growth engine concept is it creates new possibilities for worldwide linkages; it also reinforces certain advantages of proximity, which supports demand for increased localization of political power.

The financial crisis of 2008 and its rude awakening about the instability of the political economy suggest that the current elite-centered growth model and its effects on the natural resources "threatens the foundations of long-run growth and development" (OECD 2017). Given that natural resources are the key to economic growth and that the planet contains only a finite amount of them, clearly upward and onward growth is not a sustainable model (Vavrek and Chovancova 2016). Thus, seeking more inclusive and sustainable growth approaches should at the top of growth policy agenda.

The aims of this chapter are:

1. To identify the emerging urban economic models that could serve global South now and in the future
2. To explore how to utilize them to develop the diverse natural, human and technological resources
3. To explore the development impacts of the colored urban economic models

Achieving these objectives requires a careful review of the current situation, the trend and impact analysis. Given the dramatic shifts and imbalances created in the global socio-economic and geopolitical systems caused by the 2008 financial crisis (Fujita 2013), it seems unwise to rely on the largely discredited Western models to guide the future urban economies in the global South (Brown 2017).

Emerging out of the crisis perspective environment are diverse approaches to the planning of new urban economy around the world. A preliminary review of these models shows that they are identified as Green, Blue, Brown, Silver, Grey, Black, White and Colorless (Virtual) Economies. These are categorized as Grow with Nature (Green, Blue, and Silver) Economies, Grow with Human Capital (Black, Grey, and Brown) Economies, and Grow with Technology (Virtual and White) Economies. The color reflects the emphasis of resource base use whether nature, urban built physical or social environment, targeting the aging population or is based on the application of the digital technology. Each is defined, analyzed in terms of their size, global span and growth promoting characteristics and their potential in the global South are assessed.

BACKGROUND

Literature Review

The current path of economic development places human survival in jeopardy. This is due to the severe stress on the environment and human livelihood resulting from unsustainable forms of production and consumption, excessive finite resources dependency, with the impact of climate change widespread and growing. Society is responding to these threats through green growth and green economy policies seeking to develop a low-carbon, resource efficient and socially inclusive development pathway (Rödiger-Vorwerk

2015). Many arguments have been advanced in support of a green economy, among which are its enhances medium and long-term economic prospects; lessens the risks of existing economic growth; offers both short and long-term resource development prospects; advance quality of life; and attract investors interested in political prestige and economic gains (OECD 2010; Rödiger-Vorwerk 2015, GIZ 2012) .

Grow With Nature

Karlenzig, et.al. (2017) suggests shifting focus from transforming the urban economy to toward transforming the urban economy in the global South has the support of the diverse urban development specialists, using natural resources as the basis for growth. For example, many researchers (e.g. Karlenzig et al. 2017, Brown 2017) argue that the prevailing window of opportunity and business considerations in most of the rapidly growing urban centers of the global South have the chance to cost-effectively drive down carbon emissions and production of pollutants. In addition to the academics, urban policymakers at the global level are increasingly targeting cities as a key source of scalable global economic solutions, particularly in sustainable development (WWF 2010); and support is coming from the investment community, that is recognizing and alerting its members of the unprecedented opportunities in sustainable development (OECD 2010). The global banking and financing institutions receive adequate consideration, as they are turning attention away from the national level to the city level following the successes of urban investment model used in Hong Kong, Dubai, Bilbao, Barcelona, and Sydney (Wu 2005).

Grow With Human Capital

Rapid suburbanization in the global South – fed by the constant flow of human capita- poses significant challenges for municipal authorities, which typically lack the institutional and fiscal capacity to engage in effective land use planning (UN-Habitat 2009). Moreover, as Watson (2009) argues, "urban planning in many parts of the world reflects an increasing gap between current approaches and growing problems of poverty, inequality, informality, rapid urbanization and spatial fragmentation". International policy discourses led by UN-Habitat (2009) and the World Bank (2010) are thus actively exchanging new ideas and 'best' practices on how urban planning can become more effective. Regarding the debate on urban form, the compact city is widely endorsed as the best solution to the social, economic and environmental externalities of 'urban sprawl' and other unsustainable patterns of urbanization (UN-Habitat, 2009, 2010, 2011). Different problems give a standard Western compact solution as found in Barcelona (Spain) and Portland (USA), avoiding models from Global South as exemplified by Timbuktu (Benna 2013) and Sokoto (Benna 1997)

The shifting global forces are urging the world to pay attention to views of researchers like DeSoto (2000), Neuwirth (2005) and Collier (2007). They lead the hundreds of concerned academics who have drawn attention to the predicament of the urban poor and slum-dwellers in the age of globalization searching for sustainably smart cities –the "maker smart cities" built by creative forces from ground-up. They all point to the need for inclusive urban policies that allow for greater physical and digital participation in the political, social, economic and cultural life of cities in which they live.

Grow With Technology

Backed by a steady flow of innovative business models, digital technology has enhanced the competitiveness of businesses through more varieties and higher speed transactions. Attempts to enhance these speedy transactions, even more, are on-going, through various innovative smart cities and virtual cities projects. On the perceptions of public officials on smart cities, Rodríguez-Bolívar (2015) analyzes the insights of stakeholders, including city managers and politicians, concerning the incentives and role of governments in Smart Cities that enable a direct link between e-government projects and workers in smart workplaces. From the perspective of the citizens, Picon (2015) reports what happens and the intelligence gained within the infrastructure to the smartphones that connect individual citizens. Obaidat and Nicopolitidis (2016) examine the smart networks to highlighting the digital networks connecting different areas of computing, focusing of on both new and emerging computer networking systems designed to enhance the competitiveness of the city-region.

With regard to advances in virtual cities, Pinto (2013) published a book that covers a host of newly created hardware and software technology innovations in planning (both urban and regional) and architecture. Similarly, authors Dan and Crăciun (2016) Virtual cities as memory-scape using Lisbon as a case study. Rapid advances in digital technology have enabled many cities and nations to create place-branding and place-marketing strategies in order to enhance their competitiveness. Given this premise, the publication by Govers and Go (2016) under the title" Place Branding: Glocal, Virtual and Physical Identities, Constructed, Imagined and Experienced", would not need any further elaboration. Focusing on personal prosperity, BCG (2018) argues that despite GDP growth worldwide, employment size and quality has been relatively low, reflecting on the relatively low quality of life. To achieve higher and better jobs, cities and nations need to invest more in digital services, grow local knowledge, encourage young businesses to go global, digitally formalize the informal, and increase local consumption (BCG 2018).

The concepts, policy measures and action instruments presented in the above review of the current literature set the stage in this chapter's development. After a brief discussion of the conceptual framework and the methodology, the next section discusses the research findings.

Conceptual Framework

The literature review has guided the development of the conceptual framework to guide this chapter. As shown in Figure 1, the conceptual framework used here assumes that the growth of the colored urban economies is influenced by the deliberate economic policies chosen by the urban development actors. Subsequently, their development activities are in turn guided by the economic development goals of cities and nations around the world.

Methodology

This study uses mostly secondary qualitative and quantitative data to identify, define, categorize and explain each type of urban economies analyzed in this chapter. The desktop search was the primary tool used in data collection and this is a secondary data collection method that some researchers (for example Mogalakwe 2006) described by as being suited for qualitative studies. The collected data from documents, databases and scientific journals were inventoried and categorized according to the classification system of the types of urban economies.

Figure 1. Conceptual framework
Source: Author Generated

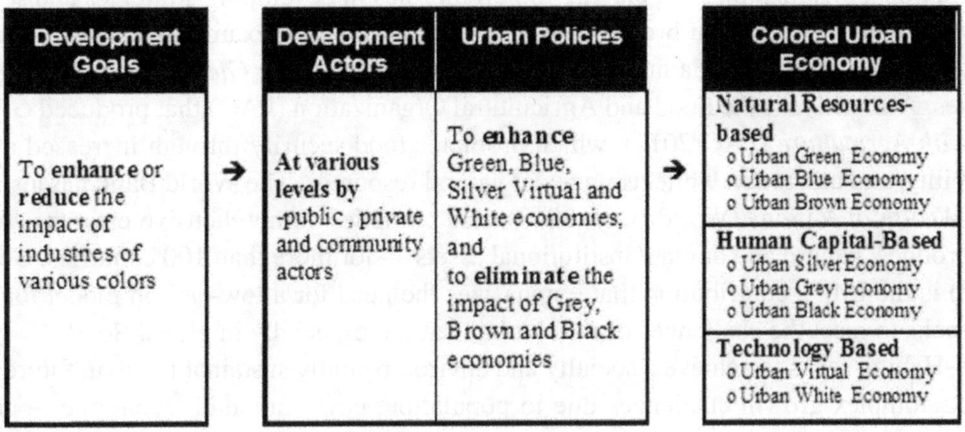

Discussion of Findings

It seems clear from the literature review that the colors used to identify various economics are not merely artificially painted. They are deeply rooted in the colors of natural and social resources and the digital technology used to undertake the production and distribution of urban goods and services. The research findings are discussed under three broad headings: natural resource-based, social resource-based and technology-based urban economies, each of which comprises a number of distinct economies that are identified by different colors. However, regardless of their distinctive colors, they all illustrate the dynamism, vitality and shifts in current economic activities, and broadly point to the future urban economic behavior worldwide.

GROW WITH NATURE

This section explores the growth of natural resources-based Green, Blue and Brown Economies in the urban areas. In particular, it focuses on the processes of using natural resources in the production, distribution, and consumption of goods and services for the growing urban population worldwide, especially in the global South.

Key Economic Actors

Public Sector Actors

The number and the capacities of public organizations seeking to promote sustainable use of natural resources to advance urban economy is on the rise. Broadly, three types of organizations may be identified: global players, including UN organizations such as the FAO, UNEP and UNDP; regional UN bodies, including UNECE; and sub-national agencies.

Global Players

Many international organizations are playing important roles in developing strategies and solutions for achieving the green economy and broader resource efficiencies. For example, the UN-Environmental Programme (2016) has produced a number of approaches, notably the *Global Environmental Outlook (GEO)* series. Also active is the Food and Agricultural Organization (FAO) that produced *Greening the Economy with Agriculture* (FAO 2012), which promotes food security through increased availability, access, stability, and utilization while using fewer natural resources. The World Bank has also produced *Changing Wealth of Nations* (World Bank 2018), that compiles comprehensive estimates of wealth - including produce, natural and human/ institutional assets — for more than 100 countries. *Going Green* (IMF 2012) is the IMF's contribution that emphasizes the need for a low-carbon model for growth as the world seeks to meet the challenges of rapid urbanization, especially in global South.

The UN-Habitat seeks to achieve a socially and environmentally sustainable urban future for all. As cities facing complex growth challenges due to population, environmental, economic, social, spatial development and rapid urbanization, this agency responds with a holistic and global approach that incorporates urban design and planning, infrastructure development, and inclusive slum upgrading to benefit all urban actors (UN-Habitat 2018).

Regional UN Actors

There are five regional UN Commissions for Sustainable Development in Africa, Arab, Asia, Europe, and Latin America with headquarters in New York (UN Regional Commission 2018). Their work on the green economy is driven mainly through the continental or regional partnership and regular environmental performance reviews. The other key regional UN player is ECOSOC (2018), which draws people and issues seeking to promote collective action for a sustainable world. It does this through conduct innovative analysis, decide on global standards and promote sustainable development solutions. The multi-lateral agencies promoting social and sustainable development include the OECD that published an Environmental Outlook to 2030 (OECD, 2008), the European Environmental Agency (EEA) that focuses on Europe, and the USAID that undertakes sustainability assessments around the world.

Urban Actors

City mayors from around the world have created a 'Global Parliament of Mayors" (GPM) to enhance intercity cooperation seeking to address the increasingly urgent global urban growth crises. Urban economic development issues form an important part of the solution to the crises (GPM 2018). Urban marketing strategies guide cities to achieve many objectives such as attracting investors, expanding industrial infrastructure, developing tourism, enhancing transport and health services that can be provided with the investments from the organized private sector such as Chamber of commerce and industry in various cities.

Private Sector Actors

A large number of private, voluntary, non-governmental organizations are involved in developing various aspects of the green economy. There are four main categories:

- Non-governmental organizations, charitable foundations and lobby groups often have a strong interest in promoting green economy causes. For example, the Living Planet Report produced by the World Wide Fund for Nature measures the health of the world's biodiversity in relation to humanity' s demands on the Earth' s natural resources (WWF, 2010).
    - Think-tanks and multinational organizations, for example, the World Resources Institute are mainly focused on new knowledge on green economy and in ensuring that the latest ideas are brought into decision-making, e.g. the climate analysis indicators tool (World Resources Institute 2018),
    - National, regional and international trade associations are usually interested in promoting specific viewpoints and influencing trade-related decision-making. For example, the role of steel in reducing energy use and greenhouse gas emissions (World Steel Association, 2010);
    - Research bodies (universities and research institutes) which may attract funding from private sector sources are also interested in promoting sustainable green behavior through research (Stockholm Environmental Institute, 2009).

There is very little consistency regarding the size or type of regions these organizations cover, as some have global span while others have continental or national perspectives.

Economic Activities

The main activities pursued by each type of economy tend to reflect the green, blue and brown colors of the economies. Table 1 shows examples of the natural resource-based colored economies.

- **Green Economy:** This seeks to develop markets for environmentally related products, incentivize innovation across the economy and strengthen green taxation. While R&D budgets are rising worldwide, the majority of green inventions (90%) have traditionally originated from OECD countries, although recently the number of contributions from China and India are rising (OECD 2017).

Table 1. Natural resource-based colored economies: objectives and activity areas

Economy	Objectives	Activity Areas
Green	Improves human well-being and social equity; reducing environmental risks and ecological scarcities (UNEP 2011).	Key activities include urban agriculture, tourism, renewable energy, gardening, climate and waste management
Blue	Sustainable use of resources from oceans and other water bodies for economic growth: enhance livelihood and jobs; promote the health of water ecosystem (ECA, 2017)	Managing ocean and lakes, fishing, tourism, renewable energy, marine transport, climate and waste management (World Bank 2017)
Brown	Relies heavily on fossil fuels and ignores the negative impacts of economic production and consumption have on the environment,(U.Deichmann 2013)	Managing wastes, renewable energy, transport and buildings especially in areas with dysfunctional infrastructure and institutions; reduce congestion and climate change concerns. (Brown 2017)
Source: varies as indicated		

- **Blue Economy:** This includes value-creation in aquatic and marine spaces, covering oceans, seas, coasts, lakes, rivers, and groundwater. It extends to a wide range of productive sectors, such as fisheries, aquaculture, tourism, transport, commerce and trade, shipbuilding, energy, protection, and restoration (ECA 2016). It also captures extractive industries, including underwater mining and offshore oil and gas.
- **Brown Economy:** The use of numerous types of polluting fuels for daily activities is central to this economy. Many estimates suggest that about half of the world's households use biomass and coal for cooking and heating using devices that generate unacceptable levels of air pollution in residential places. This pollution type is perhaps responsible for 4–5 percent of disease burden worldwide. Charcoal production and fuel-wood harvesting are the main the main causes of this burden. In workplaces, however, solid-fuel fuel cycles generate important risks for workers and this has the highest impacts on populations among all energy systems. In urban communities, fuel use in vehicles and stationary sources are the main cause of urban air pollution (IEA 2016)

The Blue Economy concept usually covers aquatic and marine spaces, including oceans, seas, coasts, lakes, rivers, and underground water, and it comprises a range of productive sectors, such as fisheries, aquaculture, tourism, transport, shipbuilding, renewable energy, bio-prospecting, and underwater mining and related activities. Table 2 shows examples of the ecosystem services and sectors of Blue Economy.

GROW WITH HUMAN CAPITAL

The human talent is a source of inexhaustible ingenuity and creativity for cities and nations to use for turning the challenges of the black, grey and silver economies into opportunities to face the issues of high population growth and rapid urbanization, especially in the global South.

Table 2. Key blue economy ecosystem services and sectors

Type of ecosystem services	Blue Economy sectors
Harvesting seafood, plant marine organisms, and marine-biotechnological products	Fishing (inland, coastal, and deep seas) Aquaculture Mariculture Pharmaceuticals, chemicals, cosmetics, genetic research
Extracting nonliving resources and generating new energy resources	Mining deep-sea and seabed; offshore oil and gas exploitation; renewable energy development; marine salt harvesting; coastal mining of sand, gravel, and other construction materials
Commerce and trade in and around the ocean and rivers	Providing maritime transport and services; port infrastructure development; shipbuilding and repairs; river transport, tourism and recreation
Protection	Coastal protection, marine ecosystem protection; water resource protection
Cultural and religious values	Cultural and religious practices
Knowledge and information	Biophysical, socioeconomic, and political research
Source: ECA 2016	

Key Human Capital Actors

- **Public Sector:** The United Nations Development Programme (UNDP) and United Nations Educational, Scientific and Cultural Organization (UNESCO) are the leading global institutions concerned with human capital development worldwide. While UNDP supports nations in their poverty reduction efforts and in implementing their employment strategies, UNESCO promotes peace through international cooperation in education, the sciences, culture, communication, and information.

The Global Human Capital Index is produced annually, and the 2017 Report ranks 130 countries on the level of their ability for human capital development on a scale from 0 (worst) to 100 (best), using four thematic dimensions and five distinct age groups to capture the full human capital potential profile of each nation. In a global perspective, the report shows that only 62% of human capital in developed and that only 25 nations have employed 70% of their people's human capital or more. In addition, the analysis produces a gap in human capital development for regions and nations and shows that global South regions have wider gaps than Global North. For example, Sub-Saharan Africa had 47% gap, South Asia 46% and Latin America and the Caribbean had 40%; by contrast, in the global North, Western Europe had 29%, and North America 26% gap (WEF 2017).

- **Private Sector:** Global digital business leaders are shifting as cloud-based business models become attractive and the largest companies on the list—Apple, Google, HP, Amazon, and Microsoft—remain at the top in terms cash value and global economic impact (Griffith 2015). These global players have footprints in all the global regions, in additions, there are regional players contributing to human capital development. In Africa, for example, regional players include Data tech, Econet, MTN and Naspers (BCG 2018).

Types of Activity Areas

The activities pursued by each type of economic actors tend to reflect the silver, grey and black economies to meet the needs of the aging population and of a greedy group willing to bend the law. Table 3 shows the main characteristics and the activity areas of the human capital-based economies.

- **Silver Economy**: According to projections, by 2020, people aged 60 and older will be greater in number than children younger than five and by 2050, the world's older adult population will reach to 2 billion (Gordon 2017). These numbers will have devastating impacts on the pension schemes, and the burgeoning health-care costs, thus creating new challenges for all urban economy actors. Some creative actors may turn these challenges into unique opportunities, such that public and private insurers monetize elderly health-care services and promote longevity as businesses.

The World Economic Forum (2016) suggests how aging impacts on human and financial well-being can be addressed. First, create "whealth-care", by examining the combined impacts of health and wealth together. Second, life-course approach- that considers the value of activities undertaken to promote health and wealth in early and later life. Third, initiate collaborative research to bridge the divide between health and wealth. Fourth, develop innovative technologies; the personalized technologies with the potential to

Table 3. Human resource-based colored economies: main characteristics and activity areas

Economy type	Main characteristics
Silver	Silver economy refers to names of places, film industry and activities to provide for the aging population. The names of many places reflect where silver mining once occurred, or places with importance to film industry. Third, it may signify places serving the needs of senior citizens, and their influence on many sectors; e. g, health and nutrition, leisure, wellbeing, finance, housing, and employment. Increasing longevity tends to enhance new openings for economic, social and cultural development by generating new jobs triggered by new technological innovations.
Grey	The Grey economy, or informal economy, is the type that is neither taxed nor monitored by governments. The color may reflect specific places or the color of a product. It may also echo the level of legality of activities Compared to Black economy, Gray economy typically is legal but it violates certain written and unwritten arrangements. Black products—such as those that are counterfeit—are illegal by the regulations of most countries (Melonakos 2011).
Black	Black economy tends to weaken the community's trust in the tax system; generates an unfair commercial environment that penalizes law-abiding businesses and individuals; enable the exploitation of susceptible workers; reduces tax income; and allow abuse of the welfare system (Melonakos 2011).

facilitate healthy aging and the prevention of financial fraud among older adults are gradually emerging. Fifth, formulate age-friendly policies that are suitable for managing aging populations.

- **Grey Economy:** Many colored economies get their names from the nature of their activities, from the color of their built environments, and from their climate or natural appearance. As Briony Harris (2017) points out, Aberdeen in the UK, for example, has s combination of energy-based activities, many of its buildings constructed granite and a climate that is often gloomy, all converge to give it the nickname "the Grey city". The second concept of the grey economy and one that is more widespread relates to the legality of the economic activities, such as the informal and black economies.
- **Informal Economy:** Also called a grey economy that is neither taxed nor monitored by governments. The activities in this economy, unlike the formal economy, are not included in a country's gross national product (GNP) or in the gross domestic product (GDP) Calbreath (2010).

The size of the urban informal sector varies in time and place, but it exists everywhere worldwide, but the level is a function of many factors. For example, the expansion of the urban informal sector closely linked to the pace of urbanization in some global regions (Charmes 2001). Secondly, the employment rate in the informal sector (as % of non-agricultural employment) is relatively high in the global South; as Charmes (2001) shows that it is about 74.8% in Sub-Saharan Africa, Latin America 56.9%, rising to 73.7 in India and in Indonesia 77.9%.

In the global North, the rate is much lower, for example, it is about 10% of GDP in the UK; 14% in Nordic countries and about 20–30% in many southern European countries. Tax and safety net, the state institutions' quality and labor market regulation are the key drivers of the shadow economy and Charmes (2001) suggests that tax burden reduction could trigger lowering the size of the shadow economy. This pattern could create a vicious circle in one direction or the other; the policymakers have to be careful in designing new policies tools.

- **Black Economy:** This is illegal and anti-social activities. The main issue is that while this economy exists everywhere worldwide, yet its exact size behavior is difficult to assess because it takes place in the dark. It is difficult to profile for the following reasons: first, it is based on the urbanization of poverty. Second, the black economy activities are considered non-citizens of the city. Third, the actors in various economic fields depend not on institutions but close friends and relatives for finance, professional support and for guidance.

GROW WITH TECHNOLOGY

Most urban economies are shifting from place-based to digital based economies. While the previous sections have focused on the former, this section deals with the latter economy. It explores how technology-based the virtual and white economies are promoted in urban areas, and how to eliminate technology impacts unsustainable to worldwide communities, especially in the global South. Table 4 provides the definitions and main characteristics of the two economies and the next subsection elaborates on how the two economies differ.

Key Technology Actors

- **Public Sector:** International Telecommunication Union (ITU) and InfoDev are the agencies closely connected with the information technology development at a global level. ITU allocates global radio spectrum and satellite orbits, establish the technical standards, which guarantees networks and technologies flawlessly interconnect, and endeavor to ensure that ICTs services are delivered to even poor remote communities worldwide. Its broad-based members include 193 nations, local ICT regulators, many leading academic institutions, as well as about **700** technology firms worldwide. It has regional offices in Africa, Asia, Latin America, Europe and the Russian Federation (ITU 2018).

Table 4. Technology-based economies: definitions and main characteristics

Economy type	Definitions and key characteristics
Virtual	The virtual economy exists mainly in a virtual world of computer. The relationship between Virtual and Actual economies is often debated: some argue that real economy is shrinking due to the expansion in the digital economy, but others stress that the real economy is hurt by lack of innovation and reform (CGTN 2017). Main strengths: 1. Production of innovative ideas and solutions using crowdsourcing, crowdfunding, blockchain technologies; 2. Digital delivery of goods and services
White	The white economy creates value by mixing the creative potentials existing in large cities like London and uses innovative technology to boost skilled jobs creation. Examples are: Italy's personal care assistance sector employs 3.8 million workers (Morningfuture 2017), and the UK's strong lead in online retail and marketing with very large digitally skilled relatively cheap workforce (McWilliams 2017). White market uses diverse human capital for legal, official, authorized, or destined market for goods and services. By contrast, black market is of illegally traded goods and the grey market uses channels that are informal, or unauthorized by the original producers.(Feige 1989).
Source; Developed by the author	

InfoDev is a World Bank Group Program designed to enhance entrepreneurship and innovation, especially in the global South where successful entrepreneurs can be powerful change agents. InfoDev has established worldwide network of business incubators and innovation hubs to promote climate for technology growth, agribusiness, and digital entrepreneurs and diverse clients in Africa, Asia, and Latin America, where its impact is greatly felt and appreciated (InfoDev 2018).

- **Private Sector:** There are many multinationals, nationals, SMEs and Startup promoting the development of various aspects of ICT in the global North but working across the world and some focusing on the global South. The main global players include Accenture (2017 revenue 6512mUS$), Deloitte (4,065mUS$), Cognizant (3,942mUS$), IBM (3490mUS$), PWC (3412mUS$) (*Statista* 2018). In the global South, the key players are Tata (387,223 workers), Samsung (275,000 workers), Infosys (200,364 workers), Huawei (180,000workers), and HCL Tech (119,291 workers) Wikipedia (2018).

Economic Activities

A **virtual economy** (or synthetic economy) is as an emergent online-based economy, for the exchange of virtual goods in the context of Internet games. However, many entrepreneurs are active online promoting virtual economies for "real" economic benefits. The digital economy consists of two types: the Virtual Economy (VE), comprising of digital transactions that take place entirely within online networks (Infodev, 2011); and the other is White Economy (WE) the activities of which physically take place and have an impact on urban the spatial systems (McWilliams 2015).

The main distinguishing features of the VE include; first, that it focuses on commodities that are digital and scarce such as virtual goods, currencies, software, and digital labor. Second, commodities demand arises from the cumulative practice of digital services in the business and leisure sectors. Third, the supply is generated by means of the human effort, which needs relatively specific digital skills or capitals. The VE has four main categories of commercially significant activities, namely: third-party online gaming services, microwork, "Cherry blossoming", and user-created virtual goods production. According to Infodev (2011), the first two of these segments are consumer-oriented production, and the last two are business oriented, but they may be managed from anywhere at any time.

The VE may be contrasted with the WE that produces content for the digital economy such as online services, communities, games, e-shopping, e-Commerce, e-Governance, and the production and distribution of information goods. The information goods include music, video, images, and news articles, and any other goods that are represented in digital form. WE also include the supply and servicing of broadband connectivity and wireless networks. As a study by McWilliams (2015) shows, WE can have a huge economic impact, and affect politics and lifestyles of cities and regions within nations and across the world.

DEVELOPMENT IMPACTS OF THE URBAN ECONOMIC MODELS

The analysis of the multi-colored urban economies in the previous sections indicates that stable conditions are essential for future urban economic activities and growth necessary to meet the needs of the billions projected to be urban citizens in the future. To assess their impact on the present and the future directions of urban development worldwide, especially the most affected regions of the global South, each of the three categories of colored-urban economies, is analyzed based on the vitality of their growth factors, the trend in cities growth index, and the level of their dominant activities in a global system.

The emergence of the colored economies suggests a change in the global economic landscape. As a result, suggests BCG (2018), growth strategies based on growing world trade in physical goods and foreign capital investment may not be effective in the future. For increased future effectiveness, urban development actors need to focus their attention and resources to target growth in the digital flow of services, cultivation local expertise, encourage SMEs to engage in global value chains, digitally empower the self-employed, and to increase personal consumption. By themselves, these strategies may not be enough to ensure the desired size, speed and direction of growth; they have to be supported with suitable tools to ease "Doing Business" (World Bank Group, 2017). These strategies will be used to assess each of the categories of urban economies.

Grow With Nature

In the normal societal development process, natural resources have been the main feedstock in industrial production. Careless industrialization created a variety of intense land, soil, water, and air pollutions. In response, policymakers and planners designed many strategies, such as industrial ecology, green growth, and others. This section explores more in the direction that seeks to grow with nature.

Growth Factors

The emerging natural resource-based green, blue and silver economies will have a potentially huge impact on jobs and growth in cities in the global South. Many publications suggest good policies; most natural resource-based economies can boost urban employment and trigger sustainable growth (OECD 2017, ECA 2017, Burkart 2009). Among their reasons are; first, sound resource-based policies that enhance environmental quality and sustain economic growth can promote overall employment. Second, these policies can be designed to enhance existing jobs, create entirely new urban economic sectors and manage the economy towards more labor-intensive services. Third, the new public revenues generated from tax reforms on natural resource-based activities, can lower labor taxes, mitigate income inequality effects and finance education and training programs to achieve positive urban employment outcomes. Fourth, the creation of innovative labor markets can be crucial to achieving a smooth reintegration of workers affected by job losses in the process of innovation. Fifth, the review of the existing labor-market policy tools may be necessary to make them more effective for use by institutions that provide workers with the skills required in future workplaces. Sixth, further research will help to quantify all employment dimensions of natural resources-based policies and the trends in their interactions with other sectors in cities.

Green Cities

To illustrate the variety of impacts of the innovative green, blue and silver economies are exerting on urban communities, it is instructive to analyze Green Cities Index research. Three green cities studies by TravelBird (2018), Arcadis (2018) and Siemens (2012) are examined. While the first studies 50 cities OECD countries considering three green space categories (namely nature, man-made and food production); the second study ranks 100 world's cities using three sustainability factors - People (social),

Planet (environmental) and Profit (Economic Health - the third study seems more comprehensive and is analyzed here in detail.

The main objective of the Siemens (2012) research is to highlight the key issues of urban environmental sustainability through benchmarking cities' achievements in green development practices and in sharing them with other cities. Evaluating more than 120 major cities worldwide, the study uses 30 indicators in nine categories, including factors such as CO2 emissions, renewable energy, land use, transport, water and sanitation, air quality and environmental management.

As expected, a worldwide comparison shows that the cities in global North are ahead of those in the global South in the areas of GDP level, CO2 emissions per capita, solid waste production, solid waste recycling rates per capita, travel by car, and water consumption (Siemens 2012). With respect to energy intensity, Europe relates positively to Asia in terms of per unit of GDP. However, in population density, water system leakage, sulfur dioxide emission, the global South cities are less efficient than their global North counterparts (Siemens 2012).

The studies by Siemens (2012) and OECD (2017) suggest seven steps to achieve a greener city. First, good governance and leadership at the metropolitan level are vital to goals achievement. Second, a holistic approach to solving urban problems is more effective. Third, while wealth creation is vital, but also important are balanced and inclusive policies, especially at the early development stages. Fourth, civic engagement and citizen participation in environmental issues enhance the city's competitiveness. Fifth, the use of right technology promotes the city's productivity and its greenness. Sixth, there need to ensure that the green and brown agendas are mutually supportive. Seventh, tackling informal settlements is important to the green agenda (Siemens 2012, OECD 2017).

Future Growth Potential

The growth potential lies on harnessing natural resources, including mineral geology, hydrology, soils, vegetation, wildlife, agricultural land, landforms and climate for development. The future lies in strategies that scale-up growth at a rate faster than the urbanization rate. The strategies with best results are: first, the Green, Blue, Silver economies that may use the digital branding and marketing strategies to sell their products and services, improve skills of the workforce and promote effective management. Second, with the steady growth of the self-employed population, its digital empowerment will cost-effectively boost local Green, Blue, and Silver economies and raise revenue. Third, boosting local personal consumption will increase demand for Green, Blue and Silver goods, services, and solutions. Fourth, formalization of the informal economic activities will transform the economy and the society. For greater effectiveness, physical and digital infrastructure; and efficient institutions, however, must accompany these strategies.

Grow With Human Capital

The impacts of silver grey and black economies are beginning to attract the attention of researchers (PWC 2017, UNDESA 2018, and Center for Cities 2015). They vary in the degree of legality governments around the world grant them based on the degree of "good" or "damage" they are perceived to do the society. Policy instruments should initially seek to achieve behavior modification from illegality to legal, from informal to formal, from shadow to light. The result can boost GDP, lift billions out of poverty, and boost consumption and production around the world. In this section, we explore the economies' growth factors, how they grow, transform and what the future may hold.

Growth Factors

The above activities are destined to impact future growth, which is projected to be predominant urban, with more than two-thirds of the world population- about 2.5 billion, 90% of which will be in Asia and Africa- is expected to live in urban areas by 2050 (UNDESA 2018). The impacts on the economy suggest more than doubling (130%) of the world economy and about 80% of it urban by 2050; this will exceed population growth, thanks to technology-driven productivity gains (PWC 2017). The role of the urban economies of the global South will be crucial, as they are set to grow twice as fast as other economies, and will produce the largest economies- China (1st), India (2nd) and Indonesia (4th). In terms of the overall rate of economic growth in Vietnam (5.1%), Philippines (4.3%) and Nigeria (4.2%) will rise the fastest by 2050 (PWC 2017).

The Rise of New Urban Economies

Long-term perspective shows that the growth of cities has benefited from a number of innovations such as containerization for the flow of goods across the oceans. The innovation on package budget flights has positive impacts on blue economies and the growth of seaside resort towns. Globalization enabled the growth of manufacturing cities in foreign countries that have cheap labor. Thus, manufacturing and low-cost services were exported to cities in the global South that have skilled but cheap labor. Moreover, the globalization strategy has forced some cities in the global South towards specializing towards more knowledge-intensive types of activities, that value the production of the idea is more important than the production of the physical goods (BCG 2018). The widespread penetration of the Internet has made the access to codified knowledge much easier, and has lowered the value of physical interactions and enabled the fast-growing new economies, such as the sharing economy and the alternative finance economy.

Turning Challenges Into Opportunities

In order to achieve these projections, the policymakers need to turn challenges into opportunities. For example, they need to resist protectionism and open doors to global trade; insist that the benefits of globalization are inclusively shared across society; innovate on green technologies to ensure that environmentally sustainable global growth is achieved.

While the policymakers turn challenges into opportunities, winning them is the responsibility of the businesses. In particular, they should focus on the more attractive as consumer and business-to-business (B2B) markets; foreign businesses need flexible strategies to respond to local customer preferences and fast-changing local market dynamics; and overseas investors should patiently try to overcome any short-term economic and political volatility in the global South (PWC 2017).

Enhancing the ability of cities to adapt is a winning strategy and that is best achieved through the improvement of the cities' knowledge stock and by addressing the implications of industrial decline (Center for Cities 2015). Efforts should target the following: first, improve the skills of the workforce, especially the high-skilled workers. Second, encourage innovation to enable high-skilled workers to cluster in strategically located cities turning them into global engines of economic growth. Third, deal imaginatively with issues of industrial legacy by encouraging compact employment alongside with malfunctioning infrastructure upgrading. The emerged multicolored cities, whose economies are deeply rooted in the development of natural resources, human capital, and digital technologies, forms part of this surge in innovation (BCG 2018).

Formalizing the Informal Economy

The size and global distribution of the informal economy is important. In some countries, it contributes about 70% of the GDP and regional distribution shows that Sub-Saharan Africa has the median contribution to GDP is 40.5%, but 38.7% in Latin America, Asia 35.8%, and OECD countries 16.0% (Schneider et al., 2010). Its job creation capacity is estimated by (UNCTAD 2018) at 1.8 billion informal jobs, and growing to 2/3 of the workforce by 2020, compared to 1.2 million working under formal employment system.

Tackling the economic and social challenges embedded in formalizing the informal requires the combined efforts of all urban economic development actors. The public sector needs to focus attention in three broad areas: explaining formalization, ease the process, and demonstrate its benefits (UNCTAD 2018). *Explaining formalization* implies defining minimum expected standards; providing clear information about the process to follow; and ensuring that information reaches the targeted population in the markets, alleyways, shantytowns, and similar places. *Ease of formalization* process by simplify the procedures; simplify tax system to ensure cost-effective collection, and creating easy to follow schemes for the emerging entrepreneurs. *Benefits demonstration* requires articulation of the tangible and intangible impacts on the entrepreneurs, strengthen the benefits with an identifiable package of social goods, enforce compliance by nudging actors towards formalization; and collaborate with empowering services providers such as business support, health, training, and access to development finance.

Growth Potential

Human capital resources are central to the growth to meet the present and future needs of citizens for social, goods, services and solutions that require the effective use of social capital and social enterprises. Among the most suitable tools, is the formalization of informal activities as suggested above, but with a particular focus on urban slum redevelopment to formalize both the social and physical environments. The second component consists of innovative public sector initiatives that put greater policy emphasis on digitally enabled services, building expertise, encouraging SMEs to go global, supporting self-employment, and stimulating domestic consumption. Carefully analyzed and implemented these strategies will turn the citizen into active participants in their physical and digital environments, but also significant actors in the global system. For actors from the global South, perhaps their contribution to the global system can come through an innovative application of mobile technology in advancing social capital and the democratization of personal finance, learning, health, and community mobilization.

Grow With Technology

Digital technologies are generating constant flow services and solutions, as exemplified by the explosive growth in e-commerce, Alternative Finance, and MOOC. As the global population gets wealthier and the cities become smarter and more connected more digitally, urban economic growth will flow from the broadband. This section seeks to explore how this could unfold in the coming decades.

Growth Factors

As organizations seek growth through changing their focus from physical assets to a digital business model, they would need to consider which aspects of their business should be optimized to achieve their growth and digital objectives. Towards this end, a clear digital transformation strategy is important and Ben Rossi (2016) recommends the following drivers for digital transformation. First, the long-term impact of digitization is needed through training and educating of the workforce. Second, the role of the CIO need should be revised toward managing the digital transition, maintaining a sense of order and laying the foundations for the future of the business. Third, the cost vs value of data should be reflected through ensuring data protection to minimize the cost of data loss while enhancing the value achieved. Fourth, as business assurance is the lifeblood of digital transformation, it needs the support of complete IT visibility to ensure unique insights into operations. Fifth, the DevOps chaos theory should keep pace with the digital transformation moving not only the global market but also workforce, infrastructure, policy, and all benefits of the digital economy.

Impact of Smart Cities

Smart cities are urban areas that apply digital technology to enable urban actors to conduct their activities to enhance productivity, ensure costs and resource savings, while increase government-citizen interactions. These applications seek to promote knowledge and innovations, enhance workplaces, and use technology to advance society.

To illustrate the impact smart cities have, we discuss studies by Juniper (2017) and Statista (2018). Juniper (2017) analyzes and rank the cities based on their progress and potential across four citizen-focused time-saving quality of life indices. They are *mobility*- comprehensives of urban transport systems and solutions; *healthcare*:- citizen-focused healthcare service delivery; *public safety:* - city safety measures and enforcement services; and *productivity*:- city policies and technologies applied to enhance citizen productivity, democracy and wealth distribution. As shown in Table 5, the study emphasizes the place of Singapore as an undisputed smart city and includes in the top league other global South cities such as Seoul, Dubai, and Rio de Janeiro.

Focusing on the smart city market, *Statista* (2018) has developed a regularly updated statistical portal providing an overview of smart cities components including smartness in areas of governance, homes, industry and connected-industries, energy, construction, health, and smart transportation. In addition, it produces a ranking of global smart cities, the names of the top ten of which are shown in Table 6. The scores were based on various different smart components, including transport and mobility, sustainability, governance, innovation economy, digitalization, living standard, and expert perception. The list is dominated by European cities, and the global South is represented by Singapore.

Growth Potential

Amidst the increased application of digital technology, rapid population growth, and rapid urbanization, tremendous social and economic shift are underway in cities, nations and global regions. Yet informal activities continue in all nations, creating problems for many governments. Since technology carries some responsibilities for creating the problem, it can form part of the solution. For the global South,

Table 5. The top ten global city performance by index, 2017

Rank	Mobility	Health	Safety	Productivity
1	Singapore	Singapore	Singapore	Singapore
2	San Francisco	Seoul	New York	London
3	London	London	Chicago	Chicago
4	New York	Tokyo	Seoul	San Francisco
5	Barcelona	Berlin	Dubai	Berlin
6	Berlin	New York	Tokyo	New York
7	Chicago	San Francisco	London	Barcelona
8	Portland	Melbourne	San Francisco	Melbourne
9	Tokyo	Barcelona	Rio de Janeiro	Seoul
10	Melbourne	Chicago	Nice	Dubai
Source: Juniper (2017)				

Table 6. Leading smart cities worldwide in 2017

Smart Cities	Score index
Copenhagen (Denmark)	8.24
Singapore (Singapore).	7.83
Stockholm (Sweden).	7.82
Zurich (Switzerland).	7.77
Boston (USA).	7.75
Tokyo (Japan)	7.59
San Francisco (USA).	7.55
Amsterdam (Netherlands).	7.54
Geneva (Switzerland).	7.53
Melbourne (Australia)	7.51
Statista (2018)	

the prime candidate is the cost-effective and democratizing mobile technology. As a development tool, mobile technology is central to the process of formalizing the informal sector as discussed above.

It also has the potentials to promote growth in digitally enabled services, building expertise, encouraging small firms to go global, and supporting self-employment. The response could take the following forms. First, the promotion of digitally enabled services will be achieved through rapid flows of digital goods, foreign direct investments, and increased level of services that are expected in connected compact cities. As these cities grow in size, number, and smarter; and as more workers join the sharing and Gig economies, so will the volume of the digital services, which may benefit the emerging digital tools such as the Internet of Things and Blockchain technology. Second, the building of local experts will be in response to the rise in the demand and supply in the digital market, whose volume and speed of flows will increase both locally and internationally. All these will require millions of skilled workers to plan, produce, price, market, and manage these hubs. Third, encouraging small firms to go global may be achieved when the growing member of multinationals encourage local small firms to use their platforms as suppliers. Some of these may grow in size and market influence to emerge as regional or global players. Fourth, supporting self-employment in an increasingly Gig Economy is achievable as there is evidence worldwide that the size of the temporary workforce and the number freelance workers are increasing. For example, there are projections that by 2020 about 40% of US workers will be freelance and the Sharing economy will be worth $500billion (BCG 2018).

Table 7 synthesizes the suitable applications and the expected outcome of these urban economies worldwide, especially in the global South. The BRICS are Brazil, Russia, India, China and South Africa emerging nations that are followed by the MINT (Mexico, Indonesia, Nigeria, and Turkey) promising states.

DIRECTION FOR FUTURE RESEARCH AND CONCLUSION

Future Research

This chapter explored how public and private actors have collaborated to chart colorful economic growth by promoting new industrial systems or to decrease the negative effects of grey, brown and black economies in response to the high population growth and rapid urbanization that are influenced by disruptive

Table 7. The application and expected outcomes of the colored urban economies

Type of Economy		Suitable for Application	Expected Outcome
Natural Resource-based	Green	Resource-rich, liberal climate regions both coastal & hinterland; low or high lands e.g BRICS & MINT nations	Long- & short- benefits but needs sustainable use approach
	Blue	Islands & Coastal regions, Near large lakes; Near manmade waterways. Island nations in strategic locations	Long- & short- benefits but needs sustainable use approach. Long- lasting benefits if tech capital is used
	Brown	Regions with fast vegetation growth, whether coast or hinterland; low or high lands. Any nation suitably located	Medium- & Short-term benefits only, For long-term: Renewable energy is needed
Human Resource-based	Silver	Activity type & age of workforce suited to large skilled & capital intensive manpower, with middle class	Rapid and long-lasting if tech capital is also used.
	Grey	This is a growth stage related: BRICS, MINT & others with policies move informal to formal growth forces	Rapid and long-lasting if tech capital is used to transform negative to positive growth
	Black	Growth stage but needs strong govts to transform private to public wealth sources	Rapid and long-lasting if tech capital is used to transform negative to positive growth.
Technology-based Economies	Virtual	Suited to all nations with digital network, & with talented human capital	Long-lasting benefits if combined with Human & Natural Capitals
	White	Suited to all nations with digital network and creative & skilled human capital	Long-lasting benefits if combined with Human & Natural Capitals

digital technologies. Other influences such as increasing economic nationalism and social tensions triggered by international migration suggest that future research direction need to consider how to:

1. Exploit the opportunities offered to balance growth in the Green, Blue and Silver economies and concerns for sustainable social and environmental development
2. Find innovative ways to define and design community spaces within slum areas for collective innovation, life-long learning and community problem-solving activities seeking to transform Black and Brown economies and uplifting Grey economy.
3. Define the structure and process through which all levels of government concerned with policymaking and implementation should collaborate among and between them and other levels to ensure the inclusive transformation of urban economies for the greater good.
4. Manage the transformation of Virtual and White Economies by creating urban databases and developing the effective policy instruments at national, local and community levels
5. Define new policies and tools that can be most effective in serving the needs of economies in the global North of the aging population and that of the global South of a youthful population.
6. Enable maker cities to develop from the bottom-up using the talent and innovative powers of slum dwellers and the crowd-sourced collaboration from the like-minded citizens.

CONCLUSION

The full impact of the high population growth and rapid urbanization global economy may be decades off, nonetheless governments at various level- especially in the global South- need to have the foresight to prepare their multi-colored urban economies and workforces for the tasks and opportunities that await them ahead. With the support of innovative enterprises as creative communities, governments should exploit the digitally integrated multi-colored urban economies by placing high policy emphasis on digitally embedded services, promoting local expertise, nurturing innovative firms, scaling up self-employed, and boosting domestic demand, among other innovative measures.

REFERENCES

ACCA. (2017). *Emerging from the shadows: the shadow economy to 2025*. Retrieved from https://www.accaglobal.com/content/dam/ACCA_Global/Technical/Future/pi-shadow- economy-report.pdf

Benna, U. G. (1997). Societal Values in development process: Place-making in Sokoto, Nigeria. In A. Awotona & N. Teymur (Eds.), *Tradition, Location and Community: Place-makin and Development* (pp. 173–187). Aldershot, UK: Averbury.

Benna, U. G. (2013). *Timbuktu, the African Medieval Knowledge City: The Role of Knowledge Development Actors*. Retrieved from http://www.worldscientific.com/doi/abs/10.1142/S0219649213500263

Boston Consulting Group. (2018). *Why Countries Need New Job Creation Strategies*. Retrieved from https://www.bcg.com/publications/2018/new-globalization-why-countries-need-new-job-creation-strategies.aspx

Brown, D. (2017). *Challenging the conceptual boundaries of the compact city paradigm in sub-Saharan Africa*. Retrieved from https://www.ucl.ac.uk/bartlett/development/case- studies/2017/mar/challengin-conceptual-boundaries-compact-city-paradigm-sub-saharan-africa

Burkart, K. (2009). How do you define the 'green' economy? *MNN: Mother Nature Network*. Retrieved from https://www.mnn.com/green-tech/research-innovations/blogs/how-do-you-define-the-green-economy

Calbreath, D. (2010). *Hidden economy a hidden danger*. Retrieved from http://www.sandiegouniontribune.com/sdut-hidden-economy-a-hidden-danger- 2010may30-story.html

Center for Cities. (2015). *A century of cities Urban economic change since 1911*. Retrieved from http://www.centreforcities.org/wp-content/uploads/2015/03/15-03-04-A-Century-of- Cities.pdf

CGTN. (2017). Real economy VS. *Virtual Economy*. Retrieved from http://en.ccg.org.cn/cgtn-dialogue-real-economy- vs-virtual-economy/

Charmes, J. (2001). *Informal Sector, Poverty And Gender A Review Of Empirical Evidence*. Retrieved from http://www.wiego.org/sites/default/files/publications/files/Charmes-Informal-Sector- Poverty.pdf

Colenbrander, S. (2016). *Cities as engines of economic growth*. Retrieved from http://pubs.iied.org/pdfs/10801IIED.pdf

Collier, P. (2007). *The Bottom Billion: Why the Poorest Countries are Failing and What Can Be Done About It*. London: Oxford University Press.

Dan, M. B., & Crăciun, C. (2016). *Space and Time Visualisation*. Retrieved from https://books.google.com.sa/books?isbn=3319249428

Deichmann, U. (2013). *Growing Green: The Economic Benefits of Climate Action (interview)*. Retrieved from http://www.worldbank.org/en/news/video/2013/06/25/uwe-deichmann-growing-green-interview

DeSoto, H. (2000). *The mystery of capital: Why capitalism triumphs in the west and fails everywhere else*. New York: Basic Books.

Duranton, G. (2008). *Cities: Engines of Growth and Prosperity for Developing Countries?* Retrieved from https://openknowledge.worldbank.org/handle/10986/28044

ECA. (2017). *Urbanization And Industrialization For Africa's Transformation*. Retrieved from https://www.uneca.org/sites/default/files/PublicationFiles/web_en_era-2017_01.pdf

Economic Commission for Africa (ECA). (2016). *Africa's Blue Economy: A policy handbook*. Retrieved from https://www.uneca.org/publications/africas-blue-economy-policy-handbook

ECOSOC. (2018). *About Us*. Retrieved from https://www.un.org/ecosoc/en/about-us

FAO. (2012). *Greening The Economy With Agriculture*. Retrieved from http://www.fao.org/3/a-ar585e.pdf

Feige, E. L. (Ed.). (1989). *The Underground Economies:Tax Evasion and Information Distortion*. London: Cambridge University Press. doi:10.1017/CBO9780511571749

Fujita, K. (2013). *Introduction: Cities and Crisis: New Critical Urban Theory*. Retrieved from http://sk.sagepub.com/books/cities-and-crisis/n1.xml

GIZ. (2012). *Green Economy in Sub-Saharan Africa – Lessons from Benin, Ethiopia, Ghana, Namibia and Nigeria*. Retrieved from www.greengrowthknowledge.org/resource/green-economysub-saharan-africa-lessons-benin-ethiopia-ghana-namibia-andnigeria

Global Parliament of Mayors (GPM). (2018). Retrieved from https://globalparliamentofmayors.org/program-2018/

Gordon, C. (2017). *A Silver Economy: The value of living longer*. Retrieved from https://www.smart-growthbop.org.nz/media/2034/silver-economy-report-final- a8179931-compressed-002-a8694352.pdf

Govers, R., & Go, F. (2016). *Place Branding: Glocal, Virtual and Physical Identities, Constructed, Imagined and Experienced*. Retrieved from https://books.google.com.sa/books?isbn=0230247024

IMF. (2012). *Going Green*. Retrieved from http://www.imf.org/external/pubs/ft/fandd/2012/06/eyraud.htm

IMF. (2018). *Changing Wealth of Nations: Building a Sustainable Future*. Retrieved from https://open-knowledge.worldbank.org/handle/10986/29001

Infodev. (2018). *About Us*. Retrieved from http://www.infodev.org/

International Energy Agency (IEA). (2006). *World Energy Outlook: Energy For Cooking In Developing*. Retrieved from https://www.iea.org/publications/freepublications/publication/cooking.pdf

International Telecommunication Union (ITU). (2018). *About ITU*. Retrieved from https://www.itu.int/en/about/Pages/default.aspx

Juniper. (2017). *Smart cities – what's in it for citizens?* Retrieved from https://newsroom.intel.com/wp-content/uploads/sites/11/2018/03/smart-cities-whats-in-it-for-citizens.pdf

Karlenzig, W., Zhenhua, Z., & Peck, M. (2017). *Transforming the Urban Economy*. Retrieved from http://www.un.org/esa/dsd/susdevtopics/sdt_pdfs/shanghaimanual/Chapter%203%20- %20Economic%20 transformation.pdf

McWilliams, D. (2015). *The Flat White Economy: How the Digital Economy Is Transforming London and Other Cities of the Future*. London: Duckworth Publishers.

Melonakos, B. (2011). *Informal Economy*. Retrieved from http://pubs.iied.org/pdfs/10722IIED.pdf

Mogalakwe, M. (2006). The Use of Documentary Research Methods in Social Research. *African Sociological Review*, *10*(1), 221–230.

Neuwirth, R. (2005). Shadow Cities: A Billion Squatters, a New Urban World. New York: Routledge.

Obaidat, M. S., & Nicopolitidis, P. (2016). *Smart Cities and Homes: Key Enabling Technologies*. Retrieved from https://books.google.com.sa/books?isbn=0128034637

OECD. (2010). *Shining Light on the Shadow Economy: Opportunities and Threats*. Retrieved from https://www.oecd.org/tax/crime/shining-light-on-the-shadow-economy-opportunities- and-threats.pdf

OECD. (2017). *Employment Implications of Green Growth: Linking jobs, growth, and green policies*. Retrieved from https://www.oecd.org/environment/Employment-Implications-of-Green-Growth-OECD-Report

Picon, A. (2015). *Smart Cities: A Spatialised Intelligence*. London: John Wiley & Sons. doi:10.1002/9781119075615

Pinto, N. N. (2013). *Technologies for Urban and Spatial Planning: Virtual Cities and Territories: Virtual Cities and Territories*. Retrieved from https://books.google.com.sa/books?isbn=1466643501

PWC. (2017). *Future: Shifts in global Urbanization & Economic Orders by 2050*. Retrieved from https://www.pwc.com/gx/en/issues/economy/the-world-in-2050.html

Rodríguez-Bolívar, M. P. (Ed.). (2015). *Transforming City Governments for Successful Smart Cities*. Retrieved from https://www.springer.com/gp/book/9783319031668

Schneider, Buehn, & Monteneg. (2010). *Shadow Economies 1999 to 2007*. Retrieved from http://www.gfintegrity.org/storage/gfip/documents/reports/world_bank_shadow_econ omies_all_over_the_world.pdf

Siemens. (2012). *The Green City Index A summary of the Green City Index research series*. Author.

Statista. (2018). *Leading digital agency networks worldwide in 2017*. Retrieved from https://www.statista.com/statistics/466411/digital-agency-networks/

Stockholm Environment Institute (SEI). (2009). *Economics of Climate Change in Kenya*. A SEI Project Report.

UN-Habitat. (2009). *Global Report on Human Settlements 2009: Planning Sustainable Cities*. Retrieved from https://unhabitat.org/books/global-report-on-human-settlements-2009-planning- sustainable-cities/

UN-Habitat. (2010). *State of the World's Cities 2010/2011- Cities for All*. Retrieved from https://unhabitat.org/books/state-of-the-worlds-cities-20102011-cities-for-all-bridging-the-urban-divide/

UN-Habitat. (2011). *Cities and Climate Change: Global Report on Human Settlements 2011*. Retrieved from https://unhabitat.org/books/cities-and-climate-change-global-report-on-human- settlements-2011/

UN-Habitat. (2018). *At a Glance*. Retrieved from https://unhabitat.org/un-habitat-at-a-glance/

UN-Regional Commissions. (2018). Retrieved from http://www.regionalcommissions.org/

UNCTAD. (2018). *How to formalize the informal sector: Make formalization easy and desirable*. Retrieved from https://businessfacilitation.org/assets/documents/pdf/formalizing-the-informal- sector.pdf

UNCTAD. (2018). *How to formalize the informal sector: Make formalization easy and desirable*. Retrieved from https://businessfacilitation.org/assets/documents/pdf/formalizing-the- informal-sector.pdf

UNDESA. (2014). *World Urbanization Prospects, 2014*. Author.

UNDESA. (2018). *Revision of World Urbanization Prospects*. Retrieved from https://www.un.org/development/desa/publications/2018-revision-of-world-urbanization- prospects.html

UNEP. (2012). *Global Environment Outlook 3*. Retrieved from https://wedocs.unep.org/bitstream/handle/20.500.11822/8609/GEO-3%20REPORT_English.pdf?sequence=7&isAllowed=y

UNESCAP. (2011). *Economic and Social Survey of Asia and the Pacific 2011*. Retrieved from https://www.unescap.org/resources/economic-and-social-survey-asia-and-pacific-2011

Vavrek, R., & Chovancova, J. (2016). *Decoupling of Greenhouse Gas Emissions from Economic Growth in V4 Countries*. Retrieved from https://www.sciencedirect.com/science/article/pii/S2212567116302957

Watson, V. (2009). *Seeing from the South: Refocusing Urban Planning on the Globe's Central Urban Issues*. Retrieved from https://www.jstor.org/stable/43198476?seq=1#page_scan_tab_contents

Wikipedia. (2018a). *List of IT Consulting Firms*. Retrieved from https://en.wikipedia.org/wiki/List_of_IT_consulting_firms

Wikipedia. (2018b). *Grey market goods are legal, non-counterfeit goods sold outside normal distribution channels*. Author.

World Bank. (2000). *Attacking Poverty*. Retrieved from https://openknowledge.worldbank.org/handle/10986/11856

World Bank. (2010). *Development and Climate Change*. Retrieved from https://siteresources.worldbank.org/INTWDR2010/Resources/5287678- 1226014527953/WDR10-

World Bank. (2018). *The Changing Wealth of Nations*. Author.

World Bank Group. (2017). *Doing Business in 2018*. Retrieved from http://www.doingbusiness.org/reports/global-reports/doing-business-2018

World Resources Institute. (2018). *What We Do*. Retrieved from http://www.wri.org/

World Steel Association. (2010). *Steel Statistical Yearbook 2010*. Retrieved from https://www.worldsteel.org/en/dam/jcr:1ef195b3-1a46-41c2-b88b-6072c2687850/Steel+statistical+yearbook+2010.pdf

World Wide Fund (WWF). (2010). *Biodiversity Loss And The Human Footprint*. Retrieved from https://www.footprintnetwork.org/content/images/uploads/CBD_2010_and_Beyond.pdf

Wu, W. (2005). *Dynamic Cities and Creative Clusters*. Retrieved from http://documents.worldbank.org/curated/en/441151468762563308/pdf/WPS3509.pdf

KEY TERMS AND DEFINITIONS

Colorful Economies: Urban economies that are based natural resources are characterized by green, blue, and silver colors; the human capital-based economies are described as black, brown, and grey; and the technology-based economies are defined as virtual and white.

Formalization: The processes of transforming informal activity or enterprise into formal types through public policy and a regulatory instrument designed to boost urban growth.

Global North: The more socio-economically developed global regions in North America, Western Europe, Japan, and others.

Global South: The less socio-economically developed global regions in Africa, Latin America, Asia, and the Middle East.

Informal: Any diversified set of socio-economic activity, enterprise, and worker that is unregulated or unprotected by the state.

Population Growth: The increase in the number of individuals in the population on city, nation, or region.

Rapid Urbanization: The speed at which the population shifts from rural to urban residency and how society adapts to this change.

Chapter 2
Avatar-Based Supply Chain Management as Expert Knowledge for Smart Solutions:
Creating Sustainable Urban Systems

Svetlana Panasenko
Plekhanov Russian University of Economics, Russia

Irina Potapova
Astrakhan State Architecture and Construction University, Russia

Lubov Belyanina
Astrakhan State University, Russia

Liliya Rozhkova
Penza State University, Russia

Dina Kharicheva
Moscow Pedagogical State University, Russia

Vardan Mkrttchian
https://orcid.org/0000-0003-4871-5956
HHH University, Australia

Alexander Bershadsky
Penza State University, Russia

ABSTRACT

This chapter discusses issues related to managing the avatar-based supply chains as expert knowledge for smart solutions in creating sustainable urban systems. Avatar-based supply chains as expert knowledge is a new term that describes the planning, search, production, distribution, and delivery of Mkrttchian's digital avatars from the place of origin to consumption. These supply chains are very different from traditional ones because they relate to a specific product-expert knowledge, which is created through electronic data distributed on the internet between business partners and value-added service providers operating in a general digital economy paradigm using blockchain technologies. This chapter focuses on the analysis of business relations and this integration into sustainable urban systems.

DOI: 10.4018/978-1-5225-7625-9.ch002

INTRODUCTION

As you know, issues related to planning, search, production, distribution and delivery, from the place where these products and services were created to the place of their consumption are expressed by the term Supply Chain Management (SCM). Currently, this term is a promised standard that is officially accepted when managing in the supply chain all the physical and informational flows of materials made of finished products and goods. Modern SCM ones consist of popular business processes that are implemented only by the latest technologies and innovative solutions. The main goal SCM is to be highly efficient and rational with the mind of supply management so that the right product or product is available where you need it, in time, and the price must be reasonable.

SCM is implemented as a technology that includes various sensors, including artificial intelligence, performing machine learning with cognitive computing, which makes it possible to have constant analytics and transformation between the cyber-physical real environment and the digital space. In fact, SCM provides the transformation of traditional linear supply chains into intelligent, scalable, customizable, and fast delivery networks based on digital transformations. But in order for the technology to work, two more components are needed: the correct economic business models that, under the conditions of the digital economy, form part of it under the name of a joint economy and mechanisms for providing trusted relations in business that are grouped around the ecosystem of blockage or Internet values. This chapter discusses issues related to managing the supply chains of avatar-based as an expert knowledge for smart solutions in creates sustainable urban systems. The supply chains of avatar-based as the expert knowledge is a new term that describes the planning, search, production, distribution and delivery of Mkrttchian's digital avatars from the place of origin to consumption (Mkrttchian, & Alershina, 2017). These supply chains are very different from traditional ones because they relate to a specific product-expert knowledge, which is created through electronic data distributed on the Internet between business partners and value-added service providers operating in a general digital economy paradigm using blockchain technologies. This chapter focuses on the analysis of business relations and this integration into sustainable urban systems. The supply chains of the 21st century are more complex and dynamic than ever before. How effectively and profitable companies can plan, deliver their products to customers - this is what separates industry leaders from the laggards. For companies that determine the real value of the business and the results in today's competitive global economy, they need to improve the management of several aspects of their business, such as inventory, costs, assets and the introduction of new products. And this, of course, cannot happen without the best in its class digital supply chain, which, working together with the technology of the block, will transform the world of modern logistics. Even the largest organizations lack the capacity, resources and knowledge to deploy end-to-end information integration in their supply networks that actually form a network. A supply chain network consists of many components, or supply chain nodes, that are connected through flow paths. Inventory and products - and information - along these flow paths to various supply chain nodes have the ultimate goal of ensuring that customers' needs are realized in the most beneficial way. Now governments and companies have an urgent need to cooperate to accelerate such integration within the framework of the Digital Supply Chain (DSC) concept, using the principles of joint economy and blockbuster technology. Collaboration in the DSC is a multi-stakeholder environment with different needs and objectives in which large companies are seen as those that are integrating with their main suppliers. Even competing companies are forced to cooperate to integrate the entire supply chain. Value-added service providers play different roles, but those cooperating with common interests should establish a trusted environment and systems through an information organization of the basic principles of this cooperation. For the success of this kind of joint activity, DSC should offer the company competitive advantages: intermediate products must be quickly integrated, logistics partners must make deliveries using the tracking and visibility functions; and information and communication technologies (ICT). Joint activities are possible only on the basis of expert knowledge, which can only be supplied Mkrttchian's digital avatars.

Within the framework of the Fourth Industrial Revolution, not only the list of end-to-end technologies is changing, but thinking and methodological approaches to the development of jerk scenes are radically transformed, which is especially noticeable in the sphere of urban economy - into sustainable urban systems. It is obvious that the actively recovering industry in the coming years will become one of the main drivers of economic growth in Russia, which will have an impact on into sustainable urban systems. The main driver of breakthrough development in these conditions will be promising fast-growing industrial companies that have the highest leadership potential on both the Russian and global markets. These are domestic private high-tech export-oriented companies, leaders in terms of development rates, potential participants of Russian-based transnational companies. In 2016 - 2017 years. Within the rating of Texas, 62 such companies were selected (Mkrttchian, et al, 2019). In 2018 it is planned to select an additional 30 companies. Despite the fact that the program "Digital Economy of the Russian Federation", the Strategy for Scientific and Technological Development of the Russian Federation, the National Technological Initiative, road maps have been developed, the "Digital Industry" program is being prepared, the priority project "National Champions" is being implemented, it should be recognized that there are no specific mechanisms and scenarios for implementing breakthrough development in priority industries. It is these circumstances that determine the relevance of the research in this chapter.

BACKGROUND

The advantages of Mkrttchian's digital avatars (Mkrttchian, et al, 2019) include profitability of services and the creation of value of joint activities that are beneficial to many ecosystem entities, including firms and their suppliers, employees and customers will be discussed below. According to Mkrttchian, (Mkrttchian, et al, 2019) the digital avatar supply chain can be defined as a set of avatars of three or more subjects (i.e. organizations or individuals) directly involved in downstream flows of products, services, finance, and / or transfer of information from source to client. This definition emphasizes the role of information flows between firms, especially in business and business areas and process levels. A digital avatar of Mkrttchian (Mkrttchian, et al, 2019) refers to the software industry or to the development of programs. As in any production, there are tools in programming that allow you to produce certain parts (blocks), platforms (development environments) for assembly, operating conditions, testing and product life cycle. And of course the combination of the virtual, digital and physical worlds that were published in the IGI Global publishing house in 2010-2018.

Since the governments of all countries today absolutely strictly support open source software development, Mkrttchian's digital avatars are written exactly with this code. The main reasons for this are to avoid software silos or create closed systems for interaction, to take advantage of the economic advantages of open source code and to clearly represent security issues. Open Source Software (OSS) is a computer software with its source code available with a license in which the copyright owner grants the rights to study, modify and distribute the software to anyone and for any purpose. Open source software can be developed in conjunction with the public. According to scientists who studied it, open source software is a prime example of open collaboration. Development of open source software or joint development from several independent sources creates an increasingly diverse field of design than any company that can develop and maintain a long-term perspective. And this is also one of the phenomena of a joint digital economy with its own and very significant indicators.

The transition to advanced digital, intelligent production technologies, robotic systems, new materials and design methods, the creation of systems for processing large amounts of data, machine learning and artificial intelligence. The foundations of the formation and development of industrial enterprises are set forth in the works of domestic scientists: e.g. Abalkin (2018), Alaev (2017), Batkovsky (2018), Bukharin (2017), Vorobyov (2016), Quint and Klimov (2017), Kostyukhin (2018), Myaskov and Sviridova (2018), Sirotkina (2016), Filatov, Fomina and Shestov (2018), Yasin (2018) etc. The systematization of the work of these scientists revealed the need to develop a conceptual framework for a methodology for managing the development of industrial enterprises at different levels. The problems of the new economic policy, the reindustrialization of industrial production are devoted to the works of Balashov, Belozerova, and Bodrunov (2018), Buzgalina, Bukhvalov, Bushmin, Valente, and Vertakova (2018), Greenberg, Dubenetsky, Karlik, and Kleiner (2018), Kolganova, Krasnyuk, Martyanova, Nevskaya, Osipova, Plotnikov (2018), Pobyvaeva, Romanova, Sorokin, Sukhareva, and Tatarkin (2018), Tolkachev, Tyukavkin, Shuisky,and Yudina (2017), and others.

The world experience of transition to a digital economy is described in the works of domestic scientists S. Glazyev (2017), Ivanova, Krivosheeva, Kuznetsov, Kurdyumov, and Malinetsky (2017), Medovnikov (2018), etc. Foreign authors, who formed theoretical ideas about the digital economy, became Bekert (2016), Brinjolfsson 2018), Cohen, Coleman, and Coyle (2017), X. Fu, K. Fun, and I. Hu (2018), Hoeves, Cahin, Leidner, and McLean (2016), Tapscott (2015), Terranova (2016), Samuelson (2017), Scholz, Smith, and Turban (2018), Wetherb (2017) and others. Questions of Industry 4.0 - the concept, which is an element of the fourth industrial revolution, within the framework of which the digital economy is realized in industry and digital production, are such scientists and researchers as Alexandrov, and Babkin (2018), Borovkov (2017), Schwab (2017), Schmid (2016), Venkatesh (2017), Mkrttchian (2011-2018) and others. Examples and analyzes of successful digital transformations are outlined in a significant number of published works on the digitization of the economy: Dobrynin, and Kupriyanovsky (2018), Namiot (2018), and others. The accumulated experience of research shows that it is from transformations or transformations of specific areas and businesses in the country that the volume of GDP of the digital economy is growing and developing, grow digital leaders.

Recognizing the high importance of the research conducted by these scientists and noting the existence of fundamental approaches to the disclosure of certain aspects of the issues under consideration, it should be noted that at the present time the key characteristics of the management of the development of industrial fast-growing enterprises have not been thoroughly investigated and theoretically substantiated, the system of development of such enterprises under conditions of reindustrialization and digitalization, the modeling and forecasting of the scientific and technological development of the in relation to the activities of industrial national champions, the scenarios for the development of industrial gazelles are unclear. In this connection, there is a need to supplement the theoretical and methodological foundations, scientific and methodological support, as well as clarify the goals, scenarios, benchmarks and KPI breakthrough development of fast-growing industrial enterprises and urban systems.

MAIN FOCUS OF THE CHAPTER

Issues, Controversies, Problems

The purpose of this chapter is to achieve a global competitiveness in high-tech markets by dynamic industrial enterprises, increase labor productivity, improve the quality of life of the population, create innovative and active human capital, and increase the number of people employed in non-primary sectors by developing methodological bases and corresponding theoretical and practical tools for developing and implementing scenarios of breakthrough development. As a result of the analysis of Issues, Controversies, Problems, we established that the main focus of our chapter will be directed to the following tasks, which will determine the purpose of our research. The purpose of the research in this chapter is predetermined the need for the formulation and solution of the following tasks:

1. To form the original concept of managing fast-growing industrial enterprises for the purpose of breakthrough development and technological breakthrough in the entire Russian industry.
2. To develop a methodology and principles for the breakthrough development of fast-growing industrial enterprises in conditions of digital transformation.
3. To propose a conceptual model and management system for the breakthrough development of fast-growing industrial enterprises.
4. To carry out a synergetic modeling of the breakthrough scientific and technological development of companies - national champions.
5. To substantiate the benchmarks, develop and test scenarios for the breakthrough development of fast-growing industrial enterprises.
6. To offer a compliance-management system for the problems-calls of industrial enterprises.
7. Propose the procedure for the introduction of digital counterparts and on their basis digital shadows in industrial enterprises.
8. Develop and test the methodology for assessing the KPI breakthrough development of fast-growing industrial enterprises.
9. Develop a program for the digital transformation of industrial enterprises.
10. The focuses on the analysis of business relations and this integration into sustainable urban systems. The supply chains of the 21st century are more complex and dynamic than ever before.

The goal of clearly articulating these tasks, according to the authors, is to help readers understand the logic of the decisions made, and if necessary, readers can refer to the list of additional readings.

Open source software has long become a ubiquitous industrial production and business. There is, for example, a tremendous amount and variety of open-source software components and third-party components that arise in every software development environment in the world. With proper use and management, these components are a huge source of energy to accelerate innovation in the digital economy. Otherwise, they are directly related to security vulnerabilities, licensing risks, huge improvements and wastes, as in any production. The digital avatars of Mkrttchian's are work only on the basis of expert knowledge. Components are delivered to organizations through supply chain software that work is with many parallel traditional production supply chains. Therefore, a huge network of component suppliers creates 1000 new projects and provides 10,000 new versions per day. The software industry has already produced as many as tens of millions of products and their number is continuously increasing. Within it,

OSS has the largest growth dynamics. The number of employees in the software industry is enormous and is estimated at tens and hundreds of millions of people. But the laws of reducing costs and improving profitability are also valid in it. We need new innovative technologies and, in structure, they should resemble a system of blockchain.

The scientific novelty of the research is the development of theoretical and practical approaches to the construction of scenarios for the breakthrough development of fast-growing industrial companies, the implementation of which will provide the necessary scientific and technological and socio-economic breakthrough in priority and promising in the context of new markets industries of Russian industry

The methodological basis for the study is the integration of the systemic and synergetic approaches, taking into account the most important dialectical regularities. The basis of this approach is the methodology of system analysis, which serves as a methodological framework combining all the necessary methods, research methods, activities and resources to solve the research problem. System analysis organizes our knowledge of the problem in such a way as to help choose the best strategy for its solution or to predict the results of several alternative strategies that seem appropriate to eliminate the contradictions that gave rise to the above-mentioned research problem. In the framework of the system approach, it is proposed to use the method of systemic potential as one of the methods of system dynamics, used to study complex adaptive systems, adapting it to study the development processes in the economic system. Theoretical and methodological basis of the research will be general scientific empirical-theoretical methods of system analysis, abstraction, analysis and synthesis, induction and deduction, analogy, modeling, concretization, historical and logical methods of research. Specific scientific methods will be applied to continuous and selective observation, expert methods, content analysis, cluster analysis, methods of detailing, comparative, factor and correlation-regression analysis, optimal solution method, predictive extrapolation method, mathematical apparatus of genetic algorithms, SimBrain neural simulator, the software product IBM SPSS Statistics Subscription, as well as standard (Evolver and Risk companies Palisade Corp.) and the original add-ins MS Excel.

The study of the processes of interaction of economic agents in the economic system necessitates the use of a neo-institutional approach, which makes it possible to institutionalize the basic incentive to strengthen the interaction of economic agents, namely, the level of transaction costs of economic activity. Reducing the level of transaction costs for economic activities, provided by the digitization of social and economic processes, will increase the efficiency of the functioning of formal institutions, and will enable the unrealized potential of the economic system to be used. Ultimately, the achievement of the optimal level of costs of economic activity will make it possible to launch the process of self-development of socio-economic systems. Thus, the use of the system approach will allow to correctly structure and establish the relationships between the elements and development factors, and also to identify bottlenecks in the development of the economic system. The synergetic approach will make it possible to take into account the dynamic aspect of the development of the innovation system, such categories as the growing complexity, uncertainties, etc., which are inalienable, which are inherent attributes of economic activity, and allows it, on the basis of cooperative interaction of its participants, to generate new criteria, components and structures that facilitate the adaptation of the system to changing conditions.

Within the framework of this methodological approach, dialectical methods of cognition will also be used, providing a comprehensive and objective character of the study of the problem, logical, structural-functional, strategic, evolutionary, factor analysis, modeling, economic-statistical and other methods.

At all stages of the study, the use of the content analysis method with appropriate tools will be appropriate. For the analysis of foreign experience, historical and logical methods of research will be used. The basis of theoretical methods is the methods of organization and functioning of systems with one of the most powerful methods of adaptation - self-organization. To collect information from economic agents on the level of transaction costs of economic activity, it is proposed to use sociological research methods. The tools for conducting a survey will be a poll program, the design of a representative sample, and the form of the questionnaire. For the assessment of transaction costs, mathematical models of fuzzy logic and metric are supposed to be used. This is necessary to evaluate the various in nature and essence of both quantitative and qualitative factors and parameters under conditions of nonlinearity and uncertainty (under conditions of ambiguous, asymmetric information). Metric methods provide the opportunity to carry out measurements under such conditions.

SOLUTIONS AND RECOMMENDATIONS

The mathematical apparatus of the theory of fuzzy sets provides new tools and possibilities for processing qualitative factors and parameters that have high uncertainty. The analysis of the collected empirical data will be carried out using the IBM SPSS Statistics application package.

Thus, the use of the integration of a number of methodological approaches to the research problem presents in aggregate a constructive tool that allows to solve the problems posed in the study:

1. The original author's concept of managing fast-growing industrial enterprises, containing classification characteristics and content characteristics, to ensure global, innovative, inclusive, proactive and sustainable breakthrough development of Russian industry.
2. Methodology for managing the breakthrough development of fast-growing industrial enterprises on the basis of laws and development principles, which includes a set of theoretical foundations in terms of hypotheses, applied theories and basic approaches, basic organizational and management mechanisms and basic efficiency assessments.
3. Conceptual model and management system for the breakthrough development of fast-growing industrial enterprises at mega-, macro-, meso- and microlevels, which allows preparing all actors of the ecosystem for effective sustainable development in accordance with the goals set.
4. Multi-variant scenario design of scientific, technological and socio-economic breakthrough development of fast-growing industrial enterprises of the Russian Federation until 2035 with justification of reference points and bifurcation zones, which helps to adjust the development option taking into account the comparison of resource projection and the projection of development results.
5. Compliance-system of management of problems-calls of the industrial enterprises, allowing the companies to resist "the big calls" and to manage the risks inevitably arising at realization of breakthrough development.
6. The procedure for the introduction of digital doubles integrated into the platform ecosystem and on their basis digital shadows in key industries as a priority direction of development under conditions of digital transformation that will allow consolidating the participants of industrial markets with the aim of introducing technological innovations.
7. The program of digital transformation of industrial enterprises as a set of key initiatives, activities and their results, including the ways of strategic development on the basis of a combination of organizational forms of activity, increased activity, development of integration.

8. Methodology for assessing KPI breakthrough development of fast-growing industrial enterprises, which allows you to measure the level of achievement of goals, identify weaknesses, conduct benchmarking at the global level.
9. Develop a structure and form an analytical review of the research problem. The analytical review should contain:
    a. Theme, subject, object, nature, purpose and objectives of the work;
    b. Systematization of information about the problem under study (key tasks, known positions, theories, premises, etc.) from the standpoint of reliability, doubtfulness, controversy;
    c. Review of scientific information sources on the subject of the problem under study;
    d. A description of the methods of performing the work;
    e. An analytical reference on the results of a review of scientific information sources on the subject of the problem under study, including at least 50 publications from domestic sources and 100 foreign publications, mostly published during the period 2013-2018.
10. Identification and justification of digitalization trends for the period up to 2030, a list of end-to-end technologies for the potential for making a technological breakthrough.
11. Determination of the rating positions of Russian industrial enterprises at the global level, global benchmarking, identification of best practices and best-in-class solutions.
12. Research of fast-developing high-tech companies in Russia. Drawing up a portrait of the company - the national champion on the basis of the analysis of the rating, the identification of fast-growing industrial companies (gazelles). 13. Comparison of the contribution of small, medium and large businesses to the growth of the economy in the Russian Federation.
13. Identification of drivers and inhibitors of breakthrough development in industrial companies.
14. Research of world and Russian experience of development of corporate accelerators.
15. Research of the best practices of innovation management in Russian companies.
16. Analysis of the market for direct and venture angel investments in industrial companies in Russia.
17. Research of behavioral and institutional preconditions of technological development.
18. Investigation of the economy as a socio-economic phenomenon.
19. Formation of the conceptual foundations for the creation of an enabling environment and a mature ecosystem for the purpose of breakthrough development and technological breakthrough by industrial companies.
20. Research of global practices of commercialization of technologies at different stages.
21. Development of a methodological approach to assessing the level of scientific and technological development of fast-growing industrial enterprises.
22. Development of a methodology for assessing the global competitiveness of fast-growing industrial enterprises.
23. Development of a methodological approach to assessing the potential for the formation of multinational Russian-based companies on the basis of fast-growing industrial enterprises.
24. Development of the original author's concept of managing fast-growing industrial enterprises for the purposes of breakthrough development and accomplishment of a technological breakthrough, containing classification characteristics and content characteristics.
25. Formation of a methodology for managing the breakthrough development of fast-growing industrial enterprises on the basis of laws and development principles, which includes a set of theoretical foundations in terms of hypotheses, applied theories and basic approaches, basic organizational and management mechanisms and basic efficiency assessments.

26. Development of a conceptual model and management system for the development of fast-growing industrial enterprises at mega-, macro-, meson- and micro levels.

All the tasks we have solved are solved using digital avatars (Mkrttchian and Aleshina, 2017). Digital Mkrttchian's avatars, more precisely the expert knowledge generated by them, enable each member of the network, called a node, to contain a chain of blocks that makes up the history of transactions performed on the network. Each block contains a set of transactions, the size of which depends on how many banks and financial institutions do not actually have an API, or have a very truncated form. Also, any financial system faces the risk of non-fulfillment or disputing by the parties of the transaction of payments made. Avoid these risks can involve a qualified financial intermediary, which checks the transaction and takes some of the risks. To solve this problem, all kinds of organizations were created: banks, clearing systems, depositories, financial information transfer systems such as Reuters or SWIFT. However, the use of intermediaries leads to a significant increase in the cost and slowdown of calculations. International transactions on time can last up to seven days. In the banking sector, there are obvious serious contradictions between the established traditional business and modern innovative technologies. These contradictions in the very near future cardinally reformat the financial market. And expertise will replace the financial intermediary and create a transaction and transfer it to the network. the transaction message includes information on the public address of the recipient, the transaction value and the digital signature, which proves the authenticity of the transaction. Nodes (computers / users) of the network, after receiving the message, confirm the authenticity and validity of the message by decrypting the digital signature. An authenticated transaction is placed in the "pool" of pending transactions. Nodes (computers / users) of the network, after receiving the message, confirm the authenticity and validity of the message by decrypting the digital signature. An authenticated transaction is placed in the "pool" of pending transactions. The nodes of the network validator receive the proposed block and work on its verification through an iterative process, which requires consensus in most networks. If digital avatars are implemented, they ensure that each transaction is valid and fraudulent transactions are not possible. If all transactions are verified, the new block - the forming expert knowledge is "chained" to the block chain (block box), and the new current status of the registrar is transferred to the network. The entire process can be completed in 3-10 seconds. "

Smart Solutions to Create Sustainable Urban Systems Use Expert Knowledge

The developed system allows to solve the following tasks based on the use of expert knowledge:

1. Assessment of the advantages and disadvantages of the institutional environment, the national economy and the legal system, and preparation of proposals on ways and mechanisms for improvement.
2. Substantiation of benchmarks of breakthrough development of dynamic industrial enterprises of medium-sized businesses.
3. Development of scenarios for the breakthrough development of fast-growing industrial enterprises. Implementation of the developed scenarios in the practice of dynamic industrial companies of medium business.
4. Identification of problems-calls of industrial enterprises. Correction of the list of large calls from the Strategy of scientific and technological development of the Russian Federation.

5. Formation of a compliance system for managing problems-calls of industrial enterprises in urban system.
6. Carrying out of synergetic modeling of breakthrough scientific and technological development of companies - national champions.
7. Formation of the concept of a communication campaign aimed at popularizing innovative activity and promoting success stories.
8. Examination of the existing list of publicly accessible information resources for the purpose of breakthrough development of industrial enterprises.
9. Development of a methodical approach to the evaluation of the startup startup cost index and the main characteristics of startups launched.
10. Development and validation of the methodology for assessing innovative demand and innovative activity of dynamic medium-sized companies.
11. Research of the dynamics of scientific communication in Russia.
12. Processing the results of the development of fast-growing industrial enterprises according to the developed scenarios for the first year of observation.
13. Development of the procedure for the introduction of digital counterparts and on their basis digital shadows in industrial enterprises.
14. Formation of the program of digital transformation of industrial enterprises.
15. Development and approbation of KPI evaluation methodology for breakthrough development of fast-growing industrial enterprises. The implementation is planned on the basis of the national champion.
16. Modeling the process of creating an industrial-technological enclave as a kind of network structure of the cluster type.

The proposed block system can be successfully applied for Smart solutions in create sustainable urban systems. These solutions provide a massive increase in efficiency for decision-makers. This also provides a new platform for open innovation without permission. The proposed chain of blocks was successful because they did not ask for permission. They were built on an idea in which central authority and supervision should be avoided, and that the network itself must be resistant to all forms of censorship. At the same time, the network time should be open to everyone, and all members should be able to make any transactions that are Smart solutions in create sustainable urban systems. This meant that Mkrttchian's idea of technology was seen as too slow and too risky for Smart Solutions in creating sustainable urban systems. As the digital avatar technology matured, however, more and more people began to see the potential of distributed accounting technology, just in a more controlled setting. If distributed book technology can be adapted to existing laws and regulations, this can lead to the elimination of a large number of costly inefficiencies and replace the basic system for Smart Solutions in create sustainable urban systems.

FUTURE RESEARCH DIRECTIONS

Many developers are rushing to develop software that can use these precedents and act as the best solution provider, often in several markets at the same time. You can imagine the winner scenario - all this because of the effect of a strong network that the largest provider will like, but it's interesting that some signs indicate that this may not be a coincidence. Relying on the technological roots of the blockade created with open source and the ideals of an open network of digital avatars, developers focused their attention on solutions for compatible registers. This means that in the future, the data can be transferred between different registers and allows the trading of assets that are not currently considered commodity. The web of web values will facilitate the trade of all forms of assets, such as currencies, stocks, goods and gold, but this will require completely different digital avatars that will come from the supercomputer. Development of the theory of digital economic security and formation of new knowledge that adequately describes emerging social threats in the digital economy and gives digital economic security the status of a scientific discipline. Digital economic security is understood by the scientific collective as an information model of synthetic knowledge, whose individual judgments, while within the boundaries of economic and information security, lose their former autonomy and, integrating with social security, become elements of a new system.

The specific fundamental task consists in the initial development of a number of new provisions derived from the theory of economic and information security theory on the basis of the hypothesis that the more the economy is digitized, the higher the level of ensuring its social security requires a person, society and the state. As such provisions the scientific team develops the following:

- The interests of the individual, society, state in the digital economy and the desired characteristics of the object of digital economic security;
- Mechanisms for ensuring digital economic security, based on effective analysis of large data for solving problems of the digital economy, including problem-oriented applied algorithms, machine learning systems and other methods of intellectual analysis;
- Coordination of new designs of digital economic security and showing links between the elements of these structures as part of a more complete system - the digital economy;
- The construction of derivative designs of digital economic security, combining approaches to ensuring the economic, information and social security of the individual, society, the state on the basis of effective analysis of large data for solving problems of the digital economy, including problem-oriented applied algorithms, machine learning systems and other methods of intellectual analysis.

CONCLUSION

- Today in the digital economy there are new digital avatars, so people can "share" unproductive assets, free rooms on Airbnb, spare seats on cars on the Uber and free time on TaskRabbit. These joint digital economies are nothing but a new intermediary, located between a buyer and a seller who seizes and uses virtually unused assets and valuables.
- Convergence with enabled blocking connection allows a seamless peer-to-peer node to exchange assets and cost, reducing the need for trust brokers as intermediaries and increasing the extracted market economic rent in a joint digital economy that. Therefore, it is doomed to successful development.
- Convergence with enabled blocking connection converts the value creation chain. Autonomous robotics, AI, IoT and block systems will digitize logistics and distribution, reducing its importance and therefore increasing the ability of companies at this stage in the value chain to profit.

- Manufacturers can get more value they create, and consumers can pay less. In the long term, technical deflation will fall into the knee of an exponential curve, since most of the production with a 3D print, as well as a virtual and augmented reality, make it cheap for design and give the opportunity to print products at home. And it will also be some kind of new technology (name), but everything will be determined by economic benefits even then.
- The concept of managing fast-growing industrial enterprises, containing classification features and content characteristics of the development environment; A distinctive feature of the author's approach is the consideration of the environment from the standpoint of the system-synergetic approach as a continuum of framework conditions, including values, institutions, maturity of industries and markets, infrastructure, technology, human capital that will achieve the goal of breakthrough development of industrial enterprises.
- Methodology for managing the breakthrough development of fast-growing industrial enterprises on the basis of laws and development principles, which includes a set of theoretical foundations in terms of hypotheses, applied theories and basic approaches, basic organizational and management mechanisms and basic efficiency assessments.
- Conceptual model and management system for the breakthrough development of fast-growing industrial enterprises, characterized by the allocation as vectors of decomposition of objects, management functions, directions of digitization at mega-, macro-, meso- and microlevels, as well as stages of innovative and production processes that allow achieving achievement global competitiveness, increasing labor productivity in industry, improving the quality of life and the number of people employed in non-primary sectors in the face of challenge problems .
- Methodological approach to the assessment of the level of technological development of industrial enterprises as an integral index with emergent properties, with the allocation of macroeconomic, investment, scientific, technological and innovative, stock, information and communication domains, which gives an idea of the influence of various factors on the change in the final indicator and build predictive estimates.

ACKNOWLEDGMENT

This research was supported by the Russian Foundation for Basic Research:

[Grant number 18-010-00204] entitled: Fundamental basis for the development of mechanisms for effective digital service-oriented interaction of participants in socio-economic systems and networks;

Professor Vardan Mkrttchian (HHH University, Australia) for supporting this chapter as a scientific leader.

REFERENCES

Arvind, N., Bonneau, J., Felten, E., Miller, A., & Goldfeder, E. (2016). *Bitcoin and Cryptocurrency Technologies. Princeton University Press.*

Babkin, A., Plotnikov, V., & Vertakova, Y. (2018). The Analysis of industrial cooperation models in the context of forming digital economy. *SHS Web of Conferences., 44*, 12. doi:10.1051hsconf/20184400012

Bitcoin Essential. (2016). Packt Publishing.

Bitcoin For Dummies. (2016). John Wiley & Sons, Inc.

Blockchain: Trust economy Taking control of digital identity. (2016). White paper. Digital Supply Chain Management 2020 Vision. SAP SE Walldorf, Germany.

Blockchain's Smart Contracts. (2016, June). Driving the Next Wave of Innovation across Manufacturing Value Chain. *Cognizant 20-20 insights*.

Digital-Disrupting Business Models, Digital Supply Networks. (2017). *Deloitte Development LLC Land Transport Regulation 2040 Technology, trends and other factors of change*. Foundation paper. NTC Australia National Transport Commission.

Emerging technology timeline 20 emergent technologies likely to disrupt our sector. (2017). ARUP.

Karapetyants, I., Kostuhin, Y., Tolstykh, T., Shkarupeta, E., & Krasnikova, A. (2017). Establishment of Research Competencies in the Context of Russian Digitalization. *Proceedings of the 30th International Business Information Management Association Conference (IBIMA)*, 845-854.

Mkrttchian, V., & Aleshina, E. (2017). *Sliding Mode in Intellectual Control and Communication: Emerging Research and Opportunities*. Hershey, PA: IGI Global. doi:10.4018/978-1-5225-2292-8

Mkrttchian, V., Palatkin, I., Gamidullaeva, L., & Panasenko, S. (2019). About digital avatars for control systems using Big Data and Knowledge sharing in virtual industries. In A. Gyamfi & I. Williams (Eds.), *Big Data and Knowledge Sharing in Virtual Organizations* (pp. 46–59). Hershey, PA: IGI Global. doi:10.4018/978-1-5225-7519-1ch.04

Technology, B. (2016). *Possibilities for the U.S. Postal Service RARC Report*. Report Number RARC-WP-16-01.

The Benefits of Blockchain to Supply Chain Networks. (2017). *Watson Customer Engagement*. IBM Corporation.

Tolstykh, T. (2018). Professional Training for Structural Economic Transformations Based on Competence Approach in the Digital Age. In Handbook of Research on Students' Research Competence in Modern Educational Contexts. IGI Global. Doi:10.4018/978-1-5225-3485-3.ch011

Tolstykh, T., Shkarupeta, E., Kostuhin, Y., & Zhaglovskaya, A. (2018). Key Factors of Manufacturing Enterprises Development in the Context of Industry 4.0. *Proceedings of the 31th International Business Information Management Association Conference (IBIMA)*, 4747-4757.

Tolstykh, T., Shkarupeta, E., Kostuhin, Y., & Zhaglovskaya, A. (2018). Digital Innovative Manufacturing basing on Formation of an Ecosystem of Services and Resources. *Proceedings of the 31th International Business Information Management Association Conference (IBIMA)*, 4738-4746.

Tolstykh, T. O., Shkarupeta, E. V., Shishkin, I. A., Dudareva, O. V., & Golub, N. N. Evaluation of the Digitalization Potential of Region's Economy. In The Impact of Information on Modern Humans. HOSMC 2017. Advances in Intelligent Systems and Computing (vol. 622, pp. 736-743). Springer. Doi:10.1007/978-3-319-75383-6

ADDITIONAL READING

Bershadsky, A., Bozhday, A., Evseeva, J., Gudkov, A., & Mkrtchian, V. (2017), Techniques for Adaptive Graphics Applications Synthesis Based on Variability Modeling Technology and Graph Theory, In A. Kravets, M. Shcherbakov, M. Kultsova, & O. Shabalina, (Eds.), *Proceedings of CIT&DS 2017*, (pp. 169–179). Springer International Publishing AG. 10.1007/978-3-319-65551-2_33

Bershadsky, A., Evseeva, J., Bozhday, A., Gudkov, A., & Mkrtchian, V. (2015), Variability modeling in the automated system for authoring intelligent adaptive applications on the basis of three-dimensional graphics, In A. Kravets, M. Shcherbakov, M. Kultsova, & O. Shabalina, (Eds.), *Proceedings of CIT&DS 2015*, (pp. 149–159). Springer International Publishing AG. DOI: 10.1007/978-3-319-23766-4

Glotova, T., Deev, M., Krevskiy, I., Matukin, S., Mkrttchian, V., & Sheremeteva, E. (2015), Individualized learning trajectories using distance education technologies, In A. Kravets, M. Shcherbakov, M. Kultsova, & O. Shabalina, (Eds.), *Proceedings of CIT&DS 2015*, (pp. 778–793). Springer International Publishing AG. DOI: 10.1007/978-3-319-23766-4

Mkrttchian, V. (2011). Use 'hhh" technology in transformative models of online education. In G. Kurubacak & T. Vokan Yuzer (Eds.), *Handbook of research on transformative online education and liberation: Models for social equality* (pp. 340–351). Hershey, PA: IGI Global; doi:10.4018/978-1-60960-046-4.ch018

Mkrttchian, V. (2012). Avatar manager and student reflective conversations as the base for describing meta-communication model. In G. Kurubacak, T. Vokan Yuzer, & U. Demiray (Eds.), *Meta-communication for reflective online conversations: Models for distance education* (pp. 340–351). Hershey, PA: IGI Global; doi:10.4018/978-1-61350-071-2.ch005

Mkrttchian, V., Amirov, D., & Belyanina, L. (2017). Optimizing an Online Learning Course Using Automatic Curating in Sliding Mode. In N. Ostashewski, J. Howell, & M. Cleveland-Innes (Eds.), *Optimizing K-12 Education through Online and Blended Learning* (pp. 213–224). Hershey, PA: IGI Global. doi:10.4018/978-1-5225-0507-5.ch011

Mkrttchian, V., Aysmontas, B., Uddin, M., Andreev, A., & Vorovchenko, N. (2015). The Academic views from Moscow Universities of the Cyber U-Learning on the Future of Distance Education at Russia and Ukraine. In G. Eby & T. Vokan Yuzer (Eds.), *Identification, Evaluation, and Perceptions of Distance Education Experts* (pp. 32–45). Hershey, PA: IGI Global; doi:10.4018/978-1-4666-8119-4.ch003

Mkrttchian, V., Bershadsky, A., Bozhday, A., & Fionova, L. (2015). Model in SM of DEE Based on Service Oriented Interactions at Dynamic Software Product Lines. In G. Eby & T. Vokan Yuzer (Eds.), *Identification, Evaluation, and Perceptions of Distance Education Experts* (pp. 230–247). Hershey, PA: IGI Global; doi:10.4018/978-1-4666-8119-4.ch014

Mkrttchian, V., Kataev, M., Hwang, W., Bedi, S., & Fedotova, A. (2014). Using Plug-Avatars "hhh" Technology Education as Service-Oriented Virtual Learning Environment in Sliding Mode. In G. Eby & T. Vokan Yuzer (Eds.), *Emerging Priorities and Trends in Distance Education: Communication, Pedagogy, and Technology*. Hershey, PA: IGI Global; doi:10.4018/978-1-4666-5162-3.ch004

Mkrttchian, V., Kataev, M., Hwang, W., Bedi, S., & Fedotova, A. (2016), Using Plug-Avatars "hhh" Technology Education as Service-Oriented Virtual Learning Environment in Sliding Mode. Leadership and Personnel Management: Concepts, Methodologies, Tools, and Applications (4 Volumes), (pp.890-902). IGI Global. Doi:10.4018/978-1-4666-9624-2.ch039

Mkrttchian, V., & Stephanova, G. (2013). Training of Avatar Moderator in Sliding Mode Control. In G. Eby & T. Vokan Yuzer (Eds.), *Project Management Approaches for Online Learning Design* (pp. 175–203). Hershey, PA: IGI Global; doi:10.4018/978-1-4666-2830-4.ch009

Mkrttchian, V., & Stephanova, G. (2013). Training of Avatar Moderator in Sliding Mode Control Environment for Virtual Project Management. In Enterprise Resource Planning: Concepts, Methodologies, Tools, and Applications (pp. 1376-1405). IGI Global. Doi:10.4018/978-1-4666-4153-2.ch074

KEY TERMS AND DEFINITIONS

Application of Blockchain Technology: Is application multifunctional and multilevel information technology designed to reliably record various assets in digital economy to help the technological challenges and created tools.

Avatar Model of High Technology: Is new model with natural intelligent for Avatar introduced in 2011 from Professor Vardan Mkrttchian.

Avatar-Based: Is a new term that describes the planning, search, production, distribution, and delivery of Mkrttchian's digital avatars from the place of origin to consumption.

Blockchain Technology: Is a multifunctional and multilevel information technology, designed to reliably record various assets in digital economy.

Digital Ecosystem: Is an independent group of actors (people, equipment, and organizations) that share the standardized digital platforms to communicate with each other to achieve commercial or social goal.

Expert Knowledge: Is a specific product-expert knowledge, which is created through electronic data distributed on the Internet between business partners and value-added service providers operating in a general digital economy paradigm using blockchain technologies.

Smart Solutions in Create Sustainable Urban System: Means that Mkrttchian's idea of technology was seen as too slow and too risky for Smart Solutions in creating sustainable urban systems. As the digital avatar technology matured, however, more and more people began to see the potential of distributed accounting technology, just in a more controlled setting. If distributed book technology can be adapted to existing laws and regulations, this can lead to the elimination of a large number of costly inefficiencies and replace the basic system for Smart Solutions in create sustainable urban systems.

Supply Chain Management: Is a formal term for managing the physical and information flow of materials and finished products and goods in the supply chain.

Chapter 3
From Chaos to Order:
Articulating the Urban Policies for Cities of Hardship

Hisham Abusaada
https://orcid.org/0000-0001-6530-7714
Housing and Building National Research Centre (HBRC), Egypt

Abeer Elshater
https://orcid.org/0000-0002-5061-6861
Ain Shams University, Egypt

ABSTRACT

This chapter uses the term urban chaos as an alternative to words such as anarchy, randomness, and disorder. It expresses the visual and behavioral failure that describes a property that was not taken into consideration when dealing with the theme of hardship cities. The terms livability and quality of life focus on measuring functional, social, economic, and political indicators, ignoring visual and behavioral indicators as not essential for creating cities of hardship. This work presents two concepts, chaos city (CC) and order city (OC) based on the reviews of livability, quality of life, and the writings of Christopher Alexander, to demonstrate the lack of standards of livability to the visual and behavioral indicators. The addition of these indicators helps to classify cities of hardship from the perspective of the relationship between chaos and order and tries to provide guidelines and proposed action plan related to urban policies (UP) that enable the transformation of CC to OC.

INTRODUCTION

In 2016, through a field survey conducted in some areas of Cairo by the authors targeting many residents and visitors of the city, the central question was as follows: How do they see their city today compared to the Western city regarding the visual aspects and the human behavior of the city? Many residents and visitors of the city see it as characterized by chaos but without referring to the distinction between the concepts of chaos, such as chaos in the political sense (anarchy), disorder, or randomness. However, they

DOI: 10.4018/978-1-5225-7625-9.ch003

stressed that chaos, for them, is the opposite of order. The majority of citizens describe chaos versus order in two levels in the public realms, the first being the visual aspects that describe the features of building blocks that make up the representations of surrounding urban spaces, open spaces, local roads, and pedestrian paths. The second is the human behavior related to the actions that take place in dealing with the traffic networks or encroaching on pedestrian sidewalks from shop owners or street vendors. Furthermore, they are describing the neglect of the application of traffic regulations, whether regarding design or protection.

Thus, at the beginning of this work, the focus was based on the fact that there are two opposing urban cities—Chaos City (CC) and Order City (OC). Later, the authors discover that these two factors (visual and behavioral) have a close relationship in the sense of chaos and order. This relationship can represent a new addition to the indicators of cities of hardship, bearing in mind that their characteristics were not included in the indicators of livability and quality of life. The contribution of this work focuses on adding indicators of the characteristics of cities of hardship to these scales so that a measure of hardship can be provided in the cities of the developing world. The work examines some of the characteristics of cities of hardship based on these two concepts: CC and OC.

The present chapter includes three steps starting from discussing the meaning of chaos and order, as well as their relation to some words, such as anarchy, randomness, and disorder. Furthermore, it focuses on the theory of order for Christopher Alexander and highlights the patterns and characteristics of OC and CC. Consequently, it searches about the reasons behind increasing urban chaos by focusing on the concept of the geometrical order impacts on the architectural styles, and the whole system of the city amidst behavioral lifestyles have been taken into consideration. The second step is to explore the essence of the term cities of hardship by tracking the causes of loss of adequate daily living standards by focusing on the visual and behavioral dimensions for the creation of OC based on concepts of quality of life, livability, and livelihood. Furthermore, it proves that the impact of hardship regarding the OC does not exist in most of the living standards indexes. Ultimately, the third step provides an action plan to reduce the hardship in CC based on this vision, and it proposed an urban planning and design policy (the guidelines) to create Livable Cities based on transforming the CC into an OC.

ANARCHY, CHAOS, RANDOMNESS, AND ORDER

Anarchy, chaos, randomness, and order are entirely different issues from each other. The anarchy does not necessarily lack the order, as supposed rather than the absence of rule (Tucker, 1897, p. 13). Meanwhile, the chaos is the absence of the base of the rule. The first term means *the opposite of geometric order; it is represented by ideal mathematical forms; and ideal relationships* (Rubinowicz, 2000, p. 197). Also, it is the science of surprises and unexpected phenomenon, which is unpredictable and covers both social and economic systems. In the beginning, minor changes happen, which lead to massive changes over time. These give definitive clues to what could happen in the future, including a glimpse into the underlying systems at work. This is different from randomness, wherein it is impossible to predict it is the next step.

Often, chaos seems to be a random response, but it is not. Further, it does not adjust the models, which are considering the chance to reach completeness. Chaos refers to an imbalance in the performance of tasks and responsibilities. It is a state of utter confusion and an absence of arrangement or order. Moreover, the word "chaos" explains various, similar elements of the phenomenon. For instance, street vendors, and marginalized people, in one context, and the spreading of informal settlements, unruly traffic, and building disturbances, in another context, are all distinct phenomena of chaos; they reflect the urban chaos in any city. Each phenomenon has elements that behave differently from any other phenomena. Experts in urban planning and design measure the visual quality by using the notion of geometrical order, which is latent behind the extent of the appropriateness of the building types by using the objective indices.

- The geometric order describes an ideal mathematical field comprising numbers and equations, which is controlling on the variety the structural products, regarding form and formation. Employing the regular order creates good art, wherein, architecture is harmonies; the current sentiment is a spirit of geometry, a spirit of construction and synthesis, exactitude and order are its essential condition.
- The perceivable order understood as a reflection of an underlying order, whether physical, social, or cognitive.
- The outer order represents inner functional order, and a lack of correspondence between them produces a clash of orders, which provides an element of disorder.
- A disorder is not the absence of all order but the clash of uncoordinated orders.
- City order is relevant to the way in which people observe or read and interpret the environment.

Figure 1 includes the timeline of architecture, order, and disorder. In the second part, 'The process of creating life', Alexander (2002) explains the differences between the structural order, physical order, organic order, deepness order, geometric order, and city order (Figure 2). The architectural context of the built environment is encompassed, created, and modified by the "order," through controlling the performance of people and place, with a focus on the designing of the buildings, and strict managing of the behavioral settings. This experience is essential to establish the order. The founder of the order should be a specialist, innovator, stakeholder, or beneficiary in the field, possesses the talent and the ability to read and analyses the facts, and have the potential to choose between the outcomes to create a new product. Any order does not replace another order; broken order requires flexibility and the ability to change in place and time according to the needs and demands.

BACKGROUNDING AND SETTINGS OF OC AND CC

This work developed its orientation around the concept of urban chaos, specifically in developing countries, based on two factors. The first is how people perceive the city, including visual and behavioral impacts and respecting other societal dimensions such as sociocultural, commercial, environmental, and governmental. The second is how the city will, firstly, meet the primary daily needs and, ultimately, reach to welfare. Thus, the intention of this work is to address ways to reduce the suffering of hardship to get satisfaction and well-being. It does not focus on gaining a high-level quality of life. Moreover, it searches for the ways the citizen lives in the city without hardship in preparation for the pursuit of a high degree of livability. In that vein, two fundamental problems are evolving: The first is linked to determining what is suitable for urban architecture by identifying the concepts of OS and CC. The second is defining the idea of the geometrical and structural order and investigating the resulting chaos that happens after the no satisfaction of an individual, a result that affects all physical elements that generate the living of hardship. The results, in these cases, come from the utilization of principles and rules. The current chapter

Figure 1. The timeline shows the temporal relationship between architecture, order, and disorder

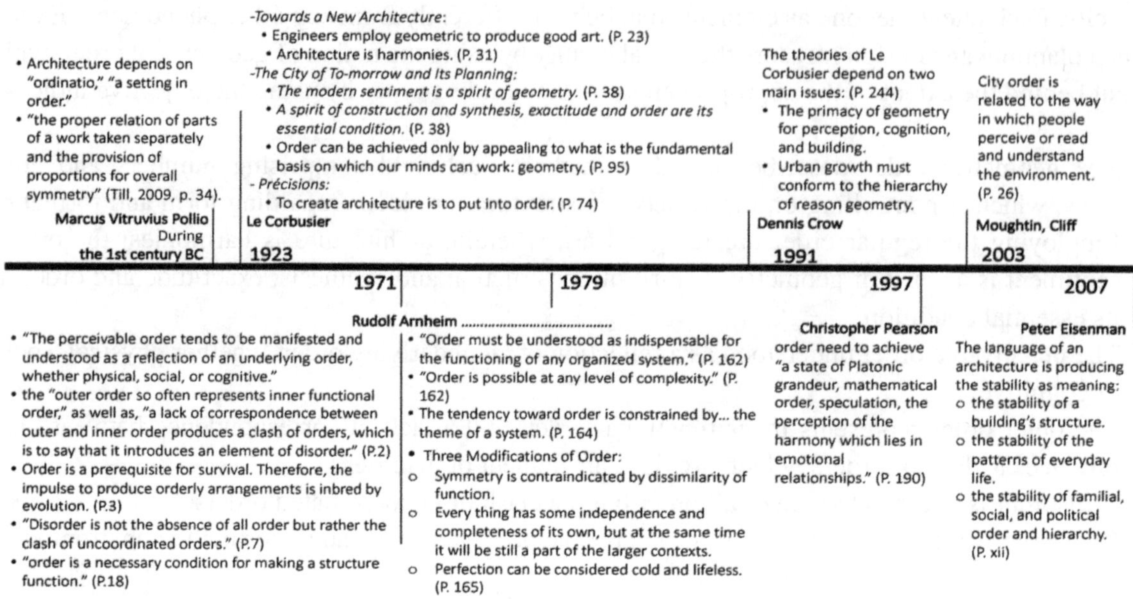

Figure 2. The differences between the type of orders (Alexander, 2002, pp. 2, 4, 62)

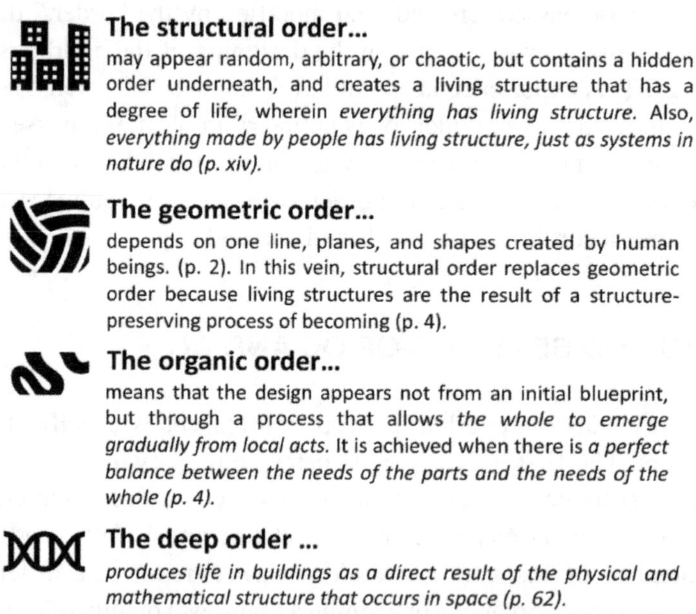

provides a conceptual background and discusses the term Cities of Hardship to describe cities that lack the characteristics of both the earlier terms and consequently inspire hardships.

This section aims to explore the characteristics of CC & OC and their explicit/ implicit relationships based on the relevant literature and direct observations in two cities in Switzerland and Egypt. The contribution focuses on the concepts of cities of hardship due to the CC which is lacking the order, Figure 3 & Table 1.

Figure 3. The differences between the quality of life, livability, and cities of hardship related to the concepts of CC and OC. The photos from the left: Vicolo Nassetta, Lugano, Switzerland, right: Heliopolis districts, Cairo, Egypt

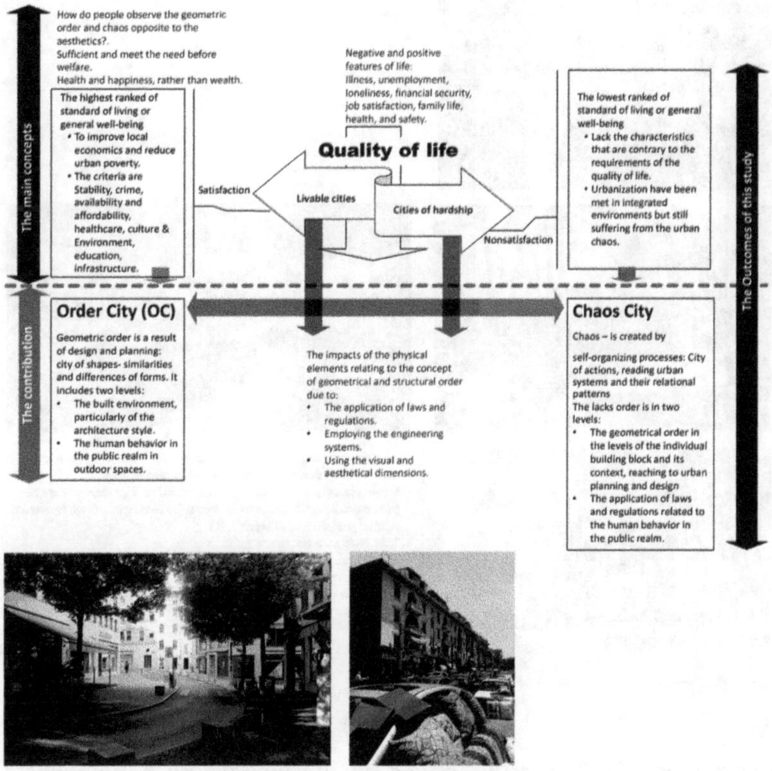

The visual comparative analysis focused on the observation of the public realm in the year 2018, regarding the design of building blocks' and human behavior. This analysis covers two different cases, indicating the characteristics of OC in the city of Lugano, Switzerland and CC in Midan El Gamaa district in Heliopolis, Cairo, Egypt. Notably, the characteristics of OC in Lugano, Switzerland are deeply embedded in the affirmative urban policy and city management. The impacts of the governmental regulations emerged in the architectural features of urban form, the individual buildings, landscape architecture, and street furniture, as well as the behavior of the people. In the context, the characteristics of CC in Heliopolis, Egypt are rooted and deeply embedded in local human behavior and non-compliance with urban policies or city management. A lack of implementation of laws is accompanied by increased violations by people. The characteristics' focus is shown in Figures 4.

LOSING SUFFICIENT LIVING STANDARDS

Nowadays, people live in cities under two concerns of living stress. The first is related to the public community services, housing, transportation, and recreation, which are measured by the socio-cultural, economic, and functional dimensions (Mohit & Iyanda, 2016, pp. 863-864). The second explores the comfort that a citizen feels sensually and emotionally under the impact of the visual-aesthetic, perceptual,

Figure 4. The characteristics of two opposite cases (OC) and (CC) in the reality, 2018, left the city of Lugano, Switzerland and right Cairo, Egypt

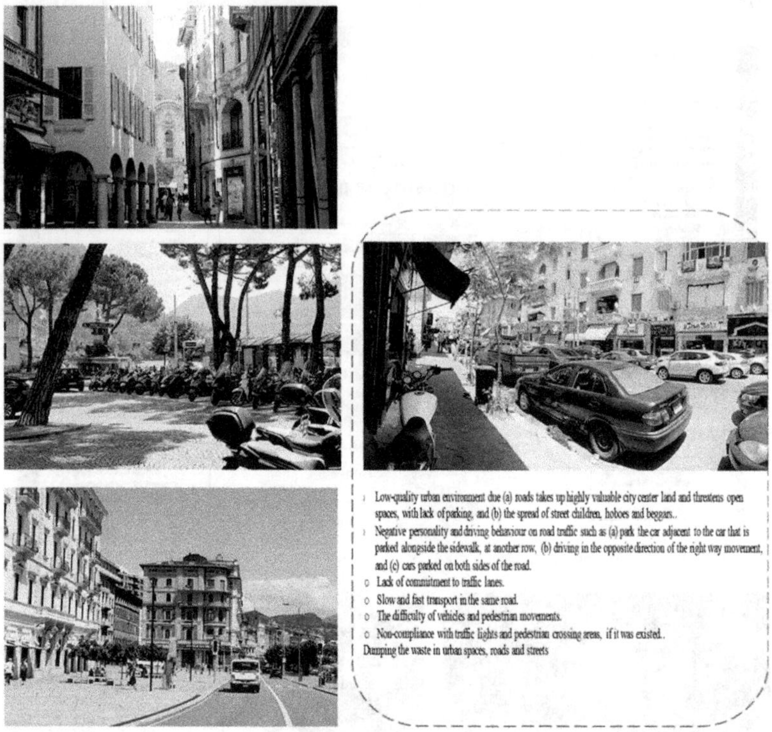

Table 1. The characteristics of CC and OC based on the visual and behavioral dimensions Source: Compiled by the authors based on (Lynch, 1960; Cullen, 1961; Meiss, 1990; Gehl, 1996; Carmona, Heath, Oc, & Tiesdell, 2010; Karimi, 2012; Ewing & Clemente, 2013; Leather, Fabian, Gota, & Mejia, 2011; White, 2015)

	Chaos City (CC)	Order City (OC)
First: the visual dimension based on the concept of geometrical order [a result of design and planning]		
A. Patterns and aesthetic order		
Architectural structures of the city and its components	- Non-organized and unplanned city. - Lack of the basic unit, and flexible composition. - Lack of congruence between urban form, distribution of activities, patterns of way binding, and the other essential constituents of the Livable city.	- Easy to organize: diversity, adaptability, connectedness, resilience, and robustness. - The homogeneous character for each district. - Controlled planning and design process. - The orthogonal street layout is more legible and most connected.
Visual complexity	- Design becomes too top-down, controlled, and predictable in modern large-scale master plans. - Wicked problems and incrementalism. - Few of the noticeable differences that viewer is exposed per unit of time.	_ Collaborative place-making _ Enough in the present scene to keep one occupied: the visual richness and variety. _ connectedness, accessibility, stability, resilience, and robustness. _ A maximum value at some midpoint between order and disorder.
Urban Design Elements	- Too few, too similar and predictable. - Too disordered to be comprehensible.	_ Works towards the creation. _ Very complex and diverse chaotic. _ Order and chaos exist in architecture.
Urban city form and shape	- Eliminated due to the development of transport technology.	_ A rich variety of geometric shape.
Scale and rhythm	- Random	_ The scale of the chosen elements is relating to the scale of the structure. _ Repetition of one or more significant detail along each facade.
Visually coherent	- Each element seems in isolation.	_ Experience respect the whole rather than the individual elements.

continued on following page

Table 1. Continued

	Chaos City (CC)	Order City (OC)
Balance and harmonic relationships	- Random	Recognition, sensitive, and the interaction of buildings is easy to observe.
Colures		_ Consistent and appropriate for the type of activity, and not too much.
Textures		_ appropriate for the type of sense of place
Public spaces and routes	- The lack of enclosure.	_ The sense of enclosure. _ Attractive and organized to everyone
Spatial organization and sequential movement		
Tissue types	- Undefined in many places	Numerous, varied, and follow the social and economic aspects.
Gestalt	- Not applicable	The recognizable similarity of parts in relations to each other, to yield an available gestalt.
Open and urban spaces	- Lost spaces if exist.	Key elements for design.
Legibility: differentiation, visual access, and layout	- Missed way finding. - Cognitive maps remain largely unexplored - Disorientation.	_ A distinctive and legible environment. _ Have the physical features to sense of orientation, way finding; and visibility. _ Recognizable paths, intersections, and visual landmarks.
Imageability	- Life in the space does not exist	_ High sense of places, dynamic experiences, distinct, recognizable, and memorable place.
Serial vision	- Haphazard movement	_ Efficient a coherent drama
- Urban architecture		
Expression	- Confusion regarding the location and arrangement of urban elements: the market square and the city hall.	_ It has a significant impact on the shape of new architectural structures. _ Depends on an arrangement of differences.
Unity & Integrity		_ In the variety
Building façades Design: city view	- An ugly and disharmonic view. - Lack of heterogeneity.	_ A part of a whole named urban space. _ Achieving an appropriate awareness. _ Allows flexibility, individuality, creativity, and artistic expression. _ signature elements within a community.
B. Street furniture		
Position	Wasted of space	Create and delineate space.
	- Impede pedestrians, vehicles, and desire lines	_ Help pedestrians to move.
Elements	- Superfluous - Confusion of arrangement	_ Incorporate the minimum of furniture. _ Integrate into a single unit. _ Suiting the quality of the environment. _ Give a coherent identity. _ Healthy complex systems.
C. Landscape architecture: hard or soft		
Character and identity	Nothing	Creating.
Legibility		Enhancing.
Aesthetic pleasure		Playing a key role.
Sense of human scale		Adding.
Sense of enclosure	- A negative an outdoor space	_ Providing: outdoor spaces seem room-like.
Appearance: what does the city look like?	Nothing	_ Regarded the context and local distinctiveness: attractive city.
Materials	Haphazard	Consider the suitability for the tasks.
Second: the behavioral dimension based on the concept of structural order [by self-organizing processes].		
A. Urban architecture		
Building façades: create the public realm	- Vulnerability of urban spaces in front of inappropriate facades. - Noise pollution: the cause of disturbance and leading to several health problems.	_ A favorable impact on improving the quality of life and prevent the emergence of adverse social interactions and develop optimal interactions. _ The welfare of outdoor pedestrian.
B. Road networks for vehicles		
Movement patterns: Entropy	Highest when the system's disorder is maximized	The system is highly ordered and thus completely predictable.

continued on following page

Table 1. Continued

	Chaos City (CC)	Order City (OC)
Urban mobility or accessibility	- Traffic focus, free-flowing, and road cognition. - Increase the environmental pollution, energy consumption, and the length of journeys and difficult to navigate. - Lack of respect or application of traffic rules. - Traffic noise: transportation systems.	_ People focus, safe, attractive, vibrant streets, and traffic calmed. _ Traffic safety, motorist awareness: Public transit systems rather than private automobiles. _ An outcome and a shaping factor of how cities take form. _ decrease collisions, and conductivity.
C. Pedestrian Activities		
Necessary activities: going to work, shopping, waiting for a bus or a person.	_ Lack of transport choices for people of all ages and abilities, especially children. _ Meet accessibility requirements and provide safety.	_ Promotes accessibility, permeability, safety, and prioritizing people to traffic. _ Creating places that connect with each other through easy routes. _ Walkability: easy walking distance. _ Street connectivity and permeability.
Optional activities:	_ Increase lights and barriers in the roads.	_ Occur with increasing frequency. _ Taking a walk to get a breath of fresh air, standing around enjoying life, and sitting.
Social activities: - Children at play, greetings, and conversations.	_ Disappearing 'shared space.' _ No amenities	_ Suitable social interaction. _ Excellent amenities such as lighting and cover from sun and rain making walking a pleasant experience.
D. Landscape architecture: hard or soft		
Pedestrians	_ Conflict between bicycles, motorcycles, and cars on the road makes walking impossible and crossing unsafely.	_ Have a concern for a welcoming atmosphere and clear directional signage. _ Giving priority to pedestrian movement in urban spaces.
Maintenance	_ Sometimes and at intervals.	_ Long term plan.
Cleansing	_ Need better cleanliness maintained	_ Ease of refuse collection, sweeping, washing, and cleaning the graffiti.
People with disabilities	_ Infrastructure is not available or sufficiently	_ Safety, convenience, removal of obstacles, and resent in good condition, and well placed.
Traffic and related matters	_ Very high crossing time	_ Consider public transport, cyclists, and pedestrians crossing the carriageways.

and behavioral dimensions; both of which affect the living standards in cities negatively or positively. Livability and hardship deal with the living standards of the cities to measure the extent of the personal satisfaction by focusing on the physical components of the city; it is based on standards, constants, and rules. While the quality of living deals with non-material elements, such as satisfaction, which is linked with urban architecture whether good or bad, this occurs through showing the extent of the application of engineering systems (Mohit & Iyanda, 2016, pp. 863-864). In the other vein, people's satisfaction focuses on the laws and regulations related to understanding human behavior in the city.

The 'Quality of Life (QoL)' and 'Livability' are discussed widely by planners and designer to create a better living for our future cities. The two terms might be used for the same objective despite the apparent differences in meaning between them. According to MERCER Index (2012), the first term focuses on the quality that is related to unfortunate personal circumstances, such as illness, unemployment, and loneliness. It deals with the amount of suffering that one bears while the second implies the highest and lowest ranked *of standard of living or general well-being of a population in some area such as a city* (Okulicz-Kozaryn, January 2013, p. 437). QoL means what people do in a day like shopping, housework, meal preparation, eating, traveling, using the telephone and internet, and taking or managing medications. Based on Index No. 1, the characteristics of livability do not include the indicators of OC and CC.

The next tracks the concepts and characteristics of livable cities and the cities of hardship as they relate to OC and CC. It is an attempt to formulate the planning and design guidelines as well as the action plans that advance the thoughts of the urban planner and designer in the early stages to deal with a growing problem over time. This problem is the result of continuous displacement within cities from a place that lacks the necessities of living to another place that has the power to let the users be free to contract the urban chaos. Chaos is also represented in the behavioral settings (or city-life systems) and moves to be discerned in urban architecture (or geometrical and structural order).

Between the years of 1976 and 2015, the two terms, livability, and livable cities, have been settled (Lash, 1976, p. 33; The National Association of Regional Councils (NARC), p. 7; Lennard & Lennard, 1995; Vuchic, 1999, p. 7; Victorian Competition and Efficiency Commission, 2008, p. xxi; The National Association of Regional Councils (NARC), p. 10; Kraftl, 2014, pp. 279-280; Mohit & Iyanda, 2016, pp. 863-864). In this context, many institutions describe these cities as having a combination of social, economic, and political factors, and enhancing the economic competitiveness. Livability is a concept that has accompanied the thought of sustainability: it implies that the ability to live includes the people's need for food, security, beauty, culture, and the sense of belonging. Livability extends to cover the disciplines of architecture, mainly, in the fields of urban planning and design. Livable cities are capable of dealing with the problems for a distinguished period to achieve the constant satisfaction of people today and to achieve a better future. The quality of urban spaces of those cities has been characterized as being physically and environmentally, socially and culturally friendly, and has environmental policies for comfort and healthy living. Moreover, the characteristics of the livable cities include the ease in the engineering of transport and traffic, walkability, cycling, and public transportation. The literature describes people in the livable cities by having the power and ability to live according to their affordability and have constant satisfaction about the better future (The European Environmental Agency EEA, 2009, pp. 5, 8, 43; Ley & Newton, 2010, pp. 191-192).

Shamsuddin & Hassanb (2012, p. 169) believe that the quality of urban spaces which are characterized by the physical, environmental aspects, and socio-cultural well-being for reaching the comfort, and healthy living. These urban spaces have the ease of use in mobility, walkability, cycling, and public transportation (Giap, Thye, & Aw, 2014, p. 177). Similarly, Peter Kraftl (2014) describes the livable cities as having attractive and exciting places for all people of different ages and doing several activities with a safe, an easy access to the green areas. Furthermore, these cities encourage the social and mental well-being, personal development, equity, dignity, and affection, and cultural and sacred enrichment (Lennard & Lennard, Livable cities observed: a source book of images and ideas for city officials, community leaders, architects, planners and all other committed to making their cities livable, 1995). The livability of these cities empowers the homeowners because of affordability and accessibility (Kraftl, 2014, pp. 279-280).

In 1967, the term 'cities of hardship' emerged to refer to two problems as Richard Nathan and Charles Adams (1976, p. 47) wrote: (a) *the seriousness of the social and economic problems which they face,* and, (b) it is *the extent of what might be called their political isolation as indicated by the population size of central cities in relation to the population of the metropolitan area of which they are apart.* Nathan and Adams are the creators of the composite index, which expresses the city-suburban relationship based on six measures: unemployment, dependency, education, income level per capita, crowded housing, and Poverty (P. 49). These scholars are the creators of the Urban Hardship Index that is *used to classify central city problems and conditions in relation to the rest of their metropolitan area (P. 50).* Suzanne W. Morse (2005) sees that the index should consider other factors such as homelessness, violent crime rates, the square acreage of the public space, access to health insurance, teenagers' pregnancy, rates of volunteerism, and rates of issuance for the new home and business loans. These items might all serve to provide an accurate picture of urban hardship. This index and suggestions do not consider the visual and aesthetic aspects that cause the hardship of living.

According to western literature, the cities of hardship are hit by different societal, architectural, and environmental impacts, which are, consequently, decreasing the living standards of the people (Myers & Jennifer, Environmental Exodus: An Emergent Crisis in the Global Arena, 1995; Nissel, Global Capital, Neoliberal Politics and Terrains of resistance in Vienna, 2010; Allen & Browne, Sustainability Strategies for City Logistics, 2010; American Renaissance, 2014; A Panel of Global Experts in Urban Environmental sustainability, 2011; Elshater, THE TEN-MINUTE NEIGHBORHOOD IS [NOT] A BASIC PLANNING UNIT FOR HAPPINESS IN EGYPT, 2016). These impacts often occur due to the decreasing efficiency of the infrastructure networks of public services and facilities, the adverse social and environmental influences, the materials hardship, and the operations of urban freight transport such as *air pollution, noise, visual intrusion, physical intimidation (of pedestrians and cyclists), road safety and accidents, and road traffic congestion/disruption* (Abusaada & Elshater, 2017, p. 47).

Cities of hardship imply the lack of the principles of proper and process of planning and designing the city and reaching the inability to deal with the current problems. Theses problem can appear in the future at all levels of the process. Based on the direct observation of an exclusive range of phenomena, which have been shown because of the real living in these cities, the characteristics can be divided into two groups. The first is related to the structure of the population and examines the nature of people and their behavior. It includes a set of human's phenomena that is related to the lifestyle (housing, health, education, social, culture, economy, policy, and city management) (Figure 5). The second is linked with the typology and morphology of the physical architectural construction (Figure 6).

The proposed term, Cities of the Hardship, discusses the levels of difficulty by giving indicators to show the levels and degrees to achieve better living. Many objective evaluation and indexes support the actions of defining and classifying the cities of the hardship. These indicators are shown in covers many

Figure 5. The first group: the non-physical constructions in chaos city (CC) (Montiel, Nathan, & Wright, 2004, p. 1; Nathan & Charles F. Adams, Four Perspectives on Urban Hardship, 1989)

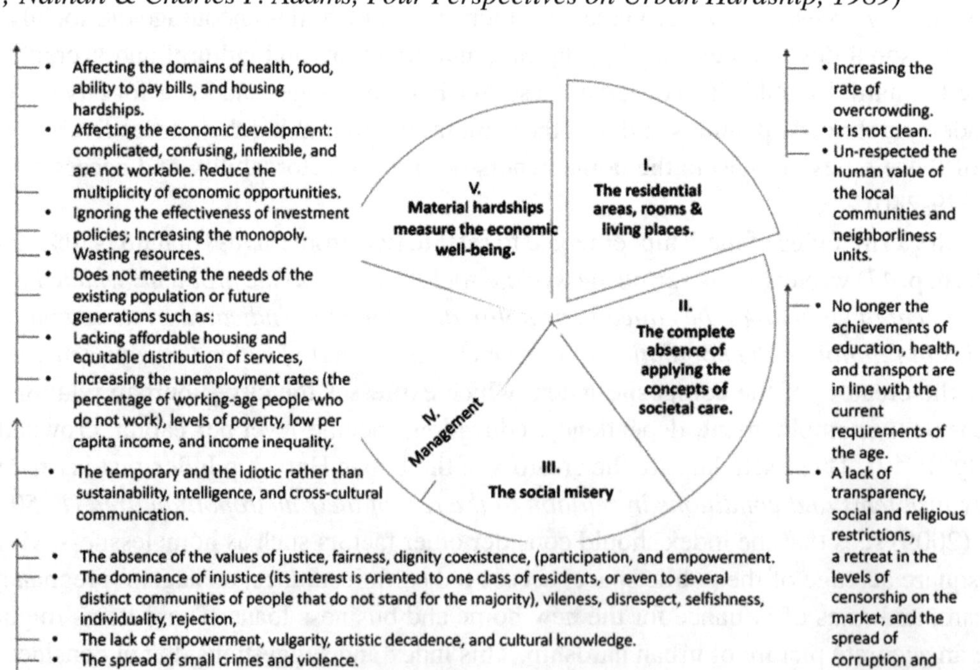

signs that are not included in the used measurement. In this, the question is related to listing the visual and behavioral factors in the indexes of livability and cities of hardship. Table 2 shows the common indexes to measure livability, explaining the elements that measure the viability, and when these elements take the less decree the cities become to cities of hardship. The most important notice that these indexes are not included. Many cities have the challenges in the living levels and an individual's lifestyle. In the field of city making, the urban planners and designers need to find benchmarks to measure the highest rates that show livable cities and the indicators that have lower values of describing standards of both the livability and hardship of the cities. There is a difference between "living competency ratings" that measures the non-material (subjective) QoL, such as freedom, tolerance, self-expression, and what steps the quality of life indicators, which include five categories: stability, healthcare, culture and environment, education, and infrastructure.

ARTICULATING UP

Similar cases might help to articulate suitable urban policies for cities of hardship while also supporting the transformation of the CC to OC. Thus, it is necessary to review some trends that are being discussed about the concept of urban growth and how to face the states of sustainability and livability. The following display focuses on two aspects. The first depends on a historical view of the stages of developing urban policies, and the second focuses on suitable growth policy and industrial policy intervention.

During the nineteenth century, urban reform emerged as a reaction against the hard-living environments of impoverished workers and inadequate housing for the poor, together with the emergence of rapid and chaotic urban growth. Afterward, urban policies were revised several times (Frisch, 1982, p. 297; UN-Habitat, 2014, pp. 19-28; Lough, 2016, p. 8) as followed:

Figure 6. The second group: the physical construction in order city (OC) and chaos city (CC)

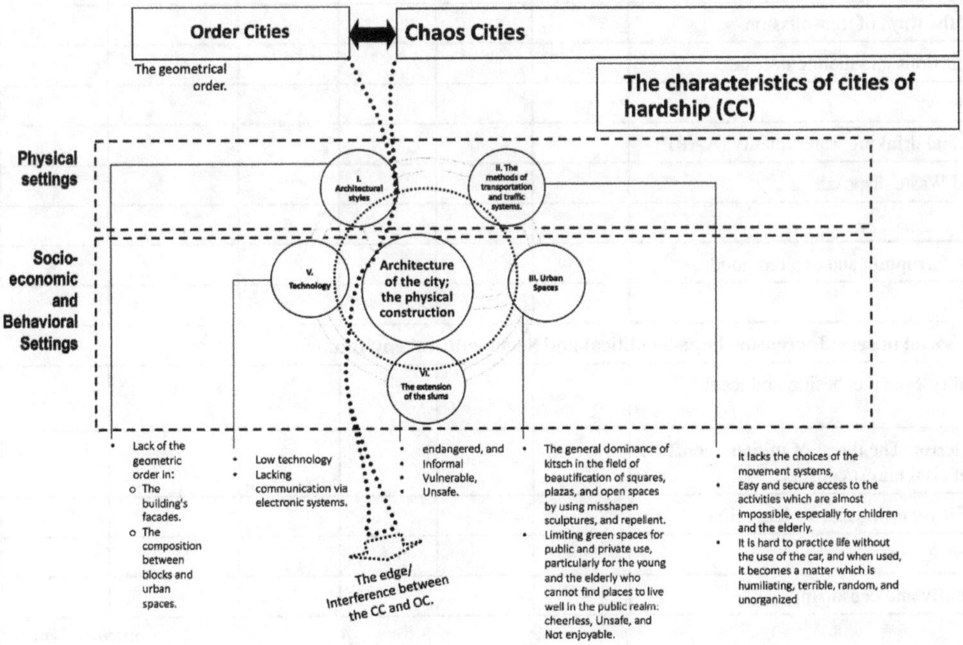

Table 2. The indexes of livability, hardship, and quality of life. Source: compiled from (The Commission on Human Rights and the General Assembly, 1998; Fielden, 2008; Brown, Boano, Vivekananda, & Walker, 2015; UNHCR, 2007; Mosel & Jackson, 2013; UN-Habitat), 2016, pp. 143-144)

Indexes / Date / The indicators	IHI	EHI	EPF	GLR	Mercer	MSSI	AARP
	1967	1967	2001	2011	2012	2013	2015
The living places: In the residential areas and rooms							
Crowded housing units (more than one person/ room).	*	*			*	*	
Population dependency (under 18 or over 64 years of age).	*	*					
Affordable housing and equitable distribution of services.							*
Applying the concepts of social care: Infrastructure, services, and the existence of networks of facilities							
Educational attainment: standards and availability of international schools, (over 25 years of age without a high school diploma), and high school graduation rate (for AARP).	*	*	*	*	*	*	*
Healthcare considerations, medical supplies, and services: infectious diseases, sewage, waste disposal, air pollution.			*	*	*	*	
Public services and transportation: electricity, water, public transportation, traffic congestion.			*		*		
Consumer goods: availability of food/daily consumption items, cars, clothing, and essential services.			*		*	*	
Transportation engineering					*	*	
Convenient transportation options: frequency of local transit service and walk trips. Accessible system design: ADA-accessible stations and vehicles (opportunity for AARP).							*
The traffic of the ways of transmission.						*	
Telecommunications and mobile networks.						*	
Public open space.					*		
Water supply and drinking water quality (AARP).						*	*
Sanitation and Waste disposal.						*	
Transparency.					*		
The spread of corruption and expired goods.						*	
Infrastructure.				*			
Decrease the social misery: Increasing hope—Political and Socio-cultural environment							
Political stability. Social cohesion and local democracy.	*		*	*	*		
The threat of terror, The threat of military conflict, and a threat of civil unrest/conflict.				*			
Prevalence of petty crime and violent crime.			*	*	*		
Law enforcement.			*				
Media availability and censorship.			*				

continued on following page

Table 2. Continued

Indexes Date The indicators	IHI 1967	EHI 1967	EPF 2001	GLR 2011	Mercer 2012	MSSI 2013	AARP 2015
Personal freedom.			*				
Recreation: restaurants, theatres, cinemas, sports, and leisure.			*			*	
Culture knowledge, environment, and leisure.				*		*	
Economic well-being: Economic environment and affecting on the economic development							
Unemployment rates (over the age of 16 years).	*	*			*		
Levels of Poverty (Income per person) (the federal level).	*	*					
Currency exchange regulations.			*				
Banking services.			*				
Nonworking-age residents % (who do not work).	*						
Jobs per worker (opportunity for AARP).							*
Income inequality (opportunity for AARP).							*
Natural environment: climate, a record of natural disasters.			*		*		

* Achieved

- Urban policy considers land-use planning and efficient public transport systems as critical factors.
- Formal urban planning systems were used as a tool for growth control and urban management, balanced regional development, and orderly urban growth.
- Local government was given potent legal instruments to regulate the character of development within its areas, to transform the urban environment, to protect open green space and to facilitate the free flow of traffic.
- Designing a city with straight arterial boulevards, long vistas, symmetrical squares and radiating roads created more space for commercial activity and new lifestyles.
- Focusing on the notions of cooperation, partnership, and participation steered private investment and growing enterprises through a combination of state controls, new infrastructure, and generous financial incentives, substantial government investment in working-class housing, government tax relief, and subsidies to encourage the growth of home-ownership and investment in the building of suburban freeways.
- Urban policies relied on attracting private investment and supporting market forces.
- The policies aim at creating and developing a rational-comprehensive approach to decision-making based on management science and operations research.

In the last revised version of the urban policy launched by the UN-Habitat (2014), the focus is on the concepts of new urbanism, growth management, new community design, sustainable development, preventing urban sprawl, creating the sense of place, development best practices, preservation development, and sustainable transport. In fact, many of them are based on urban sustainability. Urban policy in these concepts focus on the provision of essential public services and infrastructure, control, and steer growth elsewhere, ameliorate the effects of decline and poverty through social and environmental programs which have laid the basis for renewal, reinvestment and regeneration, and a new cycle of urban growth and development (UN-Habitat, 2014, p. 29).

Table 3 shows trends of three American growth management that have been emerged from the 1990s. These trends depend on sustainable urban policy intervention to raise the efficiency of cities of hardship; they focus on urban form, land use planning, and transport system.

The Intervention of Policy

The urban policy takes advantage of the chaos theory and the theory of order to resolve the urban visual and behavioral problems in general, and in the field of urban planning and design particularly. Based on the link between the reality of chaos and the nature of the order, it is not necessary to assume that each city or urban area characterized by randomness can indicate urban chaos; it might not be chaos, but just a random case. Undoubtedly, these differences should be understood before declaring that any city or part of a city is characterized by the urban chaos. A place, or a whole city, is described as being

Table 3. Three trends of urban policy intervention (Neuman, 2005; Russoa & Comib, 2012; Horn, 2015; Milana & Creutziga, 2016)

	Smart Growth	Proponents of the Compact Urban Form	Urban Renewal Initiatives or Area-Based Approaches
What	Theory for creating sustainable urban environments.	A social movement of zoning suburban.	- A popular policy instrument
What	A 'new' metropolitan governance: a global paradigm of sustainable development.	- Conveys the opposite of urban sprawl. - Redevelopment of existing cores.	- Urban form characteristics influence land-use and commuting patterns.
Urban form and land use planning: Building blocks and open space	- Mixed for a unique sense of place. - The high quality of life, social equity, urban revitalization and public health. - Distinctive, attractive, with a powerful sense of place. - Preserve open space and national areas.	- Mix uses in city centers. - Urban containment. - Concentration makes them worse. - Take advantage of compact building design. - Promotes more community-oriented social patterns. - Encourage social interaction.	- Lack of mixed-use and long commuting distances. - Compact development has never been adequately demonstrated. - Low levels of population density. - Improving the quality in the outdoor and physical environment
Sustainable transport System	- Community includes walking, biking, and mass transit. - The decrease in traffic congestion. - Create walkable communities - Minimizing the use of land without compromising the mobility of citizens. - Environmental-friendly. - Affordable and accessible. - Reduced the impacts of the automobile transportation - Reduce the impacts of urban goods movement without penalizing the life of the city.	- walkability and cycling. - Improved the public transport systems - Multimodal transportation. - The high degrees of accessibility: local/regional. - The high degrees of street connectivity. - Make public transport an attractive option due to high density and mixed land use. - Appropriate to walking, cycling, and efficient public transports. - Public transit corridors are planned in conjunction with land policies to complement each other.	- High-capacity transit systems unattractive and wasteful. - Decreasing the energy efficiency of transport networks. - Encouraging the use of more environmentally sustainable transport modes. - An incredible network of usable green space throughout the city that provides increased transportation options as well as more opportunities for physical activity and communal interaction. - Rapid Transit Network is low-carbon public transit.

characterized by the urban chaos as a result of the absence of the characteristics of order altogether. Scientific means should be used to test the characteristics of the physical structure and to distinguish clearly between randomness, disorder, non-order, and order.

In the beginning, it is necessary to explore and identify the current features and search for the underlying reasons for the non-order and disorder. Wherein, in urban areas inside cities, both of them see as an established and authoritative order to achieve livability and quality of life for wellbeing. Notably, in traditional cities, there is a constant repetition of some architectural manifestations, which describe the cities of hardship. It seems in the spread of slums and extending the informal settlements, deformity the building facades or change of its character. These manifestations seem occurred based on order; they did not appear as random as some belief. Consequently, regarding the public realm, one should recognize the efficiency of the geometric order, which apportions the building facades (masses, blocks, and clusters) that are overlooking the open areas or urban spaces. In the other levels, the priority should be in caring about the whole system concerning the designing of the urban fabrics related to the behavior of the relationship of internal geometric order over time.

The index for cities of hardship should consider the following issues:

- The aim is to highlight the concepts concerning Livability, Livable Cities, Cities of Hardship, Quality of Life, randomness, chaos, order, non-order, and disorder.
- The focus is not only on societal dimensions related to urban planning, such as population, socio-cultural, and economic factors, but rather to introduce the dimensions of urban design, particularly the visual-aesthetics and behavioral settings and considering the other aspects that relate to the plan, as well as adding them to life validity measures.
- Developing countries, due to the increasing level of hard living, should prepare the indexes based on the indicators of hardship, not based on the livability, even if the last indicators have the highest and lowest degree.
- The previous issue considers the most cities in developing countries lose any signs of livability and the quality of life. Therefore, the focus needs to be on the indexes that have been classified as the lowest level of living standards.

The index of cities of hardship should start from the concept and definition. It should include two main parts. The first is to determinate the state of the living standards of the city, divide the degree of the hardship to determine the highest and lowest standards. The second is the index of the cities of hardship that should be comprised of two issues in architecture.

A Proposed Urban Policy

In today's cities, urban policy should be used to achieve a better living standard. It should be handled by civic activities that consider both people and place. If the aim is to reduce visual chaos and urban congestion, it will be necessary to apply the principles of visual and behavioral dimensions. Therefore, the policy should involve the most concerned citizens possible in this process. All parties responsible for visual aspects must consider design aspects during implication. The educational institutions represent the first track that teaches the architects to follow requirements, principles and the criteria of the visual dimension. It is followed by the implementation engineers in the private and public sectors. As a result of this, the role of responsibilities for receiving the available works may come to reduce the irregularities. In this, the action policy includes:

- Preventing the deterioration of valuable images of traditional cities by hindering extremist interventions affecting the visual aspects. In other words, urbanization should be directed without excessive overstatement for better living through destroying historical constructions. Furthermore, new developments should consider building the cumulative order of the urban sprawl.
- Encouraging projects of national significance that contribute not only to preventing chaos but also to promoting the conservation of traditional buildings. In the city context, the conservation process moves towards applying the principles of order to improve the rules and quality standards controlled by city municipalities.
- Maintaining the required quality of communications and a smart mobility system.
- Developing the regulations and quality standards that will allow the establishment of public subsidies for this type of project to achieve a tangible effect on the city through the municipalities.
- The coordination that takes place between the vital tasks completed by the designer, the executive engineers, and the staff of the city, as well as the implementation of inter-level tasks accurately.

Urban Policy Proposals

This section provides a way for how to prepare an index for cities of hardship, related to all citizens, the residents, and visitors. It goes beyond the indexes that measuring livability based on the traditional and known aspects, socially, environmentally, economically, and politically. This index tries to focus on the issues about how to manage the common urban areas which have suffered from the collapse of its architecture and societal aspects. A focus on the dimensions of urban planning and design based on the proposed concept should be incorporated. Conclusion includes the policies, programs, and actions by the public and private actors can be in turning CC into CO. To achieve this, the transformation should consider the urban policy instruments, the urban policy actors. The following sections cover two components aimed at reducing the urban chaos in cities of hardship: the first is to develop an action plan, and the second proposes an index includes indicators of hardship cities based on the visual and behavioral features.

An Action Plan to Reduce the Urban Chaos in Cities of Hardship

As Hack, Birch, Sedway, and Silver (2009), the missing useful part of these instructions that are representing in sub-national levels or municipalities, is the main reason for creating the chaos and extend to cities of hardship. It can be said that the urban sprawl without urban management led to the difficulty in living. In so doing, for the design action, the geomatical order and structural order should be applied through the process of planning, design, and the city transformation. For management, the process should consider the communication, training, and previous experiences. Based on the urban design policy, managing the architectural products and the behavioral perspectives could help to control urban chaos in the traditional cities. The proposed action plan follows a suitable process of policy intervention that aims to transform cities of hardship to become livable cities. It should have a superior quality of living standards based on the process of transformation. The idea of transforming CC into OC should be presented to these responsible agents for managing the city and formulating recommendations. This action plan includes three aspects:

1. The determination of the groups of teamwork whose task is to turn the city from CC to OC through, first, deputies for the presidency of the city and the heads of districts and municipalities and less urban areas. The second is the stakeholders and the third is the specialists from the universities, particularly, planners and urban designers in all areas of urban development. These specialists should have a scientific background and have the knowledge of the methods of survey and articulations the recommendations.
2. The articulation of the characteristics of CC and OC that depends on the latest trends in urban planning and design with a focus on the visual dimensions as a result of the public realm where the interfaces of the behavioral system in regard to the pattern of transportation within the city.
3. Locating the level, the hardship of living in the city by using the indicators of the livability versus the non-viable cities. This can help in discovering the levels of chaos and order through the criteria concerning the visual and behavioral aspects of each city and defining to what extent the urban hardship is affected by these aspects.

For achieving the three aspects, the action plan includes six steps each one has four phases except the sixth step. The sixth step has a floating description in the scale of the four phases. The phases show the state, the objectives, types of activities, the key actors of responsibility, the key stakeholders, suitable policy intervention instruments (Table 4).

An Index for Measurement

However, the most significant problems of developing cities are the application of indicators and standards first, followed by the follow-up of laws and regulations, and both the visual and behavioral principles are based on their main problem at the level of application. The proposed action of transforming CC to be OC includes an index to measure the cities' difficulties; it will not only estimate the indexes of livability but also, collect between livability, quality of life, and cities of hardship altogether. Thus, this article intends to make politicians, decision-makers, and professionals aware of what is going on in the traditional cities, so that the pressing needs of these cities can be met. The way to do this is to enhance a group's efforts to bring the most successful political goals that encompass livability and quality of life. The role of local government in controlling the context for the citizen.

The main topic that should be related to the urban policies is the standards for dealing with life and hardship that should not only deal with the dimensions of planning but the need to be combined with the quality of life, which deals with design dimensions. Some issues that are related to the requirements of individuals cannot be measured by subjective criteria alone, such as the element of beauty, which is different from the aspects of utility, durability, and economy. Therefore, the context should be handled from the perspective of the concept of the user's appropriateness (approbation) and start providing measurable standards on the objective and subjective levels. The notion of the nature of order may help to resolve the previous issue at two levels: planning and design. Planning interests are in the management of the city, which can modify a new order for the city through different action plans, and which focus on the behavioral setting of those who live and come to live in the city, depend on the rules that govern the quality of the place. The design will be identifiable with human-made elements (form and forma-

Table 4. The four phases and six steps of the proposed action plan. Source: The Authors

Phases Steps	Phase 1	Phase 2	Phase 3	Phase 4
	Policy 'decision-making'		'Policy formulation'	'Policy implementation', 'regulation' and 'evaluation'.
Step 1: The state	Is it CC or OC?	Is it a livable city or a city of hardship?	Understanding the problem: order inside chaos.	Overview – Strategy – Emphasis: Livable cities with high daily living standards instead of cities of hardship.
Step 2: The objectives	- Identify the types of orders in the city: The geometrical, structural, and the deep order. - Describe the salient features of human behaviors for residents and newcomers of the city.	- Understanding the urban hardship. - Use the indicators of the proposed intercity hardship indexes to identify the degree of the hardship or of the cities.	- An opportunity to the authorities to put their ideas of urban policies. - Chaos and order as a root of the urban problems. - The visual and behavioral dimensions being crucial for improving environmental sustainability.	- Integral treatment: Creating new cities do not suffer from the phenomenon of chaos cities and have the characteristics of the city order. - Providing the knowledge for local governments to select the most appropriate urban policy tools.
Step 3: Types & stages of activities	- Discover the geometrical and structural order. - Identify the incompatible activities to make the structural arrangement of the city efficient. - Using the potential that offers a formal context.	- Consider the order (impacts visually and behaviorally) essentially an element among the elements of the hardship.	- Incorporate ideas of satisfaction/ dissatisfaction together with happiness/unhappiness. - Describe the relationship between the two levels of dimensions in the public realm: the visual-aesthetics dimensions and the behavioral settings to get satisfaction.	- Put a forward-looking developmental agenda for urbanization; organizational capacity building; institutional coordination. - Streamline administrative processes and evaluate progress. - Achieve a balance between the powers of the actors involved.
Step 4: The key actors of responsibility	- Students in academic institutions. - Academics and experts in the field of The professional practice.	- City mayors and representatives of the national government. - Experts: the society of The community development (individuals, inter-personal network, groups of community and society).	- The public authorities: reducing the transportation impacts: an attractive city for inhabitants and visitors. - State employees: executive architect in the smallest part in the local government in the municipalities.	- Engineers of Sub-national levels or municipalities who supervise the receipt of the work, and who follow any infractions or bad behavior. - Police responsible for law enforcement. - Enhancing the skills of planning and design.
Step 5: The key stakeholders	- Architect: supervisor in the governmental institutions. - Popular initiatives of the private sector to present the report of chaos in each segment of the city, and the whole of the city.	- Society's members discuss problems to find a solution. - Community participation is a direct pressure on the local government to integrate the order and chaos.	- The national and city government, civil community members and society. - The private sector.	- Civil society should be involved in developing and monitoring the implementation of the policies. - The national and local governments ensure that pedestrian plans are integrated with other transport development plans.
Step 6: Suitable Policy intervention instruments	- A city for all people: Long-term future livability, by considering the people's ongoing satisfaction and through understanding their day-to-day experience of living in the region. - Fit to live in: To promote one element can have unexpected impacts elsewhere develop community livability not only through raising quality of life, economic development, and social equity but also enhancing the visual image and behavioral settings: attractive and worthwhile, safe for children and elderly people, easy mobility and accessibility. - Activate the role of local government institutions in both the legislative and monitoring aspects, focusing on aesthetic and behavioral issues. - Engage stakeholders and professionals in discovering the characteristics of chaos and try to develop solutions that are appropriate to the local community. - Develop higher strategies that deal with the visual and behavioral aspects of the city while activating the role of the supervisory and security authorities to enforce the law decisively. - Economic sustainability: provide more equitable transportation choices, delivery and pick-up the goods at the lowest cost but high-quality, and transport operation and short lead-time to satisfy the best viable way the users' expectations.			

tion) by using the terms of the geometric order, which can be established through objective indices. In so doing, this work introduces a new scale that includes both dimensions. The index LCOHQ measures Livability, Cities of Hardship, and Quality of Life, it consists of six indicators and 53 factors (Figure 7).

FUTURE RESEARCH DIRECTIONS

Given that this chapter ends with the importance of widening the range of evaluating the cities between livability and hardship, the priorities need to have a further outlook. This outlook can help find answers to some questions. Do the studies of urban chaos/order represent a priority in the urban planning and design process of the city? Do the geometrical and structural order come at a later stage in planning, or should they be in the first phases of this process? In doing so, future research can revolve around the study of the influences of the aesthetic-visual and behavioral aspects using digital paragrammatical methods of urban chaos in the built environment of cities.

Figure 7. The index LCOHQ that measures cities of hardship and Quality of Life

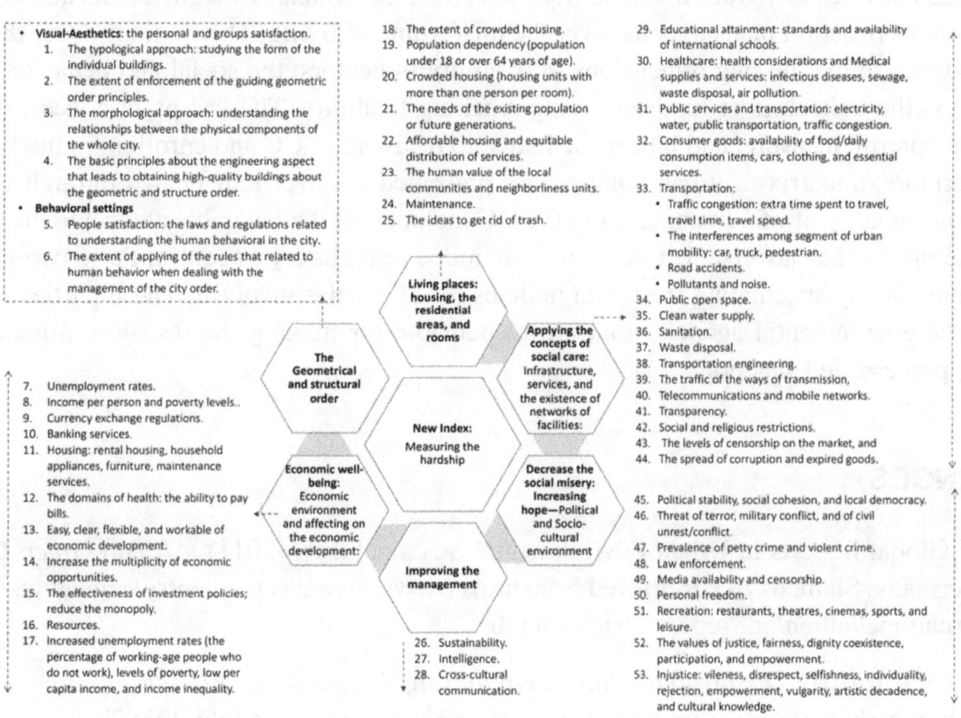

CONCLUSION

The argument of this chapter started with the concepts of urban chaos versus the livable places. The term urban chaos was used in the current work to describe the situation of cities with hard living, which do not have the characteristics of the cities in an order system. As agreed, the Order City (OC) has clear levels of livability to include not only the socio-economic, cultural and environmental aspects but also the behavioral and aesthetic values.

The following part discusses the relationship between the order and the chaotic settings. Indeed, the last is not anarchy, randomness, or disorder. Scanning the literature indicates that 'order emerges out of chaos.' To sum up, 'order,' in the present study, focuses on two types of order. The first is the regular order that gives guidance to develop characterized façades. In the architectural facades and for enhancing the visual appearance of the city, the parameter masses are arranged in a way where the street facades align the public realm to hide and obscure the private and semi-private uses in courtyards. The second is the structural order of the whole city components which control the human behavior. Meanwhile, the thought of the present authors moves toward the need to deal with the built environment from the belief that there are two characteristics of the cities changing between being an OC and a CC.

The contribution covers the need for a hardship index beside the livability indicators. As planners excluded cities of difficulty from the livability indicators, the alliance of signs of CC and OC helps in putting priorities in action plans to come over the misfortune of living. The findings cover three issues. The first extends to the missing dimensions in livability indicators: the social and behavioral settings. The second is the indicators of hardship living reaching livability. The last point concerns the urban policies that control, measure, and hinder the hardship of living in CC and enrolling in the livability of OC. Furthermore, a matrix of urban policies was presented to cover four phases through six steps in each to attain a quality of life. In conclusion, the OC includes all the favorable characteristics of livable cities, while the CC has adverse features. The concluded remarks try to control these two phenomena of the CC and OC by articulating the urban policies for all parties involved. These parties include the users and the governmental agencies that are responsible for making the decision, implementation, monitoring process, and sanctions.

REFERENCES

A Panel of Global Experts in Urban Environmental Sustainability. (2011). *African Green City Index.* Munich, Germany: Siemens AG. Retrieved from https://www.siemens.com/entry/cc/features/greencity-index_international/all/en/pdf/report_africa_en.pdf

AARP. (2015, April 20). *The Livability Index: Great Neighborhoods for All Ages.* Retrieved from Livable Communities: https://www.aarp.org/ppi/issues/livable-communities/info-2015/livability-index.html

Abusaada, H., & Elshater, A. (2017). *Back to the Order: The Chaos in the Cities of Hardship.* Saarbrücken, Germany: Lambert Academic Publishing.

Alexander, C. (2002). The Nature of Order An Essay on the Art of Building and the Nature of the Universe: Book I-The Phenomenon of Life (vol. 9). Berkeley: CA: The Center for Environmental Structure.

Alexander, C. (2002). *The Nature of Order: The process of creating life*. Taylor & Francis.

Allen, J., & Browne, M. (2010). Sustainability Strategies for City Logistics. In *Green Logistics: Improving the Environmental Sustainability of Logistics* (pp. 282–305). London: Kogan Page Limited.

American Renaissance. (2014). *2014 Quality of Living Worldwide City Rankings*. Retrieved 8 29, 2016, from http://www.amren.com/news/2014/02/2014-quality-of-living-worldwide-city-rankings/

Arnheim, R. (1971). *Entropy and Art an Essay on Disorder and Order*. Berkeley, CA: The University of California Press.

Brown, D., Boano, C., Vivekananda, J., & Walker, J. (2015). *Urban Crises and Humanitarian Responses: A Literature Review. The DFID Humanitarian Policy and Partnerships Group*. CHASE.

Carmona, M., Heath, T., & Tiesdell, S. (2010). Public Places, Urban Spaces: The Dimensions of Urban Design. Routledge.

Crow, D. (1989). Le Corbusier's Postmodern Plan. *Theory, Culture & Society*, *6*(241), 241–261. doi:10.1177/026327689006002004

Cullen, G. (1961). *Concise Of Townscape*. London: Architecture Press, Elsevier.

EEA. (2009). *Ensuring quality of life in Europe's cities and towns, Tackling the environmental challenges driven by European and global change*. Copenhagen: European Environmental Agency.

Eisenman, P. (2007). *Written into the Void. Selected Writings, 1990-2004*. New Haven, CT: Yale University Press.

Elshater, A. (2016). The ten-minute neighborhood is [not] a basic planning unit for happiness in egypt. *Archnet-IJAR*, *10*(1), 344–357. doi:10.26687/archnet-ijar.v10i1.878

Ewing, R., & Clemente, O. (2013). *Measuring Urban Design*. Washington, DC: Island Press. doi:10.5822/978-1-61091-209-9

Fielden, A. (2008). *Ignored Displaced Persons: the plight of IDPs in urban areas*. Retrieved from www.unhcr.org

Frisch, M. H. (1982). Urban Theorists, Urban Reform, and American Political Culture in the Progressive Period. *Political Science Quarterly*, *97*(2), 295–315. doi:10.2307/2149480

Gehl, J. (1996). *Life Between Buildings: Using Public Space*. Arkitektens Forlag.

Giap, T. K., Thye, W. W., & Aw, G. (2014). A new approach to measuring the liveability of cities: The Global Liveable Cities Index. *World Review of Science, Technology and Sustainable Development*, *11*(2), 176–196. doi:10.1504/WRSTSD.2014.065677

Hack, G., Birch, E. L., Sedway, P. H., & Silver, M. J. (2009). *Local Planning: Contemporary Principles and Practice*. IGMA Press.

Horn, A. (2015). Urban Growth Management Best Practices: Towards Implications for the Developing World. *International Planning Studies*, *20*(1-2), 131–145. doi:10.1080/13563475.2014.942513

Karimi, K. (2012). Are ection on 'Order and structure in urban design'. *The Journal of Space Syntax*, *3*(1), 38–48.

Kraftl, P. (2014). Liveability and urban architectures: Mol(ecul)ar biopower and the 'becoming lively' of sustainable communities. *Environment and Planning. D, Society & Space*, *32*(2), 274–292. doi:10.1068/d21012

Lash, H. (1976). *Planning in a human way: personal reflections on the regional planning experience in Greater Vancouver*. Ministry of State for Urban Affairs.

Leather, J., Fabian, H., Gota, S., & Mejia, A. (2011). *Walkability and Pedestrian Facilities in Asian Cities: State and Issues*. Metro Manila, Philippines: Asian Development Bank.

LeCorbusier. (1982). *The City of To-morrow and Its Planning*. New York: Dover.

LeCorbusier. (1991). *Précisions* (E. S. Aujame, Trans.). Cambridge, MA: MIT Press.

LeCorbusier. (2013). *Towards a New Architecture* (1931 ed.). London: Courier Corporation.

Lennard, S. H., & Lennard, H. L. (1995). *Livable cities observed: a source book of images and ideas for city officials, community leaders, architects, planners and all other committed to making their cities livable*. Southampton, UK: Gondolier Press.

Ley, A., & Newton, P. (2010). Creating and sustaining liveable cities. In S. Kallidaikurichi & B. Yuen (Eds.), Developing Living Cities: From Analysis to Action (pp. 191-230). Singapore: World Scientific. doi:10.1142/9789814304504_0008

Lough, A. W. (2016). Editor's Introduction: The Politics of Urban Reform in the Gilded Age and Progressive Era, 1870–1920. *American Journal of Economics and Sociology*, *75*(1), 8-22. doi:10.1111/ajes.12139

Lynch, K. (1960). *The Image of the City*. Cambridge, MA: The MIT Press.

Meiss, P. v. (1990). *Elements of Architecture: From Form to Place*. Taylor & Francis.

Milana, B. F., & Creutziga, F. (2016). Municipal policies accelerated urban sprawl and public debts in Spain. *Land Use Policy*, *54*, 103–115. doi:10.1016/j.landusepol.2016.01.009

Mohit, M. A., & Iyanda, S. A. (2016). Liveability and Low-income Housing in Nigeria. *Social and Behavioral Sciences*, (222), 863 – 871.

Montiel, L. M., Nathan, R. P., & Wright, D. J. (2004). *An Update on Urban Hardship*. Albany, NY: The Nelson A. Rockefeller Institute of Government.

Morse, S. W. (2005, June 27). *An Update on Urban Hardship*. Retrieved from Smart Communities: http://smartcommunities.typepad.com/suzanne/2005/06/an_update_on_ur.html

Mosel, I., & Jackson, A. (2013). *Sanctuary in the city? Urban displacement and Urban displacement and Pakistan*. Humanitarian Policy Group, Overseas Development Institute.

Myers, N., & Jennifer, J. (1995). *Environmental Exodus: An Emergent Crisis in the Global Arena*. Washington, DC: Climate Institute.

Nathan, R. P., Charles, F., & Adams, J. (1976). Understanding Central City Hardship. *Political Science Quarterly*, *91*(1), 47–62. doi:10.2307/2149158

Nathan, R. P., Charles, F., & Adams, J. (1989). Four Perspectives on Urban Hardship. *Political Science Quarterly*, *104*(3), 483–508. doi:10.2307/2151275

Neuman, M. (2005). The Compact City Fallacy. *Journal of Planning Education and Research*, *25*(1), 11–26. doi:10.1177/0739456X04270466

Nissel, H. (2010). Global Capital, Neoliberal Politics and Terrains of resistance in Vienna. In S. Banerjee-Guha (Ed.), *Accumulation by Dispossession: Transformative Cities in the New Global Order* (pp. 55–74). Delhi: SAGE Publications India. doi:10.4135/9788132105923.n4

Okulicz-Kozaryn, A. (2013). City Life: Rankings (Livability) Versus Perceptions (Satisfaction). *Social Indicators Research. An International and Interdisciplinary Journal for Quality-of-Life Measurement*, *110*(2), 433–451.

Pearson, C. (1997). Le Corbusier and the Acoustical Trope: An Investigation of Its Origins. *Journal of the Society of Architectural Historians*, *56*(2), 190. doi:10.2307/991282

Rubinowicz, P. (2000). Chaos and Geometric Order in Architecture and Design. *Journal for Geometry and Graphics*, *4*(2), 197–207.

Russoa, F., & Comib, A. (2012). City characteristics and urban goods movements: A way to environmental transportation system in a sustainable city. *Social and Behavioral Sciences*, *39*, 61–73.

Shamsuddin, S., Hassanb, N. R., & Bilyaminb, S. F. (2012). Walkable Environment in Increasing the Liveability of a City. *Social and Behavioral Sciences,* (50), 167 – 178.

The Commission on Human Rights and the General Assembly. (1998). *Guiding Principles on Internal Displacement, E/CN.4/1998/53/Add.2*. New York: United Nations.

The National Association of Regional Councils (NARC). (n.d.). *Livability Literature Review: A Synthesis of Current Practice*. Washington, DC: The National Association of Regional Councils (NARC).

Till, J. (2009). *Architecture Depends* (Vol. 55). MIT Press.

Tucker, B. R. (1897). Instead of A Book (2nd ed.). New York: Molinary Institute.

UN-Habitat. (2014). The Evolution of National Urban Policies: A Global Overview. Nairobi: United Nations of Human Settlements Programme (UN-Habitat).

UN-Habitat. (2016). *From Habitat II to Habitat III: Twenty Years of Urban Development*. UN-Habitat.

UNHCR. (2007). *Internally Displaced Persons: Questions and Answers*. UNHCR. Retrieved from http://www.unhcr.org/basics/BASICS/405ef8c64

United Nations Human Settlements Programme (UN-Habitat). (2016). *Urbanization and Development: Emerging Futures*. Nairobi, Kenya: UN-Habitat.

Victorian Competition and Efficiency Commission. (2008). *A state of liveability: An enquiry into enhancing Victoria's liveability*. Melbourne, Victoria: Victorian Competition and Efficiency Commission.

Vuchic, V. R. (1999). *Transportation for Livable Cities*. Center for Urban Policy Research.

White, J. T. (2015). Measuring Urban Design: Metrics for Livable Places, by Ewing, R. and Clemente, O. *Journal of Urban Design*, *20*(2), 291–292. doi:10.1080/13574809.2015.1008881

Chapter 4
Avatar-Based Management as Help System to Entrepreneurs in Using Emerging Tools

Svetlana Panasenko
Plekhanov Russian University of Economics, Russia

Lubov Belyanina
Astrakhan State University, Russia

Irina Potapova
Astrakhan State Architecture and Construction University, Russia

Svetlana Veretekhina
Russian State Social University, Russia

Liliya Rozhkova
Penza State University, Russia

Vardan Mkrttchian
https://orcid.org/0000-0003-4871-5956
HHH University, Australia

Sergey Vasin
Penza State University, Russia

ABSTRACT

The chapter deals with issues related to the construction and development of the digital economy in one particular region: Republic of Armenia. This country is considered the digital sector of which may become the largest in the country in the next five years. The digital revolution affects all areas of the Armenian economy. Prior to this, the Armenian economy was known as the mining industry, a food producer, and a food. Today, according to statistics, Armenia's leading mining and energy companies are already one step ahead of their colleagues in the economically successful implementation of digital technology. Naturally, in such successes of digital transformations, there are key components. The authors hope that the examples of development and thought about the driving springs of these transformations, chosen in consideration of the interests of the development of the Russian digital economy, can be interesting and useful for Russian enterprises that have started their digital transformations.

DOI: 10.4018/978-1-5225-7625-9.ch004

INTRODUCTION

Significant gains, the necessary breakthroughs over the past decades, in our understanding of the relationship between knowledge and growth, on the one hand, and entrepreneurship and growth, on the other have been made. Analogously, the researchers obtained a result that showed how entrepreneurship, innovation and knowledge are interrelated. But full understanding, that is a clear interface of all these variables: knowledge, innovation, entrepreneurship and growth, unfortunately - was not. The essential relationship between knowledge and innovation, entrepreneurship and the expected growth is very complex and depends on forces that can simultaneously influence all variables, at least in part. These are in case when other variables can expect unidirectional effects or affect only some of these variables. Therefore, the relationship between the microeconomic origin of growth and the macroeconomic position is still too unobvious to cover the entire width of these complex and overlapping variables.

Despite the successes achieved by researchers in the economy, but to date, a number of key issues related to the dynamics of the growth process and subsequent normative conclusions are not fully understood and, as a consequence, are only partially studied. This state of affairs concerns a whole series of simple but very important problems, and the definition of the basic concept of innovation is still lacking explicitly, there is no answer to the question of how they arise and by whom, that is, the connection with entrepreneurial activity. Moreover, there is no answer to the questions:

1. how does innovation contribute to new knowledge (through scientific and technological discoveries or a broader view of innovation?);
2. What knowledge bases and cognitive abilities are crucial for innovation?
3. How exactly do innovations justify growth and how do the effects dissipate spatially?
4. What policy measures should be taken to increase the likelihood of sustainable growth based on knowledge?

These are the questions that will be focused in this chapter with the help of a separate review of the literature in the background and on the examples in MAIN FOCUS OF THE CHAPTER.

We note that the lack of detailed understanding and explicit answers to the above questions shows that our knowledge of the microeconomic fundamentals of growth is not complete, but it can also be very erroneous. The conclusion is obvious that without the exact microeconomic growth model, the derived derivatives of the developed policy are in the zone of risk and perhaps they are wrong. Consequently, the growth reforms developed on them will be incompatible with time and will also change at different stages of economic development. Today's developing countries can learn from policies previously pursued by developed countries, while developed countries themselves face the more complex task of formulating growth policies for the future. Consequently, the relationship between the level of development, entrepreneurship, innovation and growth is a very important indicator, and one must know it.

The authors in this chapter show the essence, dignity, current state and development prospects of avatar-based management using blockchain technology for improving implementation of economic solutions in the framework as help system of entrepreneurs of sharing economy. The authors of this chapter set out to avoid examining the avatars based model for policy advice, but to try to assess the merits, identify avatars-based models as a new basis for policy advice based mainly on work and experience as part of a recently completed project "Triple H Avatar an Avatar-based Software Platform for HHH University, Sydney, Australia which was carried out 2008-2018" (Mkrttchian et al., 2011,2012,2013,2014,

2015, 2016, 2017, 2018). The main goal of this project is to create such a model based on avatars where there is a link between macro and micro levels that provides a single platform for solving problems in various areas of the digital economic system that is designed to assist entrepreneurs. This project was the first to create such a model implementation that allows you to scale simulations for a large number of economic avatars and provide graphical user interfaces that allow researchers at the user level not familiar with the technical details of the implementation to implement for the design of individual parts of the model, engineering and economic experiments and analysis of modeling results for the system of assistance to entrepreneurs.

BACKGROUND

Now in the digital economy, dynamic processes (theory, models, nodes, blocks), although they are understood more deeply, but they still do not take into account the influence of the entrepreneur, who acts as an independent innovator and has his direct impact on the dynamics of economic performance, important, new, higher results. Expert knowledge in the form of accumulated human and / or physical capital, can no longer explain the significance of economic development. Since Adam Smith also proposed the introduction of innovations and entrepreneur for profitable transformation of the above resources (Andersson and Tollison, 1982).

Our research has shown that politicians in many countries of the world represent from our point of view the exclusivity of the influence of both entrepreneurs and their firms. We found that there is a simplistic view that creating a new company or realizing a new project, the society receives a social benefit at the same time, which is not always so, because entrepreneurship, under certain conditions, does not accelerate economic progress, but rather reduces it. Typically, this is due to illegal entrepreneurship, when the entrepreneur spends his talents on seeking a new rent, or increases transaction costs for litigation, that is, a person violating all stimulating entrepreneur incentives. It turns out that the planned, quite progressive new enterprise at the micro level will lead to economic regression at the social level and to the unsuccessful development of micro enterprises in order to promote economic development. The foregoing suggests that at present the social consequences of the actions of individual entrepreneurs, on growth and prosperity, are not considered by researchers with selectivity, adaptation and with the necessary depth.

Our research on the phenomenon of "development" in the digital economy has shown that there really is a non-standard, adaptive-individual relationship between knowledge, innovation and entrepreneurship. These links are becoming more noticeable in the dynamics of economic development in the process of digitalization of the economy. The current view is that the introduction of innovations in the field of knowledge is always a linear process related to activities, research and development. But Mkrttchian's research (Mkrttchian et al., 2011,2012,2013,2014, 2015, 2016, 2017, 2018) showed that many other processes, such as learning, cognitive abilities, network interaction, combinatorial ideas, etc., limit public knowledge, turning the whole process of innovation into a nonlinear process. It turns out that uncertainty, search and experiments are key elements of the innovation process. It has been shown that activities to create knowledge about entrepreneurs and small firms are spreading across a range of different functional areas. Failure to comply with these aspects means that several studies ignore a significant part of the creation of knowledge relevant to innovation and economic growth. This requires a different approach, other developments, new, open software products available to all.

Currently, the level of investment sent to research, development and some other activities to create new knowledge, entrepreneurs and underserved firms make a significant contribution to the overall innovation, thanks to their innovative capabilities. Therefore, despite small investments in activities identified by research and development and other formal knowledge-building activities, entrepreneurs and small firms can still make a significant contribution to overall innovation; thanks to their entrepreneurial have built into them the very nature of the phenomenon of entrepreneurship. But at the same time Mkrttchian showed (Mkrttchian et al., 2011,2012,2013,2014, 2015, 2016, 2017, 2018) that there is no guarantee that new knowledge with commercial potential will immediately be transformed into entrepreneurial initiatives and these effects are based on these knowledge may not appear at all or appear with a delay. For this, new informal approaches are needed, which the authors of this chapter suggest, namely the application potential of blockchain technology to sliding mode in intellectual control and communication (Mkrttchian, and Aleshina, 2017). Our research on the Russian market has shown that entrepreneurship entails the actions and activities of individuals working in firms or for themselves, and important incentives are there that stimulate risky entrepreneurial activities, as well as an infrastructure that allows the transfer of knowledge from knowledge-generating subjects to knowledge that entrepreneurs use in their daily activities, introducing innovations into it. At the same time, firms and entrepreneurs are developing their strategies for balancing the slow processes of knowledge development and with instant and fleeting windows of opportunities and searching for ways to accelerate the generation and use of knowledge. However, an important role is played by the financial system, the pervasive evaluation of potential entrepreneurs, mobilization and channeling of savings for financing the most productive activities, the diversification of risks, etc. Thus, the design of financial systems affects growth, increasing the likelihood of successful innovation. The question is how this is taken into account in standard growth models based on knowledge. The technology of blockchain combined with sliding modes completely solves these challenges of the digital economy (Mkrttchian et al., 2011,2012,2013,2014, 2015, 2016, 2017, 2018).

Since the governments of all countries today absolutely strictly support open source software development, Mkrttchian's digital avatars are written exactly with this code. The main reasons for this are to avoid software silos or create closed systems for interaction, to take advantage of the economic advantages of open source code and to clearly represent security issues. We offer avatars to program open source (OSS) - since such computer software with source code available with a license in which the copyright owner grants the rights to study, modify and distribute the software to all and for any purpose is very well suited to the philosophy of our avatars, which suggests that open source avatars management software can be developed in conjunction with the public. In our opinion, open source software is a vivid example of open cooperation and consonant with the principles of the digital economy. The development of open source software or joint development from several independent sources creates an increasingly diverse field of design than any company that can develop and maintain a long-term perspective. And this is also one of the phenomena of a joint digital economy with its own and very significant indicators. Below are our campifications of the well-known truths of the digital economy to achieve the goals set in our research and outlined in this chapter. It is known that management in the digital economy is engaged in the development, implementation, monitoring and improvement of business processes. It is also known that systems that support the adoption and execution of these business processes are widely used by companies to optimize and automate intra-organizational processes. But we found out that, for between organizational processes, the problems of joint design and the lack of mutual trust hampered a wider perception of these proven management methods. In our opinion, the new blockchain technology has the potential for a radical change in the environment in which between organizational processes can interact. Blockchains offer a way to perform processes in a reliable manner even in a network without mutual trust between nodes. Key aspects are specific algorithms that lead to a consensus between the nodes and market mechanisms that motivate the nodes to promote the network. Thanks to these capabilities, this technology has the potential to transfer discourse in management research on how systems can include the acceptance, execution, monitoring or improvement of business processes within or across a business network. Using blockchain technology, unreliable parties can establish trust in true code execution. Smart contracts can be used to implement business cooperation in general and inter-organizational business processes in particular.

However, our research has shown that that the blockchain still faces numerous common technological problems. In this chapter we find and describe those main new problems and the possibilities of blockchain technology for their solution in the Digital Economy of modern Russia. Based on our earlier study (Mkrttchian et al., 2011,2012,2013,2014, 2015, 2016, 2017, 2018), in Russia, we state that most of these problems have not been resolved, although the Russian research communities in general and the block chain development communities are actively discussing some of these problems and theoretically even trying to solve their solutions offer many potential solutions. They expect that some of them can be solved using a private or consortium blockchain instead of a fully open network. But we also state that technological problems are currently limited in terms of supporting developers (lack of proper tools) and supporting end users (it is difficult to use and understand). There are two poles: there are no corresponding tools, as there are no developers of these tools, and the available tools are so complex that they are not perceived by users (Mkrttchian, and Aleshina, 2017). Our recent advances on developer support include efforts by of the towards model-driven development of blockchain applications sliding mode in intellectual control and communication, help the technological challenges and created tools) (Mkrttchian, and Aleshina, 2017)

Our research (Mkrttchian, and Aleshina, 2017) is the first to identify the application potential of blockchain technology to sliding mode in intellectual control and communication, for help the technological challenges and created tools. We are invited to describe inter-organizational processes using blockchain technology with a large flow of control and business logic, while interorganizational business processes can be compiled from process models into intellectual contracts (that is, under the control of an intelligent avatar), which ensures that the joint process will be correctly executed. The intelligent avatar is based on a trigger switch that allows you to connect these interorganizational processes to web services and implement internal processes. These triggers serve as a bridge between the block chain and enterprise applications. This concept provides the ability to implement intelligent control and built-in control at certain points in the process where it is desirable and possible (Mkrttchian, et al, 2016).

The engineering realization of this advance is still nascent at this stage, although some early efforts can be found in our previous works. For example, intelligent visualization techniques that enforce a process execution in a trustworthy way can be generated from sliding mode process models (Mkrttchian, and Aleshina, 2017).

Our study (Mkrttchian, and Aleshina, 2017) show that blockchain technology and its application to digital economy in Russia are at an important crossroads: engineering realization issues blend with promising application scenarios; early implementations mix with unanticipated challenges. It is timely, therefore, to discuss in broad and encompassing ways where open questions lie that the scholarly community should be interested in addressing. We do so in the sections that follows.

MAIN FOCUS OF THE CHAPTER

Issues, Controversies, Problems

Theoretical achievements and empirical studies seem to confirm the view that the processes of generating knowledge, innovation and entrepreneurship are localized processes. Nevertheless, no matter what flows of knowledge are largely limited in space, one can observe how knowledge, innovation and entrepreneurial initiatives are exchanged between functional urban areas and even countries. Thus, despite the fact that the regions are characterized by different internal economic and infrastructure networks, they are also connected by a multitude of such networks. Obviously, there is an important interaction between localized processes of knowledge generation, innovation and entrepreneurship, but at present there is practically no understanding of the relative importance of interregional and international networks. An increasingly global knowledge base serves to expand and diversify the local knowledge base, i.e., what was invented by "local noise and global pipelines".

From the point of view of the policy of the digital economy, this is a well-established result, according to which the market economy usually does not create a socially optimal volume of creating knowledge, innovation and entrepreneurship. However, consensus on what institutional framework and policy measures that could create such a social optimum would not be a consensus, given the imperfections of both the economic and political markets at the present time. However, this did not prevent politicians from initiating a large number of institutional changes and policies to stimulate the creation of knowledge, innovation and entrepreneurship for the digital economy. Nevertheless, the number of carefully conducted policy assessments is rather limited, which means that there is a huge knowledge gap about which politicians really work and whether they cost them. This chapter proposes the use of digital avatars for solving both local and national and over national problems of the digital economy.

Before moving on to the factors that contribute to or hinder entrepreneurship and innovation in the local region of the Republic of Armenia, we will first look at the academic view on the economic consequences of these forces. While some scholars and politicians believe from the very beginning that more entrepreneurship and innovation are good for the local area, this connection is difficult to pin down because of the endogenous nature of both forces. Despite a small discussion about the relationship between local growth and smaller, younger firms, this correlation may reflect the tendency of rapidly growing areas to attract new firms, rather than the impact of start-ups on local growth. These problems make it difficult to interpret typical data that exist at the local regional level. Moreover, it is possible to assume that in some places there are assets, such as strong research universities or pro-business policies that generate growth and attract start-ups. Some academic views give multivariate correlations between these factors, but empirical work that requires causal estimates is much smaller. We discuss the state of these academic views with hope, the most important conclusion being that much more work is required in this regard.

The intellectual tradition mentioned above and similar observations on the role of entrepreneurship in the success of the city on the example of the Republic of Armenia showed that the shortage of entrepreneurs in mining areas reflected its historical concentration in industry, which had a significant return on scale and potentially displaced more entrepreneurial activity. We expect that this evaluation of entrepreneurship is associated with both static factors (for example, with access to investment, and with financial capital for new enterprises) and dynamic factors (for example, the transfer of skills and attitudes from parents to children). In contrast, there was a vivid impulse of entrepreneurship, coming down from the city's early work in the decentralized mining industry, and we can argue that this industrial genealogy helped explain why one region grows faster than another neighboring one. Although his analysis pointed to the strength of local cultures of entrepreneurship, we refrain from making any strong policy recommendations related to this conclusion.

Moving from entrepreneurship to innovation, the relationship between innovation and efficiency of the city was focused on the model. This model especially explains the economy of cities, why cities grow or shrink, and also the movement of industries in different cities. The premise of the model is that the location of industries in cities is determined by where past breakthrough inventions occurred. This conceptual model creates models that fit well with data: for example, it predicts that industries will move around cities much faster than cities will move up and down the city size distribution.

Although there are specific studies of this process, the connection core of the model with breakthrough inventions has rarely been tested. And there are plausible reasons why one can be skeptical: why move an entire industry to a new place, and not just translate the invention itself? Some work on this topic of the model is possible on the basis of the exclusive embodiment of human capital in specialized workers in the emergence of the mining industry. A significant part of the early development of such an industry occurred in the cities where scientists and engineers of the emerging industry live, and not in places with a large number of potentially related factors, such as venture capital financing, universities, etc.

Apart from this development of breakthrough patents and the formation of new industries, work has been limited on factors that contribute to a general level of innovation and employment growth in local areas. We carefully studied the features of innovation in the "cities of companies", in which one large firm dominates. Their work shows that these large firms often become insular in their innovations, relying more on past experience of the company and less studying their efforts in the field of research and development. Based on this research and earlier work on the hypothesis of a monopolistic role, we believe that the combination of large and small firms provides the most productive environment for innovation. The study showed that the optimal mixture for patenting growth in the local area includes at least one large innovative firm, but also a sufficient mass of many small innovative firms. This mixture best reflects the benefits of innovation that come from large firms, while preserving fertile ground for new start-ups, often created by former employees of operating firms. The existing work on entrepreneurship and local innovation does not imply any natural local policy. This, however, points to the power of small start-ups, which can collectively shape the economic destiny of the region. The study showed that in the two study areas of the Republic of Armenia there was a subsequent decline in employment. However, today, one area is flourishing, unlike another, because of the large number of local entrepreneurs, some of whom grew up in the city, and others were brought into the city from outside. The key issue for local innovation policy is whether there is something that can be done to introduce more of this local business. Clusters are seen as a tool to advance this goal, and we turn to empirical data on economic clustering.

Before moving on to the Solutions and Recommendations section, we will analyze the spatial concentration for entrepreneurship and innovation, which is the same in our opinion both at the local level and at the national and global levels, as will be shown later. As discussed above, the case for cluster policy depends on the existence of strong inter-firm side effects, which naturally generate clusters and justify a spatially oriented business policy. In order for these policies to make sense, these side effects should demonstrate an increase in returns to scale (that is, 200 entrepreneurs generate more than twice as many secondary effects from 100 entrepreneurs) or are disproportionately distributed among members of a certain industrial sector. That is, even if entrepreneurs generate secondary effects, it makes sense to group these entrepreneurs if these side effects either work non-linearly in local areas, or if only entrepreneurs benefit from clustering with each other. First, we will describe a few descriptive facts about the spatial concentration of entrepreneurship and innovation in the Republic of Armenia. We do not spend too much time on this, because this common feature of the economic landscape is well known and not much discussed. Our starting point is to observe that the mining industry itself is sufficiently concentrated, even before business and innovation. A metric was developed to assess the degree to which industry is more spatially concentrated than the population as a whole. It turned out that the manufacturing industries were more spatially concentrated than was usually expected on the basis of the main population. At the same time, we found out that this clustering can represent side effects between companies or the uneven distribution of production factors throughout the space. We have established a critical issue concerning clusters and cluster policy, is the role of infrastructure. Some branches of the mining industry of the Republic of Armenia require specialized infrastructure, including physical highways and information highways. Governments have long taken on the role of supporting the provision of infrastructure, although economists and academics have discussed the merits of financing user fees. The need for a specialized infrastructure increases the value of clustering. In contrast, industry groups that do not need specific technologies provided by governments will have fewer advantages from clustering. Even if business clusters are good for local growth, it is less clear that cities or states have the ability to generate these clusters that are the same both at the local level and at the national and global levels. Now we describe the research of spatial factors related to entrepreneurship and innovation, and consider what empirically attracts entrepreneurs to specific areas. In contrast to the results of the studies discussed above, at the beginning of this section on the economic consequences of entrepreneurship and innovation, about local factors that generate or support clusters. We can draw on the results of studies that have been conducted in many countries and overlap with several academic disciplinary boundaries. Limitations on the length of the chapter do not allow mentioning each study. Instead, we will consider here some of the main topics arising from these studies, and we will try to highlight several recent results that provide special evidence of local results obtained and our compatibility with national characteristics and at the global level.

Solutions and Recommendations

Our research has shown that the process of economic development in the modern digital economy can be divided into three clearly separate stages. The first stage involves the technical discovery of new things or new ways of doing things, such as invention. At the next stage, innovation occurs, that is, the successful commercialization of a new product or service, stemming from technical discoveries or, more generally, a new combination of knowledge (new and old). The final step in this three-step process - imitation - involves more general adoption and distribution of new products or processes to markets (Mkrttchian, and Belyanina, 2018).

Obviously, there are numerous pitfalls in measuring inventions and innovations for partnership. Regardless of what scale is being applied, measurement difficulties and subjective evaluation criteria may in some way distort data about knowledge and can always be criticized. Some frequently implemented knowledge variables probably miss out on significant parts, while others tend to overstate the knowledge. The most common measure for the use of knowledge and innovation is expenditure or patents. Here we propose to manage open software resources using digital avatars (Mkrttchian et al., 2011,2012,2013,2014, 2015, 2016, 2017, 2018).

Open source software has long become a ubiquitous industrial production and business. There is, for example, a tremendous amount and variety of open-source software components and third-party components that arise in every software development environment in the world. With proper use and management, these components are a huge source of energy to accelerate innovation in the digital economy. But in such successes of digital transformations there are key components. One of them is a formalized ontology, the development of which in the world today is paid the most attention. Therefore, the authors on specific examples tried to show the digital transformations in Armenia and their moving hidden springs. Because the digital economy is nothing more than the effects of additional returns on detailed knowledge of the physical world through digital data and technology, we needed a concrete example of physical placement, and we chose two the states in Republic of Armenia – Vayk and Sunik. These two neighboring states are defeated by radical digital changes. We have chosen Lidian Gold Armenia in the mining sector - complementary use of Lydian Gold Armenia's digital technologies. We have taken a number of technical and technological measures and made recommendations, which are set out below.

The recent decline in commodity prices means for this state that such digital innovations have become mandatory for business. This caused a need for the redesign of processes, data analysis and the need for advanced research needs in which will only worsen. Formalized semantics and ontology turned out to be part of new tools for solving new economic problems through innovations that ensure transparency. The mining and energy sectors, as well as the wider ecosystem of these states, have realized that innovation thrives on cooperation as well as competition. The exchange of knowledge is necessary for the development of new solutions, and it is possible only with their ontological formalization and transparency. These states are well provided with sectorial research institutes and programs; to achieve the necessary economies of scale, this research effort will require and, as Armenia understands, cooperation at the national and global levels is also necessary to obtain formalized knowledge (Mkrttchian, and Belyanina, 2018). Digital Mkrttchian's avatars, more precisely the expert knowledge generated by them, enable each member of the network, called a node, to contain a chain of blocks that makes up the history of transactions performed on the network. Each block contains a set of transactions, the size of which depends on how many banks and financial institutions do not actually have an API, or have a very truncated form. Also, any financial system faces the risk of non-fulfillment or disputing by the parties of the transaction of payments made. Innovations in any industry depend on the ecosystem of suppliers, start-ups, research institutes, governments, service providers and asset owners. There is evidence that transformational new technologies are likely to evolve in complex, interdependent research ecosystems. The main problem of companies engaged in mining operations in states Vayk and Sunik is the lack of qualified personnel for very difficult working conditions. It is very difficult to find people who, even for a large salary (the average salary, for example, locomotive drivers there is about \$ 1,000 for a two-week watch) are willing to work in the constant stress and heat of states. Our research has shown that problems can be solved with the help of Mkrttchian's intelligent avatars (Mkrttchian, and Aleshina, 2017). The proposed blockchain system can be successfully applied for Smart solutions in create Intellectual systems use Expert Knowledge. Such solutions gave such automation a processor, which led to a number of important achievements at the company's iron mines in the region. We began to use several automated heavy trucks, focused on shared GPS and video control technologies, so that this automation helped to ensure more efficient and safe movement of mining material. In addition to the AHS trucks, seven fully autonomous drilling systems (ADS) for the drilling of wells are operating in the Iron Ore Group, and unmanned aerial vehicles are being tested to assess reserves and assist with environmental and maintenance activities. About 150 kilometers from the mines, the Armenian Operations Center acts as the "nervous center" of the system of mining enterprises in the region. Here the team of the center, numbering about 100 people, controls all the company's activity in the mines of the states in real time - up to every truck. Drivers - people need regular breaks, and AHS trucks can work almost 24 hours a day, 365 days a year, stopping only for refueling and maintenance. Since 2010, the autonomous park (fleet) at the states mines in the company has exceeded the manned fleet by an average of 24 percent, and has reduced operating costs by 18 percent. Cars without a driver are designed to more efficiently deliver their goods, minimize delays and reduce costs associated with maintenance, tire operation and fuel consumption. One of the advantages that miners get with autonomous transportation is the consistency with respect to how these machines operate. GPS technology - similar to that used in car navigation systems - is the central part of the autonomous transport system of Lydian (AHS). AHS trucks are specifically created using modern computers that perform common tasks related to driving a vehicle, such as starting an engine, acceleration and deceleration. Then the computers react to GPS routes, are controlled remotely by operators to ensure greater safety of operation. For such an automatic mining operation, Lydian made a digital map of the whole zone of activity of the mining enterprise and placed it in the system, and then the system developed how the trucks should maneuver through this zone. Trucks are programmed for the most efficient transportation of goods and equipped with proximity detection and collision avoidance systems to detect and prevent hazards. To perform these functions, the digital map must monitor the changes in the terrain and often be updated. In the energy section, we give illustrations of the sequence of applications of GIS; they have many common features, since minerals are devoted to one topic. However, we determined that it is necessary to have digital GIS data not only about the state of the surface, but also about placing the ore underground, and they must be consistent with each other. We propose to use one of the latest innovations in the program Mine of the FutureTM is the introduction of the RTVisTM system, which works just like an ultrasound or a laser scanner, and provides 3D images of ore deposits in real time located far below the surface of the earth. The combination of this technology with trucks without a driver and autonomous drilling machines led to an increase in ore mining and cost reduction. This is due to the fact that digital knowledge provides more accurate drilling and blasting, reduced use of explosives and better classification of waste. As a result, less waste and more ore are transported on trucks. All this became possible with the use of formal ontological GIS-models that are transparent with respect to other formal ontologies necessary for building working information systems, which will be discussed later. There has been a redefinition of the relationship between people and machines in the spirit of when robots take on hard and difficultly performing work functions, and a person is more intelligent. While the introduction of automation has led to the reduction of some traditional operational roles in mining, it has also created new ones - from career patrols that help drive trucks in the field, to technicians that service intelligent systems. Although we believe that there are conclusions that can be drawn at this stage - research universities have a strong influence on local development; focusing on large-scale employers can crowd out small start-ups - we need much more information before an entrepreneurial policy can reach a relatively mature status, such as a policy on international trade and monopoly. The primary need is to experiment and evaluate, especially when randomizing. For example, if a government creates an entrepreneurial cluster that overflows, it can randomize at least some of the spaces in the cluster. Comparing the results of winners and losers in the "space lottery", the government can assess the impact of politics. If the government continues to provide loan guarantees on a sustainable basis, at least some of the loans can be randomly allocated in a way that allows for an assessment of the results of these loans. Today, experimentation is taking place throughout the Republic of Armenia, as the new government at all levels (along with numerous private and non-profit organizations) is developing a policy in the hope of creating its own national silicone bunker. The problem is that this experimentation has almost no future, and it is often unclear which outcome variables (ie the number of start-ups, employment, patents) are needed for this. Moreover, most policy-makers, especially when programs are relatively inexpensive, can naturally endorse such an approach, in which every potential intervention can contribute to the development of entrepreneurship, is considered simultaneously. In fact, efforts to provide entrepreneurial education, access to capital, promotion of exports, etc. are simultaneously not possible. In the region of the Republic of Armenia considered in this chapter, it is often beneficial for beginners to undertake what makes assessing any complex political interference difficult.

FUTURE RESEARCH DIRECTIONS

Such questions remain for future research. How do we account for this dynamic in the current growth models? To what extent are the deferred effects and interaction effects included appropriately? And what is actually indigenized by the accumulation of knowledge? If knowledge should be seen as the engine of growth or it is the best metaphor for perceiving knowledge as fuel that feeds on a mechanism that converts knowledge into growth, for example: entrepreneurs, innovations, labor mobility, etc.? Was the technical balance really transformed into an entrepreneurial balance?

Many developers are rushing to develop software that can use these precedents and act as the best solution provider, often in several markets at the same time. You can imagine the winner scenario - all this because of the effect of a strong network that the largest provider will like, but it's interesting that some signs indicate that this may not be a coincidence. The future will be built by people who use their intellect and dexterity to develop solutions to the problems of everyday life. Prosperity, as a social harmony, depends on those who can create a new value, embodying successful ideas: designers, engineers and scientists. We call them thinkers. Designers in all their forms, especially technologists and engineers, are the most promising agents of long-term wealth. Engineers use technical knowledge to solve society's problems. History has shown us that engineers, volunteers and problem developers are developing solutions and technologies that actually create economic growth. Today, the Silicon Valley leads the world to wealth creation, invention and technology. It has the largest concentration of engineers in the world.

Evaluation as a concept becomes more important for regional cluster initiatives, in particular, as well as other programs that contribute to the development of entrepreneurship. The key problem here is that plausible counterfeits against which benchmarks are measured are difficult to construct and therefore rarely considered, which makes interpretation of any results difficult. This is due to the fact that the use of randomization to create research opportunities is particularly complex in this area, where politicians often deliberately target specific areas for additional funding and where "winners and losers" are very visible.

CONCLUSION

- Despite the fact that entrepreneurship is a powerful force that generates local and economic growth, it is not obvious that state policy can create entrepreneurship. Even if entrepreneurs, naturally, are grouped in narrow geographical units, it is not obvious that the government should use state policy to support such clusters. While the above-mentioned business policy usually does not require large flows of funding, it is still important to consider the shortcomings of inefficient policies. At this point, we are still just beginning to acquire sufficient wisdom to create reliable policies that absorb the externalities that may come from innovations and new start-ups.

- Thus, knowledge about microeconomic processes in the modern digital economy that lead to growth is still incomplete. In neoclassical growth models, the production of knowledge was exogenous - the technical remainder, whereas the dissemination of knowledge was either exogenous, stochastic or isolated to large firms that more closely resemble pharmaceutical companies in which research departments try to come up with the following combination of molecules that will turn into the next unit - booster.
- But knowledge is developed, applied and disseminated in many other ways, often through smaller innovative firms and entrepreneurs. The uncertainty, asymmetry and high transaction costs inherent in knowledge also give rise to a divergence in the evaluation and evaluation of the expected value of new ideas. This discrepancy in the assessment of knowledge between economic agents and in the decision-making process of existing firms can induce agents to start new firms as a mechanism for assessing the (expected) value of their knowledge. This suggests that entrepreneurship facilitates the dissemination of knowledge in the form of creating a new firm.
- Digital technologies are integrative, as they require higher levels of integration in the tracking and travel process, as well as between real-time management systems and IT business systems.
- However, developing new ways of working with the supply chain and an alternative procurement model is fundamental to transforming the network into an affordable way. This complex shift is aimed at moving from geographic specific signal updates, to an integrated package of interventions in partnership with franchises and working with suppliers to achieve the desired results based on all life cycle costs.
- In the digital economy, ontological approaches are already becoming the standard today and not only mining enterprises or railways, but digital technologies themselves are subjected to digital transformation. To ensure transparency, semantic connectivity of projects and compliance with latency requirements, formal ontological methods began to play a key role in many digital projects, allowing rapid accumulation of technological knowledge from open sources to specific physical conditions and methods used by computers and other computing devices.

ACKNOWLEDGMENT

This research was supported by the Russian Foundation for Basic Research:

[Grant number 18-010-00204] entitled: Fundamental basis for the development of mechanisms for effective digital service-oriented interaction of participants in socio-economic systems and networks ;

Professor Vardan Mkrttchian (HHH University, Australia) for supporting this chapter as a scientific leader.

REFERENCES

Anderson, G., & Tollison, R. (1982). Adam Smith's Analysis of Joint-Stock Companies. *Journal of Political Economy*, *90*(6), 1237–1257. doi:10.1086/261119

Arifovic, J., Dawid, H., Deissenberg, C., & Kostyshyna, O. (2010). Learning Benevolent Leadership in a Heterogenous Avatars Economy. *Journal of Economic Dynamics and Control.*

Belk, R. W. (2007). *Consumption, Mass Consumption, and Consumer Culture*. The Blackwell Encyclopedia of Sociology. doi:10.1002/9781405165518.wbeosc116

Bershadsky, A., Berezin, A., & Mkrttchian, V. (2018). Theoretical and Technological Perspectives on Development of Information Monitoring System for Solving Complex Problems. Academic Press.

Botsman, R. (2013). The sharing economy lacks a shared definition. *Fast Company*. Retrieved from http://www.fastcoexist.com/3022028/the-sharing-economy-lacks-a-shared-definition

Botsman, R. (2015). *Defining the sharing economy: What is collaborative economy - and what isn't?* Retrieved from https://www.fastcompany.com/3046119/defining-the-sharingeconomy-what-is-collaborative-consumption-and-what-isnt

Botsman, R. (2015). The Changing Rules of Trust in the Digital Age. *Harvard Business Review*. Retrieved from https://hbr.org/2015/10/the-changing-rules-of-trust-in-the-digital-age

Botsman, R., & Roo, R. (2011). *What's mine is yours: how collaborative consumption is changing the way we live*. London: Collins.

Chriss, A. (2015). The Disrupter Series: How the Sharing Economy Create Jobs, Benefits Consumers, and Raises Policy Questions. *Subcommittee on Commerce, Manufacturing, and Trade of the Committee on Energy and Commerce House of Representatives, 114*(80), 45-56.

Colander, D., Föllmer, H., Goldberg, M., Haas, A., Juselius, K., Kirman, A., . . . Sloth, B. (2009). *Financial Crisis and the Systemic Failure of Academic Economics*. Working paper No. 1489. Kiel Institute for the World Economy.

Contini, B., Leombruni, R., & Richiardi, M. (2004). Editorial. *Advances in Complex Systems, 7*, 125–138.

Dawid, H., & Fagiolo, G. (2008). Avatar-based models for economic policy design: Introduction to the special issue. *Journal of Economic Behavior & Organization, 67*(2), 351–354. doi:10.1016/j.jebo.2007.06.009

Dawid, H., Gemkow, S., Harting, P., & Neugart, M. (2009a). Spatial Skill Heterogeneity and Growth: An Avatar-based Policy Ananlysis. *Journal of Artificial Societies and Social Simulation, 12*(4), 5.

Dawid, H., Gemkow, S., Harting, P., & Neugart, M. (2009b). *Labor market integration policies and the convergence of regions*. Working Paper. Bielefeld University.

Deissenberg, C., van der Hoog, S., & Dawid, H. (2008). EURACE: A Massively Parallel Avatar-based Model of the European Economy. *Applied Mathematics and Computation, 204*(2), 541–552. doi:10.1016/j.amc.2008.05.116

Felson, M., & Spaeth, J. L. (1978). Community structure and collaborative consumption: A routine activity approach. *The American Behavioral Scientist, 21*(4), 614–624. doi:10.1177/000276427802100411

Gamidullaeva, L., Potapova, I., Shatokhin, M., & Mkrttchian, V. (2018). Increasing Territorial Economic Growth through Cost Optimization in the Digital Economy. In *Optimizing Regional Development Through Transformative Urbanization*. Hershey, PA: IGI Global; doi:10.4018/978-1-5225-5448-6.ch009

Gamidullaeva, L., Vasin, S., & Mkrttchian, V. (2018). *Regional Economic Growth and Open Innovation Platforms: Emerging Trends and New Opportunities*. Academic Press.

Judd, K., & Tesfatsion, L. (Eds.). (2006). *Handbook of Computational Economics* (Vol. 2). North Holland.

Khvostikova, V., Semionova, E., Chernetsov, M., Mkrttchian, V., & Potapova, I. (2017). Cost Control Strategy for the Implementation of the User Innovation Potential in the Digital Economy. InIsaias, P., & Carvalho, L. (Eds.), *User Innovation and the Entrepreneurship Phenomenon in the Digital Economy* (pp. 267–287). Hershey, PA: IGI Global. doi:10.4018/978-1-5225-2826-5.ch013

Kollman, Miller, & Page. (1997). Political institutions and sorting in a Tiebout model. *The American Economic Review*, *87*, 977–922.

Krevskiy, I. G., Bershadsky, A., & Glotova, T. (2018). Research Competence for Development of Distance Education in Russian Universities. In V. Mkrttchian, & L. Belyanina (Eds.), Handbook of Research on Students' Research Competence in Modern Educational (pp. 385-408). IGI Global. Doi:10.4018/978-1-5225-3485-3.ch020

LeBaron, B., & Winker, P. (2008). Introduction to the Special Issue on Avatar-Based Models for Economic Policy Advice. *Journal of Economics and Statistics, 228.*

McCarroll, N., & Curran, K. (2013). Social Networking in Education. *International Journal of Innovation in the Digital Economy*, *4*(1), 1–15. doi:10.4018/jide.2013010101

Mkrttchian, V. (2011). Use 'hhh" technology in transformative models of online education. In G. Kurubacak & T. Vokan Yuzer (Eds.), *Handbook of research on transformative online education and liberation: Models for social equality* (pp. 340–351). Hershey, PA: IGI Global. doi:10.4018/978-1-60960-046-4.ch018

Mkrttchian, V. (2012). Avatar manager and student reflective conversations as the base for describing meta-communication model. In G. Kurubacak, T. Vokan Yuzer, & U. Demiray (Eds.), *Meta-communication for reflective online conversations: Models for distance education* (pp. 340–351). Hershey, PA: IGI Global. doi:10.4018/978-1-61350-071-2.ch005

Mkrttchian, V. (2015). Modeling using of Triple H-Avatar Technology in online Multi-Cloud Platform Lab. In M. Khosrow-Pour (Ed.), Encyclopedia of Information Science and Technology (3rd ed.; pp. 4162-4170). Hershey, PA: IGI Global. Doi:10.4018/978-1-4666-5888-2.ch409

Mkrttchian, V., & Aleshina, E. (2017). *Sliding Mode in Intellectual Control and Communication: Emerging Research and Opportunities*. Hershey, PA: IGI Global. doi:10.4018/978-1-5225-2292-8

Mkrttchian, V., & Aleshina, E. (2017). Sliding Mode in Real Communication. In *Sliding Mode in Intellectual Control and Communication: Emerging Research and Opportunities* (pp. 22–29). Hershey, PA: IGI Global. doi:10.4018/978-1-5225-2292-8.ch003

Mkrttchian, V., Amirov, D., & Belyanina, L. (2017). Optimizing an Online Learning Course Using Automatic Curating in Sliding Mode. In N. Ostashewski, J. Howell, & M. Cleveland-Innes (Eds.), *Optimizing K-12 Education through Online and Blended Learning* (pp. 213–224). Hershey, PA: IGI Global. doi:10.4018/978-1-5225-0507-5.ch011

Mkrttchian, V., Aysmontas, B., Uddin, M., Andreev, A., & Vorovchenko, N. (2015). The Academic views from Moscow Universities of the Cyber U-Learning on the Future of Distance Education at Russia and Ukraine. In G. Eby & T. Vokan Yuzer (Eds.), *Identification, Evaluation, and Perceptions of Distance Education Experts* (pp. 32–45). Hershey, PA: IGI Global. doi:10.4018/978-1-4666-8119-4.ch003

Mkrttchian, V., Berezin, An., Berezin, A., Veretikhina, S., Bershadsky, A., & Potapova, I. (2018). Model of Benchmarking for Development of Firm's Competitive Advantage to Improve Economic Growth in Cities. In U. G. Benna (Ed.), *Optimizing Regional Development Through Transformative Urbanization*. Hershey, PA: IGI Global. doi:10.4018/978-1-5225-5448-6.ch008

Mkrttchian, V., Bershadsky, A., Bozhday, A., & Fionova, L. (2015). Model in SM of DEE Based on Service Oriented Interactions at Dynamic Software Product Lines. In G. Eby & T. Vokan Yuzer (Eds.), *Identification, Evaluation, and Perceptions of Distance Education Experts* (pp. 230–247). Hershey, PA: IGI Global. doi:10.4018/978-1-4666-8119-4.ch014

Mkrttchian, V., Bershadsky, A., Bozhday, A., Kataev, M., & Kataev, S. (Eds.). (2016). *Handbook of Research on Estimation and Control Techniques in E-Learning systems*. Hershey, PA: IGI Global. doi:10.4018/978-1-4666-9489-7

Mkrttchian, V., Bershadsky, A., Finogeev, A., Berezin, A., & Potapova, I. (2017). Digital Model of Bench-Marking for Development of Competitive Advantage. In P. Isaias & L. Carvalho (Eds.), *User Innovation and the Entrepreneurship Phenomenon in the Digital Economy* (pp. 288–303). Hershey, PA: IGI Global. doi:10.4018/978-1-5225-2826-5.ch014

Mkrttchian, V., Kataev, M., Hwang, W., Bedi, S., & Fedotova, A. (2014). Using Plug-Avatars "hhh" Technology Education as Service-Oriented Virtual Learning Environment in Sliding Mode. In G. Eby & T. Vokan Yuzer (Eds.), *Emerging Priorities and Trends in Distance Education: Communication, Pedagogy, and Technology*. Hershey, PA: IGI Global. doi:10.4018/978-1-4666-5162-3.ch004

Mkrttchian, V., Kataev, M., Hwang, W., Bedi, S., & Fedotova, A. (2016). Using Plug-Avatars "hhh" Technology Education as Service-Oriented Virtual Learning Environment in Sliding Mode. In Leadership and Personnel Management: Concepts, Methodologies, Tools, and Applications (pp. 890-902). Hershey, PA: IGI Global. doi:10.4018/978-1-4666-9624-2.ch039

Mkrttchian, V., & Stephanova, G. (2013). Training of Avatar Moderator in Sliding Mode Control. In G. Eby & T. Vokan Yuzer (Eds.), *Project Management Approaches for Online Learning Design* (pp. 175–203). Hershey, PA: IGI Global. doi:10.4018/978-1-4666-2830-4.ch009

Mkrttchian, V., & Stephanova, G. (2013). Training of Avatar Moderator in Sliding Mode Control Environment for Virtual Project Management. In Enterprise Resource Planning: Concepts, Methodologies, Tools, and Applications (pp. 1376-1405). Hershey, PA: IGI Global. Doi:10.4018/978-1-4666-4153-2.ch074

Nielsen. (2014). *Is sharing the new buying? Reputation and trust are emerging as new currencies.* The Nielsen Company. Retrieved from http://www.nielsen.com/content/dam/nielsenglobal/apac/docs/reports/2014/Nielsen-Global-Share-Community-Report.pdf

Potapova, I., Vasin, S., Gamidullasrva, L., Tolstykh, T., Belyanin, L., & Mkrttchian, V. (2018). Drivers of Urban Development in Terms of Education Based on Digital Technologies. In Optimizing Regional Development Through Transformative Urbanization. Hershey, PA: IGI Global. Doi:10.4018/978-1-5225-5448-6.ch003

Schumpeter, J. (2013). *Capitalism, socialism and democracy*. London: Routledge.

Sundararajan, A. (2016). *The sharing economy: The end of employment and the rise of crowd-based capitalism*. Cambridge, MA: MIT Press.

Tolstykh, T., Vasin, S., Gamidullaeva, L., & Mkrttchian, V. (2017). The Control of Continuing Education Based on the Digital Economy. In P. Isaias & L. Carvalho (Eds.), *User Innovation and the Entrepreneurship Phenomenon in the Digital Economy* (pp. 153–171). Hershey, PA: IGI Global. doi:10.4018/978-1-5225-2826-5.ch008

Tolstykh, T., Vertakova, J., & Shkarupeta, E. (2018), Professional Training for Structural Economic Transformations Based on Competence approach in the Digital Age. In Handbook of Research on Students' Research Competence in Modern Educational Contexts (pp. 209-229). Hershey, PA: IGI Global. Doi:10.4018/978-1-5225-3485-3.ch011

Vasin, S., & Gamidullaeva, L. (2017). About Russian Regional Users' Innovation Based on Digital Information. In P. Isaias & L. Carvalho (Eds.), *User Innovation and the Entrepreneurship Phenomenon in the Digital Economy* (pp. 304–319). Hershey, PA: IGI Global. doi:10.4018/978-1-5225-2826-5.ch015

Vasin, S. M., & Gamidullaeva, L. A. (2015). Methodical Approach and Tools to Improve the Efficiency of Managing of the Innovation Potential in the Context of Economic Globalization. *Review of European Studies, 3*, 124–139.

KEY TERMS AND DEFINITIONS

Application of Blockchain Technology: Is application multifunctional and multilevel information technology designed to reliably record various assets in Digital Economy for help the technological challenges and created tools.

Avatar Model of High Technology: Is new model with natural intelligent for Avatar introduced in 2011 from Professor Vardan Mkrttchian.

Avatar-Based Management: Is new management technology in Digital Economy introduced in 2018 from Professor Vardan Mkrttchian.

Blockchain Technology: Is a multifunctional and multilevel information technology, designed to reliably record various assets in digital economy.

Entrepreneurs to Real Using Emerging Tools: Is entrepreneurs for the real use of new tools is a new approach to the concept of entrepreneurial phenomenon in a regional digital economy that can be used both at the national and national levels introduced in 2018 from Professor Vardan Mkrttchian.

Help and Control System: Is the system of reference and control is a new system based on knowledge and used for entrepreneurial in a digital economy introduced in 2018 from Professor Vardan Mkrttchian.

Sharing Digital Resource: Is exchanged of the digital resource is a new type of cooperation between enterprises in the digital economy in the form of knowledge obtained from digital avatars introduced in 2018 from Professor Vardan Mkrttchian.

Section 2

Industrial and Urban Growth Policies at the Continental Level

On the issues of industrial and urban growth policies at the level of the continents, the contributing researchers focus on African smart cities, changing roles in the public and the private sectors, defining gaps strategies and strides of Fourth Industrial Revolution, and Sub-Saharan Africa and North Africa industrial and urban growth policies. The predominantly African researchers—but some working in the Middle East and other parts of the world—analyzed the challenges and opportunities of smart cities in Sub-Saharan Africa; the shift in the leading roles from public to private sector in African industrial urban growth; exploring the gaps, strategies, and strides of the Fourth Industrial Revolution in Africa; and a comparative analysis of industrial and urban growth policies in Sub-Saharan Africa and North Africa.

Chapter 5
Smart Cities in Sub-Saharan Africa: Opportunities and Challenges

Innocent Chirisa
University of Zimbabwe, Zimbabwe

Abraham Rajab Matamanda
University of the Free State, South Africa

ABSTRACT

The aim of this chapter is to interrogate and diagnose the concept of smart cities as it has been applied to Sub-Saharan Africa (SSA) in a bid to decrypt the opportunities and challenges characterizing its manifestation in space and actuality. The chapter is a product of the critical engagement of scholarly work that compares the best practices in the development and promotion of the smart city concept against those practices that are antithetical and retrogressive in light of this good cause. To crystallize the realities, the chapter makes use of case studies that speak to these contrasting experiences. Case studies in SSA reveal differential practices with South Africa emerging as a country doing very well relative to others in the region. Some cities, especially the small and intermediate ones, fail to break even in terms of the revenue collections. This is partly because they have failed to attract investment in the form of industries or retain them because of politically induced instabilities.

INTRODUCTION

Cities in the developed world have embraced the concept of a smart city and subsequently, have come to benefit from going smart (Zanella et al. 2014; Albino et al. 2015; Dickey, 2018). Despite the clear knowledge and appreciation of developing and managing smart cities, Africa, and SSA, in particular, continue to face challenges that may be averted by adopting smart city initiatives (Kitchin, 2015). The 'smartness' in this context, has to do with the usage of information and data through computer applications hence reducing unnecessary paperwork and traditional ways of processing data and information (Angelidou, 2015). Castells (2010) refers to the process as the scientific organization of work and means

DOI: 10.4018/978-1-5225-7625-9.ch005

of production which divert from mass production to flexible production. The smartness of the cities is mainly defined by the use of technology and Information Computer Technology (ICT). Musakwa and Van Niekerk (2014) highlight how the use of ICT is very critical towards attaining and managing smart cities. Hence, a smart city is one that the jigsaw fits the ideals of low-carbon cities (Letaifa, 2015).

On the socio-economic and political side, smart cities are better-governed cities. The citizenry can express its opinions using various platforms which are usually convenient and in this way responses are very rapid. Unlike in the traditional setup, there is little interaction between urban managers and the citizens when it comes to decision-making and urban governance. The smart city ensures good governance practices in which transparency, accountability, rule of law, trust, responsiveness, public participation are the pillars of engagement hence a functional city (Kitchin, 2015). Smart cities also engage effective utilization of information and communication platforms which make the planning and management of the cities (Angelidou, 2015). In urban planning, the use of geospatial databases, remote sensing and relate earth observation tools and platforms makes the process easy. These are spatial decision support system critical for twenty-first-century management of the built and natural environment (Musakwa, 2017). Location is an important factor in both industrial and urban policy (Dickey, 2018).

In the face of the litany of these advantages of the smart city, we ask critical questions which have baffled many scholars and practitioners. First, why are countries in SSA lagging behind when it comes to the introduction of smart cities initiatives? Second, what are the constraints which African states have to grapple with in relation to the adoption of smart cities concept? Last, how does the future look like for Africa? South Africa, Namibia, Kenya, and Botswana stand out as leading in the cause for the promotion of smart city concept in SSA. This is so because there is a general willingness by the central and local government structures to have smart cities and dividends have registered on the ground as an investment has been attracted to these countries. Smart city promotion and enhancement goes with financing which has been the case in these countries identified. For example, South Africa has made great strides with the Gau-train in Gauteng province an initiative which has been aimed at creating a smart city (Chirisa et al. 2018). On the contrary, those countries that have 'unfinished business' in terms of high corruption indices, fear of the unknown in adoption and skepticism tend to be laggards in the promotion of the smart city concept (Okeke, 2017). Fear of the unknown is partly a matter of seeking to veil shady deals by the local government officials who then fight the initiative from within. They would rather see the initiative die a still-birth than see the light of the day. Apart from resistance by the officialdom, the cost of acquisition and maintenance of the data infrastructure is high.

CONCEPTUAL FRAMEWORK

The conceptual framework guiding his study is explained in this section. In this regard, the section first outlines the concept of a smart city which is then followed by a discussion of SSA.

Despite the global use of the term smart city, there seems to be no global definition which defines what a smart city is as there are various definitions to the term (Albino et al. 2015). Providing a definition for the terms thus becomes complicated even if one tries to separate the concept and focus on the two words, that is, smart and city as outlined by Dickey (2018) that the term smart city is a composition of two words, smart and city. This implies that the definition of the term differs from region to region and from city to city (Letaifa, 2015). The definition of the smart city brings about various components that are linked to infrastructure (soft and hard) (Ahvenniemi et al. 2017). For cities to be smart they have to bear elements of technology and innovation within infrastructure (Albino et al. 2015). The smartness of a city includes components like low-carbon buildings which may be powered by solar energy or green buildings, smart transport (Gautrain), smart people and smart governance among others (Zanella et al. 2014). However, this is normally very expensive as a result when determining whether a city is smart or not, it is done on a continuum, ranging from inefficient to smart (Ahvenniemi et al. 2017). The inefficient city normally bears the poor systems, poor technology, inefficiencies in every aspect of the city (service provision and delivery) while the smart city having components like technology and data-driven infrastructural provision (Ahvenniemi et al. 2017). For the purpose of this study, however, as a smart city will be defined as "an innovative city that uses ICTs and other means to improve the quality of life, efficiency of urban operation and services and competitiveness, while ensuring that it meets the needs of present and future generations with respect to economic, social and environmental aspects."

Regions determine the qualities as well as provisions of a city (Mguni et al. 2016). Sub-Saharan Africa is a continent with fifty-four countries which are largely characterized as developing countries (Haldevang, 2016). Only two countries among the SSA nations are ranked as middle-income economies, which show the high prevalence of poverty in the region (Storeygard, 2016). Furthermore, the region has some of the highly ranked countries in terms of corruption (Pieterse and Short, 2017). Therefore, governments in SSA seek to address issues of poverty and providing the least possible services to improve the well-being of the communities in their respective countries (Dos Santos et al. 2017). Currently, 60% of the population is still rural but it is estimated that by 2050 60% of the population will be living in urban communities (Mguni et al. 2016). This presents a problem in implementing initiatives in the region as most governments will not be in a position to afford the financial need (Dos Santos et al. 2017). A few industries that are locally embedded may continue in the cities but may not be adequate to cushion the cities of the vagaries of disinvestment and industrial decline. Most African cities are victims of urban informalisation. The informal sector is thriving well in SSA. Free riding is a characteristic feature of the informal sector such that it is difficult to harness resources from it as taxation is a major source of revenue for local government business. The chapter makes critical recommendations for a study of the context of each of the selected cities so that transformative measures can be put in place for the sustainability of the practices of the smart city concept. Local authorities must fully embrace good governance as their *modus vivendi*. It is from this motif that meaningful adoption of the smart city concept can be achieved.

LITERATURE REVIEW

Smart cities exist across the globe. The characteristics, definitions, and innovations differ from region to region. The extent to which a city can be termed a smart city is depended on the level of innovation and economic development. Conceptualizing what is meant by smart cities' is different from region to region and even within a region (Albino et al. 2015). The levels of development within various regions determine the definition of a smart city. The definition of a smart city is thus normally driven by the aspirations of the citizens. In Latin America, the definition of a smart city is determined by the levels of socio-economic development (Zanella et al. 2014). Therefore, the definition of a smart city is one that embraces the notion of sustainable infrastructure (Soderstrom et al. 2014). In developed countries, the definition advances to include issues of sustainability of the infrastructure, relating to issues like green infrastructure (Dickey, 2018). In Europe and North America, the definitions are now linked to introducing technological innovations to improve the sustainability of the cities (Castells, 2010; Dickey, 2018).

Therefore, defining a smart city ranges in regions determined by the economic as well as technological development (Zanella et al. 2014).

In understanding the smart city, various terms, definitions, and classifications come into play. For a city to be termed a smart city, it has to bear traits of smartness that is smart infrastructure (hard and soft) smart governances. Smart infrastructure provides a framework for all other components of a smart city that include smart mobility, smart people, smart environment, smart economy and smart governance (Rathore, 2016). The infrastructure and smart city components are designed in a way that they generate data that will be used in managing the environment to restore equilibrium on resource use (Manville et al. 2014). A good example is the Stockholm Royal Seaport in Sweden which envisaged that by 2030 it will provide 10 000 homes and 30 000 workspaces by utilizing climate-smart and efficient infrastructure (Ericsson, 2013). In this way, the development of the city not only takes into consideration the housing needs of the community by does so through a focus on the socio-economic needs of the residents as well as the environmental considerations.

Smart buildings are the most notable elements of a smart city (Glasmeier and Christopherson, 2015). These buildings are designed in a way that they minimize and reduce energy use, waste generation and therefore can be categorized as being effective in enhancing sustainability (Kylili and Fokaides, 2015). It is presumed that such buildings increase water efficiency by 40% as well as reduce maintenance costs by approximately 30% (Mohanty et al 2016). For example, in Austria, the implementation of the plus-energy-burohochhus as a smart office building saw the construction of a building that feeds more energy into the national grid than it consumes (Glasmeier and Christopherson, 2015). Such buildings greatly reduce energy consumption which is usually the main polluter in urban areas, especially considering that most of the energy is produced using unsustainable practices.

Other elements of smart cities are smart mobility (Ning et al. 2017). This considers transport planning issues which range from greening, efficiency, and affordability (Benevolo et al 2016). The planning options are determined by the data that are collected from various transport options (Janssen et al. 2015). The transport systems are linked to issues like mass transit systems, biking and pedestrian-oriented transport (Ning et al. 2017). In Sao Paulo, Brazil, bicycle sharing has reduced carbon emissions since 2012 (Benevolo et al 2016). Furthermore, ideas like convenience technology in transport like Uber are also playing a crucial role in smart transport planning (Tussyadiah et al. 2017). The issues of reducing congestions, using modern technology make up a critical component of smart cities (Ning et al. 2017). Transport is a critical component of smart cities because it is responsible for mobility and usually accounts for economic losses through production time that may be lost by the commuters, especially when congestion is rampant. It is also in this vein that the Gau-train of South Africa comes into perspective as a means of promoting the smartness of the city.

Another component of a smart city is smart energy (Lund et al 2014). Smart energy is a system that employs modern technology like sensors, meters and renewable energy to optimize the use and distribution of energy (Alan et al. 2015). The major components of smart energy are a smart which is a system that is enhanced with ICT to improve the operations of the grid (Lund et al 2014). In Japan, the Kashiwa-no-ha smart city project has a smart electricity grid (Nastasi and Lo Basso, 2016). The system combines a home energy management system 24-hour monitoring systems and demand self-sustained energy management (Lund et al 2014).

Smart water also plays an important part in smart cities (Dickey, 2018). Considering that water is becoming a scarce resource there exist various initiatives to save water in cities (Meyer et al. 2016). The first is natural water resource management where the critical issues to be considered include smart water systems manage aimed at improving water meters and flow management (Dickey, 2018). Natural gradients may be used to promote water flow, thereby reducing the use of energy to pump water to the consumers. On the other hand, wastewater treatment sites may be decentralized while natural ecosystems like ecosystems may be used to purify such wastewater (Skiyi et al. 2016). Moreover, digital systems may be installed with the view to help reduce costs, save water as well as increase transparency and reliability of water distribution (Meyer et al. 2016). The water pipes are lined with information networks that provide data to manage water supply and demand systems (Ntuli and Abu-Mahfouz, 2016). This reduces the water wastage as the information of water leakages can be detected and corrective measures are quickly taken before more water is lost.

Smart cities also rely on components of smart waste management, smart health among others (Albino et al. 2015). These components entail integrating the data that exist within the cityscape and making the data available for manipulation. Proper manipulation of the data will ensure the increased efficiency and proper use of the available resources for the good of the city (Dickey, 2018). In this way, the city of Cape Town has made some strides in efforts to even separate the waste at the source such that those which can be recycled is recycled. The operation of smart infrastructure ideas, especially in developing countries, faces numerous challenges (Kylili and Fokaides, 2015). This section discusses some of these challenges and the role of (Science, Technology, and \Innovation) STI communities can play in overcoming them, including some policy instruments driven by STI that could help to address each challenge.

Smart city implementation requires one to localize smart infrastructure (Khatoun and Zeadally, 2016). A given smart city solution cannot easily be relocated from one geographic region to another (Scuotto et al. 2016). Smart infrastructure concepts should be made locally applicable and answer to local development needs (Boulos and Al-Shorbaji, 2014). Context, culture, and economics all play a critical role in this process (Boes et al. 2015). Cities should think through urban problems in all-inclusive manner before choosing suitable smart technology solutions (Khatoun and Zeadally, 2016). For instance, the orthodox intelligent transport systems methodology, relating a huge network of sensors and the accumulation of data, may be too costly and inappropriate for developing country needs (Boes et al. 2015). A simpler form of intelligent transport systems may leverage more universal mobile telephone data, which may be more fit to developing country contexts.

Governments can distribute research funds to smart city projects and provide enticements to make such projects a priority within their STI communities (Pierce and Andersson, 2017). Cities need to consider how best to use existing innovation infrastructure such as science parks, technology incubators, and innovation hubs to develop new smart city ideas and adapt smart city concepts (Djadel et al. 2015). For example, in Gothenburg, Sweden, a collaboration between two science parks and several other stakeholders resulted in the first modern electric bus route (Boes et al. 2015). Most importantly, cities need to create policy environments where massive amounts of small-scale innovation related to smart cities can flourish.

There is also a need to promote open data, open science models. Globally open data enterprises by Governments and the private sector have been a great motivation for smart city applications (Pierce and Andersson, 2017). For instance, the platform for open data in Singapore, endorsed by the Government, effectively uses the potential of open data in stimulating locally appropriate smart city initiatives (Scuotto et al. 2016). To make the best use of open data enterprises, as well as encourage additional innovation, civic hacking occasions have been arranged by various city governments and technology firms.

Localizing technology in making relevant smart cities has also been improved by exploiting regional innovation networks and global collaborations (Boes et al. 2015). When cities by themselves lack the capacity to conduct smart city-related research, make investments or create local adaptations, they can join with other cities confronting similar developmental challenges, as well as with technology partners, to conceptualize, finance, implement and exploit complementary competencies and share lessons learned (Khatoun and Zeadally, 2016). A successful example in this regard is the European Innovation Partnership on Smart Cities and Communities that, by pooling resources, aims to co-fund demonstration projects help coordinate existing city initiatives and projects and overcome bottlenecks to transition processes (see http://ec.europa.eu/eip/smartcities/). Similar collaborative initiatives, such as the International Summit for Smart Cities in North Africa (see http://isc-summit.org/en/) and the Asia Africa Smart City Summit held in Bandung, Indonesia

Another challenge that makes it hard to implement smart cities is the issue of skills gaps (Boes et al. 2015). For a smart city to be fruitful in its activities, human resources expertise need to be accessible to guarantee that all the diverse aspects of the city are sufficiently and efficiently addressed (Khatoun and Zeadally, 2016). For example, a digital or data layer must be added to all relevant operations, and more technology vendors and the integrated functioning of different departments must be dealt with. The skills comprise of planning and design, digital citizenship, data literacy, implementation and management (Scuotto et al. 2016). Investing in smart people, not only smart technology is essential (Pierce and Andersson, 2017). Currently, there is little research, especially in developing countries, that quantifies the exact skills deficit (Kylili and Fokaides, 2015).

To improve on the issues of skills knowledge, there is a need to accelerate education programs in science, technology, engineering and mathematics (Meyer et al. 2016). A noteworthy share of smart infrastructure creation and maintenance jobs requires a good foundation in education in science, technology, engineering and mathematics (Djadel et al. 2015). A smart city agenda gives all the more reason to accelerate and popularize education in these fields (Khatoun and Zeadally, 2016). The popularity and success of the Science of Smart Cities Program and the Urban Data School show that similar programs may help expose students to the real-life smart city applications of scientific concepts and attract more students to science, technology; engineering and mathematics at an early age (see http://engineering.nyu.edu/k12stem/sosc/ and http://urbandataschool.org/).

There is a need for curriculum reforms at the primary and secondary school levels and in higher educational institutions and technical and vocational education and training, in order to integrate the special skills requirements of smart infrastructure (Boes et al. 2015). A key characteristic of a smart city is that it is a multidisciplinary phenomenon; designing innovative smart infrastructure requires multidisciplinary teams to collaborate (Scuotto et al. 2016). Universities and schools should encourage and provide opportunities for multidisciplinary research and learning. New departments and courses related to the new urban science are already emerging in many universities (Khatoun and Zeadally, 2016). A recent analysis shows that "since 2005, more than a dozen new labs, departments, and schools have been launched with a common purpose – to pursue deeply quantitative and computational approaches to understanding the city" (Kylili and Fokaides, 2015). In addition, massive open online courses and other online training on different smart city skills may be good resources for mitigating skills gaps.

Private sector firms are actively involved in developing smart city solutions and new innovative smart applications (Djadel et al. 2015). The public sector can join with firms to provide much-needed training to its workforce (Alan et al. 2015). More courses designed and conducted by technology firms could be made available to current students through existing educational infrastructures in order to fill specific skills gaps in cities (Alan et al. 2015). Some technology vendors are already engaging in such partnerships with city governments.

Smart cities initiatives re also stifle by lack of finance and well-developed business models (Djadel et al. 2015). Smart infrastructure projects require pooling public and private resources through creative financing and public-private partnership models (Boes et al. 2015). Policies, taxation, and regulatory certainty also play an important role in this process (Khatoun and Zeadally, 2016). Governments need to address such issues in order to encourage the private sector to grow and innovate in new, thoughtful and increasingly strategic ways to invest in smart city projects (Scuotto et al. 2016). Strategically funding smart city infrastructure and technology investments is critical to the realization of smarter cities. Smart city projects are often complex undertakings, involving long time horizons, multiple stakeholders, and risks (Meyer et al. 2016). Citizens must be made aware of the costs involved, the associated benefits and the prices they will be charged before the commencement of projects. Some key policy instruments are highlighted in this section

To meet smart city financing needs there is a need to develop technology-driven innovative financing models. A smart city application allows for huge efficiency gains and less waste of resources. If efficiency gains are measured through appropriate smart technologies and monetized through business models, then a part of smart infrastructure investment costs may be recovered through such gains (Khatoun and Zeadally, 2016). Such technology-driven outcomes-based payments may be a viable financing tool for smart infrastructure projects and public-private partnerships (Boes et al. 2015). The third-party financing of projects may then be used, with the guaranteed payback of energy, water or operational cost savings. Another possibility for raising revenue is to establish customized user fees or congestion charges during peak hours in certain public spaces or city centers, enabled through sensor networks and cameras, which may help to reduce traffic congestion and promote safe pedestrian traffic (Kylili and Fokaides, 2015). In Germany, the KfW Group development bank developed a scheme to monetize the energy efficiency gains of residential buildings (Khatoun and Zeadally, 2016). Crowdfunding platforms can also help to acquire financing for smart city concepts. For example, Pakri Science and Industrial Park in Estonia conducted a successful crowdfunding campaign for its smart city expansion.

Another approach to smart city development is to monetize data (Scuotto et al. 2016). Smart infrastructure generates data, which may be transformed by city governments to generate new insights that may be monetized and sold to different stakeholders (Djadel et al. 2015). The key is to generate a suitable value chain for such data and an appropriate business model for the data at different layers (Boes et al. 2015). In addition, big data and analytics can enable increased tax collection levels by reducing tax evasion and this increase in revenue may be leveraged for smart infrastructure investments (Alan et al. 2015). However, during the process of monetizing data, the privacy and security of all citizens need to be ensured.

Governance also presents an issue in trying to develop smart cities (Meyer et al. 2016). Smart cities call for new governance models (Khatoun and Zeadally, 2016). Effective smart city management needs to balance both top-down and bottom-up governance approaches (Alan et al. 2015). On the one hand, collating the information generated by smart sensors deployed in different smart infrastructures and taking policy actions, especially during emergencies, may require strong top-level leadership and top-down execution processes (Scuotto et al. 2016). On the other hand, bottom-up governance approaches, including citizen-driven innovations and co-creation, have been the defining characteristic of much of smart city infrastructure (Boes et al. 2015). Managing a good balance between these two approaches is therefore important. Achieving such a balance helps city governments harness the synergy between various participants (such as universities, the private sector, civil society and local and municipal governments). Further, an effective governance model for smart cities requires breaking down silos across different government departments (Kylili and Fokaides, 2015). Information islands act as the greatest barrier to resource integration in the course of development, at both the technical and management levels of smart cities. Governance models need to be reformed in order that the data from smart infrastructure may be made available and used effectively in decision-making processes.

Dealing with governance issues requires one to promote platforms for bottom-up participatory governance (Scuotto et al. 2016). Several innovative and technology applications provide platforms through which city governments may actively engage with citizens in a regular manner (Boes et al. 2015). City governments are currently using various innovative platforms and technologies to actively engage with citizens in the management of cities (Khatoun and Zeadally, 2016). For example, in Amsterdam, a smart citizen kit was distributed to citizens to help create an air quality sensor network with their participation (Kylili and Fokaides, 2015). In Bangalore, India, the social enterprise Next Drop helps coordinate information between operations centers, water suppliers and customers using calls and short message services, with residents informed of any disruption in water services, and the mobile application serving as a social platform to discuss water-related issues (Alan et al. 2015).In Jakarta, city officials have used Twitter to better respond to flooding situations (Meyer et al. 2016). Such technology platforms also help create transparency and accountability, which strengthens participatory governance.

Furthermore, there is a need to establish smart city operations centers to break down administrative silos (Khatoun and Zeadally, 2016). Smart cities generate data and information that are gathered through utilities and infrastructure components and often controlled by different government entities (Scuotto et al. 2016). Without breaking down administrative silos across these entities, cities will not be able to make the best use of collected data (Boes et al. 2015). One common method for meeting this challenge, which several smart cities have adopted, is to establish a central operations center to which data from multiple sources are directly fed (Meyer et al. 2016). For example, in Rio de Janeiro, Brazil, a smart city operations center brings together the municipality's 30 departments and private suppliers in a single monitoring room (Alan et al. 2015). Operations centers allow for the efficient use of data by merging and collating different data types that help make more information available to decision makers (Alan et al. 2015). This approach is a relatively top-down one, but such centers may be game changers in times of crisis (Djadel et al. 2015). They help ensure that top-down decision-making processes are more evidence-based and transparent, as the data used to make decisions may be made public.

Another key challenge faced by the smart city concept is to ensure the engagement of all groups of citizens and to promote inclusivity (Boes et al. 2015). Smart city applications should be inclusive in terms of providing opportunities for all and ensuring that particular groups are neither left out of positive impacts nor disproportionately affected by any societal costs that may be imposed (Scuotto et al. 2016). For instance, the needs of vulnerable groups such as women, the elderly and persons with disabilities should be integrated into smart city strategies. The need to ensure inclusivity for such vulnerable groups is especially important because there is a significant possibility that they will lack the skills to use smart city applications or that their livelihoods may be the most affected by smart city applications (Khatoun and Zeadally, 2016). Promoting participatory governance in cities is a prerequisite for developing inclusive smart cities (Kylili and Fokaides, 2015).

In dealing with issues of inclusivity there is need to help formalize informal sectors through smart applications (Meyer et al. 2016). Data on informal sectors and informal settlements are missing in most countries. (Meyer et al. 2016) This is one main reason why they may often be left out of city plans and programs (Scuotto et al. 2016). However, STI-driven solutions may help in mapping informal sectors and this data can later be used to gauge the impact of various smart city projects on such sectors, as well as to design smart city infrastructures oriented to their needs (Boes et al. 2015). One of the main characteristics of informal sectors is that they do not have access to mainstream public utilities such as piped water or electricity (Meyer et al. 2016). However, smart infrastructure applications may be devised to make these basic utilities available to people in informal sectors (Scuotto et al. 2016). For example, M-KOPA Solar in East Africa uses mobile technology and solar power to make available affordable high-quality solar power solutions to people excluded from the main power grids (see http://www.m-kopa.com/). Similar applications may be crucial in ensuring inclusivity in applying smart city concepts, especially in developing countries.

The definitions, characteristics, and challenges that are associated with smart cities call for appropriate smart infrastructure design principles and policy approaches (Khatoun and Zeadally, 2016). From discussions on smart city projects worldwide some key principles that may guide smart infrastructure projects may be distilled, as follows:

1. **People-Centered and Inclusive:** While technology in the form of smart city infrastructure is an integral part of a smart city, it should only be seen as an enabler to meet the needs of the people of the city (Boes et al. 2015). Smart infrastructure development should, therefore, rely on a people-centric approach that responds to the sustainable development needs of people, and avoids a technology-centric approach (Scuotto et al. 2016). Smart infrastructure should be chosen and designed with a deep understanding of people's lifestyles, cultures, behaviors and needs.
2. **Smart Cities Should Be Resilient and Sustainable:** The convergence of climate change effects, urbanization and globalization present unprecedented challenges to cities (Khatoun and Zeadally, 2016). The notion of resilience is espoused in the Sustainable development Goals 11 which envisage cities which are able to withstand shocks of various kinds. Smart infrastructure should, therefore, be resilient to external shocks and ensure sustainability.
3. **Interoperable and Flexible:** Smart infrastructure technologies are rapidly evolving (Kylili and Fokaides, 2015). All necessary steps should be taken to ensure that smart infrastructure components are interoperable (Djadel et al. 2015). Further, infrastructure should be designed in order to be flexible with regard to future modifications and enhancements.
4. **Risk-Mitigating and Safe:** Smart city infrastructure components raise new risks and safety concerns, as smart infrastructure may be prone to hacking and illegal access (Scuotto et al. 2016). Ensuring the privacy of citizens is also an important concern (Boes et al. 2015). Therefore, smart city development should be accompanied by appropriate risk management and risk mitigation strategies. Building skills in related fields should also be a priority.

METHODOLOGY

The study is skewed more towards the interpretivism worldview. The interpretive worldview seeks to explain the phenomenon which is mainly qualitative in nature (Cresswell, 2013). Subsequently, the data collection and analysis methods used were qualitative in nature. To address the issues raised in the study, a desktop search was used as a means of data collection and this is a kind of secondary data collection method which is explained by Mogalakwe (2006) as being convenient for qualitative studies. Hence, data was collected from documents, texts and literature documents on the available subject relating to smart cities as well as for as cases from SSA. Data was then organized into themes and thematic content analysis was used to derive meanings and conclusions on the subject matter.

RESULTS AND ANALYSIS

Development of smart cities is pinned to the status quo of the study area. Sub-Saharan Africa is a region that is lagging behind in terms of technology and development. However, the region has various opportunities that make the region ripe for the implementation of smart cities. The same region has its own challenges, strategies, and strides in relation to making local cities smart cities. The following section seeks to present the findings in relation to smart cities.

Sub-Saharan Africa's GDP is expected to reach $1.6 trillion by 2020 (Parnell and Pieterse, 2014). This will represent 5% of the world's GDP compared to 2.4% in 2010 (Djurfeldt, 2015). Information and communications technology have directly contributed 7% to Africa's GDP in the last 5 years–higher than the global average (Potts, 2018). The World Bank estimates that a 10 percent increase in teledensity raises a country's Gross Domestic Product by at least 1 percent. These statistics show the potential of Africa in the implementation of the idea of smart cities in the region.

Development in Africa has been leapfrogging which is a phenomenon that brings in the idea of the underdeveloped overtaking the developed nations. To illustrate this, in SSA and Africa at large, the mobile phone networks skipped the wired era and embraced wireless (Amankwah-Amoah, 2015). This means that mobile phones are often used in new, ingenious way, more sophisticated than what can be seen in Europe or the USA (Clarfield and Rosenthal, 2017). In this context, improving urban-dwellers' access to data and social networks, and building applications on top of that could help address some of the continent's major issues. One of the interesting examples is open-source software for information collection, visualization, and interactive mapping can play a positive role and perhaps even trigger the social change (Lundgaard and Jorgensen, 2016; Musakwa, 2017). The Ushahidi project initially developed by Juliana Rotich and her team to map reports of violence in Kenya after the post-election violence in 2008, expanded across the world and is now one of the most used platforms of its kind. A sign of how innovation developed in Africa can then conquer the world (Graham and Foster, 2014).

The explosive demographic situation in many Sub-Saharan African cities has led to serious mobility issues (Ury, 2016). Upon the establishment of the city of Nairobi, the roads were developed to serve a settlement of 350,000 people, yet at the present moment, they now serve over 3 million inhabitants (Tesfaye et al. 2017). The same applies to cities in countries like Zimbabwe, Mozambique, Botswana, South Africa and others (Potts, 2018). As a result of this, congestion has become one of the major African problems (Kinai et al. 2014). In Nairobi, the TwendeTwende is a mobile phone service that was developed in IBM's research center in the Kenyan capital (ibid.). Swahili for "let's go," TwendeTwende takes images captured by existing low-cost cameras and applies network-flow algorithms to estimate traffic flow (Kinai et al. 2014). The solution does not require expensive road construction but rather uses cameras already present around the city to help facilitate traffic flows.

Another significant opportunity for smart cities in SSA is the demography of the region. Sub Saharan Africa has the largest share of the population being youths with only 3% of the average population being of people. Africa, as a continent, has the largest share of the youthful population with 62% of the population being 25 years and below (Potts, 2018). According to Ahmed et al (2015), the youths consume more internet than older people. Bearing in mind that the major characteristic of smart cities is dependence on ICT, Sun-Saharan Africa becomes a ready market for smart cities as the largest portion of the population is within the age group of internet consumers. Therefore, the population trends of the region make it ripe to develop smart cities within the region. A good example is presented for the Gautrain which was meant to enhance Johannesburg as a smart city. In trying to get useful information for analyzing the citizen's perceptions of public transit systems, social media platform was used to capture the citizens' responses (Musakwa, 2014)

The urbanization rates of the region are rocketing. In 2014, 250 million people were urban dwellers in the region. The portion of the urban population is expected to increase to go up to 55% by the year 2050 (Potts, 2018). With current traits of the African economies, urbanization seems to be a challenge at the first glances as it is characterized with urbanization without economic growth however, it presents opportunities for development and economic growth (Potts, 2018). The growth of urban population calls for the development of related infrastructure. This presents an opportunity to develop smart infrastructure and smart cities through leapfrogging (Lund et al. 2014).

Connectivity is another significant aspect of implementing smart cities. Sub-Saharan Africa is located at a strategic position as the advent of the mobile telephone networks saw an increased connectivity within the region (Lee et al. 2014).In 2014; 329 million unique subscribers became part of the network, equating a penetration rate of 38%. Consumers, governments, and businesses in SSA are rapidly adopting mobile, not only as a basic communication tool but also to access information and a growing range of new applications and services. The connections are a largely smart technology within the region implementing modern technology like 4G internet directly without having to upgrade (Friederici et al. 2017). As a result, the reduced drawbacks found in legacy cities, as well as the level of connectivity in Africa, present an opportunity for smart cities.

Having such development opportunities for smart cities in the region, certain strides have been achieved. In Ghana, a technology park was constructed at Prampram, Greater Accra Region (Owusu and Oteng-Ababio, 2015). The project was undertaken by Rlg Communications which is a mobile telecommunications company. HOPE City is an acronym for Home, Office, People, and Environment (Owusu and Oteng-Ababio, 2015). The project is expected to be complete this year (2018) and has been constructed at a cost of $US 10 billion. The project is an initiative of Mr. Roland Agambire, Group Chairman of the AGAMS Group of Companies and CEO of Rlg Communications Ltd in collaboration with the Government of Ghana, as part of the national development policy framework, turning Ghana into a knowledge-society and an active player in the global economy. This initiative opens an avenue for the development of smart cities in Ghana.

Furthermore, the emphasis has been placed on harnessing the local innovativeness. This approach entails the engagement of entrepreneurs, local universities and research centers, is key to addressing the challenge of localization. In South Africa, a collaboration between a local university and city administration led to the design of smart shacks, which respond to urban housing needs in informal settlements. Smart shacks are largely informal developments that are technologically relevant. The shacks comprise of solar panels, LED lights, satellite dishes, and other technological innovations. This has reduced the number of negative externalities that came from the shacks in South Africa. This has also met the agenda of the Sustainable Development Goals of having inclusive cities which in turn is one of the principles of a smart city.

Having sustainable smart cities require information sources and laboratories. Living labs methodologies have been introduced in the African region and SSA included. The initiatives of having technological and innovation city labs are promoted mainly through the Africa-European Union Strategic Partnership. Existing living labs networks may be used to test incubate and promote smart city innovations. Labs have been set up in South Africa, Botswana, and Rwanda. Smart city technology is beginning to sink into the Sub-Saharan region. Most countries have introduced smart electricity and water meters to reduce wastage as the user pay per use. This can be termed a technology driven financing model. An example of an innovative technology-driven financing model is the application of smart meters in Nairobi under the JisomeeMita program, which helped to sustainably finance the provision of piped water in parts of Nairobi through the use of smart meters and mobile payments. The idea of smart water meters is still primitive in Zimbabwe; however, the country has successfully installed smart electricity meters through the Zimbabwe Electricity Distribution and Transmission Company.

The major driving force hind the development of technology cities in Arica is in the African Urban Agenda (Capproti et al. 2017). The Africa Urban Agenda certified by Habitat III held in Quito, Ecuador in October 2016 commits to engaging the suitable use of new and existing technologies to improve city management (Owusu and Oteng-Ababio, 2015). While such a commitment will also need adequate infrastructure to become operational, the science, technology, innovation, and capacity-development agenda encourage an improvement in the business environment to make it more attractive to investments. This is achievable through access to digital governance solutions, as well as transparent and predictable policies and regulations (Capproti et al. 2017). In ensuring that technology is embraced in the continent, the agenda highlights that "this will require strong political will, collaborative leadership and new institutional frameworks, including a national ICT policy and e-government strategy, as well as strengthening institutions and building the capacities of the public servants besides ensuring universal access to communications and ICT."

DISCUSSION AND SYNTHESIS

The idea of developing smart cities in Sub-Saharan Africa is associated with various challenges and opportunities. The region is one of the least developed parts of the world. This presents economic challenges as well as governance issues in trying to implement smart cities in the region. Economically, the region has governments that are struggling to fund any kind of development and suffer from extreme levels of poverty. This is also linked to issues of governance. The leaders and those in power do not allow participation of the citizen in government decisions making it hard to successfully develop smart cities. The nature and the environment in Sub-Saharan Africa have led to low rates of infrastructural development. While this can be perceived as a challenge to develop smart cities in the context of the context of developing the infrastructure, it presents an opportunity for leapfrogging. This means that the region can develop smart infrastructure directly as they try to provide the infrastructure that was never built. Another significant opportunity for the development of smart cities in SSA is the demography of the region. By 2030, more than 60% of the population will be young as a result a ready market for technology and smart city opportunities. This can be seen by the statistics of mobile phones and their use in Africa. This presents an opportunity for the development of smart cities in the region as it has the cities will be in demand.

CONCLUSION, POLICY OPTIONS AND RECOMMENDATIONS

To conclude, the study identified various opportunities and potential threats to smart cities. The study identified that the demography and level of development of infrastructural development present opportunities for the development of smart cities in the sub-Saharan region. For the region to successfully overcome the challenges and harness the opportunities presented b the region to develop smart cities, there is a need to: Develop smart cities that may help to solve problems faced by African citizens. This includes issues that are presented to by urbanization which have led to increased informality, exclusion and urban poverty among others. As a result, there is a need to develop smart cities that answer to the challenges of citizens. This can be done through the consideration of the unique aspects of African Cities and managed through co-creative processes (involvement of stakeholders) – a bottom-up approach. Furthermore, Africa needs to learn from the developed world. This can be done through the leveraging of existing smart cities deployment from other parts of the world (Technology transfer). After learning from other regions, there is a need to adapt the technology to the needs of the Africans. This will help in the development of relevant smart cities that answer of the needs of the citizens. The political environment of Africa also needs to allow the free operation of technological innovations in the region. Introduction of technology reduces inefficiencies which is the major oil for all corrupt activities as a result in most cases technology is shunned. There is a need for political will to be allowing for the region to develop successful smart cities.

ACKNOWLEDGMENT

The authors are grateful for the contributions made by the editors, the anonymous reviewers as well as Mr. B Mavhima of the Department of Rural & Urban Planning, University of Zimbabwe who critiqued it and made invaluable insights towards shaping the argument.

REFERENCES

Ahvenniemi, H., Huovila, A., Pinto-Seppä, I., & Airaksinen, M. (2017). What are the differences between sustainable and smart cities? *Cities (London, England)*, *60*, 234–245. doi:10.1016/j.cities.2016.09.009

Alan, A. T., Ramchurn, S. D., Rodden, T., Costanza, E., Fischer, J., & Jennings, N. R. (2015, September). Managing energy tariffs with agents: a field study of a future smart energy system at home. In *Adjunct Proceedings of the 2015 ACM International Joint Conference on Pervasive and Ubiquitous Computing and Proceedings of the 2015 ACM International Symposium on Wearable Computers* (pp. 1551-1558). ACM.

Albino, V., Berardi, U., & Dangelico, R. M. (2015). Smart cities: Definitions, dimensions, performance, and initiatives. *Journal of Urban Technology*, *22*(1), 3–21. doi:10.1080/10630732.2014.942092

Amankwah-Amoah, J. (2015). Solar energy in sub-Saharan Africa: The challenges and opportunities of technological leapfrogging. *Thunderbird International Business Review*, *57*(1), 15–31. doi:10.1002/tie.21677

Angelidou, M. (2015). Smart cities: A conjuncture of four forces. *Cities (London, England)*, *47*, 95–106. doi:10.1016/j.cities.2015.05.004

Benevolo, C., Dameri, R. P., & D'Auria, B. (2016). Smart mobility in smart city. In *Empowering Organizations* (pp. 13–28). Cham: Springer. doi:10.1007/978-3-319-23784-8_2

Boes, K., Buhalis, D., & Inversini, A. (2015). Conceptualising smart tourism destination dimensions. In *Information and communication technologies in tourism 2015* (pp. 391–403). Cham: Springer.

Boulos, M. N. K., & Al-Shorbaji, N. M. (2014). On the Internet of Things, smart cities and the WHO Healthy Cities. *International Journal of Health Geographics*, *13*(10), 1–6. PMID:24383521

Caprotti, F., Cowley, R., Datta, A., Broto, V.C., Gao, E., Georgeson, L., Herrick, C., Odendaal, N., & Joss, S. (2017). The New Urban Agenda: key opportunities and challenges for policy and practice. *Urban Research & Practice, 10*(3), pp.367-378.

Castells, M. (2010). *The rise of the network society*. West Sussex, UK: Wiley-Blackwell.

Chirisa, I., Matamanda, A. R., & Mukarwi, L. (2018). Desired and Achieved Urbanisation in Africa: In Search of Appropriate Tooling for a Sustainable Transformation. In U. Benna & I. Benna (Eds.), Urbanization and its Impact on Socio-Economic Growth in Developing Regions. IGI Global.

Clarfield, A. M., & Rosenthal, A. (2017). Aging in Sub-Saharan Africa: Sub-par? *Journal of the American Geriatrics Society*, *65*(6), 1136–1138. doi:10.1111/jgs.14751 PMID:28176300

Dickey, T. (2018). Smart water solutions for smart cities. In *Smart Cities* (pp. 197–207). Cham: Springer. doi:10.1007/978-3-319-59381-4_12

Djahel, S., Doolan, R., Muntean, G. M., & Murphy, J. (2015). A communications-oriented perspective on traffic management systems for smart cities: Challenges and innovative approaches. *IEEE Communications Surveys and Tutorials*, 17.

Djurfeldt, A. A. (2015). Urbanization and linkages to smallholder farming in sub-Saharan Africa: Implications for food security. *Global Food Security*, *4*, 1–7. doi:10.1016/j.gfs.2014.08.002

Dos Santos, S., Adams, E. A., Neville, G., Wada, Y., de Sherbinin, A., Bernhardt, E. M., & Adamo, S. B. (2017). Urban growth and water access in sub-Saharan Africa: Progress, challenges, and emerging research directions. *The Science of the Total Environment*, *607*, 497–508. doi:10.1016/j.scitotenv.2017.06.157 PMID:28704674

Ericsson. (2015). *Laying the foundations for a smart, sustainable city*. Available online: https://www.ericsson.com/en/white-papers/laying-the-foundations-for-a-smart-sustainable-city/white-paper---laying-the-foundations-for-a-smart-sustainable-city

Friederici, N., Ojanperä, S., & Graham, M. (2017). The impact of connectivity in Africa: Grand visions and the mirage of inclusive digital development. *The Electronic Journal on Information Systems in Developing Countries*, *79*(1), 1–20. doi:10.1002/j.1681-4835.2017.tb00578.x

Glasmeier, A., & Christopherson, S. (2015). Thinking about smart cities. *Cambridge Journal of Regions, Economy and Society*, *8*(1), 3–12. doi:10.1093/cjres/rsu034

Graham, M., & Foster, G. (2014). *Geographies of information inequality in sub-Saharan Africa.* Available online: https://opendocs.ids.ac.uk/opendocs/bitstream/handle/123456789/11947/Geographies-of-Information-Inequality-in-Sub-Saharan-Africa.pdf

Haldevang, M. (2016). *Why do we still use the term "sub-Saharan Africa"?* Available at: https://qz.com/770350/why-do-we-still-say-subsaharan-africa/

Janssen, M., Matheus, R., & Zuiderwijk, A. (2015, August). Big and open linked data (BOLD) to create smart cities and citizens: Insights from smart energy and mobility cases. In *International Conference on Electronic Government* (pp. 79-90). Springer. 10.1007/978-3-319-22479-4_6

Khatoun, R., & Zeadally, S. (2016). Smart cities: Concepts, architectures, research opportunities. *Communications of the ACM, 59*(8), 46–57. doi:10.1145/2858789

Kinai, A., Bryant, R. E., Walcott-Bryant, A., Mibuari, E., Weldemariam, K., & Stewart, O. (2014, June). Twende-twende: a mobile application for traffic congestion awareness and routing. In *Proceedings of the 1st International Conference on Mobile Software Engineering and Systems* (pp. 93-98). ACM. 10.1145/2593902.2593926

Kitchin, R. (2015). Making sense of smart cities: Addressing present shortcomings. *Cambridge Journal of Regions, Economy and Society, 8*(1), 131–136. doi:10.1093/cjres/rsu027

Kylili, A., & Fokaides, P. A. (2015). European smart cities: The role of zero energy buildings. *Sustainable Cities and Society, 15*, 86–95. doi:10.1016/j.scs.2014.12.003

Lee, J. H., Hancock, M. G., & Hu, M. C. (2014). Towards an effective framework for building smart cities: Lessons from Seoul and San Francisco. *Technological Forecasting and Social Change, 89*, 80–99. doi:10.1016/j.techfore.2013.08.033

Letaifa, S. B. (2015). How to strategize smart cities: Revealing the SMART model. *Journal of Business Research, 68*(7), 1414–1419. doi:10.1016/j.jbusres.2015.01.024

Lund, H., Werner, S., Wiltshire, R., Svendsen, S., Thorsen, J. E., Hvelplund, F., & Mathiesen, B. V. (2014). 4th Generation District Heating (4GDH): Integrating smart thermal grids into future sustainable energy systems. *Energy, 68*, 1–11. doi:10.1016/j.energy.2014.02.089

Ma, Z., Lundgaard, M., & Jørgensen, B. N. (2016, November). Triple-layer smart grid business model: A comparison between sub-Saharan Africa and Denmark. In Innovative Smart Grid Technologies-Asia (ISGT-Asia), 2016 IEEE (pp. 347-352). IEEE.

Manville, C., Cochrane, G., Cave, J., Millard, J., Pederson, J. K., Thaarup, R. K., . . . Kotterink, B. (2014). *Mapping smart cities in the EU*. Available online: http://www.europarl.europa.eu/RegData/etudes/etudes/join/2014/507480/IPOL-ITRE_ET(2014)507480_EN.pdf

Meyer, D., Passenberg, C., Feldmaier, J., & Shen, H. (2016). Dynamic Programming for Smart Water Heater Control. *Integration of Sustainable Energy Conference (iSEneC) 2016*.

Mguni, P., Herslund, L., & Jensen, M. B. (2016). Sustainable urban drainage systems: Examining the potential for green infrastructure-based stormwater management for Sub-Saharan cities. *Natural Hazards, 82*(2), 241–257. doi:10.100711069-016-2309-x

Mohanty, S. P., Choppali, U., & Kougianos, E. (2016). Everything you wanted to know about smart cities: The internet of things is the backbone. *IEEE Consumer Electronics Magazine*, *5*(3), 60–70. doi:10.1109/MCE.2016.2556879

Musakwa, W. (2014). The use of social media in the Gautrain in Gauteng Province, South Africa: Analysis and Lessons learnt. REAL CORP 2014 Proceedings, 721-727.

Musakwa, W. (2017). Perspectives on geospatial information science education: An example of Urban Planners in Southern Africa. *Geo-Spatial Information Science*, *20*(2), 201–208. doi:10.1080/10095020.2017.1339403

Musakwa, W., & Van Niekerk, A. (2014). Earth observation for sustainable urban planning in developing countries: Needs, trends, and future directions. *Journal of Planning Literature*, *30*(2), 149–160. doi:10.1177/0885412214557817

Nastasi, B., & Basso, G. L. (2016). Hydrogen to link heat and electricity in the transition towards future Smart Energy Systems. *Energy*, *110*, 5–22. doi:10.1016/j.energy.2016.03.097

Ning, Z., Xia, F., Ullah, N., Kong, X., & Hu, X. (2017). Vehicular Social Networks: Enabling Smart Mobility. *IEEE Communications Magazine*, *55*(5), 16–55. doi:10.1109/MCOM.2017.1600263

Ntuli, N., & Abu-Mahfouz, A. M. (2016). A simple security architecture for smart water management system. *Procedia Computer Science*, *83*, 1164–1169. doi:10.1016/j.procs.2016.04.239

Okeke, R. C. (2017). Elitism, Local Governance and Development in Nigeria. *Specialty Journal of Politics and Law*, *2*(3), 62–72.

Owusu, G., & Oteng-Ababio, M. (2015). Moving unruly contemporary urbanism toward sustainable urban development in Ghana by 2030. *The American Behavioral Scientist*, *59*(3), 311–327. doi:10.1177/0002764214550302

Parnell, S., & Pieterse, E. A. (2014). *Africa's urban revolution*. Chicago: University of Chicago Press.

Pierce, P., & Andersson, B. (2017). Challenges with smart cities initiatives–A municipal decision makers' perspective. *Proceedings of the 50th Hawaii International Conference on System Sciences*. Available online: https://pdfs.semanticscholar.org/48fe/ed2ca255974bffd09b26aef06a4753a6b284.pdf

Pieterse, E., & Short, J. R. (2017). The city in sub-Saharan Africa. A research agenda for cities, 218-232.

Potts, D. (2018). Urban data and definitions in sub-Saharan Africa: Mismatches between the pace of urbanisation and employment and livelihood change. *Urban Studies (Edinburgh, Scotland)*, *55*(5), 965–986. doi:10.1177/0042098017712689

Rathore, M. M., Ahmad, A., Paul, A., & Rho, S. (2016). Urban planning and building smart cities based on the internet of things using big data analytics. *Computer Networks*, *101*, 63–80. doi:10.1016/j.comnet.2015.12.023

Scuotto, V., Ferraris, A., & Bresciani, S. (2016). Internet of Things: Applications and challenges in smart cities: a case study of IBM smart city projects. *Business Process Management Journal*, *22*(2), 357–367. doi:10.1108/BPMJ-05-2015-0074

Skiyi, V., Matamanda, A., & Chirisa, I. (2016). Constraints and opportunities in integrating wetland ecosystem services in urban land use planning, Harare, Zimbabwe. In *Proceedings of the 2016 ILASA Conference 55-63, Institute for Landscape Architecture in South Africa (ILASA)*. University of Pretoria (UP).

Söderström, O., Paasche, T., & Klauser, F. (2014). Smart cities as corporate storytelling. *City*, *18*(3), 307–320. doi:10.1080/13604813.2014.906716

Solanas, A., Patsakis, C., Conti, M., Vlachos, I. S., Ramos, V., Falcone, F., ... Martinez-Balleste, A. (2014). Smart health: A context-aware health paradigm within smart cities. *IEEE Communications Magazine*, *52*(8), 74–81. doi:10.1109/MCOM.2014.6871673

Storeygard, A. (2016). Farther on down the road: Transport costs, trade and urban growth in sub-Saharan Africa. *The Review of Economic Studies*, *83*(3), 1263–1295. doi:10.1093/restud/rdw020 PMID:29743731

Tesfaye, K., Kassie, M., Cairns, J. E., Michael, M., Stirling, C., Abate, T., ... Gerard, B. (2017). Potential for Scaling up Climate Smart Agricultural Practices: Examples from Sub-Saharan Africa. In *Climate Change Adaptation in Africa* (pp. 185–203). Cham: Springer. doi:10.1007/978-3-319-49520-0_12

Tussyadiah, I. P., Zach, F. J., & Wang, J. (2017). Attitudes Toward Autonomous on Demand Mobility System: The Case of Self-Driving Taxi. In *Information and Communication Technologies in Tourism 2017* (pp. 755–766). Cham: Springer. doi:10.1007/978-3-319-51168-9_54

Urry, J. (2016). *Mobilities: new perspectives on transport and society*. Routledge.

Zanella, A., Bui, N., Castellani, A., Vangelista, L., & Zorzi, M. (2014). Internet of things for smart cities. *IEEE Internet of Things Journal, 1*(1), 22-32.

KEY TERMS AND DEFINITIONS

Equipmentation: A process through which a city is capacitated with requisite equipment, usually ICT infrastructure which may be critical in promoting the establishment of a smart city.

Innovation: The process of bringing in new ideas and methods of increasing the functionality of cities and towns. More of a divergent from the traditional way of doing things and running the city.

Smart City: A city which bears the traits of smartness that is smart infrastructure (hard and soft) smart governances.

Sub-Saharan Africa: A continent with 54 countries which are largely characterized as developing countries.

Chapter 6
The Integration of Urban Growth and Industrial Policies in Africa:
Private Sector Takes Command

Muhammad Aliyu Suleiman
King Fahd University of Petroleum and Minerals, Saudi Arabia

Umar G. Benna
Benna Associates, Nigeria

ABSTRACT

Africa is the last of the major global regions to urbanize and to economically benefit therefrom largely due to centuries of the fragmented spatial system by geographic, trading zone, colonial experiences, and logistics barriers. Recently, however, the integration of African urban spatial structure was spearheaded by the private sector under the guidance of the public sector. This chapter analyzes the goals driving integration, the tools used by private and the public sectors in setting the stage for integrative urban growth through industrialization, and then identifies the future opportunities and challenges in sustaining the momentum. The chapter comprises of an introduction, a conceptual framework, the gluing elements, the review of the development guidance system, opportunities and challenges ahead, future research direction, and conclusion.

1. INTRODUCTION

Africa is viewed conventionally to be down for so long and will be very hard to ever realize and grow to its fullest potentials. It possesses 20 percent of the world's land and 15 percent of the world population but contributes little to the global economics market value (Aré, et al., 2010). From the east to a lesser degree to the west, its economy is dominated by Asia and South America respectively. Despite its endowment with natural and human resources, Africa is bewildered with poverty, health problems, geopolitical crises and imprinting effects of colonialism. However, spearheaded by the private sector

DOI: 10.4018/978-1-5225-7625-9.ch006

under the guidance of the public sector these narratives have begun to change over the last decade. Scores of African companies have been competing and rapidly expanding on the global corporate map (Aré, et al., 2010; Dupoux, Ermias, heuzé, Niavas, & Kimani, 2014). The Economist magazine in 2000, declared Africa "hopeless" (the conventional view), revised its stands in 2011 to "rising" and in the year 2013, it further revised its assessmentent of Africa to "aspiring" (Dupoux, et al., 2014).

Africa, which is largely ignored in international ranking and league tables since in the 80s is now receiving the attention and investmentent of multinational; growth rate is rising, democracy and bureaucratic confidence is gradually diminishing many long-runninging wars and conflicts. There are improvement in infrastructure and connectivity across the board (Aré, et al., 2010; Dupoux, et al., 2014). However, to sustain growth, transform economyonmy and change to higher productivity, Africa needs well-functioning urban system. Africa remains largely spatial rural areas with poor roads and logistics hubs networks transportationtion of goods and high-value services across cities, countries, and regions. Cities are central to increase in productivity as the efficiency of goods and service productions is tied to the urban system (World Bank Group, 2016). WBG (2016) gives a typical examples of the role of an effective urban systems in increasing the productivity and efficiency of goods and services, described as follow; verse area of farming are largely in a remote rural areas, this requires small cities to connect farmers to both the input and output market and as well serves as a market aggregation. Cities which are medium in size, needs an effective and efficient logistics hubs for transportport of goods and can serves as places of larger local markets. Lastly, megacitiesties play roles of connecting the economy from region to region and to the entire world serves as nodes for valued services.

Africa is the last of the major global regions to urbanize after Asia, Europe, North America and South America (Aré, et al., 2010; Dupoux, Ivers, Niavas, & Chraïti, 2018). It is also the last to economically benefit from urbanization largely due to centuries of the fragmented spatial system by geographic, trading zone, colonial experiences, and logistics barriers (Dupoux et al., 2018). Not only is Africa spatially fragmented, industrial tools as the means of transforming its cities into the engines of growth has been disconnected from urban growth policies. These two development tools are increasingly being viewed by African leaders as not complemententing each other but vital to Africa's future growth and development (Economic Commission for Africa, 2017).

Urbanization is generally recognized as a multi-facet process with profound implications for Africa's growth and transformation (Benna & Garba, 2016). The rate and scale of Africa's urbanizareion is influencing the continent's demographic profile, economic, environmental and social development (Chirisa, Maphosa, Zanamwe, Bandauko, & Mukarwi, 2016). United Nations Department of Economic and Social Affairs (2014) projects that by 2035 about half of Africa's population will be living in cities, triggering substantial demands for new jobs, urban social and physical services and infrastructure, but generating advantages for economic growth. By 2050 the projected urban population will be 60% and will be the world's youngest.

The main urban development goal is "make cities and human settlements inclusive, safe, resilient and sustainable" (Klopp & Paller, 2015; Chirisa, et al., 2016; Chirisa, Mukarwi, & Matamanda, 2017). Guided by this realization and inspired by various strategy documents of African Union, the Africa Urban Agenda (AUA) Program aims to raise the profile of urbanization as a force for the structural transformation of Africa (Habitat, 2018). The usually identifiable urban challenges include the provision of adequate and affordable urban physical infrastructures such as utilities, housing, transport systems that are safe, affordable, accessible and sustainable. Furthermore, most African cities are experiencing rising carbon, unsafe infrastructure for the majority pedestrian population in need of safe lanes for cycling and walking

(Abubakar & Dano, 2017; Klopp J. M., 2011). A more serious challenge facing urbanization in most countries in Africa is that it is happening without the industrial base to raise the income of residents and municipalities to support the financing of the desired service. This is because most African cities are "consumption cities" not the "production cities" they should be.

Recently, the integration of African urban spatial structure was spearheaded by the private sector under the guidance of the public sector. This shift is the focus of this chapter. This chapter analyzes the tools used by private and the public sectors in setting the stage for integrative urban growth through industrialization in Africa and then identifies the opportunities and the challenges ahead. The chapter comprises of an introduction, a conceptual framework, the gluing elements, the review of development guidance system, opportunities and challenges ahead, future research direction, and conclusion.

2. LITERATURE REVIEW AND CONCEPTUAL FRAMEWORK

The integration of urban growth and industrial policies to produce higher quality of urban life and lead to sustainable regions and African continent is linked to the processes of urban agglomeration, which pulls diverse resources, labor, industry, housing and transportation into urban spaces. In the process of these activities in urban spaces tension is created between the gains of improved social goods such as employment, healthcare, education, and on the other the realities of the urban "bads" in the form of crime, traffic, disease, overcrowding, poverty, inequality, ecological degradation and the collapsing infrastructure (Turok & McGranahan, 2013). The rational management of both urban growth and industrial policies appear to be the best ways to mean the needs of current urban residents and prepare for the challenge of meeting the needs of tomorrow's African urban residents.

The Boston Consulting Group (Dupoux, et al., 2018) has identified foreign direct investment, goods trade, M&A, and tourism as the tools used by African and non-African firms to achieve the integration of Africa. Trade has also been advocated by others as an effective instrument for integration. For example, ECA (2017) points out that **Trade** is an important tool for the integration large land mass like Africa, even more effective are smart trade choices. Among these choices are: making smart choices in trade agreements, using trade policy to promote industrialization, complementary policies for industrialization through trade. strengthening links among national development strategies, industrial policy and trade policy. Earlier ECA (2016), advocates a comprehensive approach that strengthens links among national development strategies, industrial policy and trade policy. The use the of the newly established Continental Free Trade Area (CFTA) is suggested for multipurpose, including as a vehicle for industrialization by committing member states liberalization agenda and developing manufacturing regional value chains that would reduce import bills for Africa (ECA, 2017).

Africa's competitive **industries (e.g.** agriculture) can also trigger widespread regional **integration** activities, connecting many coastal cities and countries with rural hinterland. On the other hand, since the start of industrial revolution, urban growth and industrial policies have been integrated to produce new towns, industrial cities, urban enterprise zones to mention just a few, with huge rewards for these clusters and for their immediate regions. The development of regional infrastructure, Potts (2012) sug-ests, can serve as an instrument for integrating regions like ECOWAS or SADC to promote urban and industrial growth and agriculture expansion. At a deep level, regional integration in Africa has its roots in the political partners' industrial interests so that goods and services are tailored to the 'protection needs' of the polity- be it city, country, region, or Africa.

2.1 Conceptual Framework: The Activity Systems Model

Building on the work of Chapin and Keiser (1979), proposed a schema for the analysis of urban and industrial growth policies for the integration of Africa. In its simplest form, the model assumes that motivated by development goals or specific objectives, the various activity agents or *actors* (individuals, households, firms and institutions), seek to take decisions or *actions* designed to promote urban and/or industrial growth that culminate in spatial and non-spatial integration of Africa. Graphically, the model may be expressed as Goals → Actors/Actions → African Integration (Benna U. G., 2013). From this simple form, the model may be modified for use whenever the identification of the socio-cultural variables of development actors and their relevant activities can be analyzed to define the pattern of integration at the regional and continental levels.

The Activity Systems Model Applied to African Integration

The Activity Systems Model sees the major urban and industrial development actors– namely key African institutions, the private sector (both African and multinational firms), and Non-government communities - as the dominant shapers of urban and industrial development through their daily decision and actions. Normally specific development tools such as policies, plans, programs, regulations and other action instruments that may be evolved overtime by the actors or their advisors guide these activities. The activities may be place-based by means of face-to-face interactions or can take place over digital networks. Thus, the resulting urban and industrial growth integration may have pattern that is physically defined or based traceable cyberspace pattern. As shown in Figure 1, the model suggests a dynamic relationship between its four main components: goals of the main urban actors, their activities, the means of carrying out the activities and the resultant patern of development integration of Africa.

This conceptual framework is used to guide the rest of this chapter's discussion. The next section explores the emerging goals for urban and industrial development at the various levels on the continent. Section 4 analyzes the key urban and industrial development actors in Africa, while the section following it focuses on the range of activities pursued by these actors to achieve the identified goals. Section 6 analyzes the emerging trends in terms of convergences, divergence, and unrelated development at subnational, national and continental levels. Future research directions and related concluding observations are presented in Section 7.

Figure 1. Conceptual framework for the integration of urban and industrial policies in Africa

Dev Goals		Key Actors		Main Activities		Dev Integration
Urban Policy	→	Public Sector Regional, National & Subnational	→	Policy Tools Investment, Regs, Incentives	→	Integration of Africa, its r, gions and cities
Industrial Policy		Private Sector (African & MNC)		Increased Investments		

3. GOALS FOR THE INTEGRATION OF AFRICAN URBAN AND INDUSTRIAL DEVELOPMENT

Africa is one of the largest global growth poles that is experiencing urbanization, which is one of the defining forces of the 21st century development. While in 1950 urban residents were only 30 percent of the world's population, but by 2050 the ration is expected to be 66 percent. Africa and Asia will generate about 90 percent of the increase (UNDESA, 2014). Urbanization alone does not necessarily drive growth, which is triggered by the concentration of economic actors and activities in cities to enable substantial productive advantages that can generate growth. As Africa is geographical, politically, economically and logistically fragmented, the integration of the continent is therefore as essential prerequisite in meeting the development needs of the projected additional population.

Goals are value-derived motivators for the activities of key urban residents, firms and institutions. Sometimes expressed as objectives or aims in qualitative and quantitative terms, the integration tools are designed to guide the decision and actions of urban actors. The focus of the goals identification will be at Africa level public institutions such as the African Union, the continental development agencies of the United Nations such as African Development Bank, Economic Commission for Africa, and the UN-Habitat. The private sector goals will be drawn from the largest study of the policies and activities of African and non-African firms that are pioneering the integration of Africa (Dupoux, et al., 2018).

Public Sector Goal for Africa

According to World Economic Forum (2017) the AU adopted Agenda: The Africa We Want – a vision for a prosperous Africa based on inclusive growth and sustainable development. Key components of this goal are:

1. the structural transformation of African economies towards achieving shared growth, decent jobs and economic opportunities for all.
2. the rejuvenating of the manufacturing system based on local value-added framework to create better-paying jobs generating high-quality life style.
3. the creation of resilient African economy that absorb shocks and
4. becoming less natural resource exports dependent by tapping into existing opportunities and mitigating its challenges.

Private Sector

Many emerging African firms have demonstrated their goal for the integration of, so far largely fragmented, African continent (Dupoux, et al., 2018). "*Their primary goal, of course, is* ***to build value for their owners****, but* ***they understand that their activities also further economic and social development, and that this dynamic creates environments in which their businesses can thrive. Integration is therefore both a strategy and a highly desirable outcome".***

The report identified 150 companies supporting integration in the continent. Among the 75 companies in Africa, 32 are based in South Africa and are contributing to integration on the continent. The remaining half are multinationals with track records in Africa. The "African pioneers" have eight characteristics which are integral to their success. This includes actively expanding their footprint across several

African countries. They make significant greenfield investments, a form of foreign direct investment where the parent company builds its operations in a foreign country. They build strong African brands. They expand using mergers and acquisitions. They innovate locally to adapt to the African consumer and invest in local talents. They build local ecosystems and connect Africa by facilitating the movement of people, goods, data and information.

4. KEY URBAN AND INDUSTRIAL DEVELOPMENT ACTORS IN AFRICA

The public sector is the key urban and industrial development actor in Africa, and is often by the municipal board and/or by a government department (Chirisa et al. 2016, 2017). However, as Dupoux et al (2018) study shows, the private sector consists of African firms and multinational corporations (MNCs) operating in Africa. Each of the two groups of companies has certain advantages, which are deployed to add their share of urban and industrial growth and African urban integration. The MNCs have advantages of scale, access to cutting-edge technology, and availability of large pool of capital but these advantages have been greatly reduced. On the other hand, African firms have grown rapidly using the following four competitive advantages that they have nurtured.

4.1 Public Sector Actors

The key public sector actors are the UN development agencies collaborating with the African Union (AU) on develpment, and include development agencies of AU, such the Regional Economic Commissions that are working to coordinate development in their regions. At the sub-national levela s are national and urban government plam and execute projects.

UN and Its Africa Development Partners

Within the UN System, UN-Habitat is the lead agency on urban planning, housing, policy and slum upgrading. Agencies such as UNFPA, UNICEF, ILO and UNEP also work on sectoral development issues in cities, offering extensive programme portfolios and experience. UNDP will help identify and document lessons and experiences as well as broker and facilitate suitable learning exchanges using design thinking and deconstruction methodologies. Development agencies and foundations such such as the World Bank, the World Resources Institute, the Ford and Rockefeller Foundations and GIZ all have extensive urban programmes and valuable insight into the latest urban development thinking.

Networks of Cities and Municipal Governments

To draw on resources for peer learning and exchange, UNDP will assist cities to connect with relevant networks and associations such as the United Cities and Local Governments (UCLG), Local Governments for Sustainability (ICLEI) and the Commonwealth Local Government. Forum (CLGF) and CityNet (CityNet). Newer global initiatives such as 100 Resilient Cities, C40 and the Compact of Mayors are mobilizing city leaders to work together on sustainability initiatives.

4.2 Private Sector Actors

*African Integration Pioneers*Some 150 companies that are blazing a trail toward a more integrated Africa, and have been active in the various sectors of development. The sample consists of 75 Africa-based companies and 75 Non-African firms with long history of operating in Africa and are contributing to further integration. The African pioneers come from 18 countries on the continent: 32 are based in South Africa and 10 in Morocco; Kenya and Nigeria are home to 6 each; 4 are from Egypt; and 2 each come from Côte d'Ivoire, Mauritius, Tanzania, and Tunisia. The MNCs are a global group, with France, the UK, and the US most strongly represented. At the same time, a dozen MNCs from China, India, Indonesia, Qatar, and the UAE are active across Africa (Dupoux et al., 2018).

Private Sector Partners

The local, national agencies engage with private sector companies and enterprises, which are critical players investing in urban spaces and are directly shaping urbanization outcomes. Some of them may be supplier of green technologies (i.e., energy) and urban infrastructure (i.e., buildings, transport, housing, roads, sewage and water supply, etc.) and of everyday commodities. The private sector also is expected to demonstrate potential to design mechanisms allowing for more citizen-driven solutions through vehicles such as the crowdsourcing of ideas and funding. These agencies are expected to make the development case' for inclusive and sustainable urban investments and develop new ways of working with the private sector, including facilitating public-private partnerships for innovation. Multinational companies have large units of capable generating solutions for city development. Many local groups, issue-based coalitions, start-ups and social enterprises are expected to pioneer solutions that can be shared and adapted for use across the region and Africa.

4.3 Community Actors

Civil Society Organizations

Many umbrella organizations of NGOs,CSOs and urban develofederations ares are expected to provide an indispensable voice for the urban poor and marginalized. UNDP will work with these networks through established partnership platforms such as Cities Alliance, as well as in direct collaborations to support their work at the country and local level where possible.

5. KEY URBAN AND INDUSTRIAL DEVELOPMENT ACTIVITIES IN AFRICA

5.1 Public Sector Activities

Regional Economic Commissions

Various regions of Africa constitutes economic blocs for the integration of Africa as listed in Table 1. Their common objectives are to facilitate the free movement and balanced integration in all fields of

Table 1. Public sector activities in urban and industrial development integration at the various levels in Africa

Agency	Some of the main activities
African Development Bank (AfDB) **Location:** Côte d'Ivoire	1. Provides loans and equity investments for the socio-economic advancement of the RMC. 2. Offers technical assistance for development projects and programs to African regions, nations & cities. 3. Promotes investment of public and private capital for development. 4. Assists in organizing the development policies of African countries and in projects to promote regional integration.
Economic Commission for Africa (ECA) Location: Ethiopia	1. Conducts research to support policymaking and programming for inclusive, equitable and sustainable development in Africa. 2. Encourages functional institutions, visionary leadership, and participatory governance mechanisms. 3. Prepares reports on economic conditions, governance and development management in Africa. 4. Promotes strategy for growth and intra-regional trade aimed at producing huge economic gains for Africa. 5. Assisting countries and Regional Economic Agencies to plan and execute new technology and innovation policies.
UN-Habitat Location: Kenya	1. Promotes the New Urban Agenda of making cities inclusive, safe, resilient and sustainable. 2. Promotes participatory urban policies linked to transparent and accountable finance mechanisms. 3. Sponsors social inclusion promoting decent, dignified, and rewarding lives for rich and poor urban residents. 4. Promotes balanced different scales of cities and towns, strengthens their role in food security and nutrition systems. 5. Seeks urban prosperity, with full and productive employment and decent work for all. 6. Advocates for sustainable social and physical environment of greater equity, less pollution and limited climate change.
Regional Economic Communities (RECs) of the African Union These are: 1. The Arab Maghreb Union (AMU/UMA). Location: Morocco 2. The Economic Community of West African States (ECOWAS). Location: Nigeria 3. The East African Community (EAC). Location: Tanzania 4. The Intergovernmental Authority on Development (IGAD). Location: Djibouti 5. The Southern African Development Community (SADC). Location: Botswana 6. The Common Market for Eastern and Southern Africa (COMESA). Location: Zambia 7. The Economic Community of Central African States (ECCAS). Location: Gabon 8. The Community of Sahel-Saharan States (CENSAD). Location: Morocco	1. Africa's RECs constitute key building blocks for economic integration in Africa. 2. They collaborate with the African Union (AU), in ensuring peace and stability in their regions. 3. Serve as the building blocks and help the African Union (AU) to execute various transformative programs of the continent, e.g. the New Partnership for Africa's Development (NEPAD), the AU's Agenda 2063, and its First Ten-Year Implementation Plan. 3. Their role in peace and security makes work with states, civil society and the AU Commission in raising the quality of life of African. 4. RECs are key to the effective regional implementation, financing, monitoring, and evaluation of Agenda 2063 and its flagship programmes. 5. Agenda 2063 provides the basis for increased activity achieve African Union's 50-year structural transformation and development plan for realizing the Pan-African vision of "an integrated, prosperous and peaceful Africa, driven by its own citizens and representing a dynamic force in the global arena,".

development among the member states such as trade, customs, transportation, monetary engagments, agriculture, information and communication, technology, industry and energy, gender and natural resources (AU, na; COMESA, na; SADC, 2012; ECCAS, 2014; ECOWAS, 2015; ECA, 2016a; ECA, 2016b; EAC, 2017; IGAD, 2018). With the support and promotion of the regional economic blocs by various member states, regional commissions provide an easy and streamlined framework for private sectors to expand their footprint in inter and intraregional trade.

5.2 National Level Agencies

The national governments are the sovereign states with power shape public life. However such power to be extended to an authority such as the African Union or delegated to the municipalities for the provision of basic services. Government support is critically needed to ensure political stability, legal protection and promote regional economic blocs (Dupoux et al., 2018). More so, as sovereign entity they can encourage developmental integration by promoting export via trade and tax policy, invest in developmental programs, provide diplomatic support, and remove barriers to investment overseas (Dupoux et al., 2018).

National Urban Policies by African Nations

National Government creating National Strategic Plans to guide public and private sector Urban Policies with Socio-Economic Policies (e.g. NationalStrategic Plan- Burundi and National Strategic Plan- Kenya). Strategic planning is an organizational management activity that is used to set priorities, focus energy and resources, strengthen operations, ensure that employees and other stakeholders are working towards a common goal. (National Strategic Plan-Rwanda). In November 2011, the law no 54/2011 of 11 November 2011 established Meteo Rwanda. The formulation of this strategic plan is to guide the activities of Meteo Rwanda in line with its mandate and the (National Strategic Plan-Tanzania). The purpose of the Plan is to have a coordinated modality of implementation of collectively agreed strategies to ensure that weather and climate services play an effective role in socioeconomic activities.

5.3 Ease of Doing Business by Cities and States in Africa

The Ease of Doing Business is an analysis to identify the extent to which the laws and regulations of cities and national governments are planned to ease the business of building sustainable cities with the collaboration and support of the private sector. The subnational level is an important level to generate sustainable cities and regions.

Africa cities and states are becoming more business-friendly, after years being associated with poor infrastructure and many bureaucratic hurdles that allowed few privileged and foreign investors from participating in economic activity. Africa accounted for 83 of the 264 total business regulation reforms in all emerging markets, Mauritius, Rwanda, Kenya, and Botswana ranked higher than most other regional averages. Also, Nigeria (+3.85), Zambia (+3.95), and Senegal (+3.75) recorded the biggest rise on the continent.

Figure 2. Comparing doing business scores across Africa and other regions

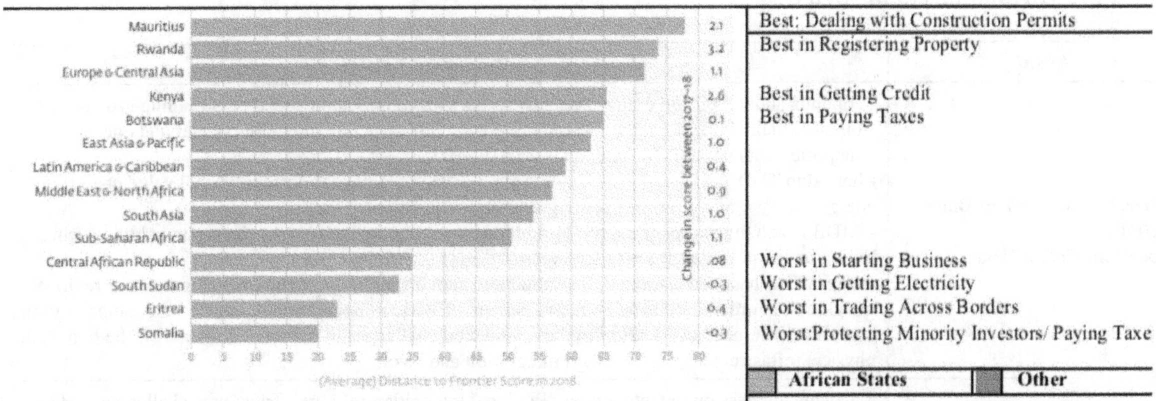

Source: World Bank, Doing Business 2018 – Reforming to Create Jobs, IFC Global Macro & Market Research, www.doingbusiness.org

6. IMPACT OF URBAN AND INDUSTRIAL ACTIVITIES

This section explores the impact of urban and industrial activities of the public and private actors towards the integration of Africa. It begins with an analysis of the effects of the public-sector activities on integration, and the some World Bank projects case studies are reviewed. Then focus turned private actors with a discussion on spatial and activity integration by the private sector, which is followed by a review of geopolitical integration strategy using Greenfield tool. The emerging African development integration and the continued growth and integration effects are analyzed, followed by a discussion on urbanization and structural transformation in Africa.

6.1 Analysis of the Impact of the Public Sector Activities

The primary function of the key UN-backed development agencies is to work with African Union's agencies to promote development in Africa in collaboration with national or sub-national governments. Among their tools are: making loans and equity investments, technical assistance, enabling investment of public and private capital for development, organizing the development policies, encouraging national and multinational projects of regional integration value. Table 2 shows the analysis of the impact of the African Development Bank (AfDB), Economic Commission for Africa (ECA) and the UN-Habitat are examples of these Africa level agencies, with headquarters in Côte d'Ivoire, Ethiopia and Kenya respectively. It is noteworthy that their headquarters are in strategic locations of the continent.

6.2 Case Studies of World Bank Development Projects

Growing populations with rising incomes across Africa are spurring demand for reliable electricity, affordable housing, good jobs, healthier environments in which to live and work, consumer goods, and higher quality, more resilient food resources. IFC, often working with the World Bank and MIGA, has intervened in multiple nations and regions to support private sector provision of such goods and services. A multitude of private and public-private initiatives across Africa—many of them assisted by IFC

Table 2. Impact by selected African public sector activities in urban and industrial development integration at the various levels in Africa

Agency	Examples of Impact
African Development Bank (AfDB) **Location:** Côte d'Ivoire	- commits about 3 billion dollars annually to African countries for social & economic growth - Initiated many in regional integration projects in infrastructure, including power and energy - supported countries in the fight against HIV/AIDS - helped in The Continental Free Trade Area (CFTA)- designed to foster regional value chains; and energize industrialization, competitiveness, and innovation - AfDB is helping address structural problems involving the lack of base-load power by investing $12 billion on the power sector over five years. • The AFDB has demonstrated commitment to supporting infrastructure development for regional integration in order to connect about 40 percent of Africa's population in landlocked countries to the rest of the continent and deals with the continental challenges in transport and energy, the poor state of physical infrastructure, weak market integration and so on.
Economic Commission for Africa (ECA) Location: Ethiopia	1. Conducted Session in Cotonou on "Regional integration in West Africa: new challenges and prospects" 2. Organized the official launching of the African Continental Free Trade Area (AfCFTA), the single sub regional currency and the situation in the Sahel. 3. In Dakar, June 26, 2018 - As part of its series of seminars, IDEP hosted a panel discussion on *Is Africa ready to invest in a green industry?* 4. Yaoundé, 26 June 2018, Congo Rep and ECA held workshop towards the formulation of Congo Vision 2047
UN-Habitat Location: Kenya	1. Invests in projects that raised the quality of life of urban residents 2. contributes to projects aimed to reduce inequalities by the provision of public goods 3. In E. Africa over 400 professionals trained, conduct 30 workshops in 8 countries, Developed tools for sustainable building design for tropical countries 4. Improved legal structure for detailed planning and land management in Egypt, with an emphasis on city densification and extension
Sources: websites of AfD, ECA and UN_Habitat	

and World Bank financing—seek to serve a region now being transformed by technological advances, urbanization, and growing middle classes.

6.3 Spatial and Activity Integration by the Private Sector

Large footprints are by firms operating mostly in cities of at least ten African countries. Naturally, these physical-based and digitally conducted activities are connected to headquarters and sometime to other other field offices. It is through this process that they contribute to the integration of the African cities and its overall spatial system. Their activities tend to range from financial, consumer and retail, industrial goods, technology, and to logistics, among others.

In the age of increased commerce, why develop a large footprint in Africa? According to Dupoux, et al (2018) many of the firms said they are motivated by the need to seek growth in new markets, the need to mitigate the risk of volatility and instability in some African countries and a multi-country footprint enables to achieve this. And thirdly, they wish to learn from the diverse cultural dynamics and customer needs shaping the continents colorful consumption patterns, trade channels, and business environments.

In its Africa study, Dupoux, et al (2018) identifies 85 out of its sample of 150 as having a large African footprint. From these private actors, 46 are African based firms, out of which 22 are South African based and others from Morocco (6), Egypt(4), Nigeria(3), 2 each from Cote d'Ivoire, Kenya and Tanzania; and one each from Angola, Botswana, Senegal, Togo and Zimbabwe. British and Franch

Table 3. Impact of World Bank-backed public sector activities in urban and industrial development integration in Africa

Industry Type	Location	Description
Azito and CIPREL	Côte d'Ivoire	IFC invested and mobilized a total of $785 million to expand independent electricity producers Azito Energie and CIPREL in Côte d'Ivoire. The result is a more competitive power market that meets growing consumer demand with improved service and lower prices. Projects included a new 300-megawatt gas-fired plant and a technology upgrade of an existing plant.Blackouts and brownouts in the country have been dramatically reduced.
Sankofa Gas Project	Ghana I	An offshore oil and natural gas project financed by IFC, the World Bank, and private lenders will producing natural gas this year, transforming Ghana's energy sector and dramatically reducing carbon emissions.The Sankofa Gas Project is expected to generate $2.3 billion in revenues for Ghana's government and provide a stable, long-term source of domestic gas that will help solve the country's chronic gas supply constraints.
Transport Eiffage Toll Road	Senegal	A partnership between government, development finance institutions including IFC and the World Bank, and the private sector brought West Africa's first public-private partnership toll road to Senegal. The 24-kilometer highway initially connected Dakar and Diamniadio, reducing commuting times dramatically and creating an important source of employment and income. It has now been extended to the nation's new international airport.
Mobisol	East Africa	Renewable energy solutions to off-grid communities in East Africa. Mobisol's high-quality systems have been conceived to meet the deep wide-ranging needs of off-grid communities by leveraging access to M mobile money and phones. obisol is a pay-as-you-go solar energy service company delivering
Caisse Régionale de	West Africa	Refinancement Hypothécaire Rapid population growth in West Africa is accelerating demand for housing and housing finance. By investing in a regional mortgage finance company and its bonds, IFC and the World Bank are helping to attract profitable, stable, and responsible institutional investors to the region's housing finance market, thereby improving the affordability home ownership
Metalco	Zambia	Once the site of a lead mine, Zambian city Kabwe suffers from dangerously high lead pollution levels and associated health problems. An IFC investment into a private recycling and waste management company is helping to dispose of lead, recycle other scrap products, and create jobs and economic growth.
Afriflora	Ethiopia	Flowers are blooming in Ethiopia. IFC client Afriflora, the East African nation's largest producer and exporter of roses, has become the world's largest rose grower, exporting 900 million roses to Europe each year. A recent IFC investment helped the company expand, install new water recycling systems, and create 5,000 new jobs.
Beef Production	Madagascar	Despite its natural beauty and biodiversity, Madagascar continues to suffer from stubborn poverty, with much of the population subsisting on less than $2 a day. Agribusiness, however, has the potential to help. IFC is supporting an investment in a local, private agriculture equipment company to help transform poultry and beef production on the island, while an IFC supported feedlot and slaughterhouse facility will create a new market for livestock farmers. The result could be better food security and resilience, and higher export revenues.
Solar Generation	Egypt	A massive solar energy park with 32 power plants in Egypt's western desert is poised to disrupt the country's energy market. The project should allow the country to generate 20 percent of its power from renewable sources within five years and dramatically lower energy costs for its 90 million residents. It is financed by IFC and a consortium of lenders, supporting 13 companies that will complete and operate the plants.

Source: (IFC, 2018).

firms (7 each) are the largest of the 39 non-African companies contributing to African integration. The rest are shared by USA(5), Switzerland (4), China (3), Germany (3), India (2), Singaporeerpore (2), and each from Belgium, Danemark, Italy, Portugal, and UAE.

Largely in response to the legacy of fragmentation in Africa that is hindering tapping its huge investments potentials triggered by population growth and rapid urbanization, these companies developed African integration strategies using diverse tools. As shown in Table 4, these strategies include Geo-politicalitical, Trading, and Logistics strategies for African integration. The *geopolitical strategy* uses the tools greenfield investments, and merger and acquisition to expand into new countries and regions and thereby help achieve African integration of urban and industrial growths. The *trade strategy* uses the brand recognition, local innovation and talent development tools to open up new operations, opportunities and create value that add to Africa's development.The *logistic strategy* applies the instruments local ecosystem dynamics, and networks of flows to connect Africa and thereby contribute to achieving 'One Africa'.

Table 4. Strategies and tools of African integration used by the private sector actors

	GEO-POLITICAL STRATEGY
Tool	**Greenfield Investments for Africa Integration**
Definition	Innovative African firms are making significant greenfield investments in manufacturing facilities and other business infrastructure. These are types of African fodirect investmentstment (FDI) where a parent company builds its operations in another Africa country from the ground up. In addition to the construction of new production facilities, these projects can also include the building of new distribution hubs, offices and living quarters. Just as encouraging, these companies are reaping attractive returns.
Actors:	9 Africa firms: South Africa (3), Morocco (2), and one each from KMauritiusittius, Nigeria, and Tog
	Non-Africafrica firms: India (3), and one eachCanadacanada, China, France, GerLuxembourgumburg, Singapore, Switzerlandthe, and USA
Activities:	Dangote Group of Nigeria, established cement factories in six African countries in 2014 and 2015, costing billions of $US and Dangote's African operations outside Nigeria contributes almost 30% of the group's revenues,. Also Groupe AddoMorocco isco is expanding in sub-Saharan Africa by investing in both building-materials factories and real estate in several countries. Other activities include banking, telecom, logistics, foods,
Spatial	The span of activities are across Africa: the South African firms invest in East and West Africa; the North Africa pioneers invest in Sub-Saharan Africa, whileAfricansricans invest in Central and East Africa.
Tool	**Merger and Acquisition for Africa Integration**
Definition	ATool of African Integration through which the ownership of companies, or other business activity units are consolidated with other entities. Both African and Non-African firms use this tool to acquire quick access to new assets, markets, and customers, and to gain new talent and skills, as well as staff with knowledge of a particular industry or sector in a new market.
Actors:	11 Africa firms: South Africa (11), Egypt (1), Morocco (1), and Tunisia (1)- thus a tool dominated by southern & northern Africa firms
	11 Non Africa firms: UK (4), France (2), USA (2), India (1), Qatar (1) and UAE (1).
Activities:	Dairy products, telecom, banking, logistics, foods, and diversified
Spatial	Danone (of France) scaled up dairy products growth in East and West Africa and by acquiring Zain Bharti (Indian) gained 42 million subscribers across 17Africa countries within five years it raised the subscribers to 76 million.
	TRADING STRATEGY
Tool:	**Brand Recognition for Africa Integration**
DefinA brand	Braan nd is important tool for pridentitydenity that often links price to durability, functionality or taste. Although global rather than regional brand is preferred, nonetheless, an African identity encourages the idea of Africa integration and helps drive cross-border sales of Africa's products. Local marketing mixed with innovation seem approachpraoch.
Actors:	7 Africa firms: South Africa (3), Nigeria (2), Kenya (1)Ugandanganda (1
	Non-Africa firms firms: US (4), France (2), UK (2), GermanIndonesiaonisia (1), Japan (1), South Korea (1), and Switzerland(1).

	GEO-POLITICAL STRATEGY
Tool	**Greenfield Investments for Africa Integration**
Activities:	Diversified, manufacturing, telecom, electronics, foods,
Sp	Predominantlynently in Southern Africa, West, frica and East Africa
Tool:	**Local Innovation for African Integration**
Definition	Africa's diversity of culture, socio-economigeopoliticalitical systems, and the difficulties of doing business, combine to generate innovations targeting local conditions and promotes continental progress as well.
Actors:	10 Africa firms: South Africa (4), Kenya (20, Nigeria (2), Morocco (1), and Togo(1
	Non-Africafrica firms: UK (3), Netherlands (2), Switzerland (2), USA (2), and France (1)
Activities:	Three examples: 1. Safaricom's Mobile money technology triggering 237 million peer-peer transactions in 2015 and other mobile activities – e.g. m-commerce, m-learning, m-governance,eVliscop'sscop;s fabric design ttastee tathe st of high-end market; and 3. Promoinnovation overcomes come the logisticinfrastructureucture frustrations to denutritionitions to children in small affordable sachets. Other areas are manufacturing, banking, telecom, logistics, foods,
Span	Predominantly in East Africa, Southern, frica and West Africa.
Name:	**Talent Development for Africa Integration**
Definition	Although in growing competitive African market, the training and retaining talents is difficult, it enriches business competence and promotes social development of Africa.
Actors:	10 Africa firms: Morocco (4), South Africa (3), Ethiopia (1), Nigeria (1), and Tanzania (1)
	Non-Africa firms firms: USA (6), UK(2), France (1), and Switzerland(1).
Activities:	Companies are hiring and training in large numbers both locally and abrothe ad in best school, packages and conditions rising to global standards. Africa's labor pool is rich, growing and better educated. Activities are diversified from manufacturing, banking, telecom, logistics, foods, to real estate
Spatial	North Africa, East Africa, South Africa and West Africa
	LOGISTICS STRATEGY
Name:	**Local Ecosystems for Africa Integration Tool**
Definition	The compleGeopoliticalitical chal ges, and diversithe ty of African market have led to the need to work through a local business ecosystem.
Actors:	12 Africa firms: Morocco (3), South Africa (3), Algeria (1), Egypt (1), Kenya (1), Nigeria (1), Tunisia (1) and Togo (1).
	8 Non-Africa firms: France (2), China (1), Japan (1), Singapore (1), Switzerland (1), UK (1the) and USA (1)
Activities:	In the African environan ment, ecosysta em is key to business expansion, and investing in it ena sures competitive advantage. For e,xample China's Huawei is seeking to reduce digital divide thru training, providing ICT access and donating computers around Africa. Morocco's OCP Group is covering the whole fertilizer value chain in most parts of Africa. Areas of activity iclude, telecom, manufacturing, banking, logistics, foods, and diversified activities
Spatial	Spanning mainly North Africa, So, thern and West Africa
Name:	**Networks of Flows for Africa Integration**
DefinA large	Large number of African and non-African firms are operating networks of flows of people, goods, information, and finance. They are large and are integrating Africa within and linking Africa to the world.
Actors:	10Africa firms: South Africa (4), Morocco (2), Ethiopia (1), KenyaMauritiusittius (1), and Rwanda (1)
	15 Non-Africa firms: France (5), USA (3), UK (2), Germany (1), Danmark (1), India (1), Italy (1), and UAE (1)
Activities:	The $70 billion worth South Africa's Naspers, has interests in television, print media, internet services, technology products, and book publishing in many countries. Similarly, the Ethiopian Airlines for decadeconnectednceted African cities and these cities to other world c ities,while still expanding the span of its influence and enhancing its services in the air and on the ground. Emirates of UAE and Maersk of Denmark are the non-African firms with air and logistics networks spread across the continent.
Spatial	The span of activities is fairly balanced towards areas of dense economic activities in the North, East, West and Southern Africa,

Source: compiled by the authors

6.4 Geo-Political Integration Strategy Using Greenfield Tool

Africa is geopolitical and economic fragmented due to its 54 sovereign countries that is highest number of in a global region. Although the continent is among the largest global land masses, most African countries have small population and economic activity. The large number of the nations and low level of economic activity some of them suggest the need for continental integration into a larger market. A key tool to achieve this integration is greenfield investment.

Tool: 'Green Field Investment'

greenfield field investment" concept refers to a situation where firms build operations in a foreign Africa market starting fresh, or a so-called green field. These foreign direct investments provide the highest level of control for the sponsoring companies when compared to foreign acquisitions or buying controlling shares in foreign firms. This tool allows the construction of a new plant to be done based on specifications of the firm that controls employees training and other project development issues.

Table 5 illustrate how in the 2014 -2017 periods; Dangote Group of Nigeria apply greenfield investments as tool for Africa integration. The Group invested in various scalable sizes of cement plants (in Senegal, Zambia, Tanzania, South Africa, Congo Brazzaville, Ethiopia and Cameroun) and terminals (Ghana, Sierra Leone, Ivory Coast, and Liberia. The cement plants are designed to serve Sub-Saharan Africa region, while the terminals are focused on the expanding West African market. The power plants investments in Tanzania and Zambia are designed to serve the cement plants surrounding communities (Benna, 2018). Figure 3 shows the locations of these greenfield investments in Africa.

Table 5. Dangote group's use of greenfield investments for African integration

Greenfield Investments in various African markets			
Activity type	**Capacity**	**Location & Market**	**Year**
Cement	o **Plants at** Senegal 1.5 million MTpa Zambia 1.5 million MTpa Tanzania 1.5 million MTpa South Africa 2.2 million MTpa Congo (Brazzaville) 1.5 million MTpa Ethiopia 3.0 million, total MTpa; Cameroun (Grinding) 1.5 million MTpa	Locations: Senegal, Zambia, Tanzania, Congo Brazzaville, South Africa, Ethiopia, Cameroun, Grinding Sierra Leone. Ivory Coast, Liberia for local and regional markets	2014-17
	o **Terminals:** Ghana 3.0 million MTpa Sierra Leone 0.5 million MTpa Ivory Coast 1.0 million MTpa Liberia 0.5 million MTpa	To serve West African market	
Power Plant	o **Tanzania:** Dangote to build coal power plant in Tanzania, a 75 MW capacity at the cost of $90 million. o **Zambia: construction** of a 30MW coal-powered electricity **generation plant,** worth US$50mn,	Located at Maura, approximately 562Km south of Dar Salam Location: Ndola factory in Zambia.	2015-17
Sources: Dangote Group Annual Reports and Press Releases over the years			

Figure 3. Dangote cement greenfield investment locations

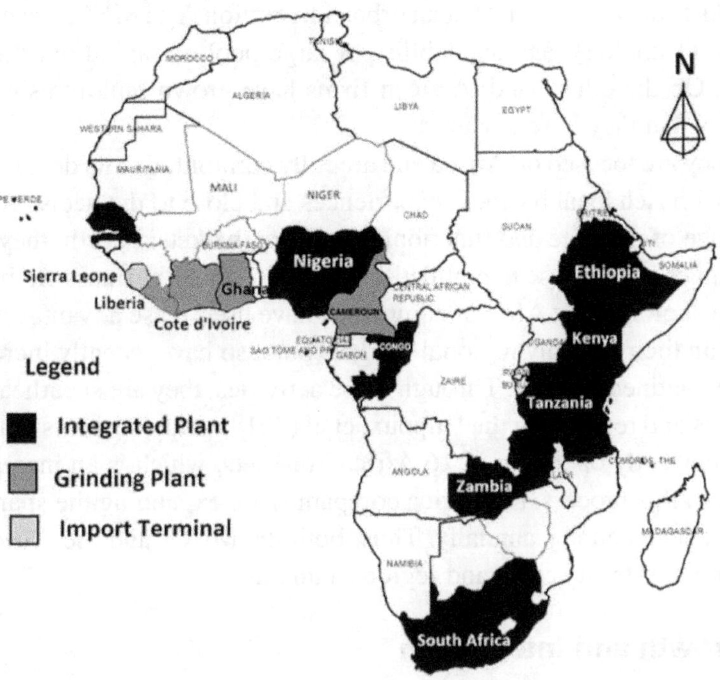

6.5 Emerging African Development Integration

The discussion in the previous section, has emphasized that among the key actors, the public sector seems focused on creating enabling environment for urban and industrial growth and investing mainly in those areas the private sector seems unwilling or unable to go. As is generally the case worldwide, the private sector consisting of emerging African firms and their multinational counterparts have been doing most of the growth-generating activities either within their borders or across the continent. The various communities and civil actors have scaled up their consumption activities, thereby turning Africa into a growing and lucrative market.

Thus, the current situation, according to the recent study by Dupoux, et al (2018), African firms are the primary drivers for growth within the continent. African investnvests more in Africa, trades more within Africa, and increasing citizens travel more to African destinations. This statement is supported by data between 2006–2007 and 2015–2016, the average annual amount of African-to-Africa direct investment almost tripled, from \$3.7 billion to \$10 billion. In the same period, the average number of annual merger and acquisition deals within African regions rose sharply from 238 to 418. Also in the same period, the average annual intra-African exports leaped from \$41 billion to \$65 billion, while the mean yearly number of intra- African tourists increased from 19 million to 30 million. In the 2015–2016 season, African tourists comprised of more than half of the total number of tourists on the continent.

As indicated above, in terms of driving urban and industrial growth in Africa, the private sector has taken the lead in the continent where once the Public Works Department (PWD) was virtually the sole driver of urban and industrial growth (Chirisa et al. 2016, 2017). However, as Dupoux, et al (2018) study shows, the private sector consists of African firms and multinational corporations (MNCs) operating in Africa. Each of the two group of companies has certain advantages, which are deployed to add their share of urban and industrial growth and African urban integration. The MNCs have advantages of scale, access to cutting-edge technology, and availability of large pool of capital but these advantages have been greatly reduced. On the other hand, African firms have grown rapidly using the following four competitive advantages that they have nurtured.

In the first place, they are focused on Africa and are fully committed to its development. Second, they rooted to the ground with rich local business experiences and close to the decision makers. Third, they have detailed knowledge of the state and functioning of local markets. Fourth, they are agile in making quick and sudden changes in response to competition from informal business environments.

As Dangote Group shows, many African companies have used these advantages to boost urban and industrial growth within their not only regional markets but also have recently increased their exposure to other regions of the continent as well. Through these activities, they are spearheading economic integration of African cities and regions. In the Dupoux, et al (2018) study, it shows that on average, the top 30 African firms are currently operating in 16 African markets, which is an increase from an average of only eight in 2008. In this process, the Africa companies are expanding the span of activities into at least one additional African country annually. Thus, both the MNCs and the African firms have been active in the integration of African cities and regions annually.

6.6 Continued Growth and Integration

The available evidence so suggests that factors of African fragmentation are waning, while the elements driving the economic integration of Africa are rising and speeding up. It increasingly becoming clear that despite the barriers of fragmentation, closer economic integration in Africa is not only taking place, but is also gathering speed. The reality of the situation is that the sources of change are springing up from within the continent, led by African private businesses and facilitated by the public sector. Under this primarily urban environment of Africa to Africa dynamics, the emerging pattern is that Africans invests more in Africa, Africans **trade** more and more with Africa, and Africans travel most to Africa (Dupoux, et al., 2018).

Table 6 presents four statistics that show the level of African integration using the following factors: foreign direct investment, goods trade, M&A, and African tourism. It is noteworthy that between 2006–2007 and 2015–2016, the average annual amount of African foreign direct investment—money that African companies invested in African countries—nearly tripled, from \$3.7 billion to \$10 billion (BCG 2018). Secondly, the BCG(2018) study shows that over the same period, the average number of yearly intraregional M&A deals jumped from 238 to 418, with African-led transactions representing more than half of all African deals in 2015. Meanwhile, average annual intra-African exports increased from \$41 billion to \$65 billion. And the average annual number of African tourists – t, hat isAfricans traveling in Africa-- rose from 19 million to 30 million. African tourists made up more than half of all tourists on the continent in 2015–2016. The overall effects of these activities in the increasing integration of African urban spaces.

6.7 Urbanization and Structural Transformation in Africa

Africa's urban transition overlaps with a demographic transition—moving from high mortality and high fertility to low mortality and low fertility—which is occurring across huge swathes of the continent.

Table 6. Progress in african integration using selected tools, 2006-2007 and 3025-2016

Africa Integration Components	Indicators	2006–2007	2015–2016
African FDI *(African invest in African)*	Intra-Africa Greenfield FDI	$3.7 billion	$10 billion
	Total Inflow to Africa (%)	6%	13%
M&A *Africa aquires in Africa*	Intraregional M &A deals	238	418
	Africa deals in total deals (%)	34%	54%
Goods Trade *Africa trades with AIntra-Africa*	nfrican Exports ($Bn)	41	65
	Total Exports from Africa (%)	12%	18%
Africa Tourism *Africa travel to Africa*	African Tourists (mitouristsourits)	19	30
	Total Tourists inflow to Africa %	46%	53%
Source: BCG 2018			

1) centersentres lead this demographic transition, with its associated demographic di asvidend a positive factor for economic development (ECA, 2017). It is therefore indispensable to harness the forces of urbanization for Africa's sustained growth and structural transformation, 2) including the economic and social challenges flagged in the previous two chapters. Multi-dimensional urbanization shapes all three pillars of sustainable development economic development, social development and environmental protection (UNDESA, 2014). And while urbanization is not a sufficient condition to generate economic growth, with the right urban form—the spatial layout of cities—and patterns, it can bring major productive advantages to industrial value chains. Managing the urban transition is thus essential for economic growth and the well-being of Africa's urban and rural populations.

Deliberate policy responses are required to optimize urbanization and minimize challenges. They involve balancing agglomeration economies and diseconomies to exploit urban scale and externalities, preventing slum forward planning and investing in infrastructure and public goods and creating jobs to absorb swelling urban populations including for women and young people. These interrelated challenges and opportunities are complex and best handled through inter-sector and multi-level governance. Policies need to be coordinated through national development planning frameworks to link urban space and economic development—as well as the public and private sectors—and to be supported by investment and urban planning at national and local levels.

6.7.1 Private Sector Impacts on African Integrative

In the previous sections have seen how the African and non-African private companies use three strategies and seven tools to integrate African cities, countries, regions and the whole continent. With the help of these companies some countries have succeeded in structural transformation are rapidly urbanizing with a consumption and production pattern driven by productive industrial and service sectors. These countries and the cities have restructured resources (including labor) from low- to high-productivity sectors, often involving industrial development. As a result, the pattern of African urban system is changing, as indicated in Figure 4, some of Africa's small and medium-sized cities are projected to show major growth by 2030. However, those cities that are failing to attract new investments to significantly reduce urban inequality and informality will remain problematic because economic growth will be largely job-

Figure 4. Urban agglomerations in 1990 and 2030

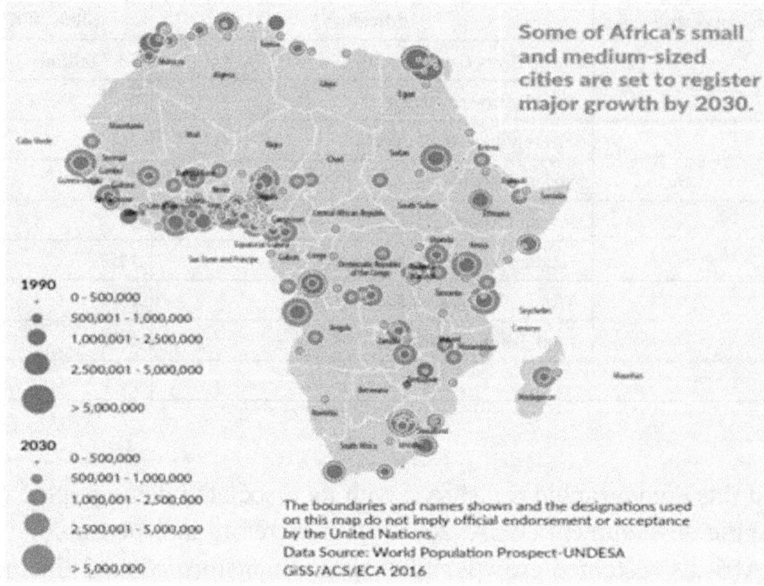

less, especially for economies heavily reliant on natural resources that tend to generate the low-level type of "consumption cities".

6.7.2 Private Sector Investments Have Displayed Continuity From the Past Into the Future

As an African proverb suggests, the Private sector investments are indicating that "the shortest cut to the future is via the past. Thus, the scale and pattern of investments in most African economies willthe show continuity of prosperity, as the following evidences indicate. First, the growth in Africa is real and enduring driven; private consumption and commodity-oriented export. Second, while theof manufacturing is steadily growing, the services sector, according to EY (2017), still forms a significant portion of most African economies. Third, the factos of consumption driven growtd and the relative rise of the manufacturing, combine to underpin the resilience that many African economies, in the face of extremely difficult global conditions. Fourth, as Figure 5 shows, the majority of African economies are essentially better position currently than they were about two decades ago, and the overall robust growth is projected to continue for at least the next decade.

6.7.3 More FDI Flows to the Hub Economies Targetting New Regional Clusters

An emerging trend in the FDI behavior of foreign investors to focus on the Africa's larger and more diverse markets. Combined these markets attracted 58% of Africa's total FDI projects in 2016. The attractiveness of that these markets is base on their positions of being the leading anchor economies in their respective spheres of influence, and in their ability to ensure investors greater and more mature market environment. From these economic hubs, the private investors would secure enough to open up new investment areas, thereby expanding the zones of African integration.

Figure 5. SSA GDP growth 1990 - 2030

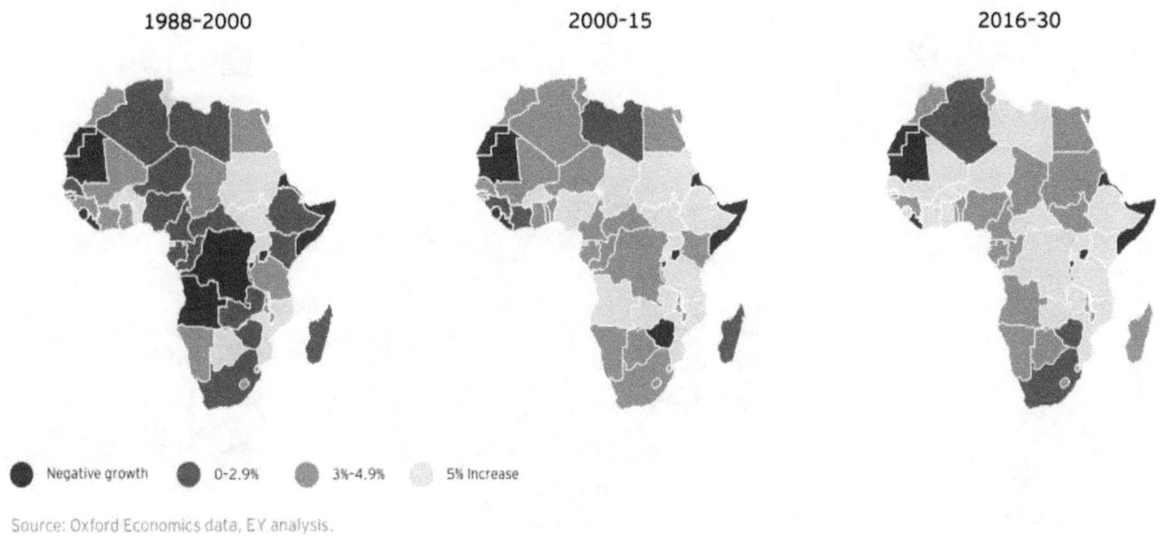

Table 7 and Figure 6 show areas of FDI flow in the emerging hub economies with their new clusters appearing in the West and East, in addition to establish ones in North and South. With almost half of the African pioneering Africa integration in the BCG (2018) survey, and in the EY (2017) report achieving 20.6% increase over 2016 in FDI projects growth and 8.1% in increase over same period in FDI amount, South Africa seems to be the most attractive place to invest in Africa, and it is also the first choice to use as a launch pad for growing across Africa.

In terms of the most favored investment sector, EY(2017) places transport & logistics became the first ranked sector in 2016. As Africa/s growth attract worldwide attention, the providers of global transport and logistics seek to be the "connectors" for Africans and markets, tapping on the huge opportunity presented by relative underdeveloped state of infrastructure in the continent. In 2016, RHC accounted for more than 40% of the capital inflow into Africa due to several large-ticket projects, including a US$20b spending by China Fortune Land Development Co. Ltd. Towards the development of Phase II of Egypt's new administrative capital.

Table 7. Africa's hub economies account for the majority of FDI 2017

Emerging African FDI Hub-economies	FDI attractive regioAfrica Afria	FDI Projects (% increase over 2016)	FDI Amount (% increase over 2016)	Jobs Created (% increase over 2016)
Morocco	North	12	7.0	19.2
Egypt	North	11.7	43.5	14.9
Kenya	East	5.9	1.2	1.5
Nigeria	West	7.5	6.7	4.9
South Africa	South	20.6	8.1	14.7
Source: EY (2017)				

Figure 6. show areas of FDI flow in the emerging hub economies, 2017

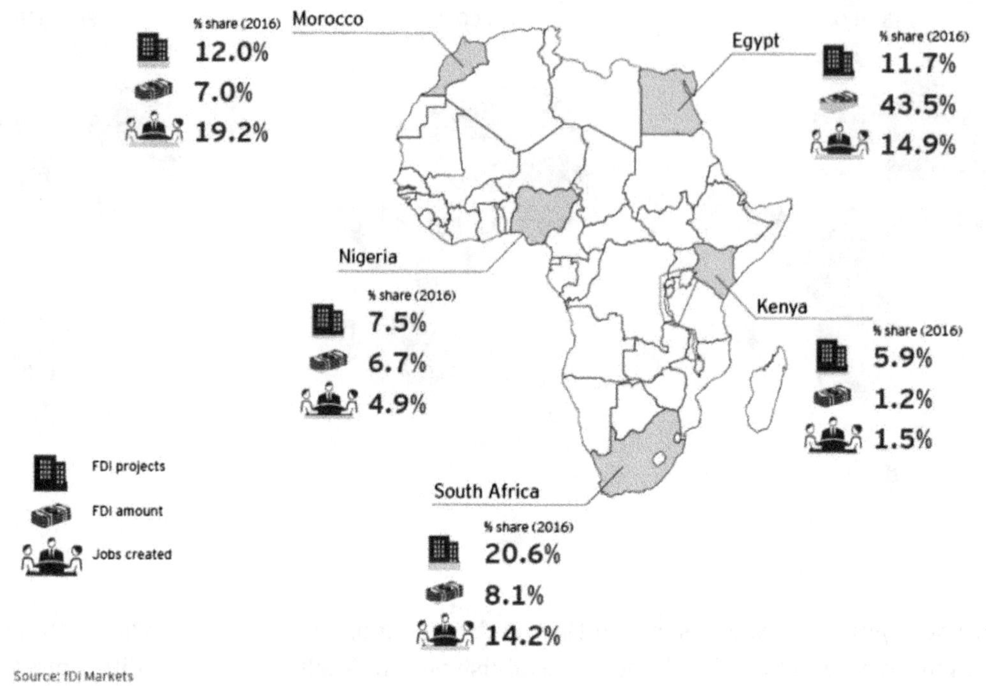

7. FUTURE RESEARCH DIRECTIONS AND CONCLUSION

There are many areas requiring further research, among which are the following:

First, multi-faceted economic linkages between urban and rural areas mean that well functioning urban economies have benefits for rural areas too. This relationship needs further research

Second, the failure of governments to deliver public infrastructure and services is at the heart of urban and industrial failures. Economically, efficient cities require early, strategic investments, particularly in energy, transport and other infrastructure, These issues need further investigations to ensure that the institutions can meet the needs of the expected much higher percentage of urban population.

Third, more research is needed on how to handle the increasingly complex Urban policies – whether in housing, sanitation or health – have economic implications.

Fourth, the economic dynamism of cities underlie their ability to achieve development goals in a host of many other areas, including human development, more research is needed to deal with the dynamism.

REFERENCES

Abubakar, I. R., & Dano, U. L. (2017). Socioeconomic Challenges and Opportunities of Urbanization in Nigeria. Hershey, PA: IGI Publishing.

Aré, L., Chabenne, S., Dupoux, P., Ivers, L., Micheal, D. C., & Morieux, Y. (2010). *The African Challengers- Global Competitors Emerge from the Overlooked Continent*. Beijing: The Boston Consulting Group.

AU. (n.d.). *CEN SAD*. Retrieved 2018, from African Union: https://au.int/en/recs/censad

Benna, U. G. (2013). Timbuktu, the African Medieval Knowledge City: The Role of Knowledge Development Actors. *Information & Knowledge Management, 12*(3).

Benna, U. G. (2016). From Rural Majority to Urban Majority Africans: Where will They Work? In U. G. Benna, S. B. Garba, U. G. Benna, & S. B. Garba (Eds.), *Population Growth and Rapid Urbanization in the Developing World* (Vol. 1, pp. 1–22). Hershey, PA: IGI Publishing. doi:10.4018/978-1-5225-0187-9.ch001

Benna, U. G., & Garba, S. B. (2016). Population Growth and Rapid Urbanization in the Developing World (Vol. 1). Hershey, PA: IGI Global.

Chapin, F. J., & Kaiser, E. J. (1979). *Urban Land Use Planning*. Urbana, IL: University of Illinois Press.

Chirisa, I., Maphosa, A., Zanamwe, L., Bandauko, E., & Mukarwi, L. (2016). Past, Present and Future Population Growth and Urban Management in Zimbabwe: Putting Institutions into Perspective. In U. G. Benna & S. B. Garba (Eds.), *Population Growth and Rapid Urbanization in the Developing World* (Vol. 1, pp. 64–81). Hershey, PA: IGI Publishing. doi:10.4018/978-1-5225-0187-9.ch004

Chirisa, I., Mukarwi, L., & Matamanda, A. R. (2017). Social Costs and Benefits of the Transformation of the Traditional Families in an African Urban Society. In U. G. Benna & I. Benna (Eds.), *Urbanization and its Impact on Socio-Economic Growth in Developing Regions* (pp. 179–197). Hershey, PA: IGI Publishing.

COMESA. (n.d.). *Overview of COMESA*. Retrieved 2018, from Common Market for Eastern and Southern Africa: http://www.comesa.int/overview-of-comesa/

Dupoux, P., Ermias, T., Heuzé, S., Niavas, S., & Kimani, M. V. (2014). Wining in Africa-From Trading Posts to Ecosystems. Boston: BCG Publishing.

Dupoux, P., Ivers, L., Niavas, S., & Chraïti, A. (2018). *Pioneering One Africa - The Companies Blazing a Trail Across the Continent.* BCG Publishing.

EAC. (2017). *About EAC*. Retrieved 2018, from East African Community: https://www.eac.int/about-eac

ECA. (2016). Macroeconomic Policy And Structural Transformation Of African Economies. Addis Ababa: Economic Commission for Africa (ECA).

ECA. (2016a). *AMU - Arab Maghreb Union*. Retrieved 7 19, 2018, from United Nation Economic Commission for Africa: https://www.uneca.org/oria/pages/amu-arab-maghreb-union

ECA. (2016b). *CEN-SAD - The Community of Sahel-Saharan States*. Retrieved 2018, from United Nations Economic Commission for Africa: https://www.uneca.org/oria/pages/cen-sad-community-sahel-saharan-states

ECCAS. (2014). *Presentation of ECCAS*. Retrieved 2018, from Economic Community of Central African States: http://www.ceeac-eccas.org/index.php/en/a-propos-de-la-ceeac/presentation

Economic Commission for Africa. (2017). *Economic Report on Africa 2017: Urbanization and Industrialization for Africa's Transformation*. Addis Ababa: ECA Publishing.

ECOWAS. (2015). *About the Commission*. Retrieved 2018, from ECOWAS Commission: http://www.comm.ecowas.int/about-ecowas/

Gollin, D., Lagakos, D., & Waugh, M. (2013). *The Agricultural Productivity Gap in Developing Countries*. Cambridge, UK: Faculty of Economics, Cambridge University. doi:10.3386/w19628

Habitat. (2018). *Africa Urban Agenda Programme*. Retrieved 07 09, 2018, from UN-Habitat: https://unhabitat.org/urban-initiatives/initiatives-programmes/africa-urban-agenda-programme/

IGAD. (2018). *About Us*. Retrieved 2018, from Peace, Prosperity and Regional Integration: https://igad.int/about-us

Klopp, J. M. (2011). *Towards a Political Economy of Transportation Policy and Practice in Nairobi*. Science and Business Media.

Klopp, J. M., & Paller, J. W. (2015, October 9). *How Africa can build inclusive, safe and sustainable cities*. Retrieved 07 09, 2018, from The Conversation: https://theconversation.com/how-africa-can-build-inclusive-safe-and-sustainable-cities-48445

Potts, D. (2012). *Whatever happened to Africa's rapid urbanization?* Counterpoints.

SADC. (2012). *About SADC*. Retrieved 2018, from Southern African Development Community: https://www.sadc.int/about-sadc/

Turok, I., & McGranahan, G. (2013). Urbanization and economic growth: the arguments and evidence for Africa and Asia. *Environment and Urbanization*.

United Nations Department of Economic and Social Affairs. (2014). *World Urbanization Prospects: The 2014 Revision*. United Nations, Department of Economic and Social Affairs/Population Division. UN-DESA.

World Bank. (2015). *Rising through cities in Ghana: urbanization review - overview report*. Washington, DC: World Bank Group.

World Bank Group. (2016). *From Oil to Cities - Nigeria's Next Transformation*. WBG Publishing.

World Bank Group. (2017). *End Extreme Poverty Boost Shared Prosperity*. World Bank Group.

World Economic Forum. (2017). *The African Union is on a mission to transform the continent by 2063. This is what you need to know*. Africa Union.

KEY TERMS AND DEFINITIONS

Business Friendly: Refers to how easy an individuals or organizations find it to do business with a state.

Development Goal: Needs to be substantial and unambiguous objectives a state or institution aspire to attain.

Development Partner: Refers to state, organization, or institution that is committed to an undertaking with another or others in the development process.

Greenfield Investment: When an institution or business organization commits capital in a state starting from scratch with a complete supply chain industrial plant.

Key Actors: Refers to various entities or stakeholders that are directly involved in the main activities.

Regional Integration: This refers to the free movement of goods and services across states within the same region creating a balanced development among member states.

Trading: Refers to an action of buying and selling of goods and services.

Chapter 7
Africa Under the Impact of the Fourth Industrial Revolution:
Gaps, Strategies, and Strides

Innocent Chirisa
University of Zimbabwe, Zimbabwe

Brilliant Mavhima
University of Zimbabwe, Zimbabwe

ABSTRACT

The chapter stresses that Africa requires a clear position of how "leapfrogging" into the FOIR should be informed by clear and unambiguous policy goals and strategies so that a sustainable development route is created. Political will, global connectivity, and straightforward pathways are fused in the menu. Africa is neither a monolithic nor a homogenous space where events and developments happen in a linear pattern. The traditional perspective about Africa perceives the region as motley of so many variations and controversies – spatial, temporal, gender, racial, and ideological. This is evident from the fact that Africa has portions of its economy that are pre-modern, modern, and post-modern. The "resource curse" phenomenon seems to hold water in both debate and practice in some circles. Countries and states should avoid falling into the proverbial trap of unequal exchange in form of transacting the natural endowments that Africa is known for.

INTRODUCTION

The chapter is linked to the discussion, in 2016 by Klaus Schwab, who is the Founder and Executive Chairman of the World Economic Forum entitled '*The Fourth Industrial Revolution (FOIR): what it means, how to respond*'. Thus, it demonstrates the gaps, and strides made by the member countries and the push that regional and sub-regional bodies are making to catch up with the diktats of the FOIR. In achieving this goal, the chapter is based on a study that reviewed a number of sources by desktop research, using content analysis and developing thematic lines of analysis in a bid to build a synthesis of critical ideas towards sustainable urban and industrial policy paradigms.

DOI: 10.4018/978-1-5225-7625-9.ch007

It is behooved of countries and regions by this discussion that must seek to catch up. It is underscored that the initial industrial revolution revolved around water and steam, the second around electricity, the third, around electronics while the fourth, that is, the FOIR is an extension and build-up of the third and digitalization is the mantra. The major gap noted with Africa, particularly Sub-Saharan Africa is confusion in trying to build its economies around the technologies of the first revolution with such ideas as social inclusion in employment being the principal departure point. Some economies, in the quest to generate jobs and create employment for their populaces, fear in engaging in meaningful industrial mechanization. In certain cases, a lot of de-industrialization is noted. In regional and urban economics, it is possible to engage the 'big push' approach, where a 'big cake' can be created, the equity policy is engaged, and everyone has a fair share of the cake. Some Asian countries including China, Malaysia, Singapore and South Korea have used this approach to massive success. The generality of African states seem to admire this but fear to immerse in it profoundly. The other quarter of the fear is explained by the fact that the countries have not meaningfully developed their democracy; promising jobs is a ritual of the cycle of election campaigning and keeping economies in some state of bad shape is a plus to the alleged 'ruling parties'.

In the context of strides, regional bodies including the African Union (AU), the Southern Africa Development Corporation (SADC), East African Community (EAC), Economic Community of West African States (ECOWAS), Middle East and North Africa (MENA) have clear statements of what they intend in form of industrialization. The Africa 2063 Agenda is there in place but its adequacy in spelling out the immersion of Africa into the FOIR is not clear, and so are the other regional bodies, policies and agendas.

CONCEPTUAL FRAMEWORK

The chapter is premised on the conceptual framework presented in Figure 1, which shows the three seemingly interlinked components relating to the FOIR. First, are the gaps which exist in any context and which national and local governments grapple with in efforts to have successful FOIR. There are arrays of gaps, which stand in the way of effective FOIR in Africa. Second, there are various strategies, which can be employed to narrow and possibly close these identified gaps. In simple terms, a strategy can be defined as a plan of action, which is intended to attain a specific action in the long-term. Strategies, therefore, are the schemes, plans, policies, schedules, and programs, which are formulated and adopted by national together with the local governments with the intention to close the gaps in different sectors. In actual essence, such strategies may refer to policies or planning and development approaches and paradigm, which take certain issues linked to the gaps and find ways to close these gaps.

Table 1, Table 2, and Table 3 highlight the indicators for gaps that African countries have, strategies that African countries have taken and strides that African countries have made in trying to reach the FOIR. The tables focus largely on technology and entrepreneurship gaps, strategies and strides in trying to increase the regional competitiveness of Africa. The innovation and entrepreneurship highlights the key components FOIR.

Lastly, there are strides, which symbolize the progress that will be made towards achieving the set strategies. Through implementing the strategies, certain strides will be made which may be perceived as the deliverables of the strategies. Hence, the strides are an indication of the headway that is made and a true reflection of moving forward from the gaps to the set goals and objectives.

Figure 1. The conceptual framework guiding the study (Authors, 2018)

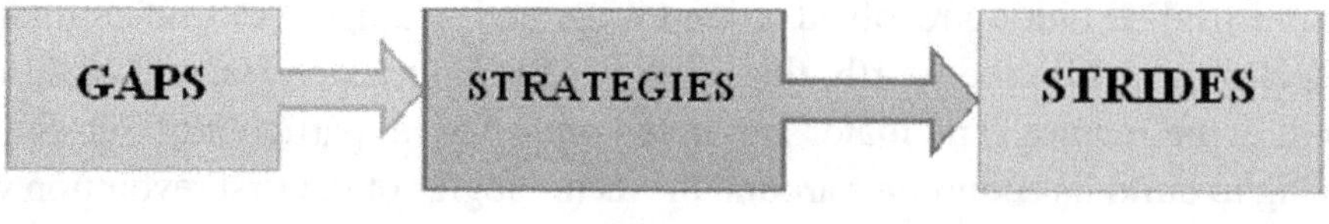

Table 1. Indicators for Gaps in trying to reach FOIR

Gaps	Indicators
• Decision-making	The extent of decision-making power within authorities. Highly centralized states shows a decision-making power gap.
• Implementation	Approaches and players that are involved in implementation. How the programs and projects are implemented
• Resources (Financial and Human)	Human and financial resources to implement FOIR fully.
• Participation	Who is involved and who is excluded/

Table 2. Indicators for strategies taken to reach FOIR

Strategies	Indicators
• Global competitiveness technology, processes, solutions	Ability to use technology in development. The approaches in which entrepreneurship and human development is promoted. The cost of production relative to continental costs.
• Socio-economic plans in relation to FOIR	Policies and plans that enhance innovation and investment.
• Sectoral Plans that focus on technology, knowledge-based development	Sectors and sector based plans that promotes regional competitiveness in FOIR. .

Table 3. Indicators for Strides made towards FOIR.

Strides	Indicators
• Investments in technology	What investment has been placed in technology to improve competitiveness in the FOIR?
• Investment in knowledge bases	What investments have been placed in human development to improve competitiveness in the region?

THEORIES UNDERPINNING THE STUDY

Development and economic enhancement are attainable through various strategies, approaches and via different stages. This can be through focusing on moving from one stage of development to the other or by leapfrogging, for instance jumping from stage two to stage five. In conceptualizing how development occurs, various theories exist. This section looks at the theory of capitalism and theory of modernization to explain how Africa is progressing in light of FOIR.

Theory of Capitalism

The theory of capitalism is often attributed to Adam Smith, who is revered as the father of modern capitalism; hence, it is critical to consider his views on capitalism in addition to other scholars such as Karl Marx. Smith argued that there exist an invisible hand, which transforms selfish motives and actions into results that promote the public good. This conceptualization of capitalism is anchored on the market forces, which relate to the laws of demand and supply. Various scholars agree with Smith in that markets mainly determine how an economy functions and determines the success or failure of means of production (O'Connor, 1974; Collins, 1980; Koslowski, 2013). In this regard, capitalism, governments and governance are perceived to distort the equilibrium of the scientific process, therefore, should not be part of the processes (Collins, 1980). This form of capitalism includes the rule by capitalists. This idea overlooks any significance of society engagement in managing the community (Berger, 1986). From this theory, capitalism developed from merely activities of economic actors under the influence of private players who bring in new ideas, which are usually innovative and geared at transforming the economy (Heywood, 2014). Capitalism is then perceived as involving human agents as the governing institution in which market forces interact. Therefore, Friedman (2009) argued that capitalism intends to achieve economic coordination as it explains how economies and economic enhancement progresses and the forces that determine its continued existence. Permitting the continued operation of market forces entail economic advancement without government disturbance, meaning that development follows a certain anticipated trajectory. Capitalism has been improving bringing into play what is called digital capitalism (Skeggs, 2018). This concept is largely capitalism as conceptualized in this paper but on the internet (). This kind of capitalism is becoming significant in the world and an essential factor of FOIR. One of such trajectories is elucidated by the modernization theory. Digital capitalism

Modernization Theory

The modernization theory posits every nation was once traditional community, which largely depended on the production of raw resources (Bernstein, 1971). The theory suggests that growth is phased and every nation has to pass through the stages to get to the modern society (Engerman, 2003). This modern society is characterized by various aspects, which include transformation from the traditional means of production to the use of technology. For example, the Silicon Valley in United States can be referred to as a highly modernized region in the world considering the high-tech industries, which exist in the region. One of the major events that have propelled modernization in the Global North has been the Industrial Revolution, which modernized almost all facets of human life from transport, manufacturing processes, food processing, and settlement types among many others. It is also quite interesting to note that modernization is highly contested in Africa, as it is a Western phenomenon (Watson, 2009). The result at times is the production of urban fantasies, which remain largely grand plans in city halls, with the realities on the ground being a far outcry from the visions (Chirisa *et al.* 2017).

The stages of modernization are elaborated by Rostow in his development model, he suggests five stages in modernization which are; traditional society, the preconditions to taking off, take off, the drive to maturity and high mass consumption (Rostow, 1960). The varied paces in development are linked to endogenous and exogenous factors. Endogenous factors include the social, political, physical and economic environment while the exogenous factors include issues international relations together with exploitations (Heywood, 2014). This theory explains the development stages in which modernization of nations occur. This process of development is not universal in terms of the exact stages that nations take to develop. Some nations leapfrog while others are failing completely to develop. However, the general development trajectory can be spelt easily with this process. FOIR can be located at the High Mass consumption stage. In this case, Africa is yet to reach FOIR.

LITERATURE REVIEW

In this section, a literature review is presented which considers the issue under discussion. Posing questions to FOIR in Africa requires the scrutiny of the various policies and strategies to be implemented in African nations for the revolution to start rolling. The FOIR has begun in Europe Asia, America and other developed nations around the globe. The technological impacts of FOIR are beginning to be felt in Africa. In the same period, the youth base is beginning to bulge while Africa is slowly losing its financial, political and economic prowess to influence the global dynamics. In light of this, this section seeks to unpack the potential changes that should be introduced to the existing urban and industrial growth policies and policy-structures to, ensure success given African youth protuberance and inadequate power, finance and weak global political & economic influence.

Development, as in the modernization theory, occurs in phases (Rostow, 1960; Friedman, 2009). In Rostow's modernization theory, five stages are identified (Rostow, 1960). The same seems to be occurring in explaining industrial growth globally. To date, four industrial revolutionary epochs have been identified (Schwab, 2017). The first industrial revolution was experienced in Europe during the period 1700-1850 and was made possible using steam and water to generate power. At the time, steam was used to generate power to support the various inventions, which were made to increase productivity mainly in the coalmines and textile industries (Wilde, 2018). The revolution in this era was thus anchored on the steam engine, which was, however, very capital intensive as well as being less efficient and effective though it somehow resulted in some significant increase in productivity.

The second revolution commenced around 1860 up to 1919 and was supported by electric power which superseded steam power. The introduction of electricity and electric power was very much appreciated in the industrial sector because it resulted in the generation of energy, which made production faster, and goods could be produced at relatively lower costs. The supply and distribution of electricity were one of the major successes which meant that light was to be provided in the streets, homes as well as use of some transport and telegrams which made communication and transportation of raw materials and finished products much easier. In this way, the industrial revolution was greatly supported by the advent of electric power in France, 2017).

The 1920s marked the inception of the third industrial revolution, which was characterized by employing microchip technology and information technology to mechanize production. The current is the fourth part of the industrial revolution, which is an appendage of the third revolution (Kemp, 2016). The current development appears to be defying the physical, economic and biological boundaries (Hawken *et al.* 2013). This presents a new set of problems to nations that are not evolving and keeping pace with these seemingly complex evolutionary changes.

FOIR has come with various impacts to nations the world over (Kemp, 2016). The negativity or positivity of the impacts largely depends on the aptitude of a nation to manipulate the technology (Blanchet *et al.* 2014). From this, FOIR has the potential to increase the well-being of the populations while it also has the ability to lower the human well-being in some instances (Steams, 2018). It is believed by many that the revolution will bring about increased efficiency and productivity in industries, reduce transport other relative costs and open new markets to drive economic growth (Schwab, 2017). Such efficiency is what scientists and professionals from different disciplines have always been trying to achieve considering that resources are always constrained, especially for countries from the Global South.

However, although the revolution is presumed to bring positive economic growth and allow free market trading, it is noted that inequalities will increase despite such progress (Steams, 2018). This may be explained by the fact that a significant number of workers are at risk of retrenchment since their duties and responsibilities will be assigned (and done immaculately) to faster and even more efficient, machines (Blanchet *et al.* 2014). It is only a few professionals with the ability to operate such machines, for example, professionals in robotics while the generality of the population will remain unemployed or under-paid. Subsequently, this will form a huge gap between incomes. These gaps are part of the greatest feared challenges associated with FOIR (Kemp, 2016). The revolution will create an economic environment that requires more talent than thus creation of two distinct groups [low-skill/low-pay" and "high-skill/high-pay] (Schwab, 2017).

The FOIR has also blurred certain industrial boundaries and challenged existing regulatory frameworks. This is so because FOIR generates a new set of challenge for policy makers to maintain the global pace (Steams, 2018). Policymaking is adaptive, human-centered, particularly inclusive and sustainable. This implies that policymaking is no longer done by the government but by various relevant stakeholders (Blanchet *et al.* 2014). This brings in the issues of agility in government and policy-making (Schwab, 2017). This permits policies to be modified as rapid as the rapid change of the policy environment. In this case, policy-making becomes focused more on achieving policy goals than being a regulatory compliance, allowing information to determine policy trajectory and permitting data input from various stakeholders (Hawken *et al.* 2013).

In trying to survive the forces of FOIR, government policies become more open to private sectors. Permitting private sector operators to be more innovative and enhancing the competitiveness (Schwab, 2017). Industrial self-regulation also promotes the growth of the industries guided by the pace of the free market (Steams, 2018). Another important aspect is that as FOIR is unfolding, certain regulatory bodies are emerging (Blanchet *et al.* 2014). Therefore, the government becomes the major regulating body, managing the unfolding of the revolutionary yields (Steams, 2018).

METHODOLOGY

This chapter employed qualitative approach. This is largely because the chapter required explanations on how the African continent is in relation to the coming of the fourth industrial revolution. The collection of relative data was done through reading various literature and documents. Therefore, a desktop review was employed to collect data that was used in developing the chapter. Data from applicable literature and documents where reviewed in order to understand Africa's position during the FOIR. Data where classified into themes and thematic content analysis was engaged in analysing the data. The themes included; gaps which were largely the vulnerabilities and the drawbacks of Africa during FOIR, Strategies which were the approaches that have been engaged by Africa to deal with the weaknesses to harness the benefits and Strides which were the successes that Africa has managed to achieve against the gaps. From the themes, synthesis was done and conclusions were made based on the collected data.

RESULTS AND ANALYSIS

Various issues that range from endogenous and exogenous forces have stifled the current environment in African cities, growth. This calls for identification of gaps in practices by the African countries together with the strategies to harvest fully the benefits offered by the FOIR. This section presents the results of the study. The section also brings about an analysis of the study findings grouped in two themes, which are gaps and strategies.

Gaps

One major gap that has dragged Africa into reaching FOIR is the decision making gap. Significant reforms and relevant decision-making powers are vested in the hands of politicians (Dibua, 2017uwira, 2017; Migdal, 2018). Just like any region in the world, Africa is not an exception as politics play an integral role in the continent's socio-economic development trajectory (Mkandawire, 2015; Kieh, 2018; Kulu *et al.* 2018). The nature in which the political leaders in Africa take power is packed with corruption and praising of the 'big man' who becomes the lifelong leader. The leaders nurture a group of worshipers who have the political protection of the leader (Kulu *et al.* 2018). This makes it impossible for any other person to implement a project without being corrupt (Mkandawire, 2015). Furthermore, the activities undertaken by those who have political positions or affiliations are susceptible by any engagement of impartial technological innovations thus; any form of innovation is resisted. This can be evidenced by innovations that have been resisted for instance the invention of a helicopter by Daniel Chingoma, the resistance of the Government of Zimbabwe to digitize the Department of Deed and Registry (Mudombi and Muchie, 2014). As a result, making decisions of significance in Africa creates a huge gap to reaching the FOIR.

Furthermore, the development of Africa is also stalled by the knowledge gap between the region and other nations globally. This gap makes it hard for the region to grow and compete into the talent and entrepreneurship based Fourth Industrial Revolution. This was left by inequalities developed by through the segregatory laws, which shaped the evolution and eventually form of towns and cities during the time with some of the footprints still visible to this day. Evidence is shown from the urban areas, which are usually more developed in terms of infrastructure availability in comparison to the rural areas (Ogunbodede *et al.* 2015). For instance, in Rwanda, Kigali is one of the most developed cities in Africa and is home to one of Africa's most expensive buildings (Caldwell, 2015). On the other side, other regions in Rwanda still lag and the percentage of the rural poor even increasing (Umubyeyi *et al.* 2016). Moreover, in South Africa, Apartheid resulted in spatial inequalities between the urban areas (white enclaves) and the Bantustans and townships (for the Africans). To this day this segregation is still in existence as there are some areas which remain deprived of basic services while cities such as Cape Town, Johannesburg and Durban state of the art infrastructure and boost of being economic hubs of Africa (Bond, 2014). These forms of disparities make it hard to develop the nations evenly as the cores that were developed by the colonial masters continue to progress and the peripheral areas continue to lag behind. Given the significant elements of FOIR, it makes it difficult to implement and benefit from the innovations of the epoch. First, FOIR largely depends on information, which is hard to access or disseminate easily in the terrain of African business. The systems make it hard, as the information gaps in Africa are huge.

The level of citizen empowerment and the ability for one to invest and venture into enterprises present another huge gap in Africa that is stalling the speed of Africa to reach the FOIR. The World Transparency Index shows that most countries that are ranked highest in corruption are located in Africa (World Transparency Index, 2018). This corruption has been institutionalized to an extent that one cannot carry out any project without being corrupt (Knutsen et al. 2017). The result is that most development initiatives, which could possibly have transformed Africa's economy in selected countries, have remained stifled due to the high prevalence of corruption (Chirisa, Bobo and Matamanda, 2017). For example, the project by Dangote to erect a cement factory in Harare, Zimbabwe hit a hard wall after one minister requested the investor to pay bribe (Akinyoade and Uche, 2016; Sutherland, 2018). Corruption is also prominent in public institutions where public officer take advantage of desperate citizens to fleece the when they want things to be done faster (Nunkoo *et al.* 2018). This is evident across Africa where institutions like immigration authorities, police and departments of motor vehicle licensing have also taken up corruption making it hard to access basic services (Aborisade, 2018). In local authorities, corruption has also seen the distributing out of land without proper town planning procedures at the same time certain significant plans have failed to be approved because of corruption (Amadi and Ekwekwe, 2014; Chirisa *et al.* 2017). This proves that corruption plays a significant part in determining the success or failure of initiatives in Africa (Efobi, 2015). This is so, as corruption leads to slowing down of developments thus reducing the efficiency and dissemination of data to the citizens. Investors lose confidence in the system and would rather have their monies somewhere where there is transparency, accountability and good governance.

Another significant gap in Africa is the policy and development gap. African governments lack the ability to develop relevant policies for technological development and investment. While local governments have been developing ideas of engaging in the ease of doing business, the efficiency is still lagging. Governance issues are proving to be problematic in the African community (Fosu, 2017; Mills, 2018). Most African cities are characterized what can make them be classified as badly governed communities. Elements like corruption, lack of transparency, citizen exclusion, inefficiencies, bureaucracies, poor service delivery together with resistance to innovation by government among others (Engels, 2017). Research has it that developed countries have better governance and low corruption whereas poor countries have poor governance and are filled with corruption (Fosu, 2017). Empirical evidence shows a strong relationship between poor governance and poor growth performance (Mills, 2018). In Nigeria, the poor performance of the economy is largely linked to problems like corruption, poor institutions and low government institutions which all points to the issue of poor governance (Okeke, 2017). This kind of economic environment makes Africa less ready to cope with the demands of FOIR. This implies that countries in Africa will continue lagging behind the developed countries since the countries are run with large inefficiencies, red tape, corruption which is not conducive for business operations. As a result, the policy gap creates a problem in FOIR.

For a nation to develop into the FOIR presents a need for a stable and growing economy. This becomes a problem in Africa. African countries are struggling economically (Mkwandawire, 2015; Cohn, 2016; Dibua, 2017). This is largely due to issues of bad governance (Mills, 2018). African economic predicaments can also be ascribed to the Structural Adjustment Programs that left most African countries in debt to the International Monetary Fund or the World Bank (Pieper *et al.* 2016). Therefore, most African countries cannot borrow capital for investment. This is a problem as the revolution that is unveiling though largely depending on information and skilled labour require huge amounts of resources to fund the technological revolutions as well as the associated researches. While countries like Rwanda, Tanzania, South Africa and Cote d'Ivoire are growing economically, the GDP is increasing at a very slow pace as compared to European, American and Asian Countries (Cohn, 2016). With the FOIR, economic competitiveness is a significant factor that African countries do not have. This implies that the significant investments that are needed to survive in the new era cannot be funded in most African countries. Furthermore, the African economies coupled with poverty have left the government failing to feed the populations (Mkwandawire, 2015). This implies that the governments cannot fund other projects rather than those linked to bread and butter.

The development finance gap also present another drawback for Africa to develop into the FOIR and reap its benefits (Chu *et al.* 2014). Most governments in Africa are broke and cannot run any activities from national coffers (Dincecco and Katz, 2016; Murithi, 2017). For instance, in 2017, the Government of Zimbabwe had a net income of $3.6 billion. The national net expenses were at $4.8 billion recording a budget deficit. Zambia had $4.895 billion and expenditures of $7.05 billion (2017 est.) recording a deficit. Tunisia had $9.397 billion revenue and expenses of $11.61 billion. The other nation was Mozambique that had revenues of $2.758 billion and expenditures of $3.607 billion recording a budget deficit (Taylor *et al.* 2017). These figures beside the budgets being small in Africa, the government are not economically capacitated leading to a failure in trying to meet the needs of the countries. This reduces efficiency in resource utilization as most of the African countries. Governments in Africa have been having financial problems as they seek external sources of funding (ESAPs). This creates a perpetual financing gap in Africa. There are attempts however, to look inwards with governments introducing ideas of crowd funding.

The term super power is linked to Europe, Asia, and America particularly the United States of America (Nye, 2015). While this is largely linked to issues of nuclear prowess, the same concept applies to financial power and the financial institutions (Nye, 2015). Africa is a powerless continent in global financial issues. African banks, the local stock exchange, and other African financial institutions are largely controlled [in terms of performance] by the super powers (Geroge *et al.* 2016). This implies that any shock to the super powers will have detrimental effects to the economy of African countries. Furthermore, in global politics, countries in Africa have had weaker influence. This is largely linked to the issue of the superiority of arsenals as well as financial resources (Asongu and De Moor, 2017). This implies that Africa becomes a voiceless voice in determining the global trajectory of development. This creates a weak peripheral environment that absorbs all negative externalities during the FOIR.

Strategies

The gaps and challenges that Africa is facing in trying to take up the demands of the FOIR, presents the need for proper strategies in managing the threats and exploiting on the opportunities. This will help in increasing the competitive advantage of Africa in the evolving world. This section seeks to elaborate the strategies that have been employed by African communities in guiding Africa in the FOIR.

The central governments have been mainly responsible for policymaking. This has had impacts as to the lucrativeness of the countries as investment destinations (Rukomoinikova, 2016). Like elsewhere in the world, governments in Africa are principally responsible for large capital investments. This explains why the failure of the government to invest has led to a failure of African countries to develop economically. Africa Agenda 2063 is a 50-year strategic plan to improve Africa's global competitiveness through regional economic improvements. The policy was adopted in the year 2015 with the view to increase efficiency in the implementation of initiatives in the African continent (African Union, 2015). The plan is anchored on seven visions, which are:

1. *A prosperous Africa based on inclusive growth and sustainable development*
2. *An integrated continent politically united and based on the ideals of Pan-Africanism and the vision of Africa's Renaissance*
3. *An Africa of good governance, democracy, respect for human rights, justice and the rule of law*
4. *A peaceful and secure Africa*
5. *An Africa with a strong cultural identity, common heritage, shared values and ethics*
6. *An Africa whose development is people-driven, relying on the potential of African people, especially its women and youth, and caring for children*
7. *Africa as a strong, united and influential global player and partner (African Union, 2015).*

This blueprint for the development of Africa lays a foundation for global competitiveness. It pursues to address certain issues that are stifling growth in the African continent. Therefore, proper implementation can lead to the improvement of the continent. In trying to meet the targets of the agenda 2063, various plans and regional policies have been placed. As a result, this has the potential to increase global competitiveness of Africa as a region as it tries to stride towards FOIR.

The African region has also engaged socio-economic regional action plans to try to improve the African continent. These plans are a step towards increasing African competitiveness in its attempt to reach the FOIR. The plans have been done under the regional nations' fraternity called the African Union. In this fraternity, African leaders have tried to improve the continent through formulation and implementation of various regional action plans. Significant efforts made were the Lagos Plan of Action. The plan was a 20-year plan that ran from the year 1980 to the year 2000. The major intention was to increase economic development. This was largely focused towards making the African continent self-sufficient through power, infrastructure and industrial development (Adedeji, 2002; African Union, 2015).

Another focus of African countries towards improving investment and economic development towards the FOIR have been through sectorial plans. The region has had various kinds of sectors largely basing on natural resources and other significant aspects of the communities. Through the sectors, Africa has been looking towards improving various sectors for example, the policy taken up with an intention to increase Agricultural productivity in the continent named the Comprehensive Africa Agriculture Development Program (Boserup, 2017). The Comprehensive Africa Agriculture Development Program (CAADP) was declared as a policy in the year 2003 (Hollinger, 2015). The policy intended to have 6% annual growth of agricultural GDP as well as growing expenditure on agriculture by assigning at least 10% of public funds to agriculture (Gebreyes *et al.* 2017). To date, the policy has been signed by 44 member states and of the forty-four; thirty-three have gone on to create agricultural plans (Hollinger, 2015). The program has also seen the regional public expenditure rising by over 7% per year to date. The highlighted uptake of the policy indicates how Africa is attempting to increase its competitiveness in the efficiency driven era of the FOIR. .Furthermore, the sectorial plans have also moved towards improving technological developments through sectors like ministry of technology that focus on technology development in Africa (Heywood, 2014). African governments have stripped off import duties on technology gadgets increasing the accessibility in the region.

Africa has now become a complex web of various regional integration initiatives. The integrations in Africa has increased regional collaborations. The collaborations have seen the development of network of power, roads, pipes and railways among others. Beira corridor is one of the example which is a corridor with rail lines, pipelines and roads that links land locked countries like Zimbabwe to sea ports (). This has seen the improvement of access to the countries increasing the efficiency by reducing the cost of production as well as regional instructiveness. Furthermore, Africa has been trying to improve the business environment through removing of various hindrances. One of the key results of integrations was the removal of travelling VISA for fellow states (Bates, 2014). This can be accredited to the Regional Integration Facilitation Forum (RIFF), which originated through the cross board initiatives in 1993. This initiative envisioned to allow free market trade in the whole of Africa. The initiative by the African Development Bank and other global financial institutions saw the engagement of fourteen African countries (Banson *et al.* 2015). The Economic Commission for Africa has been spearheading regional integration in Africa. The notion was centred towards dividing Africa into small regional blocks that would spearhead development (Asante, 2016). This saw the birth of blocks like SADC, Common Market for Eastern and Southern Africa (COMESA), Economic Community of Central African States (ECCAS), Economic Community of West African States (ECOWAS) and Arab Maghreb Union (AMU) among others (Sicurelli, 2016). The block attempted to integrate Africa through the Lagos Action Plan. This plan saw the birth of separated but overarching regional blocks.

Africa was once perceived as the Dark Continent before the discovery of the Cape of Good Hope, which is now the modern day Cape Town (Allen, 2015). This was largely because of its primitive state. Looking at the modernization theory of development, Africa was at the traditional stage. When the Europeans colonized Africa, their development was largely to ensure increased ability to continue extracting the resources without industrializing. This level of development on the African continent imply that the administrative systems are filled with inefficiencies and red tape (Koslowski, 2013). Attempts to modernize the administrative systems in Africa can be seen through the attempts by governments to try to improve the administrative processes. This can be seen through policy reform attempts like Service level benchmarking, Ease of doing business, Public Finance management Reforms, Integrated Results Based Management (Chatiza, 2017). All these strategies have been to assess how government policies and processes operate in an attempt to improve the operations.

Modernization has been the only instrument that Africa has engaged to try to improve the continent. The other approach was capitalism. The idea of a free-market economy in Africa was largely exogenous (Cohn, 2016). The Washington Consensus brought about the Economic Structural Adjustment Programs (Chon, 2016). The approach was engaged to improve government and administrative structures that were largely inefficient and filled with economically unhealthy costs. This was implemented on the African communities that were largely communal. The approach saw many African countries attempting to raise Gross Domestic Product and reduce expenditure (Obeng-Odoom, 2015). Development was largely determined by capital expenditure, which was attained through lending and borrowing from the IMF and World Bank and the countries respectively. Through this approach, governments have been largely focused on economic development by creating enabling environments. The attempts to integrate regions, the creation of regional blocks all seek to create a region that had free trade to allow ease of market operations. Governments in Africa have seized to be at the center of trade but have become players in the market and in most cases regulators through policy making.

Strides

Regardless of the environment, the attempts to improve the African continent have yielded some positive results. Various governments have made efforts within their jurisdictions to improve on development. Various government reforms, agreements and efforts have seen the creation of the regional blocks, policy reforms that has seen the development of infrastructure on the African continent. The governments and other organizations have endeavored on capacity building in public institutions as well as the citizens.

Government reforms in most African countries can also signal the achievements that Africans have attained towards development to date. African countries have been focusing more on decentralization as the major government reform (Diep *et al.* 2016; Aalen and Muriaas, 2017). This has seen various form of decentralization taking place in different African countries. The reforms have been made towards strengthening the locals. The decentralization of government powers intended towards improving the capacity of the locals from local authorities to citizens (Aalen and Muriaas, 2017). To date the governments of Ghana, Mali, Namibia, Senegal, South Africa, Uganda, Zimbabwe and Ethiopia have formally engaged decentralization as a part of their constitutions (Diep *et al.* 2016). However, the level of decentralization in Africa has been largely issues of tokenism (Dipholo and Molosi-France, 2017). Actual government powers have not yet been decentralized. In Botswana, though decentralization structures exist, powers have not yet been devolved. The same case exists in Zimbabwe, Ghana and other countries.

There are notable infrastructure development success stories, which can be narrated for Africa. The governments have engaged in various partnerships to develop infrastructure in their countries. Regional blocks like SADC, COMESA and ECOWAS have had successes in infrastructure development particularly power, road, rail and even pipe lines (Bhalla, 2016). These regional infrastructure development approaches have also been aided by country-to-country infrastructure development attempts. Rwanda and Egypt have developed the continent's most expensive buildings (Kamukama and Kakwenzire, 2017). This creates investment attractions in Africa a leading to increased economic growth. South Africa has made remarkable developments in infrastructure development (Kelly and Palmucci, 2014). This has seen the development of world-class infrastructure particularly the road, rail and building infrastructure. The infrastructure development attempts by nations as well as the regions have seen the advancement of the continent into a modernized continent (Aliyu *et al.* 2017). It is worth noting that the modernization is not evenly distributed infrastructure development in some countries is still backwards. Mozambique has started to develop infrastructure but is still lagging behind. Somalia is even failing to take off due to corruption, poverty and war.

Complementing the development of infrastructure in human development is capacity building (Aliyu *et al.* 2017). Capacity building has been done by African countries in an attempt to improve local economic development. Capacity building range from national level to village level (Chu *et al.* 2014). Various capacitating attempts have been made. At national level, the governments have been developing policies that enhance the capacities of the locals. For instance, in Zimbabwe the Prime Minister's Directive intended to capacitate the local authorities by ceding government power to the locals (Aliyu *et al.* 2017). Capacity building has also been done in form of resources. African governments have engaged in various land reform programs. These programs have seen Africans getting land and engaging in agricultural activities, which are the largest contributor in Africa's GDP (Chu *et al.* 2014).

Africa has also seen various technological and infrastructure related developments that play a significant role in preparing the region in FOIR. The major developments are in power lines and roads. African countries have developed depended infrastructure, with an average of kilometres of roads per 1000 km^2 (Johnson *et al.* 2017). Of the roads, half of the roads are paved. This network of roads evidence development stride as the global average is 944 km2. The road networks in have more than 10000 kilometres are international roads, linking nations (Sign *et al.* 2018). These networks have improved movement in Africa though there is still need to continue developing as Africa is still lying way below the global road network density average. Furthermore, the region has also been developing electricity networks that save the region. Regional blocs like SADC, ECOWAS and others, divide into power network grids. As such the region has seen exportation of power by nations that are producing excess electricity (Merem *et al.* 2017). This relationship in global infrastructure has increased the productivity of Africa as a region making it a huge stride towards FOIR.

Africa has also been taking steps in human development to improve the competitiveness of its human capital. This has been seen by the development of universities and colleges developed in the region. Programs like science development programs like STEM in Zimbabwe (Bhukuvhani, 2018n). Furthermore, ideas to promote entrepreneurship I Africa through courses of entrepreneurship in universities is also another step that has been taken to develop the human abilities in the African continent (Asongu *et al.* 2017). Furthermore, the enhancement of learning technology in universities is enhancing the technological competitiveness of the African continent. Africa has had super computers that are useful in learning and data management with the largest being situated in South Africa (Goody, 2018). As such, having such technology on the continent has been improving the technical capacity of the region through development of competent citizens. This has been improving the competitiveness of Africa.

DISCUSSION AND SYNTHESIS

Africa has had a slow start in development. This is attributed to various aspects that include the political environment, poor governance, poverty, corruption and weak institutions. Dealing with this kind of environment, governments in Africa through the African Union has attempted to redress the development issues on the African continent. The various strategies employed have led to the attainment of certain milestones in the continent, which improve Africa's capabilities in the FOIR.

The current position of Africa places the continent at a disadvantage in the form of development. The African countries have come together with a purpose to improve the competitiveness of Africa as a region against the structural weaknesses that the region is vulnerable. Africa has various inconsistencies in every aspect, ranging from policies to resources as well as a human capital, which may be inefficient at times. This has become a developmental issue on the region and can be attributed to the lagging development in the African continent.

Dealing with the issues of development has been attempted through various strategies. The attempts to integrate the region, creation of development oriented blocks as well as various free travel union present the approaches that were employed by Africa to try to enhance the regional competitiveness. It is however important to note that most on the attempts that were employed by the African continent were ideas initiated in other continents through global institutions like IMF and World Bank. Therefore, it can be used to justify why some of the strategies are not working in the African continent. The kinds of approaches that have been proposed by the global institutions do not address the regional inequalities that were created by the colonialists. As a result, development that has occurred because of the strategies still leaves huge development disparities between cities, city-rural, and individual well-being.

The plans and approaches that are being implemented in Africa are largely incompatible with Africa's current position. Most parts of Africa are still rural and the modernization approach has worked in certain part but have not reached other parts of the continent. As a result, opening the markets for free trade can only create the problem of dependency. The more modernized parts of the African continent will benefit at the expense of the less developed parts. As a result, the opening up of boarders and creating the capitalistic environment will create a good business environment for countries like South

Africa, Tanzania, Rwanda, Botswana Egypt, that have invested in infrastructure. On the other hand, less developed countries like Somalia will be left even poorer as they will not be at a strategic position to compete with the potential economies of scale.

Development strides made by Africa in the context of structural weaknesses are remarkable. Africa countries have managed to come up with proper government reforms. These have managed to improve the wellbeing of the African community. This has led to proper development of infrastructure ranging from road, rail, electricity and water. The governments in Africa have also been rolling out capacity building programs that have given Africa leverage in engagement in development. However, the strides that Africa has made in development are not even. This is largely due to differing government initiatives. An example is the AfCFTA, which has not been signed by Nigeria because the government is still assessing the potential threats that Nigeria will face after creating an open market environment. Such political environment coupled with the natural environment has usually limited the success of development. Having assessed the position of Africa as a continent in relation FOIR. There is need to further understand the ways in which technology, entrepreneurship and regional synergies can be used to enhance the competitiveness of Africa as a region.

CONCLUSION, POLICY OPTIONS AND RECOMMENDATIONS

The chapter intended to proffer a nuanced dialogue and a discourse on the meanings and practical implications of the fourth industrial revolution (FOIR) to Africa as a region. Africa has had a late start on engaging into the FOIR. This is pinned to the issue of the gaps that exist in Africa. The governments aided by the African Union have had various attempts to improve the conditions of the African continent. This has seen the engagement of various kinds of agreements that seek to integrate the continent into one development oriented unit. The attempts have led to successful development of Africa in infrastructure. However, the development implementation has not been uniform in the region. As a result, there is need to improve on the conditions to make Africa more adapted to the current environment. Africa needs to develop its own economic policies as a region and avoid implementing global ideas that are usually incompatible with the African environment. An example of one such problem is the issue of the Structural Adjustment Programs. Being a pilot project, the program was implemented on the continent without looking at the reparations. This left the whole continent being in debt and to date most African countries are still fighting towards repayment of the debts. The region also needs to develop technologically to improve the competitive advantage in global markets. Currently the African Markets are flooded with cheap products from Asia. This is so as the current production methods in Africa are less efficient thereby making the local products expensive. Having expensive products imply that Africa will have products that cannot compete at a global market. Concisely, this presents the need for technological advancement on the continent.

ACKNOWLEDGMENT

The authors are grateful for the contributions made by the editors, the anonymous reviewers as well as by Mr. Abraham R Matamanda of the Department of Urban and Regional Planning, University of the Free State, South Africa who critiqued it and made invaluable insights towards shaping the argument.

REFERENCES

Aalen, L., & Muriaas, R. L. (2017). Power calculations and political decentralisation in African post-conflict states. *International Political Science Review*, *38*(1), 56–69. doi:10.1177/0192512115615704

Abdulai, A. G., Bawole, J. N., & Sakyi, E. K. (2017). *Persistent chronic poverty in Northern Ghana: is geography to blame?* University of Ghana.

Aborisade, R. A., & Aliyyu, N. B. (2018). *Corruption and Africa. The Development of Africa*. New York: Springer.

Adedeji, A. (2002). *Keynote Address: From the Lagos Plan of Action to the New Partnership for African Development and from the Final Act of Lagos to the Constitutive Act: Whither Africa?* African Forum for Envisioning Africa, Nairobi, Kenya.

Adjibolosoo, S. (2017). *Developing civil society: social order and the human factor*. Oxon, UK: Routledge. doi:10.4324/9781351160087

African Union. (2015). *Agenda 2063: the Africa we want*. Addis Ababa: African Union Commission.

Akinyoade, A., & Uche, C. U. (2016). *Dangote cement: An African success story?* ASC working paper. African Studies Centre Leiden.

Aliyu, A. K., Modu, B., & Tan, C. W. (2017). A review of renewable energy development in Africa: A focus in South Africa, Egypt and Nigeria. *Renewable & Sustainable Energy Reviews*.

Allen, C. (2015). *Tales from the Dark Continent: Images of British colonial Africa in the twentieth century*. Routledge.

Amadi, L., & Ekekwe, E. (2014). Corruption and development administration in Africa: Institutional approach. *African Journal of Political Science and International Relations*, *8*(6), 163–174. doi:10.5897/AJPSIR2013.0634

Asante, S. K. (2016). *Regionalism and Africa's development: expectations, reality and challenges*. New York: Springer.

Asongu, S. A., Anyanwu, J. C., & Tchamyou, V. S. (2017). Technology-driven information sharing and conditional financial development in Africa. *Information Technology for Development*, 1–30. doi:10.1080/02681102.2017.1311833

Asongu, S. A., & De Moor, L. (2017). Financial globalisation dynamic thresholds for financial development: Evidence from Africa. *European Journal of Development Research*, *29*(1), 192–212. doi:10.1057/ejdr.2016.10

Awuah, K. G. B., & Hammond, F. N. (2014). Determinants of low land use planning regulation compliance rate in Ghana. *Habitat International*, *41*, 17–23. doi:10.1016/j.habitatint.2013.06.002

Banson, K. E., Nguyen, N. C., Bosch, O. J., & Nguyen, T. V. (2015). A systems thinking approach to address the complexity of agribusiness for sustainable development in Africa: A case study in Ghana. *Systems Research and Behavioral Science*, *32*(6), 672–688. doi:10.1002res.2270

Bates, R. H. (2014). *Markets and states in tropical Africa: the political basis of agricultural policies*. University of California Press.

Berger, P. L. (1986). The capitalist revolution: Fifty propositions about prosperity, equality, and liberty. New York: Academic Press.

Bernstein, H. (1971). Modernization theory and the sociological study of development. *The Journal of Development Studies*, *7*(2), 141–160. doi:10.1080/00220387108421356

Bhalla, A. S. (2016). *Regional blocs: building blocks or stumbling blocks?* New York: Springer.

Bhukuvhani, C. (2018). Towards Analysis of the Status of Science Technology Engineering and Mathematics (STEM) Education in Zimbabwe Secondary Schools: Access, Quality, Policy. *Zimbabwe Journal of Educational Research*, *30*(1), 345–452.

Blanchet, M., Rinn, T., Von Thaden, G., & De Thieulloy, G. (2014). *Industry 4.0: The new industrial revolution-How Europe will succeed*. Hg. v. Roland Berger Strategy Consultants GmbH. Retrieved from http://www. rolandberger. Com/media/pdf/Roland_Berger_TAB_Industry_4_0_2014

Bond, P. (2014). *Elite transition: From apartheid to neoliberalism in South Africa*. London: Pluto Press.

Boserup, E. (2017). *The conditions of agricultural growth: The economics of agrarian change under population pressure*. Oxford, UK: Routledge.

Caldwell, D., Dyszynski, J., & Roland, R. (2015). *2015. Climate Compatible Development in the 'Land of a Thousand Hills': Lessons from Rwanda*. CDKN.

Chambers, R. (1995). Poverty and livelihoods: Whose reality counts? *Environment and Urbanization*, *7*(1), 173–204. doi:10.1177/095624789500700106

Chambers, R. (2014). *Rural development: Putting the last first*. Oxford, UK: Routledge. doi:10.4324/9781315835815

Chatiza, K. (2016). Analysing Policy Responses to the Dilemmas of Peri-urbanity and Land Management in Zimbabwe: A Case Study of Harare. In *Peri-Urban Developments and Processes in Africa with Special Reference to Zimbabwe* (pp. 129–142). New York: Springer. doi:10.1007/978-3-319-34231-3_11

Cheteni, P., & Shindika, E. S. (2017). Ethical Leadership in South Africa and Botswana. *BAR - Brazilian Administration Review*, *14*(2), 6. doi:10.1590/1807-7692bar2017160077

Chirisa, I., Bobo, T., & Matamanda, A. R. (2017). Misplaced values, political myopia and the neglect of professional ethics: Case of human factor decay and local government rot in Zimbabwe. *Zambezia*, *44*(ii), 36–52.

Chivaura, V. G., & Mararike, C. (1998). *The Human Factor Approach to Development in Africa*. Harare: UZ Publications.

Chu, K. M., Jayaraman, S., Kyamanywa, P., & Ntakiyiruta, G. (2014). Building research capacity in Africa: Equity and global health collaborations. *PLoS Medicine*, *11*(3), e1001612. doi:10.1371/journal.pmed.1001612 PMID:24618823

Cirolia, L. R., & Berrisford, S. (2017). 'Negotiated planning': Diverse trajectories of implementation in Nairobi, Addis Ababa, and Harare. *Habitat International*, *59*, 71–79. doi:10.1016/j.habitatint.2016.11.005

Cohn, T. H. (2016). *Global political economy: Theory and practice*. New York: Routledge. doi:10.4324/9781315659695

Collins, R. (1980). Weber's last theory of capitalism: A systematization. *American Sociological Review*, *1*(45), 925–942. doi:10.2307/2094910

De Melo, J., & Tsikata, Y. (2014). *Regional integration in Africa*. New York: Springer.

De Soto, H. (2000). The Mystery of Capital: Why Capitalism Triumphs In the West and Fails Everywhere Else. New York: Academic Press.

Dibua, J. I. (2017). *Modernization and the crisis of development in Africa: The Nigerian experience*. Oxford, UK: Routledge. doi:10.4324/9781351152921

Diep, L., Archer, D., & Gueye, C. (2016). *Decentralisation in West Africa: the implications for urban climate change governance*. London: IIED.

Dincecco, M., & Katz, G. (2016). State Capacity and Long-run Economic Performance. *Economic Journal (London)*, *126*(590), 189–218. doi:10.1111/ecoj.12161

Dipholo, K. B., & Molosi-France, K. (2017). The mismatch between the theory and practice of participatory rural development in Botswana: prospects for transformative social change. *International Conference on Public Administration and Development Alternatives (IPADA)*.

Dorosh, P. A., Stifel, D., & Minten, B. (2015). *Implications of isolation for rural poverty in Madagascar. Agricultural Economics*. Easton, PA: International Association of Agricultural Economics.

Efobi, U. (2015). Politicians' attributes and institutional quality in Africa: A focus on corruption. *Journal of Economic Issues*, *49*(3), 787–813. doi:10.1080/00213624.2015.1072393

Engel, U. (2017). Introduction: The African exception: conceptual notes on governance in Africa in the new millennium. In *The African Exception* (pp. 13–26). Oxon, UK: Routledge. doi:10.4324/9781351147927-1

Engerman, D. C. (Ed.). (2003). *Staging growth: Modernization, development, and the global cold war*. University of Massachusetts Press.

ENI in France. (2017). *Electricity, the energy behind the industrial revolution: The electricity fairy*. Available from: https://www.eni.com/en_FR/products-services/electricity/electricity_energy/electricity_energy.shtml

Fosu, A. K. (2017). *Governance and development in Africa: A concise*. Africa Development Bank Group.

Fox, S. (2014). The political economy of slums: Theory and evidence from Sub-Saharan Africa. *World Development*, *54*, 191–203. doi:10.1016/j.worlddev.2013.08.005

Friedman, M. (2009). *Capitalism and freedom*. New York: University of Chicago press.

Fuchs, C. (2018). *Digital Demagogue: Authoritarian Capitalism in the Age of Trump and Twitter*. Pluto Press. doi:10.2307/j.ctt21215dw

Gebreyes, M., Zinyengere, N., Theodory, T. F., & Speranza, C. I. (2017). Introduction: Grounding Climate Change, Vulnerability, and Adaptation in Africa. In Beyond Agricultural Impacts (pp. 1-11). Academic Press.

George, G., Corbishley, C., Khayesi, J. N., Haas, M. R., & Tihanyi, L. (2016). Bringing Africa in: Promising directions for management research. *Academy of Management Journal*, *59*(2), 377–393. doi:10.5465/amj.2016.4002

Goodfellow, T. (2015). Taming the "Rogue" sector: Studying state effectiveness in Africa through informal transport politics. *Comparative Politics*, *47*(2), 127–147. doi:10.5129/001041515814224462

Goody, J. (2018). *Technology, tradition and the state in Africa*. Routledge.

Hawken, P., Lovins, A. B., & Lovins, L. H. (2013). *Natural capitalism: The next industrial revolution*. Oxford, UK: Routledge. doi:10.4324/9781315065755

Hollinger, F. (2015). *Agricultural Growth in West Africa, Market and policy drivers*. Food and Agriculture Organisation. Africa Development Bank Group

Johnson, O., Muhoza, C., Osano, P., Senyagwa, J., & Kartha, S. (2017). *Catalysing Investment in Sustainable Energy Infrastructure in Africa*. Overcoming Financial and Non-Financial Constraints (No. 3). SEI Working Paper.

Kalu, K., Yacob-Haliso, O., & Falola, T. (2018). Introduction. In *Africa's Big Men* (pp. 15–32). Oxon, UK: Routledge. doi:10.4324/9780203712870-1

Kamukama, D., & Kakwenzire, J. (2017). The Development and Consolidation of Extremist Forces in Rwanda 1990–1994. In *The Path of a Genocide* (pp. 61–92). Oxford, UK: Routledge.

Kemp, R. (2016). Fourth industrial revolution. *The Lawyer*, *31*(21), 12.

Kieh, G. K. Jr. (2018). The "Hegemonic Presidency" in African Politics. *African Social Science Review*, *9*(1), 5.

Knutsen, C. H., Kotsadam, A., Olsen, E. H., & Wig, T. (2017). Mining and local corruption in Africa. *American Journal of Political Science*, *61*(2), 320–334. doi:10.1111/ajps.12268

Koslowski, P. (Ed.). (2013). *The Theory of Capitalism in the German Economic Tradition: Historism, Ordo-Liberalism, Critical Theory, Solidarism*. New York: Springer.

Makuwira, J. (2017). *Governing the ungovernable: donor agencies and the politics of development in Africa. Africa Journal of Public Affairs*.

Martinez, C., Cummings, M. E., & Vaaler, P. M. (2015). Economic informality and the venture funding impact of migrant remittances to developing countries. *Journal of Business Venturing*, *30*(4), 526–545. doi:10.1016/j.jbusvent.2014.10.004

Menyah, K., Nazlioglu, S., & Wolde-Rufael, Y. (2014). Financial development, trade openness and economic growth in African countries: New insights from a panel causality approach. *Economic Modelling*, *37*, 386–394. doi:10.1016/j.econmod.2013.11.044

Merem, E. C., Twumasi, Y., Wesley, J., Isokpehi, P., Shenge, M., Fageir, S., ... Ochai, S. (2017). Regional Assessment of Energy Trends in West Africa Using GIS. *International Journal of Energy Engineering*, *7*(1), 1–27. doi:10.5923/j.ijee.20170701.01

Migdal, J. S. (2018). The state in society. In *New Directions in Comparative Politics* (pp. 63–79). Oxford, UK: Routledge. doi:10.4324/9780429494932-4

Mills, G. (2018). Why Is Africa Poor? In *Culture and Civilization* (pp. 52–62). Oxon, UK: Routledge. doi:10.4324/9780203794128-4

Mkandawire, T. (2015). Neopatrimonialism and the political economy of economic performance in Africa: Critical reflections. *World Politics*, *67*(3), 563–612. doi:10.1017/S004388711500009X

Mudombi, S., & Muchie, M. (2014). An institutional perspective to challenges undermining innovation activities in Africa. *Innovation and Development*, *4*(2), 313–326. doi:10.1080/2157930X.2014.921272

Muggah, R. (2016). *Urban governance in fragile cities. GSDRC Professional Development Reading Pack no. 46*. Birmingham, UK: University of Birmingham.

Murithi, T. (2017). *The African Union: Pan-Africanism, peacebuilding and development*. Oxford, UK: Routledge. doi:10.4324/9781315241470

Nunkoo, R., Ribeiro, M. A., Sunnassee, V., & Gursoy, D. (2018). Public trust in mega event planning institutions: The role of knowledge, transparency and corruption. *Tourism Management*, *66*, 155–166. doi:10.1016/j.tourman.2017.11.010

Nye, J. S. Jr. (2015). The decline of America's soft power. In *Paradoxes of Power* (pp. 39–44). Oxford, UK: Routledge.

O'Connor, J. R. (1974). *The corporations and the State: essays in the theory of capitalism and imperialism*. Oxford, UK: Harper & Row.

Obeng-Odoom, F. (2015). Africa: On the rise, but to where? *The Forum for Social Economics*, *44*(3), 234–250. doi:10.1080/07360932.2014.955040

Ogunbodede, E. O., Kida, I. A., Madjapa, H. S., Amedari, M., Ehizele, A., Mutave, R., ... Okoye, L. (2015). Oral health inequalities between rural and urban populations of the African and Middle East region. *Advances in Dental Research*, *27*(1), 18–25. doi:10.1177/0022034515575538 PMID:26101336

Okeke, R. C. (2017). Elitism, Local Governance and Development in Nigeria. *Speciality Journal of Politics and Law*, *2*(3), 62–72.

Olvera, L. D., Guézéré, A., Plat, D., & Pochet, P. (2016). Earning a living, but at what price? Being a motorcycle taxi driver in a Sub-Saharan African city. *Journal of Transport Geography*, *55*, 165–174. doi:10.1016/j.jtrangeo.2015.11.010

Pieper, H., Mkandawire, T., & Van der Hoeven, R. (2016). *Africa's recovery in the 1990s: From stagnation and adjustment to human development*. New York: Springer.

Ravallion, M. (2017). *Poverty comparisons*. Oxon, UK: Routledge. doi:10.4324/9780203985328

Resnick, D. (2014). *Urban poverty and party populism in African democracies*. Cambridge University Press.

Rizzo, M., Kilama, B., & Wuyts, M. (2015). The invisibility of wage employment in statistics on the informal economy in Africa: Causes and Consequences. *The Journal of Development Studies*, *51*(2), 149–161. doi:10.1080/00220388.2014.968136

Rostow, W. W. (1960). *The stages of economic growth: A Non-Communistic Manifesto*. Cambridge, UK: Cambridge University.

Rukomoinikova, V., Zykova, N., & Tumbaeva, I. (2016). Practical aspects of realization of the development strategy in the tourism region. *Journal of Applied Engineering Science*, *14*(1), 68–74. doi:10.5937/jaes14-10123

Schwab, K. (2017). *The fourth industrial revolution*. Oxford, UK: Crown Business.

Sengers, F., & Raven, R. (2014). Metering motorbike mobility: Informal transport in transition? *Technology Analysis and Strategic Management*, *26*(4), 453–468. doi:10.1080/09537325.2013.870991

Sicurelli, D. (2016). *The European Union's Africa policies: norms, interests and impact*. Oxford, UK: Routledge. doi:10.4324/9781315239828

Singh, A., Lund, H. G., & Barr, J. (2018). *Challenges in Building Climate-Resilient Quality Energy Infrastructure in Africa*. Resilience. doi:10.1016/B978-0-12-811891-7.00014-1

Skeggs, B. (2018). *The values and value of digital capitalism*. Cambridge, MA: MIT Press.

Stearns, P. N. (2018). *The industrial revolution in world history*. London: Routledge. doi:10.4324/9780429494475

Sutherland, E. (2018). Bribery and corruption in telecommunications–the case of Nigeria. *Digital Policy, Regulation and Governance*.

Taylor, J., Sacher, M., Barberi, M., Gendronneau, C., Stepanek, M., Hofman, J., & Hafner, M. (2017). *Synergies Between the Objectives Set Out in the Annual Growth Survey and the Contribution of the EU Budget and National Budgets*. Academic Press.

Umubyeyi, A., Persson, M., Mogren, I., & Krantz, G. (2016). Gender inequality prevents abused women from seeking care despite protection given in gender-based violence legislation: A qualitative study from Rwanda. *PLoS One*, *11*(5), e0154540. doi:10.1371/journal.pone.0154540 PMID:27152680

Wilde, R. (2018). *Steam in the Industrial Revolution*. Available from: https://www.thoughtco.com/steam-in-the-industrial-revolution-1221643

KEY TERMS AND DEFINITIONS

Capitalism: Capitalism is an indirect system of governance for economic relationships.

Gap: An existing obstacle to continuous development.

Modernization: The process of development, moving from an extractive economy towards a more manufacturing kind of economy.

Strategy: An approach used in attaining development progress.

Stride: Development progress.

Chapter 8
Industrial and Urban Growth Policies in Sub-Saharan Africa and North Africa Compared

Innocent Chirisa
University of Zimbabwe, Zimbabwe

Tariro Nyevera
University of Zimbabwe, Zimbabwe

Wendy W. Mandaza-Tsoriyo
Great Zimbabwe University, Zimbabwe

ABSTRACT

The purpose of this chapter is to compare industrial and urban growth policies in Sub-Saharan Africa (SSA) and North Africa (NA) with the aim to draw lessons and inform policy and research in the subject. The chapter advances the argument that industrial and urban growth ought to be directly related. This follows the development trajectory and urbanization trend in the Global South which was birthed and sustained by the Industrial Revolution. The case study approach has been used to develop this chapter where Africa is first divided into two broad territories, SSA and NA. Subsequently, cases are selected from Lusophone, Anglophone, and Francophone countries. The analysis considers in detail Zimbabwe, South Africa, Guinea-Bissau, Algeria, and Egypt.

INTRODUCTION

This chapter compares industrial and urban growth policies in sub-Saharan Africa (SSA) and North Africa (NA) with the aim to draw lessons and inform policy and research in the subject. The chapter advances the argument that industrial and urban growth ought to be directly related. The work of Christine Kessides (2006, 2007) *'The Urban Transitions in Sub-Saharan Africa: Challenges and Opportunities'* wields immense suggestibility to the fact that urban areas are expanding at the inexpediency of industrial growth. This is unlike the way European cities emerged, or the African cities at the time of colonization

DOI: 10.4018/978-1-5225-7625-9.ch008

in the late 19th and early 20th centuries when the industry was thriving well and attracted huge numbers of populations previously residing in the rural areas. Subsequently, industrialization became the backbone of urban growth. Ironically, this is not so for Africa. There is little success to talk of when it comes to the industrial and urban growth nexus (Newman and Page, 2017). Colonial governments were mainly proactive and took it to task to industrialize the African cities. Industrial hubs were created basing on local conditions i.e. location, resources available and the population as well. In coastal cities, for example in West Africa, fisheries industries were established and cities thrived based on such. Where agriculture was viable agro-processing industries emerged and supported the local economic and population. Even areas which were difficult to develop owing to their undulating terrain, for example, Cape Town, industries such as eco-tourism were established and these somehow played an important role in supporting the local economy and subsequently urban development and growth.

Policy is best defined as what the government decides to do or not do (Dye, 2001). On the other hand, urban policy which is an appendage of public policy refers to a tool which government at local level use to create and manage functional urban spaces. In China, creative industrial policies have been implemented to spearhead sustained urban growth through the establishment of industries that support the needs of urban residents through opportunities in the creative industries. Employment opportunities are guaranteed, residents have disposal incomes which enable them to pay rates and taxes which then makes the urban system functional and efficient. Similarly, the Government of India has made strides in promoting industrial and economic development policies that are suitable for different settlements. The policy sustains industry-led growth which supports the creation of sustainable urban settlements. Industrial corridors in India have also been developed between major cities in some parts of the world. The same is true for America and Europe where industrial hubs have been established at the city and regional level in concomitant with urban development and growth.

To ensure balanced settlement systems, at least from a point of productivity, many colonial governments institutionalized laws that ensured supremacy and dominance of white industrialists in the cities and black populations in the rural areas. This is with particular reference to Southern and Central African counties including Zimbabwe and South Africa. These countries are mainly Anglophone. The Lusophone countries, for example, Angola, Mozambique and Guinea Bissau had somewhat different experiences. So were the Francophone countries, of which it remains unclear as to the industrial and urban growth policies that have subsisted. In the post-independence era, most of the countries experienced massive de-industrialization and industrial retrogression. Much of NA is in the desert hence population concentrations are already influenced by natural and biophysical qualities of the countries.

In Africa, the situation has not been so successful for one reason or the other. First, in Africa, the meaning of 'growth' needs to be examined closely. This then leaves a lot of questions unanswered. For example, to what extent have issues of availability of raw materials, markets, location, colonial influence, government policy, among other factors, influence industrial and urban growth policies. The issue of regions and regional disparities also influence the policies considering that regions are unique and have different natural resources endowments as well as climatic conditions (Matamanda and Chirisa, 2018). Such geo-physical conditions have a strong bearing on the industrial and urban growth policies as well. It thus becomes critical to analyze the industrial potential within the region and then factor in the urban growth trends so that sustainable and progressive policies are developed.

CONCEPTUAL FRAMEWORK

Industrialization is essential for economic and urban growth as evident from cities such as Birmingham, Berlin, Amsterdam, Hong Kong and Tokyo among many others. These cities, through industrialization, have managed to attract investment from all parts of the world. However, a lot of effort has been taken in ensuring that such high standards are realised and maintained in these cities as Stiglitz et al (2013: 18) note that "economic development is a process of continuous industrial and technological upgrading in which any country, regardless of its level of development, can succeed if it develops industries that are consistent with its comparative advantage, determined by its endowment structure". It follows that industrialization is thus a pathway towards this success though it needs to be done in a gradual and befitting manner taking into consideration the local resources.

THEORIES UNDERPINNING THE STUDY

Neo-Liberalism

Neo-liberalism is when the economy is dominated by private players instead of the government. The government rather assumes a regulative role and a free market economy prevails and is considered as being the best approach towards a nation's development (Harrison, 2005). Neo-liberalism also refers to the "lamentable spread of global capitalism and consumerism, as well as the equally deplorable demolition of the proactive welfare state" (Thorsen and Lie, 2006:56). The widespread use of the neoliberal policy escalated in the 1980s and 1990s mainly as an ideology of market-based policies that are export-oriented, subject to fiscal austerity and characterized by privatization or commercialization of public sectors (Flew, 2014). The Structural Adjustment Programs (SAPs) are typical examples of neoliberal policies that were adopted in most parts of Africa during the 1990s through the influence of the World Bank and International Monetary Fund (IMF) (Caffentzis, 2002). Ironically, the negative impacts of the SAPs in SSA resulted in the concept of neo-liberalism becoming increasingly blunt and less desirable in development policies (Harrison, 2005).

Growth Pole Policy

Introduced by Franco Perroux in 1949, the growth pole policy has been incorporated in many national development plans and approaches to development (Chen Lo and Salih, 1978). Parr (1999:1247) pinpoints that the growth-pole policy seeks to rectify regional disparities through "the activation of a system of planned poles, conforming to a particular spatial configuration in terms of size, hierarchical level, frequency and location". These planned poles rest on two major conceptual pillars; agglomeration of economies and spread effects to peripheral areas (Parr, 1999). At the center of the region, Perroux envisaged a propulsive industry or sector that acts as the engine for regional development, resulting in forward and backward linkages, diversification and agglomeration. The benefits enjoyed at the center will trickle down to the peripheral centers leading to spread effects (Chen Lo and Salih, 1978).

LITERATURE REVIEW

This section presents a literature review of the broad issues raised in the paper and this includes policy for human settlement and industrial growth,

Policy Framework for Human Settlement and Industrial Growth

Africa Agenda 2063

Africa Agenda 2063 (AA) was adopted in 2013 by African heads as a blueprint to guide Africa's growth trajectory from 2013 to 2063 (African Union Commission, 2015). The agenda is an action blueprint put in place to realise African Union's vision of building an integrated, prosperous and peaceful Africa (African Union Commission, 2015). Rooted in Pan-Africanism and the vision of Africa's Renaissance, AA was adopted as a roadmap for Africa to realize full potential in peace and development. In addition, Africa is to be a flourishing and prosperous society that maintains its culture (African Union Commission, 2015). To achieve this, goals and targets have been set to among other things eradicate poverty; improve access to decent and affordable housing; industrialize economies; modernization of African agriculture; establishment of continental free trade; and tie Africa through state of the art infrastructure (African Union Commission, 2015).

New Urban Agenda

The New Urban Agenda (NUA) was adopted in October 2016 to ensure that urbanization is utilized as a tool for achieving economically, socially and environmentally sustainable development. Among the major aims of the NUA are efforts to eradicate poverty, hunger and inequalities; promote inclusive economic development; foster resilience; and preserve the environment (UN-HABITAT, 2016). The success of the NUA lies in innovative approaches which governments may initiate through readdressing the planning, design, financing, development and management of human settlements. It is in this regard that considering the rapid rates of urbanization being experienced in across the world (see Figure 1), there is a need to create and manage human settlements where citizens have opportunities to prosper. Hence, the NUA emerges as a template which may help guide governments towards achieving sustainable urban development and growth.

Sustainable Development Goals (SDGs)

The Rio de Janeiro summit of 2012 resulted in the formulation of the Sustainable Development Goals (SDGs) that were ratified by the United Nations General Assembly (UNGA) later in 2015. The SDGs are centered on three broad goals - socio-economic inclusion, poverty reduction and environmental protection. The SDGs among other things guide industrialization and urban growth. This is evident through goal 9 which aims at building resilient infrastructure and promoting sustainable industrialization. Persson, Weitz and Nilsson (2016) criticize the SDGs for being inconsistent, unpredictable, lacking concrete indicators therefore difficult to monitor and also difficult to implement. Critical to note is that the SDGs are non-binding and member states will come up with their own national and regional plans which may somewhat not be in line with SDGs (Swain, 2018).

Figure 1. Global urban population trends and projections
Source: UN-HABITAT (2016)

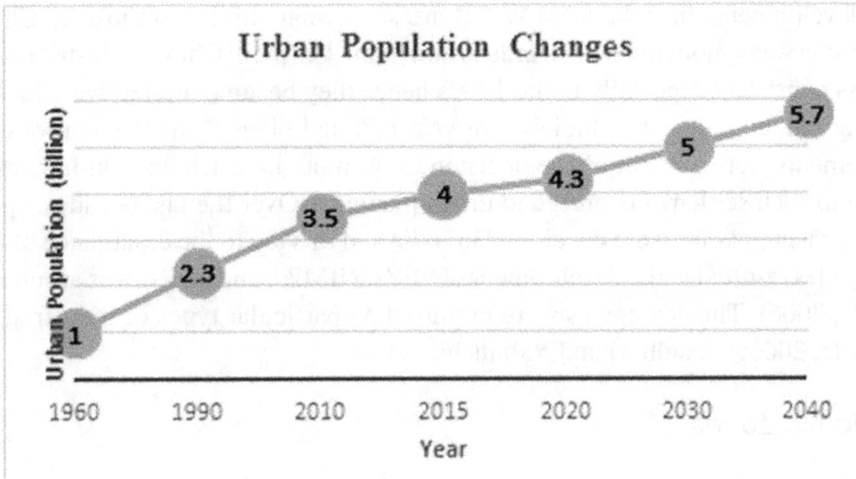

Urban Growth Policies

In countries like India, towns that that have particular industrial and economic activities are emerging (Sami and Anand, 2015). The process includes the establishment of industrial corridors with the primary emphasis being on building manufacturing and industrial centers. Such cities owe their existence and emergence to industrial policies rather than to planned urbanization (Anand et al. 2015). Manufacturing and service industries are highly concentrated in industrial clusters and cities (Newman and Page, 2017). In this way, such manufacturing activities thus act as growth poles which then help to support and sustain the local economies as well as those of areas in close proximity. Subsequently, economic growth spreads out, so does urban development as highlighted by Anand et al. (2015) that economic and industrial strategy in manufacturing cities has had notable successes in some countries in East Asia.

Urban Industrial Policies: China Cultural Diversity Industries

Anand et al. (2015) argue that it was after WWII when China started implementing a development approach that were state led and included industrialization and deliberate insulation from the world economy. The reforms paid off for China as evidenced by an increase in GDP growth rates during the 1980s and 1990s to become the highest in the world. Of importance to note is that growth was largely attributed to industrial development (ibid). Industrial reforms in China started with the opening up to foreign investors together with establishing township and village enterprises as hubs for industrial and economic growth. In the 21st century, China adopted the 'cultural industries' and since then cultural policies have been used as instrumental tools to regenerate cities (Anand et al. 2015). The focus of cultural industries is on the specific dynamics of symbolic production and circulation (Kniivila, 2006). Such industries seek to integrate the production and commercialization of creative contents which are intangible and cultural in nature. At the present moment, creative industries in China are a significant constituent of economic output and employment in many cities, more than is generally appreciated in urban plans (Kniivila, 2006).

The Case of India

The industrial developments in India after WWII are somewhat similar to those of China. Economic development in India was synonymous with industrialization. Unlike in China, industrialization strategies in India were less consistent especially in the 1990s hence they became ineffective with time. Anand et al. (2015) highlight how a review of India's five-year national plans from 1990 onwards indicate that new urban settlements were a result of the decision to promote industrialization in backward regions. Industrialization in such settlements preceded urban planning. Over the last decades, specific kinds of industrial development policies were developed in India and this led to the emergence of different urban forms. These policies resulted in the development of SEZs, NIMZs, and new towns around existent urban regions (Kniivila, 2006). The new towns were premised on particular types of industrial and economic activities (Kniivila, 2006; Chaudhuri and Yabuuchi, 2008).

Special Economic Zones

It is highlighted that SEZs are a useful instrument for a broader industrialization strategy targeted at attracting FDI and promoting exports (Newman and Page, 2017). Zeng (2012) however argue that this can only be achieved when SEZs are implemented properly in the right context. Where there are strong links between the zone and the local economy, Chaudhuri and Yabuuchi (2008) assert that SEZs can be effective strategies that can be utilised to promote industrialization and structural transformation. Particularly, Asian and Latin American countries have recorded notable successes of SEZs. In China, for instance, SEZs have recorded overwhelming success attracting the attention of the policymakers in countries like Mexico, Mauritius and India (Chaudhuri and Yabuuchi, 2008). African countries are considered as latecomers to the promotion of SEZs with progress towards promoting SEZs much recorded in the late 1990s or early 2000s (Newman and Page, 2017; Zeng, 2015). The record of SEZs in Africa lives a lot to be desired except for countries such as Mauritius, Kenya, Madagascar, and possibly Ghana (Zeng, 2015). Most of the zones in countries such as Malawi, Mali, Nigeria, Senegal, and Tanzania the zones are turning into 'white elephants' (ibid).

Players in Urban and Industrial Growth

The government, central and local, plays a critical role through setting the table for all other players and actors to participate. This is so because it is the government which shapes public policy when they decide what to do or not to do (Dye, 2001). The government may initiate policies such as decentralization which in one way or the other may propel or stifle urban development and growth (Mattingly, 1995). These policies may be aimed at reshaping settlement patterns and systems (Metropolis Commission, 2011). The government may direct investment into declining industrial cities through tax subsidies, employment incentives, improvements on infrastructure, selective public sector procurement policies and creation of SEZs, for example, enterprise zones, urban development corporations and simplified planning zones (Metropolis Commission, 2011). Local government usually comes up with their policies at the local level to operationalize central government policies. The response of local governments is typically one of accommodating new developments with services and sometimes land so as to operationalize national and regional policies.

Incentives for Urban Growth and Industrial Development

In developed countries like United States of America, incentives in the form of financial benefits have been used to encourage local industries (Parilla and Liu, 2008). Such practices have their origin in the period of the Great Depression which plagued America in the 1930s (Alix-Garcia, Schneider and Zhao, 2016). For example, during this period a small town in Mississippi called Durant developed a new type of industrial revenue bond to expand industrial activities in the city (Parilla and Liu, 2008). The strategy of incentives spread across the globe in the 1970s and 1980s when demand for firms went global. Government incentives were offered to firms and organizations so as to enhance growth in some areas and parts of urban centers. Thus it is apparent that cities may use incentives for industrial and urban growth. Where there is urban decay in certain parts of the city, incentives may be useful tools for attracting industrial and manufacturing firms that can bring back life to such areas (Porter, 1985). Firms may get tax benefits to spur economic activities in the blight and deteriorating areas. In China, incentives have worked quite well in transforming small fishing villages into vibrant towns such as Shenzhen, Zhuhai, Shantou and Xiamen (Alix-Garcia, Schneider and Zhao, 2016).

Colonial Legacy and Implications on Urban and Industrial Growth Policies

Urban development and growth crises in Africa can be viewed as a manifestation of Africa's colonial path (Feremenga, 2005). This is explained by Ekali (2005) who argues that the establishment of colonial administrative, political, economic, and social policies and structures hastened the pace of urbanization in Africa. Colonial governments were mainly proactive and took it to task to industrialize the African cities. In coastal cities, for example in West Africa, fisheries industries were established and cities thrived based on such. Where agriculture was viable agro-processing industries emerged and supported the local economic and population. However, scholars like Lushaba (2010) argue that in the process of industrialisation in Africa, industrial policies and structures altered the lifestyles of Africans, especially when the notion of modernity was put at the fore (Lushaba, 2010). The legacy that was left in Cameron was that of non-African ownership of urban economic social and economic systems that fostered urban underdevelopment (Salm and Falola, 2005). French colonial urban schemes, designs, and legislation have detrimental implications for urban growth and management for instance in transportation, housing, land tenure and the growth and development of urban centers vis-à-vis the rural areas (Herbst, 2000). In Zimbabwe, the presence of white settlers during the colonial era left legacies of urban management (Munzwa and Jonga, 2010). Prior to independence, white settlers in Zimbabwe used the military to subjugate the indigenous population and take control of the best land. This has manifested into the independent government where programs such as fast-track land reform program and Operation Murambatsvina were practiced with the use of the militia.

Drawing the strings together, colonial governments made significant strides balancing between urban growth and industrial development. Efforts were made to use comparative advantage in industrializing urban areas. It was industrial development that attracted urban growth. This is evidenced by noting that after independence in Africa, rates of urbanization increased as people were eager to enjoy the benefits of industrialized urban centers. During and soon after the colonial era in Africa, most cities were centers of attraction because of, among others employment opportunities that were created through the establishment of various industries that include fishery industries, agro-processing industries, eco-tourism industries, just to mention but a few. These industries somehow played an important role in supporting the local economy and subsequently urban development and growth.

METHODOLOGY

The chapter adopted a case study approach in a bid to explore and draw lesions of industrial and urban growth in Africa. The study used a multi-staged sampling technique to select countries and cases. The case study approach has been used to develop this chapter where Africa is first divided into two broad territories based, SSA and NA. In SSA, three countries were selected for exploration and these countries are Guinea-Bissau, South Africa and Zimbabwe. In NA, Egypt and America were explored. The study was mainly centered on extensive review and documentary analysis. For data analysis, the chapter made use of thematic and textual analysis.

RESULTS AND ANALYSIS

This section presents the results and analysis of the study and commences with the NA case studies which are then followed by the SSA context.

NORTH AFRICA

NA is basically an arid region which is characterized by longstanding and recurrent droughts (Institute of Development Studies, 2017). The region through countries such as Libya is endowed with oil reserves which significantly support the economy of the region thus closing the gaps emanating from drought effects. In NA, urban population growth is mostly attributed to natural population increase although rural-urban migration also contributes to the urban population through the youth who continue to migrate to urban areas in anticipation of greener pastures (UN-HABITAT, 2008). NA countries' economies are largely dependent on the utilization of natural endowments such as agriculture, phosphates, mineral resources, fisheries and hydrocarbons (UN-HABITAT, 2008). It is imperative to note that the agri-business sector in NA is unevenly distributed. In Algeria, the agribusiness has a sizable share of the economy. In Egypt, it is SMEs in the processing sector which predominates (Economic Commission for Africa, 2015). Urban centers in NA are the real engines of economic growth. In Egypt, Alexandria, the Mediterranean port accounts for a significant share of industrial activities. The port is home to 40% of manufacturing and 50% of the oil refining capacity in a large industrial zone west of the port area (UN-HABITAT, 2008). Another point which may help to explain the dominance of the industries in the big cities in NA is the availability of a transport infrastructure which facilitates the movement of goods and services (Anyanwu and Yameogo, 2015). For example, the existence of the large industrial zones with light industries, offices, and services which have been established and grown around Tripoli International Airport in Lydia and Tunis-Carthage International Airport in Tunisia. This is translated into improved FDI where North Africa has been dominated since 1970 right through to 2013 (Figure 2).

Figure 2. FDI Inflows to Africa's sub-regions, 2004-2013 (US$ million)
Source: Anyanwu and Yameogo (2015: 6)

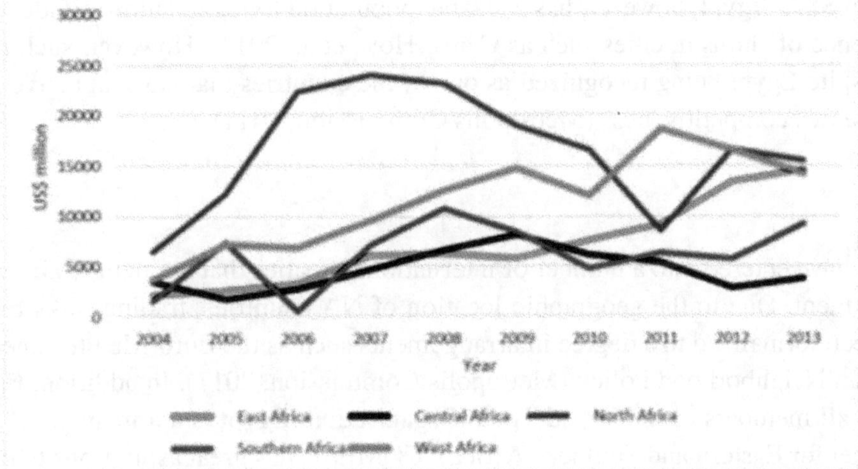

The major drivers of urban growth in Egypt are urban agglomerations, linked by development corridors. Urban agglomerations in Egypt have resulted in concentration of new housing and employment activities (UN-HABITAT, 2008). Many of Egypt's smaller urban areas are located in the Nile River Delta and this implies that any urban expansion in those urban areas will result in a significant loss in the prime agricultural land. Evidence shows that the urban area of Cairo increased from 233,78 to 557,87 square kilometers between 1973 and 1996 of which 136, 75 square kilometers of the increase were from agricultural lands (Hereher, 2012).

Looking at economic aspects, the Egyptian economy is relatively diversified between agriculture, industry and services (Institute of Development Studies, 2017). Egypt's economy witnessed a steady recovery from a low 1.8 percent in 2011 to 2.2 percent in 2014 (Economic Commission for Africa, 2016). In Algeria, The Federal Research Division (2008) pinpoints industry accounted for 61 percent of gross domestic product (GDP) in 2007 and much of the industry is dominated by the hydrocarbon industry. Petroleum products (oil and gas) account for 46.6 percent of government revenues as of 2016 (Economic Commission for Africa, 2016). Algeria, however, has faced limitations in diversifying industries from hydrocarbons. In addressing this, a novel industrial policy has just been adopted, designed to promote more competitive strategic sectors, based on the country's comparative advantages. Between 2007 and 2015, Algeria has experienced sustained economic growth rate averaging at 3.1 percent (Federal Research Division, 2008).

Policy Framework (at National and Local Level)

Settlement Development

In all NA countries, urban policy is a function that is mandated to respective ministries who are responsible for the urban development and management initiatives. Much of urban policies in NA had focused on addressing rapid urban growth for instance in Egypt in the 1950s. In Cairo for example, urban renewal, densification and in some cases de-densification has been practiced as a way of managing urban sprawl (Metropolis Commission, 2011). As such it may seem that settlement development in NA is more coordinated than SSA. Egypt, however, has a sizable population living in slums. Evidence is shown by the high prevalence of slums in cities such as Cairo (Hove et al. 2013). However, such proliferation of slums exists despite Egypt being recognized as one of the countries that have an active national urban policy that addresses competitiveness (Metropolis Commission, 2011).

Trade

Counties in NA have entered into a number of international treaties that are mainly aimed at increasing trade and investment. Due to the geographic location of NA countries, trading links between Europe and NA have been formalized to a degree in arrangements such as the Euro-Mediterranean Partnership and the European Neighborhood Policy (Metropolis Commission, 2011). In addition, Egypt, Morocco and Tunisia are all members of the World Trade Organisation. Egypt is a a member of the COMESA (Common Market for Eastern and Southern Africa). COMESA has great aspirations to establish a Free Trade Area (FTA) and customs union in the medium term (Anyanwu and Yameogo, 2015).

Industrial Growth

The NA region has made significant strides in industrial growth within the rest of the Africa region. The industrial policies such as the protection against competing imports and financial subsidies in NA countries have helped the manufacturing countries to develop. For instance, approximately 16.8 percent of Egypt's industrial activities manufacturing industry are accounted for in Alexandria Metropolitan Area (AMA) (Currie-Alder et al. 2014). The last couple of decades, AMA has experienced a significant growth in industrial development. Behind this significant growth as noted by tiglitz et al. (2013) is the existence of inter-industry linkages and also supporting infrastructure that was developed in the prime industrial center (Stiglitz et al. 2013). Industrial policies in NA cover issues that include, among other things protection against competing imports, financial subsidies, credits, and discrimination in Government procurement in favor of public sector industries (Currie-Alderet al. et al. 2014).

Investment

The implications of the absence of dynamic and robust private sectors in NA's economies have been felt especially in the area of investment. North Africa has the lowest private investment ratios among developing regions (Currie-Alder et al. 2014). However, some public sector activities can be noticed in the region. In Algeria, for example, from 2001 to 2004 an estimated US$7 billion of oil revenue was allocated to 16,000 projects in different economic sectors (UN-HABITAT, 2008). Of the 16,000 projects, 2,500 were focused on housing and urban development, strengthening of industry, the development of telecommunications, the improvement of education and the provision of youth facilities (Anyanwu and Yameogo, 2015).

Infrastructure Development

Over the past years, NA has made improvements in infrastructure quality. Between 2001 and 2005, NA had a higher than average share of paved roads (66%) (Agénor et al. 2005). Algeria and Egypt were ranked in the first top ten countries between 2007 and 2010 (African Development Bank, 2013). Countries in the NA region have occupied the top positions of the AIDI from the year 2000 to 2010.

Private Sector Industrial Development and Competitiveness Contributions

Soon after WWII, NA countries pursued state-led development initiatives with the belief that the state would help to ameliorate the effects of market and coordination failures. In Egypt, Morocco and Tunisia industrialization was pursued through central planning and large public-sector projects. Currie-Alderet et al. (2014) highlight that NA countries adopted a socialist and welfare state with efforts to create employment and promote human well-being. Though the initiative had positive outcomes with respect to economic diversification, the initiative faced challenges that include financial limitations, failing to embrace marginalized groups, and led to higher levels of unemployment (Stiglitz et al. 2013). In the 1980s and 1990s, the governments had to shift to incorporate the private sector and this period coincided with the adoption of SAPs across Africa and the rise of neoliberalism (Currie-Alder et al. 2014). However, private sector development in NA continues to face enormous challenges that emanate from, among other things limited progress in building market-oriented institutions and in integrating the region into the world economy. Stiglitz et al. (2013) note that successful transformations in industrial development should be based on policies that encompass both the state and the private sector.

Role of Sub-National Institutions (Municipalities and Local Authorities) in Enhancing 'Ease of Doing Business'

The government of Egypt has in recent years initiated on a couple of structural reforms at both national and sub-national level aimed at promoting a more stable business environment and fueling economic growth (Economic Commission for Africa, 2016). The policies focus on economic recovery and growth through mega-infrastructure development, tourism, economic policy improvements and increasing private sector investments (Economic Commission for Africa, 2016). Moreover, new laws and policies that aim at to promote and improve foreign investments through offering incentives, reducing bureaucracy, and simplifying and enhancing processes have been enacted to improve investment in Egypt (Anyanwu and Yameogo, 2015). Recently, Egypt ratified a landmark investment law that will modernize and reduce barriers to FDI in the country and this will likely increase Egypt's competitive edge across the region (World Bank, 2016). In Algeria, World Bank (2016) notes that many tax regimes and tax holidays and incentives are available to attract foreign direct investors. For example, there is a temporary exemption from for investing companies creating 100 jobs or more (World Bank, 2016). New investment law with incentives to local and foreign businessmen in the non-oil sector in Algeria's government has been drafted (Anyanwu and Yameogo, 2015).

Place Marketing Strategies and Efficiency and Effectiveness

Place marketing strategies in NA have to some extent been affected by political instabilities. Anyanwu and Yameogo, (2015) pinpoint that instabilities in the political environment and sluggish growth in NA countries have significantly resulted in a slow development of market economies in the region. More so, the Great Recession of 2007/08 and the Arab Spring revolts of 2011 had international implications on place marketing of NA countries (Currie-Alder et al. 2014). Such events have delayed the implementation of necessary reforms that are direly needed for an improvement in economic performance of North Africa (Currie-Alder et al. 2014).

Role of Cultural Diversity

Cultural offer of cities is increasingly utilized as a tool of city branding, to attract not only tourists but also FDI in NA. Egypt and Algeria share 12 World Cultural Heritage Sites. Such heritage sites are critical for local economic development (Licciardi and Bigio, 2010). They are key in the tourism industry and overall contributing to GDP. Of importance to note is that tourism is the primary source of foreign currency revenue and primary source of foreign exchange in less developed countries. NA, therefore, has a comparative advantage in that it is endowed with an exceptional cultural heritage. The distinctiveness in culture and heritage in NA makes the region ideal for tourism.

Colonialism and Its Impact on Urban Industrial Growth and Settlement Development

European models of legislation that deal with urban land use, regulatory measures and spatial design structures are commonplace throughout the region (Currie-Alderet al. et al. 2014). European colonial countries were largely responsible for championing Western urban planning concepts and models in NA. In countries such as Algeria, Tunisia, and Morocco, colonial town planners developed layouts that reflected French urban planning style as well as urban features (Currie-Alderet al. et al. 2014). There is a difference in colonization approaches between Britain, France and Italy and other European powers. Evidence from literature indicates that British institutional and cultural legacies are more conducive to urban and industrial growth than those of France, Italy and other colonizers (Lee and Schultz, 2011). Anglophone countries benefited much from the common law system that permitted greater rights and confidence to investors and property owners whereas this is not the case for Italy and France colonies that used civil law systems (Iyer, 2007). These approaches affected institutional settings of post-colonial economic development in Africa. In Anglophone countries, scholars like Baruah et al. (2017) emphasize that cities experience urban sprawl compared to Francophone ones. This is because Anglophone countries operated under an indirect rule and therefore cities developed without overall planning and coordination (Baruah et al., 2017).

SUB-SAHARAN AFRICA

The SSA region experiences varied urbanization, demographic and economic trends. Guinea-Bissau is home to a population of less than 2 million whereas Zimbabwe has a population that is estimated around 14 million and South Africa is home to 55 million people as of 2016 (Economic Commission for Africa,

2016; ZimStat, 2013). Though SSA is the least urbanized region globally, the region is urbanizing at a rapid rate and is currently second only to Asia. It is estimated that from the 1970s, the urban growth rate in SSA was the highest in the world, averaging five percent per annum (Hove et al. 2013). However, the high urbanization rates in SSA are not accompanied by industrialization (Chirisa et al. 2018). Rather, urbanization in the region has been characterized as parasitic urbanization, urbanization of poverty, or even ruralization of urban areas (Mugumbate and Nyoni, 2013; Chirisa et al., 2014).

Numerous examples of primate cities exist in SSA. Maputo, for example, is home to 83 percent of the national urban population, while Dakar, Lome, and Harare have more than 50 percent of the nations' population (Hove et al. 2013). Like the variations in urbanization trends; the economic trends in SSA have similar connotations. South Africa is among the richest countries in Africa and has some state of the art infrastructure for instance in Cape Town, Johannesburg and Durban. Yet, the country has one of the greatest Gini-coefficients in the world (Hove et al. 2013). On the contrary, Guinea-Bissau is among the poorest countries in Africa (UN-HABITAT, 2008).

Having noted the increase in urbanization in general and in-situ urbanization in peri-urban areas in SSA, the economic development in the region has not kept pace with urban population dynamics. Such a stagnant economic growth can be traced back to the policies when SSA countries became independent (Economic Commission for Africa, 2016). In the early years of independence, SSA Countries centralized administration and planning in the hope that the government itself would best address colonial inequalities legacies and deliver rudimentary services to a majority of the poor (UN-HABITAT, 2008). However, governments ignored efforts on economic development and growth. Nevertheless, since the 1990s the SSA countries have made strides in trying to improve their urban economies through fundamental transformations that are aimed at achieving reintegration and deeper entrenchment in the global economy (Hove et al. 2013). With the adoption of neo-liberal economic reforms, urban areas have pursued global-focused pro-growth initiatives to attract investment and become globally competitive. The concept of Local Economic Development (LED) has become interwoven with proactive city marketing and restructuring of local governments, for example, in South Africa (Hove et al. 2013). Of critical to note for SSA is that the informal sector remains a major source of livelihoods for the majority of people, for example, in Zimbabwe and Guinea Bissau (Economic Commission for Africa, 2016).

It is estimated that 4.9% in annual sales are lost due to electrical outages in SSA, with the corresponding cost of fuel for backup power generation estimated to be at least USD 5 billion in 2012 (Economic Commission for Africa, 2016). Power outages and shortages greatly compromise the growth of industries in most countries in SSA. For example, in Zimbabwe power cuts have reached critical stages such that some areas could receive power supply for less than 8 hours per day and usually late at night. As such industrial growth has been somewhat unsuccessful over the past years (Bhebhe, 2015). Moreover, the transport infrastructure in Zimbabwe (e.g. road and rail) has become dilapidated; movement of goods and services is increasingly becoming difficult. On the other hand, South Africa dominates the SSA region's economy. The existence of international airports such as OR International airport helps to connect South Africa to the world. This explains why South Africa is among three regional hub markets and attractive for investment destinations in SSA (Hove et al. 2013). Moreover, at the local level, the distance between the residential south of Johannesburg and its nodal industrial north is linked by an efficient public transport system so as to overcome this spatial divide. In this regard, the development of the Rea Vaya Rapid Bus Transport System in late 2013 helped in achieving this goal (Greve, 2013). Hence, the distribution of manufacturing activity is extremely skewed with just one country, South Africa, accounting for 27.3% of total MVA in SSA and registering sizable growth over the past two decades (Economic Commission for Africa, 2015).

Urban management has been compromised in urban areas where opposition parties have a majority of the elected urban councilors (Muchadenyika and Williams, 2017). However, this tends to have negative implications on urban policy consistency and thus overall stagnating urban growth and development. The reparations of political polarization in urban management include revenue allocations unbalancing program and capital expenditures, urban areas' infrastructure starvation and continued ignorance of the need for hierarchical national urban development (Mbiba, 2017). In Guinea Bissau, the economy is largely supported by the export of cashew nuts but a series of military coups coupled with the traffic of narcotics have negatively impacted on the nation's economy in recent years (Economic Commission for Africa, 2016). To make matters worse, social and political instability in the country has always stood in the way of sustained socio-economic growth since the country attained her independence from Portugal in 1974.

Policy Frameworks (National and Local Level)

Settlement Development

Settlement development in SSA is currently stifled by the proliferation of slums which has come to change the dimensions of urban planning and growth (Todes, 2011; Mbiba, 2017; see Figure 3). In Zimbabwe, for instance, municipalities have shifted from the demolition approach to encompass re-development approaches such as slum upgrading (Chirisa and Matamanda, 2016). Such an approach is informed by the statutory plans which guide settlement development in the country. However, criticisms have been pinned on statutory plans in most SSA countries on the basis that they are rigid, outdated and cumbersome (Watson, 2009; Cirolia and Berrisford, 2017). The situation is somewhat different in South Africa where integrated development plans are used by local governments to guide settlement development.

Industrial Growth

Most countries in SSA have been experiencing premature de-industrialization and this is evident from declining GDP from 15 to 10 percent between 1990 and 2008 (Xirinachs et al. 2014). Deindustrialization is mainly attributed to SAPs which were prominent during the 1990s across most SSA countries. The result has been the widespread of the informal sector, for example, cities such as Harare and Bulawayo in Zimbabwe which were once thriving industrial hubs (Dube and Chirisa, 2012). In South Africa, since the 1990s the state has been proactive in implementing policies to develop industry with the aim to improve industrial performance (Green, 2009). Such proactive initiatives paid off well for South Africa, especially in the automotive and component industry. Foreign firms such as Ford and Toyota reinvested in South Africa although retail and services sectors dominate the informal urban economies in cities such as Johannesburg, Cape Town and Durban. In Guinea-Bissau, the country is one of the largest producers of cashew nuts in the world but sadly the industry in the nation is extremely underdeveloped. Overall, the economy in most SSA countries is supported by Small and medium enterprises (SMEs).

Figure 3. Proportion of urban population living in slums in Sub-Saharan Africa
Source: Hove et al. (2013)

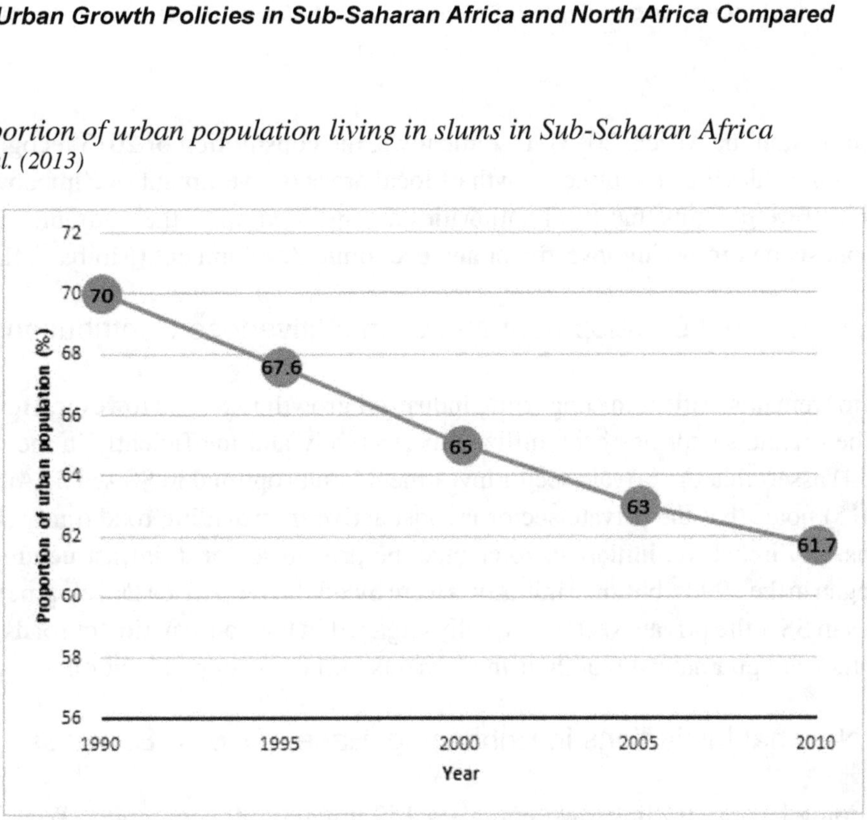

Trade

Trade in SSA is facilitated through agreements signed by AU and SADC. The policy of open trade and globalization has resulted in the improvement of trade and industry not just with fellow African countries but even with the West and East. Zimbabwe's Look East Policy opened the doors to the Chinese who have been trading with the country as well as supporting local industry. Regional integration has also resulted in the trade quotas and embargoes which facilitate the acquisition of raw materials at cheaper process in instances when they are not available locally. Currently, Africa's integration landscape contains an array of regional economic communities that are aimed at, among other things promoting trade and regional integration (Economic Commission for Africa, 2015). This is also espoused in the AA which emphasizes regional integration among African nations.

Investment

Though agriculture in SSA seems to be the major sector for economic development and growth, investment in agricultural development in SSA stands below 10% and suffers from further decline (Economic Commission for Africa, 2015; Zhou and Zvoshe, 2012). Investment in SSA is best understood in the context of political economy. This is so because investment, especially, FDI is mainly determined based on political grounds. Sanctions imposed on Zimbabwe since 2000 have been mainly attributed to the low levels of FDI in the country by the west although China has been investing in agricultural and mining sector in the country. On the other hand, local policies such as the indigenous policy have been responsible for the decline in FDI in Zimbabwe as investors felt robbed by the policy (Zhou and Zvoshe, 2012). To stimulate investment at the local level, South Africa is making use of LED in a structured manner

(Economic Commission for Africa, 2015). In Zimbabwe, the constitution of 2013 recognizes LED as a useful instrument in achieving economic growth of local areas (Government of Zimbabwe, 2013). The challenge in Zimbabwe remains that local authorities are still tied up to their administrative roles and putting less emphasis on promoting investment and economic development (Mbiba, 2017).

Private Sector Industrial Development and Competitiveness Contributions

The private sector remains critical in supporting industrial growth in SSA. However, Hove et al. (2013) observed that the private sector has been utilized ineffectively and inefficiently in most SSA. Currie-Alderet al. (2014) assert that the private sector investment is sub-optimal in SSA. The African Development Bank (2015) notes that the private sector is most active in providing road transport services and communications. In Zimbabwe, initiatives to engage the private sector in infrastructure and industrial development began in the 1990s, but such initiatives were inconclusive(Africa Development Bank, 2015). In all three cases in SSA the private sector is usually engaged in the construction of roads and real estate projects where they are guaranteed that their investments will be recouped later on.

Role of Sub-National Institutions in Enhancing 'Ease of Doing Business'

In the ease of doing business, Zimbabwe is ranked 159 among 190 economies (World Bank, 2016). This implies that establishing a business in Zimbabwe is not an easy task as the process is riddled with many procedures and protocols. In contrast, South Africa is ranked 82 out of 190 and despite noting that the business environment is challenging, it is still one of the best in the developing world. South Africa has a well-established transport infrastructure, robust macro conditions and watertight financial and legal frameworks. (World Bank, 2016). South Africa, unlike Zimbabwe and Guinea-Bissau, has a different scenario in terms of the ease of doing business. The cost of opening a business is just 0.3% of income per capita in South Africa unlike over 60% costs in other countries (World Bank, 2016). In Guinea Bissau, the establishment of the Center for the Formalization of Enterprises (CFE) which was established in 2011 has made some noticeable strides in enhancing the ease of doing business. The CFE one-stop shop integrates under one roof all essential services and activities needed to create a business. Prior to CFE, Guinea Bissau was ranked near the bottom, 181 out of 183 countries (World Bank, 2016). After the CFE, basing on the latest World Bank annual ratings Guinea Bissau is ranked 176 among 190 economies in the ease of doing business (World Bank, 2016).

Place Marketing Strategies and Efficiency and Effectiveness

Very few success stories can be reiterated with respect to place marketing strategies in SSA. South Africa is among the few countries to internationally market their nations. In 2010, South Africa hosted the FIFA World Cup tournament and the event boosted the tourism industry for her as world-class infrastructure was developed in preparation for the tournament (Africa Development Bank, 2015). The coastal cities such as Durban and Cape Town are also remarkable tourist destinations which help to market South Africa as well as register her success in eco-tourism. The notion of 'culture' is perhaps nowhere more relevant than in the development of South Africa (Africa Development Bank, 2015). There is a plurality of cultures together with different languages spoken in South Africa and this implies that adopting a bespoke approach to different regions, is crucial (Green, 2009). The country's multifaceted culture and history present some impediments for growing businesses, although recent statistics indicate that a period of consolidation has created a modern market (ibid). However, such success stories cannot be reiterated for Zimbabwe and Guinea-Bissau. In Zimbabwe, political instabilities together with policies and programs such as FTLRP and the Indigenization Policy have had negative implications in place marketing (Hove et al. 2013). Of late, the new president of Zimbabwe is making strides to put the nation back on the international radar market through his famous mantra 'Zimbabwe is open for businesses'. Like in Zimbabwe, Guinea-Bissau's political instabilities have had serious consequences that have made the nation a scary destination for investors.

Colonialism and Its Impact on Urban Industrial Growth and Human Settlement Development

Colonization had significant implications on urban and industrial growth in SSA. The colonial settlers were much concerned about developing cities that were only benefiting the minority. In that case, infrastructure development was established mainly for the purpose of supporting manufacturing and industry with which the colonial groups had interest in. In Zimbabwe and South Africa alike, the transport infrastructure was established along mineral resources (Zhou and Zvoushe, 2012). Because of selective colonial approaches in colonial development approaches, Zimbabwe still suffers challenges in reducing regional disparities. Zhou and Zvoushe (2012) argue that the colonial reality remains a decisive factor in national policy decision making in SSA. In South Africa, the Apartheid laws imposed before 1994 were instrumental in spatial segregation for South Africa, though they were instrumental for development of a vibrant industrial hub. On the contrary, after independence in 1980, the government of Zimbabwe emphasized much on addressing inequalities between blacks and whites and putting less emphasis on economic growth. Cities like Bulawayo that were industrial hubs of the country de-industrialized in alarming rates (Mbira, 2015).

DISCUSSION AND SYNTHESIS

There seems to be a relationship between the size of the city and the capacity to attract FDI. It has been observed that large cities attract FDI more than smaller cities. Currie-Alderet al. et al. (2014) assert that every year from 2004 to 2015, the top ten destination cities for FDI in Africa attracted on average more than 30% of total investment projects to the continent. As the cities grow, they become feasible and viable for investment because of the increase in the concentrated market.

Urban growth and urbanization without industrialization result in amorphous urban growth. Where there is no industrial growth, the informal economy tent to dominate in urban areas for example in Zimbabwe. The dominance of informal activities tends to cripple urban growth since the sector is usually shunned and considered as an urban ill, hence its full potentials are never realized, particularly in SSA. Informal settlements also become prominent and this occurs with the urbanization that is not supported by industrial growth. Without industrialization, the urban areas continue to develop and growth in an uncoordinated and chaotic manner.

As in the cases of India and China, policies have played a critical role in stimulating industrial growth. Industrial policies seek to address the key aspects of industrial growth that include trade, regulation, innovation and technology, education and skill formation, infrastructure and sectoral competitiveness. At the national level, policies mainly are envisaged to attract FDI because it is the national policies which set the tone for all other actors in urban and industrial growth to chip in. At the local level, operational policies should be put in place so as to operationalize national goals and targets. Local authorities for instance in South Africa have made a great impact through operationalizing LED plans. Without a clear policy framework, it is difficult to achieve smooth and coherent urban and industrial growth. In India, industrialization preceded urban policy and planning. It is ideal for industrial growth to precede urban growth. Where there is industrialization first within an area, urban growth will automatically follow through. However, it is challenging if urban growth precedes industrialization in the sense that some areas will fail to industrialize at all hence the outgrowth of ghost towns.

Infrastructure and the involvement of the private sector is key for successful industrial and urban growth. The formal private sector is still lagging and remains underdeveloped in most African countries. Governments can make use of targeted interventions as well as general policies specifically designed to remove bottlenecks, streamline procedures and protect property rights (Hove et al. 2013). In Egypt, for example, the private sector is significantly participating in the national economy with more than 50% share and it has been invited recently to invest in major infrastructural projects through the B.O.T. and B.O.O.T models (Anyanwu and Yameogo, 2015). The private sector is important especially in the development of infrastructure which is instrumental in both industrial and urban growth.

Capitalizing on comparative advantage within African nations is key for industrial growth. However, African countries have failed to fully utilize their primary resources dominating in their economies. Most African countries have failed to create industrial cities such as Shanghai in China and other manufacturing cities in India. The manufacturing cities are products of economic and industrial policies rather than of planned urbanization. Africa countries are however struggling to epitomize the industrialization of countries such as China and India. For instance, Africa is struggling to capitalize on its unique characteristics such as culture, minerals and tourism resort centers.

CONCLUSION, POLICY OPTIONS, AND RECOMMENDATIONS

Africa is a fragmented continent. The continent is composed of several ethnic groups, particularly in SSA. Most parts of SSA are characterized by culture rooted on African traditional religions. For NA countries, Islamic and Arabic culture and language dialects dominate in that region. Because of NA's geographic location, NA has joined hands with European countries, for instance the Euro-Mediterranean Partnership and the European Neighborhood Policy, in way to promote trade between NA countries and European countries. In SSA, efforts to integrate the region are evidenced by blocs such as SADC, COMESA and EAC. Efforts such as the single tripartite arrangement between COMESA, EAC and SADC are commendable as way of integrating Africa but there is still need for more integration efforts in Africa to increase the global competitiveness of the region (Brenton and Isik, 2012). Cities in SSA have experienced urbanization that has not kept pace with industrialization. Attributing to this lack of industrialization in SSA, cities in Africa are constrained by a lack of supportive infrastructure and are crowded and disconnected thereby increasing the costs of doing business (Lall et al. 2017). The inefficient spatial form of SSA cities also plays a significant role in constraining industrialization. Urban centers are the engines of industrial and economic growth. Policies needs to be put in place to foster urban and industrial growth. Policies related to infrastructure, trade, regulation, innovation and technology, education and skill formation, and sectoral competitiveness are all critical to enhancing industrial growth. Africa still has a long way to go in achieving sustainable urban and industrial growth. Hence, the need to capitalize on the competitive and comparative advantage as a way of stimulating industrial growth. This can be achieved through the use of local resources to develop local areas into competitive destinies. Moreover, African countries need to move away from over-reliance on one resource and diversify their economies. Policies that attract rather than deter FDI and the private sector should be crafted to enhance industrial and urban growth. Incentives and subsidies, including tax privileges, could be created to stimulate the adoption of large-scale investments from private players. To harness the private sector, creating forums for public-private dialogue and consultation may be useful. NA has been attracting high FDI for the past decade as compared to sub-Saharan Africa. It is therefore imperative for SSA to emphasize much on policies that attract FDI. Again incentives and subsidies remain critical in attracting FDI. More so, there is a need for structured Public-Private Partnerships in Africa.

ACKNOWLEDGMENT

The authors are grateful for the contributions made by the editors, the anonymous reviewers as well as by Professor I Chirisa and Mr. Abraham R Matamanda of the Department of Urban and Regional Planning, University of the Free State, South Africa, Mr B Mavhima of the Department of Rural & Urban Planning, University of Zimbabwe who critiqued it and made invaluable insights towards shaping the argument.

REFERENCES

Addaney, M. (2018). The African Union's Agenda 2063: Education and Its Realization. In Education Law, Strategic Policy and Sustainable Development in Africa. African Union Commission.

Alix-Garcia, J., Schneider, A., & Zhao, N. (2016). Playing Favorites: Tax Incentives and Urban Growth in China, 1978–2010. *Land Economics*, *92*(1), 1–27. doi:10.3368/le.92.1.1

Anderson, J. E., & Wassmer, R. W. (2000). Local Economic Development Incentives in the United States. In J. E. Anderson & R. W. Wassmer (Eds.), *Bidding for Business: The Efficacy of Local Economic Development Incentives in a Metropolitan Area* (pp. 1–24). Kalamazoo, MI: W.E. Upjohn Institute for Employment Research. doi:10.17848/9780585313610

Anyanwu, F., & Yameogo, J. (2015). What Drives Foreign Direct Investments into West Africa? An Empirical Investigation. *African Development Review*, *27*(3), 199–215. doi:10.1111/1467-8268.12141

Baruah, N. G., Henderson, J. V., & Peng, C. (2017). *Colonial legacies: shaping African cities*. SERC/ Urban and Spatial Programme Discussion Paper.

Bhebhe, N. (2015). *Zimbabwe Industries bear Brunt of Electricity Shortages*. Available from: http://www.theafricareport.com/Southern-Africa/zimbabwe-industries-bear-brunt-of-electricity-shortages.html

Brenton, P., & Isik, G. (Eds.). (2012). *De-fragmenting Africa: deepening regional trade integration in goods and services*. World Bank Publications.

Caffentzis, G. (2002). Neo-liberalism in Africa, Apocalyptic Failures and Business as Usual Practices. *Turkish Journal of International Relations*, *1*(3), 89–104.

Chaudhuri, S., & Yabuuchi, S. (2008). Formation of Special Economic Zone: Liberalized FDI Policy and Agricultural Productivity. *International Review of Economics & Finance*, *19*(4), 779–788. doi:10.1016/j.iref.2010.02.004

Chirisa, I., Matamanda, A. R., & Mukarwi, L. (2018). Desired and Achieved Urbanisation in Africa: In Search of Appropriate Tooling for a Sustainable Transformation. In Urbanization and Its Impact on Socio-Economic Growth in Developing Regions (pp. 88-106). IGI Global.

Cirolia, L. R., & Berrisford, S. (2017). 'Negotiated planning': Diverse trajectories of implementation in Nairobi, Addis Ababa, and Harare. *Habitat International*, *59*, 71–79. doi:10.1016/j.habitatint.2016.11.005

Currie-Alder, B., Kanbur, R., Malone, D. M., & Medhora, R. (Eds.). (2014). International Development: Ideas, Experience, and Prospects. Oxford University Press.

Dube, D., & Chirisa, I. (2012). The Informal City: Assessing its Scope, Variants and Direction in Harare, Zimbabwe. *Global Advanced Research Journal of Geography and Regional Planning*, *1*(1), 16–25.

Dye, T. (2001). *Understanding Public Policy*. Englewood, NJ: Prentice Hall Inc.

Economic Commission for Africa. (2015). *Economic Report on Africa 2015*. Available http://www.uneca.org/publications/economic-report-africa-2015

Economic Commission for Africa. (2016). *Economic Report on Africa 2015*. Available http://www.uneca.org/publications/economic-report-africa-2016

Ekali, T. N. (2005). The Fluctuating Fortunes of Anglophone Cameroon Towns: The Case of Victoria, 1858–1982. In S. J. Salm & T. Falola (Eds.), *African Urban Spaces in Historical Perspectives*. New York: University of Rochester Press.

Federal Research Division. (2008). *Country Profile: Algeria*. Washington, DC: Library of Congress.

Feremenga, D. T. (2005). Urban Planning and Development in Zimbabwe: A Historical Perspective. In S. J. Salm & T. Falola (Eds.), *African Urban Spaces in Historical Perspectives*. New York: University of Rochester Press.

Flew, T. (2014). *Six Theories of Neo-liberalism*. Queensland: SAGE.

Green, P. (2009). *Industrialisation in South Africa: The Impact of Globalisation*. Norwich: University of East Anglia.

Greve, A. (2013). Learning from Tokyo urbanism: The urban sanctuaries. *Cities (London, England)*, *30*, 98–104. doi:10.1016/j.cities.2011.12.007

Harrison, G. (2005). 'Economic faith, Social project and a misreading of African society: The travails of neo-liberalism in Africa'. *Third World Quarterly*, *26*(8), 1303–1320. doi:10.1080/01436590500336922

Herbst, J. (2000). *States and Power in Africa: Comparative Lessons in Authority and Control*. Princeton, NJ: Princeton University Press.

Hereher, M. E. (2012). Analysis of urban growth at Cairo, Egypt using remote sensing and GIS. *Nature and Science*, *4*(6), 355–361. doi:10.4236/ns.2012.46049

Hove, M., Ngwerume, E. T., & Muchemwa, C. (2013). The Urban Crisis in Sub-Saharan Africa. A Threat to Human Security and Sustainable Development. *Stability*, *2*(1), 1–14. doi:10.5334ta.ap

Institute of Development Studies. (2017). *Climate change and stability in North Africa*. London: DFID.

Iyer, L. (2007). *Direct Versus Indirect Colonial Rule in India: Long-term Consequences*. Working Paper.

Kniivila, M. (2016). Industrial development and economic growth: Implications for poverty reduction and income inequality. *Sustainable Development Perspectives.*, *1*(3), 295–333.

Lall, S. V., Henderson, J. V., & Venables, A. J. (2017). *Africa's cities: Opening doors to the world*. The World Bank. doi:10.1596/978-1-4648-1044-2

Lee, A., & Schultz, K. A. (2011). *Comparing British and French colonial legacies: A discontinuity analysis of Cameroon*. Working paper.

Licciardi, A. G., & Bigio, G. (2010). *The Urban Rehabilitation of Medinas. The World Bank Experience in the Middle East and North Africa (English). Urban Development Series No. 9*. Washington, DC: The World Bank.

Lo, C. F., & Salih, K. (Eds.). (1978). Growth Pole Strategy and Regional Development Policy: Asian Experience and Alternative Approaches. Pergamon Press.

Mbiba, B. (2017). *On the Periphery: Missing Urbanisation in Zimbabwe*. London: Africa Research Institute.

Metropolis Commission. (2011). Managing Urban Growth. Commission Report 2. Metropolis Commission II, Melbourne, Australia.

Muchadenyika, D., & Williams, J. J. (2017). Politics and the practice of planning: The case of Zimbabwean cities. *Cities (London, England)*, *63*, 33–40. doi:10.1016/j.cities.2016.12.022

Newman, C., & Page, J. (2017). *Industrial clusters: The case for Special Economic Zones in Africa*. WIDER Working Paper 2017/15. United Nations University.

Njoh, A. J. (2004). The experience and legacy of French colonial urban planning in sub-Saharan Africa. *Planning Perspectives*, *19*(4), 435–454. doi:10.1080/0266543042000268813

Njoku, O. (2006). NGOs and Africa's Development and Economic Growth. In *International Conference on the State of Affairs of Africa (ICSAA)*. International Institute of Justice and Development. Available: http://www.iijd.org/PDF%20Ogechi_njoku__NGOs-and-Africa.pdf

Parilla, J., & Liu, S. (2008). *Examining the Local Value of Economic Development Incentives: Evidence from four U.S. cities*. Washington, DC: Brookings Institution.

Parr, J. B. (1999). Growth-pole Strategies in Regional Economic Planning: A Retrospective View. Part 2. Implementation and Outcome. *Urban Studies (Edinburgh, Scotland)*, *36*(8), 1247–1268. doi:10.1080/0042098992971

Persson, A., Weitz, N., & Nilsson, M. (2016). Follow-up and Review of the Sustainable Development Goals: Alignment vs. Internalization. *Review of European Community & International Environmental Law*, *25*(1), 59–68. doi:10.1111/reel.12150

Porter, M. E. (1985). *The Competitive Advantage: Creating and Sustaining Superior Performance*. New York: Free Press.

Salm, S. J., & Falola, T. (Eds.). (2005). African Urban Spaces in Historical Perspectives. University of Rochester Press.

Sami, N., & Anand, S. (2015). *Manufacturing cities: Industrial Policy and Urban Planning in India.* Paper presented at the RC21 International Conference, Bangalore, India.

Swain, R. B. (2018). A Critical Analysis of the Sustainable Development Goals. In K. W. Leal (Ed.), *Handbook of Sustainability Science and Research.* Cham: Springer. doi:10.1007/978-3-319-63007-6_20

Thorsen, E. D., & Lie, A. (2006). *What is Neo-liberalism?* Oslo: Department of Political Science: University of Oslo.

Todes, A. (2011, May). Reinventing planning: Critical Reflections. *Urban Forum*, *22*(2), 115-133.

UN-Habitat. (2008). *The state of Africa's Cities. A framework for addressing urban challenges in Africa.* Nairobi: UN-Habitat.

UN-Habitat. (2009). *Planning Sustainable Cities: Policy Directions. Global Report on Human Settlements*. Nairobi: UN-Habitat.

UN-Habitat. (2016). *Draft outcome document of the United Nations Conference on Housing and Sustainable Urban Development (Habitat II)*. Available: http://nua.unhabitat.org/uploads/DraftOutcomeDocumentofHabitatIII_en.pdf

UN-Habitat. (2018). *Country Profile: Egypt*. Available at https://unhabitat.org/egypt/

Watson, V. (2009). 'The planned city sweeps the poor away…' Urban planning and 21st-century urbanization. *Progress in Planning*, *72*(3), 151–193. doi:10.1016/j.progress.2009.06.002

World Bank. (2016). *Doing Business: Measuring Regulatory Quality and Efficiency*. Washington, DC: World Bank.

Zeng, D.Z. (2012). *Special Economic Zones: Lessons from the Global Experience*. PEDL Synthesis Series No. 1.

Zeng, D. Z. (2015). *Global Experiences with Special Economic Zones: Focus on China and Africa.* Policy Research Working Paper. World Bank Group.

Zhou, G., & Zvoushe, H. (2012). Public Policy Making in Zimbabwe: A Three-Decade Perspective. *International Journal of Humanities and Social Science*, *2*(8), 212–222.

ZIMSTAT. (2013). *Census 2012. Zimbabwe National Report*. Harare: ZIMSTAT.

KEY TERMS AND DEFINITIONS

North Africa: Comprises seven countries that are Morocco, Algeria, Tunisia, Libya, and Egypt that are situated between the Mediterranean and the Sahara.

Policy: A government decision that is backed by a sanction.

Sub-Saharan Africa: All countries that are geographically situated south of the Sahara. The region consists of 46 countries.

Urban Growth: Improvement in industrial activities which significantly impacts on the socio-economic status of an area and is evident through employment creation and improved standard of living.

Section 3
Industrial and Urban Growth Policies at the National Level

Researchers from Mexico, Nigeria, and Russia presented chapters on national opportunities and challenges related to industrial and urban growth policies. From Mexico came three chapters dealing with the interplay of smart water, governance, and adaptive capacity to enhance the development of Mexico's green and blue city-regions; the exploration of the role of the economic and environmental factors in the dynamics of rural and urban shrinkage transformation processes in Mexico; and an institutional entrepreneurship analysis of biodiesel companies in Mexico. From Nigeria is a chapter on technology assessment of national renewable energy potentials by university academic research and development actors, and from Russia is a research making a comparative cross-cultural analysis of regions in Australia and Russia to overcome barriers across cultures and small businesses practices.

Chapter 9
Green and Blue City-Regions:
Smart Water, Governance, and Adaptive Capacity Development in Mexican Cities

Blanca C. Cecilia Garcia
El Colegio de la Frontera Norte, Mexico

ABSTRACT

Water security has been defined as the capacity of a population to safeguard sustainable access to adequate quantities of acceptable quality water. Growing populations and the increasing trend of human migration from rural to urban environments is leading to an expansion of the metropolitan/urban landscape, which threatens water security. Mexican cities are following this worldwide trend. Hence, this chapter will seek to develop theoretical understanding of the smart cities (SCs) model to meet global challenges such as water security. Seemingly, SCs are expected to deploy adaptation strategies resilient enough to secure future water quotas. Hence, the core scope of the chapter is to link water resources and social resilience strategies to social learning and governance in cities, which in some cases are featured as green and blue cities in the smart city paradigm. This linkage will explore potentials and opportunities of urban spaces and strengthen the efficacy of water networks in smart cities in Mexico, Latin America, and other developing spaces around the world.

1. INTRODUCTION

The interconnected environmental, energy, economic, and equity crises of our 21st century are posing complex and often unpredictable challenges to communities around the world. Clearly, conventional forms of urban planning, design, and governance—often centralized, hierarchical, and inflexible—are ill-suited to these new realities. Capacity development for governance in our communities is therefore setting the pace for building and strengthening our communities' resilience. Amongst those crises, water resources are characterized by connectedness, complexity, uncertainty, conflict, multiple stakeholders and intrinsically, multiple perspectives. Water resource crisis is increasingly being felt by most urban actors, although this situation is hardly reflected in the leading model for environmental planning and policy development processes. Given this background, it is unadvisable to base water management and

DOI: 10.4018/978-1-5225-7625-9.ch009

policy solutions purely on scientific knowledge alone. A strong case can be made for the inclusion of *Social learning* in this process as it offers managers and policy makers more alternative tools to understand and solve water crises problems.

On the other hand, the uniquely complex nature of water issues opens up opportunities for social science to make ground-breaking contributions to addressing the challenges that emerging green and blue cities pose. This chapter will therefore intend to explore the theoretical convergences between ***water management, social resilience*, *social learning, Smart City*** and ***Green and Blue cities*** concepts through more critical environmental issues such as water quality and water access for the urban poor. Therefore, the research focus could be placed on key characteristics such as adaptive capacity of communities. This chapter, therefore, will seek to develop a better understanding of capacity development processes through social learning processes which enable and constrain resilience, and thereby enhance communities' ability to develop and exploit their adaptive water security knowledge-base. Later in the chapter, the first steps into a research case from Oaxaca City in Mexico will help understand such processes in Mexico, Latin America and other developing spaces around the world.

2. THE SMART CITY MODEL

Emerging in late 1990s, the Smart City paradigm encompassed from digital-based urban environments; to many adjectives describing many innovative forms of digital cities (Anthopoulos, 2017). This process is being extended to defining capacity indexes (people, economy, living, environment, mobility and governance) (Giffinger et al. 2007); to enhancing the city's capacity to entice human capital; and to apply digital technology to attract this human capital in partnerships with the diverse urban development actors (Anthopoulos, 2017). "Smart City" is indeed a term which denotes a current "hype" in characterizing advanced cities being equipped with up-to-date ICT infrastructures. However, *smart city* concepts are going beyond the IT intelligence horizon. The claim evolves towards the idea of a city which is developed with a holistic framework in mind. For instance, some authors advance that a true smart city would be developed in a concerted approach covering six different aspects synchronously, namely: Smart Infrastructure, Smart Technology, Smart Mobility, Smart Economy, Smart Governance and Smart Living (Koch, 2015)

The so far discussions about smart cities are reflecting the lower level "hardware layers" offering the many functionalities a smart city is based upon, while on the other hand a *knowledge city* has been defined by the highest "soft(ware) layers" made by people, as shown in Figure 1. Additionally, professionals and academics broadly accept that concept of "smart cities" has attained mainstream acceptance by 2017, with North-American and Asian cities and towns spearheading this movement, while European communities have closely followed especially since the end of 2015.

While the term "smart city" is most frequently used, a range of other terms have been introduced by companies and institutions, such as "connected city", "resilient city", "senseable city" or "intelligent community". Other terms that are used frequently are "digital city" and "digital community". However, not all of these terms are used for the same phenomenon. But for the purposes of this chapter, the terms *smart* and *city* will not be defined from a scholar's perspective, but rather from the one advanced by practitioners; a "smart city", thus refers in this chapter to a paradigm of:

Figure 1. Smart ecosystems, smart cities, knowledge cities
Source: Koch, 2015

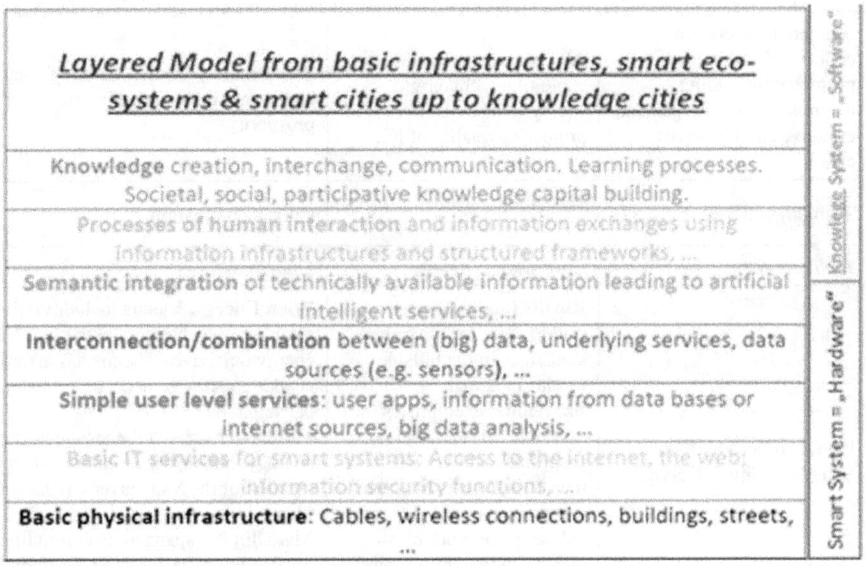

Utilizing the capacity of a city/community to create and adopt solutions for overcoming challenges and seizing opportunities that help transform "the place we call home" to a prosperous and more livable place for all stakeholders. The ecosystem of implemented solutions is what defines how smart a city/ community is (Mueller, 2017).

Generally speaking, it was the city as a unit of analysis the one that triggered the development of city administration and management concepts that were advanced through at least three generations of the Smart City paradigm, as shown in Table 1.

The Smart City models provide the interconnected ecological, energy, economic, and equity crises of our 21st century are creating multifaceted and often-unpredictable constraints to groups around the world. Obviously, conventional urban planning, design, and governance- often centralized, hierarchical, and inflexible—are unsuitable to the emerging realisms. Capacity development for resource management and governance in our communities is therefore setting the pace for building and strengthening our communities' connectedness, equity and resilience.

3. WATER MANAGEMENT PARADIGMS, SOCIAL LEARNING, AND GOVERNANCE

Relentlessly, one of the most important city´s indicators of progress and development is its water management and water governance. The characteristic connectedness, complexity, uncertainty, conflict, multiple stakeholders and thus multi-perspectives of water sources, makes it unsuitable to depend only on scientific knowledge for planning and strategies. Social learning that is based on different theoretical model, seems to offer professionals and policy-makers' new option and harmonizing potentials (Ison,

Table 1. Smart city generations

Paradigms	Smart Cities 1.0	Smart Cities 2.0	Smart Cities 3.0
Features	A technology-centric concept of smart cities promoted by leading technology firms to generate effective and innovative cities	A public-sector vision of exploiting technologic strategies as tools for promoting quality of life	A community-centric vision of smart cities founded on co-creation to enhance quality of life and produce prosperity
Nature	Techology-driven	Technology enabled, City-led	Citizen co-creation
Key Actors	***Technologists***	***Government Agents***	***Smartivists***
City Cases	PlanIT in **Portugal** Songdo in **South Korea.**	**Rio do Janeiro's** sensor grid to alleviate the role of landslides in the hillside favelas in Brazil. **Barcelona,** exemplifies the excess of 20 smart cities programs and the more than 100 projects of active smart cities with Wi-Fi in public spaces and transit places, intelligent lighting, and the electric vehicle infrastructure scheme..	**Wien Energy,** Vienna includes citizens-investors in solar power-generators in the city's 2050 renewable energy objectives. Vienna has affordable housing and gender equality projects based strong focus on citizen participation. **Vancouver** created the most determined collaborative strategy that engages 30,000 residents in the co-creation of the Vancouver Greenest City 2020 Action Plan. **Medellin** has spanned its commitment to citizen-innovators by backing the development of an impressive innovation district (Ruta N) to entice and preserve entrepreneurial talent.
Source: Cohen, B. (2015).			

Röling, & Watson, 2007). The following water management models and definitions will allow us to a better perspective of where principles of water management, water resilience, social learning, and Green & Blue cities converge.

Water Management and Social Learning

There are different definitions behind the concept of water management, but one of them, relevant to this chapter is the following: "water management includes all the activities involved in analyzing and monitoring water resources; and also developing and implementing measures to maintain the state of water resources in a desirable limit" (Pahl-Wostl, 2015:27). It has also been defined as "planning, acting or practicing determinedly to exert influence on a system, directly towards a certain direction" (Pahl-Wostl, 2009). Also, the adaptive mode of water management is defined as a "systematic process for improving management policies and practices by learning from the outcomes of implemented management strategies" (Pahl-Wostl, 2007b). However, it is clear that practice in water management and governance has "traditionally been characterized by a *command-and-control* paradigm and has not been very supportive of learning approaches (Gleick, 2003; Pahl-Wostl, 2007a; 2007c). This paradigm has led to "quite rigid regulations, large-scale technology, dominance of expert knowledge, technical approaches to risk management and engineering practices of optimal design under predictable conditions" (Pahl-Wostl, 2009) that are no longer valid.

A *water management* paradigm is understood as: "a set of basic assumptions about the nature of the systems to be managed, the management objectives and the ways in which these objectives can be achieved" (Pahl-Wostl et al., 2006:7). The paradigm is shared by what is called an epistemic community of actors involved in the management of the water. Following such line of thought, Pahl-Wostl et. al. (2006) propose that the concept of paradigm can be used to characterize the way of thinking of an epistemic community; that is, the way how researchers, managers, water makers, organized civil society, users, etc. consider that water management should be coded in the practices, laws, technologies, speech, etc. Hence, the paradigm is manifested in various forms, including technical infrastructure, planning approaches, regulations, engineering practices and management models, amongst others. In terms of this chapter, this concept is relevant because the paradigm of an epistemic community also translates into the formal and non-formal institutions which are at the core of the systems of water governance (Young, 2013). Also, this influences the epistemic community's decision-process to management issues (Pahl-Wostl, 2017). Such water management paradigm is highly relevant for this chapter purposes because it allows incorporating the cognitive (learning) dimension that underlies the process of decision making of those involved in the construction and implementation of governance regimes and water management. It could also explain why certain strategies of solution are preferred by decision-makers and link them with other factors within the system of governance, which in turn could be strengthened by cultural, economic, social and individual factors.

Two Water Management Paradigms

In recent decades a new paradigm for water management has emerged that sought to raise management alternative models to the so-called traditional model of management, such as the *Integrated Water Resources Management* (IWRM) and the *Adaptive Water Resources Management* (AWRM). It was Pahl-Wostl (2007) who characterized the paradigm behind the traditional model of water management as the one that "predicts and controls". It is characterized by the belief that any water management system is highly predictable and controllable, and it does not consider uncertainty. In contrast, Pahl-Wostl sees an "integrate-adaptive" feature in the emerging IWRM and AWRM paradigms, which indeed characterise these models. These two paradigms display six common structural dimensions within the water system (Table 2), which include the management models they advance. Such paradigms of water management include a theoretical perspective that characterises an overview of the water governance systems.

The Traditional Paradigm: Prediction and Control

The water management traditional paradigm focused on solving specific problems, such as urgent treatment processes due to rapid demographic growth and intensification of industrial and agricultural productivity characteristic of XIX and XX centuries (Pahl-Wostl, 2007a). The infrastructural solutions (dams, channels, treatment plants, irrigation systems, etc.) were developed as a successful and efficient response in the short term to solve short term problems. These solutions were associated with the development and well-being of the growing urban centres, namely: health and hygiene, flood control, food production, water pollution, water supply and power electricity to meet the ever-increasing demand of urban and industrial locations. This large-scale infrastructure also had a fundamental role in the protection, and expansion of urban communities' ability to coping with variability and climate extremes. For example, the transfer of water channels, dams, and other artificial water storage mechanisms have been used to expand the base of water availability during periods of drought (Pahl-Wostl et. al., 2007a).

The traditional water management model has been characterized by certain principles, such as a specific focus on technology and lack of water resources (supply management) as the underlying causes of the current water problem. In other words, it focuses on technology-driven solutions (Pahl-Wostl, 2007a). It does not take limitations and uncertainties imposed by climate and environmental change or the short- and long-term water availability into consideration. The traditional model focuses on control to succeed its water management goals (Pahl-Wostl, 2007a). Table 2 compares the traditional model versus other emerging models for water management, relevant for the purposes of this chapter.

The Integrated and Adaptive Paradigms: Flexibility and Effectiveness

The need for a transition towards new paradigms of management started in the early 90´s, speared by the emergence of knowledge, evidence, and consumer preferences that question the basic assumptions of the traditional water management (Pahl-Wostl et al., 2006) which consider that water crises are often a crisis of governance and not problems of scarcity of water or technological resources. Moreover, IWRM was promoted heavily as a principle more effective and efficient to manage water. Changes in preferences socially aimed toward care of the environment. Internationally, the environmental destruction caused by the hydraulic Mission gave rise to numerous protests, which began from the years 60´s and 70´s (Allan, 2003; Molle & Mollinga, 2003). Evidence has continually emerged pointing out that technical infrastructure of large scale used for the prevention of disaster risk increasingly has a limited protective effect due to the increase in the intensity and frequency of climatic extremes associated with climate change (Pahl-Wostl, 2007).

The Integrated Water Resources Management (IWRM) Model

The IWRM model has several definitions, and it is still considered amorphous concept (Biswas, 2008). The most popular definition was developed by the Global Water Partnership (GWP), (Global Water Partnership, 2000). Their definition emphasizes IWRM as a process that consists of balancing and making trade-offs between different goals and visions based on informed decision-making (Medema & Jeffrey, 2005) and need to integrate social sciences with natural sciences through an interdisciplinary approach (Bauer, 2004).

This paradigm, although integrative in its conceptualization, is operationally complex (see arguments by Medema and Jeffrey 2005, Biswas 2008, Bauer 2004, Martínez 2001). In practice, some principles of IWRM that are followed among several national, regional and basin strategies include the conviction that it is critical to a) integrate water management and environmental management; b) a systemic approach; participation of different decision makers including the communities; c) the attention to the social dimension; d) some capacity building; e) the availability of information and the ability to use it to anticipate; f) the recovery of total costs and subsidies to specific groups; g) the support of the central government through the creation and maintenance of an enabling environment; h) the adoption of the best technology and existing practices; i) the efficient use of water; j) reliable and sustained financing; k) equitable allocation of water resources; l) the recognition of water as an economic, ecological and social good; and m) the strengthening of the role of women in water management (IWA / UNEP, 2002 in GWP-TAC, 2000: 22, see also Jeffrey & Gearey, 2006, Martínez, 2001, Medema & Jeffrey, 2005). These IWRM principles clearly do not propose water management within a context of uncertainty, nor

Table 2. Traditional and emerging water resources management paradigms

Traditional Model of Water Management	Integrated Water Resources Management (IWRM)	Adaptive Water Resources Management (AWRM)
Waste waters are a problem. These must be removed after the minimum treatment required to reduce their harmful properties.	**Waste waters are a resource.** These should be captured and processed effectively, and used for agricultural and urban uses.	**Waste waters are a matter of governance.** These should be treated as part of a full water cycle and re-used for agricultural and urban needs.
Rainwater is a problem. Transport rainwater away from developed areas in the shortest time possible.	**Rainwater is a resource.** Collect rainwater as a source of supply, and conserve or infiltrate it.	**Rainwater is part of water supply.** Collect rainwater and store it as part of the community's strategy of water resources and use for community's needs.
Build according to demand. It is necessary to build more capacity as demand increases.	**Manage according to demand.** Opportunities to manage demand are real and are increasing. Take advantage of all cost-efficient options before increasing infrastructure capacity.	**Manage demand water instead of your offer.** Manage the sources of the problems and not the effects (i.e. manage the demand for water instead of its supply).
The demand as a quantity issue. The amount of water required by the end users is the only relevant parameter in the infrastructure options. Treat all water on the supply side to a drinking standard, and collect all wastewater for treatment in one system.	**The demand is multi-user.** The infrastructure options must comply with the various water characteristics required by the different end users: quantity, quality (biological, chemical, physical), level of profitability, etc.	**The demand is environment-adaptive.** It explicitly includes the environment issues in the management objectives of a community. The infrastructure options must comply with the environment characteristics and must seek to increase the integration of problems and sectors into general planning.
Water is used only once and wasted away. Water flows a unidirectional path from the source of supply to a single occasion of use, from there to be treated and disposed to the environment.	**Water re-use and recovery.** Water can be used multiple times, by cascade from the needs of higher to lower quality (i.e. use gray water for irrigation or for the discharge of toilets), and by recovery treatment to rejoin the supply infrastructure.	**Water re-use and recovery.** Water can be used multiple times, by recovery treatment to rejoin the supply infrastructure, under community and stakeholders' supervision.
Gray infrastructure. Infrastructure must be made of concrete, metal and plastic.	**Green infrastructure.** Infrastructure includes the natural capacities of soil and vegetation to absorb and treat water.	**Human Infrastructure.** More attention is given to the management of human behavior through "soft" measures, such as social learning interventions.
Large and/or centralized is better. Large systems, especially water treatment plants, entail economies of scale.	**Small and/or decentralized is possible, and often desirable.** Small-scale systems are effective and can be economical, especially when scale economies in conventional distribution and collection networks are considered.	**Management approaches are more flexible and decentralized.** Network-based systems can incorporate smaller conventional distribution and collection networks without affecting scale economies.
Limited complexity: Traditional models use standard solutions. A small number of technologies, well known to water professionals, define the range of response infrastructure options.	**IWRM Models allow different solutions.** It requires a diversity of solutions capable of adjusting to situations in increasingly complex human environments and with limited resources, which are possible thanks to new technologies and management strategies.	**AWRM Models incorporate iterative learning cycles** in the general management approach capable of triggering social learning and participation in increasingly complex human environments such as urban and rural-urban communities.
Integration by accident. The water supply, rainwater management and wastewater systems must be managed by the same agency as a matter of local-historical occurrence. However, systems must be physically separated in the territory.	**Physical and institutional integration by design.** Important connections can and must be made between the physical infrastructure of water supply, rainwater and wastewater. Realizing the benefits of integration requires highly coordinated management.	**Open and shared sources of information for water governance.** Important connections can and must be made between science and decision making for collective water resources management. It requires the intentional, coordinated participation of all community stakeholders, aiming to build water security and resilience (both social and water resilience).
Collaboration is equal to public relations. Approach to other agencies and the public when the approval of pre-selected solutions is required.	**Collaboration is equal to commitment.** Involve other agencies and the public in the search for effective solutions with multiple benefits.	**Collaboration is equal to participatory management, collaborative decision making and governance.** Agencies, Institutions, social and private sectors integrate in a social learning process of governance with common interests and benefits.
Water Resources Management as Prediction and **Control.**	**Water Resources Management** as learning rather than as control.	**Water Resources Management and Water Governance** as a Social Learning process.
Source: Adapted from Pahl-Wostl (2002, 2004, 2006:7, 2007a, 2009)		

does it explicitly propose the development of adaptive capacities as an important feature within water management strategies (Woodhouse & Muller, 2017).

The Adaptive Water Resources Management (AWRM) Model

AWRM takes the basin as the basic management unit and seeks to increase the adaptive capacity of this system (Pahl-Wostl et al., 2004, 2007a). This means in order to move to an adaptive management model, it is necessary to identify and understand those determining factors that inhibit or favour identified adaptive capacity (Pahl-Wostl et al., 2004).

AWRM has been defined as "a systematic process of continuous improvement of management policies and practices through learning from the results of the management strategies implemented" (Pahl-Wostl et al., 2005: 4). In this sense, a change towards a more adaptive management of water implies "learning to manage through managing knowledge" (Bormann et al., 1994 in Pahl-Wostl et al., 2007: 49). In this sense, this approach recognizes that there is no single or simple solution that can be prescribed to solve the complex problems of water management and governance, but that their solution is measured by a continuous learning process (Ostrom, 2007).

AWRM is a concept that has been developed to deal with management within highly connected, variable, dynamic and self-organized complex systems, such as ecosystems (Medema and Jeffrey, 2005). This perspective comes with a high level of uncertainty and complexity, which is partly explained by the wide range of perceptions and values in competition and of decisions at stake involving water management (Pahl-Wostl et al., 2007). In AWRM, the governmental authority and the administrative apparatus yield their hegemonic role in the decision-making process to give rise to a polycentric, horizontal and participatory model (Pahl-Wostl et al., 2006). Likewise, the answers to the problems involve a more integrated and systemic vision, while management strategies seek to be able to adapt and be flexible in the face of uncertainty scenarios, such as those foreseen by climate change and the current rapid socio-economic and ecological changes.(Pahl-Wostl et al., 2005, 2007). Consequently, as Jeffrey and Gaerey (2006) point out, it is characterized by policies that are constantly changing and that are flexible to adapt to surprises, given that they are inevitable. In the long term, adaptive management models aim to achieve a change in the structure of the water system (i.e. changes in crop types, in lifestyles, in water quotas allocated to certain uses) through cycles of learning (Pahl-Wostl et al., 2005). These changes in turn increase the ability of the water regime to operate in a greater range of environmental variation (Pahl-Wostl et al., 2005). Hence, two key concepts emerge from this water management literature review one is social learning and the other is governance. In fact, relevant to this chapter is to define water management and governance processes as social learning processes.

Social Learning Processes

Bandura's (1977) Social Learning Theory explains that individuals learn from each other through observation, imitation, and modeling. It is often described as bridging the behaviorist and cognitive learning theories, mainly because it includes attention, memory, and motivation concepts. However, Reed, et. al., 2006 argue that social learning has more than bridging functions; it extends to: (1) demonstrating that a cognitive change has occurred among the participating persons; (2) demonstrating that this new awareness is not limited to the participants but extends to the wider communities of practice; and (3) showing that it occurs through social exchanges between and among networked social actors. The meaning of social learning could improve our capacity to critically assess outcomes and to better appreciate the processes through which social learning takes place. In this way, it may be possible to better facilitate the desired outcomes of social learning processes (Reed, et. al., 2006).

With this in mind, our rural and urban communities, through social capital are likely to adapt to contextual changes due to a systemic coordination and cooperation through their learning processes. In order to examine possible outcomes in terms of adaptive responses to change in city systems, we will need to understand the links between water management, resilience, social learning and water governance within the rural and urban systems (Ruiu et al., 2017).

4. WATER MANAGEMENT, WATER GOVERNANCE, AND RESILIENCE IN COMMUNITIES

Milbrath (1989) was among the first researchers to link 'social learning' concept to sustainable development through the 'self-educating community' expression to define situations of mutual-learning, where actors learn from each other, and from nature. Sustainable development is viewed as a wicked problem (Rittel and Webber 1973), whose solution is function of the capacity of diverse actors to discuss, negotiate and reach collective decisions (Pahl-Wostl 2007, Schusler et al. 2003, Woodhill 2004; Muro & Jeffrey, 2008). These perspectives help considering a better view of the communities' decision-making practices, their capacity to endure change, as well as their ability to learn how to adjust toward new scenarios of governance policies about water, energy and sustainability. This chapter elicits a glimpse into these factors as possible examples of complex adaptive systems problems.

What Is Governance?

With the new millennium, the concept of governance has been extended with some "adjectives". Among others, we are talking about evolutionary governance, cooperative governance and associative governance. Some authors affirm that governance is expressed in "modes" or "ways": through hierarchies, persuasion, markets, community involvement and by association (Bell and Hindmoor, 2009). For the purposes of this chapter we have concentrated on Evolutionary Governance and Associative Governance, which have been raised from the theoretical explanation of social processes and the relationship between the State (government) and the actors around it.

For example, the theoretical position of the Evolutionary Governance Theory (EGT) is based on the explanation, from various theoretical bases, of the different stages in which the **dynamic** capacity of governability of social groups is developed as they are organized. From this perspective, governance is not something given or fixed, but something that is changing according to the elements and actors of the context. This vision is complemented by the theoretical vision of the Associative Governance, with which we try to emphasize the relationships that arise between the actors and the bonds of trust that arise from a regional context in the use of the resource (Stoker, 1998).

Thus, the contemporary concept of governance refers to an empirical phenomenon that has been impacting the **forms of state intervention and** how the state has been transformed (Dancause and Morin, 2013). It also comes from a new theoretical perspective that helps us to understand the processes of **integration and management of the social system**, as well as the role of the state in these processes (Enjolras, 2005). Indeed, the concept of governance is used to better understand "the introduction of new methods for the development of public policies based on negotiation, as well as new ways of implementing these **policies, especially through partnerships**" (Canet, 2004).

On the other hand, the concept of Associative Governance allows us to rethink the relationships between the different **economic, political and social actors, as** well as forms of public intervention. Its starting point is that the state no longer plays the same role it had been doing in the past. But above all, it notes that its fundamental characteristic is the nature of the links between the actors (Stoker, 1998). For their part, Hamel and Jouve (2006) have also rightly pointed out the ideological role played by governance, which has served to justify and legitimize the transition of governments from Keynesianism to neoliberalism (Bell and Hindmoor, 2009).

On the other hand, it is possible to link the increasingly widespread use of the concept of governance with the fact that the state has lost its central role in the formulation of public policies. Experts have pointed out that this has happened on three levels: international relations, economic regulation and the relations of the state with local powers (Canet, 2004). Some see the state as one of several actors, acting in concert with other representatives of the private sector and civil society (Duchastel and Canet, 2004). In terms of public policy and state regulation, and due to the complexity of social structures, it is observed that hierarchical, vertical and coercive relationships have gradually been replaced by more horizontal relationships, with incentives, negotiation and cooperation, which they involve a wider variety of economic and social actors (Canet, 2004, EME, 2005, Levesque, 2001). It is therefore clear that in the areas of economic development and social development, (where the social economy is at the intersection of these two) the state no longer plays the leading role. It has become, rather, a "partner" with multiple normative, human and financial resources.

The interest in governance arises from finding ourselves in a period of constant change. In which new problems are faced and new solutions are also proposed, it is no coincidence that governance is such a mentioned topic. Governance is one of the ways in which academia has found a mechanism to analyse change. (Levi-Faur, 2014, p.7). These changes arise and are institutionalized in different levels or spheres. They can be conceptualized in three directions: upward (regional, transnational, intergovernmental and global), downward (local, regional and metropolitan) and horizontally (private and civil authority spheres) (Levi-Faur, 2014, p.7). **For the purposes of this chapter, we** will understand governance as a complex social process. This means that we take the elements and interactive factors of the government structure, to analyse governance as a process of continuous improvement of the ability to direct and coordinate, and not as an immutable monolithic entity, as some previous perspectives observed. The idea of State from a governance perspective is understood in four approaches (Levi-Faur, 2014, p.11). In the first, governance is the emptying of the state, is to see that the state is not the omnipotent creator of public policy and although it is still an important actor has lost influence in various aspects of reality, since the participation of social agents strong and the ideas of a decentralized government based on interdependence, negotiation and trust (Sorensen and Torfing, 2005: 195-196 in Levi-Faur, 2014, p.10). The **secon**d perspective is degovernancing (Levi-Faur, 2014, p.11). This is based on the concept of deregulation and debureaucratization. This results in alternate areas of authority. That is, the emptying of policies as a whole, is clearly seen in the field of markets (Levi-Faur, 2014, p.11). **The third perspective** is government centered on the state, (Levi-Faur, 2014, p.11).

The state recognizes its changes and transformations in the organization of the government. Therefore, it considers its limitations in its capacity and the importance of private actors in the development of politics and governance (Levi-Faur, 2014, p.11). The last **and fourth** perspective is known as Big Governance (Levi-Faur, 2014, p.13). It seeks to have a better understanding of the role of the state in governance, studying the relationship between governments and governance, from regularization and regulation. It is perceived that regulation is what has the most significance along with governance within the structure of the political system (Levi-Faur, 2014, p.13). This expansion of the concept of governance allows the development of new forms of regulation, and the development of alternative models of governance (Levi-Faur, 2014, p.11).

However, for the purposes of this chapter, it is advanced that "governance is an ongoing process of steering or enhancing the institutional capacity to steer and coordinate" (Pierre and Peters, 2000; Kooiman, 2003). It is a "norm-generating process" (Humrich and Zangl, 2010:343) as well as a group of "practices of governing" (Bevir, 2011:1) and the exercise of public authority (Heinrich, 2011:256, in Levi-Faur, 2014). Most importantly, "the notion of governance, when applied to water refers to the capability of a social system to mobilize energies, in a coherent manner, for the sustainable development of water resources" (Rogers, 2002). Clearly, water governance refers to the range of political, social, economic and administrative systems that are in place to develop and manage water resources, and the delivery of water services, at different levels of society (Rogers & Hall, 2003). As mentioned above, relevant to this chapter is to define water management and governance processes as social learning processes, mainly because they can be linked to concepts that are embedded in collective ways of learning. One of those embedded concepts, in which water management, governance and learning converge is resilience.

What Is Resilience?

Increased water demand and the consequences of climate change, clearly pose serious risks to the provision of sustainable urban water services, e.g., drinking water, sanitation, and safe drainage, especially in cities. These challenges call for a transition toward improved water management, including considerations of "resilience." However, because the resilience concept has multidisciplinary origins it is open to multiple interpretations, which poses a challenge to understanding and operationalizing the concept. It is thought that building resilience needs to take three distinctive dimensions into consideration: socioeconomic, external hazard considerations, and larger social-ecological (regional) systems to be sustainable. Indeed, resilience as a notion adds value to understanding and addressing the complex urban water management within its three dimensions (Fath, et. al., 2015).

Resilience is a rich and complex concept. It has roots in systems theory, and it has a variety of interpretations and applications every time human agency and/or networked, collective action is involved. The concept has been defined by a number of authors as indicated in Table 3, but for the purposes of this paper we follow upon the work of the *Resilience Alliance*, one of the leading scholarly bodies working on the resilience of social-ecological systems.

They have defined *resilience* as "the capacity of a social-ecological system to absorb or withstand perturbations and other stressors such that the system remains within the same regime, essentially maintaining its structure and functions" (Holling 1973, Gunderson & Holling 2002, Walker et al. 2004). Moreover, it describes the degree to which the system is capable of self-organization, learning and adaptation, as illustrated in Figure 2.

The concept of resilience started in systems ecology, framing the resilience concept explicitly in the adaptive cycle with the observation that resilient systems are the "ones that successfully navigate all stages of growth, development, collapse, and reorientation of this cycle" (Johannessen & Wamsler, 2017). Resilience refers to the capacities, competencies, and cultures needed by social organizations to bounce back, requiring consideration of the entire life cycle for success (Johannessen & Wamsler,

Table 3. Definitions of resilience: sampler

First author, year	Domain	Definition
Kimhi, 2004	Community	Individuals' judgement of the ability of their community to successfully solve the on-going political violence
Coles, 2004	Community	A community's capacities, skills, and knowledge that enable it to engage completely in recovery from tragedies
Allenby, 2005	Community	The system's capacity to retain its function and structure in the face of internal and external transformations and to degrade graciously if it must
Gunderson, 2005	Community	The recovery time of a social-ecological system, determined by (1) that system's ability for regeneration in a active environment and (2) group's ability to learn and change (which, in turn, is mainly a function of the institutional context for knowledge sharing, learning, and management, and partly by the group's social capital)
Source: CARRI Report (2013		

Figure 2. The adaptive cycle
Source: Adapted from Holling, Gunderson and Ludwig (2002)

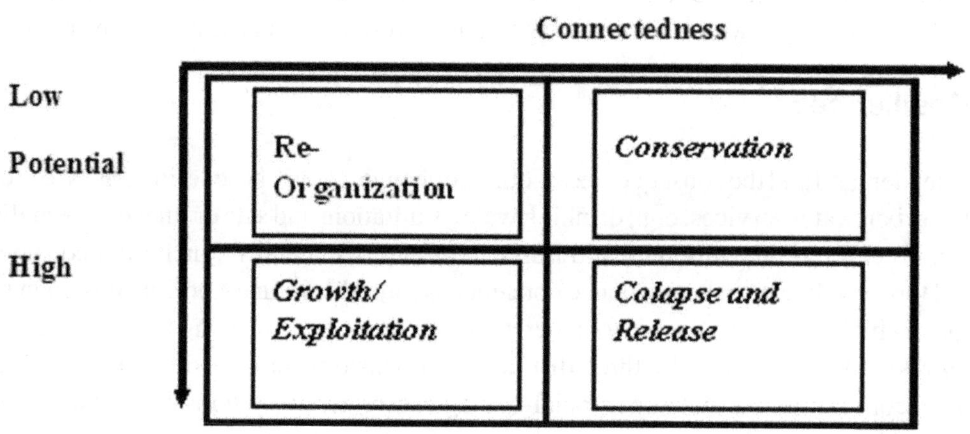

2017r). *Resilience*, is also a key concept in terms of social capital, which is relevant for the purposes for this chapter, but has the following challenges:

1. Transferring and integrating different forms of resilience across diverse communities and social settings; b) the evolution of resilience as an adaptive capacity for the institutions and practices that regulate the formation and utilization of *Smart City* strategies;
2. The complex combination of system forces, including policy, technology and city capitals, with the creation, measurement and representation of *smart water* initiatives;
3. The new role of government, which advances learning adaptive capacities and *Smart City* schemes;
4. The limited role of technology and ICTs (Information and Communication Technologies) in triggering the evolution of Smart Cities; and
5. The *Smart City* and other concepts which afford different levels of analysis, (Fath, et. al., 2015).

Amongst the multiple applications in which water management and governance, are built-in, and social learning and resilience converge, are the Green Cities and the Blue Cities schemes, which will be depicted in the next paragraphs.

5. GREEN CITIES FRAMEWORKS

Urban green areas, sometimes called ‘green infrastructure’ or ‘urban vegetation’, are critical to urban residents in their vital roles in reducing urban heat island effects, impeding climate change, and in creating multiple ecosystem services and diverse aesthetics (Ramos, 2014).

In 2009, Siemens corporation (Germany) sponsored a research led by the Economist Intelligence Unit (London), which resulted in the publication of the European Green City Index (EGCI) report, in which the environmental performance of 30 large cities in Europe was analyzed. The European Green City Index evaluates 16 quantitative and 14 qualitative indicators, under eight dimensions. One of them, and of central interest for this chapter, is Water (Water consumption, System Leakages, Wastewater system treatment and Water efficiency and treatment policies) but it also includes an Energy dimension closely tied to water management. The methodology for Europe was adapted for the other regional indexes. However, its critics underline it is important to set targets and goals, and to be aware of pitfalls that may exist in the course of a blind pursuit of a higher Green Score (Venkatesh, 2014). Fragmentation in public administration causes overlaps, conflicts and synergies that could hinder the advancement of Green City Index schemes. Despite of such hindrances, the EGCI has moved on to adapt its original dimensions and indicators as shown in Table 4 for African, Asian and Latin American city cases (Venkatesh, 2014).

On the other hand, “exploitation and degradation of urban green areas reduce their capacity to sustain ecosystem services”, as it was observed at the Stockholm National Urban Park (Ernstson, et. al. 2008). Their work showed how the core-periphery structure has facilitated collective action to protect the park, hence, they suggest incorporating social network structure of adaptive governance and co-management.

6. BLUE CITIES FRAMEWORKS

Amsterdam in the Netherlands is a good example of Blue City scheme due to its integrated water resources management (IWRM) and has earned a first place for the Water dimension in the European Green City Index (see above). In 2006, the various urban water-related services in Amsterdam were brought under one roof, culminating in Netherlands’ first water cycle company called *Waternet.* This company has responsibilities for surface water (rivers, canals, ditches and lakes), groundwater, storm water, drinking water supply and waste water treatment, which integrates its reported Blue City Index (BCI). The BCI is based on a survey as defined by Van Leeuwen et al., (2015) and is complemented with other information on water security, public involvement and regional or national estimates for local environmental quality (surface water, groundwater and biodiversity). This information is applied to give a quick preview of IWRM of cities and regions. It integrates a set of 24 indicators, listed as shown in Table 5.

There are, however, few success cases in water management and governance like Amsterdam, whose IWRM strength is the result of a strong focus on water governance (Van Leeuwen et al., 2015). The city has shown high commitments to sustainable solutions on almost all aspects of the water cycle: water efficiency, drinking water leakages, sanitation as well as energy and nutrient recovery from waste wa-

Table 4. Green cities index components

Dimension	Indicators
Environmental Governance	Green Action Plan Green Management Public Participation in Green policy
CO_2	$CO_{2\ Intensity}$ $CO_{2\ Emissions}$ $CO_{2\ Reduction\ Strategy}$
Energy	Energy Consumption Energy Intensity Renewable Energy Consumption Clean and Efficient energy Policies
Buildings	Energy Consumption of Residential Buildings Energy-efficient buildings standards Energy-efficient building initiatives
Transport	Use of non-car transport Size of non-car transport Network Green Transport promotion Congestion reduction policies
Waste and Land Use	Municipal Waste production Waste Recycling Waste Reduction Policies Green land use policies
Water	Water consumption System Leakages Wastewater system treatment Water efficiency and treatment policies
Air Quality	Nitrogen Dioxide Sulphur Dioxide Ozone Particule Matter Clean Air Policies
Source: Siemens (2012)	

Table 5. Blue cities index components

Indicators	Indicators
1. Water Footprint	13. Energy Efficiency
2. Water Scarcity	14. Energy Recovery
3. Water Self-sufficiency	15. Nutrient Recovery
4. Surface Water Quality	16. Average age sewer system
5. Ground Water Quality	17. Infrastructure separation
6. Sufficient to drink	18. Climate Commitments
7. Water System Leakages	19. Adaptation Measures
8. Water efficiency	20. Climate-robust buildings
9. Drinking Water consumption	21. Bio-diversity
10. Drinking Water quality	22. Attractiveness
11. Safe Sanitation	23. Management and action Plans
12. Sewage Sludge Re-cycling	24. Public Participation.
Source: Siemens(2012)	

ter. Could such success be replicated in cities such as in the developing Latin American context? The next paragraphs concentrate in exploring the context of a Mexican City: Oaxaca, for which a number of research projects dealing with IWRM, water governance and *Smart Water* are already in progress.

7. A CASE OF SMART WATER FOR A MEXICAN CITY

Since the adoption of dramatic national water policy reforms in 1992, Mexico's water governance has been consolidating into a national (albeit centralized), force. Apparently, a "new culture of water" focused on the three principles of efficiency, decentralization, and sustainability is advancing in order to establish a new state-citizen relationship around water policy. However, a coherent water governance strategy has yet to be achieved. The proposed research to which the theoretical framework of this chapter is intended, is an interdisciplinary investigation designed to lay the foundations for enhancing sustainable regional water security through improved integration of *Smart City* concepts as part of metropolitan design and urban landscapes. It will develop a bilateral UK-Mexico research partnership in order to diagnose the problem of water security in the metropolitan area of Oaxaca and draw possible scenarios and solutions for the future, such as blue and green infrastructure, that will help transition towards an inclusive and sustainable system of water management and distribution.

Oaxaca City

The state of Oaxaca (Mexico), classified as the most vulnerable to climate change, is located in the South-Southeast portion of the Mexican Republic. It limits to the north with the states of Veracruz and Puebla, to the west with Guerrero, to the southeast with Chiapas and to the south with the Pacific Ocean. It covers a territorial extension of 93,793.33 km2, 4.8% of the national surface. Administratively, the state is composed of 570 municipalities and is composed of 65 major hydrological basins, formed from the watershed that originates in the Sierra Madre Occidental and north of Oaxaca to the Pacific Ocean, called the coastal strip of the state of Oaxaca. Administratively, CONAGUA (2012) classifies them into 11 Planning Cells among the set of municipalities that belong to a single state within the limits of a hydrological sub-region.

The average annual rainfall in the state of Oaxaca is 1,070 mm, which produces an annual average volume of 62,475.6 hm3. The region receiving the highest rainfall is Papaloapan with an annual average of 2,840 mm and that of Coatzacoalcos that receives 3,300 mm, the Coast of Oaxaca 1,347 mm, the Coast of Chiapas with 1,633 mm, Costa Chica and Río Verde with 609 mm, Alto Balsas with 502 mm and finally Tehuantepec with 1,018 mm. The annual potential evaporation varies from 1,606 to 2,757 mm with a monthly average of 144 mm in September and 214 mm in April. It has a coastline of 568 km in whose estuaries and coastal lagoons there is a great potential for fish production, coupled with the broad tourist potential. The surface runoff of the state of Oaxaca totals an annual volume of 62,475.6 hm3 (DOF Availability of surface waters of the watersheds 2007.), of which they are destined to satisfy the demands of the various consumptive uses 1,103 hm3, from which an amount of surplus water is available for new uses of 61,372.6 hm3 / year, which represents the current supply of surface water in the state of Oaxaca, in conditions of availability, which is apparent since it occurs in a short period (June to September) and no infrastructure is available for its collection. There are 21 main aquifers in the state of Oaxaca, all underexploited, with a recharge of the order of 1,366.9 hm3 and an extraction of 310.7 hm3. However, the Valles Centrales aquifer is overexploited due to the pressure exerted by the growing population (CONAGUA, 2012). The volumes of water reserved in the state of Oaxaca for forest systems and other ecosystems are of the order of 3,040 hm3 / year in surface water and 173,63 hm3 / year of underground water.

Water Offer

Even when 61,372.6 hm3 / year are reported as available water (current supply) for new uses, due to the insufficient and deficient infrastructure for its capture and use, availability is usually apparent. Particularly to supply water to the population, there is a total supply of 201 hm3 per year; 60.4% of this volume comes from groundwater (122 hm3) and the remaining 39.6% (80 hm3) of surface water.

Water Demand

At present, the demand for the resource in the state of Oaxaca is of the order of 1.918 hm3, without taking into account the environmental flow of approximately 148 hm3; 73.9% of agriculture (1,418 hm3), 308 hm3 of the urban public sector and 44 hm3 of the industrial sector. CONAGUA (2012).

Oaxaca City-Region (Valles Centrales) Socio-Cultural and Economic Context

The regionalization of the state of Oaxaca is part of its historical, social and natural process. Its surface area of approximately 9.4 million hectares is made up of 570 municipalities, 30 districts and 8 regions: Cañada, Costa, Istmo, Mixteca, Papaloapan, Sierra Sur, Sierra Norte and Valles Centrales, where its capital city, Oaxaca (same name) is located.

The *Central Valleys* (Valles Centrales) region of Oaxaca are in the central area of the state, with an extension of 330,495 hectares and 103 municipalities. They are located between the Nudo Mixteco, the Sierra de Juárez and the Sierra Madre del Sur. The urban area is concentrated in these valleys and is the main user of the environmental services provided by the forests of the rural high areas. The urban area is mainly comprised by private property and concentrates the majority of the population. The state capital Oaxaca de Juarez is located here, and has 265,033 inhabitants (7.6% of the whole state population). The Valles Centrales aquifer is integrated by a system of four micro-basins located in Coyotepec, Tlacolula, Oaxaca and Ocotlán, part of the Atoyac River basin. In the aquifer, 143 agrarian nuclei have been identified. The region consumes 121.8 million cubic meters of water annually. The aquifer is being depleted due to excessive extraction caused by the construction of deep wells with inadequate infrastructure.

Environmental Context: This consists of the following components:

1. *Valles Centrales* contains one of the most important aquifers in the state of Oaxaca.
2. Provides water to more than half a million people.
3. The mountains of the valley include a wide variety of forests in good condition.
4. Its forests provide environmental services fundamental for the inhabitants of the city of Oaxaca and 67 municipalities of the state.

Environmental Challenges are dominated by the following issues:

1. Messy urban growth and increased pressure on natural resources
2. About groundwater extraction
3. Lack of water supply
4. Decrease in forest area due to changes in land use
5. Presence of pests and forest diseases
6. Migration of inhabitants of the mountain communities to the urban area
7. Degradation and desertification of the vegetation layer in mountain ranges
8. Lack of ecological and territorial regulations
9. Vulnerability to climate change and lack of adaptation plans.

Key Stakeholders

Comunidades locales; Centro de Acción para el Desarrollo (CODICE); Ambientare; Instituto de la Naturaleza y de la Sociedad de Oaxaca (INSO); Fundación Comunitaria Oaxaca; Secretaría de Medio Ambiente y Recursos Naturales (Comisión Nacional de Áreas Naturales Protegidas, Slim Foundation, Comisión Nacional Forestal, Instituto Nacional de Ecología, Comisión Nacional del Agua, Procuraduría Federal de Protección al Ambiente); Gobierno del estado de Oaxaca (Municipio de Oaxaca de Juárez).

Oaxaca City-Region Water Governance

In general, we can sustain that Mexico continues to rely on large scale infrastructure for water procurement rather than on integrated management practices—infrastructure that often is badly built, not maintained and not sustainable. Water conditions in Oaxaca and the state capital, Oaxaca de Juarez reflect these national trends. In a detailed draft document, Monique Segarra[1] describes in detail the socio-cultural context in the surrounding municipalities in the Central Valleys. There, chronic water shortages, poor water quality, drawn down and polluted aquifers have been precipitated by the following factors in Oaxaca City:

- **Socio-Political Context**: That includes rapid and often unplanned city growth, increasing population, and inadequate and leaking pipes.
- **The Problematic Agricultural Practices**: On the other hand include rapid deforestation, declining agricultural production and livelihoods, fluctuations in water quality and quantity inconsistent water provision, and health risks.
- **Other Issues:** All over the city those who can afford it, buy water privately to avoid waterborne diseases.

Since late 1980's, Mexico became a IWRM leader in Latin America, aiming to decentralize and pluralize water management through extensive stakeholder participation. Nonetheless, centralized organization endures, and user involvement is often restricted to larger water interests groups. Local communities, citizens groups, and environmental non-governmental organizations seldom are able to effect policy-making or organization practices. Researchers working on democracy issues and on resource management in Mexico explain this gap by noting the nation's tradition of state-created 'invited spaces' that apparently include effective social participation but in reality is mere cooption relationships (Segarra, 2012:2), as is clearly observed in Oaxaca City's case. However, to enhance water delivery and coordinate administration within the watershed, Oaxaca City has created a set of decentralized water administrations based on ecological rather than political jurisdictions.

The watershed council and micro groundwater committees (COTAS), however, remain subjugated by the national water agency, Comisiŏn Nacional del Agua (CONAGUA). Sadly, multi-stakeholder participation remain limited. Hence, the current situation in Oaxaca City's case maybe shown in the following:

Socio-political Challenges:

- Stimulated migration to the state's urban centers
- Fragmented Water management and organization
- Multiple political jurisdictions through which the water flows.
- Equity issues
- Vulnerability facing both draughts and floods.
- Vertical structures of decision-making.
- Historical authoritarian models of public administration and management.
- Initiatives

Environmental and Social Resilience

The novelty of this type of research sits in the fact that it is a multi-disciplinary team aiming to tackle two core aspects of Oaxaca City resilience simultaneously: its *environmental* and *social resilience*. The proposal advances that by following knowledge-based strategies such as *Green City* or *Blue City* models under the flag of the Smart City paradigm the foundational (hard) dimension of sustainable development is put in place with ICT infrastructure while the (soft) dimension of relational capital is being fostered during the same period of the project. For these purposes, the following definition of the Smart City paradigm has been adopted.

FUTURE RESEARCH DIRECTION AND CONCLUSION

The long-term challenge of climate change poses a threat to water security, (defined as the capacity of a population to safeguard sustainable access to adequate quantities of acceptable quality water) and must be accounted for as the water security landscape expands (CONAGUA, 2014). Mexican cities are following this worldwide trend, and a lack of sustainable water resource planning in the metropolitan design of its major cities is increasing the risk. According to emerging research within the framework of *Smart Cities* (Batty, et.al., 2012) connectivity and flow of information play a crucial role in ensuring resilience, which as mentioned, is the ability of a city or urban system to absorb disturbance while retaining identity, structure and key processes (Leichenko, 2011). In this sense, a key objective of proposed research is to collect official data and create new datasets with the help of a prototypical mini-sensor network, so that a diagnosis of how water is managed and distributed can be performed. This initial research will build on results of team' links and data management in 2019. The author of this chapter is part of the mentioned team). In addition to analyzing the main variables giving rise to the observed problems, the team will aim at identifying vulnerable groups and communities whose access to the resource is unreliable and sometimes non-existent from official sources.

In this context, we will be able to describe how social exclusion is related to poor water management, touching upon one of the Water Policy Programs three strategic aspects. This diagnosis will help us develop a transferable set of indicators to evaluate the efficiency and resilience of the water networks from an inclusive perspective. This is an objective that we intend to achieve in an iterative way. It will be constructed through models and analyses incorporating socio-economic data together with measures of vulnerability and resilience. We will introduce methodologies from statistical physics together with complex network analysis, in order to construct models that can help us define resilience in the specific theoretical context considering social exclusion. We will investigate the resilience and vulnerability of the water networks looking at the effect of the changes in the system. These will be modelled according to projected scenarios given by climate change, population growth, and extreme events, such as flooding or droughts. We will particularly measure the impact of such disturbances to vulnerable communities, and propose infrastructural changes to enhance inclusive access to quality water. This will help develop a strategy towards building resilience to extreme events and hence improve disaster prevention along with robustness and adaptability in the face of future uncertainties in population and climate change.

REFERENCES

Allan, A. (2003). *IWRM/IWRAM: A new sanctioned discourse?* SOAS Water Issues Study Group. Occasional Paper No. 50. London: School of Oriental and African Studies.

Allen, D., & Potts, J. (2015). *Why it Exists, What it Does, Who it Benefits, and How*. Available at SSRN: https://ssrn.com/abstract=2617141

Anthopoulos, L. G. (2017). *Understanding Smart Cities: A Tool for Smart Government or an Industrial Trick?* New York: Springer; doi:10.1007/978-3-319-57015-0

Antonelli, C. (2000). Collective Knowledge Communication and Innovation: The Evidence of Technological Districts. *Regional Studies*, *34*(6), 535–547. doi:10.1080/00343400050085657

Bandura, A. (1977). *Social Learning Theory*. New York: General Learning Press.

Bell & Hindmoor. (2009). *Rethinking Governance*. London: Earthscan.

Biswas, A. K. (2008). Integrated water resources management: Is it working? *International Journal of Water Resources Development*, *24*(1), 5–22. doi:10.1080/07900620701871718

CARRI Report. (2013). Retrieved from http://www.resilientus.org/wp-content/uploads/2013/08/definitions-of-community-resilience.pdf

Carrillo, F. J. (2004). Capital cities: A taxonomy of capital accounts for knowledge cities. *Journal of Knowledge Management*, *8*(5), 28–46. doi:10.1108/13673270410558738

CohenB. (2015). Retrieved from https://www.fastcompany.com/3047795/the-3-generations-of-smart-cities

CONAGUA. (2014). *Federal Government of Mexico. National Water Plan. National Development Plan 2014 - 2018*. Retrieved from http://www.conagua.gob.mx/CONAGUA07/Contenido/Documentos/PROGRAMA\

Ernstson, H., Sörlin, S., & Elmqvist, T. (2008). Social movements and ecosystem services–the role of social network structure in protecting and managing urban green areas in Stockholm. *Ecology and Society, 13*(2), 39. Retrieved from http://www.ecologyandsociety.org/vol13/iss2/art39/

Fath, B. D., Dean, C. A., & Katzmair, H. (2015). Navigating the adaptive cycle: An approach to managing the resilience of social systems. *Ecology and Society, 20*(2), 24. doi:10.5751/ES-07467-200224

Garcia, B. (2007). Working and Learning in a Knowledge City: A Framework for Knowledge Workers. *Journal of Knowledge Management, 11*(5), 18–30. doi:10.1108/13673270710819771

Hess, C., & Ostrom, E. (2007). *Understanding Knowledge as a Commons. From Theory to Practice.* Cambridge, MA: MIT Press.

Ison, R., Röling, N., & Watson, D. (2007). Challenges to science and society in the sustainable management and use of water: Investigating the role of social learning. *Environmental Science & Policy, 10*(6), 499–511. doi:10.1016/j.envsci.2007.02.008

Johannessen, Å., & Wamsler, C. (2017). What does resilience mean for urban water services? *Ecology and Society, 22*(1), 1. doi:10.5751/ES-08870-220101

Koch, G. (2015). Knowledge Cities versus Smart Cities - A discussion triggered on occasion of the case of Timisoara, Romania. In *13th NETTIES Conference (Network Entities) on "Open Data and Big Data – The Impact on Digital Society and Smart Cities"*. IAFeS.

Molle, F., & Mollinga, P. (2003). Water poverty indicators: conceptual problems and policy issues. *Water Policy, 5*(5-6), 529-544.

Mueller, T. (2017). Towards a New Paradigm of the Smart City. [Web log Post]. Retrieved from https://hub.beesmart.city/strategy/towards-a-new-paradigm-of-the-smart-city

Ostrom, E. (1990). *Governing the Commons: The Evolution of Institutions for Collective Action.* Cambridge, UK: Cambridge University Press. doi:10.1017/CBO9780511807763

Pahl-Wostl, C. (2002). Towards sustainability in the water sector: The importance of human actors and processes of social learning. *Aquatic Sciences, 64*(4), 394–411. doi:10.1007/PL00012594

Pahl-Wostl, C. (2006). The importance of social learning in restoring the multifunctionality of rivers and floodplains. *Ecology and Society, 11*(1), 10. doi:10.5751/ES-01542-110110

Pahl-Wostl, C., Moltgen, J., Ebenhoh, E., & Holtz, G. (2007a). The New Water management and transition framework—state and development process. In Adaptive and Integrated Water Management. Coping with Complexity and Uncertainty. Springer Verlag.

Pahl-Wostl, C. (2009). A Conceptual framework for analysing adaptive capacity and multi-level learning processes in resource governance regimes. *Global Environmental Change, 19*(3), 354–365. doi:10.1016/j.gloenvcha.2009.06.001

Pahl-Wostl, C. (2015). *Water governance in the face of global change: From understanding to transformation.* London: Springer. doi:10.1007/978-3-319-21855-7

Pahl-Wostl, C. (2017). An Evolutionary Perspective on Water Governance: From Understanding to Transformation. *Water Resources Management, 31*(10), 2917–2932. doi:10.100711269-017-1727-1

Pahl-Wostl, C., Craps, M., Dewulf, A., Mostert, E., Tabara, D., & Taillieu, T. (2007b). Social learning and water resources management. *Ecology and Society, 12*(2), 5. doi:10.5751/ES-02037-120205

Pahl-Wostl, C., & Hare, M. (2004). Processes of Social Learning in Integrated Resources Management. *Journal of Community and Applied Social Psychology, 14*, 193–206. Retrieved from www.interscience.wiley.com

Pahl-Wostl, C., Sendzimir, J., Jeffrey, P., Aerts, J., Berkamp, G., & Cross, K. (2007c). Managing change toward adaptive water management through social learning. *Ecology and Society, 12*(2), 30. doi:10.5751/ES-02147-120230

Ramos-González, O. M. (2014). The green areas of San Juan, Puerto Rico. *Ecology and Society, 19*(3), 21. doi:10.5751/ES-06598-190321

Reed, M. S., Evely, A. C., Cundill, G., Fazey, I., Glass, J., Laing, A., . . . Stringer, L. C. (2006). What is social learning? *Ecology and Society, 15*(4). Retrieved from http://www.ecologyandsociety.org/vol15/iss4/resp1/

Rogers, P. (2002). *Water governance in Latin America and the Caribbean*. Inter-American Development Bank (IDB). Retrieved from http://www.iadb.org, https://www.ircwash.org/sites/default/files/202.2-02WA-17802.pdf

Rogers, P., & Hall, A. (2003). *Effective Water Governance* (Vol. 7). Elanders Novum, Sweden: GWP-TEC, The Background Papers.

Siemens. (2012). *Green Index Report*. Retrieved from https://www.siemens.com/entry/cc/features/greencityindex_international/all/en/pdf/gci_report_summary.pdf

Tuomi, I. (2002). The future of knowledge management. *Lifelong learning in Europe, 7*(2), 69-79.

Tuomi, I. (2004a). *Future Challenges of the European Knowledge Society*. Paper presented at Institute for Prospective Technological Studies. Retrieved from: http://www.meaningprocessing.com/personalPages/tuomi/articles/TheFutureOfTheEuropeanKnowledgeSociety.pdf

Tuomi, I. (2004b). *Knowledge sharing and the idea of Public Domain.* Paper presented at the Unesco 21st Century Dialogue on Building Knowledge Societies. Retrieved from: http://www.meaningprocessing.com/personalPages/tuomi/articles/KnowledgeSharingAndTheIdeaOfPublicDomain.pdf

Tuomi, I. (2005). *The future of learning in the knowledge society: disruptive changes for Europe by 2020*. Paper prepared for DG JRC/IPTS and DG EAC, 17.

Van Leeuwen, K., & Sjerps, R. M. A. (2015). The City Blueprint of Amsterdam: An assessment of integrated water resources management in the capital of the Netherlands. *Water Science and Technology: Water Supply, 15*(2), 404–410. doi:10.2166/ws.2014.127

Venkatesh, G. (2014). A critique of the European Green City Index. *Journal of Environmental Planning and Management*, *57*(3), 317–328. doi:10.1080/09640568.2012.741520

Wallis, A. (1998). Social capital and community building. Building Healthier Communities: Ten Years of Learning. *National Civic Review*, *87*, 317–319. doi:10.1002/ncr.87404

Wenger, E., White, N., & Smith, J. (2009). Digital habitats: Stewarding technology for communities. Portland, OR: CPSquare.

Chapter 10
Economic and Environmental Effects of Rural and Urban Shrinkage Transformation Processes in Mexico

José G. Vargas-Hernández
University of Guadalajara, Mexico

Adam Konto Kyari
Imam Abdulrahman Bin Faisal University, Saudi Arabia

ABSTRACT

The purpose of this chapter is to analyze the empirical-theoretical approaches to shrinking cities in Mexico. The study of tendencies in economic and environmental shrinkage is tied to the expressions of substantive changes in the complexity of determinant contexts of internal and migration flows. The method used is the critical analysis of economic, social, and political tendencies in relation to the situation of shrinking cities in Mexico. The results of this analysis led to the finding that the shrinkage process in Mexico, as a developing and emerging economy, does not follow the same patterns of well developed countries, where an increase in shrinking cities has occurred since the middle of the 1950s, and the use of incentives in some localities to attract economic growth have had modest success to turn around the shrinking process. Further research on shrinking cities should be done in Mexico. Finally, this chapter analyzes some of the important issues and problems that are important to set an agenda for future research in Mexico.

INTRODUCTION

This chapter is aims to analyze the link between rural-urban migration and shrinkage transformation processes caused by the lack of urban and industrial policies in Mexico. This is important because the determinations of losers with rural economies of low productivity and scarce human capital that are being inserted in a global economy. Territorial expressions of productive structure are relevant to understand

DOI: 10.4018/978-1-5225-7625-9.ch010

patterns of spatial redistribution of population but they are not enough and not always oriented in the same direction.

Rural-urban migration predominates in developing societies and to the extent that they advance, the flow of migration decreases in absolute and relative terms. In the case of Mexico, despite the decrease in rural-urban migration after 2000, the contribution to urbanization is less than natural growth.

Similarly, migration influences the depopulation of the center of Mexico City. Within the historical processes, the dialectics between the rapid peripheral expansions are enhanced by the translation of poor population and gradual depopulation of central areas in large cities like Mexico and Guadalajara. The orientation and selectivity of this migration makes it a factor of spatial demographic and socioeconomic differentiation and create socio-spatial and residential segregation.

The rest of the chapter is divided into XXX sections. The section that follows gives an analysis of T rural migration to urban settlements in México using the new rural and urban spatial distribution as framework. The second section discusses the theoretical framework that underpins the chapter. Evidences of mining towns´ shrinkage in México together with studies on firms related to shrinking cities are examined in the third section. Finally, the forth section concludes the chapter and set an agenda for future research.

RURAL MIGRATION

The displacements from rural areas to large urban centers are determined by the transformations of regional economies. The economic, social and political development of a country is manifested as the transformation of processes of modernization of a traditional society. The analysis of the distribution and concentration of the population is related to rural migration to urban areas due mainly, among other causes, to economic reasons to improve their material life. Economic development is related to the demographic behavior that influences social relations and forms of production.

Rural economies are considered incomplete economies because the conditions for sustained economic growth do not exist due to lack of intermediaries and rural financial markets. Ledent (1982) analyzes the behavior of the movements of the population from rural to urban areas showing that this mobility increases or decreases depending on economic development. Where the rural area is economically developed, the region experiences a decrease in the migration rate. Migration from rural areas to urban centers has been considered as the main trend of the last century in México. According to the INEGI (2010), a population is considered rural when it has less than 2 500 inhabitants while the urban one is where more than 2,500 people live. The process of rural development in Mexico has undergone profound transformations in such a way that they laid the foundations for the creation of conditions that allowed the spatial mobility of the rural population with rural migration to urban centers.

Rural migration flows have an effect on the structure and dynamics of the population. Rural migration is one of the components of demographic dynamics that modifies spatial relationships giving rise to population concentrations in urban and metropolitan areas. In the mobility of the population from rural areas to urban and metropolitan areas, the friction of distance is relevant. Rural-urban migration in Mexico has implications for the decrease in the rural population and growth in the urban population.

Rural migration is a tangible resource for farmers who aspire to obtain better levels of well-being. Among other reasons, the search for better economic income, development opportunities and improvement in the quality of life have motivated the spatial changes of rural migration (Hattion and Williamson,

2005, Boyle and Halfacree, 1998, Champion, 2001, Herrera, 2006; Seto, 2001). Rural migration to cities explains the functionality of the labor reserves that result from the transformations of economic processes in the accumulation of capital. The surplus labor force and low wages in the Mexican countryside are two causes for rural migration to urban centers where there are offers for better paid jobs. Rural migration to the big cities is the main escape valve to relax and relieve the pressure of the peasants to obtain the means of subsistence for their families as a result of the agrarian and rural policy. It must be considered that the means of subsistence of rural life, apart from the productivity of working in the countryside, are also wages, remittances and government subsidies. Therefore, rural migration is related to the size of the household, the number of children, age and occupation of the farmer (Reyes Morales and Gijón Cruz, 2007). Thus, labor mobility is related to social mobility (Savage, 1988) and is explained by the differentials in family income (Mathur et al, 1988; Aroca, 2004: 106).

The displacements of population between rural municipalities and urban and metropolitan areas are mostly made up of population with low educational levels described as regional selectivity of migration because it reinforces the inequalities and differences between rural, urban and metropolitan localities (Pérez and Santos, 2008). The population of rural areas that migrates to large cities is less qualified. The population that migrates from rural areas or has it as their destination have lower educational levels, lower job qualifications and are employed in low productivity sectors which contribute to the growth of the gap that separates socioeconomic development between the city and the field which, in turn, results in greater inequalities in patterns of regional divergence in Mexico. However, the net migratory balance is positive for rural municipalities.

Rural migration is explained in the economic rationality and the roles of heads of households in the family life cycle. From the economic perspective, migration processes are investments of human capital of rational agents that seek to maximize their benefits based on the returns and economic and emotional costs of the process (Aroca, 2004: 106-109; Yue, 2008). The incorporation of the life cycle to the analysis suggests that the heads of households that can emigrate are those that do not have children or are small and cannot be incorporated into work but that also have the support of the family or a network of friendships that can pay your mobilization expenses. The migration of rural households occurs more when there are more children, with parents above the average age who continue to cultivate their plot. The agrarian reform initiated in the thirties of the last century resulted in the intensification of rural migration to large cities, including Mexico City (Tomas 1997). The mobility of the population from rural to urban areas has a strong impact on the territorial expansion of large cities, as they are the result of changes in economic policy that have reconfigured demographic relations. As soon as the large cities receiving rural migration became congested, so the new solution to the problem was rural migration from Mexico to the United States which is regulated by the Bracero Program and subsequently illegalized (Reyes Morales 1999, Duhau & Schteingart 1997). Ladent (1982) asserts that the rate of rural migration to urban centers in Mexico reached its peak in the 1970s and 80s. During these periods, the Mexican population experienced high and sustained fertility rate, decrease in the mortality rate and spatial redistribution. All of these factors have contributed to the accelerated growth of migration in search of opportunities and therefore the urbanization of the country. This process of accelerated urbanization exceeded the limits of planning and presented many challenges to development despite sustained economic growth.

Migrations are carried out by individuals who were characterized as being young and in a greater proportion by women (Cabrera, 1970). In international migration, illegal migration is greater (Cornelius, 1978). Due to the constant migration of the countryside to the cities, the number of inhabitants of urban localities has been increasing while that of rural women decreasing. In Mexico, migration flow is from the rural population to the metropolitan areas and, at the international level, to the United States. The internal rural migration from the Agrarian and International Reform from the Bracero Program became the escape valve of the peasant laborers mainly to reach better levels of life and well-being. Rural-urban migration in Mexico has implications for the decrease in the rural population and growth in the urban population. In spite of the challenges involved in urban dynamism, it has always been the focus of attraction for the rural population migrating to the urban areas Mexico has its highest growth of urban population characterised by economic, political and demographic concentration in the large metropolitan areas of Mexico City, Guadalajara, Monterrey, Puebla, Leon, and Tijuana, among others and all of which are consolidated under the new economic model instrumented by economic neoliberal reforms. This pattern of spatial growth in metropolitan areas is related to migratory flows.

The economic diversification of the cities of the North and Bajío defines the migrant population in a different way to that of the cities of the South that have tertiarization of their economies (Chávez, 1999, Chávez and Galindo, 2006, Pérez, 2007). The accelerated and expansive growth of the urban and metropolitan areas of the North and Center of the country have reconfigured the destinies of the migratory flows coming from the rural zones that attempt to fit themselves into the labor markets of the agglomeration economies which require few labor qualifications.

The displacement of the rural population of Mexico to urban cities and to the North (i.e. the United States of America) is the result of growing inequalities in socioeconomic development and the creation of opportunities. Border metropolitan areas are those that receive a greater flow of migrants with low educational levels due to the demand of the labor market that requires low labor qualifications in sectors of low productivity. However, since the eighties of the last century, Mexico has been transformed by the implementation of structural reforms to the extent that it has modified the entire economic system that has had a strong impact on the rural population. The increase in rural migration in the 1980s is associated with economic policies focused on structural reforms that discouraged small rural production and forced peasants into wage labor and the use of remittances to improve their standard of living, the possibility of financing their basic food and preserving their community organization and culture.

The economic policies of structural adjustment initiated in the eighties in Mexico have transformed the rural economies, forcing the peasants to seek complementary alternatives to obtain economic resources to alleviate their subsistence needs and improve their living standards. The number of salaried persons in the household determines the number of migrant members as part of the negative implications of structural adjustment policies in rural areas. Similarly, the structural reforms, with the aid of the technologies used in the Mexican countryside, have produced labor surpluses with displacements of day laborers mainly migrating to seek insertion in other economic sectors to improve their wages. It can, therefore, be suggested that the instrumentation of structural reforms in Mexico has had economic, political and demographic concentration effects. Although the tendency of concentration is not entirely absolutely, the urban centers that have had a greater demographic growth as a result of the migration of the countryside are precisely the cities that have had a greater economic growth.

Furthermore, the implementation of the structural reforms in Mexico has transformed the spatial occupation of the population in Mexican territory (Chávez and Lozano, 2006) with concentration in 15 metropolitan areas with more than one million inhabitants. The growth of these metropolitan areas is due to changes in migratory flows brought about by the transformations of the economic model (Ariza and Ramírez, 2004, Sobrino, 2010). The increase in international rural migration has been the result of the implementation of economic policies of neoliberal structural adjustment that forces the peasants to look for employment that requires low qualification abounds in the United States.

Although the trend of mobility of the Mexican population between metropolitan areas stabilized in the nineties (Ariza and Ramírez 2004, Pérez and Santos 2008 and Sobrino 2010), the flow of migrants from the Mexican countryside to the cities increased. As a result, the tendency of the migratory growth has been reduced. Rural migration to urban centers has decreased while urban migration to other urban centers and metropolitan areas has increased (Cabrera, 1967, Sobrino, 2010).In the last two decades, the migratory movement from rural areas of Mexico to large urban centers has decreased compared to the migratory movements between urban and metropolitan areas (Perez Campuzano and Santos Cerquera, 2013). The rates of rural-urban migration, as well as the rural population, have decreased in the last two decades, making a difference from previous historical trends. Internal migration slowed in the last two decades of the last century compared to the accelerated phase they had in the sixties and seventies. This deceleration of internal migration is explained by the effects of the crisis of the eighties and the low economic growth of the nineties. With data from the population census of the year 2000, the migration of the population from rural areas to metropolitan areas was 6.7 percent and to urban areas it was 3.9 throwing a total of 10.7 percent. In the year 2000, the urban-rural flow was 21% while urban-urban was 64%, urban-rural flow was 11% and rural-rural flow was 4%. Therefore, there is a change in the main flow of migration from rural-urban to urban-urban and urban-rural. The currents with higher balances were from rural areas and small cities to intermediate cities and large cities. Intermediate cities and large cities received positive flows from rural migrants and small cities (Sobrino, 2014).

Rural-urban migration predominates in developing societies and, to the extent that they advance, the flow of migration decreases in absolute and relative terms. In the case of Mexico, with the decrease in rural-urban migration after 2000, the contribution to urbanization is less than natural growth. In the first decade of the 2000s, with an increase in the degree of urbanization, the rural population of Mexico is lower than in previous decades in absolute terms and this brings with it a reduction in rural migration. However, it should be considered that this tendency is due largely to the statistical treatment based on a reclassification of urban and rural localities. The 2000 General Population and Housing Census (INEGI) reports that 4.35% of all households received remittances with higher percentages in households in rural municipalities that have migrants working in Mexico's Urban Center or abroad. Therefore, access to the markets of rural households largely depends on the remittances received from migrants from rural households who do not have income from other agricultural activities. Remittances from migrants to their families are received in stores by 36.7% and in remittance companies by 19.9%. On the other hand, the Population Census of 2010 presented a migration of the population from rural areas to the metropolitan areas of 10.7 and to the urban areas of 5.3, yielding a total of 16 percent. In 2010 the rural-urban and rurual migration flows decreased and remained at to 16%, and 4% respectively while urban-urban and urban-rural flows increased to 67% and 13% respectively. (Sobrino, 2014).

The migratory flow from rural areas to the Metropolitan Zone of Mexico City is relevant so is the flow of those who migrate to other urban or rural areas. In 1970, migration was predominantly rural-urban. The states where the rural population predominates generated 55% of the total emigrant population in 1970, decreasing to 43% in 2010. The population growth rate 2000-2010 in rural communities and small cities was below the national average.

In developed countries like México, mobility from urban centers to rural areas has increased (Jones, 1990) in a movement that is de-concentrating the population (Champion, 1989, 2001; Long and Nuccy, 1997; Elliot, 1997; Boyle and Halfacree, 1998; Boyle et al., 1998; Johnson et al, 2005). As a result, large migration flows of the population living in rural areas dwarf numerically in absolute and relative terms, giving space to changes in the trends of population mobility at points that were previously attractors to extractors now. The main urban destinations of rural migration are also transformed into the main centers that expel population in inter-urban migration or from urban centers to rural areas. In Mexico,, with data from the National Institute of Statistics and Geography and taking into account the political-administrative territorial delimitations, in 2007 the Social Development Secretariat (SEDESOL) and the National Population Council (CONAPO) determined 56 metropolitan areas and urban municipalities that have at least one town with more than 15 thousand inhabitants and rural municipalities that have all their towns under 2 500 inhabitants.In 1900 only 6 percent of the total population was migrants compared to 18 percent in 2000. The population concentration in a small number of cities and the population dispersion in a large number of localities with less than 2500 inhabitants are two predominant phenomena of the population distribution in Mexico. The Population census of 2000 identified 196 thousand localities with less than 2500 inhabitants with a total of 24.6 million inhabitants. The localities of less than 2 500 inhabitants are characterized by various levels of geographical, economic, political and social marginalization. However, the percentage of people living in rural communities has decreased. In 1950 it represented just over 57% of the total population of the country; in 1990 it was 29 percent, and 22% in 2010. In 1950, just fewer than 43% of the population in Mexico lived in urban areas as against 71% in 1990. By 2010, this figure increased to almost 78%. From 2010 to 2015, migrants who returned forcefully or voluntarily from the United States to rural locations represented 29% of the total population. In 2016, it was estimated that 12 million Mexican migrants resided in the United States of America (CONAPO, 2017)

With the low rates of economic growth, urban centers lose the economic and demographic attractiveness for rural migration. Migrants from rural areas are attracted by the opportunities of medium-sized cities (Geyer, 1996) when the diseconomies of large cities are presented according to the approaches of differential urbanization (Geyer and Kontuly, 1993) and the transition of mobility (Zelinsky, 1971). The territorial areas that experience decrease in their economic activities are also those that begin to experience demographic decrease due to the need of the population to seek better sources of resources to improve their living standards. In other words, the socioeconomic development of a region is related to migration phenomena. The demographic consolidation of urban centers and the geographic distribution of the population has been the result of changes in the composition of migration that is manifested in a decrease in rural migration and an increase in intra and inter-metropolitan migration. The rural population has decreased the migratory flow to the large cities while the migration from the middle cities to the rural communities is relevant.

Rural migration will continue to exist as long as the current conditions that result from the implementation of neoliberal economic policies continue. Neoliberal structural adjustment policies aimed at the agricultural sector of the Mexican countryside only try to avoid outbreaks of peasant and rural social movements.

NEW RURAL AND URBAN SPATIAL DISTRIBUTION

There are compelling evidences suggesting the presence of a clear negative correlation between the percentage growth of urban population and rural population. More precisely, the negative relationship relate to evidences for rural dispersion, instability and heterogeneity of population. In the case of Mexico, in 1995 more than 10 million people lived in almost 185 thousand localities with less than 500 inhabitants (CONAPO, 1999 Rubalcava, 2001). Thse studies concluded that the instability of these localities which increased dramatically between 1990 and 1995 were related to historical patterns of mobility for survival purposes. However, the tendency of rural – urban transference is changing nowadays. The intensity of transference of rural people to the large cities in México has an inverse relation to the urbanization levels. This means that in the near future large cities like Mexico City, Guadalajara, Monterrey, Puebla, León, among others, will have some shrinking areas as is already occurring in the downtown and commercial oriented zones of these cities due to changing of soil use.

Following the overall crisis of the Mexican economy in the early 1980s and mid 1990s and the restructuring and liberalization that ensued, a large number of smaller establishments were forced to close down as they could not keep up with foreign competitors. In parallel to these processes of de-industrialization, Mexico City has experienced uneven economic growth, stagnation and decline of formal economy, shrinkage of formal retail in relative terms, and the counterpart to this growth at the top has been the spread of micro businesses and the unprecedented expansion of the informal sector (Potkin, 2002). Even though Mexico City still represents the largest concentration of industrial activities in Mexico, the significance of this sector in the local economy has decreased significantly over the past few decades and the tertiary sector has become the driving force of the regional economy. The problematic transition of Mexico City has produced an increasingly fragmented metropolis evidencing signs of special unevenness and territorial disjointedness with the majority of the inhabitants of Mexico City stay at home rather than use the city in their free time. However, the persistence gravitation of Mexico City, although it registers natural growth rate of population below the national average is explained by sustainable immigration.

A generalized and enduring economic crisis is marked by an absence of local alternatives of employment and conditions of limited economic options. Every year, around 1.2 million people need to be incorporated to the labor force. However, in recent years, as a response to a new socioeconomic scenario, other new forms of population mobility have appeared differentiated from the traditional migration such as temporal, cyclical, seasonal and periodical movements related to the rural component. Population movements directed toward the internal frontiers or colonization's fronts attract young people and have been characterized in great proportion by being temporal. Some colonization areas suddenly experienced notable growth in rural population for a period of time, but suddenly shrunk (Reboratti, 1992 y 1990). People involved in these displacements moves from one front to a new one are always looking to improve living conditions and higher returns. Most of these displacements are caused by the effects of the new economic activities such as tourism and recreation, seasonal exports, mining and are always functions of labor flexibility that characterizes temporal agriculture activities. Some Mexican cities are considered artifacts of globalization linked to life styles and increasing global network of demographic and economic relationships as it is the case of Cancun, Acapulco, Vallarta, Mazatlán, Los Cabos, among others. Cancún in Quintana Roo registers important immigration associated to the tourism expansion. A similar situation is observed in large cities in states near the United States border such as Baja California, Sonora, Chihuahua, Coahuila, Tamaulipas and Nuevo León. These cities are already inserted in global economic and production processes. The ongoing economic globalization process is reinforcing the border economies of Mexico because of their privileged position for commercial exchange. As a result, Tijuana is the fastest growing city in México. On the other hand, in Central and Southern Mexican states, which have important concentrations of rural and indigenous populations, small concentrations of young people are registered. There is tendency that this trend will continue for years to come. Young people will have more relative representation in the urban than in rural environment in the future. However, the percentage of young urban population and the total urban population is almost close, probably as product of major urbanization processes.

Mexico City's development in the global economy is considerably vulnerable due to its lack of resilience to macroeconomic shifts and its dependent position within the international urban hierarchy. The globalized enclaves of Mexico City are functionally and territorially disconnected from the rest of the city where the most alarming sign of urban change manifests itself in the form of enormous swelling of the informal economy. From the perspective of territorial occupancy, there are manifestations of new forms of residential segregation patterns since the economic crisis of 1980, although it is an old phenomenon and not exclusive of México. In 1970, there were 4000 of these closed urbanizations and by 1996; the number has risen to 100,000.

The literature on structure of intra urban neighborhoods, colonies and suburban areas has identified opposing forces, although is marked by the real estate market behavior and population policies. Sometimes, these policies and market behavior imply the programmed virtual displacement of poor families to get rid of them from the wealthy residential areas (Villa y Rodríguez, 1997). In Mexico, while the middle class is impoverishing, the higher class looks for closed urbanizations in protected areas. Gated communities legitimize residential segregation, increase inequality and polarization of cities. The sprawling and fragmented Mexican large cities face the challenges to reintegrate the mosaic of segregated settlements and built typologies. However, they responded adequately to the mounting needs for housing and urban space which not only alleviate the still increasing housing shortage but also help at controlling metropolitan expansion. By reinforcing the existing segregation pattern of a rich west and south and a poor north and east, they are the new face of today's urban sprawl in Mexico City's metropolitan area (Potkin, 2002).

INSUFFICIENCY OF POLICIES

Research on the relationship between the emergence of small locations and communities and the economic problems of the Mexican country has been scanty over the last decade. Mexico has witnessed an increment of dispersed population in smaller rural communities and shrinkage of larger communities which put pressure on the provision of infrastructure and utilities. The dispersion of rural locations and communities had also increased in terms of poverty and internal exodus. The absence, discontinuity and quality of data on natural growth do not allow assessing correctly the future scenarios.

From the geographical perspective, the spatial concentration of these small settlements takes place in territories that have poor accessibility and a weak functional integration to important central locations. Considering the high supply costs of basic utilities to benefit all the communities, and the extreme poverty conditions of people living there, there is the need for more productive strategies toward the improvement of economic and social conditions. Another serious problem is population pressure on nonrenewable scarce resources such as water, forest, and soil, among others, related to food capacity. Greater concentration of population in a rural community diminishes the cultivable land per capita and gradually leads to supplies being sought in other regions. In this sense, the greater the urban concentrations, higher the environmental deterioration as it is the case with Central part and the Northern border line of Mexico. A good number of studies on the environmental consequences of future trends of population distribution are conducted on fragile and high vulnerable ecosystems (Gómez de León y Rabell Romero, 2001: 595).

One of the important population policies of the Mexican government is the desired for the achievement of population - territory equilibrium through programs for medium size cities such as public management decentralization, health and education services decentralization and municipal promotion. There is a territorial valorization in the strategies targeted to promote economic growth and policies to combat territorial mechanisms that reproduce poverty such as the Progresa-oportunidades program in México.

Policies as instruments for intervention must have as objectives sustainable exploit of territorial potentialities, reduced social exclusion and avoidance of natural catastrophic disasters. The dramatic effects of natural disasters are devastating and require territorial ordering plans to avoid human settlements in areas of high risks to prevent possible threats. There are not empirical evidences suggesting that the free operation of market leads naturally to better process of spatial redistribution of population and economic development. On the contrary, there is a wide consensus that the market failures can cause more troubles than solutions. Public policies are necessary to create incentives, for the transparency of costs, to compensate externalities, to avoid asymmetric information and imperfect competency in order to develop programs of territorial distribution of population and promotion of programs for sustainable economic, social and political development.

HISTORICAL APPROACHES AND RESOURCE BASED THEORY

Literature on the analysis of case studies recounting the rise and fall of mining cities and towns in Mexico strongly depend the mining firms. However, Most of these studies are historical and sociological recounts and are not necessarily sustained by a specific theoretical framework. Specifically, most of the case studies are not historiography based but instead historic interpretation, and more closely, economic history. Their limitations and the risk of misinterpretations depend of the analyses done by the historians regarding the history of mining in Mexico and the colonial history. The method of historic exploration used is the revision and compilation of studies related to the topic of shrinking cities, which have been interpreted under the optic of historic materialism, procuring to show the contradictions that characterized the mining activities as part of the colonial exploitation scheme. With the theory development of second contradiction of capitalism, O´Connor (2001) asserts that economic growth since the industrial revolution has been achieved at expensive costs for the autonomy of human communities and for the natural environment.

The resource based theory may offer a framework to further the study and research of these historical and sociological recounts in the field of shrinking cities. Resource-based theory provides the framework to explain how organizations achieve sustainable competitive advantages. A resource is a kind of production factor which is at the firms' disposal, that is, each one is controlled by the firm in spite of having no property right to it. Additionally, any resource is able to create a competitive advantage if it has certain features. Resource based theory treats enterprises as potential creators of value-added capabilities. The theory focuses on the idea of costly-to-copy attributes of the firm as sources of business returns and the means to achieve superior performance and competitive advantage (Barney, 1986; Hamel and Prahalad, 1996). As Grover Grover, Teng, and Cheon (1998:84) explain: "the essence of a resource-based theory is that given resource heterogeneity and resource immobility and satisfaction of the requirement of value, rareness, imperfect inimitability, and non-substitutability, firms' resources can be a source of sustained competitive advantage". One of the objectives of the theory is to appreciate why competences can be perceived as a firms' most valuable asset and, at the same time, to understand how those assets can be used to improve business performance. Undervaluing urban areas can unwittingly place the economic and social futures of countries at risk.

The historic roots of the urban profile are found in the logic of the conquerors that valuated urban localization for the achievement of economic, political and ideological objectives. During the colonial period in México, mining was the gravitational sector of socio economic development inserted in the primary extracting and export scheme logic under the metropolitan- periphery colonial dependency context of the capitalism in transition from the bilateral mercantilism to the multilateral industrial capital. The local economies of the different Mexican regions were more obedient to transnational interests during the different stages of development: Colonialism, economic liberalism, industrialization by import substitution and the neoliberal regimes.

The metal orientation mentality of the Spaniards is going to be the main reason of population mobility toward the exploration of new territories to find the silver and gold mines. The Iberian migrants had the mentality that the wealth was given by God through the precious metals and not as the product of work. The discovery of silver deposits in Zacatecas in 1546 is the first colonial antecedent that started the population mobilizations to form new settlements near the mines. Other natural deposits of gold and silver were discovered in Chihuahua and lately in San Luis Potosi. The Northern region of Mexico was populated and a heavy transit and traffic followed between this places and the metropolis México City.

The disarticulated internal economic structure has been more oriented toward the exploitation of natural resources more for the transnational capital than for the welfare of the Mexican population and its demographic development. Numerous cities, towns and villages were founded under this logic. When the economic gravitational centers moved to the Northern countries, following the interests of the international economic structure these cities and towns declined and shrunk, showing that the colonial heritage is the development of underdevelopment. Today, most of these affluent and wealthy cities are ghost towns or have already disappeared. These are analysis of case studies in the literature of shrinking cities, towns and villages.

The successful periods of mining exploitations are related to the population growth and the increase of economic development of the mining cities and towns. During these successful periods, distinct clusters emerged against which patterns of factors could be distinguished that appeared to account for the variations in successful adoption in the firms studied. To explain these findings a number of theories can be initially considered, but building on the recent work of others cited above, resource-based theory appears to offer possible explanations, given that the determinant factors identified are both clearly associated with the internal contexts of the firms. Moreover, resource-based theory argues that sustained advantage results from unique attributes of a firm developed over time – therefore it could explain why some firms had evolved to become more successful than others in this context.

Vargas-Hernández (2007) analyzes the shrinkage of mining towns in Mexico which are going through a shrinking and declining processes after having an enormous impact in economic development. This shrinking process of the mining towns posits a trap and a dilemma in economic development: From being ghost towns, at the turning point the inhabitants are mobilizing to defend historical and cultural heritage and environmental survival from the mining companies and to find alternative activities such as cultural tourism which may bring the needed resources.

THE EVIDENCE OF THE MINING TOWNS' SHRINKAGE IN MÉXICO

Mining had a tremendous importance to Mexico's economy. The mining industry was an economic indicator during the colonial times in Mexico. Since the pre-Hispanic times, mining has played an important role in political and economic history of Mexico. Spanish colonizers were attracted by the rich mines and with the discovery of new ones. The mining activity was the incentive for the foundation of new villages and towns far away from the large cities and with difficult access. Houses were built with adobes covered with tejamanil on the slopes of the mountains and between a dark and dense fog, without any order or sense of space according to the needs of the mines (Flores Clair, 1997). These new villages and towns were populated and had grown until reach the status of cities during the colonial times.

Starting from the discovery of the first mine in the Nueva España in 1532 it followed a giddy exploitation of precious metals all over the territory. In 1546, in the Hill of La Bufa of the State of Zacatecas, the process of colonization started centered in the indicator the location of gold and silver as the mineral resources to be exploited. The precious metal oriented mentality of the Spanish conquerors was the main cause of population mobility in the exploration of new territories and the foundation of new towns and villages mainly in the highlands (Zacatecas, Chihuahua, San Luis Potosí, etc.) and lowlands (El Bajío, Guanajuato, etc.) around the mines of gold and silver. In 1564 the mines of Guanajuato initiated activities followed by a massive migration to populate Guanajuato and the Bajío. The productive schema of Guanajuato was linked to the mining production by providing the necessary goods and services to Zacatecas and further to the North. The scattered Haciendas (Ranchs), villages and towns founded in the El Bajío were the economic units that produced the goods and services supplied. Mining activities had a sustainable growth before 1600 when the towns and villages also grew and some achieved the status of cities, such as Zacatecas and Guanajuato.

During the XVI Century, the populated areas were concentrated around the mining centers, congregations and haciendas, according to the economic activities restricted by the physical territory and oriented toward the agricultural production for self-consumption and mining for the export of gold and silver to Spain not for commercial purposes but to accumulate and treasure. The mining sector was the gravitational center of the colonial productive scheme. Villages, towns and cities founded followed this logic and also began to shrink when the mines lower or stopped production. The demographic catastrophe of the XVI and XVII Centuries caused a scarcity of manpower and the shrinking of mining cities and towns. The Crown protected the indigenous of what was considered inhuman works, such as mining, agricultural activities, and other industrial jobs. This protection to the indigenous people caused that goods and services were expensive, and thus spoliation had to be used. The indigenous population is substituted by Afro-Caribbean people who were introduced to México. The mining development established a sustainable demographic growth until the beginning of the years 1620-30 when the crisis started due to the insufficient supply of mercury necessary for the exploitation of silver. Mining cities, towns and villages also began to shrink.

There were no regulations over the civil population in the mining cities and towns. At the middle of the XVI Century, exploitation of prolific seams was the main cause of the emergence of mining towns spread all over the New Spain territory. Most of these became cities of great economic and social importance, among them Pachuca, Hidalgo, Parral, etc. The exploitation of precious metals that had achieved an outstanding growth by the end of the XVI Century represented more than 80% of total exports from the Nueva España (Estrada, 2001). Around the activities of the mining industry were the motor of the economy around which it had emerged other economic activities which provided employment, allowed commercial trade with the metropolis and gave rise to prosperity in the mining towns and cities.

There are many issues regarding the economic history of México to explain. One of these issues is the debate on the decay of the Mexican economic in the XVII and XVIII Centuries. One of the arguments has been the mining production. There is no economic evidence to prove the hypothesis that mining in Mexico had a profound crisis during the XVIII Century and also the parameters used to sustain are not the right data (Ibarra, 1995). Production of silver was multiplied for four times through the XVIII Century. To understand and comprehend the meaning of the colonial mining activity, Galeano has said: En Potosí the silver built temples and palaces, monasteries and gambling dens, offered motive to tragedy and the feast, spilled over blood and wine, inflamed greed and untied squandering and adventure (Ibarra, 1995). Life in mining cities became harsh and troubled, all type of contrasts, ambitions, concupiscence and disorder are manifested with harshness.

The decline of the mining industry originated in 1810 although it is questionable the cause: the movement of the Mexican independence and the lack of stable political and social institutions. With the independence of Mexico in 1821, the colonial production scheme based on mining lost the relevant economic role. Mining cities, towns and villages shrunk. The mining activities lost their impulse avoiding to lead an industrial revolution in México. However, during the second half of the last Century, the decline of the mining activities brought also a shrinking process of the mining cities to the level of converting them in ghost towns. It was until the era of Porfirio Diaz (1880-1910) that the mining activities had a modest growth exploited by English and American mining companies, insufficient to provide work for the expansive growth of populated areas. Recent changes in Mexican legislation have liberalized the mining sector and after the opening of North America Free Trade Agreement (NAFTA) foreign companies have increased investments.

In Mexico, some early mining towns faded into obscurity while others became centers for ranching and commerce but were abandoned after the declining of mining activities. Mining towns, containing rich Baroque architecture, generally located in mountain areas, did not follow the geometric layout but were adapted to the topographic condition of the sites. The conquest of northwest Mexico lead to the establishment, during colonial times, of towns located on the Sierra Madre Occidental where mining was the main economic activity. The State of Sonora in the northwest of Mexico is wealthy in mineral resources. It is the first producer of gold and also produces silver, cooper, and other metals. After the opening of NAFTA, more than 70 foreign mining companies have established offices in Hermosillo the capital of the State. During the XVI century, exploitation of mines located around Guadalupe de los Reyes, San José de las Bocas and Cosalá started. Cosalá was founded in 1562 and became in the XIX century the most important in this region, and in 1898 it produced 50% of the silver exported by the State of Sinaloa. Among the outstanding mining towns in the North of Mexico are La Bufa, Batopilas, Cerro Colorado, the Raramuri communities of Munérachi, La Yerbabuena, and the Jesuit mission of Satevó with important mining centers as Urique, Maguarichi, Uruachi and Ocampo, Batopilas and the veins of La Bufa reached renown of a world level. Batopilas has preserved, to a great extent, its architectural heritage from the richness of those times. In its greatest mining period at the end of the 19th century, Batopilas had up to 7,000 inhabitants. Today, the town is a community of 800 inhabitants.

The mining towns Concepción del Oro y Mazapil were far away from Real de Minas Zacatecas. In 1569, Mazapil had around 150 Spanish settlers. Both mining towns achieved economic relevance in the Province of Nueva Vizcaya during the XVII y XVIII. However, today both cities are ignored by the maps of México. In the Northeast of México, the first foundations such as San Gregorio (1577) y La Trinidad (1577) were based on the discovery of silver mines. The mines of La Iguana were discovered in 1757 near Lampazos. Similarly, Mineral de Pozos (a rough translation might be Mineral Wells) is an old mining town in the State of Guanajuato, founded in 1576, when it was built a Fort to protect the silver route, from Zacatecas to México City. During the XIX Century, the town had large periods of abandonment due to the armed movements. It became one of the richest of the colonial mining towns, reaching its peak about 1890. As 20th-century revolution closed, the town fell into poverty. Currently, Pozos is gradually reawakening from a small village trapped in the abandonment after being a prosperous city during the mining exploitation. Everywhere in the paved streets can be seen semi destroyed large colonial adobe homes and dismantled buildings that once before were sumptuous. The town was decleared in 1982 as Historic Monument of the Nation. From a population of more than 70,000, it shrank to less than 4,000 10 years ago. Today, the 8 thousand remaining inhabitants lived in misery.

San Sebastian in the State of Jalisco is one of the oldest mining towns in Mexico founded in 1605 and reached the highest rate of growth and prosperity during the 17th and 18th Centuries when more than 20, 000 inhabitants populated the town. The population fluctuated in relation to the production of gold until 1930. Nowadays, it has only 600 inhabitants retaining the colonial heritage in public buildings and houses, as an extraordinary example of the traditional living forms of labor in a remote village. Similarly, Real de Arriba in the State of Mexico is an enchanting mining town with a splendorous past. Today, some of the remaining walls and rocks within the forest are ruins that remind us of the great colonial miners' homes and infrastructure buildings which witnessed the past economic boom of the area. The city of el Oro de Hidalgo also in the State of Mexico were considered the second richest just after Transvaal, in Africa and still now shows the wealthy architecture of its mining past. Its Museum shows mineral from the mines La Esperanza, Chihuahua, Tiro México, Tiro Skip, La Calera, La Providencia, San Patricio, El Nolan, El Consuelo, La Victoria, Santo Domingo y La Aurora.

The mining district of Pachuca-Real del Monte and El Chico in the second half of the XVIII Century, the most prosperous period, has been studied by Navarrete (2004). Real del Monte received its name in 1577. An anonymous source mentions that there were 1,300 inhabitants at the end of the XVI Century. In 1610, there were 1,683 inhabitants. At the end of the XVII Century the traveler Giovanni Francesco Gemelli Carreri calculated 12, 000 inhabitants. Using parish church data of 1768, which only registered population in communion, he estimated that Real Del Monte achieved its largest population around the middle of the XVIII Century and it started a gradual drop until it reached its lowest point at the end of the first decade in the XIX Century. Real del Monte produced 10% of the silver of the Nueva Spain (Hausberger, 1995) and had a population of 7, 152 inhabitants.

The military census of 1791 reported that the Jurisdiction of Pachuca had a population of 9,615 inhabitants out of which 26.7% or 2567 persons forming 608 families belonged to Real del Monte, although the Census did not consider indigenous people, women and children under 16 years old. After 1824, Real del Monte changed its name to Mineral del Monte. In 1858 the population of Mineral del Monte was around 6,000 inhabitants and in the Census of 1854 registered 5,310. In 1865 a Census of men older than 18 years registered 1,005 hombres integrated to 700 families. Comparing the data of the Censuses of 1791 and 1865, the number of inhabitants was almost similar, which lead us to conclude that for around 7 decades the growth of population was almost null. Very good examples of these trends are Charcas, Real de Catorce, Guadalcazar y Cerro de San Pedro in San Luis Potosi, ghost towns that once were important mining cities. Nowhere in Mexico are the changing styles and fortunes of former gold and silver mining towns better displayed than in these four towns. Charcas was refunded in 1584 and had produced more than 3 million dollars' worth of silver each year.

Today, only a few old buildings and large stoned houses survived. Real de Catorce had a grandeur past with gorgeous buildings, outstanding church and beautiful Palenque. In Guadalcazar, the miners built two magnificent churches and a Casa de Moneda was founded. Cerro de San Pedro is now a ghost town where handful of old buildings has been restored reluctant to completely relinquish their hold over real estate. San Pedro, founded in 1592, was abandoned about fifty years ago.

ANALYSIS OF CASE STUDIES ON RESOURCE BASED FIRMS RELATED TO SHRINKING CITIES

There are case studies that analyze the relationships between resource based firms and the shrinking of cities, more specifically the so called "corporative city" and "Corporative town". One of such studies analyzed the environmental economic development shrinkage of Atenquique after the industrial boom of the paper mill during the second half of the last Century (Vargas-Hernandez, 2007). The town of Atenquique was settled down and grew up in terms of population, social and economic development in the same proportion that the Industrial Company of Atenquique did during the period when the company was property owned by the Mexican State. After the Company was privatized, the town started declining and shrinking in population, social and economic development, and the most disastrous aspect is the environmental hazards. The turning point of this increasing regional development was a conflict between the Union and the new owners of the Company, which represents a struggle for the survival of the old project of development welfare State oriented and the new hegemonic project, the neoliberal model of development.

The impact on the environmental and economic development has initiated the shrinking and declining of Atenquique but also of the surrounding cities and towns, while the new owners are increasing the levels of productivity and profitability. Therefore, in order to relate the findings to the core tenets of resource-based theory the focus of the analysis of the case study evidence should be contrasted where appropriate between the successful firm and the shrinkage of the town.

AN AGENDA FOR FUTURE RESEARCH

Further research on shrinking cities should be conducted in México. Some of the important issues and problems to set an agenda for future research in Mexico are:

Development of a simple hypothesis may be suggesting patterns of spatial redistribution of population. Research should provide conceptual frameworks for the analysis of relocation processes of economic activities in relation to the spatial redistribution of population to achieve more sustainable productive, economic and demographic dynamics through generation of employment.

The increasing flows of migration from rural areas to urban settlements open new challenges for research on tendencies related to residential localization and displacement of population, intra urban segmentation, socioeconomic territorial segmentation, and contra-tendencies such as suburbanization of high income groups in rural areas, etc.

Research on rural labor market and urban labor market should be conducted to analyze the impact on spatial redistribution of population. This analysis should consider the effects of erosion that represents the best qualified people who move from rural communities' settlements to large cities or to other country, leaving behind children an old people.

CONCLUSION

This chapter analyzes the link between the rural-urban migration and shrinkage transformation. Social and economic stagnation of rural areas cannot continue being postponed as the main cause responsible for the accelerated urbanization process, despite the innumerable signals of exhaustion and overuse of absorption capacity of cities and the emergent phenomena of local identity projects and dynamism should be recognized. Rehabilitation of inner areas in large cities may improve their living conditions and contribute greatly to social cohesion. Integrated preservation may have an impact on economic development and fosters employment through small scale business development.

REFERENCES

Ariza, M., & Ramírez, J. M. (2004). *Urbanización, mercados de trabajo y escenarios sociales en el México finisecular.* Princeton University.

Aroca, P. (2004). Migración interregional en Chile, modelos y resultados, 1987-1992. Notas de Población, 31(78).

Barney, J. (1986). Strategic factor markets: Expectations, luck and business strategy. *Management Science, 32*(10), 1231–1241. doi:10.1287/mnsc.32.10.1231

BBVA Bancomer the National Population Council (CONAPO). (2017). *Anuarion of migration and b remittances 2017. Yearbook of migration and remittances.* Available at: https://www.bbva.com/es/mexico-segundo-pais-mas-migrantes-mundo-12-3-millones/

Boyle, P. y Halfacree, K. (1998). *Migration into rural areas.* John Wiley and Sons.

Boyle, P., Halfacree, K., & Robinson, V. (1998). *Exploring contemporary migration.* Longman.

Cabrera, G. (1970). Selectividad por edad y sexo de los migrantes en México, 1930-1960, en Demografía y Economía, 4(12).

Castells, M. (2002). La ciudad en la nueva economía. *Tareas, 110*, 6-21.

Celade-Fnuap. (2000). *Juventud, población y desarrollo en América Latina y el Caribe. Problemas, oportunidades y desafíos. Centro Latinoamericano y Caribeño de Demografía (CELADE).* Santiago de Chile.

Champion, T. (1989). *Counterurbanization. The changing pace and nature of population deconcentration.* Routledge.

Champion, T. (2001). A changing demographic regime and evolving poly-centric urban regions: consequences for the size, composition and distribution of city populations. Urban Studies, 38(4).

Chávez, A. (1999). *La nueva dinámica de la migración interna en. Centro Regional de Investigaciones Multidisciplinarias/Universidad Nacional Autónoma de México.* Cuernavaca, México: CRIM/UNAM.

Chávez, A., & Lozano, F. (2006). *Género, migración y regiones. Centro Regional de Investigaciones Multidisciplinarias/Universidad Nacional Autónoma de México.* Cuernavaca, México: CRIM/UNAM.

CONAPO (Consejo Nacional de Población). (1999). *La situación demográfica en México, 1999.* México, D.F., México: CONAPO.

Cook, S. F., & Borah, W. (1980). Ensayos sobre historia de la población (México y California). T. III. Ed. Siglo XXI. Colección Nuestra América No. 29.

Cornelius, W. A. (1978). La migración ilegal mexicana a Estados Unidos: conclusiones de investigaciones recientes, imülica-ciones políticas y prioridades de investigación. Foro internacional, 18(17).

Duhau, E., & Schteingart, M. (1997). La urbanización popular en la Ciudad de México. In Pobreza, condiciones de vida y salud en la Ciudad de México (pp. 29-42). El Colegio de México.

Elliot, J. R. (1997). Cycles within the system: metropolisation and internal migration in the U.S. 1965-1990. Urban Studies, 34(1).

Estrada, A. (2001). *Impactos de la inversión canadiense en México: Una primera aproximación*. Fundar.

Flores Clair, E. (1997). Minería y población. Dimensión Antropològica, 11.

Geyer & Kontuly. (1993). A Theoretical Foundation for the Concept of Differential Urbanisation. *International Regional Science Review*, *17*(2), 157-177.

Geyer, H. (1996). Expanding the Theoretical Foundation of the Concept of Differential Urbanisation. *Tijdschrift voor Economische en Sociale Geografie*, *87*(1), 44-59.

Grover, V., Teng, J., & Cheon, M. (1998). Towards a theoretically-based contingency model of information systems outsourcing. In L. Willcocks & M. Lacity (Eds.), *Strategic Sourcing of Information Systems* (pp. 79–101). Chichester, UK: Wiley.

Hamel, G., & Prahalad, C. (1996). Competing for the Future. Harvard Business School Press.

Hatton, T., & Williamson, J. G. (2005). *Global migration and the world economy: two centuries of policy and performance*. Cambridge, MA: MIT Press.

Hausberger, B. (1995). La minería novohispana vista a través de los libros de cargo y data de la Real Hacienda. *Estudios de Historia Novohispana*, *15*, 36-66.

Herrera, R. (2006). La perspectiva teórica en el estudio de las migraciones. siglo XXI editores.

Hongchen, Y. (2008). *Three essays on internal migration. Tesis para optar por el Grado de Doctor en Fisología*. Universidad de Manitoba.

Ibarra, D. G. (1995). *Minería en México durante el Siglo XVIII ¿Auge o decadencia? Estudios*. Filososìa-historia-letras. Otoño.

INEGI. (2000). *General Population and Housing Census*. INEGI.

INEGI. (2010). *Volumen y crecimiento. Población total según tamaño de localidad para cada entidad federativa*. INEGI.

INEGI. (2010). *Volume and growth Total population by size of locality for each state*. INEGI.

Johnson, K., Nucci, A., & Long, L. (2005). Population trends and nonmetropolitan America: selective deconcentration and the rural rebound. Populaiton Research Policy, 24(5).

Jones, H. R. (1990). A population geography. Sage Publications Limited (Ltd).

Ledent, J. (1982). Rural-urban migration, urbanization and economic development. *Economic Development and Cultural Change*, *30*(3), 507–503. doi:10.1086/452574

León & Romero. (Eds.). (2001). *La población de México. Tendencias y perspectives demográficas hacia el Siglo XXI*. Consejo Nacional de Población-Fondo de Cultura Económica.

Long, L., & Nucci, A. (1997). The 'clean break' revisited: Is the U.S. population again deconcentrating. Environment and Planning, 29(8).

Mathur, V. K., & Stein y Kumar, S. H. R. (1988). A dynamic model of regional population growth and decline. Journal of Regional Science, 28(3).

Navarrete, D. (2004). Población y estructura ocupacional minera: Real del Monte en 1768. *II Congreso de Historia Económica Ciudad Universitaria.*

O'Connor, J. (2001). *Causas Naturales. Ensayo de marxismo ecológico*. Siglo XXI Editores.

Pérez, E. (2007). Transformación urbano-regional y migración de clases medias de la Ciudad de México hacia Querétaro. Alteridades, 17(34).

Pérez, E., & Santos, C. (2008). Urbanización y migración entre ciudades, 1995-2000. Un análisis multinivel. Papeles de Población, 14(56).

Perez Campuzano, E., & Santos Cerquera, C. (2013). Recent trends in internal migration in Mexico. Recent migratory tendencies in Mexico. Population Papers, 19(76).

Potkin, K. (2002). The incredibly shrinking cities. Convinced the world's urban populations are growing beyond control? Not so fast... *The Republic, 50.*

Reboratti, C. (1990). *Fronteras agrarias en América Latina*. Retrieved from www.ub.es/geocrit/sv-26.htm

Reboratti, C., (1992). Fronteras agrarias y población en América Latina International Union for the Scientific Study of Population (IUSSP). *El poblamiento de las Américas, Actas, 4*, 333-352.

Reyes Morales, R. G. (1999). Comparación socioeconómica de seis colonias populares de la ciudad de Oaxaca. *Alteridades (El Parque)*, *17*, 11–22.

Reyes Morales, R. G., & Gijón Cruz, A. S. (2007). Rural development, international migration and shortage of financial markets in Mexico. *Trace*, *52*, 45-62.

Rubalcava, L. N. (2001). *Localidades y hogares en un mundo de propensiones*. documento presentado en el seminario internacional: Las diferentes expresiones de la vulnerabilidad social en América Latina y el Caribe, Santiago, CELADE/CEPAL.

Ruiz Chiapetto, C. (1999). Population and rural migrations in Mexico: Hypothesis for another century (vol. 2). Academic Press.

Ruiz Chiapetto, C. (1999). Población y migraciones rurales en México: Hipótesis para otro siglo (vol. 2). Academic Press.

Savage, M. (1988). The missing link? The relationship between spatial mobility and social mobility. British Journal of Sociology, 30(4).

Seto, K. (2011). Exploring the dynamics of migration to mega-delta cities in Asia and Africa: Contemporary drivers and future scenarios. Global Environmental Change, 2.

Sobrino, J. (2014). Internal migration and size of locality in Mexico. *Demographic and Urban Studies, 3*(87), 443–479.

Sobrino, J. (2014). Migración interna y tamaño de localidad en México. *Estudios Demográficos y Urbanos, 3*(87), 443–479.

Sobrino, L. J. (2010). Migración urbana. In *La situación demográfica en México*. CONAPO.

Tomas, F. (1997). Acerca de un nuevo modelo de regularización de los asentamientos irregulares de la Ciudad de México. In El acceso de los pobres al suelo urbano (pp. 233-242). IIS-Universidad Nacional Autónoma de México, PUEC, CEMCA.

Vargas-Hernández, J. G. (2006). *Trapped development: the shrinkage of mining town Mexico. The Cerro de San Pedro Case*. Working Paper. Instituto Tecnológico de Cd. Guzmán.

Vargas-Hernández, J. G. (n.d.). Economic and environmental shrinkage of Atenquique. Instituto tecnológico de Cd. Guzmán, Jalisco.

Villa, M., & Rodríguez, J. (1997). *Dinámica sociodemográfica de las metrópolis Latinoamericanas durante la segunda mitad del siglo XX. Notas de Población, Año XXV, n° 65*. Santiago: Centro Latinoamericano de Demografía, Celade.

Zelinsky, W. (1971). The Hypothesis of the Mobility Transition. Geographical Review, 61(2), 219-249.

KEY TERMS AND DEFINITIONS

Countryside: A countryside is a broad land with land that is used for farming.

Mexican: Relating to Mexico, country of North America, or its inhabitants.

Migration: Population movement that consists of leaving the place of residence to settle in another country or region, usually for economic or social reasons.

Rural: Of the field and of the own works of the agriculture and the cattle ranch.

Shrinkage: Reduce the extent, intensity, or number of something.

Transformation: Action to transform or changing.

Chapter 11
A Technology Assessment of Renewable Energy Potentials in Nigeria:
University Academia Perspective

Yusuf Opeyemi Akinwale
https://orcid.org/0000-0003-3955-2606
Imam Abdulrahman Bin Faisal University, Saudi Arabia

Ibikunle Olalekan Ogundari
Obafemi Awolowo University, Nigeria

Adeyemi Oluwaseun Adepoju
https://orcid.org/0000-0002-2841-8092
Federal University of Technology Akure, Nigeria

John-Felix Kayode Akinbami
Obafemi Awolowo University, Nigeria

ABSTRACT

Science, technology, and innovation (STI) has become a significant factor in driving several sectors towards economic growth and development in many economies. There are several possibilities of usage for renewable energy resources in Nigeria which could be explored for solving electricity crisis especially in the growing urban centers where large population of Nigerians are moving into en masse. There is no doubt that technology capability plays a central role in the development of renewable energy. This chapter assessed the level of technology capability among the Nigerian university academia specializing in renewable energy-related disciplines. The results revealed that the level of renewable energy R&D funding is insufficient and poor university-industry interaction also abounds. Thus, there is a colossal gap between the existing and the required technology innovation capabilities. This study makes some suggestions which could be used by the policymakers to salvage the present situations in the country so as to improve the electricity generation in meeting the needs of the growing urbanization.

DOI: 10.4018/978-1-5225-7625-9.ch011

1. INTRODUCTION

The level at which urbanisation is rising in Africa has manifested in the growth of megacities and many smaller towns (Guneralp et al., 2018). Countless documented research has shown that urbanization is a necessary tool for socio-economic development across the globe. Human wellbeing and environmental protection is expected to improve through urbanization. Urbanization improves the level of socio-economic development support through industrialization, low carbon and innovative system (Cobbinah and Adams, 2018). Sub-Saharan Africa (SSA) has been considered as the world's swiftest urbanizing region and the major cities therein accounted for a combined $0.5 trillion, approximating 50 percent of the region's gross domestic product (Saghir and Santoro, 2018). Though many countries across the globe have attributed their socioeconomic growth to the benefits of urbanization, but majority of the African countries witnessing rapid urbanization continue to experience a lop-sided amount of the costs associated with it, which includes energy poverty, carbon emission, pollution and urban poverty among others (Cobbinah and Adams, 2018). This could be as a result of weak policy and poor urban planning which depict their unpreparedness for urbanization that occurred in their cities. World Bank (2016) opines that approximately eighty five million Nigerians, which is about half of the population, presently resides in urban centers; and the Nigeria's urban population is still growing rapidly at an average of 5% from 2000 to 2015.

The urbanization level increased drastically above the average urban population share of 37 percent of Sub-Saharan Africa. The population of cities of more than 300,000 residents skyrocketed from 21 to 42. The Nigerian urban residents is estimated to upsurge to 295 million by 2050 given the fertility rate and decline in mortality rate; the country would be the third largest nation by the end of this century (Bloch et al., 2015; World Bank, 2016). The over reliance on crude oil by Nigeria government where the oil sector generates 97% and 72% of her foreign exchange earnings and federally collected revenue respectively has resulted to a *resource curse* and *Dutch disease* whereby the country abandoned the manufacturing sector and service sector (Adelowo et al., 2016; Akinwale, 2012). This has further worsen the challenges of urbanization growth as many youths who moved to the urban centers remain unemployed and lack access to basic urban facilities including epileptic power supply which further cripple the business activities of small and medium enterprises (Ogundari et al, 2017). Energy demand has outstripped supply in many Sub-Saharan Africa nations with Nigeria inclusive. The total electricity demand in Nigeria is far above 10,000 MW, meanwhile the national installed electricity capacity is below 7,000 MW whereas the available capacity is averagely between 2,500 and 3,000 MW out of the installed capacity. The efforts made so far by the governments to improve the electricity generation and distribution from the national grid has not yielded significant results (Makwe et al., 2012; Ibitoye and Adenikinju, 2007). The increased in energy demand by the growing residents of urban centres has resulted into epileptic power supply which led many households and businesses to privately generate electricity through petrol and diesel powered generators. These generators are greatly contributing to carbon emission and many families have been suffocated to death in the urban centres as a result of emission from these fossil fuelled generators, hence not sustainable (Akinwale and Ogundari, 2017). However, renewable energy could be explored as a substitute source of energy to meet the need of the growing urbanization in the African continent in general, and Nigeria in particular.

Global development is essentially determined by the supply and demand of energy (Akinwale et al., 2013). Economic prosperity, global stability, and quality of life all have an intimate and essential role in the adequate supply of clean energy (Akinwale, 2018). A foremost societal challenge for the next half-century is discovering energy sources to meet the world's growing demand (WEO, 2015). Despite having various new and renewable energy resources; only about 7% of Africa's huge hydro potential has been explored (Karezeki and Kithyoma, 2003) which explains why the gap between energy demand and supply continues to widen in Africa. This has posed a lot of challenges to the life of people in many African cities and affected the level of industrialization that could have accompanied urbanization. The significance of this predominant challenge and the confounding technicalities of disentangling it require an intensive nationwide effort requiring highly advanced scientific and technological competences of the Citizens.

It is no longer news that the whole world is working towards achieving economic growth in a safer and cleaner environment, and one of the ways is generating power through renewable energy. Various kind of energy that is being replenished by natural processes at a rate that is greater or equals its rate of usage is referred to as renewable energy (Akinbami, 2001). These sources of energy can be gotten from the continuing flow of energy occurring in the natural environment which comprises resources such as hydropower, wind, biomass, solar, geothermal heat and waves among others (Moomaw *et al.*, 2011). They are not susceptible to volatility in the global oil price which makes each country to have control on its application. Nigerian government has also been making effort to harness renewable energy to solve electricity crisis in the country especially in both cities and growing rural areas, and this is termed "Operation Light Up Rural Nigeria" (Akinwale, 2018). The level of commitment of the Nigerian government towards this has not fully been established as it's still at the infancy stage. However, the government is clamouring for bringing foreign companies to carry out these renewable projects which might be a necessary condition but definitely not sufficient. There is need for the government to develop and train Nigerian citizens who can learn, acquire, assimilate, transform and apply the knowledge that has been learnt over time (Akinwale, 2016a; Akinwale et al. 2018).

Developing renewable energy (RE) resources requires skills in science, engineering and management which are equally important to develop other energy sources. Nonetheless the requisite skilfulness varies in detail for various technologies, and definite training is required for each one. Acquiring the expertise to use and maintain the renewable energy 'hardware' is extremely essential for a successful RE project (Martinot, 1998). Technology capability becomes very critical in moving the developing countries from greenhorn's situation to the expert's position (Stahl, 1990). A very crucial point to this analysis is an assessment of Nigeria's indigenous technological abilities in renewable energy from the academia perspective. Building high competence level in renewable energy technologies would foster the development, adoption and utilization of renewable energy resources which would support the growing urbanization in Nigeria.

This chapter is structured into six sections. Section one introduces the background to the study and the purpose of the research and the second section focuses on the renewable energy potentials in Nigeria. Technology innovation and renewable energy ecosystem are discussed in the third section, while methodology and results of the survey conducted are presented in fourth section. Section 5 provides direction for further research and section 6 and concludes the chapter.

2. RENEWABLE ENERGY POTENTIALS IN NIGERIA'S ENERGY SYSTEM

Energy system has the major purpose of providing energy services (Sambo, 2005). Energy services is refer to the beneficial products or services that stem from the use of energy, which includes cooking, refrigerated storage and lighting, among others. The aforementioned services could be provided by starting to extract primary energy which is afterwards transformed into energy carriers appropriate for final-users (Akinbami, 2001). These energy carriers are used to deliver the preferred energy services (Sambo, 1997). Energy not only serve as a tradable goods for generating national revenue, it also plays an important part in the nation's international diplomacy as well as bolsters the national earnings used to fund the developmental projects of the government. Energy also serves as resources used in the production of goods and services in differing industries in the country such as agriculture, health and transport. Energy therefore serves as a fundamental tool for socioeconomic development and eradicating poverty (Akinwale et al., 2015). The availability of energy influences the level of industrialization, economic growth and development (Makwe et al., 2012). While energy consumption and electricity consumption per capita in Nigeria were 769Kg of oil equivalent and 145kWh respectively in year 2014, that of South Africa were 2,696Kg of oil equivalent and 4,198kWh respectively and that of Brazil were 1,485Kg of oil equivalent and 2,601kWh (World Bank development Indicators, 2018). This shows that the level of energy and electricity poverty is still very high despite the sporadic urban growth. The sectoral usage of energy and electricity is also shown in Figures 1 and Figures 2 respectively. Residential sector (Households) accounted for the largest consumption of both energy and electricity in Nigeria compared with Brazil and South Africa. The Nigerian industrial sector consumes only 8.7% of energy and 15.8% of electricity from the national supply as against that of South Africa (35% of energy and 59.5% of electricity) and Brazil (23.4% of energy and 44.3% of electricity). The largest percentage of national energy supply apportioned to residential sector in Nigeria as against that of industry affected the energy required to drive industrialization in the urban sector. Meanwhile, the residential sector is also witnessing high level of epileptic power supply from the national grid. This engendered the micro, small, medium and large firms to buy fossil-fuelled generators to support their businesses, and this off grid energy source outstrips the supply from the national grid.

However, energy security and access to clean modern energy facilities are great challenges facing the African continent as more than 70% of the populace are inaccessible to these modern energy services (Oyedepo, 2013; Akinwale et al, 2013). Due to high level of carbon emission of fossil fuel energy source which has exposed a great number of the populace to toxic substances and unquantifiable environmental hazards, renewable energy source (RES) is then seen as a better alternative. This RES is clean, environmental friendly and easier to provide electricity for the remote areas where the grid system is not connected.

What is happening in Nigeria as regard renewable energy is similitude to what is obtainable in other Africa nations. Nigeria is a country blessed with abundance of renewable energy sources. The potentials of the country in renewable energies are as summarised in Table 1.

The renewable energy potentials of Nigeria include energy from hydro (Large and Small), solar, wind and biomass. This can be briefly explained in the subsections that follow.

2.1. Hydropower

This is a renewable energy source which relies on converting the tremendous pressure of water to electrical energy. Large hydropower presently accounted for 29% of the national electricity supply in Nigeria (Akinwale et al., 2014; Akinwale and Ogundari, 2017). Some of the sources of this hydro power include Kainji station with installed capacity of 1,376 MW both along river Niger. There are some other rivers

Figure 1.

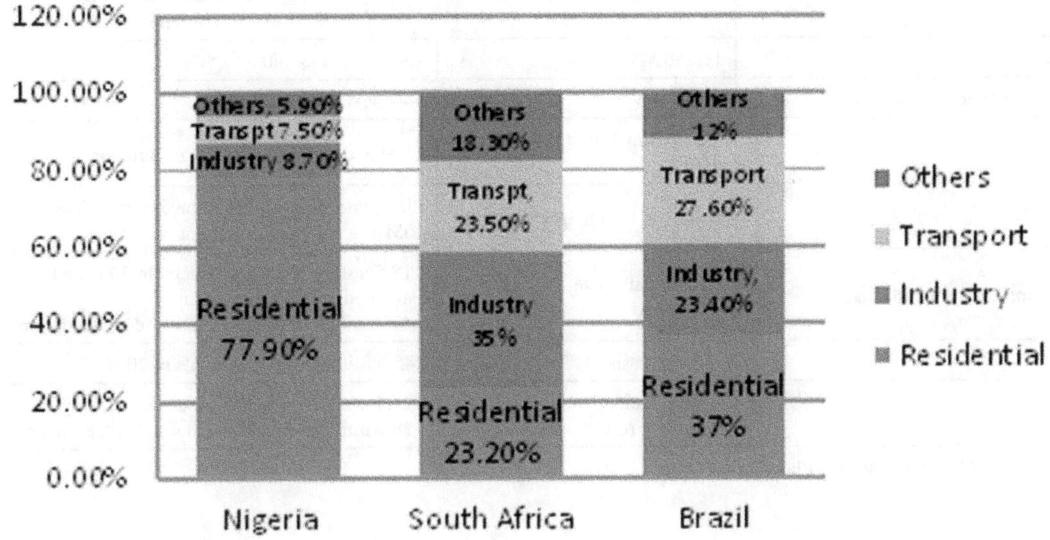

Figure 2.

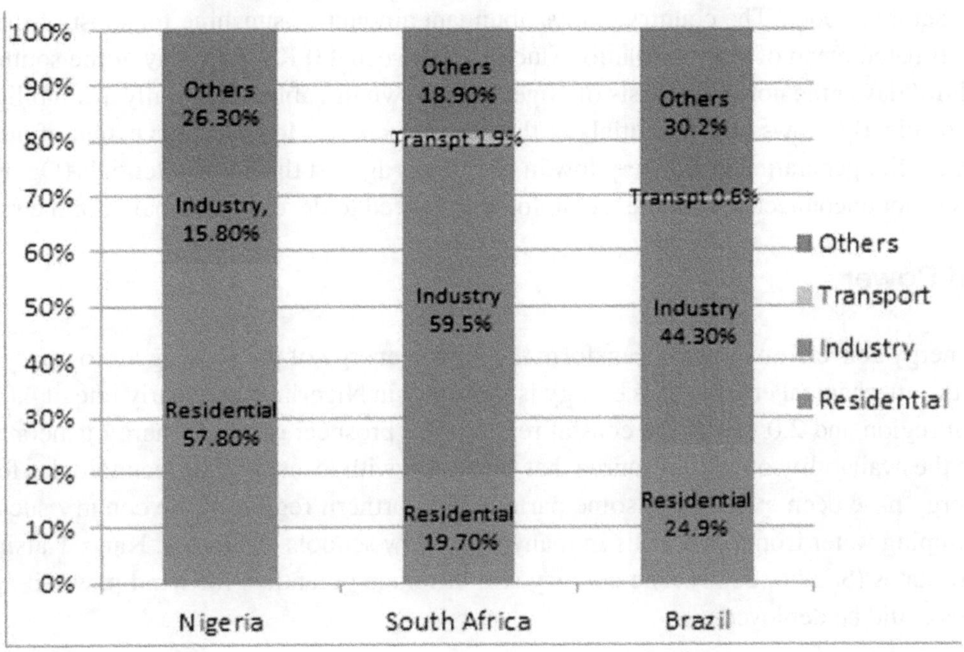

with huge potentials such as Benue and Cross River at Shiroro and river Kaduna, among others (Sambo, 2005). The total large hydropower resources possibly available in Nigeria are estimated in excess of 11,000MW out of which an average of 1,900 MW only has been exploited. Also, the country's small hydro potential is put at 3,500MW out of which only 64MW has been exploited (Renewable Energy Master Plan, 2013).

Table 1. Renewable energy potentials in Nigeria

Resource	Potential	Remark
Large Hydropower	11,250 MW	1,900 MW exploited
Small Hydropower	3,500 MW	64.2 MW exploited
Solar	4.0 kWh/m^2/day- 6.5 kWh/ m^2/day	15 MW dispersed solar PV installations (estimated)
Wind	2-4m/s @10m height mainland	Electronic Wind Information System (WIS) available; 10MW wind farm in Katsina in progress
Biomass (non-fossil organic matter)	-Municipal waste -Fuelwood	- 18.5 million tonnes produced in 2005 and now estimated at 0.5kg/capita/day - 43.4 million tonnes/yr fuelwood consumption
	Animal waste	245 million assorted animals in 2001
	-Agric Residue -Energy Crops	- 91.4 million tonnes/yr produced - 28.2 million hectares of arable land; 8.5% cultivated

Source: Renewable Energy Master Plan (Draft), 2013

2.2. Solar

Solar energy seems to be the most viable among the renewable energy as a result of its boundless potential in Nigeria (Sambo, 2008). The country enjoys abundant amount of sunshine for most of the days in a year. The estimated mean of solar insolation fluctuate between 4.0 KWh/m^2/day at the southern coasts to 6.5 KWh/m^2/day at the northern coasts of Nigeria as shown in Table 1.The daily availability of abundant sunshine clearly shows high potentials of this energy source. However, the extent of utilisation of solar for electricity generation is still very low in Nigeria as against the huge potentials (Ogundari et al., 2017). This is not unconnected with the technologies required to develop and maintain the solar power.

2.3. Wind Power

The wind energy conversion systems transform the kinetic energy of the moving air to rotary motion of a shaft, that is, mechanical energy. This energy is prevalent in Nigeria at the yearly rate of 4.0 m/s at the far northern region and 2.0 m/s at the coastal region. The prospect of wind energy generation largely depends on the availability of wind resource that fluctuates with location. The technologies for harnessing this energy have been explored in some parts in the northern region of the country such as power used for pumping water from open wells in many secondary schools of Sokoto, Kano, Katsina, Bauchi and Plateau States (Sambo, 2008). The country still has huge potentials for wind power if appropriate technologies could be deployed.

2.4. Biomass

Energy derived from biological systems including wood and wastes are referred to as Biomass energy (Sambo, 2005). Nigerian biomass resources can be recognized as wood biomass, forage grasses and shrubs, residues and wastes as well as aquatic biomass (Renewable Energy Master Plan, 2013). Nigeria has a 28.2 million hectares of arable land from which only 8.5% has been cultivated. This implies that the biomass potential of Nigeria is 8.5%. According to Akinbami et al. (2001), the identified feedstock substrate for an economically feasible biogas program in Nigeria includes water lettuce, water hyacinth, dung, cassava leaves, urban refuse, agricultural residues and sewage. They also opined that Nigeria produces approximately 227,500 tonnes of animal wastes daily. Thus, Nigeria could produce nearly 6.8 million m^3 of biogas daily. Large number of Nigeria's populace relies on fuel wood for domestic uses. The demand for fuel wood is exacerbated by the extensive use of inefficient cooking methods, which is mainly open fire. Thus, modern and high-efficient bio energy which utilises more suitable solids, liquids and gases as secondary energy carriers to generate combined heat and power (CHP), electricity, and transport fuels for several sectors should be adopted to replace the traditional biomass (Chum et al., 2011).

It is noteworthy to mention that there are huge potentials of renewable energy in Nigeria, though the distribution is more favourable in some regions than the other. For instance, Southern region has potentials to exploit sea wave, wind and hydropower because of the location to shoreline, whereas the Northern region has potential to easily harness solar, wind and hydropower due to high radiation of sun, high wind speed and many large dams. Biomass has been identified to have a greater potential of converting municipal solid waste to energy in the urban city such as Lagos, Abuja, Kano and Port Harcourt in Nigeria. Adepoju et al. (2018) analysed the economic feasibility of using solid waste to generate electricity through landfill gas in Lagos State, and the result showed a breakeven price of twenty nine naira (N29.17) per unit of electricity at a discount rate of 10%.

3. RENEWABLE ENERGY ECOSYSTEM AND TECHNOLOGY INNOVATION IN NIGERIA

Renewable energy presently accounts for a small fraction of energy mix in Nigeria despite its abundance. Huge potentials exists for utilising renewable energy resources to generate electricity in Nigeria as shown in section 2 above. The Council for Renewable Energy of Nigeria (2009) evaluates annual loss caused by power outages to be 126 billion naira (US$ 984.38 million). Poor electricity supply has caused huge income loss to various businesses, unemployment, and high cost of living leading to a decline in living conditions in the urban centres. Also various health hazards due to exposure to carbon emissions caused by constant use of 'backyard generators' in different households and business enterprises are affiliated to failure to properly harness renewable energy (Oyedepo, 2013. However, if the renewable energy potentials are properly harnessed, it will bring about achieving certain goals such as strengthening the country's manufacturing capacity, boosting the country's exports, generating employment opportunities, creating wealth leading to economic growth and development. For a country like Nigeria to achieve the aforementioned goals, there must be policies aimed at improving the indigenous renewable energy supply chain and strengthening technological skills at different levels. Nevertheless, acquisition and expanding technological capabilities is a process which has different stages. Building human capital in the areas of renewable energy requires all stakeholders in the energy ecosystem such as universities and polytechnics, research institutes, local and international donors, government and the general members of the public (Akinwale, 2018). Olaopa et al. (2018) also suggested a governance structure that strengthens and facilitates linkages among the agencies of government, research institutions and industries in order to achieve an effective and implemental national energy policy. The Evolutionary theorists opine that innovation could be seen as an outcome of a feedback circles between knowledge-producing and knowledge-using elements with differing level of collaboration within and among stakeholders (Rennings, 2000). More so, in the context of sectoral innovation system, emphasis was made on the ecosystem of related entities (education and research institutions, firms, banks and government) in efficiently harnessing the potential innovation resources in a particular sector (Nelson, 1993; Malerba, 2005; Akinwale and Surujlal, 2017). Meanwhile, education and research institution is endorsed with the responsibility of developing competence level in the innovation system (Freeman, 1995).

According to Ogbimi (2007), any nation which neglects the learning opportunities in her economy cannot experience innovations because learning, acquiring new knowledge and skills and applying these in production are the bases for achieving technological innovations. By this, transformation can be said to depend on the learning intensity and the rate at which new knowledge and skills flow into production activities of a nation. As a result of this Scientists such as Ogbimi opined that educational/learning institutions can be referred to as "economic pump". This is because the knowledge generated from these institutions can be used to transform an artisan-economy like Nigeria's into an industrialised one rapidly; just as mechanical pump can be used to inflate a good tyre rapidly. Many studies have shown that innovation capabilities are critical to the development of any sector of the economy (Romijn and Albaladejo, 2002; Vidican, 2012; Akinwale, 2016b). Innovation capabilities denote skills required to generate new products or processes, with the exact skills needed by the uniqueness of the new technology. This includes activities ranging from pure science to advanced development. Innovation capabilities are required to improve indigenous companies' involvement in more technologically inclined activities in the value chain (Vindican, 2012). From the standpoint of developing countries, innovations refers to the process by which firms understand and implement the design and production of goods and services which are new to them, regardless of whether they are new to their competitors (Mytelka, 2000). However, in emerging economies, innovation is generally concerned with not only to "new-to-the-world" technologies; rather focus on technological assimilation and adaptation of already established technologies to native environmental conditions (Akinwale, 2018). Research activities in most developing nations are scattered as a result of the absence of national technology strategy developed to direct research funds towards renewable energy. Technological change, for many developing countries, occurs largely through technological learning from the existing technologies in developed countries and not by developing cutting-edge technologies. Succinctly, in order to achieve technological advancement in developing countries absolute attention must be placed on technological catch-up through learning (UNCTAD, 2007).

There are two types of skills needed to achieve the relevant production skills required to acquire, adapt and produce new or imported technologies. These are theoretical skills(TSs) and practical skills(PSs); anyone who acquires either type alone is termed a "mediocre" (Ogbimi, 1991). Ogbimi believes that while formal education produces theoreticians (mediocre), the informal sector's apprenticeship system also produces those with limited practical skills known as artisans (mediocre). This is what is invariably predominant in most of the sectors in Nigeria including renewable energy subsector as both formal and informal manpower development efforts in Nigeria do not go through the complete cycle that equips people with both theoretical and practical skills. This can be seen in the university graduates who are well equipped in terms of theoretical knowledge (principles) only and the artisan who lack theoretical knowledge but possess limited practical skills alone. Hence, there is need for a curriculum in the Nigerian educational system that promote people to pass through both the theoretical and practical training so as to develop relevant production skills for solving problems confronting the energy sector.

Realising technology innovation and development may be likened to a ladder-climbing process (Ogbimi, 1990). This involves a gradual and a step-wise process rather than a haphazard one. In order to encourage the application of renewable energy technologies in solving electricity crisis in Nigeria particularly in the growing urban centres, the country must climb to a higher level of the technology ladder. This requires rapid development of many people who possess both theoretical and practical skills to advanced level as shown in Figure 3.

Figure 3 shows that an individual must begin acquiring training and knowledge from the lowest level of theoretical and practical skills so as to acquire technological capabilities. He must not jump steps. A country does not begin to climb the technology ladder till the indigenous people have completely understood the principles and practices associated with the existing renewable technologies. Ogbimi further stated that it is only after a nation has fully understood the fundamental theories (step 1) and practices (step 2) of existing technologies that it will attain the 'independent thinking status' where it will not rely on the thoughts of the foreign experts. Once this stage of independent thinking status has been reached, progress comes speedily because the other steps leading to innovations and technological capabilities follow readily. However, it should be noted that 'copying' (step 6) is an advanced stage of technological capability. From this we can deduce that for a country like Nigeria to copy the technologies developed in the advanced countries, sound relevant production skills must be embraced.

Some Nigeria Universities, Polytechnics and Energy Research had embarked on selected research and development activities, which have made it possible to come up with a certain number of renewable energy systems and devices which are indeed ready for implementation into the national economy (Sambo, 2005). This includes solar cooker, solar water heaters, solar dryers, photovoltaic powered pumps, wind water pumping sets, biogas digesters, and improved wood-burning stoves among others. However, some of these are at the pilot stage or under laboratory trials. For renewable energy to be fully integrated into Nigerian energy system and contribute to sustainable energy development, there is need to internalise some of the imported high-tech knowledge require to harness renewable energy.

Figure 3.

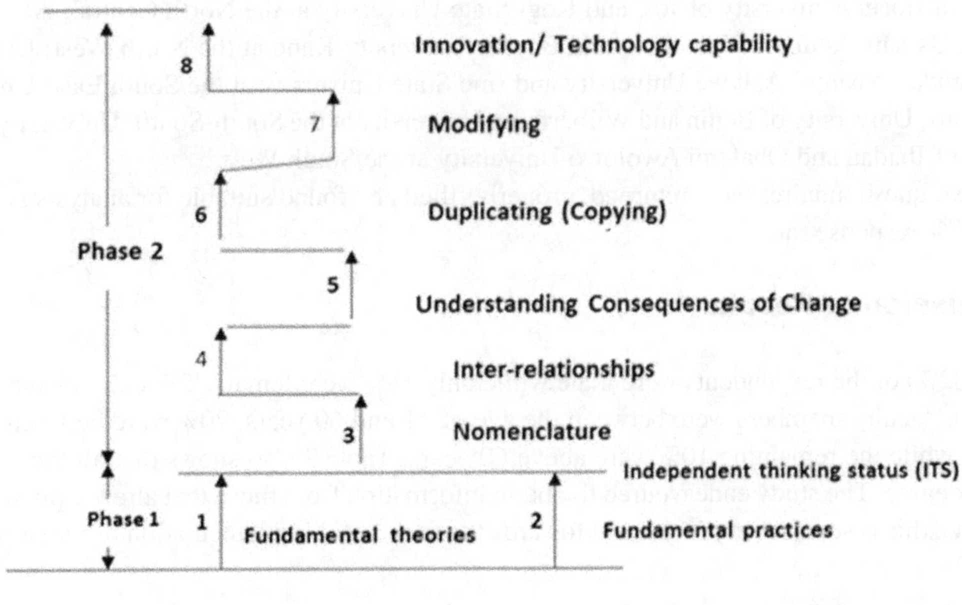

In the renewable energy ecosystem, like any other innovation system, the government is expected to provide an enabling environment through various policies; universities and research institutions are expected to play the role of the knowledge support for the system; firms are expected to produce goods and service through innovation that must have been developed; and the banks are expected to provide finance through various affordable credit. However, the objective of this study is to assess the technology innovation of renewable energy from the university academia perspective so as to be able to proffer solution to the electricity crisis facing urbanisation in Nigeria.

The next section will provide report of the survey carried out in Nigerian universities relating to renewable energy technologies development.

4. METHODOLOGY AND DISCUSSION OF RESULTS

4.1. Sample and Data Collection

This paper made use of both primary and secondary data for proper analysis. Five faculty members who specialise in the field of renewable energy were sampled from each university across 15 universities in 5 geopolitical regions in the country was purposefully selected, and the questionnaires was administered to them accordingly. The universities in the North East zone were exempted because of the insurgency on going in the zone as at the period of this study. A multistage sampling technique was initially used for categorising the universities into zones and thereafter purposive sampling technique was finally adopted to select the universities and the faculty members in the field of renewable energy from each institutions. The emphasis was science and engineering/technology faculties offering courses related to renewable energy technologies. The relevant questions on technology innovation and R&D were obtained from Oslow manual (OECD, 2005) and Frascati Manual (OECD, 2002) which are two main manuals for innovation and R&D surveys. The initial questionnaire was administered on three university faculty members at Ladoke Akintola University of Technology (LAUTECH) Ogbomosho as pre-test so as to validate the questionnaire, and few questions were revised afterwards. The universities include University of Ilorin, University of Jos, and Kogi State University at the North Central; Ahmadu Bello University, Usman Danfodio University and Bayero University Kano at the North West; University of Nigeria Nsukka, Nnamdi Azikwe University and Imo State University at the South East; University of Port Harcourt, University of Benin and Wilberforce University at the South-South; University of Lagos, University of Ibadan and Obafemi Awolowo University at the South West.

Sixty-two questionnaires were returned, properly filled and found suitable for analysis and this represents 82.7% response rate.

4.2 Discussion of Results

Majority (82%) of the respondents were male while only 18% were female. Table 2 indicates that most (70%) of the faculty members were between the age of 41 and 60 years, 20% were between the age of 26 and 40, while the remaining 10% were above 60 years. Table 2 also shows that all the respondents have Ph.D degree. The study endeavoured to obtain information from those that already possessed Ph.D degree, since this is seen as very important towards the successful implementation of renewable energy related research. Descriptive method such as frequencies, charts and mean ranking was used for proper analysis of the data collected.

Table 2 also shows that majority (72.6%) of the faculty members had their educational background in Engineering/Technology and few (27.6%) had theirs in Sciences.

The questionnaire sought views on perception about technological capabilities in the area of renewable energy and extent of linkage with the energy companies that provide renewable energy service. Table 3 shows nature of research engagements through a multiple response frequency. While 98% of the respondents claimed to engage in teaching and training research, 85% of the respondents claimed to engage in basic and scientific research and only 32% claimed to engage in applied research related to renewable energy. According to African Innovation Outlook (2010), Applied and Developmental research constitutes the lowest in the kind of research being performed in developing countries. Table 3 also shows factors driving research and development (R&D) among the University researchers using multiple responses. While 80% of the respondents claimed that their R&D activities were driven by knowledge, 75% believed that career enhancement was the main factor driving their research and the least (30%) of them claimed to be driven by demand/market.

This implied that most of the researches being carried out by the University Academia as related to renewable energy were not really driven by the demand in the market but rather to gain more knowledge as well as enhance their career through promotions in their respective Universities.

Comparison was also made between the renewable energy equipment in the University laboratories to the state-of-the-art required in the energy industry. Figure 4 shows that majority (70%) of the respondents ranked their laboratories low, 20% ranked them medium while 10% ranked them very low. This perception clearly showed that the conditions of laboratories for renewable energy in the Nigerian Universities when compared with the world standard required to develop renewable energy industries is low.

Table 2. Socio-demographic and educational characteristics of the respondents

Respondents' Characteristics	%
Gender	
Male	82
Female	18
Age	
26 – 40	20
41 – 60	70
> 60	10
Highest Academic Qualification	
MSc	-
PhD	100
Educational Background	
Engineering/Technology	72.6
Sciences	27.4
Total	**100**

Table 3. Nature of Universities' research engagements and factors driving research

Nature of research engagements	%
Nature of Research Engagements**	
Teaching and Training	98
Basic and Scientific research	85
Applied research	32
Factors driving R&D in the University**	
Knowledge driven	80
Career Enhancement driven	75
Demand/Market driven	30

** Multiple responses

Figure 4.

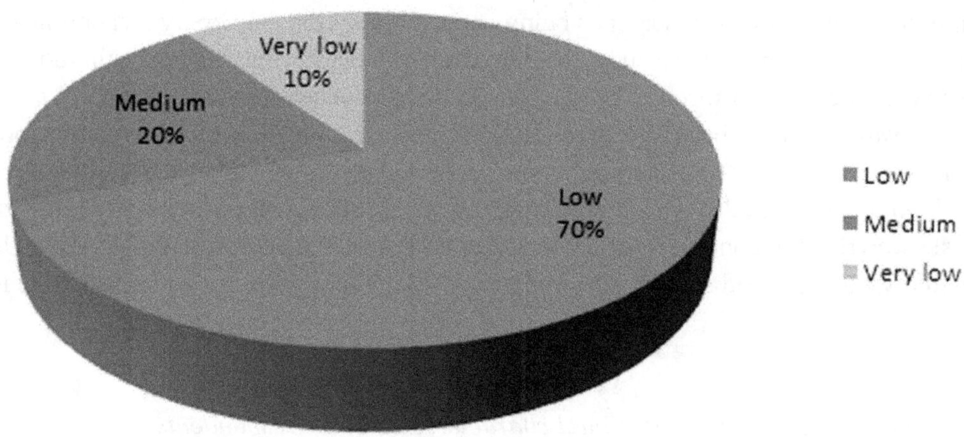

Table 4 shows that 56.5% of the faculty members indicated government fund as their primary source of finance for renewable energy research in the last three years, followed by self-financing (21%) and international/private donors (19.4%). This indicates that lots of academia funds their own research from their personal money and some received funds from the governments while others got fund from the internally generated revenue of the institutions. Table 4 also shows the adequacy of the R&D funding that the Academia received in the last 3 years. Majority (77.4%) of the respondents opined that such fund was not adequate while 14.5% and 8.1% opined that it was fairly adequate and just adequate respectively. Whereas, none of the respondents opined that the fund was very adequate.

The main setback in the development of renewable energy systems in Nigeria is the lack of technical competence (Aliyu and Bawa, 2013). They opined that the technical failures of renewable energy system could be linked with poor level of understanding of indigenous energy needs; dearth of R&D to adapt technologies to indigenous conditions and resources; lack of indigenous experts to install, operate and maintain the equipment appropriately; and inadequate access to spare parts. Akinbami (1997, 2001) also asserted that research, development and demonstration of renewable energy is still relatively low in Nigeria unlike in developed countries where they already have better scientific bases and known manu-

Table 4. Sources and appropriateness of renewable energy R&D fund in the University

Sources and Appropriateness of R&D fund	%
Sources of R&D Finance	
Government	56.5
Donor Agencies	19.4
Self-sponsored	21
Internally generated by the university/department	3.1
Adequacy of renewable energy related R&D fund	
Not Adequate	77.4
Fairly Adequate	14.5
Just Adequate	8.
Very Adequate	0

facturing capability to produce these energy systems. The application of renewable energy technologies in sub-Saharan Africa has not always been effective as a result of technical factors (Dunmade, 2002). Nevertheless, sustainable energy technologies are available and can be applied positively in Nigeria to alleviate electricity problem as well as contribute to job creation in the growing urban centres and can also contribute to job creation.

The dispersion of technology and knowledge is a prominent issue in the recent literature on technological change, innovation and growth, and the role of universities has been given special attention (Loof and Brostrom, 2006). Universities and research institutes are supposed to serve as a knowledge base for the industries. Often times, however, university research is not easily, or even effectively, transferred to industry (Markham et al., 1999). Some of the factors that may be influencing the extent of interaction with the renewable energy sub-industry were also examined. This was captured through the mean ranking of these factors ranging from 'Not at all/Very low' to 'High' extent. Table 5 shows the result with Academic papers presented and published in renewable energy related conferences being rated high (3.53). Consultancies with the industry, Technical services/Joint research between University and the industry, Prototypes developed by the Academia, Use of University laboratory facilities by the industry were all graded low with mean rank of 2.37, 2.25, 2.21 and 2.18 respectively. Other factors such as Licensing arrangement between the academia and the industry, Patent granted to the academia invention in the area of renewable energy, Spin-off firms emanated from renewable research activities were rated Very low with the mean rank of 1.22, 1.13 and 1.11 respectively. From this result, it can be deduced that the level of collaboration of the University Academia with the renewable energy sub-industry is low based on the sampled opinion.

Table 6 shows factors impeding interaction of the Academia with the industrialists through mean ranking. The higher the mean of the impeding factors, the more the factors affect the interactions of the University with the renewable energy industry. The dearth of adequate research and laboratory facilities to embark on industrially oriented research, Lack of entrepreneurial spirit among the Academia and poor R&D fund were rated high with mean of 3.56, 3.52 and 3.50 respectively. Inadequate mechanism to interact with the industry, absence of policy papers in the University geared towards interacting with the industry and Time devoted to teaching were rated medium with the respective mean of 3.21, 3.19 and

Table 5. Factors influencing the extent of interaction of university academia with the renewable energy sub-industry

Factors	Mean Rank
Academic papers presented and published in renewable energy related conferences	3.53
Consultancies with the industry	2.37
Technical services/Joint research between University and the industry	2.25
Prototypes developed by the Academia	2.21
Use of University laboratory facilities by the industry	2.18
Licensing arrangement between the academia and the industry	1.22
Patent granted to the academia renewable energy invention	1.13
Spin-off firms emanated from renewable research activities	1.11

Mean Rank: 1= Not at all/ Very low; 2 = Low; 3 = Medium; 4 = High

2.98. The only factor that was ranked very low (1.12) was that 'the academic scholars are not competent enough to undertake developmental research'.

Only 14,616 youth corps members (young graduates) studied engineering out of 187,744 total corps members in year 2008 (NBS, 2012), but the engineering youth corps members increased to 26,215 out of 189,913 in 2014 (NBS, 2017). Also, a total number of 682 citizens have been given petroleum technology development fund (PTDF) scholarship between year 2002 and 2007 while 731 citizens have been given PTDF scholarship between year 2007 and 2009 (NBS, 2012). This scholarship was given to pursue MSc and PhD in energy and oil & gas related courses both within Nigeria and Overseas. It is unfortunate that government is not monitoring how these scholars that benefitted from these scholarships are properly placed to their respective field of study to transfer the knowledge to others and as well impacted it on the economy. Nigerian government ended up training Nigerians for other countries that employ them after graduation. Akinbami (1997) opined that there is a limited reservoir of trained personnel in the country, and this will hamper the country's capability to construct, control and sustain these renewable energy systems. Hence, there is a need for an environment that will foster an efficient transfer of renewable energy technology from the industrialised countries to less developed countries as well as creating

Table 6. Factors impeding university-industry interaction

Impeding Factors to University-Industry Linkage	Mean Rank
Lack of adequate research and laboratory facilities to conduct industrially oriented research	3.56
Lack of entrepreneurial spirit among the Academia	3.52
Poor R&D funding	3.50
No adequate mechanism to interact with the industry	3.21
No policy in University towards interacting with the industry	3.19
Time devoted to teaching	2.98
Academic scholars are not competent enough to undertake developmental research	1.12

Mean Rank 1= Not at all/ Very low; 2 = Low; 3 = Medium; 4 = High an enabling environment for the less developed economies to acquire and effectively adapt such to suit local conditions (Akinwale, 2018; Lema et al., 2015; Akinbami, 2001). Although provision was made for this in the United Nations Framework Convention on Climate Change, mandating the Annex 1 Parties (the developed countries) to transfer environmentally sound technology to developing countries but this has not been effected to any reasonably significant level.

5. DIRECTION FOR FUTURE RESEARCH

Further study should take into consideration other stakeholders that are relevant to renewable energy development such as respondents from renewable energy firms, research institutes and financial institutions among others. This would provide a robust analysis of using renewable energy ecosystem to resolve the electricity crisis facing urbanisation in Nigeria. Also, further research should also take into consideration large sample size for the faculty members so as to be able to carry out some inferential statistical analysis.

6. CONCLUSION AND POLICY RECOMMENDATION

The huge renewable energy resources in Nigeria will continue to remain unexploited in the foreseeable future if nothing is consciously done to harness it. This would worsen the energy crisis as the level of urbanization is growing rapidly in Nigeria. Furthermore, the level of dependence on the developed countries for equipment, spare parts and skills required to develop such renewable energy will continue if the Nigerian government does not take a lead in the right direction. This study has been able to show the nature of renewable research that is mostly carried out in the Nigerian Universities, the factors driving research among the University faculty members as well as the status of the research laboratories when compared with that of the state-of-the-art. The level of funding R&D has been shown to be low and insufficient in the universities. The factors influencing the extent of collaboration of the University with the renewable energy sub-industry as well as factors impeding such interactions were all examined in this study. There are some recommendations which are expected to inform certain policies for the present government administration towards proper urban planning.

In spite of the large quantity of alternative energies in Nigeria, the resources are currently being poorly harnessed and represent a small fraction of energy mix. The potentials of renewable energy appear to be huge in generating electricity which will directly and indirectly boost the economy, promote urbanization, improve exports and foster development. This study has shown that the level of adequacy of fund and the laboratories required are low in the Nigerian Universities. There should be a government policy directed toward creating special fund for renewable energy research and full implementation of such policy. This will inform the academia to engage in applied and developmental researches which are market driven to solve societal problems rather than restriction to teaching within the four walls of the classrooms. This will enable the acquisition, assimilation and application of foreign technologies to the local situation. This study also showed that there is lack of entrepreneurial spirit among the University Academia. Nigerian government through policy should create a culture of academic entrepreneurship that will build a strong relationship between the academia and the industry. This will require a change in the work norms of University Scientists which will encourage mobility between University and the industry so as to develop both the academic and industrial experience required to manufacture some of these renewable energy equipment and the spare parts presently imported. There is need to establish technology transfer offices in Universities where they have not been established which should strengthen the connection between the University and the industry; however, there should be a wakeup call in the Universities where such offices are in existence because their impacts have not been felt.

In order for Nigeria as a country to develop technology and innovation capabilities in renewable energy, it is essential to introduce a policy aimed at localising the renewable energy supply chain and strengthening the technology capabilities at various levels. Nigerian government should bring together all the uncoordinated research activities scattered across various Universities under a coordinated national technology strategy which integrates all the actions of various Academicians as regards renewable energy. A sustainable educational curriculum in relevant disciplines should incorporate renewable energy at various educational levels so as to increase the knowledge and R&D capabilities needed to develop absorptive capacity which in turns make it possible to localise benefits from the foreign technologies. There should be a strong political commitment on the part of the government to ensure that all the policy put in place by her are strictly implemented. The current Science, Technology and Innovation (STI) Policy, which support building science and technology and commercialising them to innovation output, should also be fully implemented by all the stakeholders towards achieving a sustainable economic development.

REFERENCES

Adelowo, C., Olaopa, O., & Akinwale, Y. (2016). Policy Direction for Effective Interaction and Linkages among the Elements of Nigeria's National Innovation System. *Journal of Entrepreneurship and Innovation Management*, *5*(1), 1–12.

Adepoju, A., Akinwale, Y., & Ogundari, I. (2018). Feasibility economic analysis for electricity generation in internal combustion engine sets using landfill gas in Lagos State. *African Journal of Science, Technology, Innovation and Development*, *10*(5), 593–599. doi:10.1080/20421338.2018.1495285

African Innovation Outlook. (2010). *Research and Experimental Development*. Retrieved from: http//:www.nepadst.org

Akinbami, J. (1997). Comparative Environmental Effects and Cost Analysis Between Conventional and Non-conventional Energy Source – A Case for Objective Analysis and Decision Making in Nigeria's Energy Policy. *Nigerian Journal of Renewable Energy*, *5*(1&2), 131–139.

Akinbami, J., Ilori, M., Oyebisi, T., Akinwumi, I., & Adeoti, O. (2001). Biogas energy use in Nigeria: Current status, future prospects and policy implications. *Renewable & Sustainable Energy Reviews*, *5*(1), 97–112. doi:10.1016/S1364-0321(00)00005-8

Akinbami, J. F. K. (2001). Renewable Energy Resources and Technologies in Nigeria: Present Situation, Future Prospects and Policy Framework. *Mitigation and Adaptation Strategies for Global Change*, *6*(2), 155–181. doi:10.1023/A:1011387516838

Akinwale, Y. (2012). Empirical Analysis of Resource Curse in Nigeria. *International Journal of Economics and Management. The Sciences*, *1*(6), 19–25.

Akinwale, Y. (2016a). Indigenous Technology and Innovation Capability Building in Nigerian Upstream Oil and Gas Subsector: The Academia Perspective. *Advances in Management and Applied Economics, 6*(2), 49–70.

Akinwale, Y. (2016b). Harnessing science technology and innovation for enhancing marginal oil and gas field development in Nigeria: a comparative analysis. *International Journal of eBusiness and eGovernment Studies, 8*(2), 47 – 63.

Akinwale, Y. (2018). Descriptive analysis of building indigenous low carbon innovation capability in Nigeria. *African Journal of Science, Technology, Innovation and Development, 10*(5), 601–614. doi:10.1080/20421338.2017.1366131

Akinwale, Y., Akinbami, J., & Akarakiri, J. (2018). Factors influencing technology and innovation capability in the Nigerian indigenous oil firms. *International Journal of Business Innovation and Research, 15*(2), 247–268. doi:10.1504/IJBIR.2018.089146

Akinwale, Y., Ilevbare, O., & Ogundari, I. (2015). Utilising renewable energy technologies for electricity poverty reduction in South-West Nigeria: Technology adoption and psychosocial perspectives. *International Journal of Renewable Energy Technology, 6*(3), 224–244. doi:10.1504/IJRET.2015.070149

Akinwale, Y., Jesuleye, A., & Siyanbola, W. (2013). Empirical Analysis of the Causal Relationship Between Electricity Consumption and Economic Growth in Nigeria. *British Journal of Economics. Management and Trade, 3*(3), 277–295.

Akinwale, Y., & Ogundari, I. (2017). Exploration of Renewable Energy Resources for Sustainable Development in Nigeria: A Study of the Federal Capital Territory. *International Journal of Energy Economics and Policy, 7*(3), 240–246.

Akinwale, Y., Ogundari, I., Ilevbare, O., & Adepoju, A. (2014). A Descriptive Analysis of Public Understanding and Attitudes of Renewable Energy Resources towards Energy Access and Development in Nigeria. *International Journal of Energy Economics and Policy, 4*(4), 636–646.

Akinwale, Y., & Surujlal, J. (2017). A techno-economic policy framework to enhance the contribution of marginal oil and gas field to Nigeria's economic growth: A petroleum innovation system approach. *International Journal of Economics and Finance Studies, 9*(1), 132–147.

Aliyu, A., & Bawa, J. (2013). Clean Energy Technologies in Nigeria: Issues, Perspectives and Solutions. *Proceedings of the International Conference of the Nigerian Association of Energy Economics*, 134-154.

Bloch, R., Fox, S., Monroy, J., & Ojo, A. (2015). *Urbanisation and Urban Expansion in Nigeria. Research report, Urbanisation Research Nigeria*. London: ICF International.

Chum, H., Faaij, A., Moreira, J., Berndes, G., Dhamija, P., Dong, H., ... Pingoud, K. (2011). Bioenergy. In *IPCC Special Report on Renewable Energy Sources and Climate Change Mitigation* (pp. 209–332). Cambridge, UK: Cambridge University Press. doi:10.1017/CBO9781139151153.006

Cobbinah, P., & Adams, E. (2018). Urbanization and Electric Power Crisis in Ghana: Trends, Policies, and Socio-Economic Implications. In U. Benna & I. Benna (Eds.), *Urbanization and Its Impact on Socio-Economic Growth in Developing Regions* (pp. 262–284). Hershey, PA: IGI Global. doi:10.4018/978-1-5225-2659-9.ch013

Council for Renewable Energy Nigeria (CREN). (2009). *Nigeria Electricity Crunch.* Available at http://www.renewablenigeria.org

Dunmade, I. (2002). Indicators of sustainability: Assessing the suitability of a foreign technology for a developing economy. *Technology in Society, 24*(4), 461–471. doi:10.1016/S0160-791X(02)00036-2

Freeman, C. (1995). The National System of Innovation in Historical Perspective. *Cambridge Journal of Economics, 19*(1), 5–24.

GIZ. (2015). *Nigerian Energy Sector: An Overview with a Special Emphasis on Renewable Energy, Energy Efficiency and Rural Electrification* (2nd ed.). Available at https://www.giz.de/en/downloads/giz2015-en-nigerian-energy-sector.pdf

Guneralp, B., Lwasa, S., Masundire, H., Parnell, S., & Seto, K. (2018). Urbanization in Africa: Challenges and opportunities for conservation. *Environmental Research Letters, 13*, 2–8.

Ibitoye, F., & Adenikinju, A. (2007). Future demand for electricity in Nigeria. *Applied Energy, 84*(5), 492–504. doi:10.1016/j.apenergy.2006.09.011

International Energy Agency. (2013). *Key World Energy Statistics.* Available at: https://webstore.iea.org/key-world-energy-statistics-2013

Karezeki, S., & Kithyoma, W. (2003). *Renewable Energy in Africa: Prospects and Limits.* Paper presented at the Workshop for African Energy Experts on Operationalizing the NEPAD Energy Initiative, Dakar, Senegal.

Lema, R., Iizuka, M., & Walz, R. (2015). Introduction to low Carbon Innovation and Development: Insights and Future Challenges for Research. *Innovation and Development, 5*(2), 173–187. doi:10.1080/2157930X.2015.1065096

Loof, H., & Brostrom, A. (2006). *Does Knowledge Diffusion between University and Industry Increase Innovativeness?* Centre of Excellence for Science and Innovation Studies Working Paper Series No. 21.

Makwe, J., Akinwale, Y. & Atoyebi, M. (2012). An Economic Assessment of the Reform of Nigerian Electricity Market. *Energy and Power, 2*(3), 24-32.

Malerba, F. (2005). Sectoral systems of innovation: A framework for linking innovation to the knowledge base, structure and dynamics of sectors. *Economics of Innovation and New Technology, 14*(1-2), 63–82. doi:10.1080/1043859042000228688

Markham, S., Kingon, A., Zapata, M., & Baumer, D. (1999). A methodology to find assess and commercialize technologies, civilization, modern technology and sustainable development. *The Eighth International Conference on Management of Technology.*

Martinot, E. (1998). Energy efficiency and renewable energy in Russia: Transaction barriers, market intermediation and capacity building. *Energy Policy, 26*(11), 905–915. doi:10.1016/S0301-4215(98)00022-6

Moomaw, W., Yamba, F., Kamimoto, M., Maurice, L., Nyboer, J., Urama, K., & Weir, T. (2011). Introduction. In *IPCC Special Report on Renewable Energy Sources and Climate Change Mitigation.* Cambridge, UK: Cambridge University Press.

Mytelka, L. (2000). Local systems of innovation in a globalized world economy. *Industry and Innovation*, *7*(1), 33–54. doi:10.1080/713670244

NBS. (2010). *Social statistics in Nigeria.* National Bureau of Statistics.

Nelson, R. R. (1993). *National Innovation Systems: A Comparative Analysis*. Oxford University Press.

OECD. (2002). *Frascati Manual: proposed Standard Practice for Surveys on Research and Experimental Development*. Paris, France: OECD.

OECD. (2005). Oslow Manual: Guideline for Collecting and Interpreting innovation Data. Paris, France: OECD.

Ogbimi, F. (1990). Establishing a Policy Framework for Rapid Technological Advancement in Nigeria. *The Nigerian Engineer*, *25*(3), 1–8.

Ogbimi, F. (1991). Managing Education-Production Linkages: Bridging the Gap between Theoretical and Practical Skills in Nigeria. *Proceedings of the Conference jointly organized by Council for Registered Engineers of Nigeria (COREN) and Committee of Deans of Engineering and Technological Institutions (CODET) in Lagos*, 22-32.

Ogbimi, F. (2007). Solution to Mass Unemployment in Nigeria (3rd ed.). Society For Linking Education and Problems, Obafemi Awolowo University.

Ogundari, I., Akinwale, Y., Adepoju, O., Atoyebi, M., & Akarakiri, J. (2017). Suburban Housing Development and Off-Grid Electric Power Supply Assessment for North-Central Nigeria. *International Journal of Sustainable Energy Planning and Management*, *12*, 47–64.

Olaopa, O., Akinwale, Y., & Ogundari, I. (2018). Governance Institutions for Sustainable Energy Resources Management in Nigeria: Issues, Perspective and Policy Agenda for Action. In L. Asuelime & E. Okem (Eds.), *Political Economy of Energy in Sub-Saharan Africa* (pp. 82–101). London: Routledge Taylors and Francis.

Oyedepo, S. (2013). Energy in Perspective of Sustainable Development in Nigeria. *Sustainable Energy*, *1*(2), 14–25.

Renewable Energy Master Plan. (2013). *Renewable Energy Potentials in Nigeria*. Retrieved from http://www.energy.gov.ng/index.php?option=com_docman&task=cat_view&gid=39&Itemid=49

Rennings, K. (2000). Redefining Innovation – Eco-Innovation Research and the Contribution From Ecological Economics. *Ecological Economics*, *32*(2), 319–332. doi:10.1016/S0921-8009(99)00112-3

Romijn, H., & Albaladejo, M. (2002). Determinants of Innovation Capability in Small Electronics and Software Firms in Southeast England. *Research Policy*, *31*(7), 1053–1067. doi:10.1016/S0048-7333(01)00176-7

Saghir, J., & Santoro, J. (2018). *Urbanization in Sub-Saharan Africa: Meeting Challenges by Bridging Stakeholders.* Center for Strategic and International Studies. Available at http://csis.org

Sambo, A. (1997). *Energy options for sustainable national development: Resources, issues, and the position of renewable energy technologies. University Inaugural Lecture Series No. 1, Abubakar Tafawa Balewa University*. Bauchi: ATBU.

Sambo, A. (2005). Renewable Energy for Rural development: The Nigerian perspective. *ISESCO: Science and Technology Vision, 1*(5).

Sambo, A. (2008). Matching Electricity Supply with Demand in Nigeria. *International Association of Energy Economics, 4*, 32–36.

Stahl, J. (1990). A New Universal Learning Curve. *Proceedings of the Annual Conference of the ASEE in Canada*, 163-186.

UNCTAD. (2007). The Least Developed Countries Report 2007: Knowledge, Technological Learning and Innovation for Development. *United Nations Conference on Trade and Development.*

Vidican, G. (2012). *Building Domestic Capabilities in Renewable Energy. A case study of Egypt. German Development Institute / Deutsches Institut für Entwicklungspolitik.* DIE.

World Bank. (2016). *From Oil to Cities: Nigeria's Next Transformation*. Available at http://documents.worldbank.org/curated/en/711661468010811972/pdf/106150-PUB-ADD-DOI-ISBN-SERIES-OUO-9.pdf

KEY TERMS AND DEFINITIONS

Purposive Sampling Technique: This is a method of selecting a group of people base on a particular purpose.

Renewable Energy Ecosystem: This is an arrangement of interacting relationships among the stakeholders that engage in renewable energy products and services.

Renewable Energy Sources: These are the sources of power whereby the regenerating rate of such energy are higher than the depleting rate.

Sectoral Innovation System: This encompasses the network among the stakeholders in a particular sector, in this case renewable energy sector. It involves the firms that produce the energy goods and services, the government, which provides policy for an enabling environment; the financial institutions, which provide credit funds for other stakeholders; and the universities, which provide knowledge support for the industry.

Technology and Innovation Capabilities: This involves skills and competence that are required for developing new product/service or improve on the existing ones.

University Academia: These are university faculty members who teach and conduct research.

Urbanization: This is a gradual or continuous movement of people towards urban centers.

Chapter 12
The Cross-Cultural Analysis of Australia and Russia:
Cultures, Small Businesses, and Crossing the Barriers

Vardan Mkrttchian
https://orcid.org/0000-0003-4871-5956
HHH University, Australia

Svetlana Veretekhina
Russian State Social University, Russia

Olga Gavrilova
Petrozavodsk State University, Russia

Anastasiia Ioffe
Petrozavodsk State University, Russia

Svetlana Markosyan
HHH University, Australia

Serge V. Chernyshenko
Open University for the Humanities and Economics, Russia

ABSTRACT

The chapter examines the comparison of the cross-cultural analysis of the green country, Australia (NSW), and the northern country, Russia (Republic of Karelia). Based on the results of the analysis, it shows how a small business from Russia, Green Roofs, overcomes barriers in Australia through the application of blockchain technology. The authors hope that examples of development and thoughts about the driving sources of these transformations, chosen by taking into account the interests of the development of the Russian digital economy, can be interesting and useful for Russian enterprises, small businesses that have begun their digital transformations.

DOI: 10.4018/978-1-5225-7625-9.ch012

INTRODUCTION

As shown by Chernychenko (2009,2013), intercultural experience is considered a valuable contribution to personal and professional growth, especially in urban promote social growth & cohesion of HHH University (Australia, NSW), Russian State Social University, Open University for the Humanities and Economics (Russian Federation) and Petrozavodsk State University (Russian Federation, Republic of Karelia) in training teachers and social workers.

Nowadays literary review showed, in an urban environment, intercultural experience is useful in training teachers and social workers to training with students in multicultural classroom teaching. Our experience in the above mentioned team has shown that such work is especially important for the training of teachers and social workers in the city and urban environment at all levels, as Australia is recognized as a culturally diverse nation through its diverse immigration policies. Our experience in the Australian Federation has shown that Australian professional standards for graduate teachers and social workers require that teachers and graduates of social schools should have the knowledge and skills about learning strategies that meet the strengths and abilities of students in various linguistic, cultural, religious and socio-economic groups, especially in large, medium and small urban environment. In the course of our daily work, we became convinced that it is very important for teachers and social workers to be able to conduct a variety of professional experiences in different sociocultural settings and educate teachers prior to the start of training in order to understand teaching and learning in multicultural contexts and develop the student's ability to work with classes with multi-ethnic students from different cultures.

This chapter summarizes our reports on the intercultural pedagogical experience of pre-school teachers and social workers at HHH University (Australia, NSW) to three Russian Universities: Russian State Social University, Open University for the Humanities and Economics (Russian Federation) and Petrozavodsk State University (Russian Federation, Republic of Karelia). HHH University (Australia) was created in January 2001 by bringing together the resources All Armenian Internet University and Campus Armenian Catholic High School in Sydney. Our university offers higher education, social and vocational education and training on the Sydney campus. The University of HHH is an open access university, which is both regional and international. To provide teachers who have completed preliminary training, an international outlook and to enable graduates to effectively participate in studies in a multicultural class, HHH University has developed several foreign offices for teachers, which include the cities of Moscow, Petrozavodsk (Russian Federation). In accordance with the Memorandum of Understanding signed between the Petrozavodsk State University and the University of HHH, teachers and social workers of pre-school education in the third or fourth year of their undergraduate program were invited to the primary or secondary school in Petrozavodsk for three to four weeks prior to the beginning of the the main official program. During this training in the Russian Federation, we planned and implemented special, additional English lessons, attended regular training sessions for teachers and participated in joint preparatory activities for the lesson. They also had the opportunity to get acquainted with Russian culture and learn to understand the Russian education system, including strategies and approaches to teaching and teaching. Petrozavodsk is the capital of the Republic of Karelia in the northeast of the Russian Federation with a population of about one million people. Before the trip, none of the teachers before the start of the training did not have intercultural training in the classroom outside the Australian context. For four students, it was their first visit to Russia when they first saw the "big" class (with 50-60 students) taught by one teacher in the classroom, and their first experience was to start the work day before 7:00 am to prepare for the first the lesson of the day, which usually began at 8:00. For our students, these were new problems and experiences related to new opportunities in the learning and training process. The second author, a representative of the Russian-speaking university and the organizer of this placement in Russia, was in Karelia with four of his students. To study the broader picture of this international teaching practice, she interviewed four local instructors and interviewed 80 Russian students who were taught and trained by the University of HHH to find out their views and perspectives on how they felt working with Australian teachers and what they perceived as the contribution of Australian teachers in their educational environment. The survey and survey data provided valuable information for this study, not only to inform the teaching experience in the Russian Federation, but also to better understand intercultural communication and teaching and learning, especially in the context urban promote social growth & cohesion. The third author represents the Moscow Open University (a HEI, providing distant education for the entire territory of Russia) and has wide international experience in higher education. He had professorship at universities of Russia, Ukraine, Germany and Poland, was a faculty dean, a national didactic committee member, manager of about thirty international projects in the field of higher education. His contribution to the new cross-cultural training programs will be based on his wide international experience.

BACKGROUND

The work carried out by the staff of the HHH university showed that the teacher-pupils will greatly benefit from the international experience of teaching, understanding more about children and opinions, beliefs and understandings and methods of teaching and learning in different contexts, urban conditions promote social growth and rallying (Mkrttchian, et al, 2011-2018). This section was considered by us on two positions: training and small business:

The Cross-Cultural Teaching Experience of Pre-Service Teachers and Social Workers

On a broader level, research literature suggests that the advantages of international teaching experience are professional and personal growth, including increased confidence, better evaluation and respect for differences in other and other cultures, and awareness of the importance of reflection in professional cultural development. Our research on similar pedagogical education programs in other regions and other countries shows that international experience can contribute to the development of students and teachers in various ways, such as: flexibility, tolerance, patience, self-confidence, self-criticism, courtesy, independence and the ability to adapt in another culture concluded that the international experience of teaching students can potentially change the beginning of the teacher's thoughts about himself, curriculum development and strategy training; increase the skills and abilities of effective teachers; resolve and encourage the study of personal beliefs, habits and values, and encourage a commitment to openness (Mkrttchian, et al, 2011-2018). All these factors should influence, finally, on quality of the teaching process (Gorbunova, et al, 2012) and should be directly taken into account during organization of education management (Chernyshenko, et al, 2012). We have seen that there is a convergence of views on the value of foreign professional experience and evidence of the use of such programs in numerous teacher training programs in Australia and internationally. Nevertheless, there is still a need for a new, focused study to determine the full effectiveness of such programs, including specific elements of pedagogical pedagogy and identity that they help to develop the system of international exchange and training (Mkrttchian, et al, 2011-2018). We noticed that the literature focuses on the perspectives and growth of the number of students - teachers and social workers during international pedagogical practice, our studies have shown that in very few studies reviews of local instructors-mentors and local students are considered, how they relate to approaches to learning, and also to what kind of harm they bring to local schools and communities due to language barriers. Therefore, the answer to questions about the impact of the international experience of teaching students-teachers and social workers on the local context remains uncertain and needs further study. The main focus of this study was not only on how the teaching experience of the Russian Federation influenced the prospects for Australian teachers and social workers in teaching and learning, as well as their personal and professional development, but also to study that Australian student teachers and social workers bring in the local Russian context. This was achieved by studying the experience and voices of local instructors-mentors and students. (Mkrttchian, et al, 2011-2018) with using general approaches to development of international education standards (Chernyshenko, Okhrimenko, 2009).

The research proposed in this chapter was intended to answer the following questions:

1. How do Australian student teachers and social workers from the HHH university reflect their Russian experience and what is the impact of this intercultural placement on the personal and professional development of Australian student teachers and social workers?
2. How do the teachers and students of the Russian mentor perceive their experience with Australian student teachers and social workers, and how does this cross-cultural practice contribute to the local context from the point of view of teacher-mentors and students?

All the studies were organized around the study of these central issues. Based on these issues, more specific reflexive questions were developed to receive feedback from three different groups of participants. The study was approved prior to a trip to the Russian Federation by the Ethics Committee of the University of HHH, Australia.

The Small Business From Russia "Green Roofs" and Technology Green Roofs

Every year, green roofs are becoming an increasingly popular element of environmental construction. Now green roofs are covered by garages, shopping centers, they are used as playgrounds, restaurants and other recreational areas. Most green roofs are found in the southern climate, but there are also single projects in the northern conditions of Russia. The creation of green roofs in conditions with a high fluctuation of average annual temperatures is very effective.

The rapid pace of urbanization of the modern world leads to an inevitable deterioration of the ecological state of the environment. Thus, a high level of noise, dust, pollution of air emissions from road transport and industry, the reduction of optimal visual environment (a large number of homogeneous and aggressive visual fields) undermine people's health, violate the psychological balance and are generally characterized as unfavorable for living and working of the population.

The researches of the authors of the chapter, conducted in Faro (Portugal) and Petrozavodsk (Russia), showed a complicated ecological situation in the northern and southern European countries of different countries, which is connected with the lack of green spaces.

The territory of Petrozavodsk is 135 sq. M. km, including directly urban land -113 square meters. km, the rest - the city's forests. The green zone of Petrozavodsk covers an area of 48.2 thousand hectares, including 1.8 thousand hectares within the city limits. The forest park area of the green zone is 12.9 thousand hectares, the forestry part is 35.3 thousand ha. Parks, squares and street plantations occupy about 400 hectares, which is somewhat more than 14 square meters per one inhabitant.

On the territory of the city of Petrozavodsk, the main indicators of the ecological situation in the area were investigated. We studied the noise level, the level of dust pollution, the degree of gardening of the city.

The noise level was measured in the summer and autumn (after the fall of the leaves), as well as in the absence of precipitation and strong wind. A route of measurements was compiled with the selection of certain points for the study. At each point, three replicates were measured at different time intervals: in the morning (7.00 - 9.00), in the afternoon (12.00 - 15.00) and in the evening (17.00 - 20.00). For the accuracy of each result, the computation duration was at least 5 minutes. The microphone of the sound level meter was directed towards the noise source at a distance of half a meter from the observer.

In summer, the minimum noise level of 25 dBA was observed in parks and squares. This is due to the presence of green spaces. The maximum value of 52 dBA was observed on Rovio Street. In the autumn (impersonal period), the minimum noise level was fixed at 30 dB on Lisa Chaikina Street. The maximum value of 59 dBA was observed on the Lososin Highway. The maximum values in most cases adjoin the places of delay of the traffic flow (pedestrian crossing, traffic light). Also, the noise level is increased in places where illiterate landscaping is created or not created at all.

The results of studies of the dustiness of the city's atmosphere show the level of dustiness in the central district of the city. The minimum amount of dust on the Topol Siberian leaves was recorded at a distance of 0.3 km from the lake - 0.0587 g / m2, maximum at a distance of 2.08 km 0.3108 g / m2. On the leaves of Lipa large leaf, the maximum value was found at a distance of 0.5 km - 0.2375 g / m2, the minimum - at a distance of 0.08 km -0.0406 g / m2. The distance from the water area of the lake has no effect on the dust content.

The results of the studies show the level of dustiness in the central district of the city. The minimum amount of dust on the leaves of the Topol Siberian was recorded at a distance of 0.3 km from the lake - 0.0587 g / m2, maximum at a distance of 2.08 km 0.3108 g / m2. On the leaves of Lipa large leaf (Figure 5) the maximum value was found at a distance of 0.5 km - 0.2375 g / m2, the minimum - at a distance of 0.08 km -0.0406 g / m2. The distance from the water area of the lake does not affect the content of dust in the air.

This numeral indicates the need to create additional green spaces. Regardless of climatic parameters and temperature conditions, cities experience an acute shortage of gardening.

Green plants are able to neutralize the harmful effects of many negative environmental factors. The problem of gardening is complicated in conditions of dense development, when in order to save space, similar houses are being built, leaving no space between them for parks and public gardens. One of the ways to solve the problem can be the creation of green roofs, when on the roofs of buildings, depending on the required functions, an exploited or unexploited construction, including green plantations, is created.

G. Petrozavodsk is a unique city. The range of fluctuations in average annual temperatures is from -40 to +30 degrees. The amplitude of the temperature fluctuation is 70 degrees. This number is typical for a few cities, some of which are located in the south near the equator (see cities). Therefore, in part, studies conducted in Petrozavodsk can be considered model for cities with wide amplitude of average annual temperatures.

The green roof allows you to reduce the air temperature in cities in summer (up to 10 ° C), thereby reducing the effect of the thermal island; Exclude the release of hazardous to human health volatile substances; Reduce air pollution (plants on the roof can catch up to 50% dust from the air streams); ensure the supply of oxygen; Reduce the total background noise from 2 to 10 dB; increase due to the slow evaporation of moisture from the soil humidity in the cities; regulate the number of storm drains; To exclude rapid spread of fire on the roof surface during fires.

Recent studies conducted in conditions with a wide range of fluctuations in mean annual temperatures have shown that the difference in temperature in the premises under the green roof and under the usual roof is 0.76 ° C. The difference in the room temperature under the green roof and the environment was 2.45 ° C. The difference in the room temperature under the usual roof and the environment was 1.69 ° C.

The Russian company "Green roofs" is a scientific and productive branch of Petrozavodsk State University. It was very interested to work in Australia, where there is no such technology for making roofs, but it did not have success in overcoming the existing barriers. The authors of the chapter before presenting their experience of overcoming these barriers below represent the company "Green roofs".

Green plants are capable of neutralizing the harmful effects of most negative environmental factors. The problem with planting of greenery is getting more challenging in the restrained urban conditions, namely when twin houses are built to save space, leaving no room for parks and public gardens. One of the solutions to this problem could be construction of green roofs, when on the surface of regular roofs a certain design with green plants is set which is either in or out of use, depending on its purpose.

A green roof is able to lower air temperatures in cities in summer (up to 10ºC), thus decreasing the heat island effect; to prevent emissions of volatile substances which are detrimental to people's health; to decrease air pollution (rooftop plants are capable of keeping up to 50% of dust from the air flow); to provide oxygen supply; to lower the general background noise by 2-10 dB; to increase air moisture in cities because of the slow water evaporation from soil; to adjust the number of storm drains; to prevent fire from spreading fast on the surface of the roof in case of emergency. Thanks to modern technologies and materials it is now possible to create rooftop gardens with lawns, flowerbeds, ponds and fountains.

An extensive downside of industrialization is waste management. If we take into consideration the cafe-coffee culture in Australia, it creates a colossal damage. According to sustainable campus of university of Melbourne it is estimated that Australians use one billion disposable coffee cups each year. Large amount of plastic and paper use goes towards the culture of industrialized societies however we have not yet reached a point where we can handle the waste created up to the present point. When considering a further industrialization of largely populated region such as Africa the factor of waste management cannot be ignored.

A green roof (ecological roof, accessible roof, living roof, and vegetation covered roof) is a roof that is partially or completely covered with vegetation located in the upper part of a roof panel on a waterproof membrane with a growing medium.

Researchers single out two types of green roofs: intensive and extensive. There are also some transitional options: half-intensive green roofs and half-extensive green roofs. All these types are mainly differentiated by thickness of a growing medium, mounting and running costs and by species of plants used in green roofs construction.

Extensive Green Roofs

An extensive way of roof greening is the easiest one. It is often used on roofs of industrial factories as well as in greening garage, gazebo and terrace roofs and roofs of different kinds of household buildings.

It is worth mentioning that extensive green roofs are not designed for walking or recreation and are mostly used for ecological or aesthetical purposes.

Such type of roofs has a very thin growing medium and besides that it does not require much maintenance. As far as economy goes, this type of roofs is considered the least resource-intensive.

Various species of moss, succulent plants, and herbs are often used in extensive roof construction. Such roofs are typically covered with sedum, and spurge, aye-green. These plants are officially approved for green roof construction in America and Singapore.

Features of extensive green roofs:

- Limited number of plants, few opportunities for creating a composition;
- Low running costs – normally not more than two checks a year;
- The roof is not thick;
- It does not weigh much;
- Cheap installation and technical maintenance are in Solution and recommendations.

Intensive Green Roofs

Such kind of roofs has a thicker growing medium that allows to grow trees and shrubs (except for species with a taproot system).

Permanent technical maintenance, irrigation and fertilizers are necessary for enabling intensive green roofs to function properly.

Intensive greening is characterized by:

- Thick layer of soil;
- Heavy weight;
- Higher capital costs;
- Increased diversity of plants.

An intensive green roof is a real garden that gives an opportunity to grow not only plants but also shrubs and trees. According to its performance characteristics, a green roof can hold from 100 to 700 kg for 1 m^2.

The technology of green roof construction includes several important stages.

1. Pre-design stage

This stage implies analyzing the given roof, how suitable it is to be turned into a green roof. Records of the building are looked into (the building's permissible load, roof coating materials), sizes of the planned roof are measured, the roof's susceptibility to winds is found out, and also a sunlight analysis is done (unless the data is provided in the records)

The building's permissible load must be no less than 200 kg for 1 m^2 (considering an average snow load to be 100 kg for 1 m^2). In this case it is possible to construct a roof of the extensive type. An intensive green roof requires the permissible load to be more than 200 kg for 1 m^2. It is crucial to be aware of the layers of the given roofing pie in order to specify the number of layers in a future green roof. So, if the given roof has liquid roofing, it means that a green roof can be created without any deconstruction.

It is necessary to measure the inclination of the given roof to determine the type of a green roof to be constructed. The inclination being less than 8 degrees allows constructing any type of roof. The inclination about 8 degrees is believed to be the most suitable for a green roof. With a bigger inclination only an extensive green roof could be constructed with the use of a volume georgic.

A sunlight analysis, the roof's susceptibility to winds as well as the wind diagram help to find proper plants that would naturalize best on this given roof.

At this stage the green roof type is chosen (extensive, half-intensive, intensive). A landscape design project of the green roof is created depending on its type; the basic structure of the green roof is determined in accordance with the given roof. Choosing the type of the roof implies analyzing the data gathered during the previous stage. Such a comprehensive approach allows constructing the roof type that best fits the building. The construction of an extensive green roof does not differ much from the construction of an intensive green roof. In making a rooftop garden with large-sized trees it is possible to make use of extra water isolation and a blocking layer (landscape fabric) to create a better protection from root penetration. Construction of different types of roofs depends on how thick the layer of the soil is.

It is advisable to use the following construction materials:

- VA pour barrier – Izospan A, Izospan B;
- Thermal covering – glass wool;
- Surface cast - cement-sandy mixture;
- Water isolation – liquid rubber;
- Drain membrane – graded membrane PLANTER TechnoNicol;
- Landscape fabric – polymeric nonwoven material 200 gr/m^2.

The water drain installation scheme is shown in figure 1.

Figure 1. The water drain installation scheme

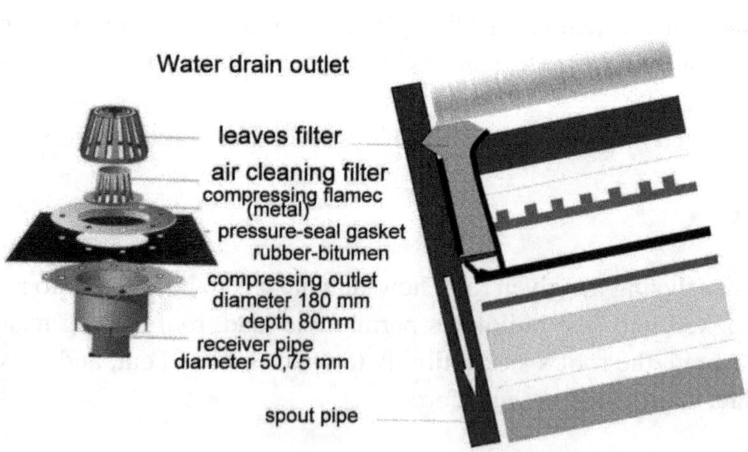

A water drain outlet is used for this purpose; it is also waterproofed with a layer of liquid rubber. The water drain outlet is attached to the spout pipe of the roof. The outlet is put between the layer of green plants and water isolation in the lowest part of the roof. To provide the best water drain the inclination of the green roof must be 8 degrees.

The design of a green roof depends on certain conditions (insolation, exposure to winds, and the wind diagram). A set of documents is prepared: a general layout, a dendrological plan, a layout drawing, a plants drawing, and a lighting and watering plan (if necessary)

At this stage the green roof construction is carried out, its landscape design is created and the whole green roof construction process is supervised.

Upon finishing the construction of a green roof it is important to take a range of measures to take care both of the roof and the plants that are growing on it. So that the green roof could function properly, the following requirements must be met:

1. Monitoring leaks 2 times a year (in autumn and in spring after pouring rains and snow melting).
2. Using supplementary fertilizers or bio compost in the ground coat in order to provide better nutrition for green plants and help them naturalize - at least once a year.
3. Monitoring the plants' condition regularly. As the first symptoms of freezing or different diseases appear it is necessary to provide good quality treatment and care.
4. Conducting technical maintenance of water drain outlets at least two times a year (in autumn and in spring).
5. If applicable, conducting technical maintenance of automatic irrigation and illumination systems before and after use.
6. Immediate removal of weeds and other undesirable plants.
7. During construction and use of intensive and half-intensive roofs it is necessary to protect them against pests.
8. During construction and use of intensive and half-intensive roofs such measures are necessary as timely lawn mowing, repairing lawns, decorative and anti-age trimming of trees and shrubs.

The proposed technology should be based on theoretical understanding of the processes from the point of view of population ecology and mathematical modeling. The authors have an approach to consider the green technology as a population development process (Belozyorov, Chernyshenko, 2014), forming a succession, which leads to sustainable ecosystems (Chernyshenko, Ruzich, (2013).

MAIN FOCUS OF THE CHAPTER

Issues, Controversies, Problems

The main focus of the research, the results of which are outlined in this chapter, is how to solve the problems, disagreements and problems of the experience of intercultural students / teachers, and the business of green roofs and how these decisions are related to urban policies and / or urban growth in Australia and Russia. Proceeding from the foregoing, it is necessary to combine the results obtained in the Russian Federation on the experience of intercultural students / teachers, and the business of green roofs. To do this, we need to develop new, special principles and create a practice of qualitative case study by all the numerous participants engaged in this research project. The need to develop and create such a qualitative approach was dictated by the fact that the research of case studies is focused on the development of large descriptions of specific phenomena (events, experiences and meanings that are attributed to them) in the epistemology of the concrete. Therefore, we used the traditions of case studies, as our research was intended to provide a detailed, holistic and descriptive description of how Australian student teachers interpreted their experience in the Russian Federation and how the teachers and pupils of the Russian mentor perceived their experience with Australian students teachers, and how the Russian green roof business integrated into the Australian reality, breaking all intercultural barriers, The created opportunity are related to urban policies and / or urban growth in Australia and Russia. The study was also based on the belief that a case study is the preferred strategy when:

1. The question "how" or "why" is asked about a modern set of events, according to which the researcher has practically no control;
2. Researchers are interested in insight, discovery and interpretation, not in testing hypotheses;
3. The type of data required is what people tell you and what they do, which allows the researcher to understand the meaning of what is happening;
4. Using this approach of qualitative case study, we organized this research project so that we could hear the voices of the participants.

Using this approach of qualitative case study, we organized a poll so that the participants could hear the voices of both the Russian Federation and the Australian Federation. To protect the anonymity of participants, aliases were used during the study. Four students of the fourth year undergraduate education voluntarily participated in the study. These pedagogical students and social workers have already successfully completed more than 70 days of vocational training in primary and secondary schools in Australia. The minimum requirement for registration by the Victorian Teachers Institute in Australia is 80 days of supervised training. At the beginning of the trip they did not have the skills of the Russian language. During a three-week international training in the Russian Federation, they were already able to work with local journals that contained statistical information and that included daily experience in the school and other details of cultural experiences and excursions. Students, educators and social workers described what they observed in the school, and how they felt about Russian educational concepts, student training activities, strategies and approaches to learning, and about the lessons they taught. They also included observations and reflections on weekend activities outside the school. At the end of the trip, the student teachers completed the final analytical work, which was the main source of data for this study. In addition, records of researchers of class observation in the Russian Federation and e-mail messages from the teachers and social workers' judges were also used as sources of data. As noted above, the Russian company "Green Roofs", this scientific and productive division of Petrozavodsk State University was very interested in working in Australia, where there is no such technology for making roofs, but was not successful in overcoming the existing barriers. The authors of the chapter have developed a new on Solutions and Recommendations overcoming this barrier, which is described below decisions, are related to urban policies and / or urban growth in Australia and Russia.

SOLUTIONS AND RECOMMENDATIONS

To present the results of the research, we organized data on three broad topics; first, a valuable cultural experience for all participants; secondly, differences in educational concepts and learning strategies, and thirdly, student-teachers and social workers reflect on their personal and professional development. We recognize that these individual topics can be interpreted in several ways and distributed in different categories. Where possible, for the purposes of this document, we focus on the initial voices of the participants.

In general, Australian student teachers, local tutor teachers and local students appreciate this cross-cultural experience and consider it an unforgettable and meaningful life experience. Some of the basic values in traditional Russian culture, such as respect for teachers, hospitality and friendliness, impressed the Australians very much. The warm reception and friendly attitude of teachers and pupils of the school was repeatedly noted. Valuable cultural experiences and attitudes for Australian student teachers and social workers, as well as Russian teachers and students, along with the green roof business project, provided an interesting, new solution to the issues of urban and / or urban growth in Australia and Russia. In everything, everything was mentioned, how stimulating and exciting cultural experiences were for themselves and how they were warmly welcomed in schools and culture.

The goal is to link the barriers and style of management of intercultural communication (Gerald, 2000), the communication system and the behavior of employees of the Russian firm Green Roofs in Australia. Highlights define the basis of the conceptual model and hypothesis to achieve this goal (Huselid, et al, 1997; Becker et al, 1999; Wright, et al 1999). Therefore, we developed and tested six hypotheses, the verification of which served as a test for the purpose of the study, namely, is described below decisions, are related to urban policies and / or urban growth in Australia and Russia. These hypotheses are expressed as follows:

Hypotheses

- National culture does not influence the style of management of Russian companies
- National culture influences the style of management of Russian companies.
- The national culture does not affect the communication management system of Russian companies.
- National culture influences the communication system of management of Russian companies.
- National culture does not affect the behavior of Russian companies
- The national culture influences the behavior of Russian companies.
- National cultural values affect the productivity of the team in Russian companies.

Testing the Hypothesis

Based on the purpose of this study, three hypotheses were mainly proposed. Each hypothesis was tested using correlation analysis and multiple linear regression analysis and variance analysis. As for obtaining significant items related to the values of the national culture, intercultural communication barriers and efficiency, factor analysis was conducted. All variables, with the exception of communication systems, are positively and significantly correlated with Team Management. The style of behavior and management of personnel in terms of choosing hiring is up to 20% of the difference in the company's performance (R2 = 0.2). To test the mitigating effect of the communication barriers measured by the power distance on the relationship between the management style and personnel behavior, the coefficient of determination (R2) obtained when the cultural orientations were in the regression equation and when they were not compared. Communication barriers and national culture account for 30% of the total productivity of the group. We conducted a study in which we developed a conceptual model linking all variables by introducing intercultural communication barriers to mitigate the relationship between national culture and management style, communication system and staff behavior. Their joint influence on the work of the team earlier, before us was not considered in Russian firms operating in Australia.

The conceptual model of the small Russian company "Green Roof" to overcome existing barriers in Australia is shown in Figure 2.

We found that the structure assumes that the relationship between the national orientation to culture, the style of management, the communication system and the behavior of personnel. It is proved that there is a direct link between the national culture and the teams. Our research put forward the hypothesis of a direct link between national culture and the work of the team. It was shown that existing intercultural barriers, a moderate relationship between national culture and managerial consequences in a multinational firm. It can be argued that the national cultural values do not directly lead to team productivity, but they affect the process, for example, motivate the work of employees, and these processes ultimately lead to the achievement of the team. As a result of our research, we emphasize a fundamental understanding of how the Russian company Green Roof is facing cultural barriers in communicating with the leadership of teams in Australia. Moreover, the result was influenced by the index of national cultural values (power distance, individualism / collectivism, masculinity / femininity and long-term orientation) to command management. From the analysis of the results, these communication barriers are associated with the influence of national culture on the workplace and the behavior of people with different identities (boss and subordinates). However, all the recommendations and decisions in today's conditions, namely, in the digital economy, require a digital transformation, only in this case it is possible that the results obtained were relevant for urban and / or urban growth in Australia and Russia. Therefore, based on the published works of Professor Mkrttchian (2018), technical solutions were summarized that are universal in nature and are given below.

Figure 2. A conceptual model of small Russian company "Green Roof" for overcoming the existing barriers in Australia

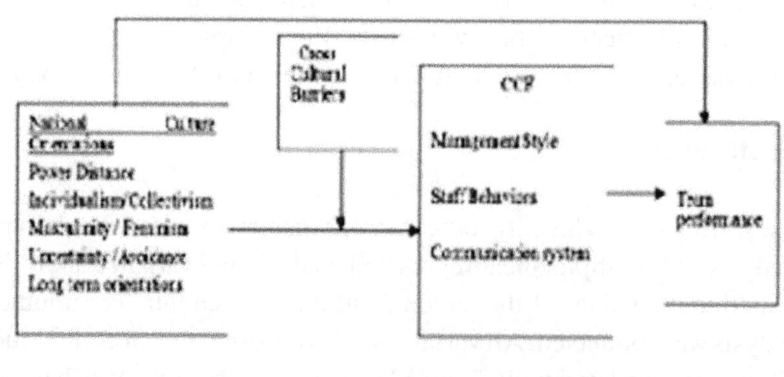

Digital Economy and Digital Transformation

The analysis would be incomplete without mentioning the results of comparing the state of the digital economy and Green Roof in Australia and the Russian Federation, especially on digital transformation. As a result of the implementation of our project, it was established that Australia, developed by the level of the digital economy, can adopt the Russian experience of teaching the basics of digital transformation of participants in this process. We have established how the learning process takes place.

The two sides of digital transformation are centered on local hardware, software and infrastructure for a distributed virtual machine model, software as a service and cloud IT. This is the transition from the physically grounded world to the digital one. This is a digital transformation. This transformation consists of two parts: the technological side and the human side. Most business and IT leaders already have a technological side, but they do not pay attention to the human side: the understanding that effective digital transformation is related to how people adopt and use technology, at least as well as in technology itself. And this applies not only to people at the top of your organization, but to everyone who works for you, especially if they interact directly with customers.

The digital approach should help in forming a proper legal environment for the considering educational transformations including green roof, particularly, of international standards (Chernyshenko, Okhrimenko, 2009) and qualification frameworks (Mitrofanova, et al, 2105). According to the research (Mlrttchian, et al, 2018) the achievement of a complete and successful digital transformation depends not only on the right technology, but also on:

- From the leaders. People at the top of your organization must lead the way through digital transformations, for example, using the same tools that they expect everyone else will use;
- From managing an employee's trip, exactly the way you manage your customer's trip. Each user expects that the online experience will be as smooth as that of the world's leading digital companies.

These are small tasks, but they are much easier to accomplish with an integrated, seamless and secure solution. Just like cloud IT solutions can help you improve the quality of customer service, it will also help you provide the best experience with employees. This can become a real impact on the business when first-line employees feel able to help their clients in new and exciting directions.

Two Critical Business Effects

Collaboration uses the collective mental capacity of your employees. Two main components are basic for collaborative technologies: the ability to work from virtually anywhere and the ability to work with simple intuitive solutions on almost any device. Premium solutions offer integrated tools that help everyone to contribute. They are easier to adapt to your specific needs and culture, they are easily scaled, they have more life cycles, and their creators usually offer better long-term support. And since they are more common, new employees may already know how to use them, which reduces the time and cost of training.

Creativity depends on the ability to find innovative solutions to existing problems. From there, it expands the possibilities of finding these solutions, finding and fixing problems and testing them again. Creativity in business is not just a series of wild ideas, ideas must also work. Thus, the necessary tools for working together also help you stimulate creativity, simplifying the experiment and finding ideas that really work.

Security and Management

Digital transformation has opened up new opportunities, but it has also raised increased security concerns. Triple H-Avatar helps protect data that has been trusted with intelligent, permanent protection that protects data on many devices and scenarios. A simplified IT environment also allows your IT team to create and manage employees' devices and services, which reduces the burden on members of your IT team.

Business creativity depends on the ability to find innovative solutions to existing problems. Fortunately, there is a simple answer: Triple H-Avatar meets the needs of the enterprise. It integrates all existing technologies and equipment to help employees be more creative and work together safely, namely;

- Unlock creativity, helping its people to work with documents, voice and touch, all backed up by tools using AI and machine learning.
- Provides the widest and deepest applications and services, as well as a universal tool for collaboration, giving its people the flexibility and choice in how they connect exchange and communicate.
- Simplifies IT by integrating management of users, devices, applications and services.
- Helps protect customer data, company data and intellectual property with built-in intellectual protection.

Triple H-Avatar is designed for businesses with up to 50 users, but this is not limited, if necessary, the number of users can be increased to 3000. It combines all available resources with individual security and management functions. It also helps to expand the capabilities of employees, protect your business and simplify the management of IT. Namely;

- Helps your teams achieve more by better connecting employees, customers and suppliers.
- Helps your employees work anywhere on any device.
- Protects data on all devices with permanent protection.
- Simplifies the configuration and management of employees' devices and services using a single IT console.

Example of Industrial Internet in sharing use Triple H-Avatar technology from Small Russian Company "Green Roof" for overcoming the existing barriers in Australia show in fig.3

FUTURE RESEARCH DIRECTIONS

Future research on our chapter are related to intercultural progress on the part of countries and their institutions, green roof policies and urban growth policies will be aimed at studying the interaction of people, sensors, composing Internet of things, Internet sing, analysis and storage of Big Data and cyber physical systems.

Figure 3. Industrial internet in sharing use triple H-avatar technology from a small Russian company "green roof" for overcoming the existing barriers in Australia

Industrial Internet

WORLD MARKET	PILOT PROJECTS IN RUSSIA
IBM PTC GE Microsoft SAP Amazon Cisco	System integrators Foreign solution provider Software engineer
SCENARIOS OF USE	
User	**Goal**
Plants	Serviceability monitoring and optimization of equipment load
Logistic and transport companies	Transport optimization
Services and trade organizations	Analysis of clients' behavior, development of personal
Agricultural producers	Fields' monitoring, monitoring of cattle's health
Oil and gas companies	Percent increase in hydrocarbons' extraction

CONCLUSION

- As a result of our research, we underline a fundamental understanding of how the Russian firm "Green Roofs" faces cross cultural barriers to communication while managing teams in Australia. Moreover, the result was influenced by the index of national cultural values (power distance, individualism / collectivism, masculinity / femininity and long-term orientation) to command management. From the analysis of the results, these communication barriers are associated with the influence of national culture on the workplace and the behavior of people with different identities (bosses and subordinates).
- We have established that the structure assumes that the relationship between the national orientation to culture, the style of management, the communication system and the behavior of personnel. It is proven that there is a direct link between national culture and teams. Our research put forward the hypothesis of a direct link between national culture and the work of the team. It was shown that existing intercultural barriers, a moderate relationship between national culture and managerial consequences in a multinational firm. It can be argued that the national values of culture do not directly lead to team productivity, but they influence the process, for example, to motivate the work of employees, and it is these processes that ultimately lead to the achievement of the team.
- At the same time, a study of the problem of cyber-physics system for Digital Transformation showed that is section of information security, within the framework of which the processes of formation, functioning and evolution of cyber-physics objects are studied, to identify sources of

cyber-danger formed while determining their characteristics, as well as their classification and formation of regulatory documents, implementation of Digital Transformation in future. This also is certainly true, and this truth has again never been questioned. However, working in the application of Machine Learning for Digital Transformation with the using the author's Avatars-Based Management techniques, we came to the conclusion that this is not so, and the built-in cyber-physics systems can be destroyed by the same artificial intelligence.

- Example of Industrial Internet in sharing use Triple H-Avatar technology from Small Russian Company "Green Roof" for overcoming the existing barriers in Australia

ACKNOWLEDGMENT

This research was supported by the Russian Foundation for Basic Research –

[Grant number 18-010-00204] entitled: Fundamental basis for the development of mechanisms for effective digital service-oriented interaction of participants in socio-economic systems and networks.

REFERENCES

Adler N J (1997). A typology of management studies involving culture. *Journal of International Business Studies*, 29-47.

AFDB Policy Brief. (2010). *Chinese trade and investment activities in Africa*. African Development Bank Group, Chief Economist Complex.

Asheghian, P., & Ebrahimi, B. (1990). *International business: economics, environment and strategies*. New York: Harper Collins Publishers.

Baregu, M. (2008). The three faces of the dragon: Tanzania-China relation in historical perspective. In *Crouching tiger, hidden dragon? Africa and China*. University of KwaZulu-Natal Press.

Barney, J. B., & Wright, P. M. (1998). On become a strategic partner: The role of Human resource in gaining competitive advantage. *Human Resource Management*, *37*(1), 31–46. doi:10.1002/(SICI)1099-050X(199821)37:1<31::AID-HRM4>3.0.CO;2-W

Becker, B. E., & Huselid, M. A. (1999). Overview: Strategic human resource management in five leading firms. *Human Resource Management*, *38*(4), 287–301. doi:10.1002/(SICI)1099-050X(199924)38:4<287::AID-HRM2>3.0.CO;2-L

Belozyorov, V. Ye., & Chernyshenko, S. (2014). Quadratic model of inter-population interaction: Investigation of stability areas. *Applied Mathematics and Computation*, *230*, 43–56. doi:10.1016/j.amc.2013.12.095

Benet, M. J. (1988). Intercultural communication: A current perspective. In M. J. Bennet (Ed.), Basic Concepts of intercultural communication: selected readings. Yarmouth, ME: Intercultural Press.

Bennet, M. J. (1998). Intercultural communication: A current perspective. In M. J. Bennet (Ed.), *Basic concepts of intercultural communication: Selected readings* (pp. 1–34). Yarmouth, ME: Intercultural Press.

Bershadsky, A., Berezin, A., & Mkrttchian, V. (2018). Theoretical and Technological Perspectives on Development of Information Monitoring System for Solving Complex Problems. In U. G. Benna (Ed.), Optimizing Regional Development Through Transformative Urbanization. Hershey, PA: IGI Global. Doi:10.4018/978-1-5225-5448-6.ch006

Burke, C., & Corkin, L. (2006). *China's interest and activity in Africa's Construction and infrastructure sectors*. Centre for Chinese Studies, Stellenbosch University.

Chaponniere, J. R. (2009). Chinese aid to Africa, origins, forms and issues. In The New Presence of China in Africa. Amsterdam University Press.

Chernyshenko, S. V., Demchyk, O. I., & Chernyshenko, V. S. (2012). Regional system of higher education management: Information support of interaction with stakeholders. *J. of Pedagogical Informatics, 18*(1-2), 134–146.

Chernyshenko, S. V., & Okhrimenko, O. A. (2009). Formalisation of international education standards: Design of information models with use of computer technologies. *Proceedings of International Conference "Actual Problems of International Cooperation in the Field of Science and Education"*, 257-264.

Chernyshenko, S. V., & Ruzich, R. V. (2013). Bifurcation Model of Successions in Ecosystems. *Proceedings of 27th European Conference on Modelling and Simulation. ECMS-2013*, 169-174.

Foster, V., Butterfield, W., Chuan, C., & Pushak, N. (2008). *Building bridges; China's growing roles as infrastructure financier for sub-Saharan Africa*. Washington, DC: World Bank.

Fua, Y., & Kamenou, N. (2011). The Impact of Chinese values on Human resource policies and practices within transnational corporations in China. *The International Journal of Human Resource Management, 22*(16), 3270-3289.

Gamidullaeva, L., Potapova, I., Shatokhin, M., & Mkrttchian, V. (2018). Increasing Territorial Economic Growth through Cost Optimization in the Digital Economy. In U. G. Benna (Ed.), Optimizing Regional Development Through Transformative Urbanization. Hershey, PA: IGI Global. Doi:10.4018/978-1-5225-5448-6.ch009

Gamidullaeva, L., Vasin, S., & Mkrttchian, V. (2018). *Regional Economic Growth and Open Innovation Platforms: Emerging Trends and New Opportunities*. Academic Press.

Gerald, M. J. (2000). Cross-cultural Industrial and Organizational psychology: introduction to the special issue. *Journal of Applied Psychology: An International Review*, 191-123.

Gorbunova, Yu. N., Bykova, A. V., & Chernyshenko, S. V. (2012) Social and psychological aspects of education process quality as a factor of forming competitiveness of a manager in labour market. *Human Resources Management in the Russian Innovation Economy. Conference Proceedings*, 106-112.

Hitt, M. A., Keats, B. W., & DeMarie, S. M. (1998). Navifating in the new competitive landscape:Building competitive advantage flexibility in the 21st century. *The Academy of Management Executive, 12*, 22–42.

Hofsetde, G. (2001). Culture Consequences: Comparing values, Behaviors, Institutions and Organizations across Nations, Thousand Oaks California. *Sage (Atlanta, Ga.), 2001*, 25–40.

House, R. J., Wright, N. S., & Aditya, R. N. (1997). Cross-Cultural research on organizational leaderhip: a critical analysis and a proposed theory. In New Perspectives in international industrial Organizational Psychology. New Lexington Press.

Kwani, Y.A., & Ofori, G. (2001). Chinese Culture and Successful Implementation of partnering in Singapore's Construction Industry. *Construction Management and Economics, 19*, 619–632.

Merkin, R. S. (2006). Uncertainty avoidance and face work: A test of the Hofstede Model. *International Journal of Intercultural Relations, 30*(2), 213–228. doi:10.1016/j.ijintrel.2005.08.001

Mitrofanova, E.A., Afanasyev, V.Y., & Chernyshenko, S.V. (2015). *Development of sectoral qualification framework: methodology and practice*. Moscow: Publishing House of State University of Management.

Mkrttchian, V. (2011). Use 'hhh" technology in transformative models of online education. In G. Kurubacak & T. Vokan Yuzer (Eds.), *Handbook of research on transformative online education and liberation: Models for social equality* (pp. 340–351). Hershey, PA: IGI Global. doi:10.4018/978-1-60960-046-4.ch018

Mkrttchian, V. (2012). Avatar manager and student reflective conversations as the base for describing meta-communication model. In G. Kurubacak, T. Vokan Yuzer, & U. Demiray (Eds.), *Meta-communication for reflective online conversations: Models for distance education* (pp. 340–351). Hershey, PA: IGI Global. doi:10.4018/978-1-61350-071-2.ch005

Mkrttchian, V. (2015). Modeling using of Triple H-Avatar Technology in online Multi-Cloud Platform Lab. In M. Khosrow-Pour (Ed.), Encyclopedia of Information Science and Technology (3rd ed.; pp. 4162-4170). Hershey, PA: IGI Global. Doi:10.4018/978-1-4666-5888-2.ch409

Mkrttchian, V., & Aleshina, E. (2017). *Sliding Mode in Intellectual Control and Communication: Emerging Research and Opportunities*. Hershey, PA: IGI Global. doi:10.4018/978-1-5225-2292-8

Mkrttchian, V., & Aleshina, E. (2017). Sliding Mode in Real Communication. In *Sliding Mode in Intellectual Control and Communication: Emerging Research and Opportunities* (pp. 22–29). Hershey, PA: IGI Global. doi:10.4018/978-1-5225-2292-8.ch003

Mkrttchian, V., Amirov, D., & Belyanina, L. (2017). Optimizing an Online Learning Course Using Automatic Curating in Sliding Mode. In N. Ostashewski, J. Howell, & M. Cleveland-Innes (Eds.), *Optimizing K-12 Education through Online and Blended Learning* (pp. 213–224). Hershey, PA: IGI Global. doi:10.4018/978-1-5225-0507-5.ch011

Mkrttchian, V., Aysmontas, B., Uddin, M., Andreev, A., & Vorovchenko, N. (2015). The Academic views from Moscow Universities of the Cyber U-Learning on the Future of Distance Education at Russia and Ukraine. In G. Eby & T. Vokan Yuzer (Eds.), *Identification, Evaluation, and Perceptions of Distance Education Experts* (pp. 32–45). Hershey, PA: IGI Global. doi:10.4018/978-1-4666-8119-4.ch003

Mkrttchian, V., & Belyanina, L. (Eds.). (2018). *Handbook of Research on Students' Research Competence in Modern Educational Contexts*. Hershey, PA: IGI Global. doi:10.4018/978-1-5225-3485-3

Mkrttchian, V., Berezin, An., Berezin, A., Veretikhina, S., Bershadsky, A., & Potapova, I. (2018). Model of Benchmarking for Development of Firm's Competitive Advantage to Improve Economic Growth in Cities. In U. G. Benna (Ed.), *Optimizing Regional Development Through Transformative Urbanization*. Hershey, PA: IGI Global. doi:10.4018/978-1-5225-5448-6.ch008

Mkrttchian, V., Bershadsky, A., Bozhday, A., & Fionova, L. (2015). Model in SM of DEE Based on Service Oriented Interactions at Dynamic Software Product Lines. In G. Eby & T. Vokan Yuzer (Eds.), *Identification, Evaluation, and Perceptions of Distance Education Experts* (pp. 230–247). Hershey, PA: IGI Global. doi:10.4018/978-1-4666-8119-4.ch014

Mkrttchian, V., Bershadsky, A., Bozhday, A., Kataev, M., & Kataev, S. (Eds.). (2016). *Handbook of Research on Estimation and Control Techniques in E-Learning systems*. Hershey, PA: IGI Global. doi:10.4018/978-1-4666-9489-7

Mkrttchian, V., Bershadsky, A., Finogeev, A., Berezin, A., & Potapova, I. (2017). Digital Model of Bench-Marking for Development of Competitive Advantage. In P. Isaias & L. Carvalho (Eds.), *User Innovation and the Entrepreneurship Phenomenon in the Digital Economy* (pp. 288–303). Hershey, PA: IGI Global. doi:10.4018/978-1-5225-2826-5.ch014

Mkrttchian, V., Kataev, M., Hwang, W., Bedi, S., & Fedotova, A. (2014). Using Plug-Avatars "hhh" Technology Education as Service-Oriented Virtual Learning Environment in Sliding Mode. In G. Eby & T. Vokan Yuzer (Eds.), *Emerging Priorities and Trends in Distance Education: Communication, Pedagogy, and Technology*. Hershey, PA: IGI Global. doi:10.4018/978-1-4666-5162-3.ch004

Mkrttchian, V., Kataev, M., Hwang, W., Bedi, S., & Fedotova, A. (2016). Using Plug-Avatars "hhh" Technology Education as Service-Oriented Virtual Learning Environment in Sliding Mode. In Leadership and Personnel Management: Concepts, Methodologies, Tools, and Applications (pp. 890-902). Hershey, PA: IGI Global. doi:10.4018/978-1-4666-9624-2.ch039

Mkrttchian, V., & Stephanova, G. (2013). Training of Avatar Moderator in Sliding Mode Control. In G. Eby & T. Vokan Yuzer (Eds.), *Project Management Approaches for Online Learning Design* (pp. 175–203). Hershey, PA: IGI Global. doi:10.4018/978-1-4666-2830-4.ch009

Mkrttchian, V., & Stephanova, G. (2013). Training of Avatar Moderator in Sliding Mode Control Environment for Virtual Project Management. In Enterprise Resource Planning: Concepts, Methodologies, Tools, and Applications (pp. 1376-1405). Hershey, PA: IGI Global. Doi:10.4018/978-1-4666-4153-2.ch074

Potapova, I., Vasin, S., Gamidullasrva, L., Tolstykh, T., Belyanin, L., & Mkrttchian, V. (2018). Drivers of Urban Development in Terms of Education Based on Digital Technologies. In U. G. Benna (Ed.), Optimizing Regional Development Through Transformative Urbanization. Hershey, PA: IGI Global. Doi:10.4018/978-1-5225-5448-6.ch003

Roberstson, C. J. (2000). The global dispersion of Chinese values: A three-country study of Confucian dynamism. *Management International Review*, *40*(3).

Rozkwitalska, M. (2010). Barriers of Cross-cultural Interactions According to Research Findings. *Journal of Intercultural Management*, *2*(2), 37–52.

Schuler, R. S., Dowling, P. J., & De Cieri, H. (1993). An intergrative framework of strategic international human resource management. *International Journal of Human Resource Management*, *4*(4), 717–764. doi:10.1080/09585199300000056

Shree, S. (2011). Challenges Before Management with Reference to Cross Cultural Issues and Communication. *The IUP Journal of Soft Skills*, *V*(3), 7–11.

Sonja, A. S., & Philips, M. E. (2004). Contextual influence on Culture Research Shifting: Assumptions for New Workplace Realities. *Applied Psychology*, *49*(1), 192–221.

Tanzania Investment Centre. (2008). *Chinese trade and Investment in Tanzania*. Author.

Tolstykh, T., Vasin, S., Gamidullaeva, L., & Mkrttchian, V. (2017). The Control of Continuing Education Based on the Digital Economy. In P. Isaias & L. Carvalho (Eds.), *User Innovation and the Entrepreneurship Phenomenon in the Digital Economy* (pp. 153–171). Hershey, PA: IGI Global. doi:10.4018/978-1-5225-2826-5.ch008

Tolstykh, T., Vertakova, J., & Shkarupeta, E. (2018). Professional Training for Structural Economic Transformations Based on Competence approach in the Digital Age. In Handbook of Research on Students' Research Competence in Modern Educational Contexts (pp. 209-229). Hershey, PA: IGI Global. Doi:10.4018/978-1-5225-3485-3.ch011

Triandis, H. (1988). Collectivism vs individualism: a reconceptualization of a basic concept in cross-cultural psychology. In G. Verma & C. Beyley (Eds.), *Cross-cultural studies of Personality Attitudes and Cognition. Macmillan*. doi:10.1007/978-1-349-08120-2_3

Tsui, J., & Windsor, C. (2001). Some cross-cultural evidence on ethical reasoning. *Journal of Business Ethics*, *31*(2), 143–150. doi:10.1023/A:1010727320265

Vasin, S., & Gamidullaeva, L. (2017). About Russian Regional Users' Innovation Based on Digital Information. In P. Isaias & L. Carvalho (Eds.), *User Innovation and the Entrepreneurship Phenomenon in the Digital Economy* (pp. 304–319). Hershey, PA: IGI Global. doi:10.4018/978-1-5225-2826-5.ch015

Vasin, S. M., & Gamidullaeva, L. A. (2015). Methodical Approach and Tools to Improve the Efficiency of Managing of the Innovation Potential in the Context of Economic Globalization. *Review of European Studies*, *3*, 124–139.

Wright, P. M., & Snell, S. A. (1991). Toward an integrative view of strategic human resource management. *Human Resource Management Review*, *1*(3), 203–335. doi:10.1016/1053-4822(91)90015-5

KEY TERMS AND DEFINITIONS

Comparison: Special tools for cross-cultural analysis.

Cross-Cultural Analysis: Discussing some aspects of cross-cultural experiences, touching the rapidly changing small business in Australia and Russia, its cultural connection.

Cross-Cultural Communication Barriers: Understanding differences in communication systems, management practices, and decision making.

Digital Transformation: Application of multifunctional and multilevel information technology designed to reliably record various assets in the digital economy to help with technological challenges and created tools.

Green Country (Australia): Traditional international identification name of Australian Federation.

North Country (Russia): Traditional international identification name of Russian Federation.

Chapter 13
An Institutional Entrepreneurship Analysis of Biodiesel Companies in Mexico

José G. Vargas-Hernández
University of Guadalajara, Mexico

Juan José Esparza-López
Universidad de Guadalajara, Mexico

Adam Konto Kyari
Imam Abdulrahman Bin Faisal University, Saudi Arabia

ABSTRACT

The objective of this chapter is to analyze the role of the institutions in the biodiesel industry in order to know if there is a relationship with the quality and maturity of the same with the ventures. Starting from a literary review, the framework of the current situation is identified, covering aspects related to formal institutions, laws, rules, regulatory bodies, and the theory that supports the relationship between institutions and entrepreneurship. The chapter concludes that the institutions in Mexico have increased their maturity and incentive to increase the number of producers and distributors of biodiesel, thus taking advantage of the growing market.

INTRODUCTION

To reverse the current shortage of natural resources needs new breeds of innovative enterprises in the productive sectors of the economy is required. This research, therefore, seeks ways to promote the stability of the biodiesel markets that enhance competitiveness and preservation of the urban environment, and ensure a steady growth. The global biodiesel consumption is expected to rise to over 40 million liters by 2023. By which time, countries such as the United States, Germany, Netherland, Argentina, Brazil, Colombia and Chile, among others, would have come up with better approaches for the protection of the urban environment (OECD 2017). This emerging consumption trend among development actors

DOI: 10.4018/978-1-5225-7625-9.ch013

generates new markets that can be exploited by the developed economies at the expense of emerging economies that have the essential resources for the manufacture and supply of biodiesel.

Biodiesel is an emerging source of energy that creates entrepreneurial opportunities. Among the many factors driving entrepreneurship are unique opportunities and innovations that meet specific new needs that were unfelt previously. These are the types of creative entrepreneurs emerging nations need because they generate a large number of benefits, including new employment creation, and sustainable economic growth. The unexpected rising demand for biodiesel at the global level is an important and rare opportunity that must be seized. The recognition of the opportunities embedded in a growing market alone does not. However, success is ensured because facing challenges of planning and knowledge of the terrain in which entrepreneurs seek to enter the market are critical. As the biodiesel market is a relatively new market, very few entrepreneurs have the essential information to plan for entry or be competitive in the bioenergy market.

Formal institutions such as laws or agencies that oversee the demeanor of industry can be tools that help entrepreneurs to have the guidance of the actions that are possible to carry out that can be used as a knowledge, which the institutions can transfer to the entrepreneurs so as to help them to achieve success. In addition to the existence of recognized organization's sufficient quality and maturity as can be easy to use legal frameworks and regulatory agencies sound planning and implementation of actions are good examples for minimizing payable taxes. While offering fiscal support and development it may trigger a greater degree of entrepreneurship in a defined sector that may have all the needed incentives.

Preliminary investigation has shown that there was a clear problem of lack of rules governing the behaviors of actors in biodiesel sector, and this made the market in Mexico unable to consolidate. There are, however, any agencies seeking to develop enough regulations that will provide a clear roadmap for those interested in entering this rapidly emerging new market. Therefore, in this study, a theoretical analysis will be carried out to compare the evolution of the biodiesel production companies in urban Mexico to determine if there is an association with the formal institutions and how they would solve the inefficiency inherent in the sector since 2008.

BACKGROUND OF THE PROBLEM

To solve the twin problems of cleaner fuel and cleaner urban environment, the Mexican government promotes the production, distribution and consumption of biofuels in several plants. Included among the varieties of the biodiesel are those that promote the use of clean and renewable energies as alternatives to fossil fuels, consistent with the global emphasis on climate change.

Biodiesel is a mixture of monoalkyl esters of fatty acids that is obtained through processes such as the "transesterification" of industrial waste oils and fats. As a mixture of methyl esters of fatty acids, biodiesel t can replace diesel and is obtained from the reaction of vegetable oils or fats with methanol. Glycerin is obtained as a byproduct. Biodiesel is used mainly in Europe and the USA in mixtures with 5% or 20% diesel (B5, B20) or as pure biodiesel (B100). In Brazil and Argentina B5 is used.

In Mexico, the Prospective for the use of bioenergy was designed in 2003. The prospective highlights that the infrastructure used by Pemex to produce diesel can be used, considering that diesel engines would require minor adjustments to use pure biodiesel. In addition, it is considered that there has been an increase in the cultivation of oil producing plants in tropical and temperate climates and that there are fiscal incentives and subsidies to promote biodiesel. In 2007, the first study on the possibilities of bioethanol and biodiesel as transportation fuels in Mexico was conducted (SENER / BID / GTZ (Edit.), 2007).

The Investment Plan of the Clean Technology Fund (CTF) for Mexico was approved by the fiduciary committee in 2009. On June 18, 2009, the Regulation of the Law of the Federal Government was published in the Official Gazette of the Federation (DOF). Promotion and development of Bioenergetics (LPDB), which entrusts the Inter-Secretarial Commission of Bioenergetics to establish, review and evaluate a strategy to develop the input market and promote energy security, food security and sovereignty and environmental sustainability. In 2009 Biotop, that was a project for the assessment of technical opportunities and research requirements for Latin America, mentioned how the Mexican monitoring framework for the development of biofuels was just beginning and was still in the process of development. Restrictive for biodiesel businesses in Mexico could be due to formal organizations that did not function in the best way or efficiently.

Among the major limitations of the development of production, distribution and consumption of biodiesel is the performance of formal and informal institutions of the Mexican market, mainly in aspects related to the existence of limited information, energy legislation in transition processes, structures of market, prices, and costs, among others The knowledge of this failure in the Mexican market is seeking solution which, according to Rembio (2009), could be achieved by acknowledging the fact of non-existing specific promotion policies for the second generation of biofuels. However, this is likely to be included in a new biofuels research program, which will be developed by The National Council and Technology (CONACYT).

The production of biodiesel is a very complex task for companies and is characterised by high rate of failures. the Plant in Cadereyta is a good example of company that failed in biodiesel production. This company which is located in Nuevo León was established in 2005 by Grupo Energéticos and the Itesm Campus Monterrey with an annual installed capacity of 18 thousand cubic meters that produced biodiesel from animal fats and vegetable oils was closed down in 2011. Similarly, In Lázaro Cárdenas, Michoacán, in 2007 a plant attached to a vegetable oil factory was installed, with a capacity of 9 thousand cubic meters of annual production of biodiesel from castor oil but shortage castor oil caused it to be closed a year later. In the same vein, the Institute of Bioenergetics of Chiapas installed a biodiesel production plant in 2010 from Jatropha but stopped operating in 2011 due to lack of seeds.

In 2013, the Secretariat of Energy developed the Mexican Atlas of Biomass, with information on the production potentials of the different types of biomass that could be used for energy purposes (Riegelhaupt, Odenthal and Janeiro 2016).The biomass resources used as inputs to produce biodiesel, according to their origin and technology are divided into three generations. Riegelhaupt, Odenthal, and Janeiro (2016) develop this characterization considering that the first generation resources are fatty acids which is contained in the lipids synthesized by plants and animals mainly the vegetable oils of the seeds and oleaginous fruits. The second-generation plants are plant lignocellulosic, residual or cultivated, whose carbohydrates can be transformed to C10 to C12 alkanes by various technological ways, such as Fischer-Tropsch synthesis, hydrolysis followed by reform or isomerization and hydrotreatment.

The third generation consists of cultures of microorganisms selected or modified to produce certain biodiesel precursor molecules, such as lipids and fatty acids. The current degree of uncertainty about the inputs and production processes of 3rd generation biodiesel, its costs and technological viability is very high. For this reason, there are no certain or probable values to perform the necessary calculations and to be able to formulate production scenarios and prices of 3rd generation biodiesel.

The potential for production of first generation biodiesel from oil seed crops is growing. However, the use of animal fats as an input for the production of biodiesel is technically feasible for the production of biofuels.

Biodiesel is produced in Mexico with crude vegetable oils whose commercial production has not been able to be sustained due to the lack of competitive costs of the inputs or with used oils and fats that gives rise to a value chain. In this value chain, according to Riegelhaupt, Odenthal and Janeiro (2016), several agents intervene and participate. These include the producers of the raw material who use the oils for the kitchen, such as the traces, greaseries, processors of pork derivatives, and others, but such practices delimit the levels and quality of recovery. Others are the harvesters of the cooked oil- such as the fat collectors of butcher shops- and who can contribute their efficiency in the organization for the collection to reduce the costs. The collectors and processors help to collect and refine the used oils, contribute to the conversion, distribution and sale of biodiesel and finally the biodiesel processors who convert the oils into biodiesel, co-products and waste such as glycerin that they also distribute commercially.

Currently, in Mexico, the agents of both chains operate for the production of biodiesel, mostly informally. The information related to the capacity, type of inputs and processed volume of the companies that operate in the processing and preparation of biodiesel can be obtained from the same companies, but the information related to their marketing processes, prices and customers is unreliable and limited. Riegelhaupt, Odenthal and Janeiro, (2016) reported four companies that collect used cooking oil as the main input for the production of biodiesel:

- Reoil Mexico collects Used Residual Cooking Oil and produces "Pre TPO" or Pre-technical plant oil that it exports to the European Union where it is processed in two biodiesel plants.
- MORECO collects used cooking oil and transforms it into biodiesel in three plants installed in Michoacán, Guanajuato and Querétaro.
- Biofuels de México collects used cooking oil and produces biodiesel in Puebla, Toluca, Cuernavaca, Tlaquepaque, Zapopan, Tonalá, Veracruz, Cordoba, Xalapa, Boca del Rio, Queretaro, Cancun, Playa del Carmen, Chetumal.
- SOLBEN, from Monterrey, Nuevo León, collects used cooking oil, produces biodiesel, sells biodiesel plants and provides services such as characterization of seeds and oils, technical support, automation and biodiesel quality analysis.

Although used cooking oils have few alternative uses, some authors maintain that there is an informal collection circuit with operators that filter discolor and package the recycled oil to sell it as edible oil. The technical potential for obtaining cooking oils and animal fats to be used as inputs in the production of biodiesel is only theoretical because there are currently concurrent uses for many of these sources of fats, and in many cases the capacity and willingness to pay of concurrent users would be higher than that of potential biodiesel users. This is the case of animal fats which have high demand as inputs for soap, food additives, pet food and other end uses. To determine the production potential of biodiesel from animal fats, the use of chicken fat, beef tallow (bovine fat) and pork fats, among others, can be considered. These fats are obtained in the traces, as co-products of the slaughter of animals, and also in plants that reprocess butcher's fats.

Based on official statistics of SAGARPA (2017, 2010), obtained through consultations with the Agrifood and Fisheries Information Service (SIAP) to determine the potential for biodiesel production from current oilseed crops, they are considered to be the most important sources of fatty acids at the global level. Seed to oil conversion factors are an average of industrial performance for pressure extraction technology. For soybean and sunflower, two sequential extractions are carried out by pressure and by organic solvent. Riegelhaupt, Odenthal and Janeiro (2016) analyze that for the case of those considered in group 1, as new crops, it is integrated by the Mexican pinion (Jatropha curcas) and the castor bean (Ricinus communis). Their contributions to the national production of oils are minimal, and their trends are still undefined.

The minor crops considered in-group 2, is composed of canola (Brassica Rapa) and sunflower (Heliantus annuus). The canola has low yields but the sunflower has experienced a significant increase in its cultivation and found a market niche of better prices as a specialty. The third group, is considered as dynamic crops and it is integrated by coconut (Cocos nucifera), oil palm (Elaeis guineensis) and soybean (Glycine max), crops that have had a clear tendency to increase the harvested area and / or the production.

The potential of agricultural residues, esquilmos and stubbles considered as the parts of the vegetables, usually stems and leaves that are not removed from the field during the harvest, is estimated at 15 million tMS / year. Riegelhaupt, Odenthal and Janeiro, (2016) assume a conversion rate of 0.25 m3 of biodiesel / tMS based on the average of the values reported for pilot plants and plants projected according to the European Biofuels Technology Platform (EBTP, 2016). Assume a technically sustainable production level of about 3.75 million m3 of biodiesel per year. However, the authors consider that this potential is not economically feasible for the production of biodiesel in the short and medium terms since the conversion technologies known as 2nd generation have not yet reached the degree of technical maturity to be applied on a commercial scale.

The largest potential source of woody forest biomass in Mexico as a raw material for second-generation biodiesel is the native forest vegetation. The estimate of sustainable annual production excludes wood of species and qualities that can be used by the sawmill, cellulose and panel industries, and includes only wood that is useful for energy. The total potential national production calculated by Riegelhaupt, Odenthal and Janeiro (2016), includes components of forests and jungles located less than 3 km from a road, area with land slopes of less than 30%. Others are outside protected natural areas and/or areas of high value for the conservation of biodiversity is 112 million tMS / a, but some 22 million tMS / a currently used as domestic fuel and 3 million tMS / a destined to manufacture charcoal should be deducted.

The net potential is thus about 87 million tMS / a. This potential is found in almost all the states of the country, and its annual harvestable increase ranges from 2.0 to 4.2 tMS / ha / a. It is therefore similar to the harvesting rates of field residues or agricultural residues, but it has the advantage that the growth can be accumulated in cycles of 10 to 15 years, to harvest from 30 to 50 tMS / ha in an operation at the end of each cycle. As with agricultural wastes, Riegelhaupt, Odenthal and Janeiro (2016) argue that the conversion of woody biomass into biodiesel is technically possible, but there are no economically viable industrial processes so far.

For the development of future scenarios for the introduction of biodiesel in Mexico, several elements have to be analyzed along the biofuel value chain, from the production of inputs to the commercialization of the fuel market up to the conversion of infrastructure of biofuels inputs to biodiesel. The level of future penetration of biodiesel in the Mexican fuel market depends on a large number of economic, technological and institutional factors as well as political decisions. It has been noted in the empirical review that a major problem in Mexico for entrepreneurs interested in the renewable energy markets in specific biodiesel is that the institutions are not clear enough in their actions that help the understanding of the market.

For SMEs producers of biofuels to survive in the market they have to fight against their main competitors, that is the PEMEX emporium, producer and marketer of fossil fuels. However, the excessive increase in the price of gasoline, alternative fuels, such as biodisel, are becoming more competitive in the market. As a result, the biggest challenges for SMEs producing biodiesel are marketing processes.

Analysing the demand of the fuel market will enable the determination of the price buyers would be willing to pay for biodiesel. Biodiesel is a substitute for diesel of fossil origin, and for this reason the existence of demand for biodiesel depends mainly on the reference price of diesel of fossil origin defined as the price before the application of taxes. If biodiesel can be produced (or imported) and marketed at prices lower than the diesel reference price, there will be demand for biodiesel in the market. If, on the other hand, the reference prices of diesel of fossil origin are lower than those of biodiesel, there will be no demand for alternative renewable fuel. If there is no demand for biodiesel in the market, this can be induced through economic and fiscal support policies to achieve a certain level of penetration of biodiesel in the market or, alternatively, determine the market share that can be obtained and sustained with a certain level of spending on support policies.

There is uncertainty about the supply of bioenergy and biofuels based on renewable resources in the market as a consequence of the lower price of fossil fuels. This situation means that there are few economic incentives to invest in alternative fuel technologies. To make the production, distribution and consumption of biofuels more efficient and cheaper, institutional aspects such as the legal framework and the supply chain must be resolved. If reached by 2030, the greatest impact will be on the capacity to generate a significant reduction in carbon emissions.

The existence of demand for biodiesel in the fuel market is complemented by the evaluation of the evolution of the installed capacity of infrastructure for the conversion of inputs to biodiesel. In order to determine that, it is sufficient to satisfy the demand at all times. Finally, if there are both demands for biodiesel in the market and conversion capacity, it is required to evaluate the availability of inputs as well as their production costs, or import to produce the biodiesel demanded in the market.

DELIMITATION OF THE PROBLEM

In view of the growing market for biodiesel consumption in Mexico and the clear absence of firms seeking to monopolize production, a solid manufacturing base can be created in key urban centers to boost the nation's economic growth. So far, there is no solid evidence suggesting the promotion of a sustained marketing strategy.

This is further complicated by absence of firms seeking to monopolized production and the existence of only natural factors aiding the production of raw materials in Mexico. In addition, as there are clear indications that the demand for biodiesel is increasing couple with the weakness of the industry,, it would be expected that by complying with the theory of resources and capabilities, the biodiesel production sector would grow. These facts can lead to the conclusion that there are some other factors inhibiting growth. Hence, the background of the lack of institutions to promote the initiatives of productive companies in biodiesel generates the following question:

How have formal organizations influenced the creation of biodiesel producing companies particularly in urban Mexico?

JUSTIFICATION

As the biodiesel sector is a growing market that is expanding in sustained volume demand over the past years, there is an opportunity for Mexico to consolidate its manufacturing facilities in ways that make it among the leading global competitive players.

As Figure 1 shows, beginning from 2014 the average biodiesel production of 1436 per year was exceeded by the average consumption of 1454.6 per year. This led to the general conclusion that with the continuation of this trend demand will outstrip the production, a situation clearly opening new opportunities for entrepreneurs in this sector. The rational for this conclusion based on the estimators of the variations in the independent variable are sound because the coefficient of determination (r^2) is more than 0.6, which normally is an acceptable parameter. There is, however, the concern that institutions have been able to provide a clear picture, so that investors in this sector can have a conducive environment to make informed decisions. According to the Energy Regulatory Commission (2014), which is in charge of energy regulatory framework, other institutions also contribute in the regulation processes. They include the National Hydrocarbons Commission (CNH), the Secretary of Energy SENER), the Ministry of Finance and Public Credit (SHCP), the Federal Economic Competition Commission (COFECE), and the Security, Energy and Environment Agency (ASEA).As Energy Regulatory Commission (2015) points out, the main objective of these institutions is to establish environments for the efficiency of the energy markets. There clear improvement in the regulatory framework of bioenergetics, however, it is necessary to know if the stability in the regulatory framework achieved has helped in creating the stability of the market, as well as to know if the institutions have contributed to the growth of viable companies in biodiesel sector. The nature of the relationship between institutions and entrepreneurs around the world in 2015 was highlighted in a relevant research report that:

Figure 1. Projection of biodiesel production and consumption from 2013 to 2023
Source: Prepared by the Organization for Economic Co-operation and Development (OECD Stats, 2017).

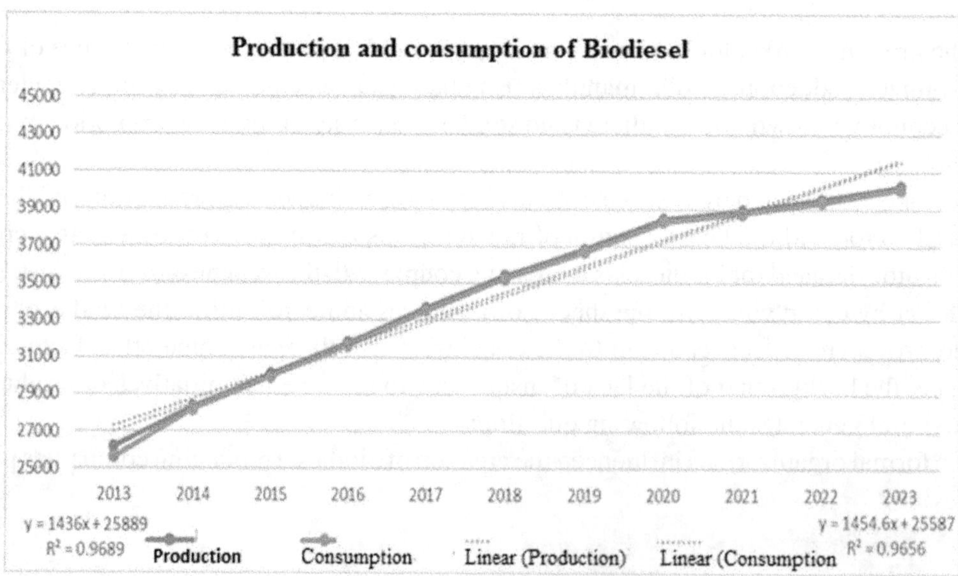

"To the extent that the entrepreneur carries out his activity in an environment where the rules of the game are well-defined (i.e. that there is good protection of property rights, that the judicial system functions properly, that governments are stable or that there is no corruption, among other factors) the entrepreneur will enjoy greater security that will positively contribute to the success of his company". (Fuentelzas and Gonzalez, 2015).

THEORETICAL ASSUMPTION

Institutions, understood as the limitations to the behavior of an individual or a society, have a very important role in the creation and consolidation of MSME's biodiesel companies concerned. Any entrepreneur must abide by them for the proper functioning of their organization. Leaving the institutional framework entails tangible and intangible sanctions for the organization. First, the institution is defined as the humanly constructed constraint that structure human interaction (North, 1990). On the other hand, the institutional framework is described by Peng (2012) as the set of formal and informal organizations which are responsible for regulating the human behavior of people and companies based on three pillars, namely; regulators, normative and cognitive.

Institutions are divided into both formal institutions and informal institutions. Within formal institutions are found the laws, regulations and rules to which every individual who interacts in a society must be subject otherwise be sanctioned as described in the regulations and laws. As for formal institutions, all MSME's that are established in Mexico will be subject to the Federal Law of mercantile companies. The Federal Law regulates anonymous companies while state laws and municipal regulations take care of the opening of establishments which, in turn, depend on the geographical location where the MSME's biodiesel company is established. Such state laws, which differ from state to state, include: Income Tax Law (ISR), Single Tax Rate Business Act (IETU), Value Added Tax (VAT), Industrial Property Law, Federal Data Protection Act, Federal Labor Law, Social Security, and Law of the Institute of the National Housing Fund for workers. Each law has a particular objective which seeks the regulation of all companies in Mexico.

Institutional framework, on the other hand, is informal institutions which include norms, culture and ethics that apply to companies. According to Peng (2012) these formal institutions have two supports: normative and cognitive. The first refers to how the behavior of people and in this case of companies is influenced in terms of their values, beliefs and actions. On the one hand, of the cognitive pillar, refers to the internal values and beliefs that guide the behavior of individuals and companies. Some of the informal institutions are covered by the culture, beliefs and values of a society and that in some ways affects the functioning of MSME's in Mexico as they help in generating cleaner fuel for the urban environment.

Culture can be defined as the collective programming of the mind of individuals. This programming or way of thinking distinguishes the members of one group or category of people from another (Hofstede, 2011). Ethics is also part of all informal institutions, defined as "Norms, principles or standards of conduct that govern the individual behavior of organizations" (Vargas, et al. 2005, p.133). Although the importance of social norms and culture in the functioning of the economic system is well explained, it should be understood that all human beings are socially designed to behave in a certain way respecting the social norms that exist (Basu, 2013). Accordingly, as all the social norms in which action delimit our behavior and, in this case, delimit the action of the MSME's, so does each regulation or law limits the possible actions that the companies can carry out.

The central question: is what do institutions do? Or why are they so necessary? According to Peng (2012) the role of institutions is to reduce uncertainty because they indicate the legitimate and illegitimate channels. What institutions do is to delimit actions to only acceptable limits leaving out those outside this range and thus reduce transaction costs. Reducing uncertainty leads to a reduction in transaction costs which are vital for the proper functioning of any economy. The less transaction costs, the more effective economy of a country or a locality functions. Transaction costs were introduced by Coase and are defined as the costs of market use (Salgado, 2003). Transaction costs are only the costs of information search, negotiation costs, decision making, formulation costs, and policy implementation. Another definition for transaction costs is the one proposed by Peng (2012) which defines this concept as: the costs associated with economic transactions, or the costs of conducting negotiations.

Institutions, both formal and informal, play vital role in the reduction of transaction costs without which the operation of each transaction in the economy would be much greater. In developed economies, transaction costs tend to be zero, while in developing economies these costs are much higher. This is explained by the weakness of the institutions which makes uncertainty high, and this explains the necessity of signature in contracts between individuals.

In the framework of informal institutions, as noted by Peng (2012), institutions reduce uncertainty in various ways. The first is related to relationship contracts, known as "personalized exchanges", informal and based mainly on relationships. Robert Putnam's theory of social capital brings much to the subject of reducing transaction costs through informal institutions. Social capital is understood as "the characteristics of social organization, such as networks, norms and trust, which facilitates coordination and cooperation for mutual benefit" (Urteaga, 2013, page 45). These networks of confidence through expected behavior cause confidence among economic agents to be high so that transaction costs will be null because of expected behavior.

One concept that helps the understanding of the importance of informal institutions is "The Culture of Confidence: one can trust the given word because that is the social norm, so people follow it by instinct" (Basu, 2013, p. 167). The main reason why the culture of trust is important is because it is needed to rely on the other's word on multiple occasions. It is not feasible to sign any contract at any time and then go to court if the other party does not comply with the agreement because of the high costs that the operation will have. That is why the culture of trust between two parties is important.

Another important concept within the theoretical review of formal and informal institutions is institutional transactions which are defined as major changes that are incorporated into the formal and informal rules of the game that affect organizations as players (Peng, 2012). Property rights are another type of formal institutions that influence business. These rights are social institutions that define the range of privileges granted individuals to specific resources. In other words, it is the right of individuals to direct or indirect power on an object or a good (Mahoney, 2010). The theory of property rights was developed by various theorists including Ronald Cease to explain the social and economic relationships that people should consider when using scarce resources.

From the discussions above, the following assumption is developed:

Formal institutions positively impact the entrepreneurship of biodiesel companies in Mexico.

THEORETICAL CONCEPTUAL FRAMEWORK

The emergence of the power of industrial revolution brought with it rapid urban growth around the world. According to Agarwal (2007), some of the emerging problems faced by humanity include the issues of environmental deterioration, especially in the urban areas, and the crisis in the energy industry. Among the main causes of air pollution is the burning of fossil fuel, and this is because the combustion of air produces large amounts of greenhouse gases (carbon dioxide, oxides of nitrogen), sulfur oxides, unburned hydrocarbons and ash thin (Agarwal, 2007). Furthermore, it important to note that hydrocarbon-based fuel is a non-renewable good, and since it is finite on the planet, it is therefore essential to reduce its depletion by resorting to energies that can be renewable and friendlier to the urban environment.

Many researchers have identified many suitable energy sources as Medina, Chavez and Jauregui (2012:63) state as thus:

"Recent studies indicate that there are other sources of energy, which have extremely low emissions and appear to have the potential to become energy sources for automotive propulsion, including alcohols, natural gas, hydrogen and biodiesel" (Medina, Chávez and Jáuregui, 2012, 63).

The conclusion drown from this is that an alternative for this destructive path to economic growth and one which is unfriendly to the environment, may be turned to using fuels that are substitutes for conventional fuels such as biodiesel which is locally produced and is more urban environment friendly..

The following is the definition of biodiesel adopted for this study:

It is a mixture of methyl esters of fatty acids (FAMEs) that is obtained by a process of transesterification, mainly from vegetable oils and animal fats and, more recently from algae. It can be used as a substitute for conventional diesel, as it has similar properties, reducing pollution and extending the life of the vehicle's engine. In its production, glycerin is obtained as a by-product, with multiple industrial applications. (Molina, 2012, 7)

Theories of Entrepreneurship

In recent decades, entrepreneurs are increasingly becoming important urban development actors in many emerging economies. To adequately assess the entrepreneurship function in this situation, it is essential to explain the meaning of the concept of entrepreneurship. To some analysts an entrepreneurship is the search for constant useful change, generation of ideas, speculation of projects that generate beneficial effects for the economy and society (Contreras and González, 2010). To others, the concept is given a broader meaning. For example, Sánchez and Pérez (2015) define entrepreneurship as those initiatives of business nature that relate to the way of thinking, reasoning and acting, along with the constant search for a business opportunities, which results in inventiveness that generate value not only in an economic sense. The concept is also concerned with social development issues in which all the actors participate in the initiatives that are inclusive of owners, employees, customers, suppliers and the general beneficiary community.

Some analysts are concerned with the quality of entrepreneurship. Baumol (1990), for example, makes a distinction between entrepreneurial activities that are productive, unproductive and destructive. The productive enterprise is one in which there is clearly identifiable innovation, economic growth and can be related to the discovery of viable commercial opportunities. There are also clear distinctions between entrepreneurships relationship; for example *opportunity* and *necessity* entrepreneurship. In the case of an opportunity enterprise, there is greater opportunity for growth in the economy because that innovation has found a new and exploitable niche market. In the necessity entrepreneurship, however, the development of employment and growth of the economy is not with the same rate of acceleration (Reynolds et al 2003)

The World Economic Forum emphasizes the tremendous benefits of entrepreneurship. It has recently defined high-impact entrepreneurship as one that generates greater benefits for the customers by means of the fruits of innovations which, in turn, also produce more employment opportunities and more wealth for the entrepreneurs (Economic Forum World, 2014).

There seems to emerge a consensus conceptualizing entrepreneur as one who manages to find opportunities that generate greater benefits and the use of innovations that sustain and exploit the opportunity in space and time. Targeted impact is important in this activity because the entrepreneurs who focus on their clients are the ones who generate the greatest wealth for their owners (Hitt, Ireland, Sirmon and Trahms, 2011). These entrepreneurs tend to have strategies for success. First, they have clear and detailed business plans and to enter the market early. Second, they usually participate in markets with which they have already had previous interaction. Third, take measure through enhanced application of their knowledge of the local markets in their planning. (Liñán, Fernández, Romero, 2013).

Many economic historians such as Schumpeter (1934), have observed that entrepreneurship is an indispensable mechanism for the development of economies, and that it is essential for every economy to develop enterprises that can foster the growth of valuable employment and innovations. However, these views have tend to encourage political institutions to focus on favoring the growth of the more established companies with the greatest potential for growth at the expense of small firms and start-up enterprises (Friar and Meyer 2003). The political decision-makers who are responsible for the development of public policies, which Bazua and Valenti (1993) explain, are the references to any social decision which can be taken by an individual or an organization or the state.

Governments at all levels- from federal, state, and local- have clear appreciation of the importance of firms on the economy, social and political issues and focused on creating the policies needed to support entrepreneurship. In this process, however, they face the decision whether policies should target supporting the leading national companies, helping existing firms achieve survival, or focusing on the formation of new enterprises (Stam, Studdle, Hessels and Stel, 2009).

Theories of Formal and Informal Institutions

Both formal and informal institutions have important roles to play in the urban and industrial policies of most countries. North (1990) defines institutions as the humanly constructed organizations that structure human interaction, which many researchers call the "rules of the game". These rules guide the behavior of the firms in surveying the terrain of the markets to enter to understand how to conduct their business activities to achieve desired profits. The institutions themselves and the rules they formulate are intended to achieve a reduction in uncertainty, encourage investment to enhance productivity, but in nations with weak institutions, the effect is the opposite (North 1990).

According to Peng (2012), the institutional framework is constituted by both formal and informal organizations that will mark the actions that can be taken individually and collectively. Formal organizations are institutions that are constituted in writing and are expected to follow explicitly rigorous rules and comply with the defined pattern of behavior, which are in the form of the laws, the regulations and the rules. Many researchers suggest that, in addition to the formal institutions, when entering new markets entrepreneurs should also consider informal institutions which may have many important lessons to teach, even though documentary knowledge about them is limited or nonexistent.

It is generally accepted that the levels of entrepreneurship in a given nation or region are, undoubtedly, influenced by the local conditions in which entrepreneurship is carried out. This is because such an environment can facilitate or discourage the creation of new viable initiatives (Fuentelsaz, González and Macías 2015). More importantly, such an environment promotes the growth of formal institutions that have laws or regulations that help the visualization of how processes of business should be carried out and thus making the management of business easier and also helps in ensuring that well-structured businesses achieve considerable success. Furthermore, the inception and development of new companies are influenced by such factors as proprietary rights, commercial legislation, constitution procedures, ideas, cultural beliefs, gender, attitudes towards the entrepreneur, etc (Marulanda and Morales, 2016, 18).

Using the theory of institutions, Urbano and Diaz (2009) suggest that the business environment in each country is usually a decisive factor in terms of quality business opportunities that are available. Also important is the perception about these opportunities and their ability or capability for adaptation to generate greater incentives for the creation of new companies. Since they lack the necessary experience in, or knowledge of, the new environment in which new start-ups seek to penetrate, they may encounter many problems such as limited access to finance, difficulty of employing high-quality personnel, and accept higher transaction costs (Aldrich and Auster, 1986). Fuentelzas (2015), with a focus on startup enterprises, explains how the existence of experienced institutions can simplify the resolution of complications of inexperience, uncertainty, access to resources essential for full functioning, and the stability in developing new business activities. Experienced institutions can easily and quickly simplify access to resources and offer the essential stability for the sustained growth of the activities that could greatly enhance changes of business survival.

The foregoing clearly demonstrates that the quality of institutions has not only strong influence on business competitiveness and development, influences investment decisions, the planning of production; but also significantly influence the way societies allocate profits and the costs of evolving strategies and policies. An unstable institutional atmosphere, on the other hand, creates an even more difficult behavior among companies, hampers their collaborative efforts and distortions the vision of growth in the short term, in ways that negatively affects the quality and success of companies in the long run (Fuentelzas and González, 2015).

The uncertainty faced by new enterprises suggests that the number of successful businesses is reduced. Not all is doom and gloom; however, because as Vargas, Guerra, Bojórquez and Bojórquez (2014) pointed out, the main role of institutions is to reduce uncertainty. They are also to distinguish between uncertainties in a) policy related to ethnic turbulences that can cause problems for companies, and b) economic related to the transaction costs that, if used wisely, can generate greater opportunities for firms.

CONTEXTUAL FRAMEWORK

The industrial and urban growth policies driving the national development of Mexico are based on its key regulatory framework derived the political constitution of the United Mexican States. This document establishes the outline of action of the authorities and the governed, through principles, rights and obligations that govern the rest of the national legal system. Article 4 of the Constitution explains that "Everyone has the right to a healthy environment for their development and well-being". "The damage and environmental deterioration will generate responsibility for who provokes it in terms of the provisions of the law" which has been added as Decree of the Official Gazette of the Federation on February 08, 2012. In article 25, the constitution mentions, "the State is responsible for national development to ensure that it is comprehensive and sustainable." Thus, this clause demonstrates the concerns for the environment within the framework of the national urban and industrial policies.

The law dealing specifically with the renewable energy is the Law on the promotion and development of bioenergetics that seeks "to promote the production of inputs for bioenergetics from agricultural activities, forestry, algae, biotechnological processes and sovereignty food". Thus, its main responsibility under this law is to encourage the use of bio energies in Mexico. Article 8 of this urges that "the Bioenergetics Committee is created, which will be composed of the members of SAGARPA, SENER, SEMARNAT, the Secretary of Economy and the Secretary of Finance and Public Credit", along with which many public agencies are involved in the promotion of bioenergy manufacture and research.

The energy agency in Mexico, the Secretary of Energy (2017), likewise reporting the process made by 2017 states as follows: 7 permits are granted for the production of bioenergetics, 41 bioenergy marketing permits, 5 transport permits and 21 permit exemption notices for Production of bioenergetics.

Along similar lines, the National Commission for Science and Technology in February 2017 reports that the Secretary of Energy launches a call for the creation of development projects in sustainable energy technologies with the full backing of the Bank of Mexico. In the competition for these projects, the first prizes will be awarded with cash of up to 2 million dollars, some 500 thousand dollars for the second place and 100 thousand dollars for the third place. These are just part of many competitions that encourage the research and development initiatives in alternative energy for the purpose of encouraging firms that want to create enterprises but lack financing. This type of competition tends to provide an incentive to emerging businesses in ways that encourage the sustainable development of creative pursuits every year.

Similarly, the Ministry of Agriculture, Livestock, Rural Development, Fisheries and Food (SAGARPA) (2016) has reported that in the period since 2013 it has promoted 960 projects related to the production of biofuels in Mexico. In the four years prior to 2017, incentives have been granted of around 275 million pesos, which has produced a total investment of 529 million pesos. The Ministry had also made possible the installation of 7 biofuel plants, six of which are devoted to the production of biodiesel that is 4 plants more than they existed in 2009.

METHOD

This chapter is intended as a qualitative research that relies on a review of the literature on studies applied in Mexico and globally about the characteristics, factors and relevant variables related to biodiesel industrial growth and its influence of the urban growth. The Mexican biodiesel companies are expected to comply with the collection of their data as required by the laws and regulations governing their establishment. Such data is analyzed and used in comparing with the applied theories of entrepreneurship and institutionalism to see if appropriate innovation and new forms of administration suited to the needs of 21st century situations are achieved.

The nature of the research is exploratory and descriptive through the analysis of previous researches trying to provide quality and flexibility that allow researchers to use multiple data collection methods with the aim to analyze the role of the institutions in the biodiesel industry, to explain and describe the phenomenon under study and to determine if there is a relationship with the quality and maturity of the same with the entrepreneurial ventures.

ANALYSIS OF RESULTS

Biodiesel is undoubtedly emerging to be an attractive market. However, it needs a sufficiently strong regulatory framework to encourage the consolidation of the existing companies as well as nurture the emergence of new entrepreneurs seeking to enter into competition for the market. Achieving this would require not only public intervention with the right tools at the right time, but also regular collaborative interaction between the firms, both new and old. The lack of competitiveness in the sale prices of biodiesel with the reference price marked by diesel fuel of fossil origin calls for the demand for biodiesel to be induced through different formal institutions and support policies. For example, the analysis of Riegelhaupt, Odenthal and Janeiro (2016) point out, among other options, the establishment of a legal obligation in the form of a quota to certain actors in the market, generally fuel trading companies, to guarantee that a fraction of the total consumption of diesel is replaced with biodiesel. There are different possible designs for the quotas depending on who are the obligated parties, the obligation to mix in the final product or if different mixtures of fossil diesel-diesel are allowed as long as the quota is met globally. An important element in the design of the obligation is the price of the penalty established in case of default to the obligated parties. The price per liter of fuel that the obligated party must pay in case it cannot provide evidence of having marketed the volume established in the obligation. The establishment of a quota guarantees the achievement of a certain penetration of biodiesel in the market. However, the legal obligation by itself does not control the unit cost of support needed per liter of biodiesel introduced in the market,

Another support policy option proposed in the analysis of Riegelhaupt, Odenthal and Janeiro (2016) - which can be implemented independently or in combination with a quota - is to provide economic incentives to improve the competitiveness of biodiesel in the market. In Mexico there are no recent statistics on the production and use of biodiesel but it is possibly expected to increase due t to the increase in the price of fossil diesel. Although fiscal incentives would be needed, that was what triggered the development of the biodiesel market in other countries.

The mechanism can be the reduction of production costs (for example through subsidies or tax exemptions to farmers or producers of biodiesel) or the reduction of final marketing prices through monetary support or tax reductions. Whether the economic incentive is established as a subsidy to biodiesel producers or as a tax exemption, the result sought in both cases is to increase the competitiveness of biodiesel in the market. In this study we refer to this type of political instruments as "economic incentives". The establishment of an economic incentive (e.g. a tax reduction) allows in principle to control the level of support per liter of biodiesel but does not guarantee by itself the control of the volume of biodiesel introduced in the market.

The two support options described result in additional direct costs to society. These are calculated as the differential between the costs of introducing a certain amount of biodiesel in the market versus that of continuing to use fossil diesel. However, both instruments differ from the point of view of the distribution of said costs among different actors. The establishment of the mandatory quota generally transfers the additional cost of acquisition to suppliers, who in turn transfer the cost to the final consumers. In the case of economic incentives, these usually leave the state budget in the form of tax reductions, tax exemptions or subsidies. To meet a certain demand for biodiesel in the market, not only the necessary inputs must be available but also sufficient production capacity in the supply chain. A key element of the supply chain is the facilities for converting inputs to biodiesel.

The production of biodiesel requires institutions to consolidate the creation of an agency responsible for regulating and facilitating the development of the biodiesel industry in Mexico. Small producers of biodiesel such as Smart Recycling of Puebla, have the permits from the Ministry of Energy for the production, sale and transportation of biofuel and certification processes for the quality of biofuel values such as viscosity, density and pH parts per million glycerin and some waste.

Due to the risks to sustainability that biofuel production could present if not done correctly, several initiatives have been developed to certify liquid biofuels produced in a sustainable manner, among them are the RSB3 and the GBEP4 which establish principles and criteria such as: conservation of biodiversity, non-deforestation, GHG mitigation, good use of water resources, respect for human and worker rights, among others. In Mexico, the Ministry of Environment and Natural Resources (SEMARNAT) is developing the voluntary NMX standard for the certification of the production of liquid biofuels of plant origin based on the principles of RSB.

There is the technical possibility of expanding some oil crops more intensively in palm oil, coconut, soy, sunflower, castor and jatropha to produce biodiesel respecting the principles established in the LPDB and considering that the marginal costs of biodiesel production are increased as the aptitude of the land is reduced. The increase in second-generation biodiesel production can be obtained from the abundant available ligno-cell resources, such as agricultural residues or agroindustrial and forestry co-products, when the conversion technologies have reached commercial maturity and become competitive. The conversion infrastructure of crude oils to biodiesel is limited for the moment to a small number of demonstration plants of very small scale.

The companies producing biodiesel in Mexico for the years 2008-2009 represent the pioneers of the Mexican biofuel market. Due to the initial confusion and instability resulting from lack of public encouragement and general uncertainty, it became necessary to arrange for massive intervention by formal institutions. Thus, the government came up with new institutional and regulatory frameworks with the objectives of stabilizing and developing the sector.

After the review of events on how to change the institutional landscape in Mexico, it was considered essential to solidify and support the emerging entrepreneurship initiatives in the biofuel sector. Particularly targeted are the biodiesel companies and operations and the results show double growth in recent years. These results help to strengthen the argument advocating for a collaborative relationship not only between formal institutions but also among and between well-established companies and the growing start-up of enterprises. This approach is well supported in the theoretical basis and particularly in a study undertaken by Fuentelzas (2015) which shows how institutions are an important factor for successful ventures in their sectors.

FUTURE RESEARCH DIRECTION

The growing entrepreneurship of biodiesel companies is greatly contributing to the broader industrial development of Mexico and industrial clusters in the form of industrial towns, parks, or estates which, in turn, are increasingly shaping the spatial forms of cities and affecting the quality of urban environment. Efforts regarding future research should be viewed from this perspective. The future research on entrepreneurship of biodiesel companies in Mexico from the perspective, of the institutions, which is arguably a reasonable option in the short-term, should consider the impact of the institutions in the design and implementation of a program geared towards the promotion of the economic forms of biodiesel. This institutional impact must consider the different combinations of institutional incentives such as economic, fiscal, subsidies, among others, that allow biodiesel to compete in a range of costs similar to that of fossil diesel at current oil prices. Analyze and evaluate the possibility of introducing a larger-scale program after a detailed analysis of the impact on the Mexican economy as a whole, including the direct costs of support, the positive impacts of the investment, indirect tax revenues, trade balance, and generation of employment, among others.

Another line of relevant research is the analysis, design and implementation of structural programs to strengthen institutional capacities that allow the acquisition of institutional and technical experience for the development of the biofuels and biodiesel market.

Further research should also be directed toward the impact of investments in biofuels and biodiesel on the generation of additional income in the agricultural sector and investments in production infrastructure in the industrial sector. Research in this area is important as the likely finding might impact on a country's level of employment and income from taxes.

Similarly, further research should be conducted on the impacts of formal institutions on national and local economies by encouraging the choice of biodiesel against diesel of fossil origin and consider that in addition to the urban environmental benefits of reducing greenhouse gas emissions, there are other positive economic impacts derived of the introduction of biodiesel.

Also research evaluating the cost-benefits of adopting an institutional program that stimulates the production, distribution and consumption of technically viable biofuels and biodiesel based on the potential availability of resources is suggested.

Finally, further research is required to estimate the institutional capacity for the production of biodiesel with national resources with reductions in biodiesel imports, in such a way that they contribute to improve the country's trade balance and to mitigate the negative effect of high oil prices.

CONCLUSION AND RECOMMENDATIONS

There is an emerging industry in biodiesel production in Mexico based on cooking oils as raw materials which are accompanied by processes of processing, collection, distribution and marketing mainly carried out in institutions that operate informally. However, because the potential for the expansion of biodiesel production is broadly based on increase on the production of other types of inputs such as fats of animal origin and vegetable and oil-based oils such as soybean, palm and coconut, There is the requirement for the establishment of more formal market institutions to carry out the distribution and commercialization of the product. The establishment of market mechanisms in formal institutions will not allow reaching higher recovery rates with lower costs but also allows covering in greater percentage the current demand for biodesel.

In view of the above, it is important to face the issue of competitive growth if the growth rate of the Mexican economy is to match or even surpass its global peers that are now achieving much faster growth rates. Given this premise, it is necessary to understand that creating and energizing formal institutions is a way by which entrepreneurs create effective businesses that exploit thriving markets and do so in manner that is commercially and environmentally sustainable within an urban context.

In addition, all those who seek to generate projects in the renewable energy sector -as well as in any other sector of the economy- need to look for countries with better formal institutions. In case of entering emerging markets that usually do not have established institutions that are guided by laws, regulations and regulatory agencies, they have to anticipate the systemic failures and unexpected costs increases. Alternatively, such companies must be prepared to enter the market with proactive strategies to be applied when faced with unsustainable situations.

REFERENCES

Agarwal, A. K. (2007). Biofuels (Alcohols And Biodiesel) Applications As Fuels For Internal Combustión Engines. *Progress in Energy and Combustion Science*, *33*(3), 233–271. doi:10.1016/j.pecs.2006.08.003

Aldrich, H., & Auster, E. R. (1986). Even Dwarfs Started Small: Liabilities Of Age And Size And Their Strategic Implications. *Research in Organizational Behavior*, *8*, 165–198.

Basu, K. (2013). *Más allá de la mano invisible*. Fondo de Cultura Económica.

Baumol, W. J. (1990). Entrepreneurship: Productive, Unproductive, And Destructive. *Journal of Political Economy*, *98*(5), 893–921. doi:10.1086/261712

Bazua, F. Y., & Valenti, G. (1993). Hacia Un Enfoque Amplio De Política Pública. *Revista de Administração Pública*, 84.

Comisión Reguladora De Energía. (2015). *Desarrollo Del Marco Regulatorio Mexicano En Materia Energética*. Author.

Constitución Política De Los Estados Unidos Mexicanos, Diario Oficial De La Federación. (2017). *Constitución Política De Los Estados Unidos Mexicanos*. Author.

Contreras Comeche, R., & González García, N. (2010). La Medición Del Valor Social Y El Impacto De Los Emprendedores Sociales. In Emprendimiento, Economía Social Y Empleo. IUDESCOOP, Instituto Universitario De Economía Social Y Cooperativa Dela Universidad De Valencia.

Foro Económico Mundial. (2014). *The Bold-Ones High-Impact Entrepreneurs Who Transform Industries*. Foro Económico Mundial.

Friar, J. H., & Meyer, M. H. (2003). Entrepreneurship and start-ups in the Boston region: Factors differ- entiating high-growth ventures from micro-ven- tures. *Small Business Economics*, *21*(2), 145–152. doi:10.1023/A:1025045828202

Fuentelsaz, L., & Gonzáles, C. (2015). El Fracaso Emprendedor A Través De Las Instituciones Y La Calidad Del Emprendimiento. *Universidad Bussiness Review*.

Fuentelsaz, L., González, C., & Maícas, J. P. (2015). ¿Ayudan Las Instituciones A Entender El Emprendimiento? *Economía Industrial*.

Hitt, M. A., Ireland, R. D., Sirmon, D. G., & Trahms, C. A. (2011). Strategic Entrepreneurship: Creating Value For Individuals, Organizations, And Society. *The Academy of Management Perspectives*, *25*(2), 57–75.

Hofstede, G. (2011). *Culture's consequences* (1st ed.). Thousand Oaks, CA: Sage Publ.

Ley De Promoción Y Desarrollo De Los Bionergéticos. (2008). *Ley De Promoción Y Desarrollo De Los Bionergéticos*. Publicado En El Diario Oficial De La Federación El Primero De Febrero De.

Liñán, F., Fernández, J., & Romero, I. (2013). Necessity And Opportunity Entrepreneurship: The Mediating Effect Of Culture. *Revista de Economía Mundial*, *33*, 21–47.

Mahoney, J. (2012). *Property rights theory. In Economic Fundations of Strategy* (pp. 158–199). Academic Press.

Marulanda, F. Morales, S. (2016). Entorno Y Motivaciones Para Emprender. *Revista Escuela De Administración De Negocios,* 8.

Medina, I., Chavez, N. Y., & Jauregui, J. (2012). Biodiesel, Un Combustible Renovable. *Investigación Y Ciencia, 20*, 62-70.

Molina, C. (2012). Estudio de la composición y estabilidad de biodiesel obtenido a partir de aceites vegetales limpios y procedentes de aceites de fritura. Servicio de publicaciones de la Universidad de la Laguna.

North, D. (1990). *Institutions, Institutional Change and Economic Performance*. Cambridge, UK: Cambridge University Press. doi:10.1017/CBO9780511808678

OECD. (2017). *OECD Stats FAO Agricultura*. Retrieved from Http://Stats.Oecd.Org/Viewhtml.Aspx?Queryid=58648&Vh=0000&Vf=0&L&Il=&Lang=En#

Peng, M. (2012). *Enfatizando Las Instituciones, La Cultura Y La Ética*. Gestión Estratégica. Editoral Cengage Learning.

Rembio. (2009). *Expert Opinion Based On Delivered Questionnaire*. Author.

Reynolds, P., Bygrave, W. D., Autio, E., Cox, L. W., & Hay, M. (2003). *Global Entrepreneurship Monitor 2002 executive report*. Wellesley, MA: Babson College.

Riegelhaupt, E., Odenthal, J., & Janeiro, L. (2016). *Diagnóstico de la situación actual del biodiésel en México y escenarios para su aprovechamiento*. Informe Final (CONFIDENCIAL red Mexicana de Bioenergía. Ecofys 2016 por orden de: Banco Interamericano de Desarrollo para SENER).

Rutz, D., Thebaud, A., Janssen, R., Segura, S. A., Riegelhaupt, E., & Ballesteros, M. … Bravo, G. (2009). *Biofuel Policies And Legislation In Latin America*. WIP Renewable Energies, Report Of The EU Project Biotop (FP7); Contract No.: 213320.

SAGARPA. (2010). *Monografía de cultivos: palma de Aceite*. Subsecretaría de Fomento a los Agronegocios.

SAGARPA. (2016). *Direccion General de Fibras Naturales y Biocombustibles. BIODIÉSEL 06052016. Presentación realizada en el Taller de Biodiésel.* Paquete Tecnológico de Higuerilla y Paquete Tecnológico de Jatropha.

SAGARPA. (2017). *Impulsa SAGARPA Producción De Biocombustibles En México*. Author.

Salgado, C. E. (2003). *Teoría de costos de transacción: una breve reseña. Cuadernos de Administración*. Recuperado de http://www.redalyc.org/articulo.oa?id=20502604

Sánchez, L. A., & Pérez, E. (2015). Las Entidades De Economía Social Como Protagonistas De Un Nuevo Modelo De Emprendimiento Y Medidas Legales De Apoyo Al Emprendimiento, CIRIEC-España. *C.I.R.I.E.C. España*, *84*, 35–62.

Schumpeter, J. A. (1934). The Thory Of Economic Development: An Inquiry Into Profits, Capital, Credit, Interest And The Business Cycle. Harvard Economic Studies, 46.

Stam, E., Suddle, K., Hessels, J., & Van Stel, A. J. (2009). High-Growth Entrepreneurs, Public Policies, And Economic Growth. In J. Leitao & R. Baptista (Eds.), Public Policies For Fostering Entrepreneurship: A European Perspective. International Studies In Entrepreneurship. Academic Press.

Tapia, P. (2017, February 12). Biodiésel, a la espera de brillar en México. *Milenio*.

Urbano, D. Y., & Díaz, J. C. (2009). Creación De Empresas E Instituciones: Un Modelo Teórico. In M. F. R. Hernández (Ed.), Creación De Empresas. Aproximación Al Estado Del Arte. Lisboa: Juruá.

Urteaga, E. (2013). *La teoría del capital social de Robert Putnam: Originalidad y carencias. Reflexión Política*. Recuperado de http://www.redalyc.org/articulo.oa?id=11028415005

Vargas, J., Guerra, E., Bojórquez, A. Y., & Bojorquez, F. (2014). Gestión Estratégica De Organizaciones. Elaleph, 134.

KEY TERMS AND DEFINITIONS

Biodiesel: Biodiesel is a liquid biofuel that is obtained from lipids of natural origin, such is the case of vegetable oils or animal fats that have had or not previous use, subjected to the transesterification process.

Company: A company is an enterprise or business that has been organized as a business and commercial society including capital and labor and whose main purpose is to obtain an economic benefit.

Entrepreneurship: It is the ability of people to create new businesses. It is the person who knows how to discover, identify a specific business opportunity and then will arrange or get the necessary resources to start it and then take it to fruition.

Formal Institutions: Are the institutions related to constitutions, codes, laws, contracts, and other legal elements.

Informal Institutions: Are extensions, interpretations, and modifications of formal rules, rules of behavior, agreements, codes of conduct, or conventions and all those aspects that are related to culture.

Mexico: A country located in North America.

Section 4

Industrial and Urban Growth Policies at the Sub-National Level

Researchers from Russia and Nigeria analyze themes such as the Fourth Industrial technologies, smart city, industrial opportunities for sub-national development, and a possible shift from oil to cities as development tools. The Russian contributors analyzed three themes: the emergence of Industry 4.0 technologies to provide leapfrogging opportunity for the Russian Federation, the use of "smart city" as a tool of resolving the contradiction between production and urban life, and an analysis of the emerging trends and opportunities for industry development at the sub-national level in Russia. Similarly, the Nigeria study put to test the transformative role of cities shifting from dependent on oil export to finance sub-national development.

Chapter 14
Emergence of Industry 4.0 Technologies:
Leapfrogging Opportunity for the Russian Federation

Leyla A. Gamidullaeva
https://orcid.org/0000-0003-3042-7550
Penza State University, Russia

Sergey M. Vasin
Penza State University, Russia

Elena V. Shkarupeta
https://orcid.org/0000-0003-3644-4239
Voronezh State Technical University, Russia

Tatyana O. Tolstykh
NUST MISIS, Russia

Alexey G. Finogeev
Penza State University, Russia

Galina V. Surovitskaya
K. G. Razumovsky Moscow State University of Technologies and Management, Russia

Sergey Kanarev
Penza State University, Russia

ABSTRACT

Innovations in the modern world are not simply connected with the opportunities of digital technologies but also largely based on them. This is exactly why the full-fledged successive industrial sector's digitization will become a platform for qualitative changes of the economy and long-term opportunities. Thus, the transition to digital technologies is inevitable, but from another perspective, this very transition cannot be the absolute goal. In this chapter, the authors aimed at providing a better understanding for Industry 4.0 concept and its application benefits for Russia. The main problem is how the Russian Federation acts against the economically developed countries, which are the creators of Industry 4.0. This chapter mainly focuses on presenting the authors' views on how to sustain and increase competitive advantage of the Russian Federation by catching and implementing Industry 4.0. With Industry 4.0, Russian Federation gets a bigger share of the world manufacturing value chain.

DOI: 10.4018/978-1-5225-7625-9.ch014

INTRODUCTION

Recent trends of globalization are faced with the need to meet the constant global demand for new production technologies. To overcome this problem, the industry must ensure sustainable production. It is expected that, within the framework of the fourth stage of industrialization, a new approach in the industry 4.0 will ensure a greater integration of information and communication technologies (ICT) with industry. It leads to the intelligent and self-organized industry as well as, more flexible and efficient industrial goods.

During the first industrial revolution with the help of water and steam, the production was mechanized. The main driver of the second industrial revolution was electricity, which helped create mass production. At the center of the third revolution was electronics and information technologies that automated production. Due to the third industrial revolution there began a wide use of information technologies in the industry. The industry 4.0 is related with the development of Cyber Physical Systems.

The fourth industrial revolution is the blending of technologies of the physical, digital and biological world, which creates new opportunities and affects political, social and economic systems.

The fourth industrial revolution fundamentally transforms modern production, thanks to new technological achievements, including digitalization and robotization, artificial intelligence and the Internet of things (IoT), new materials and biotechnology. Due to these changes, production in developed countries again becomes the main source of prosperity and creation of new jobs.

In this chapter, the authors aimed at providing a better understanding for Industry 4.0 concept and its application benefits for Russia. The main problem is how the Russian Federation acts against the economically developed countries, which are the creators of Industry 4.0. This chapter mainly focuses on presenting the authors views on how to sustain and increase competitive advantage of the Russian Federation by catching and implementing Industry 4.0. With Industry 4.0, Russian Federation get a bigger share of the world manufacturing value chain.

BACKGROUND

By rapid implementation of information and communication technologies in manufacturing, the industrial processes becomes smart and enables mass customization. Many researches today are devoted to the investigation of the technologies and processes concerned with Industry 4.0 and its impact on economic development.

Industry 4.0 supposes the use of network approach that is based on the ability of creating smart products and components *(Kohlberg & Zühlke, 2015)*. According to the authors *(Kohlberg & Zühlke, 2015)* Industry 4.0 enables new implementation areas through the potential of Industry 4.0 technologies such as powerful, flexible and affordable Cyber Physical Systems applications or extended applicability of Lean Production with various production types.

Bughin and Manyika *(2015)* assumed that the crucial impact factor in competition is related with the Internet of Things (IoT) which means that senior managers and company's members must act at the system level in order to be able to solve the challenges coming from the technological disruption.

Industry 4.0 technologies' application has proved their effectiveness in terms of increasing European firm's competitive advantage not only in manufacturing sectors, but also in service fields such as retail, healthcare, travel and financial services *(Piercy & Rich, 2009)*.

Further, we should consider the main approaches to the identification of milestones in the development of industrial systems.

INDUSTRIAL REVOLUTIONS: FROM INDUSTRY 1.0 TO INDUSTRY 4.0.

During the first industrial revolution with the help of water and steam, the production was mechanized. The main driver of the second industrial revolution was electricity, which helped create mass production. At the center of the third revolution was electronics and information technologies that automated production. Due to the third industrial revolution there began a wide use of information technologies in the industry.

We are at the beginning of a new era, the era of artificial intelligence. But this is not only new technologies, but also cardinal changes in the very foundations of our civilization, the way of thinking of all the inhabitants of the Earth. The founder of the World Economic Forum Klaus Schwab (called it the "Fourth Industrial Revolution" *(Schwab, 2017)*. Determination is inevitable and society is involved in changes regardless of the individual's desire: the decision to grant a loan in a bank or to invite to a new job takes artificial intelligence. The media was overwhelmed with a wave of reports about new successes of neural networks or investments in their creation, in amounts comparable to the budget of cities with million inhabitants.

Artificial intelligence technologies are actively being introduced in the retail and banking sectors, but the introduction of technologies into the real economy is still at an initial level. Most large enterprises still can not decide on the transition from traditional methods of managing customer or production management to technologies based on data analysis and fully automatic decision making. However, those few who have already made up their mind declare real effectiveness from the introduction.

The fourth industrial revolution seems to come out of the third, which is also called "digital" and which began in the middle of the last century. It was characterized by the merging of technologies and the blurring of the facets between the physical, digital and biological spheres.

The fourth industrial revolution is the blending of technologies of the physical, digital and biological world, which creates new opportunities and affects political, social and economic systems *(Schwab, 2017*). The fourth industrial revolution fundamentally transforms modern production, thanks to new technological achievements, including digitalization and robotization, artificial intelligence and the Internet of things, new materials and biotechnology. Due to these changes, production in developed countries again becomes the main source of prosperity and creation of new jobs. The leading developed and developing countries are now implementing their own initiatives aimed at developing the future production, and the leading foreign regions play an active role.

The features of the fourth technological revolution include the following:

- Rates of development. Development is not linear, but rather exponential. The new technology itself synthesizes more and more advanced and efficient technologies;
- Breadth and depth. It changes not only what and how we do, but also who we are;
- Systemic exposure. Integral external and internal transformations of all systems are envisaged in all countries, companies, industries and society as a whole;
- Methodological changes. The harmonization and integration of a large number of different scientific disciplines and discoveries is growing.

With the term fourth technological revolution, the term Industry 4.0 (Industry 4.0) is associated (Figure 1).

The digital economy in industry is realized within the framework of the concept Industry 4.0, which is an element of the fourth industrial revolution. The concept Industry 4.0 was first presented at the Hanover Fair in 2011 by German scientists and politicians H. Kagerman, V.-D. Lucas, W. Valster (Kagermann, et al., 2011). In 2012, the Government of the Federal Republic of Germany within the framework of the "Strategy for High Technologies 2020" adopted an innovative development program - Industrie 4.0.

The basis of the program Industry 4.0 is the creation of "smart" enterprises (factories). These enterprises / factories have three types:

- Digital enterprises;
- Smart enterprises;
- Virtual enterprises.

The scale, depth and speed of the transformations that are occurring allow us to speak about the humanitarian and technological revolution (Ivanov, 2017). In this situation, technology comes to the forefront. The possession of high technologies and, especially, leadership in them means a strategic advantage in the modern world. It is technologies that become the leading variables, order parameters that determine the place of the state in the world and attract capital from countries in which there are none or insufficient (Ivanov and Malinetsky, 2017).

TECHNOLOGICAL WAYS OF LIFE

Determining the genesis of the development of the PC is impossible without the hypothesis put forward a quarter of a century ago, according to which the long-term technical and economic development in its

Figure 1. Large-scale trends in Industry 4.0

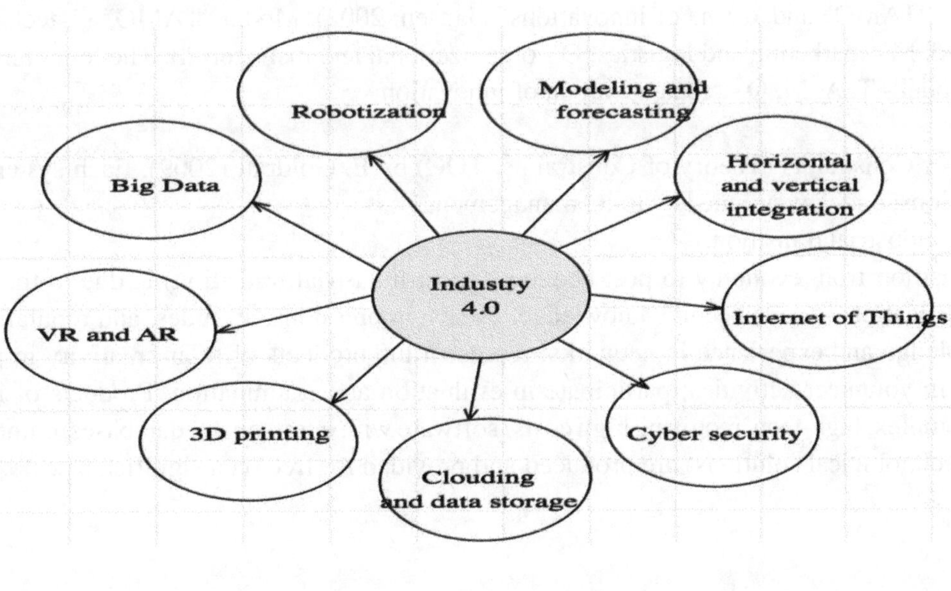

content represents a change in the technological structures (Lvov, 1986; Glaziev, 1993). This structuring of the process of global technical and economic development has shown its effectiveness in a number of works on measuring technological changes in the modern economy.

According to the most common point of view, the technological way is "a combination of technologies characteristic of a certain level of production development; in connection with scientific and technical and technological progress, there is a transition from lower orders to higher, progressive ones" (Glaziev, 1990).

To date, economists have identified five existing ways and talk about the onset of the sixth. In the Russian economy, there are several technological structures (Ermakova, 2013). It is conventionally assumed that the duration of the technological order is 50-60 years.

If we follow the theory of Kondratiev cycles and technological structures, then computer technologies are not related to tomorrow, but, rather, to today's and even to yesterday's day. The core of the sixth technological order, according to some scientists, may be NBIC-convergence, based on the union and synergistic enhancement nano achievements, bio-, information and cognitive technologies. The result of SCBIC-convergence will be a complete merger of these technologies into a single scientific and technological area of knowledge (Schummer 2009).

EVOLUTION OF MODELS AND CONCEPTS OF THE INNOVATION PROCESS

Modern concepts of innovation development include:

- "Open" innovations, which in 2003 proposed G. Chesbrough (2003). The model assumes that the company, when developing new technologies and products, not only relies on its own internal corporate R & D, but also actively draws innovations and competences from the outside;
- "Disruptive" innovations - K. Christensen theory (2016), which he introduced for the first time in 1997. This model can be used to describe the impact of new technologies on the functioning of a company: everything changes at a time when subversive technologies find their buyer who is ready to put up with the shortcomings of a new product and who need new properties of this product;
- Model "TAMO" and "arena of innovations" (Jansen, 2002). Model "TAMO" (T-technology, A - applied, M - marketing and logistics, O - organizational and managerial). The four components of the model - T, A, M, O - create an arena of innovation;

Theory of Constraints (Theory of Constraints, TOC) by E. Goldratt (2009). Each system has very few restrictions, and they are the key to its management.

IV. Post-industrial transition.

The transition from economy to post economy (post-industrial transition) is due to the expansion of commodification - goods become knowledge, events, impressions, attitudes, and reputation. People share knowledge and experience in networks; represent the products of their creativity in public use; participate in volunteer activities; participate in evaluation and examination. Products of intellectual activity - complex, high-tech, requiring high costs (software with open source, databases, communication channels, technological solutions) are produced and provided for free on a significant scale.

MAIN FOCUS OF THE CHAPTER

Issues, Controversies, Problems

The "old economy" relied on the industrial revolution and the management of industrial branches. In an effort to reduce costs, manufacturers standardized products and aimed to continuously increase their market shares and increase efficiency from the growth of production scale. Thinking about efficiency, they copied successful processes and policies in each geographic market and managed operations, according to the hierarchy, when the chief executive instructed middle managers who in turn gave orders to employees. Standard organizational structures were developed that corresponded to the types of production, the planning system and the commercial activities associated with it. Unified methods of motivation were used, depending on the output and quality of products.

The new economy, called digital, in the already saturated consumer market is based on digital technologies and other approaches to managing information about customers, products, prices, competitors and all other aspects of the marketing environment. Information can be infinitely changed, analyzed, personalized and sent electronically to a large number of addressees in a short period of time. Having public information, for example, such as a message about the proposed price, and a feedback system with the seller, consumers and corporate customers can make more informed decisions about the purchase. Thus, the information age offers more precise levels of production, targeted communication and a balanced pricing policy.

Evolution of Types of the Economy

A.V. Babkin *(2017)* outlines the following concepts for the formation of a modern economy:

- Post-industrial,
- new,
- innovative,
- Information,
- knowledge economy,
- Competencies,
- network interaction,
- digital.

Over the past half century in Russia, several types of economies have changed from the industrial economy to the information economy, the digital economy and the knowledge economy.

The main feature of the information economy is the ratio of the rate of development of individual subsystems of the economic system. Denoting S, T, P, I, F - respectively, the rate of development of science, technology, production (product), information sector and finance, we can write the ratio in the rate of dynamics of different subsystems (elements) of the economy for different historical periods *(Sukharev, 2015)*:

$$\frac{\partial P}{\partial t} > \frac{\partial T}{\partial t} > \frac{\partial S}{\partial t} \tag{1.1}$$

$$\frac{\partial I}{\partial t} \geq \frac{\partial F}{\partial t} > \frac{\partial S}{\partial t} > \frac{\partial T}{\partial t} > \frac{\partial P}{\partial t} \tag{1.2}$$

The information economy can also develop without the influence of digital technologies, which has been observed so far. However, the use of digital technologies clearly expands its capabilities, as it improves the processing, storage of information, facilitates the information choice, by reducing the transaction capacity of decisions made.

Analysis of Different Views on the Concept of "Digital Economy"

The term "digital economy" was introduced by D. Tapscott *(1996)*. In 2009, co-authored with E. Williams, he introduced the term "Wikinomics", implying a massive collaboration under it, which is based on such competitive principles as openness, sharing and actions at the global level *(Tapscott and Williams, 2009)*.

The system of views on the concept of "digital economy" is presented in Figure 2.

In fact, in the modern concept of "digital economy" it is a matter of changing the technological base of the economy, which will automate routine operations. G.G. Malinetsky believes that it is worth talking about the digital economy, referring to the computer economy *(Ivanov and Malinetsky, 2017)*.

The Government of the Russian Federation has developed and in July 2017 approved a program for the development of the digital economy until 2024, which defines five basic areas: regulation, personnel and education, the formation of research competencies and technical facilities, information infrastructure and information security. This is not about a separate autonomous project, but about creating a fundamentally new way of life, a new basis for the development of the system of public administration, economy, business, the social sphere, the whole society. Obviously, these tasks can not be solved from above, it is necessary to interact with all participants in this process. In accordance with the program "Digital

Figure 2. System of views on the concept of "digital economy"

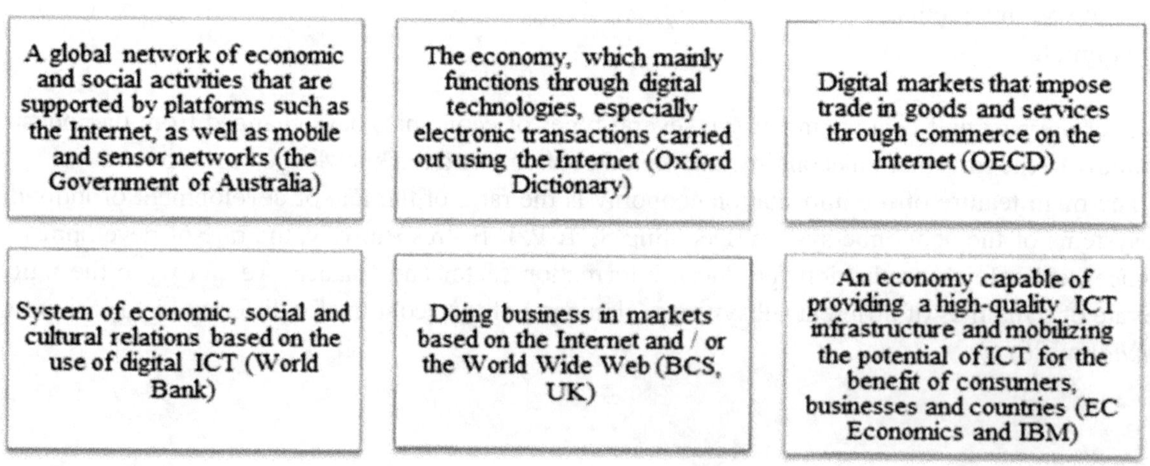

Economy of the Russian Federation", the digital economy is "economic activity, the key factor in the production of which is data in digital form, and contributes to the formation of an information space, taking into account the needs of citizens and society in obtaining quality and reliable information, the development of information infrastructure Russia, the creation and application of Russian ICT, as well as the formation of a new technological basis for social and economic spheres *(State program "Digital Economy in the Russian Federation", 2017).*

The digital model will increase the competitiveness of the Russian economy in global markets, provide the conditions for a gradual transition to the level of the innovation economy and knowledge economy, and improve the quality and standard of living of the population (for example, by reducing harmful emissions and improving the environmental performance of industrial production).

The digital economy has great potential to promote economic development. The Internet "explodes" the established markets for goods, services and labor, as well as the principles of the functioning of the public sector. Russia needs to take advantage of the current scientific and technological situation in the world economy in order to ensure globally competitive positions in the market *(Babkin, 2017).* Thus, the problem of managing the development of industrial companies in the context of reindustrialization and digitalization comes to the fore and becomes archival.

According to S.P. Kurdyumov (2018) under the term "digital transformation" the authors understand:

- A change of the model of economic management from program-target to program-prognostic;
- A change in the economic structure, the change in traditional markets, social relations, public administration associated with the penetration of digital technologies into them;
- A fundamental change in the main source of value added and the structure of the economy through the formation of more efficient economic processes provided by digital infrastructures;
- A transition of the function of the leading mechanism of economic development to institutions based on digital models and processes.

The notion of "digitalization" is closely related to the concept of digital economy.

In the broad sense, the process of "digitalization" is usually understood as a socio-economic transformation initiated by the massive introduction and assimilation of digital technologies, i.e. technologies of creation, processing, exchange and transfer of information.

Digitalization is also understood as the introduction of technologies needed to create new business models, processes, systems and software that will increase profits, increase competitiveness and business efficiency. Digitalization is the use of the possibilities of online and innovative digital technologies by all participants in the economic system from individuals to large companies and states. Digitalization is the most complete disclosure of the potential of digital technologies through their use in all aspects of business - processes, products and services, approaches to decision-making. It is important to emphasize that in order for the digitalization process to be complete, clearly defined business tasks and data.

Current Problems of Digitalization in Russia: Building Knowledge Economy

The movement along the way of managing the development of industrial companies requires the joint efforts of all participants. It is necessary to overcome a significant number of barriers. Only in this way the industrial complexes and the national economy of Russia as a whole will be able to move to a new stage in the development of the digital economy, to ensure the competitiveness of products of national production, both on the domestic and global markets.

Thus, the development environment under digital transformation changes its state to the "digital environment for the development of industrial companies" due to infrastructure and institutional changes.

Under the digital environment, the authors propose to understand a set of interrelated subjects of the production process and a digital infrastructure characterized by the use of information technology, high innovative activity and receptivity, operating in a favorable climate, which allows implementing scientific, technological, innovative and digital potential through proactive behavior. The digital environment for development is the most important prerequisite for scientific, technical and humanitarian progress.

The development of ICT infrastructure was noted by the Government of Russia as one of the priority directions in the construction of the digital economy. Access to high-quality ICT infrastructure positively affects GDP growth and the possibility of developing digital services. Providing broadband Internet access for small settlements, medical and educational institutions, the creation of domestic digital platforms, the deployment of 5G networks is an incomplete list of tasks planned by the Digital Economy of the Russian Federation program.

Thus, the knowledge economy is the goal of the development of the digital economy in Russia. The urgency of the formation of the knowledge economy is confirmed by the state and business. The knowledge economy is an economy in which knowledge is a market product. It is characterized by a high share of services, a high share of investment in innovation, developed information and communication sphere, building partnerships, cooperation of various companies. The economy of knowledge becomes a factor of innovative development, without which it is impossible to imagine modern society. The key characteristics of the knowledge economy are shown in Figure 3.

In Figure 4, the presence or absence of a digital economy is determined through E-Intensity, the index developed by The Boston Consulting Group, which tracks the development of the digital component of the global economy in 85 countries.

The index of the economy's digitization is calculated as the weighted average of three subindexes: infrastructure development, online costs, user activity.

The subindex "Infrastructure Development" reflects the degree of infrastructure development and the availability and quality of Internet access (fixed and mobile). The subindex "Online costs" includes the costs of online retail and online advertising. The subindex "User activity" is calculated as a weighted average of subindexes of a lower level: the activity of companies, the activity of consumers and the activity of state institutions. All subindexes are formed from the weighted averages of several parameters underlying them.

Figure 5 shows that Russia's position in the rating of BCG for the past five years has not actually changed, and the country ranks 39th out of 85 in the development of the digital economy. In 2011, it was on the 43rd place, in 2012 - on the 39th, in 2013 - on the 40th line. At the same time, the RF index (e-Intensity) grew at an average annual rate of 24% and in 2015 was 113. The leader of the rating Denmark is characterized by the value of the index of 213. The top 3 also includes Luxembourg and Sweden (212 and 208 respectively). Singapore ranks first in digital competition. However, China's indicators are growing very fast, on average by 33% per year - and by 2025 it can take the first place in the ranking (URL: https://www.rbc.ru/economics/10/06/2016/5759aed19a79470d3392e05d). Technologically, China stands at the forefront of development in the most key industries, especially in the development of the Internet, applied developments, and is ahead of the US. Many institutions in Beijing do not accept cash or credit cards, they only accept aliexpress checks. It is already clear that the way Asian countries

Figure 3. Key characteristics of the knowledge economy (Adapted from: Russia 2025: from talent to cadres, 2017)

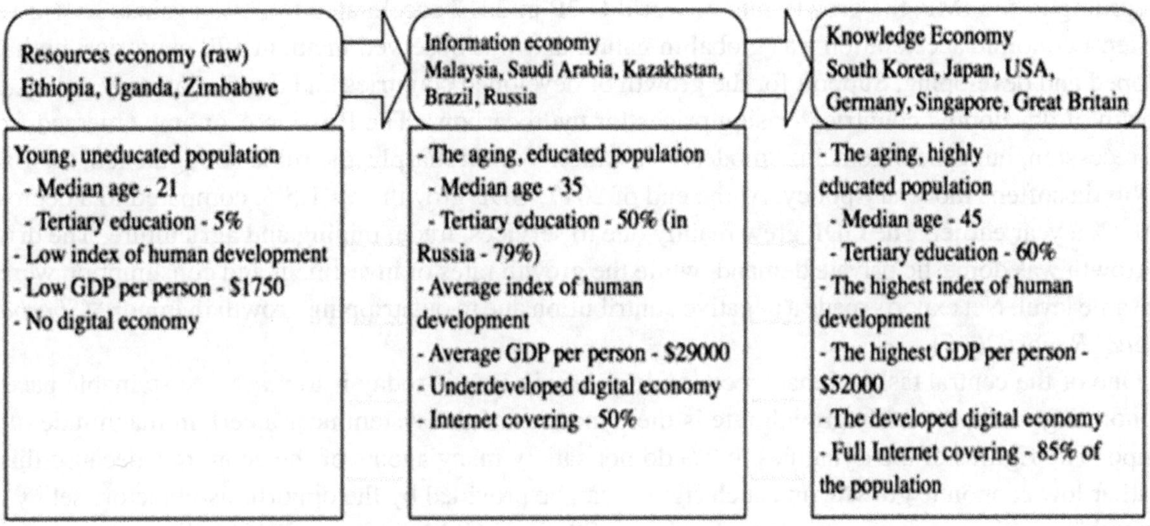

Figure 4. The index of the development of the digital economy of the countries of the world in 2015 (Boston Consulting Group, 2018)

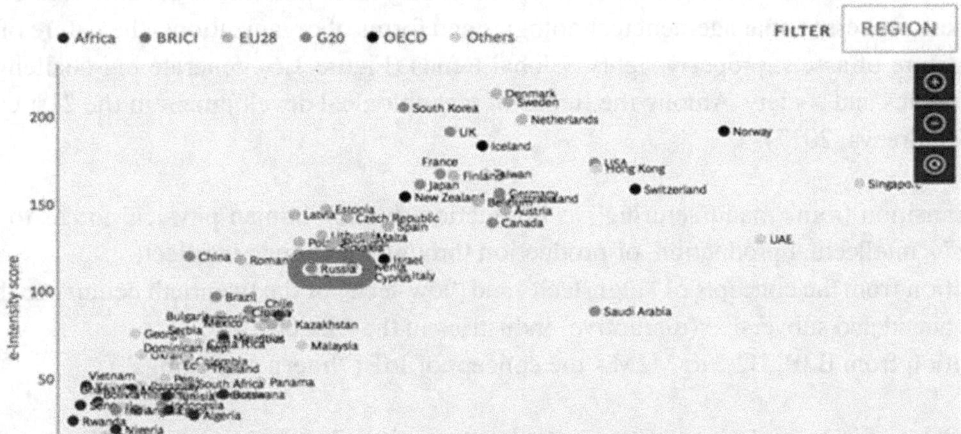

respond to global challenges, at what pace they will be set, will largely affect the further development of the world economy. However, the USA is the only digitally developed country in the world where there is no regulatory framework for digital politics.

The advantages that developing countries have so far demonstrated: high growth rates, cheap labor, are no longer a systemic factor that provides economic growth. Russia will need the industrial policy that will promote inclusive and smart economic growth.

Challenges and Opportunities in Leap-Frogging Strategies in Russia

According to the IMF, the growth rate of world GDP in 2017 accelerated to 3.7% against 3.1% a year earlier. Economic acceleration was global in nature and was observed in about 120 countries, both developed and developing. Support for the growth of developed countries had a soft monetary policy, the growth of developing countries - rising prices for hydrocarbons. The Russian economy emerged from the recession, but growth remains "modest". Inflation slowed sharply, the ruble strengthened, the Bank of Russia softens monetary policy. At the end of 2017, GDP growth was 1.5%, compared to a decrease of 0.2% a year earlier. The GDP grew mainly due to services, trade, mining and agriculture. The driver of growth was domestic private demand, while the growth rates of investment and consumption were at the same level. Net exports made a negative contribution due to outstripping growth in import[s] (*Sberbank Annual Report 2017).*

One of the central tasks of macroeconomic policy in Russia today is to reach a sustainable pace of economic growth. A steady growth rate is the dynamics of the system near a certain magnitude of its tempo. The figures of the dynamics to 2% do not satisfy many agents of the economy, because this is a rather low economic growth, and such figures can be provided by the opportunistic factors set by the dynamics of prices in foreign markets (Sukharev, 2018). G.G. Malinetsky (2015) believes that "to seriously talk about modernization and, even more so, to implement it, Russia needs to have its own big project, to master the possibilities of a new technological order and to ensure rapid economic growth (by more than 10% a year)".

In the conditions of rapid changes in society, everything is transformed - the structure of the workforce, business processes, management technologies and forms of organizations, the nature of creativity and the structure of assets, property rights. Global trends (Figure 1.6) generate big challenges for the economy, politics and society. Among the trends of technological development in the 21st century, the following (Andreeva, 2017):

- The transition from "manufacturing" as production through human physical forces to "brainfacturing" - intellectual production, or production through the human intellect;
- Transition from the concepts of "high-tech" and "low-tech" of the twentieth century to the concept of advanced and subversive (disruptive) industries in the 21st century;
- Transition from B2B, B2C to M2M - the concept of IoT ("Internet of things").

Management of industrial companies can not keep up with all global trends. In these conditions, the issue of prioritization comes first. The organization that can prioritize and concentrate efforts wins, which understands that no company can cope with all trends, it is necessary to be open to the world. The key quality of PC management in the modern world is collaboration, cooperation.

The concept and characteristics of Russia's major challenges are presented in the Strategy for Scientific and Technological Development of the Russian Federation until 2025 (Decree of the President of the Russian Federation dated 1 December 2016, No 642). In recent decades, Russia has entered a wave of deep technological and social changes, characterized by the emergence of new ones and the strengthening of the following aspects:

- The origin of the digital revolution - the massive use of digital technology, personal computers, laptops, tablets, smartphones, cameras, digital video and sound;

Figure 5. Global development trends (adapted from Chulok, 2017)

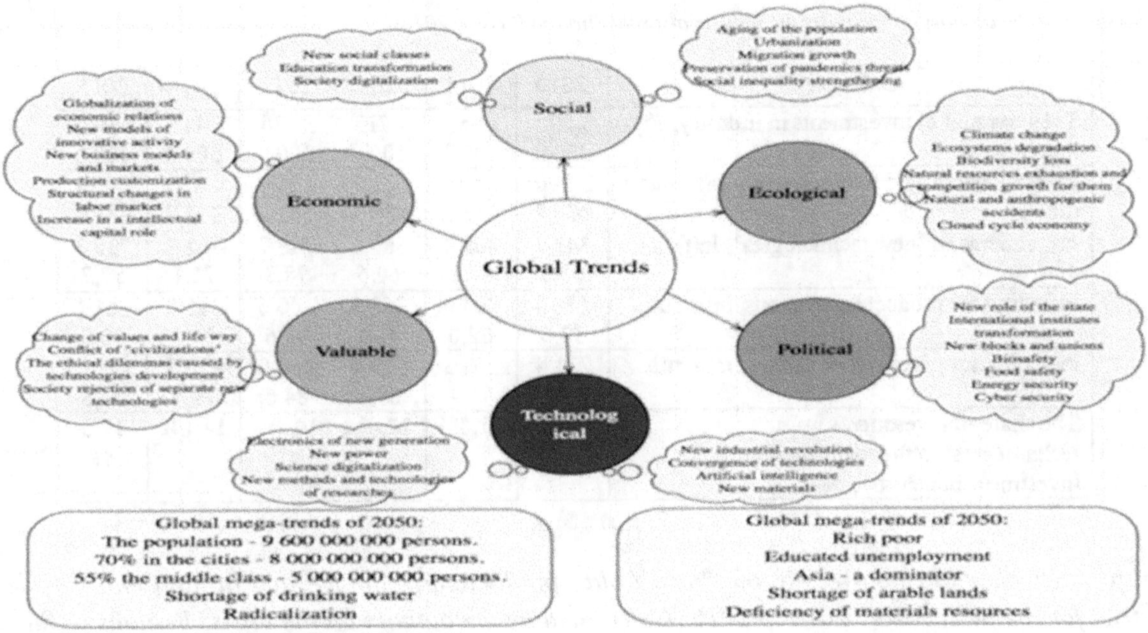

- Explosion of the communicative revolution - cellular communications, broadband Internet, social networks, GPS navigation;
- Manifestation of the consumption revolution - retail chains, supermarkets and shopping and entertainment centers, fitness centers, symbolic and glamorous consumption.

Further we will analyze the changes in the structure of the "old / new" technologies of Russian industry. By new technologies we mean technological innovations, under old technologies we mean the available traditional technologies. If a new production is mentioned, then it means production on new technologies, that is, when implementing technological innovations (Tatarkin, et al., 2017).

We consider the value of the costs of technological innovation as the cost of new technologies *In(t)*, and the total amount of expenditures in fixed capital - as all investments *I(t)*. Then, the difference between the value of all investments in fixed assets and the costs of technological innovation in the form of costs for old technologies, labeled *Is (t)*, is calculated in Figure 6.

As we can see, the total amount of investments in the Russian industry is growing: increase as the cost of technological innovation (investment in "new technology" (*In(t)*) in absolute terms, and their share in the structure of investments. For the period 2010-2015. the amount of investment in "new" technology has increased 2.1 times, and in "old" - 1.8 times without inflation, which is explained by the policy of stimulating innovation activities of enterprises.

Next, we will analyze the changes in the structure of "old / new" technologies by the number of employees in production on new and old technologies (Figure 7). The number of employed in the development will be taken as the number of employees in the "new" technologies *Ln(t)*. The difference between the number of all employed and employed in development is the number of people working on "old" technologies *Ls(t)*.

Figure 6. Dynamics of investments in "old / new" technologies of industrial complexes of the Russian Federation for 2010-2015
(Calculated by the authors on the basis of: Industrial production in Russia, 2016)

Indicator	2010	2011	2012	2013	2014	2015
Total amount of investments in industry, I(t), mln. rub.	3 290 400,0	3 969 500,0	4 713 100,0	5 136 900,0	5 415 600,0	5 970 100,0
Investments in "old technologies", Is(t), mln. rub.	2 940 636,7	3 500 057,8	4 129 439,4	4 390 121,7	4 652 825,9	5 234 342,3
Investments in "new technologies", In(t), mln. rub.	349 7 63,3	469 4 42,2	583 6 60,6	746 7 78,3	762 7 74,1	735 7 57,7
including for product innovations, mln. rub.	138 3 33,0	203 0 67,0	263 9 75,6	260 6 93,6	291 8 04,5	264 1 80,8
including for process innovations, mln. rub.	211 4 30,3	266 3 75,4	319 6 85,1	486 0 84,6	470 9 79,5	471 5 76,8
The share of investments in "new technologies" in the total amount of investment in industry, %	10,6%	11,8%	12,4%	14,5%	14,1%	12,3 %

Figure 7. Number of employees in the "new / old" production in the RF and in the Central Federal District for the period from 2010 to 2016 (Calculated by the authors on the basis: Regions of Russia. Socio-economic indicators. 2017).

Indicator	2010	2011	2012	2013	2014	2015	2016
The number of employed in the industry of the Russian Federation, people.	13 25 5 200	13 23 8 500	13 19 6 800	13 07 5 400	12 84 8 800	13 38 0 100	13 35 7 500
The number of employed in the industry of the Central Federal District, people.	3 428 600	3 419 100	3 384 500	3 343 300	3 305 400	3 578 000	3 613 800
Number of employees in the "new" production of the Russian Federation, people.	736 5 40	735 2 73	726 3 18	727 0 29	732 2 74	738 8 57	722 2 91
Number of employees in the "new" production of the Central Federal District, people.	381 7 95	380 3 63	373 4 61	375 0 87	381 0 47	380 1 40	372 2 93
Number of employees in the "old" production of Russia, people.	12 51 8 660 ,0	12 50 3 227 ,0	12 47 0 482 ,0	12 34 8 371 ,0	12 11 6 526 ,0	12 64 1 243 ,0	12 63 5 209 ,0
Number of employees in the "old" production of the Central Federal District, people.	3 046 805, 0	3 038 737, 0	3 011 039, 0	2 968 213, 0	2 924 353, 0	3 197 860, 0	3 241 507, 0
The share of employed in the "new" production of the Russian Federation,%	5,56 %	5,55 %	5,50 %	5,56 %	5,70 %	5,52 %	5,41 %
The share of employed in the "new" production of the Central Federal District,%	11,14 %	11,12 %	11,03 %	11,22 %	11,53 %	10,62 %	10,30 %

In 2015, we managed to overcome this negative trend a little: there was an increase in employed in industry, both throughout the Russian Federation and in the Central Federal District. This trend in 2016 remained only in the Central Federal District, where the increase in employed in industry amounted to a negligible amount of 35,700 people. In the Russian Federation in 2016, there was again a reduction in employed in industry. The number of employees in new and old production is also declining over the past seven years both for Russia and the Central Federal District. At the same time, the share of research and development personnel is also decreasing with a general reduction in labor productivity (as shown before).

Consequently, the key competencies for innovation development in Russia are as follows: new materials, devices, the human factor, information technologies, biotechnology.

SOLUTIONS AND RECOMMENDATIONS

Lessons From De-Industrialization and Re-Industrialization

The modern condition of the Russian industry provided there was a drop of production volumes in 2015 and a slight growth in 2016 and 2017 with the cumulative deficit of fixed capital expenditures (Figure 8), is characterized by a set of attributes *(Sukharev, 2014):*

- High level of de-industrialization and technological lagging of Russian productions;
- Fragmentation of the industrial system: sectoral (branch) breaks, including vertical and horizontal links;
- Localization (spatial) of productions by regions with the emerging effect of monopolization and spatial segmentation of industrial markets;
- The effect of scouring for orders, technical solutions, sometimes personnel, as information systems of management fail to find necessary solutions and auxiliary processes (therefore sometimes import is inevitable);
- Problems with product competitiveness due to a low technological level of production;
- Underdeveloped institutions of industrial development promotion, lack of favorable development environment and organizational forms.

Let us briefly analyze the dynamics of the most significant parameters determining the Russian industrial development.

The index of industrial production (Figure 9) shows a drop in the dynamics in 2010-2014, a negative value of the rate in 2015 and a weak growth in 2016-2017.

The yield on capital investments for the last 5 years decreased from 0,125 in 2011 to 0,117 in 2014, in 2015 there was a slight increase to 0,12 (Figure 11).

Figure 8. Annual increase rates of industrial production and fixed capital investments

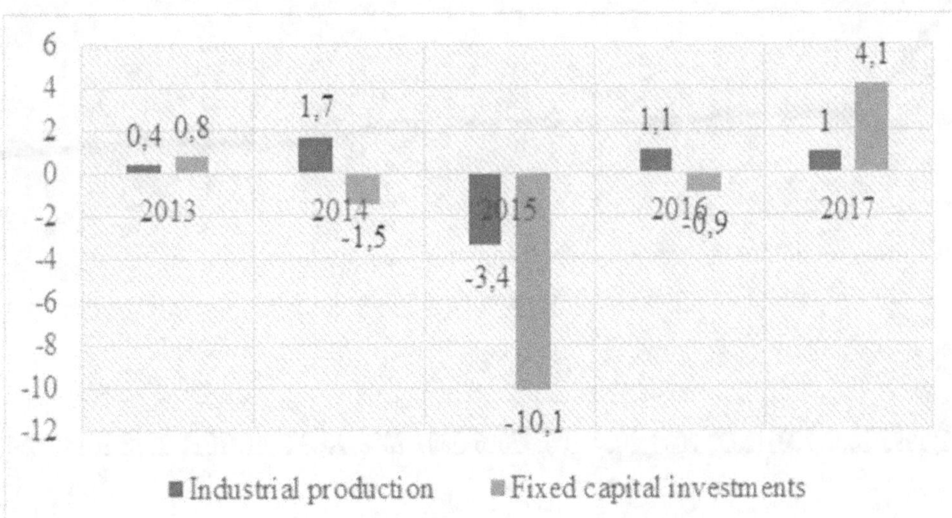

Figure 9. The index of industrial production from 1992 till 2017, in % with resect to the previous year. The general dynamics for the last 7 years may be evaluated as descending (from 107,3% in 2010 to 101% in 2017). Changes of the financial results display extremely unstable functioning of the industry as a system due to major fluctuation from year to year. The number of employees in the industrial field (figure 1.3) was constantly decreasing from 21,3 mill. of people in 1992 to 12,8 mill. in 2015.

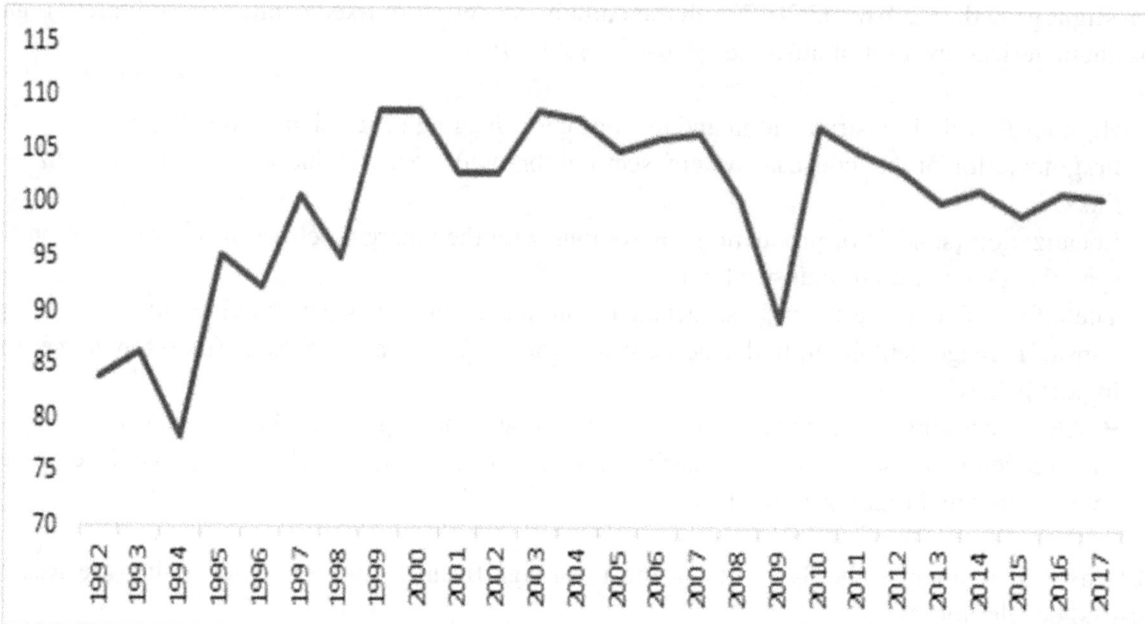

Figure 10. The average annual number of employees in the industry from 1992 till 2015, mill. of people

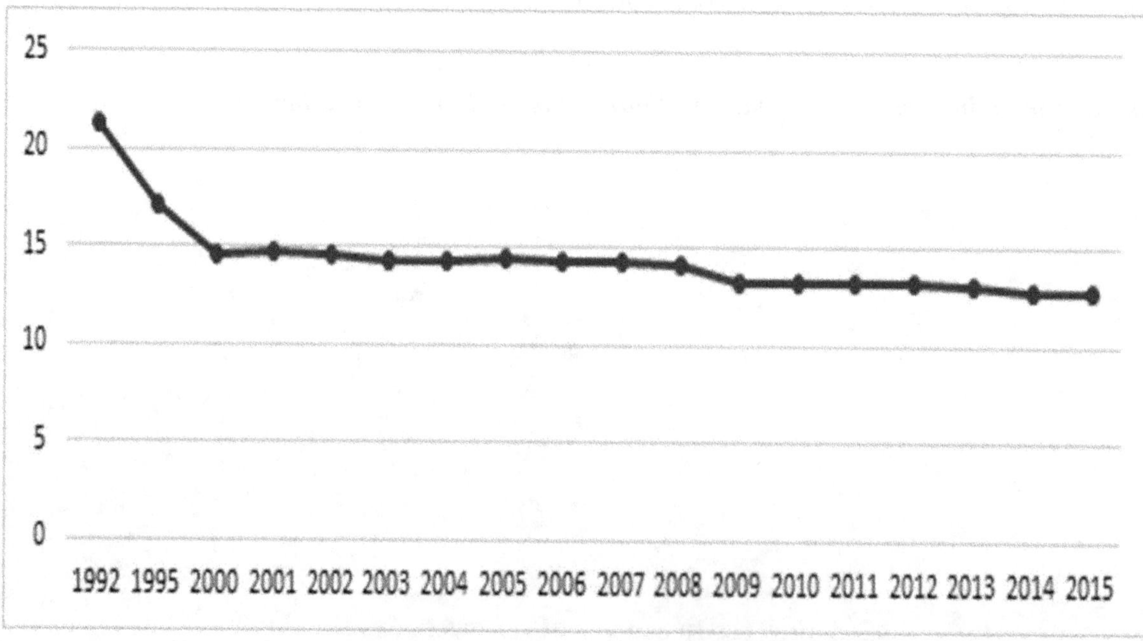

Figure 11. The yield on capital investments in the industrial production from 1995 till 2015

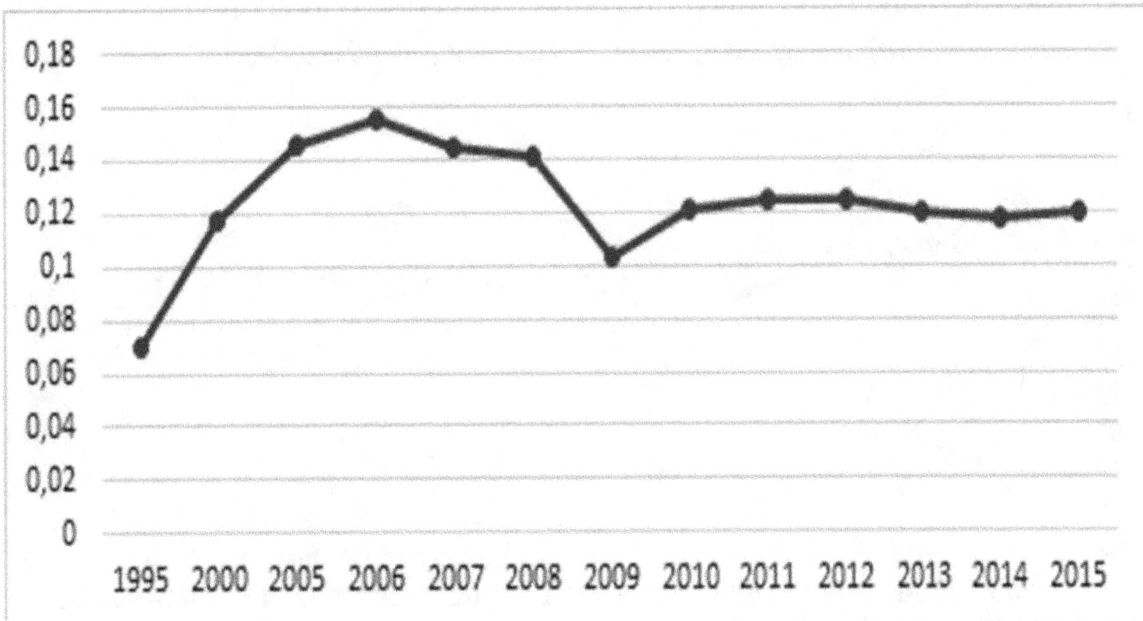

The labor and industrial productivity (Figure 12) was falling from 2009 till 2013, and in 2015 reduced critically.

These alerting figures are the evidence of the necessity to change approaches in the industrial policy.

The experience of economic reforms in Russia from 2000s shows that the measures focused on Russian industry development promotion have included the following initiatives:

- Establishment of special economic zones since 2005;
- In the period of economic growth in 2005 Russia realized top priority national projects;
- Establishment of development institutions in 2006;
- Introduction of technological platforms in Russia from 2010;
- From early 2012 innovation territorial clusters have been organized;
- In late 2014 the legislation fixed special forms of socioeconomic development specifically for Dalnevostochniy region (Far East region) – "territories of priority development" (TPD);
- In December 2014 in his message to the Federal Assembly the President of Russia set an objective to implement National Technological Initiatives (NTI);
- Following the changes of the geopolitical situation and some restraints on the import of certain technologies in 2014 the attention was drawn to elaboration of the Russian industrial policy;
- In December 2015 the objective was set to create a national project office to support priority socioeconomic development projects;
- In 2016 there was launched the development program of the economy of new generation – digital economy;
- In 2018 12 national priority projects have been launched (demography; healthcare; education; accommodation and municipal environment; ecology; safe and high-quality highways; labor pro-

Figure 12. The labor productivity in the industry from 2005 till 2015, in % with respect to the previous year

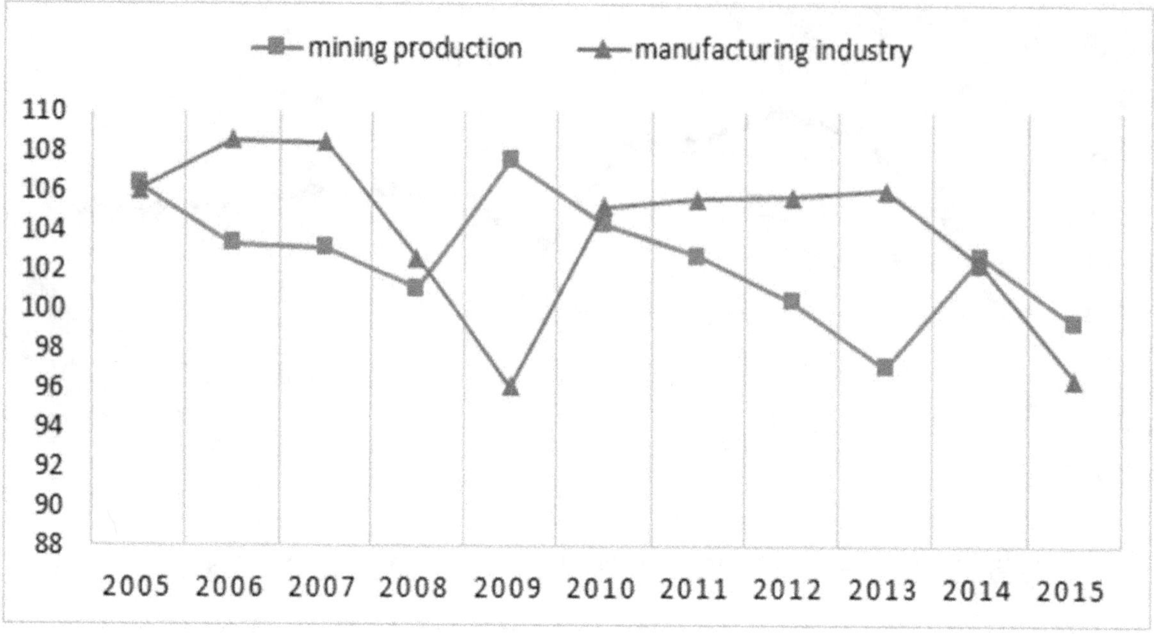

ductivity and employment support; science; digital economy; culture; small and medium entrepreneurship and individual entrepreneurial initiative support; international cooperation and export).

- Some principal problems of the inefficiency of implementation of some initiatives include the following:
- Lack of feedback in the system of initiators and conductors of the said initiatives. The key condition of success in the innovation economy is the development of positive feedback. The presence of idea exchange, an innovation-receptive environment, many ambitious people coming from all over the world provides positive feedback between economic agents engaged in the knowledge-intensive field;
- Lack of coordination between initiators and conductors of the said initiatives. Cooperation and symbiosis should become more important than traditional logic of economic competition;
- Inactivity, lack of motivation and low innovation activity. It is favorable to increase the innovation activity till the level of the Soviet times (approximately 20 times). It is necessary to have a flow of ideas, projects, inventions, proposals, initiative; it is important to value the new, the original, the unusual.

Let us highlight the main problem to be resolved by the present study. To be considered the main, a problem should be of system nature for all industrial systems and have such a difficulty that it would be impossible to solve it within the existing managerial models.

We believe that this sort of problems includes deep de- industrialization of the Russia industrial system, which has led to systemic negative socioeconomic consequences. The external factors of the socioeconomic stagnation (sanction in particular) in this case served only as a catalyst of problem aggravation. In this situation the negative effect of de-industrialization is not reduced only to absolute and relative (industrial share in GDP) reduction of industrial production volumes. According to O.S. Sukharev *(2014),* at de-industrialization the share of industrial production doesn't just reduce, it becomes more primitive; the technological level drops down, the production infrastructure collapses/curtails.

De-industrialization is a process of socioeconomic changes caused by decreased or absolutely ceased industrial activities in a region or a country, especially in heavy industry and industrial production *(The program of economic re-industrialization of Novosibirsk region).*

To describe the above-mentioned negative consequences there was defined the "two Ds effect" (de-industrialization and de-qualification), which has been later transformed into the "three Ds effect" (de-industrialization, de-qualification, dysfunction of management), as well as into the "four Ds effect"1 (from some analogy with the "four Is effect" *(Bodrunov, 2016):*

- *Disorganization* of production (decreasing organization and management of production);
- *Degradation* of technologies applied (falling technological level of production);
- *De-Qualification* of labor in production (includes not just a loss of skills and competences, but also simplification of the labor content, destruction of labor motivation etc.);
- *De-Complication* (simplification) of products.
- To our point of view this effect can be supplemented with such components as:
- *Disintegration* of production, education and science;
- *Deficiency* of investments and sanctions in the economy;
- *De-Structuring* of sectors.

At the present time the Russian economy is at the crossroads: to develop following the innovation path and to try and keep pace with the developing economies, or to lose the ability to compete with highly-developed countries forever. Thus, lagging is the main threat for Russia. It is crucial to reverse such situation and to ensure the development dynamics.

The experience of post-soviet development shows that the main problem lies not in ideas, but in their implementation. For the last quarter of the century the country has undergone a series of innovatory and bold initiatives (from creation of Special economic zones to RAS transformation), which, according to the authors' concept, are intended to provide the transition to the innovation path of development, as well as the economic development and life-quality improvement. However, in practice, such solutions haven't always led to the predicted effects. According to some scholars *(Ivanov and Malinetsky, 2017),* such situation is to a great extent caused by application of the approach known as "innovation without science", as the bulk of such decisions have been made on the basis of common views without sufficient expert examination.

V.V. Ivanov and G.G. Malinetsky *(2017)* notice in arguments on development ways the dividing line in the following question: "Human for economy or economy for human?" If "human is for economy", than the greatest achievements are the growth of high-tech export, the number of employees in non-resource-based sectors of industry, the growth labor productivity etc. If "economy is for human", than it is natural to evaluate the quality of life in real indicators important for people: health, education quality, social protection, prosperity, food, energy etc. The authors proceed from the requirements to follow the "economy for human" paradigm. It is necessary to speak about the quality of people's lives, because obviously every next phase of economic development or changes of socioeconomic setups increases the role of the person. Therefore, the creation of high living standards is the key factor for the economy to change and to grow; for the best talents to remain in Russia.

Besides the person's role in the innovation economy, the preservation and restoration of the environment are the objectives of the modern world that require close attention and timely and efficient decisions both in the applied context and in the legal field. The commercial or paid approach to nature management seems to be just, and socially responsible and far-sighted industrial companies are ready to invest considerable funds into environmental events. At the present time the legislation provides for several types of compensation of negative impacts on the environment: payment for negative impacts, as well as indemnification for infliction of damage to environmental components, introduction or improvement of new technologies and holding of nature-conserving events. It is obvious that modernization of production, construction and reconstruction of treatment facilities has a great positive effect in comparison with payment of fees, and the state goal is to stimulate these and similar events. Companies holding nature-preserving events have the right to decrease fees, but the mechanism of funds offsetting has not been properly defined by laws, and in practice the balance is achieved through courts.

J. Stiglitz *(1997)*, famous American economist and Nobel Prize winner, has come up with the theory of "The Great Divide". He convincingly demonstrated that the American economy had been developing for quite some time in favor of 1% of the richest US citizens, which could lead to a social catastrophe: «The top 1 percent have the best houses, the best educations, the best doctors, and the best lifestyles, but there is one thing that money doesn't seem to have bought: an understanding that their fate is bound up with how the other 99 percent live. Throughout history, this is something that the top 1 percent eventually do learn. Too late» (Stiglitz, 1997). At the present time the separation between countries and inside them is continuing to grow. Although the inequality has been acknowledged as a great threat to the world stability, nowadays the 1% of the richest control 50% of the world wealth against 43% in 2010 *(BCG)*.

We believe that programs and strategies of scientific and technological development, re-industrialization of the Russian industry, the program of digital economy, as well as other state programs of modern Russia must be carried out in the interests of 99% of its population.

De-Industrialization, Re-Industrialization, and Neo-Industrialization

At the present time all developed countries are reconsidering post-industrial conceptions. Such terms as "modernization", "new industrialization" (neoindustrialization), "re-industrialization" have become permanent on the agenda. The views of researchers on the said terms are introduced below.

According to Feldman *(2001)* modernization is creation of an industrial base with structure, branches and technical equipment of the international level; establishment of mutual autonomy of social spheres (including creation of advanced systems of social protection); development of human rights protection.

In general understanding, re-industrialization is a new economic policy devoted to modernization and innovative development of the Russian economy. Economic re-industrialization presupposes establishment of new and development of existing high-tech enterprises, production of new goods and services, creation of new work places, growth of labor productivity and industrial and economic competitiveness in whole. It is reflected in accelerated technological development of the economy, in modernization of existing productions on the basis of absolutely new technologies and in establishment of new high-tech sectors and productions *(The program of economic re-industrialization of Novosibirsk region)*.

From the point of view of O.S. Sukharev *(2014)*, industrialization is a substitution of manual labor with the machine one, which leads to staff disengagement. Nowadays industrialization is reduced to *a sharp increase of production manufacturability* (the share of industrial production is subject to change, drop or

Figure 13. Views on the term "industrialization"

Source	Definition
Sukharev, 2014	Industrialization is the process of switching primitive labor scarcely equipped with technology to the machine based one
Sanzharevsky, 2010	Industrialization is a process of establishment of large-scale machine production and the transition on the basis thereof from the agrarian society to the industrial one
Epishkin, 2010	Industrialization is country's industrial development; introduction of large machinery into country's national economy
Financial dictionary, Finam.	Industrialization is a period of priority development of production characterized by the establishment of large-scale machine production standard goods on the basis of the following: - complex division of labor and specialization; - utilization of various types of energy; - application of science and technology in production organization.
Black, 2000	Industrialization is a process of transferring the resources into the industrial sector.
Dictionary of business terms. Academic.ru.	Industrialization is committed development of industry, establishment of large-scale machine production in the economy or in a certain economic branch, considerable growth of the share of industrial production in the economy.
Usoltseva, 2017	Under industrialization one understands the process of transition to the industrial stage of development associated with considerable growth of the share of industry in the economy, with development of new technologies

Figure 14. Definition of "new industrialization" (neoindustrialization)

Source	Definition
Primakov, 2012	«New industrialization» (or neoindustrialization) is a policy characterized by the following features: - economic structure diversification to achieve a growing share of industrial production; - providing the said process with personnel possessing the corresponding skills; - modernization of country's financial system for the needs of re-industrialization; - establishment of "channels", "lifts" linking scientific development with industrial production; - systemic import of high technology: through acquisition of technological assets abroad; - by attracting direct investments into the Russian industry provided technology transfer

Figure 15. Views on the term "re-industrialization"

Source	Definition
Sukharev O. S. Re-industrialization of the Russian economy and technological development //National interests: priorities and security. – 2014. – №. 10.	Re-industrialization is restoration of production and technological systems, individual sectors and types of production taking place along with settlement of principal objectives concerning stock, technological and staff foundations of the industry with the general focus on creation of national qualitative values in use
	Re-industrialization is an economic policy representing a set of measures broader than in standard variants of the industrial policy. It is devoted to planned restoration (creation, change) of the industrial and technological base of the economic system by applying macroeconomic, institutional and organizational, legal, structural and investment measures effecting not just industrial organization, but the auxiliary infrastructure, financial and banking systems etc.
Re-industrialization: How can we organize industrial development? A verbatim of a direct conversation with the Chairman of the Development Party Yuri Krupnov, 3rd November, 19:10, "Govorit Moskva" radio 92FM	Re-industrialization is designing, creation of an absolutely new industrial system that would be competitive in the world and, most importantly, that would give people, the country's population (in this case, Russia's population) a sufficient number of high skill-demanding jobs
Putin V.V. On our economic problems //Bulletin. – 2012. – Vol. 30. – №. 15. – P. 5.	Re-industrialization is considered as intensive development of the Russian industry by means of large investments into development (including acquisition abroad) of new technologies and equipment for the account of reorganization of recipients of such investments — the industry in whole, its base elements and subjects
The decision of the Scientific Expert Council under the Chairman of the Council of the Federation of the Federal Assembly of Russia on the issue "Re-industrialization of Russia: opportunities and constraints" [Online resource] – URL: http://www.council.gov.ru/media/files/41d477365af5651386f7.pdf (address date: 11.10.2016)	Re-industrialization should be interpreted as a process coordinated by authorized bodies and devoted to creation and development of the model of Russian industry, which should be implemented in the following areas: organization and development of target sectors of the country's innovation complex, in particular, bioeconomics, nano-industry, cognitive technologies; modernization of the manufacturing industry using enhanced innovation technologies; introduction of cutting-edge technologies into the development of mineral and raw-material sectors
Bodrunov S.D. Economic re-industrialization: shall we begin with import substitution? //Economic revival of Russia. – 2014. – №. 3. – P. 5-7.	Re-industrialization is a process of intensive economic growth by means of increasing the efficiency of resource utilization for the purpose of production and realization of competitive goods. These products should be developed on the basis of Russian knowledge-intensive technologies. To achieve these goals it is necessary to modernize the production and technological base of the national industry
Romanova O.A., Bukhvalov N.Y. Re-industrialization as a determinative trend of economic development of industrial areas //Fundamental research. – 2014. – №. 6-1.	Re-industrialization is a simultaneous process of creation of not just new high-tech sectors of the economy, but also efficient innovative renewal of its traditional sectors together with coordinated qualitative changes between economic, technical, social and institutional spheres, carried out by means of interactive technological, social, political and managerial alterations. As for this definition it is reasonable to highlight not just the interconnection of all sphere of public life in the country for the purpose of implementing the program of re-industrialization, but also "the functional-catalytic industrialization" as a special type of re-industrialization

even grow like in China). The comparison of the processes of industrialization and de-industrialization is shown in Figure 16.

D.E. Sorokin and S.A. Tolkachyov *(2015)* propose to characterize the upcoming changes of industrial foundation as neoindustrialization. From their point of view, neoindustrialization is large-scale introduction of a complex of breakthrough of NBICs (Nano-Bio-Info-Cogno-technologies) into the production process, cardinal alteration of the essence of the industrial way of production enabling as follows:

- To sharply increase labor productivity in manufacturing sectors;
- To create new markets (at the same time some traditional activities will vanish);
- To form global centers of rapid industrial growth;
- To reduce the need for low-skilled labor, thus exacerbating the global unemployment problem;
- To amplify the technological leadership of the developed countries over the rest of the world.
- D.P. Frolov and M.M. Babkin *(2016)* study the term "NBIC-convergence" as integration of nano-, bio-, information technologies and their combinations. According to these scholars, convergence of nano-, bio-, information technologies and their combinations as an objective process of development of a complex of new widely used technologies originates and develops locally within individual research centers and innovation clusters, and then spreads over the territories of other regions: from more innovatively developed to less ones. Centralized management of individual branches of NBIC-convergence creates incentives and impulses for the authorities, scientific and business communities that lead to industrial complex modernization.

To our mind, rapid development of NBICs obliges to correct priorities. At the present time it is more appropriate to discuss another abbreviation - SCBIN (Socio-Cognito-Bio-Info-Nano) and the decisive role of social technologies, without which prominent inventions and scientific achievements won't be apprehended and implemented by the modern society.

Figure 16. Comparison of the processes of industrialization and de-industrialization

Parameters/ Process	Industrialization	de-industrialization
The share of industry in FGP (number of factories, sectors)	Grows	Drops
Assets	Quite rapid renewal, wear reduction, introduction of new technologies	Massive wear and aging, low pace of renewal, immanent barriers to introduction of new technologies
Staff skills	Grow	Drop
Technological level (mechanization, automation, raw material processing extent)	Grows	Drops
The share of imported components, nodes, spare parts	Drops	Grows
Effective life span of developments (products)	Drops	Initially gradually rises, then sharply drops due to product wear
Technological operation complexity	Grows	Drops
Development costs and time	Grow (according to plan) on a short period of time and drop on a long one	Considerably and quite rapidly grow blocking the appearance of new products and technologies
Development institutions (institutional conditions)	Efficient as they ensure financing (crediting) of production and emerging of new technologies	Low efficiency, short resources and reduction of the resource base for the development of new technologies and industry

A number of researchers and practitioners speak about the presence of digital disruption (Schmidt and Cohen, 2010) in the modern Russian economy, about so-called "digital vortex", when digital technologies destroy the existing ways of production and consumption of goods and create new ones, and digitization in various fields in inhomogeneous and resembles a vortex. Traditional companies have advantages in capital, renowned brands and accumulated client bases. New companies-destabilizers have advantages in innovations (actively utilize new technologies), maneuverable response and organizational readiness for experiments and risks.

O.V. Krivosheev *(2017)* attributes the following principles to digital disruption:

1. Everything that can be digitized should be digitized.
2. Value chains mean nothing for consumers; what matters is value consumed.

Opportunities and Threats From Digitalization of the Russian Economy

Intensive development of the society of digital economy inevitably implies solution of problems in the field of knowledge management. Information and knowledge obtained through experience are becoming the priority resources. And such competences as innovation, competence, creativity and cognitive endeavor are becoming competitive advantages in the market. Therefore, the transition from physical to digital economy requires absolutely new approaches not just in industrial sectors and productions, but in formation of the personnel potential for the digital economy: education, personnel training, development and management of innovative human resources, management of talents.

We shall characterize the depth of digital economy penetration in Russia using the statistics. In 2017 over 62% of business were registered online, 92% of patients were registered before the ambulance arrived to the E.R. due to the access to their personal data, 92% of prescriptions were issued in electronic form, the cost of tutors' services dropped by 30%: 80% of students relied on personal educational paths created on the basis of artificial intelligence. As for the financial sector, over 50% of customers do not attend offices and receive services remotely. It is the average figure in the world. Public satisfaction with the quality of state services today has exceeded 86% *(Statistical data of the Gaydar Forum)*.

Business transformation on the basis of digital models will make it possible to reach an absolutely different level of product and services creation and promotion, to provide the optimal quality of services to clients and the efficiency to companies and enterprises (Kupriyanovsky, et al., 2017). However, such transformation necessitates substitution of traditional managerial approaches, principles and values to the models with priority goals and economic system's success criteria being not the profit or short-term efficiency, but client focus, innovation, new project realization rate, cooperation with suppliers and partners.

All the above-mentioned phenomena fundamentally change the structure of the global economic system – opportunities for consumers, the structure of sectors, the role of the state (Figure 17).

Besides the benefits from digitization described in figure 1.9 transformation processes in the course of re-industrialization constitute some threats to economic and social development (Figure 18).

Thus, describing the digital economy O.S. Sukharev *(2017)* uses the term "irrational optimism". "Irrational optimism" occurs among agents not only from financial markets, but also from markets on high-tech products. They encounter a similar, but more reserved speculative effect. Such effect may provide high pace of the economic growth, however the quality can be disappointing for most agents. In the course of time it will lead to the occurrence of interconnected bubbles (technological, financial and/or mortgage) provoking an economic crisis. New technologies reproduce irrational optimism regarding

Figure 17. Sources of benefit from digitization at different levels

Benefits from digitization at macro- and meso – levels	
Effect for the country in whole	**Benefits for the public sector**
New GDP growth source	Process efficiency growth (for example, tax collection and data management)
Creation of new work places and employees' productivity growth	Reduced chance for fraud and misuse of state services
Expansion of trade, more effective use of capital and intensified competition	Identification and analysis of social trends using Big Data
Accumulation of the potential of governments and their ability to react in current situation	More effective interaction with citizens and the private sector

Benefits from digitization at the microlevel	
Benefits for economic subjects	**Benefits for consumers**
Simplified expansion to other markets – revenue growth	Opportunity to purchase better goods and services at favorable prices
Enhanced efficiency of internal prices (for example, supply chain management)	Opportunity to use products unavailable earlier (for example, through joint consumption)
Access to the best labor resources through digital communication channels	Obtainment of information on the most interesting opportunities for employment
Increased transparency and simplicity of interaction with the public sector	Simplified access to state services through digital portals

Figure 18. Threats from digitization

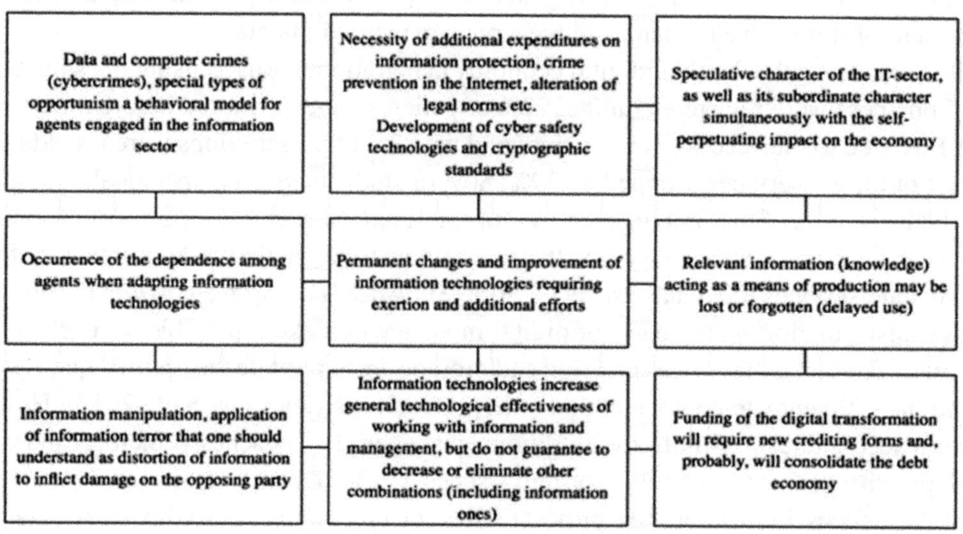

the granting of resources for their development and dissemination, including the very resource that is allocated by state funding programs.

The drop of efficiency is becoming inherent into the very plot of speculative human reaction (including the state level of administration as well). Standardization and unification in IT, on the one hand, will decrease development rates, and on the other - they will eliminate the impact of the speculative element in these sectors demonstrating a growing output. Probably, in this case the output growing effect may be ceased or reduced.

Thus, the progress (modernization), transformation processes in the course of re-industrialization entail not only positive effects. Despite a great number of successful examples, the impact of new technologies on the productivity across the globe and on the Russia's scale, on the broadening of opportunities for the poor and the middle class, as well as on the dissemination of the principles of administrative accountability have yet failed to meet expectations (Figure 19).

The forced introduction of computers into various spheres of life has given no considerable effect *(Ivanov and Malinetsky, 2017)*. The data on multifactor productivity (labor and capital) in the USA demonstrate that this crucial indicator was been growing for the last quarter of the century 2,5% per year only from 1958 to 1968. Such growth rate gave three explosive innovations – universal adoption of production lines, new materials (chemistry), mass use of combustion engines (and total motorization of the country). In the period from 2010 to 2015 the growth rate of multifactor productivity dropped 10 times to 0,25% per year *(Gurov and Poluni, 2017)*.

In Russia the markets associated with the digital economy have grown 5,5 times from 2011 from 5 to 27,7 trillion of rubles, the volume of digital economy and online commerce market is increasing (simultaneously with digital economy share stagnation starting from 2014) (Figure 21), although the level of labor productivity is significantly lower (more than two times) than the foreign countries under consideration, especially the countries with developed economies (Figure 22).

The observed dynamics of the labor productivity index in Russia in 2010-2015 (according to OECD) in combination with the remaining low level of labor productivity appears to be quite a dangerous phenomenon in terms of stable economic growth and digital economy formation, and from the point of view of country's social development provision, including people's life quality improvement (*Labor productivity in Russia*).

Figure 19. Pessimism caused by adoption of digital technologies in the world (The visuals display distribution of digital technologies determined by the Index of digital technologies adoption)

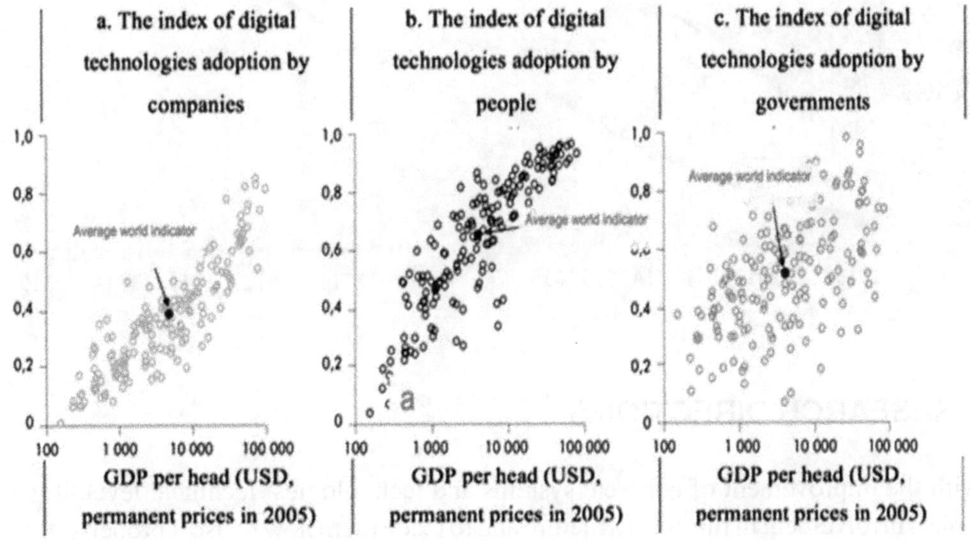

Figure 20. Pessimism caused by adoption of digital technologies in the world

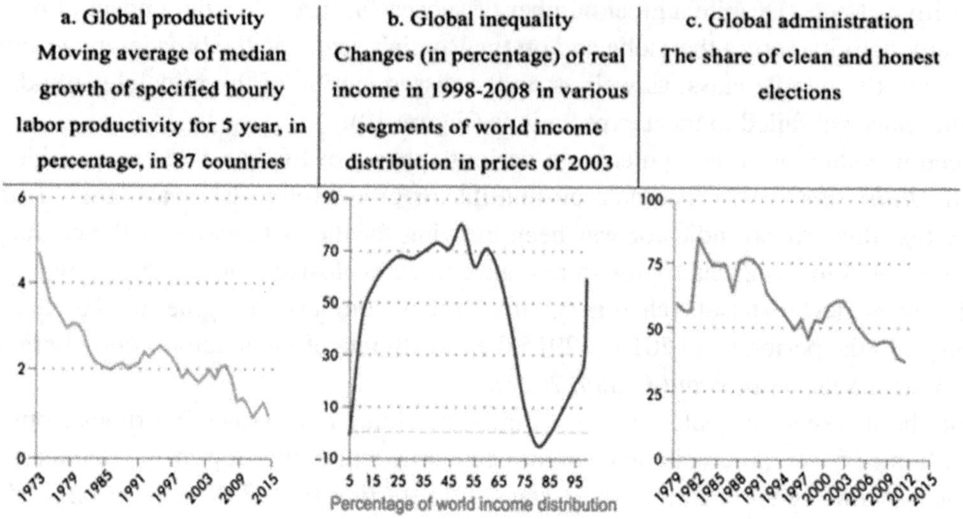

Figure 21. The volume of digital economy and online commerce market in Russia, billions of rubles; digital economy's contribution to GDP, % (BCG; https://www.insales.ru/blog/2015/09/30/ecommerce_services_report_2015/)

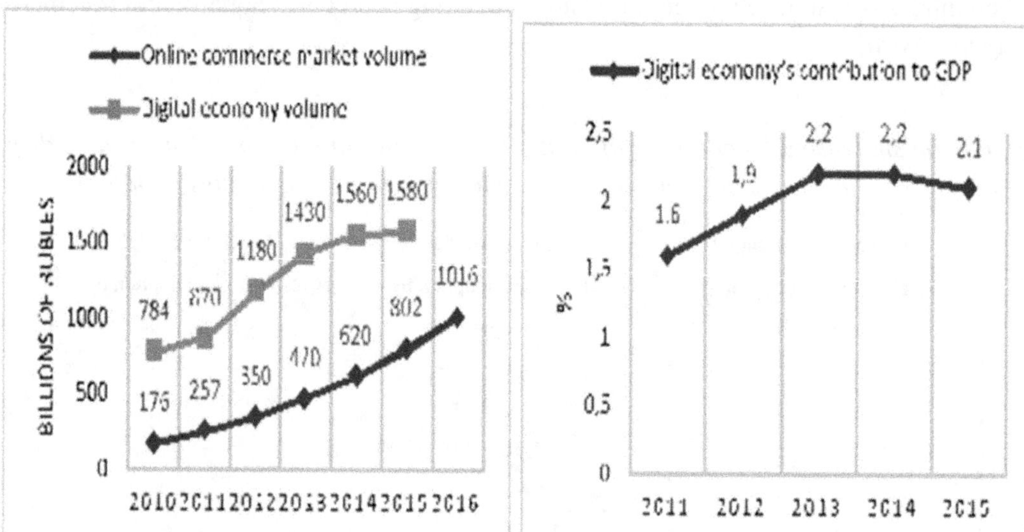

FUTURE RESEARCH DIRECTIONS

Together with the improvement of concrete systems and technologies' technical level, it is required to expand people's involvement in this infrastructure and to teach them how to use it properly. Besides, given the significance of information processing, the creation of the information is of primary importance. In other words, the digital technology itself is incapable of providing inventions in physics, chemistry or engineering sciences *(Sukharev, 2017)*.

Figure 22. The labor productivity index in Russia, EU countries, G7 and OECD in 2005–2015, % (ILO)

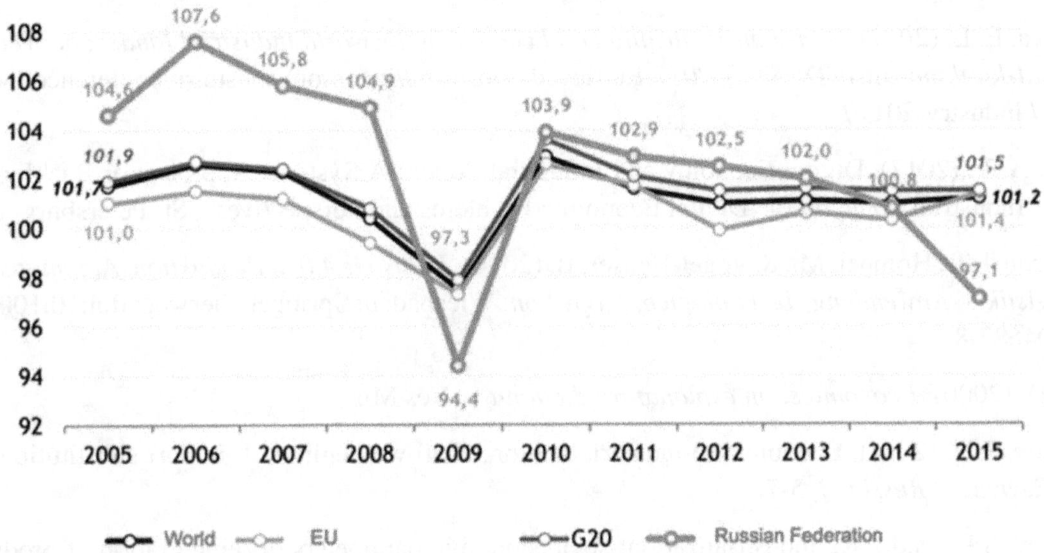

Innovations in the modern world are not simply connected with the opportunities of digital technologies, but largely based on them. This is exactly why the full-fledged successive industrial sector's digitization will become a platform for qualitative changes of the economy and long-term opportunities. Thus, the transition to digital technologies is inevitable, but from another perspective, this very transition cannot be the absolute goal. The financing of such transition will require new crediting forms and may consolidate positions of the debt economy.

CONCLUSION

In this chapter, the authors aimed at providing a better understanding for Industry 4.0 concept and its application benefits for Russia. The main problem is how the Russian Federation acts against the economically developed countries, which are the creators of Industry 4.0. This chapter mainly focuses on presenting the authors views on how to sustain and increase competitive advantage of the Russian Federation by catching and implementing Industry 4.0. With Industry 4.0, Russian Federation get a bigger share of the world manufacturing value chain.

ACKNOWLEDGMENT

The reported study was funded by RFBR according to the research project No. 18-010-00204.

REFERENCES

Andreeva, E. L. (2017). *Non-industrialization and change of the world industrial landscape: vectors of industrial development. INDUSTRY-2017*. Retrieved from http://inecprom.spbstu.ru/conference/industry/archive / industry-2017 /

Babkin, A. V. (2017). Digital Economy and Industrial Policy: A Systems Approach or Backlog. Conference "Industrial Policy in the Digital Economy: Problems and Perspectives", St. Petersburg, Russia.

Bauernhansl, T., Hompel, M., & Vogel-Heuser, B. (2014). *Industrie 4.0 in Produktion, Automatisierung und Logistik — Anwendung, Technologien, Migration*. Wiesbaden: Springer Vierweg; doi:10.1007/978-3-658-04682-8

Black, D. (2000). *Economics: an explanatory dictionary*. Ves Mir.

Bodrunov, S.D. (2014). Economic re-industrialization: shall we begin with import substitution? *Economic Revival of Russia, 3*, 5-7.

Bodrunov, S.D. (n.d.). Re-industrialization: socioeconomic parameters of reintegration of production, science and education. *Sociological Research, 2*, 20-28.

Boston Consulting Group (BCG). (n.d.). Retrieved from https://www.bcgperspectives.com

Bughin, J., & Chui, M. (n.d.). The Internet of Things. *Advances in E-Business Research*, 111–125. doi:10.4018/978-1-5225-2104-4.ch006

Chesbrough, H. (2003). Open Innovation: The new Imperative for Creating and Profiting from Technology. Boston: Harvard Business School Press.

Chulok, A. A. (2017). *Megatrends of the future: where do we wait for threats and how to open the windows of opportunities?* International Scientific and Educational Foresight Center.

Decree of the President of the Russian Federation dated 1 December 2016 N° 642 "About the strategy of scientific technology development of the Russian Federation". (n.d.). Retrieved from https://www.extech.ru/info/docs/ukaz_642.pdf

Epishkin, N. I. (2010). Historical Dictionary of the Gallicisms of the Russian Language. Academic Press.

Feldman, M. A. (2001). *Employees at large industrial facilities of the Ural in 1914-1941 //Ekaterinburg*. Ural University publishing.

Financial Dictionary Finam. (n.d.). Retrieved from https://www.finam.ru/dictionary/

Glazyev, S. Y. (1990). Economic theory of technical development. Moscow: Nauka.

Glazyev, S. Y. (1993). Theory of long-term technical and economic development. Moscow: Vlada Dar.

Gurov, G., & Polunin, Y. (2017). The attack of "blue collars". *Expert, 3*, 12–17.

ILO. Analytical center's calculations. URL: http://ac.gov.ru/files/publication/a/13612.pdf (address date: 05/01/2018)

Ivanov, V. V. (2017). Global humanitarian and technological revolution: Preconditions and prospects. *Innovations*, *6*(224), 11–16.

Ivanov, V.V., & Malinetsky, G.G. (2017). Digital Economy: Myths, Reality, Opportunities. Russian Lvov D.S. Theoretical and Applied Aspects of NTP Management. *Economics and Mathematical Methods, 1986*(5).

Jansen, F. (2002). *The Age of Innovation.*. INFRA-M.

Kagermann, H., Lukas, W. D., & Wahlster, W. (2011). Industrie 4.0: Mit dem Internet der Dinge auf dem Weg zur 4. industriellen Revolution. VDI Nachrichten, 13.

Kagermann, H., Helbig, J., Hellinger, A., & Wahlster, W. (2013). *Recommendations for Implementing the Strategic Initiative INDUSTRIE 4.0: Securing the Future of German Manufacturing Industry*. Final Report of the Industrie 4.0 Working Group.

Kolberg, D., & Zühlke, D. (2015). *Lean automation enabled by industry 4.0 technologies*. Academic Press.

Krivosheev, O.V. (2017). *Digital economy in Russia. Technological backlogs*. Academic Press.

Kupriyanovsky, V. P., Dobrynin, A. P., & Sinyagov, S. A. (2017). A holistic model of transformation in digital economy – how to become digital leaders. *International Journal of Open Information Technologies*, *5*(1), 26–33.

Kurdyumov, S. P. (n.d.). *Development of the digital economy in Russia*. Retrieved from http://spkurdyumov.ru/digital_economy/razvitie-cifrovoj-ekonomiki-v-rossii-programma-do-2035-goda/

Labor productivity in Russia. A social bulletin for July 2017. (n.d.). The Analytical Center of the Government of the Russian Federation. Retrieved from http://ac.gov.ru/files/publication/a/13612.pdf

Lasi, H., Fettke, P., Kemper, H. G., Feld, T., & Hoffmann, M. (2014). Industry 4.0. *Business & Information Systems Engineering*, *6*(4), 239. doi:10.100712599-014-0334-4

Lee, J., Kao, H. A., & Yang, S. (2014). Service innovation and smart analytics for industry 4.0 and big data environment. *Procedia CIRP*, *16*, 3–8. doi:10.1016/j.procir.2014.02.001

Malinetsky, G. G. (2015). *To make a fairy tale happen ... High technology is Russia's way to the future* (3rd ed.). Moscow: LENAND.

Piercy, N., & Rich, N. (2009). The implications of lean operations for sales strategy: From sales-force to marketing-force. *Journal of Strategic Marketing*, *17*(3-4), 237–255. doi:10.1080/09652540903064738

Primakov, E. M. (2012). *Country's new industrialization. – A report on a meeting of "Mercury club"*. Retrieved from http://www. tpp-inform. ru/official/2393. html

Putin, V. V. (2012). On our economic problems. *Bulletin*, *30*(15), 5.

Re-industrialization of Russia: opportunities and constraints. (n.d.). Retrieved from http://www.council.gov.ru/media/files/41d477365af5651386f7.pdf

Regions of Russia. (2017). *Socio-economic indicators.* Retrieved from http://www.gks.ru/wps/wcm/connect/rosstat_main/rosstat/ru/statistics/science_and_innovations/science/

Romanova, O.A., & Bukhvalov, N.Y. (2014). Re-industrialization as a determinative trend of economic development of industrial areas. *Fundamental Research,* 6.

Russia 2025: From talent to cadres. (2017). The Boston Consulting Group (BCG).

Sanzharevsky, I. I. (2010). *Political science: Dictionary-reference book.* Retrieved from http://www.glos.virmk.ru/

Sberbank Annual Report. (2017). Retrieved from http://www.sberbank.com/ru/investor-relations/reports-and-publications/annual-reports

Schmidt, E., & Cohen, J. (2010). The Digital Disruption-Connectivity and the Diffusion of Power. *Foreign Affairs*, *89*, 75–88.

Schummer, J. (2009). From Nano-Convergence to NBIC-Convergence: "The best way to predict the future is to create it". Governing Future Technologies, 57-71.

Schwab, K. (2017). *The Fourth Industrial Revolution.* Publishing House "E".

Sorokin, D.E., Tolkachev, S.A. (2015). Conditions and factors of efficient re-industrialization and industrial policy in Russia. *Economic Revival of Russia*, *4*(46), 87 – 99.

State Program. (n.d.). *Digital Economy in the Russian Federation.* Retrieved from http://government.ru/docs/28653/

Statistical data of the Gaydar Forum. (2018). Retrieved from Official Telegram-channel of the Forum: https://t.me/gaidarforum

Stiglitz, J. (1997). Economics of the public sector. Moscow University Publishing.

Sukharev, O. S. (2014). Re-industrialization of the Russian economy and technological development. *National interests: priorities and security, 10.* Retrieved from https://cyberleninka.ru/article/n/reindustrializatsiya-ekonomiki-rossii-i-tehnologicheskoe-razvitie

Sukharev, O.S. (2015). *Information Economy: Knowledge, Competition and Growth*. Finance and Statistics.

Sukharev, O. S. (2018). Strategy of growth and renewal of industrial and technological base. *Metals of Eurasia*, *2*, 2–5.

Sukharev, O. S. (n.d.). *Digital economics – «irrational optimism» of management*. Retrieved from http://www.osukharev.com/images/present/21-11-2017.pps

Tapscott, D. and Williams, E. (2009). *Wikinomics. How mass cooperation changes everything*. Best-BusinessBooks.

Tatarkin, A. I., Sukharev, O. S., & Strizhakova, E. N. (2017). The definition of the vector of the new industrial policy based on the neo-Schumpeterian theory. *Bulletin of Perm University*, *12*(1), 5–22.

The program of economic re-industrialization of Novosibirsk region till 2025. (n.d.). Retrieved from https://www.nso.ru/page/15755

Usoltseva, A.V. (2017). Re-industrialization of industry as a state's priority objective. *NovaInfo*, *3*(62), 198-202.

Yermakova, Zh. A. (2013). Scientific and technical progress as a basis of social and economic development of the region. *Bulletin of the OSU*, *3*(152), 202–208.

KEY TERMS AND DEFINITIONS

NBICs (Nano-Bio-Info-Cogno-Technologies): "Breakthrough" innovation technologies in the field of convergence of nanotechnologies, ICT, biotechnologies, and cognitive technologies. Many modern technologies are at the interface of NBIC, for example, construction of cellular and fabric structures, new information interfaces (info+cogno), bioinformatics (nano+info+bio).

Chapter 15
"Smart City": The Concept of Resolving the Contradiction Between Production and Urban Life

Vardan Mkrttchian
https://orcid.org/0000-0003-4871-5956
HHH University, Australia

Yulia Vertakova
Southwest State University, Russia

Yuri Treshchevsky
Voronezh State University, Russia

Natalya V. Firsova
Voronezh State Technical University, Russia

Vladimir Plotnikov
St. Petersburg State University of Economics, Russia

Dmitry Y. Treshchevsky
Voronezh State University, Russia

ABSTRACT

The chapter proposes the correction of the concept of "smart city." It is substantiated that the specificity of the redistribution of the population and economic resources to the major cities of Russia, mainly to regional centers, requires the modification of the concept of "smart city." In accordance with this concept, a number of principles are proposed, among which the most important are the principles: integration, metabolism, architectural quality of the urban environment. The most important functional goals are defined: the creation of a new production structure, formation of a modern transport and logistics infrastructure, modernization of the road-street network, development and modernization of the rolling stock of urban transport, development and modernization of communal infrastructure, provision of safe and comfortable living conditions for citizens, improvement of the ecological condition of the urban district, improvement of the state of objects of cultural heritage and improvement of the urban district. Three levels are singled out, each of which requires solutions.

DOI: 10.4018/978-1-5225-7625-9.ch015

INTRODUCTION

The future of intelligent cities («smart city") - in 2025 the population of our planet will reach 8 billion people, and more than half of them will live in cities. At the same time, municipal infrastructure, electricity networks and water supply systems of cities often have an age of more than a hundred years and desperately need modernization in conditions of economic growth and population. Effective energy and water supply is the foundation for the development and prosperity of any modern city. To provide the population with access to these critical resources and other new opportunities, it is important to ensure the competent management of them using innovative technologies and tools for joint work. To understand how utilities affect the shaping of the city's image of the future, we undertook a global study of the sphere of public utilities in the Russian Federation. A unique study involved more than 20,000 managers of utilities and their clients from all major cities of the country. Based on the results of the study, a report was compiled containing key analytical data on the utilities industry, including information on the need for technology application, effective joint work and innovations for the transformation of energy supply and water management systems.

The idea of Innovative Technologies One of the most important results of our research was that 74% of the managers of utilities and 76% of their customers said the need for transformations in the industry. Moreover, 50% of executives and 60% of customers believe that at the moment the industry is not working efficiently. The good news is that the technologies that make it possible to bring the utility industry to a qualitatively new level already exist. Innovative technologies open up new opportunities for us, paving the way for the intellectual cities of the future. However, for this, the city needs a solid technological foundation, on the basis of which new applications will be built. Utilities investments in smart metering systems and transmission networks help to improve the overall efficiency of the city and the quality of services provided to the population through a bilateral mechanism for interaction and data collection and analysis on energy and water consumption in real time. This allows us to lay a solid groundwork for the effective use and conservation of valuable resources. In case of successful implementation, this strategy will allow building intellectual cities, opening up new prospects for effective use of resources.

However, the technologies themselves do not give the desired effect. It all depends on how effectively people can work with each other, you need to have Effective cooperation. Especially important is cooperation in solving energy, transport problems and urbanization problems. It is impossible to overcome these problems with a single point solution. To create a new resource-saving reality, effective interaction between all stakeholders is required.

An excellent example of this is the city of Voronezh, the capital of the Voronezh region of the Russian Federation. The city authorities implement a unique public-private partnership program aimed at sustainable economic development that could serve as a model for all other aspects of society. For this purpose, the mayor of the city is developing a program for the conservation of energy and water resources, aimed at reducing operating costs. The main objective of the program is to ensure a balanced development of the city center, provide the necessary information to change behavior and simplify making informed decisions. The key to the success of the program is cooperation. Technology companies, local enterprises, municipal services, city government and non-governmental organizations share the balanced development of the city center.

In the new century, the city's efficiency will largely depend on whether we are able to competently manage energy and water resources. Now it is necessary to rebuild the entire industry in such a way as to ensure that available resources meet ever-increasing demand. Together, we will be able to modernize the power grid, build intelligent cities, open up new opportunities for interaction with the population and improve the management of such valuable resources as gas, water and electricity, using innovative technologies. This will allow not only to attract new companies to the city, but also to strengthen its reputation as a center for sustainable and balanced development. Thanks to innovative technologies and joint work, we will be able to create intelligent cities and open new economic opportunities for people around the world.

The concept of "smart city" is very popular. It is continuously developing. This development is due both to the enhancement of the experience of the "smart city" projects, and to the expansion of the theoretical basis of this concept. In the article, the correction of the concept of "smart city" is proposed.

The authors' proposals are based on an analysis of the experience of forming "smart cities" in Russia. At the same time, the tendencies of the social and economic development of Russian cities and the country as a whole were taken into account. The authors have proved that the specificity of the redistribution of the population and economic resources to the large cities of Russia (mainly regional centers) requires the modification of the concept of "smart city". A number of new principles were proposed. They are the principles: integration, metabolism, architectural quality of the urban environment.

The creation of "smart cities", taking into account the new principles, requires an orientation towards achieving the strategic goals of urban development. The authors showed that the priority goals are: to achieve the city's leadership positions in the development of human capital; sustainable development of the city's economy based on the innovation sector; effective spatial development. Key functional objectives have also been identified: the creation of a new production structure; formation of a modern transport and logistics infrastructure; modernization of the road-street network; development and modernization of the rolling stock of urban transport; development and modernization of communal infrastructure, provision of safe and comfortable living conditions for citizens; improvement of the ecological state of the urban environment; improvement of the state of objects of cultural heritage and improvement of the city.

The chapter identifies three levels of zoning for "smart cities". For each city zone, separate decisions are needed to implement the author's concept. These zones are: the historical center; city as a whole; city agglomeration. For each of the zones, important tasks have been justified, which are being solved in the sphere of industrial sector transformation; construction; transport, logistics infrastructure.

This chapter is proposes the correction of the concept of "smart city". It is substantiated that the specificity of the redistribution of the population and economic resources to the major cities of Russia, mainly to regional centers, requires the modification of the concept of "smart city". In accordance with this concept, a number of principles are proposed, among which the most important are the principles: integration, metabolism, architectural quality of the urban environment.

The implementation of the concept requires an unconditional orientation towards achieving strategic goals aimed at: achieving the city's leadership positions in the development of human capital; sustainable economic development based on the innovation sector; effective spatial development. As the most important functional goals are defined by the creation of a new production structure; formation of a modern transport and logistics infrastructure; modernization of the road-street network; development and modernization of the rolling stock of urban transport. The development and modernization of communal infrastructure, are important and so are the provision of safe and comfortable living conditions for citizens; improvement of the ecological condition of the urban district; improvement of the state of objects of cultural heritage and improvement of the urban district. Three levels are singled out, each of which requires separate solutions for the implementation of the concept: the historical center; city as a whole; city agglomeration. Proposals on the composition of tasks to be solved in the sphere of industrial sector reform are substantiated; construction; transport, transport and logistics infrastructure. On the example of one of the cities of Russia it was shown that the formation of the concept of "smart city" arising in the process of transformation of the old large city requires abandoning the traditional vision of its spatial and functional characteristics.

The concept of "smart city" has become widespread in the theory of strategic planning of administrative-territorial entities. The basis for it was the mass dissemination of information and communication technologies (ICTs) in the management of housing and communal services (utilities), transport, warehousing, trade, etc. Almost all large cities of Russia announced the adherence to this concept in the process of forming their strategies for a long-term perspective. At the same time, the emphasis is mainly on the formation of a comfortable urban environment as a place of residence for the population. It is implicitly assumed that the population will at the same time be provided with jobs that fully correspond to the quality of this environment. However, there is reason to believe that the implementation of the concept in a significant number of cities will face a contradiction between the technical possibilities of urban environment and the provision of a sufficient number of high-tech jobs. With respect to Russia and a significant number of developing countries, whose production is based on the fourth technological order, it can be argued that "smart cities" will be formed as large recipients of economic resources in a strong redistributive economy. With a weak redistribution system, they generally cannot exist as a mass phenomenon. If we look at the wide space for the formation of "smart cities" in Russia, then there is clearly a very strong potential competition (yet not fully manifested) between cities for the right to be "smart". In particular, there are dozens of fairly large cities in Russia - regional centers. Among them are Moscow and St. Petersburg, which have a special status and have concentrated half of the country's production and economic resources. In addition, there are 13 cities with a million populations, which also accumulate a significant amount of resources. In the country there is an intensive redistribution of the population from rural areas and small towns to regional centers. ICTs that are hoped for as a technological basis for "smart" cities will be able to provide high technology for their living conditions, but will (and already lead) to deindustrialization and a sharp reduction in jobs that require high skills. In the future this can lead to "qualitative degradation" of the population of "smart" cities.

PROBLEMS AND PROSPECTS FOR THE DEVELOPMENT OF "SMART CITIES"

Studying the problem of smart cities is quite a new phenomenon. In the scientific literature there is no unequivocal opinion on this phenomenon. This is noted in particular (Hollands, 2008; Gil-Garcia, Pardo, & Nam, 2015), pointing to the uncertainty of the concept of "smart city", consider it necessary to ensure the conjugation of scientific research of a smart city as an object of academic research, with management tools, implemented in practice.

A number of scientists singled out "critical factors of smart city initiatives" as key components of the smart city concept: management and organization, technology, management, politics, context, people and communities, economics, construction, infrastructure and the natural environment (Chourabi et al., 2012).

The authors note that it is possible to influence the approach to planning a "smart city" based on intellectual initiatives and understanding the role of various economic, urban, demographic, and geographical factors. The results of the studies of these authors indicate that local conditions are of great importance for the implementation of the concept of "smart city". Among them: intra-party, economic development, structural parameters of cities, geographical position, population density (Neirotti, De Marco, Cagliano, Mangano, & Scorrano, 2014).

Often, scientists pay attention to the need for "smart cities" of "smart governments" that provide effective governance (Gil-Garcia, Zhang, & Puron-Cid, 2016). Scientists rightly point out that "smart cities" are quickly forming and introducing new practices and services in the sphere of functioning of urban facilities. There are quantitatively measurable relationships between the "smart city" and urban planning. The architectural layers of smart cities (Anthopoulos & Vakali, 2012) are of great importance.

Many Russian researchers pay attention, first of all, to creating a comfortable urban environment. "Smart City" should be linked to its goals, ensuring sustainable development, improving the quality of life and efficient use of resources for its residents (Ruhlandt, 2018). In general, this is the development of ideas for the creation of a comfortable habitat as the main goal (Drozhzhinov, Kupriyanovskii, Namiot, Sinyagov, & Kharitonov, 2017).

The idea of "smart city", according to some researchers, can be realized on the basis of using mathematical methods for optimal allocation of resources on the basis of information and communication technologies infrastructure and methods of mathematical programming (Salomatin, 2016; Bozhenov, 2012), in fact, characterizes a smart city as an efficiently managed, providing high quality of the urban environment. Thus, it is necessary to take into account the different purposes of the functional subsystems of the city. So, for residents, first of all, the convenience of obtaining various services and their payment, including housing and communal services, transport, parking, medical and public services, and, of course, fast internet. For city authorities, the cornerstone is public safety, effective management of emergency and operational services, management up to and planning of expenses and incomes, environmental monitoring, transparent provision of educational and medical services, and provision of a "one-stop-shop" regime for residents and organizations in obtaining public services. For managers and resource-supply organizations, priorities are different: automated collection data from metering devices, issuance and control of bill payment, forecast of resource consumption and energy saving technologies, weather-oriented behavior engineering systems, provision of automatic and dispatching systems shutdown in the event of natural or man-made disasters, repair planning and de-bureaucratization of interaction with city authorities.

CONCEPT OF "SMART CITY"

In this section, we view the city of Voronezh as one of the promising from the point of view of realizing the concept of a smart city. At the same time, the state of Voronezh largely reflects the specifics of the development of cities with a million population of Russia. In the economy of the region, Voronezh occupies a significant share; transport hub of the city - the most important in the Central Black Earth region of the Russian Federation - in the immediate vicinity of the city is the international airport; the city is the largest city of the Central Federal District after Moscow, it is included in the sixth (highest) hierarchical level of settlement systems, plays a strong role in the geopolitical situation in the system of resettlement of Russia. On the outskirts of the city and the territory adjacent to it, the industrial (industrial parks "Maslovskiy" and "Perspektiva"), logistic construction, major shopping centers (Metro, Castorama, Grad, Leroy-Merlin and etc.). There is agglomeration of the regional center, the space of its influence on adjacent settlements is expanding. This implies not only positive effects for residents, but also a number of negative effects.

The street-road network of the urban district does not cope with the existing traffic flow and has significant length of fate with the non-normative cover; there is a shortage of education and health facilities in terms of capacity indicators, and in terms of pedestrian (transport) accessibility indicators; there are problems (quantitative and qualitative) in engineering support of the city's territories. The number of floors in the residential building is increased to 17-25 floors. In this connection, the area of yard space is reduced, the area of green areas is reduced; there is the problem of parking.

Emerging negative effects require the use of traditional mechanisms for regulating spatial and socio-economic development used in the concept of "smart cities". Among them - the change in the production profile of the city on the basis of identifying inefficiently used territories, the re-profiling of a number of production zones. First of all, we are talking about the reorientation of industry in the production of the fifth and sixth technological order, based on the leadership of information technology. In connection with this, the reconstruction and reduction of production areas in the central zone of Voronezh is required. The complete elimination of the production use of this territory is not ruled out. The liberated territories must acquire a new functional purpose (public and business centers, science parks, technology parks, including IT parks.

It is necessary to carry out dispersed functional division of industrial zones with the introduction into their territory of service elements of the population and the system of gardening as part of the ecological framework of the citywide structure. The change in the production structure requires an increase in the efficiency of resource consumption and environmental management in the territories of development zones that have reserve's for spatial development, technological measures to reduce negative loads to the permitted standards.

A separate problem is the development of residential areas that emerged and developed spontaneously as a result of changes in the industrial dominant - enterprises of the machine building complex, which required a significant number of workers living in the immediate vicinity of the place of employment.

Spatial isolation of production sites and residential areas required a fundamental change in the system of engineering support for streets and yard territories. In this regard, the first priority was the formation of an economical and comfortable environment, requiring the following actions:

- The introduction of a centralized street lighting control system;
- The introduction of a management system for street lighting networks via the Internet;
- The creation of a "single data center and management of activities in the sphere of housing and communal services of the city" using fiber-optic technologies, GSM and GPRS terminals, wireless modules;
- Creation of smart quarters - territories, on which the most progressive world technologies in life support sphere (smart infrastructure, house, garbage disposal, improvement, etc.) should be introduced.

Fundamentally, these problems can be solved through the creation of a technology consortium with participation of the call, construction organizations, telecommunication organizations, business incubators, technology parks offering effective technological solutions for the municipal economy

As a pilot project, it is possible to propose the creation of a modern multifunctional quarter in the central part of the city (the main business, cultural and public part of the city).

An important problem of a large city is the organization of traffic, requiring the introduction of advanced technology and vehicle upgrades. Among the main events, with reference to the city of Voronezh and most of the million-million cities in Russia, it is possible to propose:

- The introduction of an adaptive traffic management system at traffic lights;
- Creation of a single intellectual system for managing the parking space of the city with the arrangement of paid urban parking facilities on the basis of a concession agreement for the creation and operation of a paid parking management system;
- Purchase of urban passenger road transport of a new generation;
- Modernization of the dispatching system for passenger transport using navigation systems;
- The introduction of an electronic payment system for travel in public transport;
- Creation of a network of "smart" stops of public transport.

Organizationally, the solution of these problems is possible, given the inadequacy of the financial resources of most cities, by involving business structures, city residents and civil society institutions in city projects and programs.

Among the organizational measures, a significant effect can be brought:

- actualization of the master plan, local standards of town-planning design, land use rules and development of the urban district of the city of Voronezh, taking into account the possible changes in its boundaries;
- Improving the quality of urban planning;
- Development of a policy of active territorial marketing at the municipal level;
- The implementation of an active cultural policy and the development of a cultural industry that creates one of the strong motives for visiting the city;
- "Counter initiative", i.e. the active position of local authorities in the search for and attraction of investors, defending the interests of the city in the implementation of private projects in urban areas;
- Creation of a favorable investment climate, where a special resource is the image of the city and the business reputation of the city authorities responsible for the Formation of investment infrastructure;

Furthermore, it important to ensuring the flexibility of the management system in order to take into account the rapid changes in the situation, technological structures, the emergence of new industries, etc. on the basis of the wide spread of the project approach.

Assistance to investors in the integrated development and development of built-up areas, is important ensuring compliance with the requirements of regulatory provision of such territories with educational, health, engineering and transport facilities.

- Creation of a single municipal geo-information system;
- creation and improvement of the complex automated information system of the local government authorized in the field of architecture and town planning, including an electronic database for the implementation of design regulations, the placement of advertising structures on the facades of

buildings, as well as the technical support for the updating of digital topographic plans and monitoring of engineering communications.

Improving the mechanisms for reviewing and agreeing on project documentation for the construction, reconstruction, decorative, advertising and information design of buildings and structures;

- Improving the quality of project documentation;
- Improvement of the monitoring and control system in the construction industry;
- Ensuring the coherence of city plans and municipalities forming part of the urban agglomeration, implementing investment projects, housing, social, infrastructure construction through the creation of inter-municipal consultative and coordinating forms of management, including the adjustment of development plans, taking into account the principles of creating a comfortable urban environment and real the needs of the population, the transition from quantitative indicators in construction to quality;
- Intellectualization of the economy and spatial development: promotion of "smart" and environmentally friendly technologies, "smart" environments, "smart" systems and "smart" industries, including transport, houses, neighborhoods, etc. ; participation in the implementation of pilot federal projects in this area.

SOLUTIONS AND RECOMMENDATIONS

1. Implementation of the Concept of Three-Level Spatial Development of the City

Most of the cities with a million populations in Russia are developing quite intensively, which determines the formation of agglomerations around them. Given the historical roots of the emergence and development of these cities for many centuries, it can be argued that they require a three-level spatial development.

At the first level (the historical center), it is necessary to raise the level of architectural solutions and functional saturation of the historic part of the city in combination with preserving historical and cultural monuments, improving the organization of traffic, landscaping, planting a network of pedestrian and bicycle routes.

The problems of urban centers development in cities with a million population include typical and characteristic of the state and development of large and largest cities, as well as specific, specific to a particular city, connected with the peculiarities of the landscape structure and historical development.

Essential are: the features of urban planning, urban context, scale, silhouette, proportions, coloring the objects of the city center among other urban sites. Among the main shortcomings can be identified: the wrong general and local urban planning, inconsistency with the context; violation of the stylistic integrity and historical appearance of buildings; flaws in the silhouette; violation of scale; unsuccessful proportions, silhouette and color solutions; an unsuccessful combination of architecture, design and monumental art.

Problems of the central part of such cities are: the presence of transit traffic of vehicles, the contrast of high-density and low-density buildings, the limited space of public spaces, the violation of architectural and compositional development, the limited planning relationships of different territories.

Nevertheless, the central part of the city is rated traditionally high, despite the presence of transport problems (including a shortage of parking spaces), congestion of social infrastructure and urban networks, a high level of physical deterioration of buildings. The center of the city retains the appeal for both living and for short visits, which is an ambiguous factor: today there is an extensive use of the territorial resource of the center and unification of its functional and imaginative characteristics.

When implementing the concept of three-level spatial development, it is necessary to proceed from the need for optimization in the center of transport and pedestrian links; the formation of public spaces; historical continuity; multifunctionality of urban space. For cities with a million populations, the expansion of historically established centers is characteristic. In this regard, the composition of the center sets the task of forming the main and secondary centers and the basic principles of the formation of visual sites.

Spatial-territorial reserves of city centers are usually inhomogeneous. In this regard, it is expedient to identify and reconstruct the territories of urban centers that are promising from the point of view of complex development of cities. The problem often lies in the fact that not only architectural ensembles of historical and cultural significance are concentrated in the historical centers of million-million cities, but also quite dilapidated buildings with courtyard structures. This problem is not so much town-planning as social content, since the buildings belong to individuals who historically live in the central part of the cities. This requires careful treatment of the social and institutional characteristics of residents living in the central part of the city. However, the solution must be found on the basis of a compromise of interests, which will ensure:

- The possibility of expanding the functional saturation of the center, due to the very nature of the central core of the city, which will always be attractive for the development of new and existing functions:
- Development of urban ensembles;
- Development of landscape and recreational structure;
- Expansion of the territorial influence of the city center, usually limited by the natural boundaries of the territories;
- Development of the transport network, including the development of underground parking and parking;
- The development of pedestrian space in all landscaping and urban areas.

It should be noted that the main trend of spatial development of urban centers today is the development of pedestrian areas, among which it is expedient to distinguish nine types: citywide pedestrian zones; pedestrian streets; pedestrian areas; intra-quarter pedestrian areas; pedestrian areas of local level (interquarter). The trend includes pedestrian streets connecting the upper and lower plateaus; recreational and pedestrian zones of the coastal part; pedestrian and transport streets; transport and pedestrian streets.

The development of such pedestrian spaces requires significant restrictions on the city from many other functions, including the reduction of workplaces in the central part of the city, the restriction of the volume of new construction, which leads to a conflict of interest between the various functional subsystems of the city. The authors did not succeed in observing the actual resolution of the problems of Russian urban centers. We believe that this is largely due to the fact that they are solved outside of connection with two other levels - citywide and aglomarational.

The second level (the city as a whole) requires a qualitative organization and a positive reorganization of the urban environment with priority development of urban municipal services, modernization of the street network, housing stock, improvement of residential and public areas.

Implementation of the concept of three-level spatial development at the city level as a whole is designed to create conditions for the effective development of the economy and social sphere, human development, preservation of cultural heritage and rational nature management, which implies a qualitative change in the urban environment.

Practical implementation of the concept provides:

- Elimination of disproportions in providing the city with transport, engineering and social infrastructure;
- Consistent optimization of built-up areas;
- Increase of aesthetic qualities of new architectural complexes and open urban spaces;
- Preservation of territorial reserves for the subsequent transformation of the urban environment in accordance with modern challenges, in the first place - technical and technological, aimed at the formation and use of qualitatively new competencies of the population;
- Preservation and development of the territories of the natural complex;
- The preservation of historical heritage in the sphere of culture, architecture and urban planning.

In terms of organizational decisions, the most significant for the implementation of the concept at the city level as a whole are the most significant:

- The formation of the functional and planning structure of the city in accordance with the city's place in the system of resettlement of the Russian Federation, regional and local settlement systems;
- Formation of the city district as the central core of the agglomeration (in this case, the Voronezh agglomeration) with the main centers of adjoining administrative-territorial entities (in the case of the city of Voronezh, the village of Novaya Usman, Ramon town, Semiluki city);
- The formation of the territorial organization of the city, taking into account the specific economic, functional and spatial development of the adjacent centers of the Voronezh agglomeration (in the case of Voronezh it is the left-bank transport and production cluster, the Northern agricultural-recreational, the Southern production);
- Formation of planning and voluminous-spatial organization of the city on the basis of the main compositional and planning axis of the city (in Voronezh its role is performed by the Voronezh reservoir with adjoining natural complexes and historically formed building of the central part of the city);
- Selection of sites for placement of new places of employment;
- Formation of a system of public centers of planning areas, residential areas and neighborhoods;
- Accounting for the nature of the city's development (for example, because of intensive and disproportional spatial development, Voronezh needs a transit-oriented development of the city, implying that the objects of new construction should be built within walking distance from stops of public transport and transport-transfer points).

Other important decisions include the creation of specialized public centers, corresponding to the needs of the population and corresponding to the existing urban development conditions;

- The formation of multifunctional public-business and residential areas, including office centers, exhibition, fair, trade and hotel complexes, by reforming the areas including non-functioning production and non-production facilities;
- The formation of functional-town planning clusters (planning patterns), combining education, production, science (technical, natural science, humanitarian clusters);
- Historical continuity in the development of the central part of the city;
- The formation of a unified system of public spaces, including public centers, sub-centres, local centers and pedestrian areas of the city;
- Optimization of the general system of recreational areas on the basis of the main landscape and city planning axis of the city (in Voronezh - the Voronezh reservoir in conjunction with the forests of the Usman bora and the Right-bank oak grove);
- Preservation and development of unique landscape and town-planning complexes (in Voronezh - the northern landscape and town-planning complex of the Voronezh State Agrarian University and Voronezh State Forestry University);
- Optimization and town-planning development of the system of children's health camps in remote neighborhoods from the center (in Voronezh – micro districts Somovo and Borovoe);
- Reformatting the places of mass recreation of the population in various spatially localized recreational zones (in Voronezh - in the left-bank and right-bank parts of the city);
- Expansion of the typology of urban and suburban parks;
- Creation of new intra city and suburban recreational zones;
- Preservation and identification of panoramic urban development within and outside the city (in Voronezh - panoramas of the right and left coasts, panoramic perception of the Kominternovsky region from the right-bank part of the Don, South-West micro district from the federal highway Voronezh-Kursk);
- Preservation and development of valuable urban planning ensembles in the central part of the city and individual urban fragments;
- Active involvement of residents in the processes of territorial and architectural-spatial development through the introduction of the principle of "participatory design."

The development of these measures will ensure: increasing the level of comfort of the urban environment, increasing the economic efficiency of operating enterprises and institutions, reducing the time for transport and pedestrian travel, improving the level of the provision of territories with transport, engineering and cultural and domestic infrastructure. They will also be strengthening the positive image of the city; increase of investment and tourist attractiveness of the urban district, increase of the city's competitiveness in attracting investors, professional staff, tourists and students. The infrastructure development of adjacent territories will increase the economic potential of the city and the region as a whole, preservation and revitalization of cultural heritage sites and public spaces, entertainment and recreation at long-term and short-term mass recreation facilities within the city Voronezh county and Voronezh agglomeration, At this level also important are increase of the level of provision with public infrastructure, increase in the quality index of the urban environment (in Voronezh it is planned to increase it to 80% in 2035).

The third level (urban agglomeration) is the development of the agglomeration as a zone of interrelated relations, the joint solution of questions of economics, transport, engineering, social well-being, ecology, use of territorial, labor, natural-resource potential.

To implement the three-level concept of city development at the agglomeration level, it is necessary to improve the modern transport and logistics infrastructure that ensures accessibility, continuity and security of transport and pedestrian connections in the main directions of population movement and freight flows, necessitating the formation of a rationally organized transport and logistics framework of the territory, including transport, pedestrian communications and transport nodes.

Practical implementation of the concept provides:

- Integrated development of transport and logistics infrastructure, including road, rail, air, pedestrian and transport hubs;
- Optimization of transport and pedestrian traffic;
- Provision of conditions for the system development and operation of all modes of transport in order to maximize the satisfaction of the requirements for passenger and freight traffic;
- Creation of conditions for the introduction of alternative modes of transport (rail, electric, air, bicycle);
- Decrease in the level of accidents on the roads of the city.
- In terms of organizational decisions, the most significant for the implementation of the concept at the agglomeration level are the most significant:
- Implementation of the program for the development of the agglomeration transport infrastructure;
- Alignment of the ring and diametric mains, the construction of roads-doubles of the main city highways. For Voronezh, it is actual, in particular, to build a ring railway;
- Creation of transport and transfer points in the city system to limit the impact of external traffic flows within the city limits;
- Construction of transport interchanges, bridges, overpasses;
- Reconstruction and repair of existing highways and roads;
- Reservation of land for the construction of transport infrastructure facilities;
- Construction of high-speed passenger transport;
- Optimization of the urban route network of the city;
- The formation of a system of pedestrian areas of the city, including pedestrian areas and pedestrianstreets;
- Formation of the structure of the rolling stock of urban public passenger transport meeting the requirements of a comfortable urban environment;
- Orientation to environmentally friendly types of vehicles;
- Modernization of road infrastructure engineering infrastructure;
- Organization of development of the project of an intelligent transport system and installation of its elements for the collection and processing of data on vehicles and road infrastructure, including: traffic flow detectors; adaptive (smart) traffic lights; parking lots; information boards; automated lighting control
- Systems; GPS / GLONASS systems; other elements;
- Creation of a single intellectual system for managing the parking space of the city with the arrangement of paid urban parking lots;
- Development of alternative types of public and individual transport;

- Implementation of a set of measures aimed at reducing accidents and deaths from road traffic accidents;

The organization of an integrated system of professional training of personnel for the transport and logistics industry, seeks the harmonization of such a training system with world practice. It includes the renewal of the rolling stock of urban passenger transport, bringing it in line with the standards of security, modernization of the rolling stock structure, taking into account its economic, environmental characteristics, accessibility for persons with disabilities; and reconstruction and development of a network of street storm sewers.

The implementation of these measures will ensure:

- Increase mobility of city residents and agglomeration;
- Increase the share of public transport in passenger transportation. In Voronezh, it is promising to build public high-speed passenger transport lines, the length of which will be 20 km by 2030;
- The length of the ring road will reach 71 km by 2030;
- The length of the ring suburban railway is planned to be increased to 65.3 km in 2035;
- Length of public roads of local importance, completed by construction (reconstruction) should increase by 2020 by 76.0 km;
- The level of road facilities in the system for collecting and processing data on vehicles and road infrastructure is planned to be increased by 30% by 2035;
- In addition, three transport-transfer nodes should be introduced by 2030;
- An increase in the proportion of roads corresponding to regulatory requirements in their total length is planned to increase to 85 percent by 2035;
- Increase in the provision of rolling stock of passenger transport in 100-seat calculation per 1,000 inhabitants (the standard is 1,327 per 1,000 inhabitants) to 90% of the standard by 2035;
- The annual renewal of rolling stock should be 20% for small capacity buses and 14% for medium and large capacity buses;
- Increase in the share of the rolling stock of urban passenger transport equipped for the transport of low-mobility groups in the total number of rolling stock to 100% by 2035;
- Reducing travel time and turn at intersections by 15%;
- Improving the city's ecology, reducing the number of harmful substances and noise levels by 5-10%.
- Achievement of connectedness of suburban settlements.

The implementation of a polycentric, three-level model requires the use of three basic principles in city management. The principle of integration, ensuring the transition from a cruel functional delineation to an integrated environment based on a compromise and perspective composition of the subsystems of the city and its surroundings (city and adjacent agglomeration areas, urban development and natural environment, historical and new parts of the city.

The principle of metabolism is providing expediency, efficiency, safety of functioning of city systems and improvement of quality of a life of townspeople. The principle of the architectural quality of the urban environment, included providing a combination of cultural and historical heritage of the city with a new urban landscape, harmoniously blending into the national and international notions of the aesthetics of a comfortable environment and focused on the target image of the international (Eastern European) city.

The implementation of a polycentric, three-level model requires the use of three basic principles in city management (Aditya & Laksono, 2017). The principle of integration, ensuring the transition from a cruel functional delineation to an integrated environment on the basis is of a compromise and perspective composition of the subsystems of the city and its surroundings (city and adjacent agglomeration areas, urban development and natural environment, historical and new parts of the city).

The principle of metabolism, providing expediency, efficiency, safety of functioning of city systems and improvement is of quality of a life of townspeople (Garau, Ghiani, Celli, & Pilo, 2017). The principle of the architectural quality of the urban environment, providing a combination of cultural and historical heritage of the city are with a new urban landscape, harmoniously blending into the national and international notions of the aesthetics of a comfortable environment and focused on the target image of the international (Eastern European) city.

2. Refusal From the Traditional: The Search for Fundamentally New Spatial Solutions

The concept of "smart city" assumes that not only its territory is realized not only new technological solutions in industry transport, housing and communal services, but also new ideas are formulated in spatial solutions. The problem is that the familiar environment is seen as a necessary part of the city, its mandatory part (Bibri, 2018). This inevitably leads to a narrowing of the possibilities of spatial and functional development. Refusing to accept the inevitability of the existing, it is possible to significantly expand the horizon of the decisions made. In this connection, let us turn to the possibility of forming a natural-anthropogenic complex on the territory of the Voronezh reservoir. It arose in 1973 in the process of closing the Voronezh River to provide water to industrial enterprises. At present, due to the change in the structure of production in the city, the need for it has disappeared. But for most residents of the city the reservoir is already part of the unchanging landscape. At best, there are projects aimed at creating separate reclaimed islands for recreational purposes. But they do not solve the problem of spatial development. Refusing to think of the immutability of the landscape, we can offer a solution that radically changes the approach to the spatial development of the city. Naturally, it is necessary to take into account four circumstances: why this is needed (grounds for a new spatial concept); what needs to be done; emerging positive effects; predicted negative effects.

In our example, these circumstances look like this.

The Basis for the Formation of a New Spatial Concept

The city consists of two planning elements that differ in many characteristics and are poorly connected, the left-bank part represents a closed system, a "city in the city", and consisting of the same closed spatial units, separated by a railway line and the federal highway M4;

- In the city center of the city are concentrated and constantly increasing the flow of cars;
- There are no real and potential sites for new development, except for sloping and coastal areas that are not in demand due to transport and economic reasons.
- The northern part of the city develops as a new city center of the city, which includes large public and recreational facilities, but is weakly connected with the left-bank part of the city.

Directions of Action

It is necessary to deepen the Voronezh reservoir to improve the quality of water and increase its volume;

- Clean the bottom of the reservoir;
- To equip the banks of the reservoir for recreational activities;
- Deepen the bottom of the reservoir and narrow the water area to increase the rate of water exchange;
- Limit the area of the reservoir and restore the Voronezh River in historical landscape boundaries.

Positive Effects

- The re-creation of the natural landscape in the urban environment, which corresponds to the ideas of urban urbanism;
- The creation of an extensive recreational zone with visually rich spatial qualities;
- Purification of the contaminated bottom of the Voronezh reservoir;
- The reconstruction of the Voronezh river bed with a certain speed of water flow and a high level of water exchange;
- New architectural scale of the building adjacent to the floodplain part of the river;
- creation of a well-organized, visually rich recreational area for the left-bank part of the city that does not possess the landscape diversity inherent in the right-bank part;
- Creating fundamentally new opportunities for urban transport and logistics infrastructure in general, including solving the problems of interconnection of the right-bank and left-bank part of the city.

Negative Effects

- Technological and sanitary and hygienic hazards of the descent of the reservoir waters into the Voronezh River and further to the Don;
- High cost of justification, design, construction, monitoring and maintenance of the facility, reclamation of the bottom of the reservoir;
- The need to restructure the entire transport and logistics network in the area of the reservoir;
- A new stage in the change in the bio-synopsis, which has now been adapted to a high level of standing of groundwater in the coastal zone;
- The formation of the riverbed and floodplain of the Voronezh River within the boundaries of the urban district and the re-creation of all hydro-mechanical, hydrogeological and hydro-chemical processes inherent in all river systems (flooding, flooding, waterlogging, shallowing, erosion of shores, etc., etc.);
- The need to find solutions to the drainage of storm and sewage from the slope of the reservoir, bypassing the left-bank treatment facilities;
- Inevitable morphological changes in the lower tail of the reservoir and small rivers (Peschanka, Tavrovka);
- Reducing the development potential of water sports popular in the city;
- Destruction of the city's water area, corresponding to the scale of the city of a million people and creating numerous interesting visual effects of the perception of urban development.

FUTURE RESEARCH DIRECTIONS

In future formation of the concept of "smart city" arising in the process of transformation of the old large city requires abandoning the traditional vision of its spatial and functional characteristics.

The results of the study will be informative for future researchers to expand the scope of the study or to consider supplementing the results with qualitative data to achieve a better understanding of how to break down barriers in intercultural organizations and enhance their organizational effectiveness. At present, the most prestigious and highly paid is the work in the sphere of international business, in connection with which the migration of labor resources cannot be avoided. International labor migration is an inter-state movement of labor resources with a change of permanent residence. It includes two counter phenomena: emigration and immigration. Emigration is the departure of a country's population abroad; immigration is the entry of the population of other countries into the territory of a given country. These multidirectional flows of labor resources form an international labor market that unites similar markets at the level of states and regions and represents a separate scientific interest for this chapter authors, requires new innovative solutions, new tools to use Intelligent Visualization Techniques for Big Data Analytics in the future. It would be reasonable to conduct phenomenological research to provide empirical evidence based on perceptions and experiences of the top and middle managers in Russian corporations; conduct semi structured interviews with predetermined questions. For the interviews, future researchers could collect the data needed for in-depth understanding of cross-cultural communication process and main barriers in the process.

CONCLUSION

The contradiction between the needs of the population in a comfortable and high-tech urban environment on the one hand, and the simplification of labor functions and the growth in the number of active residents (including those coming from rural areas and small towns) that are not in demand by the labor market can be resolved on the basis of the following principles for the transformation of a large city in the "smart".

The principle of integration, ensuring the transition from a cruel functional delineation to an integrated environment on the basis is of a compromise and perspective composition of the subsystems of the city and its surroundings (city and adjacent agglomeration areas, urban development and natural environment, historical and new parts of the city.

The principle of metabolism, providing expediency, efficiency, safety of functioning of city systems and improvement is of quality of a life of townspeople.

The principle of the architectural quality of the urban environment, providing a combination of cultural and historical heritage of the city with a new urban landscape, harmoniously blending into the national and international notions is of the aesthetics of a comfortable environment and focused on the target image of the international (Eastern European) city.

The model of the "smart city" concept realization necessitates the implementation of their three-level spatial development aimed at achieving the three strategic goals: "to achieve the city's leadership positions in terms of the level of human capital development and the quality of life of the population, and the reduction of socio-economic inequality"; "Maintenance of sustainable development of the economy on the basis of the development of the innovation sector and improvement of the business environment"; "Effective spatial development, formation of aesthetically attractive, friendly, comfortable urban environment."

At the first level (the historical center) is an increase in the level of architectural solutions and functional saturation of the historic part of the city, combined with the preservation of historical and cultural monuments, improving the organization of traffic, landscaping and landscaping, the formation of a system of pedestrian and bicycle routes.

At the second level (the city as a whole) is a qualitative organization and a positive reorganization of the urban environment with priority development of urban municipal services, modernization of the street-road network, housing stock, and improvement of residential and public areas.

At the third level (urban agglomeration) - development of agglomeration as a zone of interrelated relations, joint solution of issues of economics, transport, engineering, social welfare, ecology, use of territorial, labor, natural-resource potential.

The most important spheres of the large Russian "smart city" are:

- Development of large, stable production complexes that are not subject to reduction as a result of the introduction of new technologies (production is understood in a broad sense, including services);
- The introduction of progressive elements of a new production structure that is adequate to the state of the scientific and innovative potential of the city;
- Stabilization of perspective elements of traditional production segments in the medium term;
- Formation of efficient transport and transport and logistics infrastructure, expanding the geographical and functional space of the city;
- Ensuring a high level of public safety;
- Formation of a comfortable urban environment on the basis of combining the functions of spheres of culture, the consumer market, recreational facilities.

The volume of these cities is mainly limited to build a technological park, which converts industrial property in modern information technology using the evolution of telecommunications and IP networks, including a minor asset management automation system. The basis of the development is the creation of a working platform that will manage power consumption and operating resources to reduce overall operating costs. This paper will discuss the principles of developing intelligent infrastructures and topographic location accuracy of assets as a basis for the intellectual development of the city architecture, integrated with all objects and systems associated with the smart city. The paper also will address the fundamental advantages of the proposed architecture, including quantitative and unquantifiable benefits.

ACKNOWLEDGMENT

This research was supported by the Russian Foundation for Basic Research –

[Grant number 19-010-00534] entitled: Service-oriented interaction in the management of smart cities: the elaboration of theoretical foundations and methods to increase their effectiveness

REFERENCES

Aditya, T., & Laksono, D. (2017). LOD 1: 3D CityModel for Implementing SmartCity Concept. In *Proceedings of the 2017 International Conference on Information Technology*. Singapore: ACM. 10.1145/3176653.3176734

Anthopoulos, L. G., & Vakali, A. (2012). Urban planning and smart cities: Interrelations and reciprocities. In F. Álvarez (Ed.), *The Future Internet Assembly* (pp. 178–189). Berlin: Springer. doi:10.1007/978-3-642-30241-1_16

Bibri, S. E. (2018). Backcasting in futures studies: A synthesized scholarly and planning approach to strategic smart sustainable city development. *European Journal of Futures Research*, *6*(1), 13. doi:10.118640309-018-0142-z

Bozhenov, S.A. (2012). Clever city in the development strategy of Belgorod. *City Management: Theory and Practice, 1*(4), 3-10.

Chourabi, H., Nam, T., Walker, S., Gil-Garcia, J. R., Mellouli, S., Nahon, K., & Scholl, H. J. (2012). Understanding Smart Cities: An Integrative Framework. In *Proceedings of the 2012 45th Hawaii International Conference on System Sciences*. Maui, HI: IEEE. 10.1109/HICSS.2012.615

Drozhzhinov, V. I., Kupriyanovsky, V. P., Namiot, D. E., Sinyagov, S. A., & Kharitonov, A. A. (2017). Smart cities: Models, tools, ranking and standards. *International Journal of Open Information Technologies*, *5*(3), 19–47.

Garau, M., Ghiani, E., Celli, G., & Pilo, F. (2017). *Tecno-economic and environmental assessment of a full electric smart city eco-district*. Paper presented at the 2017 AEIT International Annual Conference, Cagliari, Italy. 10.23919/AEIT.2017.8240566

Gil-Garcia, J. R., Pardo, T. A., & Nam, T. (2015). What makes a city smart? Identifying core components and proposing an integrative and comprehensive conceptualization. *Information Polity*, *20*(1), 61–87. doi:10.3233/IP-150354

Gil-Garcia, J. R., Zhang, J., & Puron-Cid, G. (2016). Conceptualizing smartness in government: An integrative and multi-dimensional view. *Government Information Quarterly*, *33*(3), 524–534. doi:10.1016/j.giq.2016.03.002

Hollands, R. G. (2008). Will the real smart city please stand up? Intelligent, progressive or entrepreneurial? *City*, *12*(3), 303–320. doi:10.1080/13604810802479126

Neirotti, P., De Marco, A., Cagliano, A. C., Mangano, G., & Scorrano, F. (2014). Current trends in Smart City initiatives: Some stylized facts. *Cities (London, England)*, *38*, 25–36. doi:10.1016/j.cities.2013.12.010

Ruhlandt, R. W. S. (2018). The governance of smart cities: A systematic literature review. *Cities (London, England)*, *81*, 1–23. doi:10.1016/j.cities.2018.02.014

Salomatin, E. V. (2016). Resource approach to the concept of "smart city". *Reports of Tomsk State University of Control Systems and Radio-electronics, 19*(3), 115–120. doi:10.21293/1818-0442-2016-19-3-115-120

ADDITIONAL READING

Khvostikova, V., Semionova, E., Chernetsov, M., Mkrttchian, V., & Potapova, I. (2017). Cost Control Strategy for the Implementation of the User Innovation Potential in the Digital Economy. In P. Isaias & L. Carvalho (Eds.), *User Innovation and the Entrepreneurship Phenomenon in the Digital Economy* (pp. 267–287). Hershey, PA, USA: IGI Global; doi:10.4018/978-1-5225-2826-5.ch013

Liu, Y., Wang, H., & Tzeng, G. H. (2018). From measure to guidance: Galactic model and sustainable development planning toward the best smart city. *Journal of Urban Planning and Development, 144*(4), 04018035. doi:10.1061/(ASCE)UP.1943-5444.0000478

Mkrttchian, V., & Aleshina, E. (2017). *Sliding Mode in Intellectual Control and Communication: Emerging Research and Opportunities*. Hershey, PA, USA: IGI Global. doi:10.4018/978-1-5225-2292-8

Mkrttchian, V., & Belyanina, L. (Eds.). (2018). *Handbook of Research on Students' Research Competence in Modern Educational Contexts*. Hershey, PA, USA: IGI Global. doi:10.4018/978-1-5225-3485-3

Mkrttchian, V., Bershadsky, A., Bozhday, A., Kataev, M., & Kataev, S. (Eds.). (2016). *Handbook of Research on Estimation and Control Techniques in E-Learning Systems*. Hershey, PA, USA: IGI Global. doi:10.4018/978-1-4666-9489-7

Mkrttchian, V., Bershadsky, A., Finogeev, A., Berezin, A., & Potapova, I. (2017). Digital Model of Bench-Marking for Development of Competitive Advantage. In P. Isaias & L. Carvalho (Eds.), *User Innovation and the Entrepreneurship Phenomenon in the Digital Economy* (pp. 288–303). Hershey, PA, USA: IGI Global; doi:10.4018/978-1-5225-2826-5.ch014

Mkrttchian, V., & Potapova, I. (2018). Professors of Innovative Implementations in Sliding Mode Digital Technology for Enhancing Students Competence. In V. Mkrttchian & L. Belyanina (Eds.), *Handbook of Research on Students' Research Competence in Modern Educational Contexts* (pp. 189–204). Hershey, PA, USA: IGI Global; doi:10.4018/978-1-5225-3485-3.ch010

Tolstykh, T., Vasin, S., Gamidullaeva, L., & Mkrttchian, V. (2017). The Control of Continuing Education Based on the Digital Economy. In P. Isaias & L. Carvalho (Eds.), *User Innovation and the Entrepreneurship Phenomenon in the Digital Economy* (pp. 153–171). Hershey, PA, USA: IGI Global; doi:10.4018/978-1-5225-2826-5.ch008

Tolstykh, T., Vertakova, J., & Shkarupeta, E. (2018). Professional Training for Structural Economic Transformations Based on Competence approach in the Digital Age. In V. Mkrttchian & L. Belyanina (Eds.), *Handbook of Research on Students' Research Competence in Modern Educational Contexts* (pp. 209–229). Hershey, PA, USA: IGI Global; doi:10.4018/978-1-5225-3485-3.ch011

KEY TERMS AND DEFINITIONS

Avatar-Based Management: Innovation management technique for human intellectual control.

Big Data Analytics: The mathematical and software techniques for examining large and varied data sets to uncover hidden patterns, unknown correlations, market trends, customer preferences, and other useful information that can help organizations make more-informed business decisions.

Competitiveness: Pertains to the ability and performance of a firm, sub-sector, or country to sell and supply goods and services in a given market, in relation to the ability and performance of other firms, sub-sectors, or countries in the same market.

Data Mining: The computing process of discovering patterns in large data sets involving methods at the intersection of machine learning, statistics, and database systems.

DSS: A decision support system is a computer-based information system that supports business or organizational decision-making activities.

ETL: Extract, transform, load refers to a process in database usage and especially in data warehousing.

Feedback: Occurs when outputs of a system are routed back as inputs as part of a chain of cause-and-effect that forms a circuit or loop.

Innovations: Production or adoption, assimilation, and exploitation of a value-added novelty in economic and social spheres; renewal and enlargement of products, services, and markets; development of new methods of production; and establishment of new management systems. It is both a process and an outcome.

Intelligent Visualization Techniques: The process of presenting data in the form of an image in order to maximize the convenience of understanding them, giving a visible form to any conceivable object, subject, process, and so on.

OLAP: Online analytical processing is an approach to answering multi-dimensional analytical (MDA) queries swiftly in computing.

Principles of Development: Progresses in a step-by-step fashion. It is orderly, sequential, and proceeds from the simple to the complex. Each achieved behavior forms the foundation for more advanced behaviors.

Response to Intervention (RTI): A multi-tier approach to the early identification and support of students with learning and behavior needs; service for management educational process for corrections.

Smart City: An urban area that uses different types of electronic data collection sensors to supply information which is used to manage assets and resources efficiently.

State-Owned Corporation (SOE): A business enterprise where the state has significant control through full, majority, or significant minority ownership.

System-Synergetic Approach: For analysis of complex social-economic systems in organization field.

Chapter 16
The Role of Industrial Development in Nigeria's Transformation From Oil to Cities:
The Case of Birnin Kebbi

Rabiu Abdullahi Bena
Waziri Umaru Federal Polytechnic, Nigeria

ABSTRACT

Nigeria, as the giant of Africa, is in a state of limbo because of its overreliance on oil money, which retarded its level of growth and development. The discovery of crude oil forced the Nigerian government to shift attention away from agriculture. This neglect of agriculture negatively affected Nigeria as both agriculture and manufacturing activities were halted. Ironically, the growth created by oil revenue was not sustained and directed to the other sectors of the economy for widespread multiplier effects. As declining oil prices reveal the economic weaknesses of the country, there is pressure for Nigeria to seek an alternative means of revenue. Nigeria is now transitioning from oil to industrial cities. It is against this background that this chapter is illustrating how the economy's overdependence on oil is transitioning to a more diversified alternative by transforming cities. This chapter focuses on Birnin Kebbi as a case study for a medium-size city that has huge growth potential.

INTRODUCTION

The Discovery of crude oil made Nigerian government to shift attention away from agriculture. Ironically, the growth created by oil revenue was not sustained and directed to the other sectors of the economy for wide spread multiplier effects. The ongoing recession coupled with the decrease in global oil prices and its attendant consequences has forced the government to look inward for diversification of the economy. In Nigeria, the overdependence on oil has led to underdevelopment of other revenue sources and prevented improvements in governance.

DOI: 10.4018/978-1-5225-7625-9.ch016

According to a report, 'in 2012 the share of oil revenue in the national budget was 75 percent and state governments received over 63 percent of their revenue from oil. Reliance on oil-based fiscal transfers to states provides few incentives to boost local revenue generation and weakens urban planning and financing', (World Bank, 2016).

In Nigeria consumption-based cities have arisen because of oil wealth, but these have not increased economic productivity or urban employment, or reduced poverty, as they have in many other parts of the developing world. Now, as declining oil prices reveal the economic weaknesses of the country, pressure for a new economic model is growing. Urbanization, which to date has *followed* wealth creation, can instead, if reformed, help *drive* economic growth and poverty reduction (World Bank, 2016). It is against this background that this study aimed at reviewing the effects of over-dependence of Nigeria's economy on oil to a more diversified alternative solution through industrial (economic) transformation of Nigerian cities using Birnin Kebbi, a medium-size city that has huge growth potential that is masked by the existing reality as a case study.

THEORETICAL REVIEW

An overview of urbanization in Nigeria, a brief early history of industrialization, role of industrial policy in the national transformation and the structure of Nigeria's industrial policy are discussed hereunder to provide the backdrop against which the country's urban and industrial growth policies should be seen.

Urbanization in Nigeria: An Overview

Urbanization is generally used to mean demographic concentration of people in an area over a given period. Urbanization is a continuous population increase, a phenomenon that is astronomically influencing the spatial growth of cities particularly in Africa. This is in accordance with a World Bank report (2017) that… Africa, with the most recent urban tradition and experience of city life, is currently urbanizing at more than 4% annually. In 1995 only 28 cities on the continent had populations exceeding 1 million, by 2005 this has grown to 43 cities, and it is expected that by 2015 there will be 59 African cities with populations exceeding 1 million. In the region, the urban population of 413(40%) in 2010 is expected to rise to 569 million (45%) in 2020. Moreover many definitions of urbanization have several consistent features as sum up by Mediel Hove, et' al (2013). Urbanization is characterized as a: (i) demographic process, (ii) necessary element of economic and industrial development, (iii) driving force behind social change and (iv) universal phenomenon. Within the field of critical urban research, the urban phenomenon is considered the dynamic result of a complex process of articulation of interactive and often conflicting economic, political, legal and cultural forces. Through this process cities and rural areas in developing countries have been redefined by the changing nature of capitalism and more recently, by the process of economic globalization (Fernandes 1998, in, Mediel Hove et'al,(2013) .

The growth in population here refers to domestic migration and immigration. Nigeria as the largest country south of the Sahara witnessed rapid urbanization after the discovery of oil in the 1970s after the civil war. Rapid urbanization is not only concentrated on mega cities such as Lagos, smaller cities like Birnin Kebbi, Sokoto Gusau and others face enormous growth rates as well.

Spatially, many urban settlements and urbanized areas have appeared in various parts of the country, they have witnessed greater intensity of the urbanization process, as some of the older bigger cities such as Lagos, Ibadan Enugu and Kano have their population sizes increased more than quadrupled between 1960 to date. Thus, the stimulus for, and the tempo of, urbanization have continued and, have become much higher since independence. There is fairly even spread of middle and lower cities in the country, this connotes any form of investments into these categories of cities would bring about wider spread of development in the country.

In fact Nigeria's urban s are becoming more in number and getting bigger in size and should be of concern and interest for both the challenges they pose and prospects they present as substitute to oil by providing industrial base for urban development. In essence, Nigeria's urbanization is in many places accompanied by a growing consumer class with more purchasing power and preferences for manufactured goods, and changing consumption patterns have already created opportunities for domestic industry. This shift is now examined as it relates to the food, housing, infrastructure and business service sectors hence transformation process sets in as examined in this discourse.

Inception of Industrialization in Nigeria

Historically, the pre-colonial era, that is, the pre-1900 economy of Nigeria featured considerable craft industries in the various clans and kingdoms when modern factory activity was then hardly known. Prominent among these craft industries that featured in local and inter-regional trade, were artifacts of wood, brass and bronze, leather, hand woven textiles and bags, iron workings and fire burnt pottery from local clay. The various zones specialized in different crafts closely linked with the available raw materials (Ajayi, 2011, P713).

Nigeria's industrial development could be traced back to early 1960 when much of the industrial sector was dominated by agriculture. At that period, agriculture was the mainstay of the Nigerian economy providing food and employment for the populace, raw materials for the industrial sector, and generating the bulk of government revenue and foreign exchange earnings for the much needed infrastructure and health facilities.

The post-colonial period of 1960-1965 was characterized by vigorous import substitution and the beginning of decline for the export-oriented processing of raw materials (Ajayi, ibid, P714). Much of the development projects like manufacturing industries, railway lines, seaports, roads, universities, and hospitals among others at that period were financed from foreign exchange earned from export of agricultural produce such as groundnuts, cotton rubber and palm oil and other mineral deposits. The post war economic boom in raw material export and a sharp increase in government revenue and explicit investment potentials of indigenous businessmen brought about rapid growth in the number of manufacturing establishments in the country. Ironically, the discovery of oil and its exploration and exportation in commercial quantities after the war, the fortunes of agriculture gradually diminished while crude petroleum replaced it as the dominant source of revenue. Moreover during the "oil boom" era in the 70s, Nigeria neglected virtually all other sectors and focused on oil for her main source of revenue. Since then, oil has become the mainstay of the Nigerian economy, with oil export as a percentage of total national exports from 1981 to 2010 reaching an average of 95 percent as noted by Harry(2016, P24).

Succinctly put, the trend in the industrial development in Nigeria is categorized into five distinct periods. These periods are:

1. Immediate post-independence period starting from independence in 1960 to the advent of the first military regime in 1966 was dominated by agro-allied industries;
2. Post-civil war oil economy starting from the end of the 30-month civil war in 1970 to the hand-over of government by the military to civilians in 1979 was a period of reconciliation, redevelopment and rehabilitation of people and the economy;
3. Transition to an austere economy that emerged in the second republic and the subsequent adoption of the World Bank/IMF-led economic SAP in 1986 a period characterized by inconsistency in policies deregulation of the economy in totality and;
4. The era of SAP and guided economic liberalization starting from 1986 to the advent of the new democratic dispensation in 1999 which rejuvenate and rekindle the economy; and
5. The regime of further economic liberalization starting from 1999 and resulting in emergent macroeconomic stability and transformation and consolidation of privatization policies (adapted after Chete, et' al. 2016, P15)

Nigeria Industrial Policy an Impetus for the Transformation

In coastal cities, for example in West Africa, fisheries industries were established and cities thrived based on such. Where agriculture was viable, agro-processing industries emerged and supported the local economic and population. Even areas which were difficult to develop owing to their undulating terrain, for example, Cape Town, industries such as eco-tourism were established and these somehow played an important role in supporting the local economy and subsequently urban development and growth.In Nigeria, the urban s have been seen as synonymous with modernization and development. They have functioned as the hubs of the economy of the country at various levels, viz national, regional, states and local levels and with neighboring countries. It is obvious that Nigerian cities have acted and are still acting as economic nerve s for investments, production and distribution because they held a stock of manpower that supply industries with the needed skilled and unskilled labor. They also serve as consumption base of manufactured goods and services by the industries. Similarly, the cities housed governments and private sector institutions as well as non-governmental organizations (centers of knowledge and innovations). Many of these cities are centers of transport and communication nerve centers from where all parts of the country are connected and reached. In view of the above roles enumerated and many more, the government re-designed industrial policy that would transform the cities into revenue generating entities to serve as substitute to monopolistic oil sector.

The Nigeria's Industrial Policy

Conventionally, an industrial policy has been defined in the words of Mailafia (2016), as a set of actions executed by interventionists or mixed-economy countries in order to affect the way in which factors of production are being distributed across national industries. He opined that, 'as a nation of almost 200 million people, it is clear that Nigeria can no longer trudge along the same trajectory as an oil-dependent monoculture rentier economy'(Mailafia 2016),.Hence the clarion calls for renewed industrial policy that will lead to diversification of the economy.

The Nation's industrial policy package stem from the vision 20:20 committee inaugurated by the Federal Government in 1997 tagged 'Nigeria Vision 2020' in the year 2020. The focus here shall be to review the portion that concerns industrial growth, diversification and urban development.

The NV20:2020 industrialization strategy aims at achieving greater global competitiveness in the production of manufactured goods by linking industrial activity with primary sector activity, domestic and foreign trade, and service activity. A key component is the promotion of a comprehensive policy of cluster development in the manufacturing and processing industries. This includes the development of industrial parks, industrial clusters and enterprise zones, and incubator facilities.

Industrial parks, aimed at large manufacturers, are expected to cover areas of more than 3,050 km^2. The parks will be based on the comparative and competitive advantage of each geographical zone. The following business activities have been identified for each of the zones (Nigeria Vision 20:2020).

- **North East:** Agriculture and solid minerals e.g. gypsum, biomass, ethanol, biodiesel, tropical fruits, etc.;
- **North West:** Gum Arabic, livestock and meat processing, tanneries, biofuel, etc.;
- **North Central:** Fruit processing, cotton, quarries, furniture and minerals, boards, plastic processing, leather goods, garments, etc.;
- **South East:** Palm oil-refining and palm tree-processing into biomass particle boards, plastic processing, leather goods, and garments;
- **South West:** Manufacturing (especially garments, methanol, etc.), distributive trade, general goods, plastic, etc.;
- **South Central:** Petrochemicals, manufacturing (plastic, fertilizer, and fabrications, etc.), oil services, and distributive trade 'TINAPA' (Author's emphasis).

The provision contained in the policy statement can be elaborated further in the following manner:

The Industrial Clusters

This will be established with the participation and assistance of states and local governments will cover areas of between 100 and 1,000 ha. They will be exclusively devoted to the organized private sector. The location of the clusters will take into account access to roads, railways, sea ports, cargo airports, and proximity to a city and management will be through a private cluster company. Industrial incentives similar to those in industrial parks will also be provided, while each cluster will have a skill acquisition/training center.

In addition, the Nigeria Industrial Revolution Plan (NIRP) was designed to facilitate the development of industrial cities, parks, and clusters while focusing on making hard infrastructure available within these industrial zones. The current administration is fully committed to implementing the NIRP.As a sign of commitment; the Acting President Professor Osinbajo has inaugurated the board of the Nigerian Industrial Policy and Competitiveness Advisory Council. The council is expected to plan and supervise policies that will speed up Nigeria's industrialization bid (Culled from www.naija.com).

Enterprise Zones

These are platforms of 5–30 ha, targeted at incorporating the informal sector into the organized private sector. Located in state capitals and local government areas, they will enable farmers and SMEs to feed their products into the value chain of large-scale industries. These centers will accommodate mechanics, block makers, small-scale furniture manufacturers, timber merchants, and other vocational workers who constitute over 70 per cent of Nigeria's private sector. Skills acquisition/training centers will also be located in each enterprise zone, while management will be handled by the private sector.

The Incubators

The incubators will be start-up centers for new and inexperienced entrepreneurs, graduates of tertiary institutions, investors, and vocational workers wishing to set up their own businesses. In these centers, prospective start-up companies will be equipped with entrepreneurial skills and resources aimed at nurturing them from formation to maturity.

Other agencies play important roles in the trade and industrial sectors in Nigeria. For instance, the Bank of Industries, Small & Medium Enterprises Development Agency of Nigeria (SMEDAN), NEPZA, Nigeria Export Promotion Council, and Nigerian Investment Promotion Commission (NIPC) are parastatals of the Federal Ministry of Industry, Trade and Investment. The Raw Material Research and Development Council is an agency of the Federal Ministry of Science and Technology and the Nigerian Customs Service is a Parastatal of the Federal Ministry of Finance. The setting-up of these teams and the designation of the finance minister as coordinator of economic policy have improved the implementation of economic policy in the country.

Implementation of the policy provisions would set a giant stride in the growth of industries and physical expansion of cities and towns where such industrial clusters are established particularly in northern parts of Nigeria.

TRANSFORMATION OF THE NIGERIAN ECONOMY

The structure of the present-day Nigerian spatial economy can trace its origins to the colonial period and the economic system that developed even before the colonial rule. Patterns of internal and cross-border trade can trace their origins back even further as noted by Mabogunje in Chete, L.N. et'al (2016, P9). Nigeria enjoys a historical legacy of north-south trading relations dating to the pre-colonial era. In this period, a complex system of trade and urban economies existed, and was particularly evident in the north. The Hausa states and the Kanem Empire, ed on Borno, were part of a trade network stretching across South Sudan northwards to ports in North Africa and on to Europe. As a drive towards economic transformation, cities are gradually taking their place as base for industrial development. Cities as engine of growth and subsequent development accommodates industrial establishment because they possess all the necessary infrastructure and manpower needed by the industries to operate and survive.

However, some of the impediments to smooth transformation include among others, congestion, expensive transport, and border barriers are most relevant for the tradable sectors. In other words, while Nigeria's poor business environment affects all firms, it has a disproportionate impact on the productivity of manufacturing firms.

Considerably, Chete, et'al, (2016) identified some of these obstacles, namely bureaucratic trade barriers and infrastructure, play a lesser role as obstacles to the development of high productivity sectors such as ICT; real estate and construction; professional, scientific, and technical services; entertainment; and finance and insurance, which have been important drivers of GDP growth over the past two decades. Growth of these sectors attests to the resilience and ingenuity of urban entrepreneurs who have successfully developed their businesses in these sectors in the face of severe challenges.

As stated in the report, 'most states have improved their business environment since 2010—some despite significant security challenges. However, 5 states stand out: Ogun, Niger, Cross River, Ekiti and Rivers introduced several high-impact reforms that narrowed the gap to best practices the most (Chete, L.N, et' al. 2016, P8). He added that added '...an emerging sector in Nigeria is the information and communications technology (ITC) sector. A key example is the Otigba Computer Village which started in 1995 involving over 392 SMEs, employing more than 3,000 workers. The formation of this cluster has given Nigeria a foothold in skills-intensive computer repair and 'clone' production. The village is located in Lagos and covers an area of some 325 km². It deals with the sale, service, and repair of ICT products and components which are targeted at the Lagos industrial axis. The cluster development has been characterized by significant inter-firm co-operation and joint action as stated by Chete, et'al (2016, P14). Many of such computer villages are spring up in the northern states of Kano, Kaduna Sokoto and Jos. Moreover, there is an ICT hub in Birnin Kebbi located along Ahmadu Bello Way which employed hundreds of youths similar to the Otigba village.

The youth restiveness and crude oil pipelines vandalism coupled with kidnapping of foreigners (working in the oil drilling companies) for ransom and other social vices that characterized the oil producing areas in the Niger Delta calls for re-think as to explore economic transformation through city mechanism for the overall development of the country. According to the plans contained in the powers bestowed on Nigerian Export Processing Zone Authority the following incentives are provided to boost export processing activities as substitute to oil in foreign earnings (this is supported by the contents in **Table 1** as benefits derived from the policy incentives).

Incentives for Non-Oil Industries

Incentives are important tools used to promote industrial development. The following are the incentives used by the various governments in Nigeria to promote the growth and development of the manufacturing, agriculture and agro-industries.

- ***Manufacturing***
    - Companies with turnover of less than NGN1 million are taxed at a low rate of 20 percent for the first five years of operation if they are in the manufacturing sector;
- Dividends from companies in the manufacturing sector with a turnover of less than NGN1 million are tax-free for the first five years of operation;
- Dividends derived from manufacturing companies in the petrol chemical, and liquefied natural gas sub-sector are exempt from tax.
- ***Agriculture and Agro-Industry***
    - Companies in the agro-allied business do not have their capital allowance restricted. It is granted in full i.e. 100 per cent;
    - The payments of minimum tax by companies that make small or no profits at all.

Arguably, Nigeria's manufacturing consists largely of assembly plants with little or no backward linkage in the economy. The few industries that have any form of backward linkage are 'rooted' industries such as tin smelting in Jos, timber and plywood factories at Sapele, leather factories and plastics in Kano, cement factories at Kalambaina in Sokoto, canned vegfru in Dadin Kowa-Gombe, rice mills in Birnin Kebbi among others. Table 1 below summarizes the free trade zones in the country that are aimed at facilitating smooth transformation of the Nigerian economy from oil to non-oil. More of these EPZ are being considered for operation especially in Kamba to facilitate trades between Sokoto, Kebbi and Zamfara states in the North-west Zone with Benin and Niger republics.

Moreover, the spatial economy developed along the same patterns post-independence, though at that point the economy was based on manufacturing supported by the policy of import substitution. Kano and the surrounding area emerged as the most industrialized region of the country. Leather, textiles, and food production were the dominant industries. By the 1980, before the onset of structural adjustment, 2,500 manufacturers were located in Kano. At its height, the textiles industry employed over 350,000 workers in over 175 businesses that exported fabrics throughout West Africa. Throughout this period, manufacturing was concentrated primarily in four areas of the country:

Table 1. Free trade zones in Nigeria

Name	Location	Status	Ownership
1 Calabar free trade zone	Cross River State	Operational	Federal gov.
2 Kano free trade zone	Kano State	Operational	Federal gov.
3 Onne oil and gas free zone	River State	Operational	Parallel Auth.
4 Tinapa free zone and tourism resort	Cross river State	Operational	Private/public
5 Snake island integrated	Lagos	Operational	Private
6 Maigatari border free zone	Jigawa State	Operational	State
7 LADO free zone	Lagos	Operational	Private
8 Airline services export proc. zone	Lagos State	Operational	Private
9 ALSCON export processing zone	Akwa Ibon	Operational	Private
10 Ogun Guangdong free trade zone	Ogun State	Operational	Public/private
11 Sebore farms export process zones	Adamawa State	Operational	Private
12 Ibom science and tech. park free zone	Akwa Ibom	Under construct.	Public/private
13 Living spring free zone	Osun State	Under construct.	State Gov
14 Lekki free zone	Lagos State	Under construct.	State/private
15 Brass liquefied natural gas free zone	Bayelsa	Under construct.	Public/private
16 Abuja technological village free zone	Abuja	Under construct.	Public/private
17 Specialized railway industrial free trade zone Kajola	Ogun State	Under construct.	Public/Private
18 Imo Guangdong free trade zone	Imo State	Under construct.	Public/private
19 OK free trade zone	Ondo and Ogun	Under construct.	States/private
20 Lagos free zone	Lagos State	Under construct.	Private
21 Kwara free zone	Kwara State	Declaration	State gov.
22 Oluyole free trade zone	Oyo State	Declaration	State gov.
23 Koko free trade zone	Delta State	Declaration	State gov.
24 OILSS logistics free zone	Lagos	Declaration	Private
25 Banki border free zone	Borno State	Declaration	State gov

Source: Chete, L.N. et'al (2016)

- Southwest corridor between Lagos and Ibadan
- Southeast industrial zone: Onitsha, Port Harcourt, Enugu, Aba, Umuahia, and Calabar
- Northern industrial zone: Kano, Kaduna, Jos, and Zaria
- Midwest industrial zone: Benin City, Sapele and Warri

However Chete, et'al (2016) postulates that, the failure of import substitution, the deterioration of infrastructure, poor governance, and a dysfunctional business climate has taken a heavy toll on the manufacturing sector across the country. It is expected that industrial development when pursue juxtaposed with adequate policy package would transform revenue base from oil to manufacturing activities in Nigeria similar to that of Asian Tigers (China Indonesia, Singapore, Thailand and Malaysia among others).

Transformation by Special Economic Zones

A prominent feature of the industrial sector in Nigeria is the existence of a number of special economic zones. There are approximately 25 free trade zones licensed by the federal government. These are documented in Table 2. However, less than 13 of them are currently operational. Some are under construction and in the early phases of development. Two types of free trade arrangement operate in Nigeria – the specialized and the general-purpose trade/export zones, which are managed by two bodies – the Nigerian Export Processing Zone Authority for the general-purpose zones and the Oil & Gas Free Zone Authority for the oil and gas zone. They have the mandate to approve new zones, modify existing ones, grant permits and approvals for operators in the EPZs, and manage the zones.

Economic activity is clustered in this way to create a controlled environment for industrialization to flourish especially in the presence of chronic infrastructural deficits. This has traditionally taken the form of industrial estates or parks. The main benefit of the localization of firms in this way is that it allows for infrastructural provisions to be prioritized and to give firms a competitive edge while offering access to raw materials, skilled labor, technology and materials. Nigeria has a number of large industrial estates and complexes but has also witnessed the spontaneous development of small clusters across the country. The latter includes the computer village in Otigba, Lagos, the auto and industrial spare parts fabricators in Nnewi, the leather tannery in Kano and the footwear, leatherworks, and garment cluster in Aba.(Chete, et'al. 2016)

Lyankurwa (1991) as mentioned by Harry (2016,P27), argued that export diversification is important because it reduces the variability of the export earnings of developing countries and raises the growth rates of both exports and domestic output. Accordingly, the import of diversification of the economy can be established by citing Madagascar as a case. In a study on export diversification in EPZs in sub-Saharan Africa during the 1990s, Cling, et' al (2005) found Madagascar to be the most successful, by increasing the number of its products worth over US $ 1 million in exports from 38 percent to 70 percent. Even today, it is difficult to find EPZs in the region that will surpass that feat. According to Cling, et al (20050, diversification was important in making Madagascar's zone Franche "the only successful EPZ in an African LDC..."(Harry 2016, P35). In Nigeria much is expected from the EPZs to be able to transform the economy away from oil dominated.

THE NEED FOR TRANSFORMATION FROM OIL TO CITIES

The need for the transformation of Nigeria's development from oil-based to city-based had been advocated by many including by Chete, L.N. et'al (2016), World Bank (2016), and Ajayi (2011). This is especially so given the nations privatization and commercialization policies, and the development of the Export Processing Zones (EPZs) in Kano, Lagos, Port Harcourt and Calabar. This will further encourage the local sourcing of industrial raw materials given the ongoing privatization and commercialization policies in the industrial development Nigeria as indicated in the table above. This was expected to increase its share of the GDP to slightly over these targets and expected to be achieved through improvement in capacity utilization in existing industries and increased investment in new ones, as well as more effective implementation of relevant policy reform measures.

Potentially, Nigeria accounts for nearly one-fourth of Sub-Saharan Africa's population and is the seventh most populous country in the world. The country is known to possess the following potentialities;

- As of April 2014, Nigeria's economy it is recognized as Africa's largest economy.
- Ranking 13th in the world for its oil production, Nigeria is Africa's largest producer and holds the second highest proven oil reserves on the continent, after Libya.
- Since embarking on the path of democracy in 1999, the country has enjoyed consistent and high economic growth rates—in the range of 6% -8% annually in recent years.
- With its large reserves of human capital and natural resources, a large domestic market, and strong economic fundamentals, Nigeria is well positioned to join the group of large emerging markets and be the Africa's powerhouse.
- Nigeria has already been identified as one of the promising "MINT" economies (an acronym for Mexico, Indonesia, Nigeria and Turkey), following the BRICs on the path to develop rapidly (World Bank, 2014, P6).

An Overview of The Key Trends in The Economy

It has been stated severally that Nigeria recently became the largest economy in Africa, overtaking South Africa, which has roughly a third of Nigeria's estimated 170 million people (Najiet'al, 2015)... The country's economic output is outpacing population growth. GDP increased from $31 billion in 1990 to $522 billion in 2013 (averaging an annual growth rate of 5.9 percent), whilst the population increased from 96 million to 170 million during the same period. Similarly, the gross domestic product (GDP) per capita has increased from just $321 in 1990 to $3,010 in 2013, being the second highest in the Economic Community of West African States (ECOWAS) region after Cape Verde. Nigeria in fact accounts for 77 percent of the total GDP of ECOWAS. It also accounts for about 53 percent of the total population and 59 percent of the urban population. It is arguably that over half (51 percent) of the country's population now live in urban settlements, a similar percentage as Ghana and Cote d'Ivoire, the two next largest economies in the region. More so, Nigeria has become increasingly integrated into the regional and global economy in recent years, as evidenced by increasing levels of foreign direct investment (FDI) inflows and trade. FDI inflows have increased more than fivefold from $1 billion in 1990 to $5,6 billion in 2013, averaging over $7,2 billion over the last five years with a peak of $8,9 billion in 2011 as quoted by Naji, M. et'al (2015).

The import of the above review is to appreciate how the economy is fairing internationally which signifies the need for diversification through economic transformation.

The Urban Development Policy

Present day urbanization in Nigeria is witnessed by speedy expansion which is influenced by rapid urban population growth. Accordingly, the rapid population is expected to continue vis-a-vis land cover is expected to double by the year 2030. The need to fashion out new urban development policy that will guide the spatial expansion of urban areas in the country becomes imperative.

The Federal Executive Council approved the New National Urban Development Policy in June 2012. The new policy on access to land has the stated goal isto "ensure that land is made available for the purposes of promoting controlled and orderly development in the urban s." However, it laments the bottlenecks process of land acquisition by both individuals and corporate bodies for building purposes under the Land Use Act, linking the inefficiencies of the law to the lack of judicial clarification, and speedy and well-controlled urban development.

The policy also identifies the major impediments to land acquisition as high rates of land speculation, poor administration of land records, lack of cadastral maps, high cost of obtaining certificate of occupancy, and high land values, which the poor and their vulnerable groups cannot afford. The policy lists six strategies for the federal government to accelerate the growth of urban s through easy access to large tracts of land with secure title, and also to ensure access to land in suitable and planned locations to reduce the social and economic costs of unplanned development and the continued proliferation of slums and shanties at periphery of the urban areas:

- Facilitate cooperation and ensure the collaboration between state governors and appropriate federal agencies to facilitate easy access to land for development by individuals and corporate bodies.
- Build and strengthen the capacities of the ministries, departments, and agencies in charge of land administration to facilitate and ensure that private sector developers have easy access to land for real estate development.
- Provide necessary support and incentives to the private sector to effectively participate in urban development programs.
- Promote public-private partnership to ensure rapid and effective urban development.
- Review existing town planning regulations and practices, and remove bottlenecks, to facilitate private sector participation in urban development.
- Build and strengthen the capacities of state planning boards and local planning authorities to implement the provisions of the urban and regional planning laws to achieve orderly and sustainable development of cities and towns.(Source: World Bank, 2012,P137)

However, there is the need to integrate modern and customary systems of land and land tenure in society which must be recognized and rationalized. Therefore, support should be provided to strengthen the nexus between the formal land development process, the informal process, and the planning system. It is equally important for the government to take a holistic actions that will bring about 'ease of doing business' at urban or city levels. This implied improvement in infrastructure and services, effective and efficient information and communication technology and facilities.

A Review of Industrial Investment Policy

State like Lagos and Ogun, Kebbi State has so far limited success in establishing manufacturing industries. There are many opportunities in establishing agro-based manufacturing thereby creating backward linkages. Besides the high quantity and quality rice production, as will be shown later in this chapter, the state is rich in mineral resources and animal husbandry raw materials. The institutional support can be provided by the Nigerian Investment Promotion Commission and the Kebbi State Investment Company Limited as follows;

- Establish skill acquisition s, for the out of school youths of both genders, in various trades such tailoring welding maintenance and repairs of motor vehicles and computer systems among others. The institutional support can be provided by the Federal Polytechnic, National Directorate of Employment, and NGOs,
- Establish Industrial Parks and Business Clusters such as motor mechanics, steel and other metal fabrications. The administrative institutional support is from the ministries, agencies and organized trade associations in the state
- Sustainable infrastructure like power, water and road shoud be provided by state government in collaboration with banks to be charged to the consumers at an initially subsidized rate.
- Encourage foreign small and medium scale investors to locate in the state to provide new technology and transfer same to other businesses in the state
- Assist macro small and medium scale enterprises to access small and medium industries. Equity investment scheme fund by providing guidance through the state ministry of commerce and industry
- Corporate with small and Medium Enterprises Development Agency of Nigeria to reach out and assist small and medium scale enterprises in the state
- Partner with development partners and donors such as United Nations Development Program and other to assist small and medium scale enterprises in the State.

OIL TO CITIES: THE CASE STUDY-BIRNIN KEBBI

Kebbi State is among the 6 states created by President Abacha in 1991. It was created from the southwestern half of Sokoto state. Kebbi borders the nations of Niger to the west and Beninto the southwest and it borders the Nigerian states of Sokoto and Zamfara to the north and east and Niger to the south. Kebbi area consists of short-grass savanna that is drained southwestward by the River Niger and its tributary, the Sokoto (Kebbi) River. Most of the Kainji Reservoir, formed by the Kainji Dam further downstream on the Niger River, lies in the southern portion of the state as potential for dry season farming.

Location Advantage

Birnin Kebbi is the capital city of Kebbi State. It is located 12.45' latitude and 4.20^0 longitudes and it is situated at elevation 234 meters above sea level. Birnin Kebbi has a population of 268,620 by 2006 Census, thus the biggest city in the state; spreading over 954.75 sq. kilometers and is located within Sudan savanna zone of the state. It operates on the WAT time zone. Upon the creation of Kebbi State in 1991, Birnin Kebbi not only remained the seat of Gwandu Emirate as well as the administrative headquarters of Birnin Kebbi Local Government but also became the state capital; the triple role it has been playing till date.

Although Kebbi State is largely rural, Birnin Kebbi witnessed rapid rate of urbanization because of its administrative, economic and commercial functions. Because of its administrative and political role, therefore, Birnin Kebbi has become the centre of educational and industrial investments in the far north.

The town is also approximately 150km southwest of Sokoto and 500km northwest of Abuja. The town is connected by road and air transport. It is sandwiched between large areas of fadama land located to the north and southeast of the town which provide good irrigation opportunities for the inhabitants. The Federal government is currently utilizing this opportunity through a program called "Anchor Borrower" that seeks to encourage farmers to improve rice production. This is not only to ensuring food security but also improvement on the economic and social status of the farmers.

A leapfrog development adjoining the forest reserve to the south in order to accommodate heavy industries is in progress. A critical observation indicates that, although there is Bulasa shelter belt, that is almost gone between the granary and livestock breeding center. The Bulasa industrial area on the other side of the Jega road has been partially serviced by the government, only few industries have been actually established on the site.

Physical developments also proceeded northeastwards where low cost houses have been constructed first by the Federal Government but later taken over by the State Government for completion. However, that the construction of the eastern bypass has greatly influenced the attraction of developments towards that direction. This is coupled with presence of natural barriers to the north and west of the town and the forest reserve including the Livestock Improvement and Breeding (LIBC) to the south. The commercial land use, which constitutes 4.8% of the total land use, is dominated by the central market and cattle/timber markets as the central focus of economic activity. Various shopping outlets, hotels and neighborhood markets located along major streets and neighborhood s compliment this. (Master Plan, 2005)

Apart from most of them being located in the direction of growth of the town, Birnin Kebbi is observed to exert a lot of influence on the socio-economic activities of the villages. It is important to point out that the villages are surrounded by fertile agricultural lands that support the growth of maize, guinea corn, millet, beans, tomatoes and other vegetables. But as Birnin Kebbi continues to expand towards this direction, most of these agricultural lands would be taken over by urban developments. This would certainly raise the question of trade-off between supply of land for urban development and utilization of same land for production of food to feed the urban population.

The Local Agro-Based Economy

It is important to point out that the various opportunities available to the people of Birnin Kebbi have been determined principally by its economic base. Performance of the town's economy in the last fifteen (25) years that is from 1991 to 2015 has exerted great influence on population growth, employment structure, physical expansion and development of the town. Birnin Kebbi is thus now serving triple functions as the State Capital and Local Government Headquarters including the seat of Gwandu Emirate. Owing to these functions it has now become of trade and commerce, serving the whole sub-region of the far North West Zone including the neighboring Niger and Benin Republics. As envisaged in the extant master plan (2005-2015), the local economy has attracted (Table 2 below depicts the picture of the informal service providers randomly surveyed), and is still attracting growth and development of the town induced by the change in its status.

The Growing Commerce and Trade

Most intensive economic activities are located indiscriminately. Wholesaling of manufactured products are carried out in built up areas along Ahmadu Bello way, Sultan Abubakar, Abdullahi Mayaki roads and other major roads inform of lock-up shops abutting roads. Few of these activities are also found; along Emir Haruna Road close to the old Motor Park (this constituted the first Central Business District). There is however, inadequate truck parking space which is evidenced by the persistent on-street parking for loading and off-loading.

The new modern market, which is located along the Eastern by-pass, close to the motor park, is emerging as the nerve of intensive economic activities in the day time. It has a total area of about 5 hectares accommodating about 182 lock up stalls with extra space for additional shops and stalls. It is well linked to the major roads, connected to electricity and water mains with police out-post station, court, fire service and refuse bunkers strategically located. The market has central administration with formal hierarchical set up under the Ministry of Lands, Housing and Urban Development.

Birnin Kebbi like other Northern Nigerian cities has in addition to the central market, other smaller markets, otherwise called local or neighborhood' markets located at 'Yar Yara in old town, Badariya and shiyar Fada popularly known as 'Yar dole'. Each of these markets specializes in perishable food items, fresh food and some edible oil among others. The recent relocation to new market has, however, made some textiles and other manufactured items to relocate to these minimarkets and along streets to display their wares. Thus, this has seen the emergence of numerous shopping complexes-departmental or super markets and kiosks located along major streets in the town. In addition to the neighborhood markets, there is the specialized market for grains, timber and cattle (popularly called the 'kara' market) located across the eastern bypass opposite the new central market. Because of the intense business and other economic activities, therefore, the area encompassing the new market, Motor Park and cattle/timber market is fast emerging as a new central business district for the town.

It is obvious that services, as tradable, have the potential to play a leading role in the growth productivity- transformation nexus as confirmed by a study conducted by Bernard et'al. (2017), therefore submits that services play a vital role in economic transformation and job creation in poor countries, but the effects are different from those in agriculture or manufacturing. Services affect developing countries, directly in the form of significant shares in gross domestic product, trade and foreign exchange, but also indirectly through productivity growth and enabling linkages with other sectors. It is necessary for Nigeria to use trade in services to support economic transformation and enjoy notable examples of successful expansion of trade in services include the development of diversified financial services hubs in Kenya, health and business tourism in Mauritius, information and communication technology services in India, air transport in Ethiopia, and hydropower transmission services in Lesotho (Bernard et'al. 2017).

DEVELOPMENT POTENTIALS OF BIRNIN KEBBI

The siting of the state capital in Birnin Kebbi has greatly increased investment in roads, public services, agriculture and industry with wider sub-regional and even regional impact. These investments have thus cumulatively made Birnin Kebbi a potential centre for direct investment in industries, commerce and trade. It behooves the government to therefore, harness these external and internal investments for effective development of Birnin Kebbi and its sub-region. This is possible through Transformation by increased Federal and State financed institutions with high recurrent expenditure in education, health and administrative establishments including the creation of a large intensive industry with high industrial products for domestic and regional markets. This would provide revenue base as substitute to oil.

The Birnin Kebbi Airport

One of the single-largest investments is the newly constructed airport for Birnin Kebbi which is located at Ambursa (14 kilometres from Birnin Kebbi Town). The location of the state capital at the far northwest corner of the country requires that it should be properly served with fast and modern means of transport. One of the most important socio-economic gains witnessed from the airport is in the generation of employment, increase in income, investments particularly of the foot-loose industries, and subsequent physical expansion of Ambursa settlement. Although the state is abundantly blessed with raw materials, the inadequate and sometimes poor road network has hampered speedy industrial take-off of the state. With the construction of the airport, additional economic gain is also expected from boost in tourism. These activities surely create employment, contributing significantly to local and national economy.

Economic Transformation Potentials

Birnin Kebbi is sandwiched between two fertile fadama lands; Shella river fadama which is situated approximately 3km south east of the town and averages about 1.5km in width. The area extends continuously in an easterly direction before turning due south into the permanent water of the Shella river and Rima river fadama situated North West of the town, which runs southerly and finally empties into the river Niger. The Rima river valley consist of the largest fadama land in Kebbi state made up of 525,000 hectares out of which about 142,000 hectares remain after the flood as dry season pools of stagnant water. The two expanses of fadama lands (Rima and Shella) thus provide important area of high value agricultural soils for planting of floating rice as well as other crops (such as onion, sorghum and millet) in the retreating flood waters. The mass rice production programme launched by the Federal Government gave birth to 'LAKE RICE' an acronym meaning Lagos Kebbi joint venture project for mass production of home grown rice in the country. Establishments of Labana Rice Mills and allied industries in Bulasa has increased employment opportunities to the youths and increased the local production of rice, onions and other crops within the State capital. International Onion Market at Aleiro, cattle markets at Ambursa, Makera and Bunza, coupled with grain markets in Bena, Dadin Kowa and Bunza. Potentials The impact of this project is visibly seen in the local market where the home grown rice is sold in large quantity; number of people that are engaged in both rain fed and dry season rice production has increased tremendouslyas well as establishment of more rice mills in the town.

Industrial Growth Programs

In pursuance of the state's policy of industrialization, directed towards accelerated industrial development and transformation to boost revenue base for the State, various programmes were designed and pursued. Among the programs includes the following;

1. Community seed development program
2. National accelerated industrial crops production program (NAICPP)
3. African Development Support Programs
4. Meat Processing and Preservation Projects
5. Gum Arabic Processing Programs
6. Leather Products Processing Projects
7. Onion and Tomato dehydration and Preservation Projects
8. Cotton ginning and textiles Projects
9. Sheanut butter processing projects
10. Industrial products processing project

Minerals Industrial Potentials

In addition to the projects and programmes listed above, the State is blessed with the following identified mineral deposits in commercial quantities ready for extraction and processing under the guidance and supervision of the relevant agencies in the State.

1. Industrial Clay (Kaolin)
2. Gold
3. Salt
4. Gypsum
5. Limestone
6. Granite
7. Glass sand and
8. Graphite

The projects and programmes mentioned above have corresponding projects and industry provision made. Some of which are in existence and operating either at Bulasa industrial estate, Jega, Yauri and Aliero.

Institutions for Industrial Manpower Development

A number of higher educational institutions have been established to produce manpower for the industrial development of the capital city and the state. Among these are the Federal University, Kebbi State University, Federal Polytechnic, College of Basic And Advanced Studies, Adamu Augie College of Education, and the National Teachers Institute Study Centre. Among these, perhaps the most important is the Federal University, the location of which falls within the planning area of Birnin Kebbi has impact on physical growth and development of the town. Host communities to universities have experienced rapid physical development as no University in Nigeria currently has the capacity to accommodate the surge in students and staff population. This therefore is a good omen for the expansion of the physical extent of Birnin Kebbi town. This provides opportunity for research, innovation, fabrications and complements the existing polytechnic and incubation centre at Bulasa. The take-off site of the university has pulling-effect on other facilities such as the new Hospital, Housing development and private nursery and primary schools.

Bulasa Industrial Area

This is the major manufacturing industrial landuse established in the capital, and is situated at Goru, along Birnin Kebbi- Kalgo road to the east. The Industrial area was established in 1993 and was designed to accommodate three types of industries viz heavy, medium and light. The site is 1000m^2 dedicated for industrial development in the town. The effect of the industrial area on urban growth and development instrument is identified by agglomeration and emergence of associated landuses around the Bulasa industrial estate. This goes to concord with the assertion that, many cities in the world today owe their landuse growth to the rapid development of industrial areas.

Therefore, the government should desire to encourage the establishment of more industries in Bulasa in order to use it as litmus for transformation from oil to cities using industrialization as the platform. The layout is designed to accommodate 84 factories of different sizes from small, medium and high with provision for ancillary services that complements industrial development. As of October 2018, 17 factories are in various stages of development, and three operating. However, the estate is inadequately serviced with infrastructure and utilities.

The challenge here is for government to incentivized industrialization so that the vast areas allocated to industries are utilized optimally. Consequently, these measures would translate into convergence of residential, economic and social activities around the estate. Presently, the few villages like Sabaran Kwara, Kwamawa, Unguwan Dembo and Mairago are found within the estate that may call for resettlement in due course.

An assessment of the industrial areas revealed an appalling situation. There is poor accessibility, inadequate power and water supply and no landscape put in place to make the environment conducive for work. There is no any recreational facility within the estate or nearby. The tax holiday and free land promised to industrialists by the present State government is a welcome development. The present effort put in by the state government in internally revenue generation derive requires serious commitment on industrialization which has multiplier effect on the people, city region and national economy at large.

THE CASE OF ICT TRANSFORMATION IN BIRNIN KEBBI

The concept of a digital economy is essentially a new economy stream that brings with it a new momentum. As ICT technologies develop rapidly and become integrated into more verticals, the digital economy is becoming the fastest growing, most innovative and widest-reaching economy. Nigeria's drive to transforming the ICT sector forecasts that optimizing the use of digital skills and technologies would generate $2tn of additional global economic output by 2020. It is established that the vast role digital technologies play in economic activity, with more than one-fifth of the world's GDP attributable to digital skills, capital, goods, and services (Frank Li, 2018).

As conceived in the ICT master plan tagged, 'SMART Digital Nigeria' it has been proposed as the required panacea to bridge the uneven growth presently dominating the ICT sector. The plan observed that Nigeria's longstanding focus mostly over the last seventeen years on Information Technology infrastructure development and also other areas in the industry, including the promotion of ICT local content, ICT deployment in Government and expansion of ICT access to Nigerians(The ICT, Nigeria, 2018).The Nigerian Entrepreneurs and start-ups demonstrated their business acumen, talents, creativity and all it takes to make the kind of difference that can be done in the ICT sector

Birnin Kebbi as state capital has provided increasing opportunities to people from different walks of life within and outside the Country. Birnin Kebbi Urban Area is the largest city in Kebbi State and therefore most urbanized. As indicated in **Table 2** below, the streets studied revealed a significant figure of 1,762 as employed by the sampled informal ICT service providers in the city. It is also important to note that the informal sector is more pragmatic and not only the domain of the urban poor. Many middle-class people in urban areas (and indeed in developing countries) greatly benefit from economic activities carried out outside the formal sectors. The manner in which ICT Informal Service Providers move about indiscriminately selling recharge cards along the streets in Birnin Kebbi Town covered major streets across length and breadth of the town.

From Table 2 above, it is obvious that informal service providers in Birnin Kebbi are scattered along the streets, of various types with varying sizes of employees, and space requirements. The figure of 1257 self employed people is significant number when consideration is made of the negative effect of unemployment in Nigeria. This is confirmed by Emmanuella (2011).

However, Nigerian government is seen as not doing much to help informal traders to help themselves. It is necessary, to find a practicable planning solution to this problem, so that the ICT trade can continue to fulfill the economic needs of the population by transforming the sector to more revenue generating and employment capacity-widening platforms. With ICT at the heart of national development, Nigeria can enhance the wellbeing of the people by forging closer cooperation with the African countries of Niger and Benin using the enhance ICT infrastructure and institutions in Kebbi State.

DIRECTION FOR FUTURE RESEARCH

Successive governments of Nigeria have hardly tapped the huge potentials of industry in employment generation, wealth creation, economic growth and physical growth and development of the cities. In practice, government officials generally drum up the campaigns to diversify the country's economy though industrialization when the overall national and global economy were in jeopardy or following a fall in oil prices resulting in reduced government revenue. Naturally, such campaigns were usually abandoned once the economic fortunes of the country improve.

Nigeria will greatly benefit from further research that focuses on the following:

1. Define the impact of industrialization on employment, urbanization and revenue generation.
2. Define the structure of industrial employment or industrial structure of Nigerian cities, focusing on the opportunities and challenges.
3. Define the role of industrial areas on urbanization, urban growth and development of the industrial cities throughout Nigeria.
4. Define the actual spatial distribution of industries and the potential growth opportunities that maximizes the talents and youthful nature of Nigeria's human capital in the next five decades.

Table 2. Random population of ICTs along major streets in Birnin Kebbi Town

S/N	Location (Along Major Streets)	Registered Premises	Stationed Vendor (umbrella stand)	Street Hawkers*	Total
1	Ahmadu Bello Way	24	12	16	52
2	Emir Haruna Road	7	12	8	27
3	Murtala Mohammed Way	7	3	7	17
4	Adamu Aleiro Road	8	2	4	14
5	Sani Umar Kalgo Road	3	1	3	7
6	Haliru Abdu Road	8	5	5	18
7	Muhd Bandi Road (k/ sabuwa-yayyara)	4	7	4	15
8	Badariya Road up to Mopol Barra	24	18	8	50
10	Jega Road by Stadium	3	5	6	14
11	Liman Zangina Road	17	13	10	40
12	Barrack Road	4	7	6	17
13	Haliru Abdu Area	2	6	5	13
14	CID–Uban Doma Abdullahi Rd	2	3	6	11
16	Sultan Bello Road	5	3	5	13
17	Rafin Atiku Road (by Gesse Hotel)	5	5	16	26
18	Id Praying Ground Rd	5	4	3	12
20	GRA-Jos Road/club Road	3	2	5	10
21	Illela Yari Road (along Nagari College)	3	5	6	14
22	Mai'ahu Road (Kofa Sabuwa to old prison)	3	5	12	20
23	Makera Road (along Dukku Hill)	2	4	8	14
25	School of Nursing to GRA	-	-	4	4
26	Kofar Kola –T/Wada Rd	3	2	5	10
27	Go slow Road	3	2	5	10
28	Argungu-Birnin Kebbi Road	3	11	18	32
29	Sani Abacha Bye pass	5	7	25	37
30	Patrick Aziza Rd (behind poly)	1	2	3	6
	TOTAL	154	146	203	----

Source: Bena, (2015)

CONCLUSION

In view of the potentials possessed by Nigeria to diversify the economy utilizing urbanization and industrial impetus coupled with the reviewed policies, the following conclusions are made. The Kebbi state government is conscious of the importance of industries as engine of growth and development hence the provision of one kilometer square of land for industrial development at Bulasa. Birnin Kebbi is fast growing urban area in terms of population growth and physical expansion. This calls for the need to review the extant master plan of the town especially to address the import of developmental transformation suggested above. Emphasis should be on agribusiness using the 'Anchor Borrower's approach, and empowerment of small scale businesses through the Cash Loans to SME productive businesses, N-Power program and industrial development. An enabling environment should be created for attracting and retaining skilled manpower with operational experience to foster growth in industry and internal revenue generation derives should be intensified. Kebbi State should use its industrial collaboration with Lagos to enhance industrial transformative initiatives that should widen and deepen the range of industrial activities seeking to lift high percentage of people out of poverty, and increase the size of middle class. Through this, the government can raise move revenue to ensure sustained provision of social, political, and economic facilities for the well-being of its citizens.

REFERENCES

Adediran, A. (2017). *Dialectics of Urban Planning in Nigeria. Paper delivered at the 5th Urban Dialogue of the Department of Urban and Regional Planning, University of Lagos.*

Adeniyi, E. O. (1982). *Administrative Framework for Physical Planning in Nigeria in Sada and Oguntoyibo. In Urbanization Processes and Problems in Nigeria.* New York: McGraw Hills Publishers.

Ajayi, D. D. (2011). *Nigeria's industrial development: issues and challenges in the new millennium.* Retrieved from https://www.witpress.com/Secure/elibrary/papers/SDP11/SDP11059FU1.pdf

Bena, A. R. (2015). *Planning for the Informal Service Providers in Nigerian Cities: Case Study of Birnin Kebbi Urban Area, Kebbi State.* Paper Presented at 4th National Conference of the Academic Staff Union of Polytechnics, Birnin Kebbi.

Bernard, H., & Dirk, W. V. (Eds.). (2017). *Trade in Services and economic transformation- A new development policy priority.* Essay Series Supporting Economic Transformation (SET). Accessed at http://set.odi.org

CES-Development Consortium. (2004). *Review of Birnin Kebbi Master Plan (2005-2015).* Waziri Umaru Federal Polytechnic.

Chete, L. N. (2016). *Industrial development and growth in Nigeria: Lessons and challenges* (Learning to Complete, working paper No. 8). Retrieved from www.brookings.edu/wp-content/uploads/2016/./L2C-wp8-Chete-et-al-1-pdf Retrieved 22/9/2018

Chete, L. N., Adeoti, J. O., Adeyinka, F. M., & Ogundele, O. (2014a). *Industrial Policy in Nigeria: Opportunities and Challenges in a Resource-rich Country*. Doi:10.1093/acprof:oso/9780198776987.003.0006

Chete, L. N., Adeoti, J. O., Adeyinka, F. M., & Ogundele, O. (2014b). *Industrial Development and Growth in Nigeria: Lessons and Challenges*. WIDER Working Paper 2014/019. Helsinki: UNU-WIDER.

Federal Republic of Nigeria. (2005). National Urban Development Policy (2005). Federal Government Press.

Federal Republic of Nigeria. (2012). World Bank Report.

Harry, D. M. (2016). Export Processing Zones and Economic Diversification in Nigeria, 2001 – 2013. *Journal of Political Science and Leadership Research, 2*(2). Retrieved from www.iiardpub.org

Kebbi State Government. (2006). *Kebbi State Economic Empowerment and Development Strategy-KB-SEEDS*. Kebbi State Government Printing Press.

Kebbi State Government. (2014). *Transformation the Journey so far. Kebbi State Ministry of Information, Youth, Sports & Culture.*

Li, F. (2018). Retrieved from https://punchng.com/exploring-the-impacts-of-digital-transformation-on-nigerian-economyRetrieved 27/7/2018

Mailafia, O. (2016). *Industrial Policy and the Path to Mass Industrialization in Nigeria*. Available from http://www.businessdayonline.com/industrial-policy-and-the-path-to-mass-industrialisation-in-nigeria/ https://papers.ssrn.com/sol3/papers.cfm?abstarct id=1266633 Retrieved 15/6/2018

Naija. (2018). Retrieved from https://www.naija.com/1107405-osinbajo-dangote-peterside-34-appointments-see-full-list-html

Naji, M., Robin, B., Yunusa, M-B., & Matthew, C. (2015). *Economic Development in Urban Nigeria Technical Report*. Retrieved from www.researchgate.net/profile/publication/economic-development-in-urban-Nigeria

Ogunbanjo. (2015). Spatial Variations in Residential Property Development. *Ethiopian Journal of Environmental Sciences & Management.* doi:10.4314/ejesm.v81210

The ICT. (n.d.). *Nigeria*. Retrieved from www.theintelligencer.com.ng/tag/nigeria

World Bank. (2016). *From Oil to Cities: Nigeria's Next Transformation. Directions in Development.* Retrieved from http://documents.worldbank.org/curated/en/711661468081l972/pdf/106150/PUB-ADD-DOI-ISBN-SERIES-OUO-9.pdf

KEY TERMS AND DEFINITIONS

Bulasa: Is a name of a place on the outskirts of Birnin Kebbi where industrial the area is located.

Export-Free Zones: These are designated areas for free trades where no tax is applicable for any export and import by manufacturing industries operating in that zone.

Growth: This is persistent increase in the economic production of a local economy.

Industries: These are units of production based in the Bulasa industrial area.

Policy: This refers to government decisions backed by an act of legislation.

Urban Centers: These are places of modernity with secondary social and infrastructural facilities.

Urbanization: This is the increase in number of people in a given town or city.

Chapter 17
Emerging Trends and Opportunities for Industry Development at the Sub-National Level in Russia

Leyla A. Gamidullaeva
https://orcid.org/0000-0003-3042-7550
Penza State University, Russia

Natalia S. Merkulova
Kursk State University, Russia

Ludmila I. Kryachkova
Financial University Under the Government of the Russian Federation – Kursk, Russia

Zoya A. Kondratieva
Financial University Under the Government of the Russian Federation – Kursk, Russia

Yulia A. Efimova
https://orcid.org/0000-0001-5226-257X
Financial University Under the Government of the Russian Federation – Kursk, Russia

Sergey V. Matukin
Penza State University, Russia

ABSTRACT

The authors believe that the transition to Industry 4.0 will have a strong impact on the level of urbanization in Russia. The level of urbanization is influenced by many factors, which include the level of economic development of the country, migration of the population, natural and climatic conditions. The highest level of urbanization is typical for industrialized regions. This suggests that it is necessary to develop industry and move to Industry 4.0. The purpose of this chapter is to show the relationship between urbanization and Industry 4.0, as well as to increase the level of knowledge about digital production, the internet of things, the Industry 4.0, and urbanization. The chapter explains the role of Industry 4.0 in the current changing environment. The chapter deals with the most important problems and opportunities of the fourth industrial revolution.

DOI: 10.4018/978-1-5225-7625-9.ch017

INTRODUCTION

In this chapter the authors search for trends, which occur in the traditional sectors of the economy as a result of digitalization, and above all in the labor market, industry and agriculture, financial services and education. Modern information and communication technologies substantially change all social relations, in connection with the notes that now it's the formation of a new, information society, which is called the "digital economy". Despite the somewhat similar properties with traditional economic relations, it differs in some respects from them, which makes its relevance from the point of view of the interest of the scientific community. One of the key areas of the state development is economic. We should understand the "digital economy" as a lever of economic structure and the environment in general. Horizons are expanding, a window of opportunity is opening by the younger generation, which can realize their ambitions and knowledge, creating favorable secure social environment for our future.

BACKGROUND

Contributions to the development of the digital economy have been made by foreign researchers such as Stephen M. Mutula (2010), Ari-Veikko Anttiroiko (2008), Georgios Doukidis, Nikolaos Mylonopoulos, Nancy Pouloudi (2003), Ionica Oncioiu (2013), Elena Druicã (2017).

The use of digital economy in industries has been reflected in the science. In the world of scientific literature, this area of knowledge is presented with such authors as: Nikolaos Mylonopoulos (2003), Bob Ritchie, Clare Brindley, Pedro Isaias (2017), Di Francesco Virgilio (2017), Ionica Oncioiu (2017), Elena Druicã (2017).

However despite the large number of works devoted to digital economy, the specifics of applying it in different industries haven't been given due attention. Innovation and the impact of the digital economy on society provided the theoretical and practical approaches for its development, increasing the awareness of understanding the term "digital economy" and what advantages there are to ensure the information technologies and innovations as basic resources. The publication of Elena Druicã (2017) focuses on rethinking of classical economic theory in the context of new technologies, information and innovation that makes her publication the best research for economists and social researchers, academicians, professionals and practitioners. In the opinion of Ionica Oncioiu (2017) digital technologies support an important tool in the modern economy business. As the economy continues to change, companies are looking for solutions for the expansion and development of its organization.

In the information economy, handling and the exchange of information and knowledge are the basis of its activities. The U.S. economy, works well, because it was due to the revolutions in the field of information technology (IT), which influenced the growth, employment, inflation, and labor productivity. Fundamental factors, driving growth in these new economies include technological innovations, e-commerce and digital conversion, higher education and skills in the IT field, open trade and a balanced budget. According to Pedro Isaias, digital economy is the main driving force of change, innovation and competitiveness for different companies and entrepreneurs. Study of the development of these initiatives can be used as a basic tool for future business success (Isaias, 2017).

According to Di Francesco (2017) in the digital age, numerous technological tools are available to improve business processes. In case of effectively using, knowledge sharing and organizational success increase significantly. According to analysts of Microsoft, a key role in the further development of the world IT industry must be played by a mass adoption of the so-called "The technology platforms" - sets of compatible technologies, products and channels of distribution, as well as the ecosystems of their distribution and usage. The main elements of the new technology platforms are now considered: cloud computing, mobility, Internet of Things technology, big data analytics, business intelligence, and machine learning. Thanks to the cumulative effects of these advanced platform technologies there has been a gradual "transformation of products into services" and the expansion of the chains of value creation, delivery of goods and services, as well as the extension of the supply chains of human capital."(The term used by the chief economist of Microsoft Preston McAfee, 2017).

The world is constantly changing, and recently one can hear about the growing role of advanced technologies and innovations in the development of the economy. New technologies allow increasing the efficiency of production and business processes. Traditional approaches and methods of work are changing as the penetration of advanced technologies in all new industries and spheres of human activity.

The influence of digital technologies is at both the global and the local level. On the one hand, the digital economy as a collection of new industries is the fastest growing part of the world economy in the traditional sense. Recent years the development of new technologies has led to the emergence of huge markets for cellular communication, Internet services, online gaming industry and others. On the other hand, new technologies have transforming impact on some aspects of the work of the established economic entities that basically is replacing the analog working mechanisms - whether it is the means of communication or industrial machines - to digital or semidigital elements, as well as the further modernization - for example, the already existing.

The growth of the digital economy follows the growth a number of markets, directly related with digital and mobile technologies. The digital economy during at least 10-15 years will be heavily dependent on traditional one. At the current stage of technology development and the current status of the markets for digital economy should not be seen as a goal, but as a means to improve the efficiency of economic activity. In the age of computerization and high technology digital economy affects every aspect of life: health, education, Internet banking and government *(Vasin and Gamidullaeva, 2018).* Digital Economy has received stimulus in all developed countries including Russia. On the basis of foreign policy developments and global trends, Russia is solving the problem of global competitiveness and national security, and a digital economy development in the country plays a great role in this issue. Some elements of the digital economy have been already successfully operated. For today the process of making digital documents and data, the resolution of the electronic signature, the communication with the state also goes on the electronic platform.

MAIN FOCUS OF THE CHAPTER

Issues, Controversies, Problems

In 2018 there are several trends in the digital economy development in Russia:

Cyber Security

The issue of cybersecurity goes to a new level in the context of the growth of IoT and robotics, as well as the increasing cyber attacks. The budget for cybersecurity by 2017 has been raised to $19 billion, and worldwide amounted to more than $80 billion. The proportion of Russian costs is more than 55 billion rubles. According to Gartner, the world market turnover of cybersecurity by 2018 will be close to $100 billion. They discuss the possibility of banks in Russian system in coding and encryption. At the conference in Munich the Head of Communications of the Russian Federation Nikolay Nikiforov proposed to develop a common regulatory framework and international standards for advanced technologies. Russian companies, leading the activities on the international market, since May of this year must comply with the updated rules for the processing of personal data according to the rules of the GDPR.

Cross-Border Cooperation

Russian companies are actively integrated in international alliances that define the technological standards in the years ahead. In May 2017, the head of the company "Russian export" Igor Chaika signed an agreement of cooperation with Alibaba, under which the Chinese trading platform will open the Russian national pavilion for the implementation of food products and household chemicals. The prospect of such undertakings is obvious. Thus in 2017 by the initiative of the Russian export center the playground "Made in Russia" (sector B2B) began to work. Requests for products from the catalog come from different parts of the world: Africa, Asia and South America. As a result long-term international partnerships with participation of Russian manufacturers develop.

The Establishment of Common IT Platforms

This allows you to synchronize the digital solutions that stimulate the emergence of associations that are interested in the qualitatively different technology solutions. So in the summer of 2017 "Sberbank" and "Yandex" agreed on the establishment of a joint platform of electronic commerce based on aggregator of goods and services "Yandex.Market". The total cost of the updated project is estimated up to 60 billion rubles *(Gamidullaeva, et al., 2019).*

Another striking example is association of the Russian "Uber" and "Yandex.Taxi" into a single site online taxi, the deal will have been closed in 2019.

The Digitalization of Public Services

Setting a course for the digitalization, the state motivates the company to develop high-tech Resource and sets a plate of IT. Within the framework of the "digital economy" Russia plans to hold the internet in remote areas of the country, place the state docs in cloud storage facilities, to ensure that by 2025 it will provide 80% of the public services in electronic format. Also there is a plan for the establishment of 50 smart cities, the launch of the 10 sectoral platforms in the figure and the transition 10 enterprises in the high-tech format. For comparison a Denmark digitalization program was adopted in 2001. Population and business interact with the State primarily through online services, due to which the country annually saves $136 million.

B2B-Marketplaces

They replace morally obsolete electronic platform where everything can be sold by everyone. Aggregators of goods and services are the trend of the past 10 years; retail consumers are already accustomed to use them. Businesses also need comfortable conditions for online purchases and variability of methods of payment for goods and services category. So on the site Yorso there is convenient search for large amounts of seafood. Agro24 is a modern online platform to buy food. Such services appear increasingly, they're different in convenience and variety of search parameters of products.

In Russia, nowadays most of the issues arising in the use of information and telecommunication technologies in various spheres of activity are resolved. However, the regulatory environment has a number of disadvantages, which stop the formation of the new institutions of the digital economy, development of information and telecommunication technologies and related economic activities. The huge number of citizens of the Russian Federation recognizes the need for the possession of the digital competencies, but the level of use of personal computers and the Internet in Russia is still lower than in Europe, and there is a serious gap in digital skills between separate groups of the population.

The doubtfulness of program (mentioned above) is proved with the following:

- The successful functioning of more than 10 companies (operators of ecosystems), competitive in global markets", while maintaining focus on the export of oil and gas seems very unlikely;
- The successful functioning of more than 500 small and medium-sized enterprises in the field of digital technologies and platforms and provide digital services" is not typical for Russia, when all of the innovations come from small and medium-sized businesses.
- The number of graduates of higher education in the areas of information and telecommunications technologies is 120 thousand people per year" looks unbelievable. Now days there are 5000 students in Information Security, and 36.1 thousand students in Informatics and computer engineering. That is to achieve the target of 120 thousand we need to increase graduates in three times.

There are some advantages. How, for example, it can be that the digitalization will help accelerate the optimization of the cost of sectors of the economy, minimizing the deficit of services. More than there was a reduction of the number of hospitals and doctors. And for encouraging the patients, telemedicine is proposed for consultation, when the doctor, starting with the second reception, can give advice to the patient via the Internet. Time, money, the cost of logistics is saved, but the number of physicians can be discharged. It leads to the growth of unemployment. Similar innovations will affect and educational sector.

Risks and Problems

The following are just a few:.

- The threat of "digital sovereignty" of the country and the redefinition of the role of the State in a transboundary world of "Digital" Economy;
- Violation of privacy / potential surveillance of citizens;
- Reducing the level of data security;
- Reducing the number of employment of low and medium professional skills;
- Increasing the level of complexity of business models and patterns of interaction;
- Change in the behavior of producers and consumers;
- Need in reviewing the administrative and tax codes.

In such socio-economic conditions the development of different spheres must be implemented with the use of information and telecommunication technologies of a qualitatively new level that allows use data in digital form as a key factor of production; the information technology industry should provide the necessary platform and services. Undoubtedly the plan of development (spoken earlier) is very faithful. Indeed there are problems in industry such as: staff shortage, "brain drain", the lack of a unified environment, in which the technological leaders would unite the efforts to establish new platforms and etc. All this points are important tasks throughout the state.

Qualitatively and quantitatively opportunities to do through a computer almost everything will increase; for example, receiving a variety of services. It is cheaper and more efficient within adequate measures of protection. The digital economy is both advantage (compared with classical way), and the threat to society, because in many respects we should deal with data security. Therefore you need to plan at the same time, substantial costs, for example, to ensure the safety of money on accounts of people, their personal data. The central bank, for example, could create a special institute which would ensure the safety of financial information of physical and juridical persons. Within the framework of the Eastern Economic Forum (September 13, 2018) Experts called the problem of Russian digital economy and this is lack of normative-legal base.

THE INFLUENCE OF DIGITAL ECONOMY ON THE LABOR MARKET

The development of the digital economy has an impact on the labor market: changing the structure of employment, new requirements for professional competence and the growing demand for IT professionals in the field of information and communication technologies (ICT). At the same time, people working in all sectors of the economy, must have a digital literacy and digital information skills, using modern telecommunication and software products.

The digital skills – they're the competence of the population in the use of personal computers, the Internet and other ICT, as well as the intention of the people to acquire relevant knowledge and experience.

Depending on the purpose of the use of ICT there are two categories of persons with digital skills:

- **A Professional:** Professional skills are necessary for the development, operation and maintenance of the information and communication systems (preparation of specification, design, development, installation, operation, support, maintenance, management, evaluation, research and development in the field of ICT).
- **A User:** The skills are necessary for the effective use of ICT skills for work, study or personal purposes.

In 2015, the number of software developers and applications, databases and networks, specialists on ICT and ICT users, support of telecommunications and broadcasting - is estimated to be 1.2 million (approximately 2%). Specialists in information and communication technologies are relatively young: 38% below the age of 30, one third - 30-39 years. The total number of staff in these age groups is 22 and 27%. A quarter of IT professionals (23%) are working in the IT industry, 10% in the communications sector, about 20% in the financial sector, trade and public administration (6-7% of the total population are ICT specialists in communication technologies).

Information and communication technologies have become a part of our lives: four fifths of the population of the world (81%) aged 15 to 72 years has used a personal computer, the same situation concerns with the Internet. The quantity of daily network users comes closer to 60%. According to The Boston Consulting Group (BCG), the share of the digital economy (also called web or internet transition) to the GDP of developed countries has grown since 2010 up to 1 point and is now 5.5%. In developing countries this figure increased from 3.6% to 4.9% of GDP.

The UK is a world leader in the proportion of the digital economy in GDP. Sector which includes the IT and telecom, online trading, government spending associated with the internet, takes the second place in the economy of the country in the wake of the real estate and telecommunications manufacturing and trade.

Dissemination of digital technologies in everyday life alters the path of access to services, information and knowledge. Rapid technological changes should make maximum use of the new opportunities offered by information and communication technologies, expanding the usage of digital technology to increase the demand for new skills. At the same time the key of effective implementation is the basic skills in the use of information and communication technologies that allow a person to deal with digital activities and adapt quickly to the new and precarious work.

Over the next 30 years the technology will overcome the biological limitation of human potential. The available devices that are connected through the Internet, will be able to transfer context sensitive information, which is directly related to our emotions. Exoskeleton and prosthetics in combination with the brain can make rights stronger and return mobility of older persons and persons with disabilities. The sensors and computers, embedded in contact lenses and the permanent implants will allow you to

Figure 1.

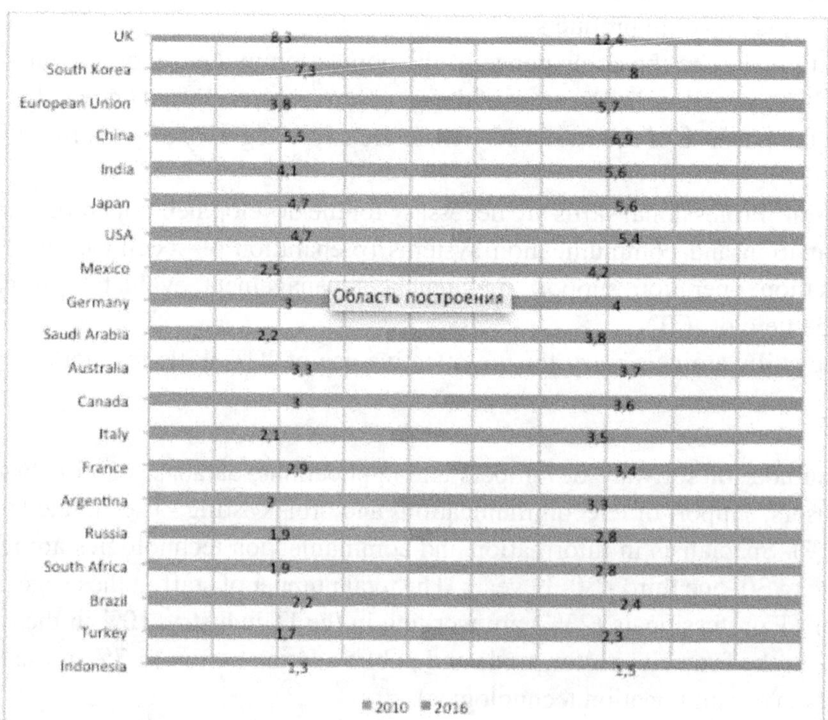

hear the whisper from the distance, give a natural night vision and allow you to immerse yourself in a virtual and supplemented by reality. Neurometabolic drugs increase the cognitive ability of the people and transform work and education.

In addition there is the evident global trend to robotizaion. Robots will be entrusted with the care of patients, procurement of supplies, the harvest, the maintenance of the company's infrastructure and providing many other services. Bots headed by the terabytes of data will be responsible for the automation of the business processes, training and the provision of services - functions and roles have traditionally been inherent in man. However, the expanding technologies are quite expensive, and those who cannot afford such upgrades, will not be able to compete in the augmented economy. Network accessories will also become an attractive target for hackers who want to control the mind and body. Robotics may lead to an increase in unemployment.

The population survey on the use of information technologies and telecommunications networks, conducted by the National Statistical Service, showed that the most common computer skills are related to the text editor (Used 42% of the respondents), transfer files between computer and peripheral devices (29%), work with tables (23%). The proportion of "advanced" users who can change the configuration of the software, is not more than 3%, the same data applies to people who have the possibility to install or reinstall your operating system. The task to write software, using the power of programming languages, is normal for only 1% of the population in this age group.

The skills to use the software for editing photos, video and audio (21% of the population), show that Russia is almost at the same level as Ireland (23%), Czech Republic (21%), Cyprus (20%). In Luxembourg, Denmark, Finland and the United Kingdom, these computer operations can perform every second. At the level of the development of the digital literacy it is possible to estimate data on the total population using the network for various purposes that require a certain skill level when you work with content, the search engines and software products.

The fact that the vast majority of Internet users has the ability to communicate over the network, demonstrates the importance of social networks (76% of the population aged 15-72 years via the Internet in the past three months). More than two fifths of the three-month Internet population (42-44%) use the network to find information about products and services, and phone calls and video, electronic letters. Nearly one-third has personal experience of the upload files to the web-sites, social networking, cloud storage for general access.

The main reason for the failure occurs from the use of the Internet, is the lack of skills. In 2017 it was registered every fourth respondent (from those who have not enjoyed the network). In comparison with the 2015 this figure had increased by 3 percentage points (from 22% to 25%).

The technology is transforming the relationship between people and their work. Freelance market increases, with access to the internet resources and tools work together. Companies are making rapid innovation technologies such as 3D-printing and application programming interface (API). In the coming years, these trends will change the structure and principles of work as a whole. For some participants, businesses reduce the barriers will bring new opportunities. On the other hand, competition in the "free earnings" will mean lower wages, lack of benefits and economic uncertainty.

THE DIGITAL TRANSFORMATION OF AGRICULTURE

Innovative development of agriculture in the world economy has now reached a high level and sustainable growth. While there are hidden reserves, the use of which will give a new impetus to its development in the third millennium. One of them is the digital economy.

Currently each country in transition to a digital economy, depending on the level of economic development, the level of education, the readiness of the normative-legal base, technology development of state and application of information systems, focuses on the strategy of digital transformation to achieve a positive effect. Digital Economy in agriculture will be able to ensure the sustainability of agricultural development, the development of the agrarian science, agricultural education, compliance with environmental regulations.

Digital Economy in agriculture will allow the development of a model agricultural growth in developing countries, oriented at both the domestic and external markets. This will ensure the growth of the main product groups, aimed at both the export demand and for domestic consumption. Sustainable development is an organization of agricultural production, in which the new generation would have access to the resources and could lead agriculture in scale, ensuring the needs of the population for food.

To avoid global problems in the field of food and bio-safety humanity needs a new kind of agriculture, which corresponds to the model of circular economy (without the waste) and the principles of sustainable development. The heads of international organizations and national governments are increasingly devote themselves to the transition to a new economic model and "smart" agriculture as an integral part of it.

"Smart" agriculture is based on the use of automated decision-making systems of complex automation and industrial robotics, as well as the technologies of designing and modeling of ecosystems. It includes minimizing the use of external sources (fuel, fertilizers and agrochemicals) with the maximum use of local factors of production (renewable energy, biofuels, organic fertilizers, etc.).

Advanced Intelligent technology agriculture provides effective protection from pests, restoration and protection of beneficial properties of soils and groundwater and remote end-to-end monitoring compliance with the requirements of certification of organic agriculture. These technologies include the use of biopesticides to integrated pest management, Nano biotechnologically clean water and soil, integrated farm management, etc.

The Innovative Development of the agricultural sector, in turn, requires the use of information and communication technologies. They can ensure effective communication, interaction in the online mode. In the conditions of the network economy technological platform should become one of the major elements of digital ecosystems. For agrarian digital ecosystems it can become of main idea a technology platform of the food and processing industry, and complementary: space and geo-informational technology - products of global competitiveness.

The development of information systems and computerization of the opens up new opportunities for agriculture by improving the quality of work and improve performance. The important role played by the enterprise, producing agricultural machinery and equipment. At the same time this development in the field of software processes control spraying and tillage, fertilizer for the crops.

Recently the market of consulting services in the agrarian sector is gaining popularity all over the world. The reasons for this were: increased interest in the implementation of information technologies and the need for practical experience in this area. Farmers need advice because they do not pay sufficient attention to the tracking of recent advances in technological progress, since for them, the quantity and quality of manufactured goods much more important. Consulting is focused on business activities, focused on projects, which allows you to pursue an independent assessment of the effectiveness of new information technologies. In this case the consultant, who regularly visits the farm, and makes recommendations to improve production and introduction of innovative technologies, comes to the rescue. This support helps farmers to spend money not only on the purchase of traditional, but new information technologies. In addition, advisory, management and organizational centers are made to help agriculture through their financial and investment projects. World-wide network of new technologies is the basis for the creation of uniform information space, but new technologies are rapidly developing and implemented with high-tech developments.

In addition, there is a need for economic and legal basis for the definition of the rights and responsibilities of individuals when creating information resources and the objective of stimulating their regulators.

An example of the development of the digital economy in agriculture is a factory "Kuban". It within the program "Electronic agriculture" the integrated program implemented a powerful plant subsystem by the creative team from various industry crop NRU and cybernetics RESEARCH INSTITUTE OF AGRICULTURE on a single methodological basis has been implemented integration of knowledge of different ICS organization (offline). The requirement of integration of information, its modes of processing, as well as the requirement of functional completeness served as a basis for compiling the list of tasks and their classification (340 automation tasks), as well as to the structure of the logical database (151 type of records), common to all crop enterprises.

In modern conditions when implementing the model site for agricultural enterprises this logical structure of the database can become an integral part of all systems of precision farming, spatial monitoring of soil and other ICS from one position. This will allow realizing the standard solutions, almost for free for manufacturers of the goods. This logical structure and classification of these tasks of automation can become the basis for the standardization of the platform digital sector of agricultural crops. Such an approach for other industries, including animal husbandry, while placing certain databases in a particular cloud, for example, a powerful database system (DBMS), extends a digital platform in all sectors of agriculture. It is clear that these databases will be integrated with each other.

As shown in the domestic and international practice, with the introduction of a typical farm plot and mandatory reflection in the overall cloud statistical information, the system of statistical accounting must be substantially changed. The integration of a single information field of the agricultural knowledge with typical locations of agricultural organizations, agricultural research institutes and universities; the standard ICS and primary accounting system, implemented through Internet technology, are the basis of the digital platform, a logical structure which is ready for the future integration with various digital devices.

Digital Economy in agriculture will form a new structure of digital ecosystems of the agrarian sector. Together with the digital assets of the agricultural sector in the technology platforms there will be innovative projects. For the establishment and operation of digital the agrarian sector of the global economy of the twenty-first century requires coordinated actions of all participants, specialists, with new competencies, high financial costs, developed the IT structure, methodical and legal support.

FINANCIAL SERVICES AND E-COMMERCE

Electronic commerce is meaningful institute of digital economy, penetrates into a growing number of legal relations in the sphere of trade, and covers the entire spectrum of relations - direct interaction with consumers-to-consumers (C2C), the interaction of sellers-to-consumers (B2C), the interaction between businesses (B2B), the interaction of business and the state in digital form (B2G), etc.

The Internet commerce is one of the most dynamically developing technology markets in the world. The rapid growth of the market due to, first of all, fast enough the global spread of broadband (fixed and mobile) access to the Internet. In the e-commerce the segment "m-commerce" slows down the increase (in 2016 he grew to 63.8%), but is still developing more dynamic market as a whole. The market of electronic commerce "m-commerce" is presented in Figure 2.

With the development of the gadget industry the proportion of purchases that users commit by means of mobile devices gradually increases; thanks to this mobile commerce becomes a separate segment of e-commerce. According to eMarketer, sales in the segment of m-commerce in the world grew by 40.3% in 2017 up to 1 357 billion dollars, which is 6.0% of the total volume of retail sales. For comparison, in 2017 the total sales of retail e-commerce throughout the world reached 2 304 billion dollars, on the segment share of m-commerce accounted for 58.9% of online sales.

It is worth noting that the increase in the market of e-commerce (+24,8% in 2017) was markedly lower than that of sales through mobile devices. It is expected that the dynamics of growth of mobile sales will remain high, but will gradually slow down to 22.2% in 2021, when the sales volume in the segment will be at the level of 3 556 billion around the world.

"Globality" in internet is fully exposed to trading platforms in all countries. In 2017 cross-border trade is one of the main drivers for the growth of e-commerce around the world. Local giants go to foreign markets, steadily being transformed in the global players, looking for business opportunities in new regions. While the buyers are motivated with the opportunity to is guaranteed to obtain a high-quality product at the right price from anywhere in the world, internet retailers cross-border electronic commerce provides tremendous opportunities for the expansion of the market for their products and attracting new clients. The number of online purchases at foreign websites will increase from year to year. Consumers from different countries are looking at foreign sites goods unavailable in their region or price and quality which are more attractive.

Trade in the Internet is gradually becoming an integral part of the world economy. However, the development of a new direction in theaters is different pace. Asian region is situated in the absolute leaders in segment, almost twice as overtaking North America on drug Internet commerce (mainly at

Figure 2.

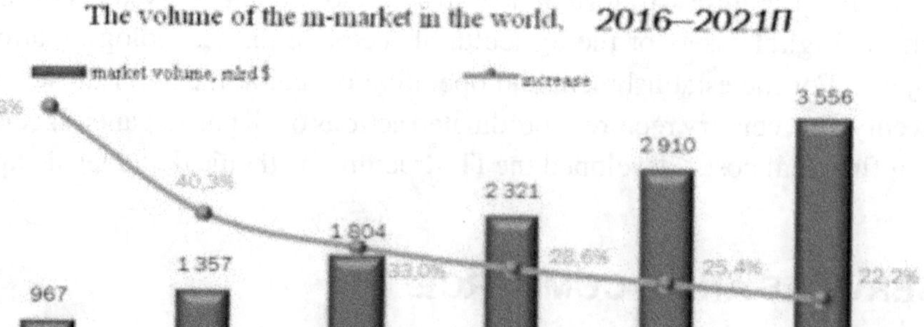

the expense of China). This trend is due to the strong economic growth in developing Asian countries and informatization.

However, the new market is less true and transparent in comparison with traditional retail due to the specifics of existing virtual technologies. But it is the global nature of the trade is at the same time as a powerful driver of growth and a key barrier to creating the necessary legal and financial instruments for legalization of the sector. In some cases, the emerging commodity-money relations is already becoming difficult to regulate the rules in force in the territory of one country (in particular, allowed to sell goods - for example, medicines, and ways of delivery), it becomes evident that the necessity of regulation of the internal and cross-border Internet-trade on the basis of uniform principles, regardless of jurisdiction, is needed.

However, the common practice for regulation at this point has not happened yet. While there was a clear trend related to the popularization of protectionist measures (except for the United States and several other countries where taken on the course of market self-regulation) in most developed and developing countries in the world in order to stimulate the national Internet retailers and manufacturers. The commodity structure of the e-commerce market includes a lot of various categories - from the spare parts for cars, hazard appliances to perfumes and art objects (practically all that is presented in a traditional retail).

The trend of e-commerce will be the mobile commerce. Now more and more users prefer to make purchases on their way in a convenient for them at the appropriate time. Retailers constantly improve applications for customers convenience and easy to execute orders through smartphones. According to the Statist, income from sales of mobile is growing steadily. In 2017 it amounted to $550 billion, an increase of 30% compared to 2016 year.

As expected, in 2018 this figure will increase by 20% and will reach $670 billion. Easy to pay for goods with smartphones (buying in one click), the use of new technologies (payment by fingerprint or payment authentication using selfie), as well as push notifications, showing greater efficiency compared to the e-mail broadcast, contribute to the growth of mobile transactions. So, the day of the Chinese sale of “Singles Day” (90% of sales was implemented with mobile phones, and in the United States in the popular network Starbucks coffee 10% of orders been decorated with smartphones.

The ability to directly buy goods on social platforms, a growing number of bots and services artificial intelligence, the popularity of instant messengers and IoT devices with voice operated control will promote the development of mobile commerce. Consumers prefer to use different devices when making a purchase - to search for goods and read reviews about it with smartphones, and execute the order with the desktop. It is important to monitor the sale, committed with different devices and make the transition from one to another smooth and integrated. The ability to identify the buyer allows companies to have recourse to it personally at the right time, bearing in mind the preferences and needs. The technology of the cross-tracking device can help you to explore user behavior and to understand its “path” to purchase, as well as to develop client-oriented marketing strategy at different devices.

Thus, each customer will be able to receive individual recommendations and will see the ads, based on his past purchases and preferences, geolocation and the trends of the market. According to the largest news portal Business Insider, by 2020 80% of the companies planning to introduce chat bots and other automated systems, in order to understand the intentions of users and to ensure a positive customer experience. Another trend of e-commerce is a social commerce. Recently “influencers” are gaining more popularity, capable to influence its target audience and unobtrusively to promote those or other goods and services.

According to the consulting and auditing firm PwC, for 50% of the respondents social networks are the main platform, enabling them to make purchases. According to a study conducted by the company, BrightLocal specializing in CEO, 85% of users' degree of confidence to online reviews as great as to personal recommendations from friends and acquaintances. Influencers generate traffic, drawing on the target page visitors. More than 40% of the companies represented online, have the significant increase in traffic from social media. One of the problems facing e-commerce is the use of blockers of advertising.

According to eMarketer, by the end of 2018, 30% of internet users will block your ads. Most ad blockers installed on the desktop and PC, but their application on mobile phones increases gradually. The USA and China will determine the trends in e-commerce. China is the undisputed leader, taking first place in the turnover and providing 40% of the world retail e-commerce. The country sets the global trends - the Chinese sale Bachelor's Day on the quantity of sales overtook the American Black Friday and Cyber Monday.

The USA, in turn, occupies a leading position in the field of technological innovation, American users have a wealth of experience of online shopping and have a high purchasing power. To understand how e-commerce will develop in the coming years, we draw our attention to these countries. The role of e-commerce in the development of the world economy, in turn, necessitates the task of the development of statistical indicators and appropriate methods of calculation and analysis.

Currently, we are witnessing rapid growth of financial services, at the same time as a stimulus for the intensive development of technological solutions for the industry. Under the Financial Technologies (hereinafter - The FinTech) we understand the application of innovative technologies in order to provide financial services. However, with a lot of technologies, used in the financial industry, boundaries of the term "branch of Financial Technologies" are blurred.

The main segments of the financial technologies at the moment are: payments and transfers, crowd-funding, asset management, the financial marketplace, the blockchain. In this regard, we see the growing trend to create a fully digital bank, which, in its activities focuses mainly on those who prefer using online banking services.

In the first half of 2017, the volume of investment around the world in this branch of economy has increased by 49% compared to the same period of the previous year and reached the level of 15 billion US dollars. Banks and large financial groups embarked on the path of technological development, the consequence of which the provision of their clients was more extensive with financial services. The consequence of the rapid development of financial technologies worldwide the number of fraudulent crimes in the area has been increasing. In this regard, the first place outside the security not only of the transaction, but also the identity management of users.

According to some estimates, currently there are many prerequisites for significant changes in the sphere of FinTech, the consequence of which we see its evolution and beyond the standard payments and credits. A new stage in the development of financial technologies is based on cloud computing technology, which gives much more opportunities for critical infrastructure changes, and the functioning of the financial sector of the economy. The widespread introduction of artificial intelligence in the area of financial technologies is having the place. Among them there are the chat bots for customer service, robotic players on the stock market, machine learning and big data for decision on the loan for the client.

THE TRANSFORMATION OF THE INDUSTRY INTO THE DIGITAL ECONOMY

The modern world business is now at an important stage of transformation - moving to the digital economy. At the same time, the steak holder queries are becoming more and more difficult, acquiring the complex and resource-intensive in nature. At the same time, political interests often have a very significant pressure, substantially limiting the ability of many entrepreneurs and corporations to fulfill the expectations of stakeholders and the realization of the principles of sustainable development at the microeconomic level. In these circumstances, the formation of new mechanisms for sustainable development of business organizations that meet the requirements of the digital economy becomes significantly important *(Gamidullaeva, et al., 2019)*. The main "end-to-end technology" for business organizations is represented at the Figure 3.

All of these processes are global in character, which is at the root of the transform approaches and mechanisms for sustainable development of business organizations. The world's largest producers of fossil fuels, oil and gas had limits, and it's required of new solutions to create highly integrated intelligent systems for generation and distribution of electric networks of the new generation Smart Grid.

Smart Grid has the following aspects of the functionality presented in Figure 4.

Smart Grid currently serves the concept of intellectual active adaptive network, which can be described with the following features:

- The saturation of the active network elements, allows you to modify the topological network parameters;
- A large number of sensors, which measure the current operating parameters for assessing the status of the network in different modes of operation of energy systems;
- The system of collection and processing of data (program-technical complexes), as well as check the active network elements and electrical installations of consumers;
- Availability of executive bodies and mechanisms in real time to change topology network parameters and the interaction with the neighboring energy objects;

Figure 3.

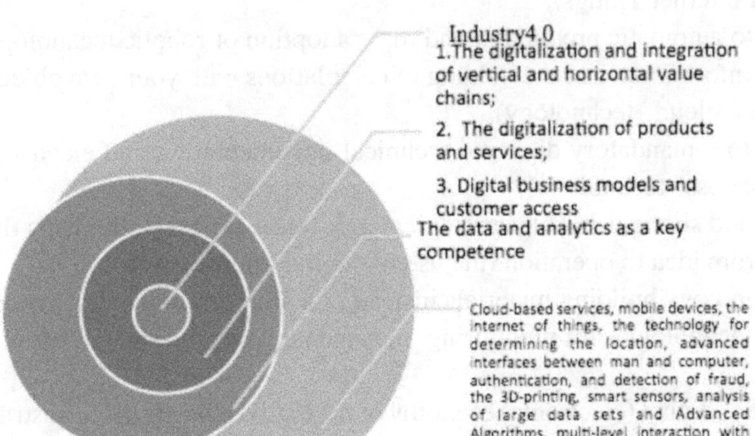

Figure 4.

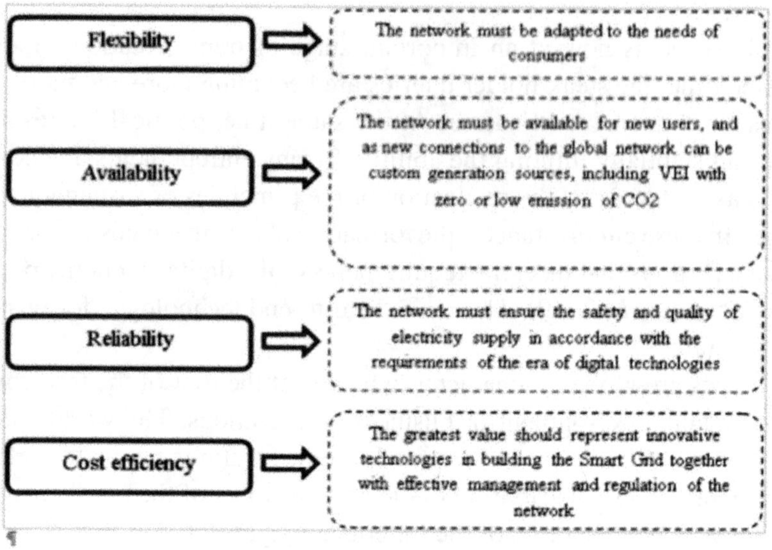

- Tools for automated assessment of the current situation and the forecast of buildings for work in the network.

It's a high-speed control system and information exchange. Based on the above-mentioned characteristics of the network, it may be defined as a file attached to the source for the creation and installation of software and hardware for consumers, as well as for the analysis of information and management systems to ensure reliable and high-quality power transmission from the source to the receiver at the right time and in sufficient quantity.

The major technological trends in the field of digital transformation of the industry are as follows:

- The mass introduction of intelligent (quantum) sensors in equipment and production lines technology (Industrial Internet Things);
- The transition to automatic production and mass adoption of robotic technologies;
- The storage of information and the holding of calculations with your own objects on the resources made available ("cloud" technology);
- The transition to a mandatory digitized technical documentation and electronic document management ("Paperless" technology);
- Digital design and simulation of technological processes, facilities, products throughout their entire life cycle from idea to operation (the use of engineering software);
- The use of technology building materials instead of a slice ("additive technology, 3d printing);
- Use of mobile technologies for monitoring, management of processes in life and at work.

The development of digital (electronic) economy of the load on the digital infrastructure, based on the communications and telecommunications, is greatly increasing. Users need access to various platforms, services and services in electronic form. The very notion of "user" is fundamentally changing, because in the digital transformation in this category there are not only people, but also representatives of the "Internet of Things" (connected devices), the number of which already exceeds the number of people in the times, and will soon exceed the already and by orders of magnitude. Thus, we are talking about loads on the communications and telecommunications and their bandwidth, surpassing the existing by several orders of magnitude.

Obviously, building communication systems and telecommunications, due to such requirements, through the traditional hardware realization of network functions will lead to the exorbitant costs and networks or obstruct their surplus equipment, which is a dead-end path. To solve the problem one can use a digital transformation of the communications systems and telecommunications, the transition to a software implementation of network functions.

"Digital Logistics" emerges as a response to the global challenges of the digital economy for the traditional sector of transport and logistics, such as the rapidly changing, globalized and super competitive trading environment, the complexity of supply chains, rapid changes in customer expectations, the limited resources of the infrastructure. So, the digital economy, in particular, electronic commerce increases the availability of information on the demand and supply. However, the conclusion of the electronic trade transactions and retail sales can be hindered the logistics problems of delivery of goods, works or services. The problem of logistics in e-commerce is associated primarily with a faster pace of formation and realization of supply chains of goods compared with traditional trade. This feature of e-commerce determines the need to improve the mechanisms for Predicting demand, which should contribute to a more rational planning of the stock of goods in warehouses in different geographic regions, reducing the time the movement of goods and cost of delivery. Within the framework of the development of e-commerce, it is necessary to develop and deploy the technologies analysis of data on demand for the planning of the distribution logistics.

Perspective directions of the development of the digital logistics are also linked with the development of the Internet of Things (use of automatic order supplies and raw materials for the production and automatic delivery of finished products to the consumer, bypassing the intermediaries) and unmanned technologies in transport systems.

Education in the Digital Economy

Technology is changing education. Schools and universities currently offer online courses; the teacher online offer new ways to study the training materials; schools regularly integrate tablet computers and other technology to the class. Education, science, research, culture and the media are key areas that implement new digital backup and serve as major factors contributing to the further development and digital technologies. This means that all citizens can take advantage of the huge opportunities in these areas for learning, development and participation in economic and social life *(Potapova, et al., 2019).*

The education system should better equip people skills and knowledge to meet the needs of the digital working environment and society of knowledge. It should also increase the level of literacy in the media. It's of great need to promote wider use of digital media in education throughout life. Together with all stakeholders in the field of education, they will strive to develop a strategy for digital learning, which systematically uses, expands and realizes the possibilities of digital media to provide high-quality education. However, the problem of social adaptation of the population to the challenges of the digital economy, associated with the constant improvement of skills and the development of new skills in the online space of digital ecosystems remain. In this regard, especially important active labor market policies, support income, continuous training and more flexible education system *(Tolstykh, et al., 2018).*

In the system of modern education it is necessary to introduce new technologies, as required by the needs of society, to teach today that will need tomorrow. Education should contribute to the development of society, the growth of its capabilities. It is necessary to shape the identity, fostering they thought, and who can realize their creativity in a broad sense of the word. Creativity is a process of searching, adoption and implementation of the complex, complicated problems. Creativity is a process (purposeful work) turning the impossible into the possible.

In spite of the digital transformation of the educational process, changes in forms and methods of training, competencies, the classic fundamental education remains important for the formation of the modern system of professional education. The educational trajectory of today changes under the influence of the external environment, under the influence of the digital environment, taking into account the requirements to the new professions, change the value orientations of people, predominantly focus on applied science and practice. The profession appears faster than they are being developed and formed educational programs. Therefore, the system of additional professional education has a key role to provide advanced training programs or professional retraining on the popular professions that will help you to be competitive in the modern information environment. Digital economy, based on digital technologies, suggests a new way of technological production, requiring new skills and new conditions of development.

To the modern specialist a number of major requirements are produced:

1. IT literacy. In modern society, the establishment of digital competences and the use of information and communication technologies in professional activity.
2. Language and mobility. The Specialist is able to learn different foreign languages, as it requires the professional suitability.
3. The desire to learn. Motivational component in the modern world expresses the ability and readiness for teaching and training has played a leading role in the development of the personality, including self-education. High motivation is generated when the person is in search for the satisfaction of their needs for creativity. In the development of the concept of "Industry 4.0" is formed by the society of continuous learning, able to learn throughout their lives.
4. Labor migration. A person is able to master the different professions and in the retraining throughout life.

Currently, the formation of the so-called digital society, in which the interaction between subjects of the economy decided by a number of production issues. This interaction is based on three components: information, knowledge, communication. A number of difficulties related to the transformation of the state mechanisms to the Cyberspace of socio-economic systems raises in the digital era in all sectors of the economy of the country. The Russian educational system at the stage of the formation of the digital society faces a number of problems, the main of which are:

1. The transfer of knowledge, the formation of skills and abilities to own is carried out using the digital and information technologies that is associated with the need to use all the opportunities of electronic, remote and interactive learning.
2. The world economic space defines the demand for new types of competencies.

Currently, education of the future is undergoing a digital transformation that goes beyond the time frame of life, beyond the educational institutions using the unique capabilities of network and digital technologies, with involvement in the educational process all direct and indirect participants. The role of the teacher in the age of digital economy is changing; there are new forms of interaction between the teacher and the students, the so-called network interaction.

Recently, in terms of digital public relations, the leading role in the pedagogical process belongs to the electronic educational technologies. One of the most popular pedagogical trends is the formation of massive open online courses (MOOCs)for systems level and additional education. Coordinating the governing body of the education in most states now approved by the order of application of educational organizations of e-learning and distance education programs. According to this document the organizations which are carrying out educational activities, have the right to implement educational programs or their parts with the use of e-learning, distance education technologies, organizing training sessions in the form of online courses, and students who mastered the educational programs in the form of online courses, provided the appropriate document, and gives the right to allow the learner to the intermediate appraisal in other educational organization.

One of the innovative projects in education is considered to be the MOOCs, which allow solving a number of problems facing the modern education. Open Educational Resources to help in the digital pedagogy to ensure the mass education (the number of registered on different courses comes to hundreds of thousands of people), the availability of each learning in any territorial in the world and the high quality of education, as these courses are the best Russian and foreign teachers. These modern digital technologies allow you to integrate Russia into the world educational environment and shape the lives of new professions for digital organizations. One of the priority directions in the trajectory of digital pedagogy is the formation of digital educational environment in which success will be implemented MOOCs. This promising form of distance education gives you the freedom to learning, gives you the opportunity to self-select their future profession, and improves the motivation of learners in the acquisition of skills to be competitive in the digital space. MOOC removes the spatio-temporal limitations in the study of the educational course or its parts are beyond the scope of one of the educational organization.

Nowadays the largest platform for MOOCs is operated by global electronic educational services; including Coursera platform, KHAN, edX Udacity, and others. This indicates that the information educational environment is available, and the training becomes a global process using the structure of the MOOCS – including lectures-Video, training exercises, homework, and references. During the period of the digital transformation the role of the university instructor- who must use all possible techniques, methods, tools of electronic and distance learning,- is vital to the innovative growththe business communities. The teachers are the authors of the online courses that enhance students creativity to enable them to manage the processes of sustainable socio-economic development in the context of digital transformation.

RESULTS

1. It's noted that the modern digital economy is the postindustrial, characteristics of postindustrial economy are presented.
2. The definition of digital economy is submitted, its essence is revealed, the main objectives and indicators of the digital economy evaluation and development are mentioned.
3. The education in the digital economy is examined.

4. The transformation of the industry in the digital economy is analyzed.
5. The financial services and e-commerce is considered.
6. A digital transformation of Agriculture is examined.
7. The influence of the digital economy on the labor market is considered.

FUTURE RESEARCH DIRECTIONS

To sum up our excursion into the "Digital" economy, we would like to stress once again that the total digitalization, automation and the introduction of appropriate technology is a natural process, and therefore inevitable. At the same time, today there is no picture of the future (neither the nearest, nor the distant), which means that the result of forthcoming changes isn't determined. Because of the fateful circumstances the beginning of the digitalization coincided with the end of globalization and the Global Economic Crisis.

The end of the extensive development model of capitalism will inevitably require revision of many of the fundamental tenets of contemporary world order. This means that under the auspices of the digitalization completely new world can be created; such a world which will become a staple of other than today's one, system of values, management paradigm, social norms and economic laws. Of course, such a sight already has both supporters and opponents, whose violent confrontation we will all be able to witness in the near future.

From feasibility, the intensity and the coherence of action it depends how quickly our digital future will come, what are the social, economic and other problems we face on this path, and, finally, whether our future represent digital slavery or triumph of humanism, spirit and intellect over all the difficulties and problems.

The most important phase of the upcoming struggle will be not economic or technological rivalry, but the formation of a new civilizational paradigm capable to unite humanity, give it intuitive and attractive image of the future and outline the main milestones toward its construction.

CONCLUSION

So, digital technology is rapidly changing the familiar forms and methods of economic life around the world. The business is changing not only the individual companies - are changing the industry, regions and entire states. The development of the digital economy starts to go beyond the changes in the technologies and even in business - it becomes a factor in the macroeconomic and political. Not only the engineers, scientists and entrepreneurs, but also policy, philosophers and social activists are trying to reflect the changes. Some see it as a tool of fundamental changes in public life, the others, on the contrary, hope that the digitalization of economy will become an alternative to painful reforms.

In this sense, the experience of developed states gives food for thought, first and foremost, of what can speak the macroeconomic effects of the mass use of digital technologies. It turns out that the effect of this is expressed not so much in a quantitative increase of labor productivity, but in the qualitative changes of industries, agriculture, labor market, finance, education, their manageability and flexibility. In addition, the leading foreign analysts expect that as the expansion of the presence of digital technologies in different segments of the economy, there will be enormous transition indicators of economic efficiency of their application to a new, higher level. And now the world is on the threshold of such a leap.

The digital economy is a new type of economic relations in all sectors of the world market, which is now growing at a rapid pace and already in the near future, with the growth of high technology, can become the main type of commodity-money exchanges in the global world. The establishment and improvement of new technologies is happening so quickly that it's not possible to follow it. Therefore it is necessary to be included in the general information and technological flow of updates and try to apply them effectively.

ACKNOWLEDGMENT

The reported study was funded by RFBR according to the research projects No. 18-010-00204, 18-310-00253\18.

REFERENCES

Anttiroiko, A.-V. (2008). *Electronic Government: Concepts*. Methodologies, Tools, and Applications. doi:10.4018/978-1-59904-947-2

Boston Consulting Group. (2016). Retrieved from http://files.runet-id.com/2016/itogi2016/presentations/14dec.itogi2016-1-12-30-13-30-- rydih.pdf

Di Virgilio, F. (2017). *Social Media Application for knowledge management in modern organizations*. Retrieved from https://www.igi-global.com/book/social-media-knowledge-management-applications/179197

Doukidis, G., Mylonopoulos, N., & Pouloudi, N. (2003). *Social and Economic Transformation in the Digital Era*. Retrieved from https://www.igi-global.com/book/social-economic-transformation-digital-era/905

Druică, E. (2017). *Driving Innovation and Business Success in the Digital Economy*. Retrieved from https://www.igi-global.com/book/driving-innovation-business-success-digital/165239

Gada, K. (2016). *Digital Economy in 5 minutes*. Retrieved from https://www.forbes.com/sites/koshagada/2016/06/16/what-is-the-digitaleconomy/#74c40ef77628

Gamidullaeva, L. A., Potapova, I., & Shatokhin, M. (2019). Increasing Territorial Economic Growth Through Cost Optimization in the Digital Economy. In U. Benna (Ed.), *Optimizing Regional Development Through Transformative Urbanization* (pp. 225–250). Hershey, PA: IGI Global. doi:10.4018/978-1-5225-5448-6.ch011

Gamidullaeva, L. A., Vasin, S. M., & Mkrttchian, V. (2019). Regional Economic Growth and Open Innovation Platforms: Emerging Trends and New Opportunities. In U. Benna (Ed.), Optimizing Regional Development Through Transformative Urbanization (pp. 163-184). Hershey, PA: IGI Global. doi:10.4018/978-1-5225-5448-6.ch008

Isaias, P. (2017). *Innovation in the digital economy.* Retrieved from https://www.igi-global.com/book/user-innovation-entrepreneurship-phenomenon-digital/178736\

Isaias, P., & Carvalho, L. (2017). *User Innovation and the Entrepreneurship Phenomenon in the Digital Economy.* Retrieved from https://www.igi-global.com/book/user-innovation-entrepreneurship-phenomenon-digital/178736

Mahesh, S. R. (2003). *Business Intelligence in the Digital Economy: Opportunities, Limitations and Risks.* Retrieved from https://www.igi-global.com/book/business-intelligence-digital-economy/117

Mahesh, S. R. (2008). *Handbook of Research on Global Information Technology Management in the Digital Economy.* Retrieved from https://www.igi-global.com/book/handbook-research-global-information-technology/472

Mutula, S. M. (2010). *Growth In the digital economy.* Retrieved from https://www.igi-global.com/chapter/growth-digital-economy/361010

Oncioiu, I. (2013). *Business Innovation, Development, and Advancement in the Digital Economy.* Retrieved from https://www.igi-global.com/book/business-innovation-development-advancement-digital/70671

Oncioiu, I. (2013). *Business Innovation.* Development, and Advancement in the Digital Economy. doi:10.4018/978-1-5225-5448-6.ch003

Oncioiu, I. (2017). *Driving Innovation and Business Success in the Digital Economy.* Retrieved from https://www.igi-global.com/book/driving-innovation-business-success-digital/165239

Potapova, I., Vasin, S. M., Gamidullaeva, L. A., Tolstykh, T., & Belyanina, L. (2019). Drivers of Urban Development in Terms of Education Based on Digital Technologies. In U. Benna (Ed.), *Optimizing Regional Development Through Transformative Urbanization* (pp. 48–70). Hershey, PA: IGI Global. doi:10.4018/978-1-5225-5448-6.ch003

Tapscott, D. (1995). *The Digital Economy.* Retrieved from http://dontapscott.com/books/the-digital-economy/

Tolstykh, T. O., Vasin, S. M., Gamidullaeva, L. A., Nedelko, S., Eremina, E., Ko-shevoj, O., & Mkrttchian, V. (2018). The Control of Continuing Education Based on the Digital Economy. In P. Isaias & L. Carvalho (Eds.), *User Innovation and the Entrepreneurship Phenomenon in the Digital Economy* (pp. 153–171). Hershey, PA: IGI Global. doi:10.4018/978-1-5225-2826-5.ch008

Vasin, S. M., & Gamidullaeva, L. A. (2018). About Russian Regional Users' Innovation Based on Digital Information. In P. Isaias & L. Carvalho (Eds.), *User Innovation and the Entrepreneurship Phenomenon in the Digital Economy* (pp. 304–319). Hershey, PA: IGI Global. doi:10.4018/978-1-5225-2826-5.ch015

KEY TERMS AND DEFINITIONS

B2B (Business-to-Business): Is a term that defines the type of information and economic interaction, classified by type of interacting actors, in this case juridical persons which deal with the other business.

B2C (Business-to-Consumer): Is a term that refers to the commercial relationship between the business and the private, the so-called "end" consumer; also a form of electronic commerce, the purpose of which is direct sales to the consumer.

B2G (Business-to-Government): Is the relationship between business and the state. Usually the term is used for the classification of e-commerce sites. An example B2G-systems can serve as a system of electronic procurement.

C2C: Is a term that refers to the scheme of electronic commerce between final consumer (consumer) and the end-user, in which the buyer and seller are entrepreneurs in the juridical sense of the word.

Digital Economy: Is economic activities, based on the digital technologies related to e-business and e-commerce, produced and marketed their electronic goods and services. Payments for goods and services are often produced by electronic money.

E-Commerce: Is the scope of the economy which includes all the financial and trade transactions, carried out with the aid of computer networks, and business processes related to such transactions.

ICT: Is information and communication technologies.

Compilation of References

A Panel of Global Experts in Urban Environmental Sustainability. (2011). *African Green City Index*. Munich, Germany: Siemens AG. Retrieved from https://www.siemens.com/entry/cc/features/greencityindex_international/all/en/pdf/report_africa_en.pdf

Aalen, L., & Muriaas, R. L. (2017). Power calculations and political decentralisation in African post-conflict states. *International Political Science Review*, *38*(1), 56–69. doi:10.1177/0192512115615704

AARP. (2015, April 20). *The Livability Index: Great Neighborhoods for All Ages*. Retrieved from Livable Communities: https://www.aarp.org/ppi/issues/livable-communities/info-2015/livability-index.html

Abdulai, A. G., Bawole, J. N., & Sakyi, E. K. (2017). *Persistent chronic poverty in Northern Ghana: is geography to blame?* University of Ghana.

Aborisade, R. A., & Aliyyu, N. B. (2018). *Corruption and Africa. The Development of Africa*. New York: Springer.

Abubakar, I. R., & Dano, U. L. (2017). Socioeconomic Challenges and Opportunities of Urbanization in Nigeria. Hershey, PA: IGI Publishing.

Abusaada, H., & Elshater, A. (2017). *Back to the Order: The Chaos in the Cities of Hardship*. Saarbrücken, Germany: Lambert Academic Publishing.

ACCA. (2017). *Emerging from the shadows: the shadow economy to 2025*. Retrieved from https://www.accaglobal.com/content/dam/ACCA_Global/Technical/Future/pi-shadow- economy-report.pdf

Addaney, M. (2018). The African Union's Agenda 2063: Education and Its Realization. In Education Law, Strategic Policy and Sustainable Development in Africa. African Union Commission.

Adedeji, A. (2002). *Keynote Address: From the Lagos Plan of Action to the New Partnership for African Development and from the Final Act of Lagos to the Constitutive Act: Whither Africa?* African Forum for Envisioning Africa, Nairobi, Kenya.

Adediran, A. (2017). *Dialectics of Urban Planning in Nigeria. Paper delivered at the 5th Urban Dialogue of the Department of Urban and Regional Planning, University of Lagos.*

Adelowo, C., Olaopa, O., & Akinwale, Y. (2016). Policy Direction for Effective Interaction and Linkages among the Elements of Nigeria's National Innovation System. *Journal of Entrepreneurship and Innovation Management*, *5*(1), 1–12.

Adeniyi, E. O. (1982). *Administrative Framework for Physical Planning in Nigeria in Sada and Oguntoyibo. In Urbanization Processes and Problems in Nigeria*. New York: McGraw Hills Publishers.

Adepoju, A., Akinwale, Y., & Ogundari, I. (2018). Feasibility economic analysis for electricity generation in internal combustion engine sets using landfill gas in Lagos State. *African Journal of Science, Technology, Innovation and Development*, *10*(5), 593–599. doi:10.1080/20421338.2018.1495285

Aditya, T., & Laksono, D. (2017). LOD 1: 3D CityModel for Implementing SmartCity Concept. In *Proceedings of the 2017 International Conference on Information Technology*. Singapore: ACM. 10.1145/3176653.3176734

Adjibolosoo, S. (2017). *Developing civil society: social order and the human factor.* Oxon, UK: Routledge. doi:10.4324/9781351160087

Adler N J (1997). A typology of management studies involving culture. *Journal of International Business Studies*, 29-47.

AFDB Policy Brief. (2010). *Chinese trade and investment activities in Africa.* African Development Bank Group, Chief Economist Complex.

African Innovation Outlook. (2010). *Research and Experimental Development.* Retrieved from: http//:www.nepadst.org

African Union. (2015). *Agenda 2063: the Africa we want.* Addis Ababa: African Union Commission.

African Union. (2018). *Agenda 2063.* Retrieved from https://au.int/en/agenda2063

Agarwal, A. K. (2007). Biofuels (Alcohols And Biodiesel) Applications As Fuels For Internal Combustión Engines. *Progress in Energy and Combustion Science*, *33*(3), 233–271. doi:10.1016/j.pecs.2006.08.003

Ahvenniemi, H., Huovila, A., Pinto-Seppä, I., & Airaksinen, M. (2017). What are the differences between sustainable and smart cities? *Cities (London, England)*, *60*, 234–245. doi:10.1016/j.cities.2016.09.009

Ajayi, D. D. (2011). *Nigeria's industrial development: issues and challenges in the new millennium.* Retrieved from https://www.witpress.com/Secure/elibrary/papers/SDP11/SDP11059FU1.pdf

Akinbami, J. (1997). Comparative Environmental Effects and Cost Analysis Between Conventional and Non-conventional Energy Source – A Case for Objective Analysis and Decision Making in Nigeria's Energy Policy. *Nigerian Journal of Renewable Energy*, *5*(1&2), 131–139.

Akinbami, J. F. K. (2001). Renewable Energy Resources and Technologies in Nigeria: Present Situation, Future Prospects and Policy Framework. *Mitigation and Adaptation Strategies for Global Change*, *6*(2), 155–181. doi:10.1023/A:1011387516838

Akinbami, J., Ilori, M., Oyebisi, T., Akinwumi, I., & Adeoti, O. (2001). Biogas energy use in Nigeria: Current status, future prospects and policy implications. *Renewable & Sustainable Energy Reviews*, *5*(1), 97–112. doi:10.1016/S1364-0321(00)00005-8

Akinwale, Y. (2016b). Harnessing science technology and innovation for enhancing marginal oil and gas field development in Nigeria: a comparative analysis. *International Journal of eBusiness and eGovernment Studies*, *8*(2), 47 – 63.

Akinwale, Y. (2012). Empirical Analysis of Resource Curse in Nigeria. *International Journal of Economics and Management. The Sciences*, *1*(6), 19–25.

Akinwale, Y. (2016a). Indigenous Technology and Innovation Capability Building in Nigerian Upstream Oil and Gas Subsector: The Academia Perspective. *Advances in Management and Applied Economics*, *6*(2), 49–70.

Akinwale, Y. (2018). Descriptive analysis of building indigenous low carbon innovation capability in Nigeria. *African Journal of Science, Technology, Innovation and Development*, *10*(5), 601–614. doi:10.1080/20421338.2017.1366131

Akinwale, Y., Akinbami, J., & Akarakiri, J. (2018). Factors influencing technology and innovation capability in the Nigerian indigenous oil firms. *International Journal of Business Innovation and Research*, *15*(2), 247–268. doi:10.1504/IJBIR.2018.089146

Akinwale, Y., Ilevbare, O., & Ogundari, I. (2015). Utilising renewable energy technologies for electricity poverty reduction in South-West Nigeria: Technology adoption and psychosocial perspectives. *International Journal of Renewable Energy Technology*, *6*(3), 224–244. doi:10.1504/IJRET.2015.070149

Akinwale, Y., Jesuleye, A., & Siyanbola, W. (2013). Empirical Analysis of the Causal Relationship Between Electricity Consumption and Economic Growth in Nigeria. *British Journal of Economics. Management and Trade*, *3*(3), 277–295.

Akinwale, Y., & Ogundari, I. (2017). Exploration of Renewable Energy Resources for Sustainable Development in Nigeria: A Study of the Federal Capital Territory. *International Journal of Energy Economics and Policy*, *7*(3), 240–246.

Akinwale, Y., Ogundari, I., Ilevbare, O., & Adepoju, A. (2014). A Descriptive Analysis of Public Understanding and Attitudes of Renewable Energy Resources towards Energy Access and Development in Nigeria. *International Journal of Energy Economics and Policy*, *4*(4), 636–646.

Akinwale, Y., & Surujlal, J. (2017). A techno-economic policy framework to enhance the contribution of marginal oil and gas field to Nigeria's economic growth: A petroleum innovation system approach. *International Journal of Economics and Finance Studies*, *9*(1), 132–147.

Akinyoade, A., & Uche, C. U. (2016). *Dangote cement: An African success story?* ASC working paper. African Studies Centre Leiden.

Alan, A. T., Ramchurn, S. D., Rodden, T., Costanza, E., Fischer, J., & Jennings, N. R. (2015, September). Managing energy tariffs with agents: a field study of a future smart energy system at home. In *Adjunct Proceedings of the 2015 ACM International Joint Conference on Pervasive and Ubiquitous Computing and Proceedings of the 2015 ACM International Symposium on Wearable Computers* (pp. 1551-1558). ACM.

Albino, V., Berardi, U., & Dangelico, R. M. (2015). Smart cities: Definitions, dimensions, performance, and initiatives. *Journal of Urban Technology*, *22*(1), 3–21. doi:10.1080/10630732.2014.942092

Aldrich, H., & Auster, E. R. (1986). Even Dwarfs Started Small: Liabilities Of Age And Size And Their Strategic Implications. *Research in Organizational Behavior*, *8*, 165–198.

Alexander, C. (2002). The Nature of Order An Essay on the Art of Building and the Nature of the Universe: Book I-The Phenomenon of Life (vol. 9). Berkeley: CA: The Center for Environmental Structure.

Alexander, C. (2002). *The Nature of Order: The process of creating life*. Taylor & Francis.

Alix-Garcia, J., Schneider, A., & Zhao, N. (2016). Playing Favorites: Tax Incentives and Urban Growth in China, 1978–2010. *Land Economics*, *92*(1), 1–27. doi:10.3368/le.92.1.1

Aliyu, A. K., Modu, B., & Tan, C. W. (2017). A review of renewable energy development in Africa: A focus in South Africa, Egypt and Nigeria. *Renewable & Sustainable Energy Reviews*.

Aliyu, A., & Bawa, J. (2013). Clean Energy Technologies in Nigeria: Issues, Perspectives and Solutions. *Proceedings of the International Conference of the Nigerian Association of Energy Economics*, 134-154.

Allan, A. (2003). *IWRM/IWRAM: A new sanctioned discourse?* SOAS Water Issues Study Group. Occasional Paper No. 50. London: School of Oriental and African Studies.

Allen, C. (2015). *Tales from the Dark Continent: Images of British colonial Africa in the twentieth century*. Routledge.

Allen, D., & Potts, J. (2015). *Why it Exists, What it Does, Who it Benefits, and How*. Available at SSRN: https://ssrn.com/abstract=2617141

Allen, J., & Browne, M. (2010). Sustainability Strategies for City Logistics. In *Green Logistics: Improving the Environmental Sustainability of Logistics* (pp. 282–305). London: Kogan Page Limited.

Amadi, L., & Ekekwe, E. (2014). Corruption and development administration in Africa: Institutional approach. *African Journal of Political Science and International Relations*, *8*(6), 163–174. doi:10.5897/AJPSIR2013.0634

Amankwah-Amoah, J. (2015). Solar energy in sub-Saharan Africa: The challenges and opportunities of technological leapfrogging. *Thunderbird International Business Review*, *57*(1), 15–31. doi:10.1002/tie.21677

American Renaissance. (2014). *2014 Quality of Living Worldwide City Rankings*. Retrieved 8 29, 2016, from http://www.amren.com/news/2014/02/2014-quality-of-living-worldwide-city-rankings/

Anderson, G., & Tollison, R. (1982). Adam Smith's Analysis of Joint-Stock Companies. *Journal of Political Economy*, *90*(6), 1237–1257. doi:10.1086/261119

Anderson, J. E., & Wassmer, R. W. (2000). Local Economic Development Incentives in the United States. In J. E. Anderson & R. W. Wassmer (Eds.), *Bidding for Business: The Efficacy of Local Economic Development Incentives in a Metropolitan Area* (pp. 1–24). Kalamazoo, MI: W.E. Upjohn Institute for Employment Research. doi:10.17848/9780585313610

Andreeva, E. L. (2017). *Non-industrialization and change of the world industrial landscape: vectors of industrial development. INDUSTRY-2017*. Retrieved from http://inecprom.spbstu.ru/conference/industry/ archive / industry-2017 /

Angelidou, M. (2015). Smart cities: A conjuncture of four forces. *Cities (London, England)*, *47*, 95–106. doi:10.1016/j.cities.2015.05.004

Anthopoulos, L. G. (2017). *Understanding Smart Cities: A Tool for Smart Government or an Industrial Trick?* New York: Springer; doi:10.1007/978-3-319-57015-0

Anthopoulos, L. G., & Vakali, A. (2012). Urban planning and smart cities: Interrelations and reciprocities. In F. Álvarez (Ed.), *The Future Internet Assembly* (pp. 178–189). Berlin: Springer. doi:10.1007/978-3-642-30241-1_16

Antonelli, C. (2000). Collective Knowledge Communication and Innovation: The Evidence of Technological Districts. *Regional Studies*, *34*(6), 535–547. doi:10.1080/00343400050085657

Anttiroiko, A.-V. (2008). *Electronic Government: Concepts*. Methodologies, Tools, and Applications. doi:10.4018/978-1-59904-947-2

Anyanwu, F., & Yameogo, J. (2015). What Drives Foreign Direct Investments into West Africa? An Empirical Investigation. *African Development Review*, *27*(3), 199–215. doi:10.1111/1467-8268.12141

Aré, L., Chabenne, S., Dupoux, P., Ivers, L., Micheal, D. C., & Morieux, Y. (2010). *The African Challengers- Global Competitors Emerge from the Overlooked Continent*. Beijing: The Boston Consulting Group.

Arifovic, J., Dawid, H., Deissenberg, C., & Kostyshyna, O. (2010). Learning Benevolent Leadership in a Heterogenous Avatars Economy. *Journal of Economic Dynamics and Control*.

Ariza, M., & Ramírez, J. M. (2004). *Urbanización, mercados de trabajo y escenarios sociales en el México finisecular*. Princeton University.

Arnheim, R. (1971). *Entropy and Art an Essay on Disorder and Order*. Berkeley, CA: The University of California Press.

Aroca, P. (2004). Migración interregional en Chile, modelos y resultados, 1987-1992. Notas de Población, 31(78).

Arvind, N., Bonneau, J., Felten, E., Miller, A., & Goldfeder, E. (2016). *Bitcoin and Cryptocurrency Technologies. Princeton University Press.*

Asante, S. K. (2016). *Regionalism and Africa's development: expectations, reality and challenges*. New York: Springer.

Asheghian, P., & Ebrahimi, B. (1990). *International business: economics, environment and strategies*. New York: Harper Collins Publishers.

Asongu, S. A., Anyanwu, J. C., & Tchamyou, V. S. (2017). Technology-driven information sharing and conditional financial development in Africa. *Information Technology for Development*, 1–30. doi:10.1080/02681102.2017.1311833

Asongu, S. A., & De Moor, L. (2017). Financial globalisation dynamic thresholds for financial development: Evidence from Africa. *European Journal of Development Research*, *29*(1), 192–212. doi:10.1057/ejdr.2016.10

AU. (n.d.). *CEN SAD*. Retrieved 2018, from African Union: https://au.int/en/recs/censad

Awuah, K. G. B., & Hammond, F. N. (2014). Determinants of low land use planning regulation compliance rate in Ghana. *Habitat International*, *41*, 17–23. doi:10.1016/j.habitatint.2013.06.002

Babkin, A. V. (2017). Digital Economy and Industrial Policy: A Systems Approach or Backlog. Conference "Industrial Policy in the Digital Economy: Problems and Perspectives", St. Petersburg, Russia.

Babkin, A., Plotnikov, V., & Vertakova, Y. (2018). The Analysis of industrial cooperation models in the context of forming digital economy. *SHS Web of Conferences.*, *44*, 12. doi:10.1051hsconf/20184400012

Bandura, A. (1977). *Social Learning Theory*. New York: General Learning Press.

Banson, K. E., Nguyen, N. C., Bosch, O. J., & Nguyen, T. V. (2015). A systems thinking approach to address the complexity of agribusiness for sustainable development in Africa: A case study in Ghana. *Systems Research and Behavioral Science*, *32*(6), 672–688. doi:10.1002res.2270

Baregu, M. (2008). The three faces of the dragon: Tanzania-China relation in historical perspective. In *Crouching tiger, hidden dragon? Africa and China*. University of KwaZulu-Natal Press.

Barney, J. (1986). Strategic factor markets: Expectations, luck and business strategy. *Management Science*, *32*(10), 1231–1241. doi:10.1287/mnsc.32.10.1231

Barney, J. B., & Wright, P. M. (1998). On become a strategic partner: The role of Human resource in gaining competitive advantage. *Human Resource Management*, *37*(1), 31–46. doi:10.1002/(SICI)1099-050X(199821)37:1<31::AID-HRM4>3.0.CO;2-W

Baruah, N. G., Henderson, J. V., & Peng, C. (2017). *Colonial legacies: shaping African cities*. SERC/Urban and Spatial Programme Discussion Paper.

Basu, K. (2013). *Más allá de la mano invisible*. Fondo de Cultura Económica.

Bates, R. H. (2014). *Markets and states in tropical Africa: the political basis of agricultural policies*. University of California Press.

Bauernhansl, T., Hompel, M., & Vogel-Heuser, B. (2014). *Industrie 4.0 in Produktion, Automatisierung und Logistik — Anwendung, Technologien, Migration*. Wiesbaden: Springer Vierweg; doi:10.1007/978-3-658-04682-8

Baumol, W. J. (1990). Entrepreneurship: Productive, Unproductive, And Destructive. *Journal of Political Economy*, *98*(5), 893–921. doi:10.1086/261712

Bazua, F. Y., & Valenti, G. (1993). Hacia Un Enfoque Amplio De Política Pública. *Revista de Administração Pública*, 84.

BBVA Bancomer the National Population Council (CONAPO). (2017). *Anuarion of migration and b remittances 2017. Yearbook of migration and remittances.* Available at: https://www.bbva.com/es/mexico-segundo-pais-mas-migrantes-mundo-12-3-millones/

BCG. (2018). *Why Countries Need New Job Creation Strategies.* Retrieved from https://www.bcg.com/publications/2018/new-globalization-why-countries-need-new-job-creation-strategies.aspx

Becker, B. E., & Huselid, M. A. (1999). Overview: Strategic human resource management in five leading firms. *Human Resource Management, 38*(4), 287–301. doi:10.1002/(SICI)1099-050X(199924)38:4<287::AID-HRM2>3.0.CO;2-L

Belk, R. W. (2007). *Consumption, Mass Consumption, and Consumer Culture.* The Blackwell Encyclopedia of Sociology. doi:10.1002/9781405165518.wbeosc116

Bell & Hindmoor. (2009). *Rethinking Governance.* London: Earthscan.

Belozyorov, V. Ye., & Chernyshenko, S. (2014). Quadratic model of inter-population interaction: Investigation of stability areas. *Applied Mathematics and Computation, 230*, 43–56. doi:10.1016/j.amc.2013.12.095

Bena, A. R. (2015). *Planning for the Informal Service Providers in Nigerian Cities: Case Study of Birnin Kebbi Urban Area, Kebbi State.* Paper Presented at 4th National Conference of the Academic Staff Union of Polytechnics, Birnin Kebbi.

Benet, M. J. (1988). Intercultural communication: A current perspective. In M. J. Bennet (Ed.), Basic Concepts of intercultural communication: selected readings. Yarmouth, ME: Intercultural Press.

Benevolo, C., Dameri, R. P., & D'Auria, B. (2016). Smart mobility in smart city. In *Empowering Organizations* (pp. 13–28). Cham: Springer. doi:10.1007/978-3-319-23784-8_2

Benna, U. G. (2013). Timbuktu, the African Medieval Knowledge City: The Role of Knowledge Development Actors. *Information & Knowledge Management, 12*(3).

Benna, U. G. (2013). *Timbuktu, the African Medieval Knowledge City: The Role of Knowledge Development Actors.* Retrieved from http://www.worldscientific.com/doi/abs/10.1142/S0219649213500263

Benna, U. G., & Garba, S. B. (2016). Population Growth and Rapid Urbanization in the Developing World (Vol. 1). Hershey, PA: IGI Global.

Benna, U. G. (1997). Societal Values in development process: Place-making in Sokoto, Nigeria. In A. Awotona & N. Teymur (Eds.), *Tradition, Location and Community: Place-makin and Development* (pp. 173–187). Aldershot, UK: Averbury.

Benna, U. G. (2016). From Rural Majority to Urban Majority Africans: Where will They Work? In U. G. Benna, S. B. Garba, U. G. Benna, & S. B. Garba (Eds.), *Population Growth and Rapid Urbanization in the Developing World* (Vol. 1, pp. 1–22). Hershey, PA: IGI Publishing. doi:10.4018/978-1-5225-0187-9.ch001

Bennet, M. J. (1998). Intercultural communication: A current perspective. In M. J. Bennet (Ed.), *Basic concepts of intercultural communication: Selected readings* (pp. 1–34). Yarmouth, ME: Intercultural Press.

Berger, P. L. (1986). The capitalist revolution: Fifty propositions about prosperity, equality, and liberty. New York: Academic Press.

Bernard, H., & Dirk, W. V. (Eds.). (2017). *Trade in Services and economic transformation- A new development policy priority.* Essay Series Supporting Economic Transformation (SET). Accessed at http://set.odi.org

Bernstein, H. (1971). Modernization theory and the sociological study of development. *The Journal of Development Studies, 7*(2), 141–160. doi:10.1080/00220387108421356

Bershadsky, A., Berezin, A., & Mkrttchian, V. (2018). Theoretical and Technological Perspectives on Development of Information Monitoring System for Solving Complex Problems. Academic Press.

Bershadsky, A., Berezin, A., & Mkrttchian, V. (2018). Theoretical and Technological Perspectives on Development of Information Monitoring System for Solving Complex Problems. In U. G. Benna (Ed.), Optimizing Regional Development Through Transformative Urbanization. Hershey, PA: IGI Global. Doi:10.4018/978-1-5225-5448-6.ch006

Bhalla, A. S. (2016). *Regional blocs: building blocks or stumbling blocks?* New York: Springer.

Bhebhe, N. (2015). *Zimbabwe Industries bear Brunt of Electricity Shortages*. Available from: http://www.theafricareport.com/Southern-Africa/zimbabwe-industries-bear-brunt-of-electricity-shortages.html

Bhukuvhani, C. (2018). Towards Analysis of the Status of Science Technology Engineering and Mathematics (STEM) Education in Zimbabwe Secondary Schools: Access, Quality, Policy. *Zimbabwe Journal of Educational Research, 30*(1), 345–452.

Bibri, S. E. (2018). Backcasting in futures studies: A synthesized scholarly and planning approach to strategic smart sustainable city development. *European Journal of Futures Research, 6*(1), 13. doi:10.118640309-018-0142-z

Biswas, A. K. (2008). Integrated water resources management: Is it working? *International Journal of Water Resources Development, 24*(1), 5–22. doi:10.1080/07900620701871718

Bitcoin Essential. (2016). Packt Publishing.

Bitcoin For Dummies. (2016). John Wiley & Sons, Inc.

Black, D. (2000). *Economics: an explanatory dictionary*. Ves Mir.

Blanchet, M., Rinn, T., Von Thaden, G., & De Thieulloy, G. (2014). *Industry 4.0: The new industrial revolution-How Europe will succeed*. Hg. v. Roland Berger Strategy Consultants GmbH. Retrieved from http://www. rolandberger. Com/media/pdf/Roland_Berger_TAB_Industry_4_0_2014

Bloch, R., Fox, S., Monroy, J., & Ojo, A. (2015). *Urbanisation and Urban Expansion in Nigeria. Research report, Urbanisation Research Nigeria*. London: ICF International.

Blockchain: Trust economy Taking control of digital identity. (2016). White paper. Digital Supply Chain Management 2020 Vision. SAP SE Walldorf, Germany.

Blockchain's Smart Contracts. (2016, June). Driving the Next Wave of Innovation across Manufacturing Value Chain. *Cognizant 20-20 insights*.

Bodrunov, S.D. (2014). Economic re-industrialization: shall we begin with import substitution? *Economic Revival of Russia, 3*, 5-7.

Bodrunov, S.D. (n.d.). Re-industrialization: socioeconomic parameters of reintegration of production, science and education. *Sociological Research, 2*, 20-28.

Boes, K., Buhalis, D., & Inversini, A. (2015). Conceptualising smart tourism destination dimensions. In *Information and communication technologies in tourism 2015* (pp. 391–403). Cham: Springer.

Bond, P. (2014). *Elite transition: From apartheid to neoliberalism in South Africa*. London: Pluto Press.

Boserup, E. (2017). *The conditions of agricultural growth: The economics of agrarian change under population pressure*. Oxford, UK: Routledge.

Boston Consulting Group (BCG). (2017). *New business models for a new global landscape*. Retrieved from https://www.bcg.com/publications/2017/globalization-new-business-models-global-landscape.aspx

Boston Consulting Group (BCG). (n.d.). Retrieved from https://www.bcgperspectives.com

Boston Consulting Group. (2016). Retrieved from http://files.runet-id.com/2016/itogi2016/presentations /14dec.itogi2016-1-12-30-13-30-- rydih.pdf

Boston Consulting Group. (2018). *Why Countries Need New Job Creation Strategies*. Retrieved from https://www.bcg.com/publications/2018/new-globalization-why-countries-need-new-job-creation-strategies.aspx

Botsman, R. (2013). The sharing economy lacks a shared definition. *Fast Company*. Retrieved from http://www.fastcoexist.com/3022028/the-sharing-economy-lacks-a-shared-definition

Botsman, R. (2015). *Defining the sharing economy: What is collaborative economy - and what isn't?* Retrieved from https://www.fastcompany.com/3046119/defining-the-sharingeconomy-what-is-collaborative-consumption-and-what-isnt

Botsman, R. (2015). The Changing Rules of Trust in the Digital Age. *Harvard Business Review*. Retrieved from https://hbr.org/2015/10/the-changing-rules-of-trust-in-the-digital-age

Botsman, R., & Roo, R. (2011). *What's mine is yours: how collaborative consumption is changing the way we live*. London: Collins.

Boulos, M. N. K., & Al-Shorbaji, N. M. (2014). On the Internet of Things, smart cities and the WHO Healthy Cities. *International Journal of Health Geographics*, *13*(10), 1–6. PMID:24383521

Boyle, P. y Halfacree, K. (1998). *Migration into rural areas*. John Wiley and Sons.

Boyle, P., Halfacree, K., & Robinson, V. (1998). *Exploring contemporary migration*. Longman.

Bozhenov, S.A. (2012). Clever city in the development strategy of Belgorod. *City Management: Theory and Practice*, *1*(4), 3-10.

Brenton, P., & Isik, G. (Eds.). (2012). *De-fragmenting Africa: deepening regional trade integration in goods and services*. World Bank Publications.

Brown, D. (2017). *Challenging the conceptual boundaries of the compact city paradigm in sub-Saharan Africa*. Retrieved from https://www.ucl.ac.uk/bartlett/development/case- studies/2017/mar/challengin-conceptual-boundaries-compact-city-paradigm-sub-saharan-africa

Brown, D., Boano, C., Vivekananda, J., & Walker, J. (2015). *Urban Crises and Humanitarian Responses: A Literature Review. The DFID Humanitarian Policy and Partnerships Group*. CHASE.

Bughin, J., & Chui, M. (n.d.). The Internet of Things. *Advances in E-Business Research*, 111–125. doi:10.4018/978-1-5225-2104-4.ch006

Burkart, K. (2009). How do you define the 'green' economy? *MNN: Mother Nature Network*. Retrieved from https://www.mnn.com/green-tech/research-innovations/blogs/how-do-you-define-the-green-economy

Burke, C., & Corkin, L. (2006). *China's interest and activity in Africa's Construction and infrastructure sectors*. Centre for Chinese Studies, Stellenbosch University.

Cabrera, G. (1970). Selectividad por edad y sexo de los migrantes en México, 1930-1960, en Demografía y Economía, 4(12).

Caffentzis, G. (2002). Neo-liberalism in Africa, Apocalyptic Failures and Business as Usual Practices. *Turkish Journal of International Relations*, *1*(3), 89–104.

Calbreath, D. (2010). *Hidden economy a hidden danger*. Retrieved from http://www.sandiegouniontribune.com/sdut-hidden-economy-a-hidden-danger- 2010may30-story.html

Caldwell, D., Dyszynski, J., & Roland, R. (2015). *2015. Climate Compatible Development in the 'Land of a Thousand Hills': Lessons from Rwanda*. CDKN.

Caprotti, F., Cowley, R., Datta, A., Broto, V.C., Gao, E., Georgeson, L., Herrick, C., Odendaal, N., & Joss, S. (2017). The New Urban Agenda: key opportunities and challenges for policy and practice. *Urban Research & Practice, 10*(3), pp.367-378.

Carmona, M., Heath, T., & Tiesdell, S. (2010). Public Places, Urban Spaces: The Dimensions of Urban Design. Routledge.

CARRI Report. (2013). Retrieved from http://www.resilientus.org/wp-content/uploads/2013/08/definitions-of-community-resilience.pdf

Carrillo, F. J. (2004). Capital cities: A taxonomy of capital accounts for knowledge cities. *Journal of Knowledge Management*, *8*(5), 28–46. doi:10.1108/13673270410558738

Castells, M. (2002). La ciudad en la nueva economía. *Tareas*, *110*, 6-21.

Castells, M. (2010). *The rise of the network society*. West Sussex, UK: Wiley-Blackwell.

Celade-Fnuap. (2000). *Juventud, población y desarrollo en América Latina y el Caribe. Problemas, oportunidades y desafíos. Centro Latinoamericano y Caribeño de Demografía (CELADE)*. Santiago de Chile.

Center for Cities. (2015). *A century of cities Urban economic change since 1911*. Retrieved from http://www.centreforcities.org/wp-content/uploads/2015/03/15-03-04-A-Century-of- Cities.pdf

CES-Development Consortium. (2004). *Review of Birnin Kebbi Master Plan (2005-2015)*. Waziri Umaru Federal Polytechnic.

CGTN. (2017). Real economy VS. *Virtual Economy*. Retrieved from http://en.ccg.org.cn/cgtn-dialogue-real-economy-vs-virtual-economy/

Chambers, R. (1995). Poverty and livelihoods: Whose reality counts? *Environment and Urbanization*, *7*(1), 173–204. doi:10.1177/095624789500700106

Chambers, R. (2014). *Rural development: Putting the last first*. Oxford, UK: Routledge. doi:10.4324/9781315835815

Champion, T. (1989). *Counterurbanization. The changing pace and nature of population deconcentration*. Routledge.

Champion, T. (2001). A changing demographic regime and evolving poly-centric urban regions: consequences for the size, composition and distribution of city populations. Urban Studies, 38(4).

Chapin, F. J., & Kaiser, E. J. (1979). *Urban Land Use Planning*. Urbana, IL: University of Illinois Press.

Chaponniere, J. R. (2009). Chinese aid to Africa, origins, forms and issues. In The New Presence of China in Africa. Amsterdam University Press.

Charmes, J. (2001). *Informal Sector, Poverty And Gender A Review Of Empirical Evidence*. Retrieved from http://www.wiego.org/sites/default/files/publications/files/Charmes-Informal-Sector- Poverty.pdf

Chatiza, K. (2016). Analysing Policy Responses to the Dilemmas of Peri-urbanity and Land Management in Zimbabwe: A Case Study of Harare. In *Peri-Urban Developments and Processes in Africa with Special Reference to Zimbabwe* (pp. 129–142). New York: Springer. doi:10.1007/978-3-319-34231-3_11

Chaudhuri, S., & Yabuuchi, S. (2008). Formation of Special Economic Zone: Liberalized FDI Policy and Agricultural Productivity. *International Review of Economics & Finance, 19*(4), 779–788. doi:10.1016/j.iref.2010.02.004

Chávez, A. (1999). *La nueva dinámica de la migración interna en. Centro Regional de Investigaciones Multidisciplinarias/Universidad Nacional Autónoma de México*. Cuernavaca, México: CRIM/UNAM.

Chávez, A., & Lozano, F. (2006). *Género, migración y regiones. Centro Regional de Investigaciones Multidisciplinarias/Universidad Nacional Autónoma de México*. Cuernavaca, México: CRIM/UNAM.

Chernyshenko, S. V., & Okhrimenko, O. A. (2009). Formalisation of international education standards: Design of information models with use of computer technologies. *Proceedings of International Conference "Actual Problems of International Cooperation in the Field of Science and Education"*, 257-264.

Chernyshenko, S. V., Demchyk, O. I., & Chernyshenko, V. S. (2012). Regional system of higher education management: Information support of interaction with stakeholders. *J. of Pedagogical Informatics, 18*(1-2), 134–146.

Chernyshenko, S. V., & Ruzich, R. V. (2013). Bifurcation Model of Successions in Ecosystems. *Proceedings of 27th European Conference on Modelling and Simulation. ECMS-2013*, 169-174.

Chesbrough, H. (2003). Open Innovation: The new Imperative for Creating and Profiting from Technology. Boston: Harvard Business School Press.

Chete, L. N. (2016). *Industrial development and growth in Nigeria: Lessons and challenges* (Learning to Complete, working paper No. 8). Retrieved from www.brookings.edu/wp-content/uploads/2016/./L2C-wp8-Chete-et-al-1-pdf Retrieved 22/9/2018

Chete, L. N., Adeoti, J. O., Adeyinka, F. M., & Ogundele, O. (2014a). *Industrial Policy in Nigeria: Opportunities and Challenges in a Resource-rich Country*. Doi:10.1093/acprof:oso/9780198776987.003.0006

Chete, L. N., Adeoti, J. O., Adeyinka, F. M., & Ogundele, O. (2014b). *Industrial Development and Growth in Nigeria: Lessons and Challenges*. WIDER Working Paper 2014/019. Helsinki: UNU-WIDER.

Cheteni, P., & Shindika, E. S. (2017). Ethical Leadership in South Africa and Botswana. *BAR - Brazilian Administration Review, 14*(2), 6. doi:10.1590/1807-7692bar2017160077

Chirisa, I., Matamanda, A. R., & Mukarwi, L. (2018). Desired and Achieved Urbanisation in Africa: In Search of Appropriate Tooling for a Sustainable Transformation. In U. Benna & I. Benna (Eds.), Urbanization and its Impact on Socio-Economic Growth in Developing Regions. IGI Global.

Chirisa, I., Matamanda, A. R., & Mukarwi, L. (2018). Desired and Achieved Urbanisation in Africa: In Search of Appropriate Tooling for a Sustainable Transformation. In Urbanization and Its Impact on Socio-Economic Growth in Developing Regions (pp. 88-106). IGI Global.

Chirisa, I., Bobo, T., & Matamanda, A. R. (2017). Misplaced values, political myopia and the neglect of professional ethics: Case of human factor decay and local government rot in Zimbabwe. *Zambezia, 44*(ii), 36–52.

Chirisa, I., Maphosa, A., Zanamwe, L., Bandauko, E., & Mukarwi, L. (2016). Past, Present and Future Population Growth and Urban Management in Zimbabwe: Putting Institutions into Perspective. In U. G. Benna & S. B. Garba (Eds.), *Population Growth and Rapid Urbanization in the Developing World* (Vol. 1, pp. 64–81). Hershey, PA: IGI Publishing. doi:10.4018/978-1-5225-0187-9.ch004

Chirisa, I., Mukarwi, L., & Matamanda, A. R. (2017). Social Costs and Benefits of the Transformation of the Traditional Families in an African Urban Society. In U. G. Benna & I. Benna (Eds.), *Urbanization and its Impact on Socio-Economic Growth in Developing Regions* (pp. 179–197). Hershey, PA: IGI Publishing.

Chivaura, V. G., & Mararike, C. (1998). *The Human Factor Approach to Development in Africa*. Harare: UZ Publications.

Chourabi, H., Nam, T., Walker, S., Gil-Garcia, J. R., Mellouli, S., Nahon, K., & Scholl, H. J. (2012). Understanding Smart Cities: An Integrative Framework. In *Proceedings of the 2012 45th Hawaii International Conference on System Sciences*. Maui, HI: IEEE. 10.1109/HICSS.2012.615

Chriss, A. (2015). The Disrupter Series: How the Sharing Economy Create Jobs, Benefits Consumers, and Raises Policy Questions. *Subcommittee on Commerce, Manufacturing, and Trade of the Committee on Energy and Commerce House of Representatives, 114*(80), 45-56.

Chu, K. M., Jayaraman, S., Kyamanywa, P., & Ntakiyiruta, G. (2014). Building research capacity in Africa: Equity and global health collaborations. *PLoS Medicine, 11*(3), e1001612. doi:10.1371/journal.pmed.1001612 PMID:24618823

Chulok, A. A. (2017). *Megatrends of the future: where do we wait for threats and how to open the windows of opportunities?* International Scientific and Educational Foresight Center.

Chum, H., Faaij, A., Moreira, J., Berndes, G., Dhamija, P., Dong, H., ... Pingoud, K. (2011). Bioenergy. In *IPCC Special Report on Renewable Energy Sources and Climate Change Mitigation* (pp. 209–332). Cambridge, UK: Cambridge University Press. doi:10.1017/CBO9781139151153.006

Cirolia, L. R., & Berrisford, S. (2017). 'Negotiated planning': Diverse trajectories of implementation in Nairobi, Addis Ababa, and Harare. *Habitat International, 59*, 71–79. doi:10.1016/j.habitatint.2016.11.005

Clarfield, A. M., & Rosenthal, A. (2017). Aging in Sub-Saharan Africa: Sub-par? *Journal of the American Geriatrics Society, 65*(6), 1136–1138. doi:10.1111/jgs.14751 PMID:28176300

Cobbinah, P., & Adams, E. (2018). Urbanization and Electric Power Crisis in Ghana: Trends, Policies, and Socio-Economic Implications. In U. Benna & I. Benna (Eds.), *Urbanization and Its Impact on Socio-Economic Growth in Developing Regions* (pp. 262–284). Hershey, PA: IGI Global. doi:10.4018/978-1-5225-2659-9.ch013

CohenB. (2015). Retrieved from https://www.fastcompany.com/3047795/the-3-generations-of-smart-cities

Cohn, T. H. (2016). *Global political economy: Theory and practice*. New York: Routledge. doi:10.4324/9781315659695

Colander, D., Föllmer, H., Goldberg, M., Haas, A., Juselius, K., Kirman, A., . . . Sloth, B. (2009). *Financial Crisis and the Systemic Failure of Academic Economics*. Working paper No. 1489. Kiel Institute for the World Economy.

Colenbrander, S. (2016). *Cities as engines of economic growth*. Retrieved from http://pubs.iied.org/pdfs/10801IIED.pdf

Collier, P. (2007). *The Bottom Billion: Why the Poorest Countries are Failing and What Can Be Done About It*. London: Oxford University Press.

Collins, R. (1980). Weber's last theory of capitalism: A systematization. *American Sociological Review, 1*(45), 925–942. doi:10.2307/2094910

COMESA. (n.d.). *Overview of COMESA*. Retrieved 2018, from Common Market for Eastern and Southern Africa: http://www.comesa.int/overview-of-comesa/

Comisión Reguladora De Energía. (2015). *Desarrollo Del Marco Regulatorio Mexicano En Materia Energética*. Author.

CONAGUA. (2014). *Federal Government of Mexico. National Water Plan. National Development Plan 2014 - 2018.* Retrieved from http://www.conagua.gob.mx/CONAGUA07/Contenido/Documentos/PROGRAMA\

CONAPO (Consejo Nacional de Población). (1999). *La situación demográfica en México, 1999.* México, D.F., México: CONAPO.

Constitución Política De Los Estados Unidos Mexicanos, Diario Oficial De La Federación. (2017). *Constitución Política De Los Estados Unidos Mexicanos.* Author.

Contini, B., Leombruni, R., & Richiardi, M. (2004). Editorial. *Advances in Complex Systems*, *7*, 125–138.

Contreras Comeche, R., & González García, N. (2010). La Medición Del Valor Social Y El Impacto De Los Emprendedores Sociales. In Emprendimiento, Economía Social Y Empleo. IUDESCOOP, Instituto Universitario De Economía Social Y Cooperativa Dela Universidad De Valencia.

Cook, S. F., & Borah, W. (1980). Ensayos sobre historia de la población (México y California). T. III. Ed. Siglo XXI. Colección Nuestra América No. 29.

Cornelius, W. A. (1978). La migración ilegal mexicana a Estados Unidos: conclusiones de investigaciones recientes, imülica-ciones políticas y prioridades de investigación. Foro internacional, 18(17).

Council for Renewable Energy Nigeria (CREN). (2009). *Nigeria Electricity Crunch.* Available at http://www.renewablenigeria.org

Crow, D. (1989). Le Corbusier's Postmodern Plan. *Theory, Culture & Society*, *6*(241), 241–261. doi:10.1177/026327689006002004

Cullen, G. (1961). *Concise Of Townscape.* London: Architecture Press, Elsevier.

Currie-Alder, B., Kanbur, R., Malone, D. M., & Medhora, R. (Eds.). (2014). International Development: Ideas, Experience, and Prospects. Oxford University Press.

Dan, M. B., & Crăciun, C. (2016). *Space and Time Visualisation.* Retrieved from https://books.google.com.sa/books?isbn=3319249428

Dawid, H., Gemkow, S., Harting, P., & Neugart, M. (2009b). *Labor market integration policies and the convergence of regions.* Working Paper. Bielefeld University.

Dawid, H., & Fagiolo, G. (2008). Avatar-based models for economic policy design: Introduction to the special issue. *Journal of Economic Behavior & Organization*, *67*(2), 351–354. doi:10.1016/j.jebo.2007.06.009

Dawid, H., Gemkow, S., Harting, P., & Neugart, M. (2009a). Spatial Skill Heterogeneity and Growth: An Avatar-based Policy Ananlysis. *Journal of Artificial Societies and Social Simulation*, *12*(4), 5.

De Melo, J., & Tsikata, Y. (2014). *Regional integration in Africa.* New York: Springer.

De Soto, H. (2000). The Mystery of Capital: Why Capitalism Triumphs In the West and Fails Everywhere Else. New York: Academic Press.

Deaton, A. (2013). *The Great Escape Health, Wealth, and the Origins of Inequality.* Retrieved from https://press.princeton.edu/titles/10054.html

Decree of the President of the Russian Federation dated 1 December 2016 N° 642 "About the strategy of scientific technology development of the Russian Federation". (n.d.). Retrieved from https://www.extech.ru/info/docs/ukaz_642.pdf

Deichmann, U. (2013). *Growing Green: The Economic Benefits of Climate Action (interview)*. Retrieved from http://www.worldbank.org/en/news/video/2013/06/25/uwe-deichmann-growing-green-interview

Deissenberg, C., van der Hoog, S., & Dawid, H. (2008). EURACE: A Massively Parallel Avatar-based Model of the European Economy. *Applied Mathematics and Computation*, *204*(2), 541–552. doi:10.1016/j.amc.2008.05.116

Deloitte. (2017). *Rewriting the rules for the digital age*. Retrieved from https://www2.deloitte.com/content/dam/Deloitte/global/Documents/About- Deloitte/central-europe/ce-global-human-capital-trends.pdf

DeSoto, H. (2000). *The mystery of capital: Why capitalism triumphs in the west and fails everywhere else*. New York: Basic Books.

Di Virgilio, F. (2017). *Social Media Application for knowledge management in modern organizations*. Retrieved from https://www.igi-global.com/book/social-media-knowledge-management-applications/179197

Dibua, J. I. (2017). *Modernization and the crisis of development in Africa: The Nigerian experience*. Oxford, UK: Routledge. doi:10.4324/9781351152921

Dickey, T. (2018). Smart water solutions for smart cities. In *Smart Cities* (pp. 197–207). Cham: Springer. doi:10.1007/978-3-319-59381-4_12

Diep, L., Archer, D., & Gueye, C. (2016). *Decentralisation in West Africa: the implications for urban climate change governance*. London: IIED.

Digital-Disrupting Business Models, Digital Supply Networks. (2017). *Deloitte Development LLC Land Transport Regulation 2040 Technology, trends and other factors of change*. Foundation paper. NTC Australia National Transport Commission.

Dincecco, M., & Katz, G. (2016). State Capacity and Long-run Economic Performance. *Economic Journal (London)*, *126*(590), 189–218. doi:10.1111/ecoj.12161

Dipholo, K. B., & Molosi-France, K. (2017). The mismatch between the theory and practice of participatory rural development in Botswana: prospects for transformative social change. *International Conference on Public Administration and Development Alternatives (IPADA)*.

Djahel, S., Doolan, R., Muntean, G. M., & Murphy, J. (2015). A communications-oriented perspective on traffic management systems for smart cities: Challenges and innovative approaches. *IEEE Communications Surveys and Tutorials*, 17.

Djurfeldt, A. A. (2015). Urbanization and linkages to smallholder farming in sub-Saharan Africa: Implications for food security. *Global Food Security*, *4*, 1–7. doi:10.1016/j.gfs.2014.08.002

Dorosh, P. A., Stifel, D., & Minten, B. (2015). *Implications of isolation for rural poverty in Madagascar. Agricultural Economics*. Easton, PA: International Association of Agricultural Economics.

Dos Santos, S., Adams, E. A., Neville, G., Wada, Y., de Sherbinin, A., Bernhardt, E. M., & Adamo, S. B. (2017). Urban growth and water access in sub-Saharan Africa: Progress, challenges, and emerging research directions. *The Science of the Total Environment*, *607*, 497–508. doi:10.1016/j.scitotenv.2017.06.157 PMID:28704674

Doukidis, G., Mylonopoulos, N., & Pouloudi, N. (2003). *Social and Economic Transformation in the Digital Era*. Retrieved from https://www.igi-global.com/book/social-economic-transformation-digital-era/905

Drozhzhinov, V. I., Kupriyanovsky, V. P., Namiot, D. E., Sinyagov, S. A., & Kharitonov, A. A. (2017). Smart cities: Models, tools, ranking and standards. *International Journal of Open Information Technologies*, *5*(3), 19–47.

Druică, E. (2017). *Driving Innovation and Business Success in the Digital Economy*. Retrieved from https://www.igi-global.com/book/driving-innovation-business-success-digital/165239

Dube, D., & Chirisa, I. (2012). The Informal City: Assessing its Scope, Variants and Direction in Harare, Zimbabwe. *Global Advanced Research Journal of Geography and Regional Planning*, *1*(1), 16–25.

Duhau, E., & Schteingart, M. (1997). La urbanización popular en la Ciudad de México. In Pobreza, condiciones de vida y salud en la Ciudad de México (pp. 29-42). El Colegio de México.

Dunmade, I. (2002). Indicators of sustainability: Assessing the suitability of a foreign technology for a developing economy. *Technology in Society*, *24*(4), 461–471. doi:10.1016/S0160-791X(02)00036-2

Dupoux, P., Ermias, T., Heuzé, S., Niavas, S., & Kimani, M. V. (2014). Wining in Africa-From Trading Posts to Eco-systems. Boston: BCG Publishing.

Dupoux, P., Ivers, L., Niavas, S., & Chraïti, A. (2018). *Pioneering One Africa - The Companies Blazing a Trail Across the Continent*. BCG Publishing.

Duranton, G. (2008). *Cities: Engines of Growth and Prosperity for Developing Countries?* Retrieved from https://openknowledge.worldbank.org/handle/10986/28044

Dye, T. (2001). *Understanding Public Policy*. Englewood, NJ: Prentice Hall Inc.

EAC. (2017). *About EAC*. Retrieved 2018, from East African Community: https://www.eac.int/about-eac

ECA. (2016). Macroeconomic Policy And Structural Transformation Of African Economies. Addis Ababa: Economic Commission for Africa (ECA).

ECA. (2016a). *AMU - Arab Maghreb Union*. Retrieved 7 19, 2018, from United Nation Economic Commission for Africa: https://www.uneca.org/oria/pages/amu-arab-maghreb-union

ECA. (2016b). *CEN-SAD - The Community of Sahel-Saharan States*. Retrieved 2018, from United Nations Economic Commission for Africa: https://www.uneca.org/oria/pages/cen-sad-community-sahel-saharan-states

ECA. (2017). *Urbanization And Industrialization For Africa's Transformation*. Retrieved from https://www.uneca.org/publications/economic-report-africa-2017

ECA. (2017). *Urbanization And Industrialization For Africa's Transformation*. Retrieved from https://www.uneca.org/sites/default/files/PublicationFiles/web_en_era-2017_01.pdf

ECCAS. (2014). *Presentation of ECCAS*. Retrieved 2018, from Economic Community of Central African States: http://www.ceeac-eccas.org/index.php/en/a-propos-de-la-ceeac/presentation

Economic Commission for Africa (ECA). (2016). *Africa's Blue Economy: A policy handbook*. Retrieved from https://www.uneca.org/publications/africas-blue-economy-policy-handbook

Economic Commission for Africa. (2015). *Economic Report on Africa 2015*. Available http://www.uneca.org/publications/economic-report-africa-2015

Economic Commission for Africa. (2016). *Economic Report on Africa 2015*. Available http://www.uneca.org/publications/economic-report-africa-2016

Economic Commission for Africa. (2017). *Economic Report on Africa 2017: Urbanization and Industrialization for Africa's Transformation*. Addis Ababa: ECA Publishing.

ECOSOC. (2018). *About Us*. Retrieved from https://www.un.org/ecosoc/en/about-us

ECOWAS. (2015). *About the Commission.* Retrieved 2018, from ECOWAS Commission: http://www.comm.ecowas.int/about-ecowas/

EEA. (2009). *Ensuring quality of life in Europe's cities and towns, Tackling the environmental challenges driven by European and global change.* Copenhagen: European Environmental Agency.

Efobi, U. (2015). Politicians' attributes and institutional quality in Africa: A focus on corruption. *Journal of Economic Issues, 49*(3), 787–813. doi:10.1080/00213624.2015.1072393

Eisenman, P. (2007). *Written into the Void. Selected Writings, 1990-2004.* New Haven, CT: Yale University Press.

Ekali, T. N. (2005). The Fluctuating Fortunes of Anglophone Cameroon Towns: The Case of Victoria, 1858–1982. In S. J. Salm & T. Falola (Eds.), *African Urban Spaces in Historical Perspectives.* New York: University of Rochester Press.

Elliot, J. R. (1997). Cycles within the system: metropolisation and internal migration in the U.S. 1965-1990. Urban Studies, 34(1).

Elshater, A. (2016). The ten-minute neighborhood is [not] a basic planning unit for happiness in egypt. *Archnet-IJAR, 10*(1), 344–357. doi:10.26687/archnet-ijar.v10i1.878

Emerging technology timeline 20 emergent technologies likely to disrupt our sector. (2017). ARUP.

Engel, U. (2017). Introduction: The African exception: conceptual notes on governance in Africa in the new millennium. In *The African Exception* (pp. 13–26). Oxon, UK: Routledge. doi:10.4324/9781351147927-1

Engerman, D. C. (Ed.). (2003). *Staging growth: Modernization, development, and the global cold war.* University of Massachusetts Press.

ENI in France. (2017). *Electricity, the energy behind the industrial revolution: The electricity fairy.* Available from: https://www.eni.com/en_FR/products-services/electricity/electricity_energy/electricity_energy.shtml

Epishkin, N. I. (2010). Historical Dictionary of the Gallicisms of the Russian Language. Academic Press.

Ericsson. (2015). *Laying the foundations for a smart, sustainable city.* Available online: https://www.ericsson.com/en/white-papers/laying-the-foundations-for-a-smart-sustainable-city/white-paper---laying-the-foundations-for-a-smart-sustainable-city

Ernest & Young (EY). (2017). *EY Global Information Security Survey 2017-18.* Retrieved from https://www.ey.com/gl/en/services/advisory/ey-global-information-security-survey-2017-18

Ernst & Young (EY). (2014). *Global View 2014.* Retrieved from https://www.ey.com/Publication/vwLUAssets/EY_Global_review_2014/$FILE/Global_review_2014.pdf

Ernstson, H., Sörlin, S., & Elmqvist, T. (2008). Social movements and ecosystem services–the role of social network structure in protecting and managing urban green areas in Stockholm. *Ecology and Society, 13*(2), 39. Retrieved from http://www.ecologyandsociety.org/vol13/iss2/art39/

Estrada, A. (2001). *Impactos de la inversión canadiense en México: Una primera aproximación.* Fundar.

Ewing, R., & Clemente, O. (2013). *Measuring Urban Design.* Washington, DC: Island Press. doi:10.5822/978-1-61091-209-9

FAO. (2012). *Greening The Economy With Agriculture.* Retrieved from http://www.fao.org/3/a-ar585e.pdf

Fath, B. D., Dean, C. A., & Katzmair, H. (2015). Navigating the adaptive cycle: An approach to managing the resilience of social systems. *Ecology and Society, 20*(2), 24. doi:10.5751/ES-07467-200224

Federal Republic of Nigeria. (2005). National Urban Development Policy (2005). Federal Government Press.

Federal Republic of Nigeria. (2012). World Bank Report.

Federal Research Division. (2008). *Country Profile: Algeria*. Washington, DC: Library of Congress.

Feige, E. L. (Ed.). (1989). *The Underground Economies:Tax Evasion and Information Distortion*. London: Cambridge University Press. doi:10.1017/CBO9780511571749

Feldman, M. A. (2001). *Employees at large industrial facilities of the Ural in 1914-1941 //Ekaterinburg*. Ural University publishing.

Felson, M., & Spaeth, J. L. (1978). Community structure and collaborative consumption: A routine activity approach. *The American Behavioral Scientist*, *21*(4), 614–624. doi:10.1177/000276427802100411

Feremenga, D. T. (2005). Urban Planning and Development in Zimbabwe: A Historical Perspective. In S. J. Salm & T. Falola (Eds.), *African Urban Spaces in Historical Perspectives*. New York: University of Rochester Press.

Fielden, A. (2008). *Ignored Displaced Persons: the plight of IDPs in urban areas*. Retrieved from www.unhcr.org

Financial Dictionary Finam. (n.d.). Retrieved from https://www.finam.ru/dictionary/

Flew, T. (2014). *Six Theories of Neo-liberalism*. Queensland: SAGE.

Flores Clair, E. (1997). Minería y población. Dimensión Antropològica, 11.

Foro Económico Mundial. (2014). *The Bold-Ones High-Impact Entrepreneurs Who Transform Industries*. Foro Económico Mundial.

Foster, V., Butterfield, W., Chuan, C., & Pushak, N. (2008). *Building bridges; China's growing roles as infrastructure financier for sub-Saharan Africa*. Washington, DC: World Bank.

Fosu, A. K. (2017). *Governance and development in Africa: A concise*. Africa Development Bank Group.

Fox, S. (2014). The political economy of slums: Theory and evidence from Sub-Saharan Africa. *World Development*, *54*, 191–203. doi:10.1016/j.worlddev.2013.08.005

Freeman, C. (1995). The National System of Innovation in Historical Perspective. *Cambridge Journal of Economics*, *19*(1), 5–24.

Friar, J. H., & Meyer, M. H. (2003). Entrepreneurship and start-ups in the Boston region: Factors differ- entiating high-growth ventures from micro-ven- tures. *Small Business Economics*, *21*(2), 145–152. doi:10.1023/A:1025045828202

Friederici, N., Ojanperä, S., & Graham, M. (2017). The impact of connectivity in Africa: Grand visions and the mirage of inclusive digital development. *The Electronic Journal on Information Systems in Developing Countries*, *79*(1), 1–20. doi:10.1002/j.1681-4835.2017.tb00578.x

Friedman, M. (2009). *Capitalism and freedom*. New York: University of Chicago press.

Frisch, M. H. (1982). Urban Theorists, Urban Reform, and American Political Culture in the Progressive Period. *Political Science Quarterly*, *97*(2), 295–315. doi:10.2307/2149480

Fua, Y., & Kamenou, N. (2011). The Impact of Chinese values on Human resource policies and practices within trans-national corporations in China. *The International Journal of Human Resource Management, 22*(16), 3270-3289.

Fuchs, C. (2018). *Digital Demagogue: Authoritarian Capitalism in the Age of Trump and Twitter*. Pluto Press. doi:10.2307/j.ctt21215dw

Fuentelsaz, L., & Gonzáles, C. (2015). El Fracaso Emprendedor A Través De Las Instituciones Y La Calidad Del Emprendimiento. *Universidad Bussiness Review.*

Fuentelsaz, L., González, C., & Maícas, J. P. (2015). ¿Ayudan Las Instituciones A Entender El Emprendimiento*? Economía Industrial.*

Fujita, K. (2013). *Introduction: Cities and Crisis: New Critical Urban Theory*. Retrieved from http://sk.sagepub.com/books/cities-and-crisis/n1.xml

Gada, K. (2016). *Digital Economy in 5 minutes*. Retrieved from https://www.forbes.com/sites/koshagada/2016/06/16/what-is-the-digitaleconomy/#74c40ef77628

Gamidullaeva, L., Vasin, S., & Mkrttchian, V. (2018). *Regional Economic Growth and Open Innovation Platforms: Emerging Trends and New Opportunities*. Academic Press.

Gamidullaeva, L. A., Potapova, I., & Shatokhin, M. (2019). Increasing Territorial Economic Growth Through Cost Optimization in the Digital Economy. In U. Benna (Ed.), *Optimizing Regional Development Through Transformative Urbanization* (pp. 225–250). Hershey, PA: IGI Global. doi:10.4018/978-1-5225-5448-6.ch011

Gamidullaeva, L., Potapova, I., Shatokhin, M., & Mkrttchian, V. (2018). Increasing Territorial Economic Growth through Cost Optimization in the Digital Economy. In *Optimizing Regional Development Through Transformative Urbanization*. Hershey, PA: IGI Global; doi:10.4018/978-1-5225-5448-6.ch009

Gamidullaeva, L., Vasin, S., & Mkrttchian, V. (2018). *Regional Economic Growth and Open Innovation Platforms: Emerging Trends and New Opportunities*. Academic Press.

Garau, M., Ghiani, E., Celli, G., & Pilo, F. (2017). *Tecno-economic and environmental assessment of a full electric smart city eco-district*. Paper presented at the 2017 AEIT International Annual Conference, Cagliari, Italy. 10.23919/AEIT.2017.8240566

Garcia, B. (2007). Working and Learning in a Knowledge City: A Framework for Knowledge Workers. *Journal of Knowledge Management, 11*(5), 18–30. doi:10.1108/13673270710819771

Gebreyes, M., Zinyengere, N., Theodory, T. F., & Speranza, C. I. (2017). Introduction: Grounding Climate Change, Vulnerability, and Adaptation in Africa. In Beyond Agricultural Impacts (pp. 1-11). Academic Press.

Gehl, J. (1996). *Life Between Buildings: Using Public Space*. Arkitektens Forlag.

George, G., Corbishley, C., Khayesi, J. N., Haas, M. R., & Tihanyi, L. (2016). Bringing Africa in: Promising directions for management research. *Academy of Management Journal, 59*(2), 377–393. doi:10.5465/amj.2016.4002

Gerald, M. J. (2000). Cross-cultural Industrial and Organizational psychology: introduction to the special issue. *Journal of Applied Psychology: An International Review*, 191-123.

Geyer & Kontuly. (1993). A Theoretical Foundation for the Concept of Differential Urbanisation. *International Regional Science Review, 17*(2), 157-177.

Geyer, H. (1996). Expanding the Theoretical Foundation of the Concept of Differential Urbanisation. *Tijdschrift voor Economische en Sociale Geografie, 87*(1), 44-59.

Giap, T. K., Thye, W. W., & Aw, G. (2014). A new approach to measuring the liveability of cities: The Global Liveable Cities Index. *World Review of Science, Technology and Sustainable Development, 11*(2), 176–196. doi:10.1504/WRSTSD.2014.065677

Gil-Garcia, J. R., Pardo, T. A., & Nam, T. (2015). What makes a city smart? Identifying core com-ponents and proposing an integrative and comprehensive conceptualization. *Information Polity, 20*(1), 61–87. doi:10.3233/IP-150354

Gil-Garcia, J. R., Zhang, J., & Puron-Cid, G. (2016). Conceptualizing smartness in government: An integrative and multi-dimensional view. *Government Information Quarterly, 33*(3), 524–534. doi:10.1016/j.giq.2016.03.002

GIZ. (2012). *Green Economy in Sub-Saharan Africa – Lessons from Benin, Ethiopia, Ghana, Namibia and Nigeria.* Retrieved from www.greengrowthknowledge.org/resource/green-economysub-saharan-africa-lessons-benin-ethiopia-ghana-namibia-andnigeria

GIZ. (2015). *Nigerian Energy Sector: An Overview with a Special Emphasis on Renewable Energy, Energy Efficiency and Rural Electrification* (2nd ed.). Available at https://www.giz.de/en/downloads/giz2015-en-nigerian-energy-sector.pdf

Glasmeier, A., & Christopherson, S. (2015). Thinking about smart cities. *Cambridge Journal of Regions, Economy and Society, 8*(1), 3–12. doi:10.1093/cjres/rsu034

Glazyev, S. Y. (1990). Economic theory of technical development. Moscow: Nauka.

Glazyev, S. Y. (1993). Theory of long-term technical and economic development. Moscow: Vlada Dar.

Global Parliament of Mayors (GPM). (2018). Retrieved from https://globalparliamentofmayors.org/program-2018/

Gollin, D., Lagakos, D., & Waugh, M. (2013). *The Agricultural Productivity Gap in Developing Countries.* Cambridge, UK: Faculty of Economics, Cambridge University. doi:10.3386/w19628

Goodfellow, T. (2015). Taming the "Rogue" sector: Studying state effectiveness in Africa through informal transport politics. *Comparative Politics, 47*(2), 127–147. doi:10.5129/001041515814224462

Goody, J. (2018). *Technology, tradition and the state in Africa.* Routledge.

Gorbunova, Yu. N., Bykova, A. V., & Chernyshenko, S. V. (2012) Social and psychological aspects of education process quality as a factor of forming competitiveness of a manager in labour market. *Human Resources Management in the Russian Innovation Economy. Conference Proceedings*, 106-112.

Gordon, C. (2017). *A Silver Economy: The value of living longer.* Retrieved from https://www.smartgrowthbop.org.nz/media/2034/silver-economy-report-final- a8179931-compressed-002-a8694352.pdf

Govers, R., & Go, F. (2016). *Place Branding: Glocal, Virtual and Physical Identities, Constructed, Imagined and Experienced.* Retrieved from https://books.google.com.sa/books?isbn=0230247024

Graham, M., & Foster, G. (2014). *Geographies of information inequality in sub-Saharan Africa.* Available online: https://opendocs.ids.ac.uk/opendocs/bitstream/handle/123456789/11947/Geographies-of-Information-Inequality-in-Sub-Saharan-Africa.pdf

Green, P. (2009). *Industrialisation in South Africa: The Impact of Globalisation.* Norwich: University of East Anglia.

Greve, A. (2013). Learning from Tokyo urbanism: The urban sanctuaries. *Cities (London, England), 30*, 98–104. doi:10.1016/j.cities.2011.12.007

Grover, V., Teng, J., & Cheon, M. (1998). Towards a theoretically-based contingency model of information systems outsourcing. In L. Willcocks & M. Lacity (Eds.), *Strategic Sourcing of Information Systems* (pp. 79–101). Chichester, UK: Wiley.

Guneralp, B., Lwasa, S., Masundire, H., Parnell, S., & Seto, K. (2018). Urbanization in Africa: Challenges and opportunities for conservation. *Environmental Research Letters*, *13*, 2–8.

Gurov, G., & Polunin, Y. (2017). The attack of "blue collars". *Expert*, *3*, 12–17.

Habitat. (2018). *Africa Urban Agenda Programme*. Retrieved 07 09, 2018, from UN-Habitat: https://unhabitat.org/urban-initiatives/initiatives-programmes/africa-urban-agenda-programme/

Hack, G., Birch, E. L., Sedway, P. H., & Silver, M. J. (2009). *Local Planning: Contemporary Principles and Practice*. IGMA Press.

Haldevang, M. (2016). *Why do we still use the term "sub-Saharan Africa"?* Available at: https://qz.com/770350/why-do-we-still-say-subsaharan-africa/

Hamel, G., & Prahalad, C. (1996). Competing for the Future. Harvard Business School Press.

Harrison, G. (2005). 'Economic faith, Social project and a misreading of African society: The travails of neo-liberalism in Africa'. *Third World Quarterly*, *26*(8), 1303–1320. doi:10.1080/01436590500336922

Harry, D. M. (2016). Export Processing Zones and Economic Diversification in Nigeria, 2001 – 2013. *Journal of Political Science and Leadership Research, 2*(2). Retrieved from www.iiardpub.org

Hatton, T., & Williamson, J. G. (2005). *Global migration and the world economy: two centuries of policy and performance*. Cambridge, MA: MIT Press.

Hausberger, B. (1995). La minería novohispana vista a través de los libros de cargo y data de la Real Hacienda. *Estudios de Historia Novohispana*, *15*, 36-66.

Hawken, P., Lovins, A. B., & Lovins, L. H. (2013). *Natural capitalism: The next industrial revolution*. Oxford, UK: Routledge. doi:10.4324/9781315065755

Herbst, J. (2000). *States and Power in Africa: Comparative Lessons in Authority and Control*. Princeton, NJ: Princeton University Press.

Hereher, M. E. (2012). Analysis of urban growth at Cairo, Egypt using remote sensing and GIS. *Nature and Science*, *4*(6), 355–361. doi:10.4236/ns.2012.46049

Herrera, R. (2006). La perspectiva teórica en el estudio de las migraciones. siglo XXI editores.

Hess, C., & Ostrom, E. (2007). *Understanding Knowledge as a Commons. From Theory to Practice*. Cambridge, MA: MIT Press.

Hitt, M. A., Ireland, R. D., Sirmon, D. G., & Trahms, C. A. (2011). Strategic Entrepreneurship: Creating Value For Individuals, Organizations, And Society. *The Academy of Management Perspectives*, *25*(2), 57–75.

Hitt, M. A., Keats, B. W., & DeMarie, S. M. (1998). Navifating in the new competitive landscape:Building competitive advantage flexibility in the 21st century. *The Academy of Management Executive*, *12*, 22–42.

Hofsetde, G. (2001). Culture Consequences: Comparing values, Behaviors, Institutions and Organizations across Nations, Thousand Oaks California. *Sage (Atlanta, Ga.)*, *2001*, 25–40.

Hofstede, G. (2011). *Culture's consequences* (1st ed.). Thousand Oaks, CA: Sage Publ.

Hollands, R. G. (2008). Will the real smart city please stand up? Intelligent, progressive or entrepreneurial? *City*, *12*(3), 303–320. doi:10.1080/13604810802479126

Hollinger, F. (2015). *Agricultural Growth in West Africa, Market and policy drivers*. Food and Agriculture Organisation. Africa Development Bank Group

Hongchen, Y. (2008). *Three essays on internal migration. Tesis para optar por el Grado de Doctor en Fisología*. Universidad de Manitoba.

Horn, A. (2015). Urban Growth Management Best Practices: Towards Implications for the Developing World. *International Planning Studies*, *20*(1-2), 131–145. doi:10.1080/13563475.2014.942513

House, R. J., Wright, N. S., & Aditya, R. N. (1997). Cross-Cultural research on organizational leaderhip: a critical analysis and a proposed theory. In New Perspectives in international industrial Organizational Psychology. New Lexington Press.

Hove, M., Ngwerume, E. T., & Muchemwa, C. (2013). The Urban Crisis in Sub-Saharan Africa. A Threat to Human Security and Sustainable Development. *Stability*, *2*(1), 1–14. doi:10.5334ta.ap

Ibarra, D. G. (1995). *Minería en México durante el Siglo XVIII ¿Auge o decadencia? Estudios*. Filososìa-historia-letras. Otoño.

Ibitoye, F., & Adenikinju, A. (2007). Future demand for electricity in Nigeria. *Applied Energy*, *84*(5), 492–504. doi:10.1016/j.apenergy.2006.09.011

IGAD. (2018). *About Us*. Retrieved 2018, from Peace, Prosperity and Regional Integration: https://igad.int/about-us

ILO. Analytical center's calculations. URL: http://ac.gov.ru/files/publication/a/13612.pdf (address date: 05/01/2018)

IMF. (2012). *Going Green*. Retrieved from http://www.imf.org/external/pubs/ft/fandd/2012/06/eyraud.htm

IMF. (2018). *Changing Wealth of Nations: Building a Sustainable Future*. Retrieved from https://openknowledge.worldbank.org/handle/10986/29001

INEGI. (2000). *General Population and Housing Census*. INEGI.

INEGI. (2010). *Volume and growth Total population by size of locality for each state*. INEGI.

INEGI. (2010). *Volumen y crecimiento. Población total según tamaño de localidad para cada entidad federativa*. INEGI.

Infodev. (2018). *About Us*. Retrieved from http://www.infodev.org/

Institute of Development Studies. (2017). *Climate change and stability in North Africa*. London: DFID.

International Energy Agency (IEA). (2006). *World Energy Outlook: Energy For Cooking In Developing*. Retrieved from https://www.iea.org/publications/freepublications/publication/cooking.pdf

International Energy Agency. (2013). *Key World Energy Statistics*. Available at: https://webstore.iea.org/key-world-energy-statistics-2013

International Telecommunication Union (ITU). (2018). *About ITU*. Retrieved from https://www.itu.int/en/about/Pages/default.aspx

Isaias, P. (2017). *Innovation in the digital economy*. Retrieved from https://www.igi-global.com/book/user-innovation-entrepreneurship-phenomenon-digital/178736\

Isaias, P., & Carvalho, L. (2017). *User Innovation and the Entrepreneurship Phenomenon in the Digital Economy.* Retrieved from https://www.igi-global.com/book/user-innovation-entrepreneurship-phenomenon-digital/178736

Ison, R., Röling, N., & Watson, D. (2007). Challenges to science and society in the sustainable management and use of water: Investigating the role of social learning. *Environmental Science & Policy, 10*(6), 499–511. doi:10.1016/j.envsci.2007.02.008

Ivanov, V.V., & Malinetsky, G.G. (2017). Digital Economy: Myths, Reality, Opportunities. Russian Lvov D.S. Theoretical and Applied Aspects of NTP Management. *Economics and Mathematical Methods, 1986*(5).

Ivanov, V. V. (2017). Global humanitarian and technological revolution: Preconditions and prospects. *Innovations, 6*(224), 11–16.

Iyer, L. (2007). *Direct Versus Indirect Colonial Rule in India: Long-term Consequences.* Working Paper.

Jansen, F. (2002). *The Age of Innovation..* INFRA-M.

Janssen, M., Matheus, R., & Zuiderwijk, A. (2015, August). Big and open linked data (BOLD) to create smart cities and citizens: Insights from smart energy and mobility cases. In *International Conference on Electronic Government* (pp. 79-90). Springer. 10.1007/978-3-319-22479-4_6

Jedwab, R., Gollin, D., & Vollrath, D. (2014). *Urbanization with and without Industrialization.* Working Papers. 2014-01. Retrieved from https://ideas.repec.org/p/gwi/wpaper/2014-01.html

Johannessen, Å., & Wamsler, C. (2017). What does resilience mean for urban water services? *Ecology and Society, 22*(1), 1. doi:10.5751/ES-08870-220101

Johnson, K., Nucci, A., & Long, L. (2005). Population trends and nonmetropolitan America: selective deconcentration and the rural rebound. Populaiton Research Policy, 24(5).

Johnson, O., Muhoza, C., Osano, P., Senyagwa, J., & Kartha, S. (2017). *Catalysing Investment in Sustainable Energy Infrastructure in Africa.* Overcoming Financial and Non-Financial Constraints (No. 3). SEI Working Paper.

Jones, H. R. (1990). A population geography. Sage Publications Limited (Ltd).

Judd, K., & Tesfatsion, L. (Eds.). (2006). *Handbook of Computational Economics* (Vol. 2). North Holland.

Juniper. (2017). *Smart cities – what's in it for citizens?* Retrieved from https://newsroom.intel.com/wp-content/uploads/sites/11/2018/03/smart-cities-whats-in-it-for-citizens.pdf

Kagermann, H., Helbig, J., Hellinger, A., & Wahlster, W. (2013). *Recommendations for Implementing the Strategic Initiative INDUSTRIE 4.0: Securing the Future of German Manufacturing Industry.* Final Report of the Industrie 4.0 Working Group.

Kagermann, H., Lukas, W. D., & Wahlster, W. (2011). Industrie 4.0: Mit dem Internet der Dinge auf dem Weg zur 4. industriellen Revolution. VDI Nachrichten, 13.

Kalu, K., Yacob-Haliso, O., & Falola, T. (2018). Introduction. In *Africa's Big Men* (pp. 15–32). Oxon, UK: Routledge. doi:10.4324/9780203712870-1

Kamukama, D., & Kakwenzire, J. (2017). The Development and Consolidation of Extremist Forces in Rwanda 1990–1994. In *The Path of a Genocide* (pp. 61–92). Oxford, UK: Routledge.

Karapetyants, I., Kostuhin, Y., Tolstykh, T., Shkarupeta, E., & Krasnikova, A. (2017). Establishment of Research Competencies in the Context of Russian Digitalization. *Proceedings of the 30th International Business Information Management Association Conference (IBIMA)*, 845-854.

Karezeki, S., & Kithyoma, W. (2003). *Renewable Energy in Africa: Prospects and Limits*. Paper presented at the Workshop for African Energy Experts on Operationalizing the NEPAD Energy Initiative, Dakar, Senegal.

Karimi, K. (2012). Are ection on 'Order and structure in urban design'. *The Journal of Space Syntax, 3*(1), 38–48.

Karlenzig, W., Zhenhua, Z., & Peck, M. (2017). *Transforming the Urban Economy*. Retrieved from http://www.un.org/esa/dsd/susdevtopics/sdt_pdfs/shanghaimanual/Chapter%203%20- %20Economic%20transformation.pdf

Kebbi State Government. (2006). *Kebbi State Economic Empowerment and Development Strategy-KB-SEEDS*. Kebbi State Government Printing Press.

Kebbi State Government. (2014). *Transformation the Journey so far. Kebbi State Ministry of Information, Youth, Sports & Culture*.

Kemp, R. (2016). Fourth industrial revolution. *The Lawyer, 31*(21), 12.

Khatoun, R., & Zeadally, S. (2016). Smart cities: Concepts, architectures, research opportunities. *Communications of the ACM, 59*(8), 46–57. doi:10.1145/2858789

Khvostikova, V., Semionova, E., Chernetsov, M., Mkrttchian, V., & Potapova, I. (2017). Cost Control Strategy for the Implementation of the User Innovation Potential in the Digital Economy. InIsaias, P., & Carvalho, L. (Eds.), *User Innovation and the Entrepreneurship Phenomenon in the Digital Economy* (pp. 267–287). Hershey, PA: IGI Global. doi:10.4018/978-1-5225-2826-5.ch013

Kieh, G. K. Jr. (2018). The "Hegemonic Presidency" in African Politics. *African Social Science Review, 9*(1), 5.

Kinai, A., Bryant, R. E., Walcott-Bryant, A., Mibuari, E., Weldemariam, K., & Stewart, O. (2014, June). Twende-twende: a mobile application for traffic congestion awareness and routing. In *Proceedings of the 1st International Conference on Mobile Software Engineering and Systems* (pp. 93-98). ACM. 10.1145/2593902.2593926

Kitchin, R. (2015). Making sense of smart cities: Addressing present shortcomings. *Cambridge Journal of Regions, Economy and Society, 8*(1), 131–136. doi:10.1093/cjres/rsu027

Klopp, J. M., & Paller, J. W. (2015, October 9). *How Africa can build inclusive, safe and sustainable cities*. Retrieved 07 09, 2018, from The Conversation: https://theconversation.com/how-africa-can-build-inclusive-safe-and-sustainable-cities-48445

Klopp, J. M. (2011). *Towards a Political Economy of Transportation Policy and Practice in Nairobi*. Science and Business Media.

Kniivila, M. (2016). Industrial development and economic growth: Implications for poverty reduction and income inequality. *Sustainable Development Perspectives., 1*(3), 295–333.

Knutsen, C. H., Kotsadam, A., Olsen, E. H., & Wig, T. (2017). Mining and local corruption in Africa. *American Journal of Political Science, 61*(2), 320–334. doi:10.1111/ajps.12268

Koch, G. (2015). Knowledge Cities versus Smart Cities - A discussion triggered on occasion of the case of Timisoara, Romania. In *13th NETTIES Conference (Network Entities) on "Open Data and Big Data – The Impact on Digital Society and Smart Cities"*. IAFeS.

Kolberg, D., & Zühlke, D. (2015). *Lean automation enabled by industry 4.0 technologies*. Academic Press.

Kollman, Miller, & Page. (1997). Political institutions and sorting in a Tiebout model. *The American Economic Review*, *87*, 977–922.

Koslowski, P. (Ed.). (2013). *The Theory of Capitalism in the German Economic Tradition: Historism, Ordo-Liberalism, Critical Theory, Solidarism*. New York: Springer.

Kraftl, P. (2014). Liveability and urban architectures: Mol(ecul)ar biopower and the 'becoming lively' of sustainable communities. *Environment and Planning. D, Society & Space*, *32*(2), 274–292. doi:10.1068/d21012

Krevskiy, I. G., Bershadsky, A., & Glotova, T. (2018). Research Competence for Development of Distance Education in Russian Universities. In V. Mkrttchian, & L. Belyanina (Eds.), Handbook of Research on Students' Research Competence in Modern Educational (pp. 385-408). IGI Global. Doi:10.4018/978-1-5225-3485-3.ch020

Krivosheev, O.V. (2017). *Digital economy in Russia. Technological backlogs*. Academic Press.

Kupriyanovsky, V. P., Dobrynin, A. P., & Sinyagov, S. A. (2017). A holistic model of transformation in digital economy – how to become digital leaders. *International Journal of Open Information Technologies*, *5*(1), 26–33.

Kurdyumov, S. P. (n.d.). *Development of the digital economy in Russia*. Retrieved from http://spkurdyumov.ru/digital_economy/razvitie-cifrovoj-ekonomiki-v-rossii-programma-do-2035-goda/

Kwani, Y.A., & Ofori, G. (2001). Chinese Culture and Successful Implementation of partnering in Singapore's Construction Industry. *Construction Management and Economics, 19*, 619–632.

Kylili, A., & Fokaides, P. A. (2015). European smart cities: The role of zero energy buildings. *Sustainable Cities and Society, 15*, 86–95. doi:10.1016/j.scs.2014.12.003

Labor productivity in Russia. A social bulletin for July 2017. (n.d.). The Analytical Center of the Government of the Russian Federation. Retrieved from http://ac.gov.ru/files/publication/a/13612.pdf

Lall, S. V., Henderson, J. V., & Venables, A. J. (2017). *Africa's cities: Opening doors to the world*. The World Bank. doi:10.1596/978-1-4648-1044-2

Lash, H. (1976). *Planning in a human way: personal reflections on the regional planning experience in Greater Vancouver*. Ministry of State for Urban Affairs.

Lasi, H., Fettke, P., Kemper, H. G., Feld, T., & Hoffmann, M. (2014). Industry 4.0. *Business & Information Systems Engineering*, *6*(4), 239. doi:10.100712599-014-0334-4

Leather, J., Fabian, H., Gota, S., & Mejia, A. (2011). *Walkability and Pedestrian Facilities in Asian Cities: State and Issues*. Metro Manila, Philippines: Asian Development Bank.

LeBaron, B., & Winker, P. (2008). Introduction to the Special Issue on Avatar-Based Models for Economic Policy Advice. *Journal of Economics and Statistics, 228*.

LeCorbusier. (1982). *The City of To-morrow and Its Planning*. New York: Dover.

LeCorbusier. (1991). *Précisions* (E. S. Aujame, Trans.). Cambridge, MA: MIT Press.

LeCorbusier. (2013). *Towards a New Architecture* (1931 ed.). London: Courier Corporation.

Ledent, J. (1982). Rural-urban migration, urbanization and economic development. *Economic Development and Cultural Change*, *30*(3), 507–503. doi:10.1086/452574

Lee, A., & Schultz, K. A. (2011). *Comparing British and French colonial legacies: A discontinuity analysis of Cameroon*. Working paper.

Lee, J. H., Hancock, M. G., & Hu, M. C. (2014). Towards an effective framework for building smart cities: Lessons from Seoul and San Francisco. *Technological Forecasting and Social Change*, *89*, 80–99. doi:10.1016/j.techfore.2013.08.033

Lee, J., Kao, H. A., & Yang, S. (2014). Service innovation and smart analytics for industry 4.0 and big data environment. *Procedia CIRP*, *16*, 3–8. doi:10.1016/j.procir.2014.02.001

Lema, R., Iizuka, M., & Walz, R. (2015). Introduction to low Carbon Innovation and Development: Insights and Future Challenges for Research. *Innovation and Development*, *5*(2), 173–187. doi:10.1080/2157930X.2015.1065096

Lennard, S. H., & Lennard, H. L. (1995). *Livable cities observed: a source book of images and ideas for city officials, community leaders, architects, planners and all other committed to making their cities livable.* Southampton, UK: Gondolier Press.

León & Romero. (Eds.). (2001). *La población de México. Tendencias y perspectives demográficas hacia el Siglo XXI.* Consejo Nacional de Población-Fondo de Cultura Económica.

Letaifa, S. B. (2015). How to strategize smart cities: Revealing the SMART model. *Journal of Business Research*, *68*(7), 1414–1419. doi:10.1016/j.jbusres.2015.01.024

Ley De Promoción Y Desarrollo De Los Bionergéticos. (2008). *Ley De Promoción Y Desarrollo De Los Bionergéticos.* Publicado En El Diario Oficial De La Federación El Primero De Febrero De.

Ley, A., & Newton, P. (2010). Creating and sustaining liveable cities. In S. Kallidaikurichi & B. Yuen (Eds.), Developing Living Cities: From Analysis to Action (pp. 191-230). Singapore: World Scientific. doi:10.1142/9789814304504_0008

Li, F. (2018). Retrieved from https://punchng.com/exploring-the-impacts-of-digital-transformation-on-nigerian-economyRetrieved 27/7/2018

Licciardi, A. G., & Bigio, G. (2010). *The Urban Rehabilitation of Medinas. The World Bank Experience in the Middle East and North Africa (English). Urban Development Series No. 9.* Washington, DC: The World Bank.

Liñán, F., Fernández, J., & Romero, I. (2013). Necessity And Opportunity Entrepreneurship: The Mediating Effect Of Culture. *Revista de Economía Mundial*, *33*, 21–47.

Lo, C. F., & Salih, K. (Eds.). (1978). Growth Pole Strategy and Regional Development Policy: Asian Experience and Alternative Approaches. Pergamon Press.

Long, L., & Nucci, A. (1997). The 'clean break' revisited: Is the U.S. population again deconcentrating. Environment and Planning, 29(8).

Loof, H., & Brostrom, A. (2006). *Does Knowledge Diffusion between University and Industry Increase Innovativeness?* Centre of Excellence for Science and Innovation Studies Working Paper Series No. 21.

Lough, A. W. (2016). Editor's Introduction: The Politics of Urban Reform in the Gilded Age and Progressive Era, 1870–1920. *American Journal of Economics and Sociology, 75*(1), 8-22. doi:10.1111/ajes.12139

Lund, H., Werner, S., Wiltshire, R., Svendsen, S., Thorsen, J. E., Hvelplund, F., & Mathiesen, B. V. (2014). 4th Generation District Heating (4GDH): Integrating smart thermal grids into future sustainable energy systems. *Energy*, *68*, 1–11. doi:10.1016/j.energy.2014.02.089

Lynch, K. (1960). *The Image of the City*. Cambridge, MA: The MIT Press.

Ma, Z., Lundgaard, M., & Jørgensen, B. N. (2016, November). Triple-layer smart grid business model: A comparison between sub-Saharan Africa and Denmark. In Innovative Smart Grid Technologies-Asia (ISGT-Asia), 2016 IEEE (pp. 347-352). IEEE.

Mahesh, S. R. (2003). *Business Intelligence in the Digital Economy: Opportunities, Limitations and Risks.* Retrieved from https://www.igi-global.com/book/business-intelligence-digital-economy/117

Mahesh, S. R. (2008). *Handbook of Research on Global Information Technology Management in the Digital Economy.* Retrieved from https://www.igi-global.com/book/handbook-research-global-information-technology/472

Mahoney, J. (2012). *Property rights theory. In Economic Fundations of Strategy* (pp. 158–199). Academic Press.

Mailafia, O. (2016). *Industrial Policy and the Path to Mass Industrialization in Nigeria.* Available from http://www.businessdayonline.com/industrial-policy-and-the-path-to-mass-industrialisation-in-nigeria/https://papers.ssrn.com/sol3/papers.cfm?abstarct id=1266633 Retrieved 15/6/2018

Makuwira, J. (2017). *Governing the ungovernable: donor agencies and the politics of development in Africa. Africa Journal of Public Affairs.*

Makwe, J., Akinwale, Y. & Atoyebi, M. (2012). An Economic Assessment of the Reform of Nigerian Electricity Market. *Energy and Power, 2*(3), 24-32.

Malerba, F. (2005). Sectoral systems of innovation: A framework for linking innovation to the knowledge base, structure and dynamics of sectors. *Economics of Innovation and New Technology, 14*(1-2), 63–82. doi:10.1080/1043859042000228688

Malinetsky, G. G. (2015). *To make a fairy tale happen ... High technology is Russia's way to the future* (3rd ed.). Moscow: LENAND.

Manville, C., Cochrane, G., Cave, J., Millard, J., Pederson, J. K., Thaarup, R. K., . . . Kotterink, B. (2014). *Mapping smart cities in the EU.* Available online: http://www.europarl.europa.eu/RegData/etudes/etudes/join/2014/507480/IPOL-ITRE_ET(2014)507480_EN.pdf

Markham, S., Kingon, A., Zapata, M., & Baumer, D. (1999). A methodology to find assess and commercialize technologies, civilization, modern technology and sustainable development. *The Eighth International Conference on Management of Technology.*

Martinez, C., Cummings, M. E., & Vaaler, P. M. (2015). Economic informality and the venture funding impact of migrant remittances to developing countries. *Journal of Business Venturing, 30*(4), 526–545. doi:10.1016/j.jbusvent.2014.10.004

Martinot, E. (1998). Energy efficiency and renewable energy in Russia: Transaction barriers, market intermediation and capacity building. *Energy Policy, 26*(11), 905–915. doi:10.1016/S0301-4215(98)00022-6

Marulanda, F. Morales, S. (2016). Entorno Y Motivaciones Para Emprender. *Revista Escuela De Administración De Negocios,* 8.

Mathur, V. K., & Stein y Kumar, S. H. R. (1988). A dynamic model of regional population growth and decline. Journal of Regional Science, 28(3).

Mbiba, B. (2017). *On the Periphery: Missing Urbanisation in Zimbabwe.* London: Africa Research Institute.

McCarroll, N., & Curran, K. (2013). Social Networking in Education. *International Journal of Innovation in the Digital Economy, 4*(1), 1–15. doi:10.4018/jide.2013010101

McKinsey & Company. (2017). *Jobs lost, jobs gained.* Retrieved from https://www.mckinsey.com/featured-insights/future-of-organizations-and-work/jobs-lost-jobs-gained-what-the-future-of-work-will-mean-for-jobs-skills-and-wages

McKinsey& Company. (2016). *Urban world: Meeting the demographic challenge in cities.* Retrieved from https://www.mckinsey.com/featured-insights/urbanization/urban-world-meeting-the-demographic-challenge-in-cities

McWilliams, D. (2015). *The Flat White Economy: How the Digital Economy Is Transforming London and Other Cities of the Future*. London: Duckworth Publishers.

Medina, I., Chavez, N. Y., & Jauregui, J. (2012). Biodiesel, Un Combustible Renovable. *Investigación Y Ciencia, 20*, 62-70.

Meiss, P. v. (1990). *Elements of Architecture: From Form to Place*. Taylor & Francis.

Melonakos, B. (2011). *Informal Economy*. Retrieved from http://pubs.iied.org/pdfs/10722IIED.pdf

Menyah, K., Nazlioglu, S., & Wolde-Rufael, Y. (2014). Financial development, trade openness and economic growth in African countries: New insights from a panel causality approach. *Economic Modelling, 37*, 386–394. doi:10.1016/j.econmod.2013.11.044

Merem, E. C., Twumasi, Y., Wesley, J., Isokpehi, P., Shenge, M., Fageir, S., ... Ochai, S. (2017). Regional Assessment of Energy Trends in West Africa Using GIS. *International Journal of Energy Engineering, 7*(1), 1–27. doi:10.5923/j.ijee.20170701.01

Merkin, R. S. (2006). Uncertainty avoidance and face work: A test of the Hofstede Model. *International Journal of Intercultural Relations, 30*(2), 213–228. doi:10.1016/j.ijintrel.2005.08.001

Metropolis Commission. (2011). Managing Urban Growth. Commission Report 2. Metropolis Commission II, Melbourne, Australia.

Meyer, D., Passenberg, C., Feldmaier, J., & Shen, H. (2016). Dynamic Programming for Smart Water Heater Control. *Integration of Sustainable Energy Conference (iSEneC) 2016.*

Mguni, P., Herslund, L., & Jensen, M. B. (2016). Sustainable urban drainage systems: Examining the potential for green infrastructure-based stormwater management for Sub-Saharan cities. *Natural Hazards, 82*(2), 241–257. doi:10.100711069-016-2309-x

Migdal, J. S. (2018). The state in society. In *New Directions in Comparative Politics* (pp. 63–79). Oxford, UK: Routledge. doi:10.4324/9780429494932-4

Milana, B. F., & Creutziga, F. (2016). Municipal policies accelerated urban sprawl and public debts in Spain. *Land Use Policy, 54*, 103–115. doi:10.1016/j.landusepol.2016.01.009

Mills, G. (2018). Why Is Africa Poor? In *Culture and Civilization* (pp. 52–62). Oxon, UK: Routledge. doi:10.4324/9780203794128-4

Mitrofanova, E.A., Afanasyev, V.Y., & Chernyshenko, S.V. (2015). *Development of sectoral qualification framework: methodology and practice*. Moscow: Publishing House of State University of Management.

Mkandawire, T. (2015). Neopatrimonialism and the political economy of economic performance in Africa: Critical reflections. *World Politics, 67*(3), 563–612. doi:10.1017/S004388711500009X

Mkrttchian, V. (2015). Modeling using of Triple H-Avatar Technology in online Multi-Cloud Platform Lab. In M. Khosrow-Pour (Ed.), Encyclopedia of Information Science and Technology (3rd ed.; pp. 4162-4170). Hershey, PA: IGI Global. Doi:10.4018/978-1-4666-5888-2.ch409

Mkrttchian, V., & Stephanova, G. (2013). Training of Avatar Moderator in Sliding Mode Control Environment for Virtual Project Management. In Enterprise Resource Planning: Concepts, Methodologies, Tools, and Applications (pp. 1376-1405). Hershey, PA: IGI Global. Doi:10.4018/978-1-4666-4153-2.ch074

Mkrttchian, V., Kataev, M., Hwang, W., Bedi, S., & Fedotova, A. (2016). Using Plug-Avatars "hhh" Technology Education as Service-Oriented Virtual Learning Environment in Sliding Mode. In Leadership and Personnel Management: Concepts, Methodologies, Tools, and Applications (pp. 890-902). Hershey, PA: IGI Global. doi:10.4018/978-1-4666-9624-2.ch039

Mkrttchian, V. (2011). Use 'hhh" technology in transformative models of online education. In G. Kurubacak & T. Vokan Yuzer (Eds.), *Handbook of research on transformative online education and liberation: Models for social equality* (pp. 340–351). Hershey, PA: IGI Global. doi:10.4018/978-1-60960-046-4.ch018

Mkrttchian, V. (2012). Avatar manager and student reflective conversations as the base for describing meta-communication model. In G. Kurubacak, T. Vokan Yuzer, & U. Demiray (Eds.), *Meta-communication for reflective online conversations: Models for distance education* (pp. 340–351). Hershey, PA: IGI Global. doi:10.4018/978-1-61350-071-2.ch005

Mkrttchian, V., & Aleshina, E. (2017). *Sliding Mode in Intellectual Control and Communication: Emerging Research and Opportunities*. Hershey, PA: IGI Global. doi:10.4018/978-1-5225-2292-8

Mkrttchian, V., & Aleshina, E. (2017). Sliding Mode in Real Communication. In *Sliding Mode in Intellectual Control and Communication: Emerging Research and Opportunities* (pp. 22–29). Hershey, PA: IGI Global. doi:10.4018/978-1-5225-2292-8.ch003

Mkrttchian, V., Amirov, D., & Belyanina, L. (2017). Optimizing an Online Learning Course Using Automatic Curating in Sliding Mode. In N. Ostashewski, J. Howell, & M. Cleveland-Innes (Eds.), *Optimizing K-12 Education through Online and Blended Learning* (pp. 213–224). Hershey, PA: IGI Global. doi:10.4018/978-1-5225-0507-5.ch011

Mkrttchian, V., Aysmontas, B., Uddin, M., Andreev, A., & Vorovchenko, N. (2015). The Academic views from Moscow Universities of the Cyber U-Learning on the Future of Distance Education at Russia and Ukraine. In G. Eby & T. Vokan Yuzer (Eds.), *Identification, Evaluation, and Perceptions of Distance Education Experts* (pp. 32–45). Hershey, PA: IGI Global. doi:10.4018/978-1-4666-8119-4.ch003

Mkrttchian, V., & Belyanina, L. (Eds.). (2018). *Handbook of Research on Students' Research Competence in Modern Educational Contexts*. Hershey, PA: IGI Global. doi:10.4018/978-1-5225-3485-3

Mkrttchian, V., Berezin, An., Berezin, A., Veretikhina, S., Bershadsky, A., & Potapova, I. (2018). Model of Benchmarking for Development of Firm's Competitive Advantage to Improve Economic Growth in Cities. In U. G. Benna (Ed.), *Optimizing Regional Development Through Transformative Urbanization*. Hershey, PA: IGI Global. doi:10.4018/978-1-5225-5448-6.ch008

Mkrttchian, V., Bershadsky, A., Bozhday, A., & Fionova, L. (2015). Model in SM of DEE Based on Service Oriented Interactions at Dynamic Software Product Lines. In G. Eby & T. Vokan Yuzer (Eds.), *Identification, Evaluation, and Perceptions of Distance Education Experts* (pp. 230–247). Hershey, PA: IGI Global. doi:10.4018/978-1-4666-8119-4.ch014

Mkrttchian, V., Bershadsky, A., Bozhday, A., Kataev, M., & Kataev, S. (Eds.). (2016). *Handbook of Research on Estimation and Control Techniques in E-Learning systems*. Hershey, PA: IGI Global. doi:10.4018/978-1-4666-9489-7

Mkrttchian, V., Bershadsky, A., Finogeev, A., Berezin, A., & Potapova, I. (2017). Digital Model of Bench-Marking for Development of Competitive Advantage. In P. Isaias & L. Carvalho (Eds.), *User Innovation and the Entrepreneurship Phenomenon in the Digital Economy* (pp. 288–303). Hershey, PA: IGI Global. doi:10.4018/978-1-5225-2826-5.ch014

Mkrttchian, V., Kataev, M., Hwang, W., Bedi, S., & Fedotova, A. (2014). Using Plug-Avatars "hhh" Technology Education as Service-Oriented Virtual Learning Environment in Sliding Mode. In G. Eby & T. Vokan Yuzer (Eds.), *Emerging Priorities and Trends in Distance Education: Communication, Pedagogy, and Technology*. Hershey, PA: IGI Global. doi:10.4018/978-1-4666-5162-3.ch004

Mkrttchian, V., Palatkin, I., Gamidullaeva, L., & Panasenko, S. (2019). About digital avatars for control systems using Big Data and Knowledge sharing in virtual industries. In A. Gyamfi & I. Williams (Eds.), *Big Data and Knowledge Sharing in Virtual Organizations* (pp. 46–59). Hershey, PA: IGI Global. doi:10.4018/978-1-5225-7519-1ch.04

Mkrttchian, V., & Stephanova, G. (2013). Training of Avatar Moderator in Sliding Mode Control. In G. Eby & T. Vokan Yuzer (Eds.), *Project Management Approaches for Online Learning Design* (pp. 175–203). Hershey, PA: IGI Global. doi:10.4018/978-1-4666-2830-4.ch009

Mogalakwe, M. (2006). The Use of Documentary Research Methods in Social Research. *African Sociological Review, 10*(1), 221–230.

Mohanty, S. P., Choppali, U., & Kougianos, E. (2016). Everything you wanted to know about smart cities: The internet of things is the backbone. *IEEE Consumer Electronics Magazine, 5*(3), 60–70. doi:10.1109/MCE.2016.2556879

Mohit, M. A., & Iyanda, S. A. (2016). Liveability and Low-income Housing in Nigeria. *Social and Behavioral Sciences,* (222), 863 – 871.

Molina, C. (2012). Estudio de la composición y estabilidad de biodiesel obtenido a partir de aceites vegetales limpios y procedentes de aceites de fritura. Servicio de publicaciones de la Universidad de la Laguna.

Molle, F., & Mollinga, P. (2003). Water poverty indicators: conceptual problems and policy issues. *Water Policy, 5*(5-6), 529-544.

Montiel, L. M., Nathan, R. P., & Wright, D. J. (2004). *An Update on Urban Hardship*. Albany, NY: The Nelson A. Rockefeller Institute of Government.

Moomaw, W., Yamba, F., Kamimoto, M., Maurice, L., Nyboer, J., Urama, K., & Weir, T. (2011). Introduction. In *IPCC Special Report on Renewable Energy Sources and Climate Change Mitigation*. Cambridge, UK: Cambridge University Press.

Morse, S. W. (2005, June 27). *An Update on Urban Hardship*. Retrieved from Smart Communities: http://smartcommunities.typepad.com/suzanne/2005/06/an_update_on_ur.html

Mosel, I., & Jackson, A. (2013). *Sanctuary in the city? Urban displacement and Urban displacement and Pakistan.* Humanitarian Policy Group, Overseas Development Institute.

Muchadenyika, D., & Williams, J. J. (2017). Politics and the practice of planning: The case of Zimbabwean cities. *Cities (London, England), 63*, 33–40. doi:10.1016/j.cities.2016.12.022

Mudombi, S., & Muchie, M. (2014). An institutional perspective to challenges undermining innovation activities in Africa. *Innovation and Development, 4*(2), 313–326. doi:10.1080/2157930X.2014.921272

Mueller, T. (2017). Towards a New Paradigm of the Smart City. [Web log Post]. Retrieved from https://hub.beesmart.city/strategy/towards-a-new-paradigm-of-the-smart-city

Muggah, R. (2016). *Urban governance in fragile cities. GSDRC Professional Development Reading Pack no. 46.* Birmingham, UK: University of Birmingham.

Murithi, T. (2017). *The African Union: Pan-Africanism, peacebuilding and development.* Oxford, UK: Routledge. doi:10.4324/9781315241470

Musakwa, W. (2014). The use of social media in the Gautrain in Gauteng Province, South Africa: Analysis and Lessons learnt. REAL CORP 2014 Proceedings, 721-727.

Musakwa, W. (2017). Perspectives on geospatial information science education: An example of Urban Planners in Southern Africa. *Geo-Spatial Information Science*, *20*(2), 201–208. doi:10.1080/10095020.2017.1339403

Musakwa, W., & Van Niekerk, A. (2014). Earth observation for sustainable urban planning in developing countries: Needs, trends, and future directions. *Journal of Planning Literature*, *30*(2), 149–160. doi:10.1177/0885412214557817

Mutula, S. M. (2010). *Growth In the digital economy.* Retrieved from https://www.igi-global.com/chapter/growth-digital-economy/361010

Myers, N., & Jennifer, J. (1995). *Environmental Exodus: An Emergent Crisis in the Global Arena.* Washington, DC: Climate Institute.

Mytelka, L. (2000). Local systems of innovation in a globalized world economy. *Industry and Innovation*, *7*(1), 33–54. doi:10.1080/713670244

Naija. (2018). Retrieved from https://www.naija.com/1107405-osinbajo-dangote-peterside-34-appointments-see-full-list-html

Naji, M., Robin, B., Yunusa, M-B., & Matthew, C. (2015). *Economic Development in Urban Nigeria Technical Report.* Retrieved from www.researchgate.net/profile/publication/economic-development-in-urban-Nigeria

Nastasi, B., & Basso, G. L. (2016). Hydrogen to link heat and electricity in the transition towards future Smart Energy Systems. *Energy*, *110*, 5–22. doi:10.1016/j.energy.2016.03.097

Nathan, R. P., Charles, F., & Adams, J. (1976). Understanding Central City Hardship. *Political Science Quarterly*, *91*(1), 47–62. doi:10.2307/2149158

Nathan, R. P., Charles, F., & Adams, J. (1989). Four Perspectives on Urban Hardship. *Political Science Quarterly*, *104*(3), 483–508. doi:10.2307/2151275

Navarrete, D. (2004). Población y estructura ocupacional minera: Real del Monte en 1768. *II Congreso de Historia Económica Ciudad Universitaria.*

NBS. (2010). *Social statistics in Nigeria.* National Bureau of Statistics.

Neirotti, P., De Marco, A., Cagliano, A. C., Mangano, G., & Scorrano, F. (2014). Current trends in Smart City initiatives: Some stylized facts. *Cities (London, England)*, *38*, 25–36. doi:10.1016/j.cities.2013.12.010

Nelson, R. R. (1993). *National Innovation Systems: A Comparative Analysis.* Oxford University Press.

Neuman, M. (2005). The Compact City Fallacy. *Journal of Planning Education and Research*, *25*(1), 11–26. doi:10.1177/0739456X04270466

Neuwirth, R. (2005). Shadow Cities: A Billion Squatters, a New Urban World. New York: Routledge.

Newman, C., & Page, J. (2017). *Industrial clusters: The case for Special Economic Zones in Africa.* WIDER Working Paper 2017/15. United Nations University.

Nielsen. (2014). *Is sharing the new buying? Reputation and trust are emerging as new currencies.* The Nielsen Company. Retrieved from http://www.nielsen.com/content/dam/nielsenglobal/apac/docs/reports/2014/Nielsen-Global-Share-Community-Report.pdf

Ning, Z., Xia, F., Ullah, N., Kong, X., & Hu, X. (2017). Vehicular Social Networks: Enabling Smart Mobility. *IEEE Communications Magazine*, *55*(5), 16–55. doi:10.1109/MCOM.2017.1600263

Nissel, H. (2010). Global Capital, Neoliberal Politics and Terrains of resistance in Vienna. In S. Banerjee-Guha (Ed.), *Accumulation by Dispossession: Transformative Cities in the New Global Order* (pp. 55–74). Delhi: SAGE Publications India. doi:10.4135/9788132105923.n4

Njoh, A. J. (2004). The experience and legacy of French colonial urban planning in sub-Saharan Africa. *Planning Perspectives, 19*(4), 435–454. doi:10.1080/0266543042000268813

Njoku, O. (2006). NGOs and Africa's Development and Economic Growth. In *International Conference on the State of Affairs of Africa (ICSAA).* International Institute of Justice and Development. Available: http://www.iijd.org/PDF%20 Ogechi_njoku__NGOs-and-Africa.pdf

North, D. (1990). *Institutions, Institutional Change and Economic Performance.* Cambridge, UK: Cambridge University Press. doi:10.1017/CBO9780511808678

Ntuli, N., & Abu-Mahfouz, A. M. (2016). A simple security architecture for smart water management system. *Procedia Computer Science, 83,* 1164–1169. doi:10.1016/j.procs.2016.04.239

Nunkoo, R., Ribeiro, M. A., Sunnassee, V., & Gursoy, D. (2018). Public trust in mega event planning institutions: The role of knowledge, transparency and corruption. *Tourism Management, 66,* 155–166. doi:10.1016/j.tourman.2017.11.010

Nye, J. S. Jr. (2015). The decline of America's soft power. In *Paradoxes of Power* (pp. 39–44). Oxford, UK: Routledge.

O'Connor, J. (2001). *Causas Naturales. Ensayo de marxismo ecológico.* Siglo XXI Editores.

O'Connor, J. R. (1974). *The corporations and the State: essays in the theory of capitalism and imperialism.* Oxford, UK: Harper & Row.

Obaidat, M. S., & Nicopolitidis, P. (2016). *Smart Cities and Homes: Key Enabling Technologies.* Retrieved from https://books.google.com.sa/books?isbn=0128034637

Obeng-Odoom, F. (2015). Africa: On the rise, but to where? *The Forum for Social Economics, 44*(3), 234–250. doi:10.1080/07360932.2014.955040

OECD. (2002). *Frascati Manual: proposed Standard Practice for Surveys on Research and Experimental Development.* Paris, France: OECD.

OECD. (2005). Oslow Manual: Guideline for Collecting and Interpreting innovation Data. Paris, France: OECD.

OECD. (2010). *Shining Light on the Shadow Economy: Opportunities and Threats.* Retrieved from https://www.oecd.org/tax/crime/shining-light-on-the-shadow-economy-opportunities- and-threats.pdf

OECD. (2017). *Employment Implications of Green Growth: Linking jobs, growth, and green policies.* Retrieved from https://www.oecd.org/environment/Employment-Implications-of-Green-Growth-OECD-Report

OECD. (2017). *OECD Stats FAO Agricultura.* Retrieved from Http://Stats.Oecd.Org/Viewhtml.Aspx?Queryid=58648&Vh=0000&Vf=0&L&Il=&Lang=En#

OECD. (2018). *Economic Outlook for Southeast Asia, China and India 2018.* Retrieved from http://www.oecd.org/dev/economic-outlook-for-southeast-asia-china-and-india-23101113.htm

Ogbimi, F. (1991). Managing Education-Production Linkages: Bridging the Gap between Theoretical and Practical Skills in Nigeria. *Proceedings of the Conference jointly organized by Council for Registered Engineers of Nigeria (COREN) and Committee of Deans of Engineering and Technological Institutions (CODET) in Lagos,* 22-32.

Ogbimi, F. (2007). Solution to Mass Unemployment in Nigeria (3rd ed.). Society For Linking Education and Problems, Obafemi Awolowo University.

Ogbimi, F. (1990). Establishing a Policy Framework for Rapid Technological Advancement in Nigeria. *The Nigerian Engineer*, *25*(3), 1–8.

Ogunbanjo. (2015). Spatial Variations in Residential Property Development. *Ethiopian Journal of Environmental Sciences & Management.* doi:10.4314/ejesm.v81210

Ogunbodede, E. O., Kida, I. A., Madjapa, H. S., Amedari, M., Ehizele, A., Mutave, R., ... Okoye, L. (2015). Oral health inequalities between rural and urban populations of the African and Middle East region. *Advances in Dental Research*, *27*(1), 18–25. doi:10.1177/0022034515575538 PMID:26101336

Ogundari, I., Akinwale, Y., Adepoju, O., Atoyebi, M., & Akarakiri, J. (2017). Suburban Housing Development and Off-Grid Electric Power Supply Assessment for North-Central Nigeria. *International Journal of Sustainable Energy Planning and Management*, *12*, 47–64.

Okeke, R. C. (2017). Elitism, Local Governance and Development in Nigeria. *Speciality Journal of Politics and Law*, *2*(3), 62–72.

Okeke, R. C. (2017). Elitism, Local Governance and Development in Nigeria. *Specialty Journal of Politics and Law*, *2*(3), 62–72.

Okulicz-Kozaryn, A. (2013). City Life: Rankings (Livability) Versus Perceptions (Satisfaction). *Social Indicators Research. An International and Interdisciplinary Journal for Quality-of-Life Measurement*, *110*(2), 433–451.

Olaopa, O., Akinwale, Y., & Ogundari, I. (2018). Governance Institutions for Sustainable Energy Resources Management in Nigeria: Issues, Perspective and Policy Agenda for Action. In L. Asuelime & E. Okem (Eds.), *Political Economy of Energy in Sub-Saharan Africa* (pp. 82–101). London: Routledge Taylors and Francis.

Olvera, L. D., Guézéré, A., Plat, D., & Pochet, P. (2016). Earning a living, but at what price? Being a motorcycle taxi driver in a Sub-Saharan African city. *Journal of Transport Geography*, *55*, 165–174. doi:10.1016/j.jtrangeo.2015.11.010

Oncioiu, I. (2013). *Business Innovation, Development, and Advancement in the Digital Economy.* Retrieved from https://www.igi-global.com/book/business-innovation-development-advancement-digital/70671

Oncioiu, I. (2017). *Driving Innovation and Business Success in the Digital Economy.* Retrieved from https://www.igi-global.com/book/driving-innovation-business-success-digital/165239

Ostrom, E. (1990). *Governing the Commons: The Evolution of Institutions for Collective Action.* Cambridge, UK: Cambridge University Press. doi:10.1017/CBO9780511807763

Owusu, G., & Oteng-Ababio, M. (2015). Moving unruly contemporary urbanism toward sustainable urban development in Ghana by 2030. *The American Behavioral Scientist*, *59*(3), 311–327. doi:10.1177/0002764214550302

Oxford Economics Research Team. (2017). *The World's Most Competitive Cities.* Retrieved from https://www.oxfordeconomics.com/recent-releases/the-worlds-most-competitive-cities

Oyedepo, S. (2013). Energy in Perspective of Sustainable Development in Nigeria. *Sustainable Energy*, *1*(2), 14–25.

Pahl-Wostl, C., & Hare, M. (2004). Processes of Social Learning in Integrated Resources Management. *Journal of Community and Applied Social Psychology, 14*, 193–206. Retrieved from www.interscience.wiley.com

Pahl-Wostl, C., Moltgen, J., Ebenhoh, E., & Holtz, G. (2007a). The New Water management and transition framework—state and development process. In Adaptive and Integrated Water Management. Coping with Complexity and Uncertainty. Springer Verlag.

Pahl-Wostl, C. (2002). Towards sustainability in the water sector: The importance of human actors and processes of social learning. *Aquatic Sciences*, *64*(4), 394–411. doi:10.1007/PL00012594

Pahl-Wostl, C. (2006). The importance of social learning in restoring the multifunctionality of rivers and floodplains. *Ecology and Society*, *11*(1), 10. doi:10.5751/ES-01542-110110

Pahl-Wostl, C. (2009). A Conceptual framework for analysing adaptive capacity and multi-level learning processes in resource governance regimes. *Global Environmental Change*, *19*(3), 354–365. doi:10.1016/j.gloenvcha.2009.06.001

Pahl-Wostl, C. (2015). *Water governance in the face of global change: From understanding to transformation*. London: Springer. doi:10.1007/978-3-319-21855-7

Pahl-Wostl, C. (2017). An Evolutionary Perspective on Water Governance: From Understanding to Transformation. *Water Resources Management*, *31*(10), 2917–2932. doi:10.100711269-017-1727-1

Pahl-Wostl, C., Craps, M., Dewulf, A., Mostert, E., Tabara, D., & Taillieu, T. (2007b). Social learning and water resources management. *Ecology and Society*, *12*(2), 5. doi:10.5751/ES-02037-120205

Pahl-Wostl, C., Sendzimir, J., Jeffrey, P., Aerts, J., Berkamp, G., & Cross, K. (2007c). Managing change toward adaptive water management through social learning. *Ecology and Society*, *12*(2), 30. doi:10.5751/ES-02147-120230

Parilla, J., & Liu, S. (2008). *Examining the Local Value of Economic Development Incentives: Evidence from four U.S. cities*. Washington, DC: Brookings Institution.

Parnell, S., & Pieterse, E. A. (2014). *Africa's urban revolution*. Chicago: University of Chicago Press.

Parr, J. B. (1999). Growth-pole Strategies in Regional Economic Planning: A Retrospective View. Part 2. Implementation and Outcome. *Urban Studies (Edinburgh, Scotland)*, *36*(8), 1247–1268. doi:10.1080/0042098992971

Pearson, C. (1997). Le Corbusier and the Acoustical Trope: An Investigation of Its Origins. *Journal of the Society of Architectural Historians*, *56*(2), 190. doi:10.2307/991282

Peng, M. (2012). *Enfatizando Las Instituciones, La Cultura Y La Ética*. Gestión Estratégica. Editoral Cengage Learning.

Perez Campuzano, E., & Santos Cerquera, C. (2013). Recent trends in internal migration in Mexico. Recent migratory tendencies in Mexico. Population Papers, 19(76).

Pérez, E. (2007). Transformación urbano-regional y migración de clases medias de la Ciudad de México hacia Querétaro. Alteridades, 17(34).

Pérez, E., & Santos, C. (2008). Urbanización y migración entre ciudades, 1995-2000. Un análisis multinivel. Papeles de Población, 14(56).

Persson, A., Weitz, N., & Nilsson, M. (2016). Follow-up and Review of the Sustainable Development Goals: Alignment vs. Internalization. *Review of European Community & International Environmental Law*, *25*(1), 59–68. doi:10.1111/reel.12150

Picon, A. (2015). *Smart Cities: A Spatialised Intelligence*. London: John Wiley & Sons. doi:10.1002/9781119075615

Pieper, H., Mkandawire, T., & Van der Hoeven, R. (2016). *Africa's recovery in the 1990s: From stagnation and adjustment to human development*. New York: Springer.

Pierce, P., & Andersson, B. (2017). Challenges with smart cities initiatives–A municipal decision makers' perspective. *Proceedings of the 50th Hawaii International Conference on System Sciences*. Available online: https://pdfs.semanticscholar.org/48fe/ed2ca255974bffd09b26aef06a4753a6b284.pdf

Piercy, N., & Rich, N. (2009). The implications of lean operations for sales strategy: From sales-force to marketing-force. *Journal of Strategic Marketing*, *17*(3-4), 237–255. doi:10.1080/09652540903064738

Pieterse, E., & Short, J. R. (2017). The city in sub-Saharan Africa. A research agenda for cities, 218-232.

Pinto, N. N. (2013). *Technologies for Urban and Spatial Planning: Virtual Cities and Territories: Virtual Cities and Territories*. Retrieved from https://books.google.com.sa/books?isbn=1466643501

Porter, M. E. (1985). *The Competitive Advantage: Creating and Sustaining Superior Performance*. New York: Free Press.

Potapova, I., Vasin, S., Gamidullasrva, L., Tolstykh, T., Belyanin, L., & Mkrttchian, V. (2018). Drivers of Urban Development in Terms of Education Based on Digital Technologies. In Optimizing Regional Development Through Transformative Urbanization. Hershey, PA: IGI Global. Doi:10.4018/978-1-5225-5448-6.ch003

Potkin, K. (2002). The incredibly shrinking cities. Convinced the world's urban populations are growing beyond control? Not so fast... *The Republic, 50.*

Potts, D. (2012). *Whatever happened to Africa's rapid urbanization?* Counterpoints.

Potts, D. (2018). Urban data and definitions in sub-Saharan Africa: Mismatches between the pace of urbanisation and employment and livelihood change. *Urban Studies (Edinburgh, Scotland)*, *55*(5), 965–986. doi:10.1177/0042098017712689

Primakov, E. M. (2012). *Country's new industrialization. – A report on a meeting of "Mercury club"*. Retrieved from http://www. tpp-inform. ru/official/2393. html

Putin, V. V. (2012). On our economic problems. *Bulletin, 30*(15), 5.

PWC. (2017). *Future: Shifts in global Urbanization & Economic Orders by 2050*. Retrieved from https://www.pwc.com/gx/en/issues/economy/the-world-in-2050.html

PWC-Global. (2017). *Reimagining the possible*. Retrieved from https://www.pwc.com/gx/en/about/global-annual-review-2017.html

Ramos-González, O. M. (2014). The green areas of San Juan, Puerto Rico. *Ecology and Society*, *19*(3), 21. doi:10.5751/ES-06598-190321

Rathore, M. M., Ahmad, A., Paul, A., & Rho, S. (2016). Urban planning and building smart cities based on the internet of things using big data analytics. *Computer Networks*, *101*, 63–80. doi:10.1016/j.comnet.2015.12.023

Ravallion, M. (2017). *Poverty comparisons*. Oxon, UK: Routledge. doi:10.4324/9780203985328

Reboratti, C. (1990). *Fronteras agrarias en América Latina*. Retrieved from www.ub.es/geocrit/sv-26.htm

Reboratti, C., (1992). Fronteras agrarias y población en América Latina International Union for the Scientific Study of Population (IUSSP). *El poblamiento de las Américas, Actas, 4*, 333-352.

Reed, M. S., Evely, A. C., Cundill, G., Fazey, I., Glass, J., Laing, A., . . . Stringer, L. C. (2006). What is social learning? *Ecology and Society, 15*(4). Retrieved from http://www.ecologyandsociety.org/vol15/iss4/resp1/

Regions of Russia. (2017). *Socio-economic indicators*. Retrieved from http://www.gks.ru/wps/wcm/connect/rosstat_main/rosstat/ru/statistics/science_and_innovations/science/

Re-industrialization of Russia: opportunities and constraints. (n.d.). Retrieved from http://www.council.gov.ru/media/files/41d477365af5651386f7.pdf

Rembio. (2009). *Expert Opinion Based On Delivered Questionnaire.* Author.

Renewable Energy Master Plan. (2013). *Renewable Energy Potentials in Nigeria.* Retrieved from http://www.energy.gov.ng/index.php?option=com_docman&task=cat_view&gid=39&Itemid=49

Rennings, K. (2000). Redefining Innovation – Eco-Innovation Research and the Contribution From Ecological Economics. *Ecological Economics, 32*(2), 319–332. doi:10.1016/S0921-8009(99)00112-3

Resnick, D. (2014). *Urban poverty and party populism in African democracies.* Cambridge University Press.

Reyes Morales, R. G., & Gijón Cruz, A. S. (2007). Rural development, international migration and shortage of financial markets in Mexico. *Trace, 52*, 45-62.

Reyes Morales, R. G. (1999). Comparación socioeconómica de seis colonias populares de la ciudad de Oaxaca. *Alteridades (El Parque), 17*, 11–22.

Reynolds, P., Bygrave, W. D., Autio, E., Cox, L. W., & Hay, M. (2003). *Global Entrepreneurship Monitor 2002 executive report.* Wellesley, MA: Babson College.

Riegelhaupt, E., Odenthal, J., & Janeiro, L. (2016). *Diagnóstico de la situación actual del biodiésel en México y escenarios para su aprovechamiento.* Informe Final (CONFIDENCIAL red Mexicana de Bioenergía. Ecofys 2016 por orden de: Banco Interamericano de Desarrollo para SENER).

Rizzo, M., Kilama, B., & Wuyts, M. (2015). The invisibility of wage employment in statistics on the informal economy in Africa: Causes and Consequences. *The Journal of Development Studies, 51*(2), 149–161. doi:10.1080/00220388.2014.968136

Roberstson, C. J. (2000). The global dispersion of Chinese values: A three-country study of Confucian dynamism. *Management International Review, 40*(3).

Rodríguez-Bolívar, M. P. (Ed.). (2015). *Transforming City Governments for Successful Smart Cities.* Retrieved from https://www.springer.com/gp/book/9783319031668

Rogers, P. (2002). *Water governance in Latin America and the Caribbean.* Inter-American Development Bank (IDB). Retrieved from http://www.iadb.org, https://www.ircwash.org/sites/default/files/202.2-02WA-17802.pdf

Rogers, P., & Hall, A. (2003). *Effective Water Governance* (Vol. 7). Elanders Novum, Sweden: GWP-TEC, The Background Papers.

Romanova, O.A., & Bukhvalov, N.Y. (2014). Re-industrialization as a determinative trend of economic development of industrial areas. *Fundamental Research, 6.*

Romijn, H., & Albaladejo, M. (2002). Determinants of Innovation Capability in Small Electronics and Software Firms in Southeast England. *Research Policy, 31*(7), 1053–1067. doi:10.1016/S0048-7333(01)00176-7

Rostow, W. W. (1960). *The stages of economic growth: A Non-Communistic Manifesto.* Cambridge, UK: Cambridge University.

Rozkwitalska, M. (2010). Barriers of Cross-cultural Interactions According to Research Findings. *Journal of Intercultural Management, 2*(2), 37–52.

Rubalcava, L. N. (2001). *Localidades y hogares en un mundo de propensiones.* documento presentado en el seminario internacional: Las diferentes expresiones de la vulnerabilidad social en América Latina y el Caribe, Santiago, CELADE/ CEPAL.

Rubinowicz, P. (2000). Chaos and Geometric Order in Architecture and Design. *Journal for Geometry and Graphics, 4*(2), 197–207.

Ruhlandt, R. W. S. (2018). The governance of smart cities: A systematic literature review. *Cities (London, England), 81*, 1–23. doi:10.1016/j.cities.2018.02.014

Ruiz Chiapetto, C. (1999). Población y migraciones rurales en México: Hipótesis para otro siglo (vol. 2). Academic Press.

Ruiz Chiapetto, C. (1999). Population and rural migrations in Mexico: Hypothesis for another century (vol. 2). Academic Press.

Rukomoinikova, V., Zykova, N., & Tumbaeva, I. (2016). Practical aspects of realization of the development strategy in the tourism region. *Journal of Applied Engineering Science, 14*(1), 68–74. doi:10.5937/jaes14-10123

Russia 2025: From talent to cadres. (2017). The Boston Consulting Group (BCG).

Russoa, F., & Comib, A. (2012). City characteristics and urban goods movements: A way to environmental transportation system in a sustainable city. *Social and Behavioral Sciences, 39*, 61–73.

Rutz, D., Thebaud, A., Janssen, R., Segura, S. A., Riegelhaupt, E., & Ballesteros, M. … Bravo, G. (2009). *Biofuel Policies And Legislation In Latin America.* WIP Renewable Energies, Report Of The EU Project Biotop (FP7); Contract No.: 213320.

SADC. (2012). *About SADC.* Retrieved 2018, from Southern African Development Community: https://www.sadc.int/about-sadc/

SAGARPA. (2010). *Monografía de cultivos: palma de Aceite.* Subsecretaría de Fomento a los Agronegocios.

SAGARPA. (2016). *Direccion General de Fibras Naturales y Biocombustibles. BIODIÉSEL 06052016. Presentación realizada en el Taller de Biodiésel.* Paquete Tecnológico de Higuerilla y Paquete Tecnológico de Jatropha.

SAGARPA. (2017). *Impulsa SAGARPA Producción De Biocombustibles En México.* Author.

Saghir, J., & Santoro, J. (2018). *Urbanization in Sub-Saharan Africa: Meeting Challenges by Bridging Stakeholders.* Center for Strategic and International Studies. Available at http://csis.org

Salgado, C. E. (2003). *Teoría de costos de transacción: una breve reseña. Cuadernos de Administración.* Recuperado de http://www.redalyc.org/articulo.oa?id=20502604

Salm, S. J., & Falola, T. (Eds.). (2005). African Urban Spaces in Historical Perspectives. University of Rochester Press.

Salomatin, E. V. (2016). Resource approach to the concept of "smart city". *Reports of Tomsk State University of Control Systems and Radio-electronics, 19*(3), 115–120. doi:10.21293/1818-0442-2016-19-3-115-120

Sambo, A. (2005). Renewable Energy for Rural development: The Nigerian perspective. *ISESCO: Science and Technology Vision, 1*(5).

Sambo, A. (1997). *Energy options for sustainable national development: Resources, issues, and the position of renewable energy technologies. University Inaugural Lecture Series No. 1, Abubakar Tafawa Balewa University.* Bauchi: ATBU.

Sambo, A. (2008). Matching Electricity Supply with Demand in Nigeria. *International Association of Energy Economics, 4*, 32–36.

Sami, N., & Anand, S. (2015). *Manufacturing cities: Industrial Policy and Urban Planning in India*. Paper presented at the RC21 International Conference, Bangalore, India.

Sánchez, L. A., & Pérez, E. (2015). Las Entidades De Economía Social Como Protagonistas De Un Nuevo Modelo De Emprendimiento Y Medidas Legales De Apoyo Al Emprendimiento, CIRIEC-España. *C.I.R.I.E.C. España*, *84*, 35–62.

Sanzharevsky, I. I. (2010). *Political science: Dictionary-reference book*. Retrieved from http://www.glos.virmk.ru/

Savage, M. (1988). The missing link? The relationship between spatial mobility and social mobility. British Journal of Sociology, 30(4).

Sberbank Annual Report. (2017). Retrieved from http://www.sberbank.com/ru/investor-relations/reports-and-publications/annual-reports

Schmidt, E., & Cohen, J. (2010). The Digital Disruption-Connectivity and the Diffusion of Power. *Foreign Affairs*, *89*, 75–88.

Schneider, Buehn, & Monteneg. (2010). *Shadow Economies 1999 to 2007*. Retrieved from http://www.gfintegrity.org/storage/gfip/documents/reports/world_bank_shadow_econ omies_all_over_the_world.pdf

Schuler, R. S., Dowling, P. J., & De Cieri, H. (1993). An intergrative framework of strategic international human resource management. *International Journal of Human Resource Management*, *4*(4), 717–764. doi:10.1080/09585199300000056

Schummer, J. (2009). From Nano-Convergence to NBIC-Convergence: "The best way to predict the future is to create it". Governing Future Technologies, 57-71.

Schumpeter, J. A. (1934). The Thory Of Economic Development: An Inquiry Into Profits, Capital, Credit, Interest And The Business Cycle. Harvard Economic Studies, 46.

Schumpeter, J. (2013). *Capitalism, socialism and democracy*. London: Routledge.

Schwab, K. (2017). *The Fourth Industrial Revolution*. Publishing House "E".

Schwab, K. (2017). *The fourth industrial revolution*. Oxford, UK: Crown Business.

Scuotto, V., Ferraris, A., & Bresciani, S. (2016). Internet of Things: Applications and challenges in smart cities: a case study of IBM smart city projects. *Business Process Management Journal*, *22*(2), 357–367. doi:10.1108/BPMJ-05-2015-0074

Sengers, F., & Raven, R. (2014). Metering motorbike mobility: Informal transport in transition? *Technology Analysis and Strategic Management*, *26*(4), 453–468. doi:10.1080/09537325.2013.870991

Seto, K. (2011). Exploring the dynamics of migration to mega-delta cities in Asia and Africa: Contemporary drivers and future scenarios. Global Environmental Change, 2.

Shamsuddin, S., Hassanb, N. R., & Bilyaminb, S. F. (2012). Walkable Environment in Increasing the Liveability of a City. *Social and Behavioral Sciences*, (50), 167 – 178.

Shree, S. (2011). Challenges Before Management with Reference to Cross Cultural Issues and Communication. *The IUP Journal of Soft Skills*, *V*(3), 7–11.

Sicurelli, D. (2016). *The European Union's Africa policies: norms, interests and impact*. Oxford, UK: Routledge. doi:10.4324/9781315239828

Siemens. (2012). *Green Index Report*. Retrieved from https://www.siemens.com/entry/cc/features/greencityindex_international/all/en/pdf/gci_report_summary.pdf

Siemens. (2012). *The Green City Index A summary of the Green City Index research series.* Author.

Singh, A., Lund, H. G., & Barr, J. (2018). *Challenges in Building Climate-Resilient Quality Energy Infrastructure in Africa.* Resilience. doi:10.1016/B978-0-12-811891-7.00014-1

Skeggs, B. (2018). *The values and value of digital capitalism.* Cambridge, MA: MIT Press.

Skiyi, V., Matamanda, A., & Chirisa, I. (2016). Constraints and opportunities in integrating wetland ecosystem services in urban land use planning, Harare, Zimbabwe. In *Proceedings of the 2016 ILASA Conference 55-63, Institute for Landscape Architecture in South Africa (ILASA).* University of Pretoria (UP).

Sobrino, J. (2014). Internal migration and size of locality in Mexico. *Demographic and Urban Studies, 3*(87), 443–479.

Sobrino, J. (2014). Migración interna y tamaño de localidad en México. *Estudios Demográficos y Urbanos, 3*(87), 443–479.

Sobrino, L. J. (2010). Migración urbana. In *La situación demográfica en México.* CONAPO.

Söderström, O., Paasche, T., & Klauser, F. (2014). Smart cities as corporate storytelling. *City, 18*(3), 307–320. doi:10.1080/13604813.2014.906716

Solanas, A., Patsakis, C., Conti, M., Vlachos, I. S., Ramos, V., Falcone, F., ... Martinez-Balleste, A. (2014). Smart health: A context-aware health paradigm within smart cities. *IEEE Communications Magazine, 52*(8), 74–81. doi:10.1109/MCOM.2014.6871673

Sonja, A. S., & Philips, M. E. (2004). Contextual influence on Culture Research Shifting: Assumptions for New Workplace Realities. *Applied Psychology, 49*(1), 192–221.

Sorokin, D.E., Tolkachev, S.A. (2015). Conditions and factors of efficient re-industrialization and industrial policy in Russia. *Economic Revival of Russia, 4*(46), 87 – 99.

Stahl, J. (1990). A New Universal Learning Curve. *Proceedings of the Annual Conference of the ASEE in Canada,* 163-186.

Stam, E., Suddle, K., Hessels, J., & Van Stel, A. J. (2009). High-Growth Entrepreneurs, Public Policies, And Economic Growth. In J. Leitao & R. Baptista (Eds.), Public Policies For Fostering Entrepreneurship: A European Perspective. International Studies In Entrepreneurship. Academic Press.

State Program. (n.d.). *Digital Economy in the Russian Federation.* Retrieved from http://government.ru/docs/28653/

Statista. (2018). *Leading digital agency networks worldwide in 2017.* Retrieved from https://www.statista.com/statistics/466411/digital-agency-networks/

Statistical data of the Gaydar Forum. (2018). Retrieved from Official Telegram-channel of the Forum: https://t.me/gaidarforum

Stearns, P. N. (2018). *The industrial revolution in world history.* London: Routledge. doi:10.4324/9780429494475

Stiglitz, J. (1997). Economics of the public sector. Moscow University Publishing.

Stockholm Environment Institute (SEI). (2009). *Economics of Climate Change in Kenya.* A SEI Project Report.

Storeygard, A. (2016). Farther on down the road: Transport costs, trade and urban growth in sub-Saharan Africa. *The Review of Economic Studies, 83*(3), 1263–1295. doi:10.1093/restud/rdw020 PMID:29743731

Sukharev, O. S. (2014). Re-industrialization of the Russian economy and technological development. *National interests: priorities and security, 10.* Retrieved from https://cyberleninka.ru/article/n/reindustrializatsiya-ekonomiki-rossii-i-tehnologicheskoe-razvitie

Sukharev, O. S. (n.d.). *Digital economics – «irrational optimism» of management.* Retrieved from http://www.osukharev.com/images/present/21-11-2017.pps

Sukharev, O.S. (2015). *Information Economy: Knowledge, Competition and Growth.* Finance and Statistics.

Sukharev, O. S. (2018). Strategy of growth and renewal of industrial and technological base. *Metals of Eurasia, 2,* 2–5.

Sundararajan, A. (2016). *The sharing economy: The end of employment and the rise of crowd-based capitalism.* Cambridge, MA: MIT Press.

Sutherland, E. (2018). Bribery and corruption in telecommunications–the case of Nigeria. *Digital Policy, Regulation and Governance.*

Swain, R. B. (2018). A Critical Analysis of the Sustainable Development Goals. In K. W. Leal (Ed.), *Handbook of Sustainability Science and Research.* Cham: Springer. doi:10.1007/978-3-319-63007-6_20

Tanzania Investment Centre. (2008). *Chinese trade and Investment in Tanzania.* Author.

Tapia, P. (2017, February 12). Biodiésel, a la espera de brillar en México. *Milenio.*

Tapscott, D. (1995). *The Digital Economy.* Retrieved from http://dontapscott.com/books/the-digital-economy/

Tapscott, D. and Williams, E. (2009). *Wikinomics. How mass cooperation changes everything.* BestBusinessBooks.

Tatarkin, A. I., Sukharev, O. S., & Strizhakova, E. N. (2017). The definition of the vector of the new industrial policy based on the neo-Schumpeterian theory. *Bulletin of Perm University, 12*(1), 5–22.

Taylor, J., Sacher, M., Barberi, M., Gendronneau, C., Stepanek, M., Hofman, J., & Hafner, M. (2017). *Synergies Between the Objectives Set Out in the Annual Growth Survey and the Contribution of the EU Budget and National Budgets.* Academic Press.

Technology, B. (2016). *Possibilities for the U.S. Postal Service RARC Report.* Report Number RARC-WP-16-01.

Tesfaye, K., Kassie, M., Cairns, J. E., Michael, M., Stirling, C., Abate, T., ... Gerard, B. (2017). Potential for Scaling up Climate Smart Agricultural Practices: Examples from Sub-Saharan Africa. In *Climate Change Adaptation in Africa* (pp. 185–203). Cham: Springer. doi:10.1007/978-3-319-49520-0_12

The Benefits of Blockchain to Supply Chain Networks. (2017). *Watson Customer Engagement.* IBM Corporation.

The Commission on Human Rights and the General Assembly. (1998). *Guiding Principles on Internal Displacement, E/CN.4/1998/53/Add.2.* New York: United Nations.

The ICT. (n.d.). *Nigeria.* Retrieved from www.theintelligencer.com.ng/tag/nigeria

The National Association of Regional Councils (NARC). (n.d.). *Livability Literature Review: A Synthesis of Current Practice.* Washington, DC: The National Association of Regional Councils (NARC).

The program of economic re-industrialization of Novosibirsk region till 2025. (n.d.). Retrieved from https://www.nso.ru/page/15755

Thorsen, E. D., & Lie, A. (2006). *What is Neo-liberalism?* Oslo: Department of Political Science: University of Oslo.

Till, J. (2009). *Architecture Depends* (Vol. 55). MIT Press.

Todes, A. (2011, May). Reinventing planning: Critical Reflections. *Urban Forum, 22*(2), 115-133.

Tolstykh, T. (2018). Professional Training for Structural Economic Transformations Based on Competence Approach in the Digital Age. In Handbook of Research on Students' Research Competence in Modern Educational Contexts. IGI Global. Doi:10.4018/978-1-5225-3485-3.ch011

Tolstykh, T. O., Shkarupeta, E. V., Shishkin, I. A., Dudareva, O. V., & Golub, N. N. Evaluation of the Digitalization Potential of Region's Economy. In The Impact of Information on Modern Humans. HOSMC 2017. Advances in Intelligent Systems and Computing (vol. 622, pp. 736-743). Springer. Doi:10.1007/978-3-319-75383-6

Tolstykh, T., Shkarupeta, E., Kostuhin, Y., & Zhaglovskaya, A. (2018). Key Factors of Manufacturing Enterprises Development in the Context of Industry 4.0. *Proceedings of the 31th International Business Information Management Association Conference (IBIMA)*, 4747-4757.

Tolstykh, T., Shkarupeta, E., Kostuhin, Y., & Zhaglovskaya, A. (2018). Digital Innovative Manufacturing basing on Formation of an Ecosystem of Services and Resources. *Proceedings of the 31th International Business Information Management Association Conference (IBIMA)*, 4738-4746.

Tolstykh, T., Vasin, S., Gamidullaeva, L., & Mkrttchian, V. (2017). The Control of Continuing Education Based on the Digital Economy. In P. Isaias & L. Carvalho (Eds.), *User Innovation and the Entrepreneurship Phenomenon in the Digital Economy* (pp. 153–171). Hershey, PA: IGI Global. doi:10.4018/978-1-5225-2826-5.ch008

Tomas, F. (1997). Acerca de un nuevo modelo de regularización de los asentamientos irregulares de la Ciudad de México. In El acceso de los pobres al suelo urbano (pp. 233-242). IIS-Universidad Nacional Autónoma de México, PUEC, CEMCA.

Triandis, H. (1988). Collectivism vs individualism: a reconceptualization of a basic concept in cross-cultural psychology. In G. Verma & C. Beyley (Eds.), *Cross-cultural studies of Personality Attitudes and Cognition. Macmillan.* doi:10.1007/978-1-349-08120-2_3

Tsui, J., & Windsor, C. (2001). Some cross-cultural evidence on ethical reasoning. *Journal of Business Ethics, 31*(2), 143–150. doi:10.1023/A:1010727320265

Tucker, B. R. (1897). Instead of A Book (2nd ed.). New York: Molinary Institute.

Tuomi, I. (2002). The future of knowledge management. *Lifelong learning in Europe, 7*(2), 69-79.

Tuomi, I. (2004a). *Future Challenges of the European Knowledge Society.* Paper presented at Institute for Prospective Technological Studies. Retrieved from: http://www.meaningprocessing.com/personalPages/tuomi/articles/TheFutureOfTheEuropeanKnowledgeSociety.pdf

Tuomi, I. (2004b). *Knowledge sharing and the idea of Public Domain.* Paper presented at the Unesco 21st Century Dialogue on Building Knowledge Societies. Retrieved from: http://www.meaningprocessing.com/personalPages/tuomi/articles/KnowledgeSharingAndTheIdeaOfPublicDomain.pdf

Tuomi, I. (2005). *The future of learning in the knowledge society: disruptive changes for Europe by 2020.* Paper prepared for DG JRC/IPTS and DG EAC, 17.

Turok, I., & McGranahan, G. (2013). Urbanization and economic growth: the arguments and evidence for Africa and Asia. *Environment and Urbanization.*

Tussyadiah, I. P., Zach, F. J., & Wang, J. (2017). Attitudes Toward Autonomous on Demand Mobility System: The Case of Self-Driving Taxi. In *Information and Communication Technologies in Tourism 2017* (pp. 755–766). Cham: Springer. doi:10.1007/978-3-319-51168-9_54

Umubyeyi, A., Persson, M., Mogren, I., & Krantz, G. (2016). Gender inequality prevents abused women from seeking care despite protection given in gender-based violence legislation: A qualitative study from Rwanda. *PLoS One*, *11*(5), e0154540. doi:10.1371/journal.pone.0154540 PMID:27152680

UNCTAD. (2007). The Least Developed Countries Report 2007: Knowledge, Technological Learning and Innovation for Development. *United Nations Conference on Trade and Development.*

UNCTAD. (2018). *How to formalize the informal sector: Make formalization easy and desirable*. Retrieved from https://businessfacilitation.org/assets/documents/pdf/formalizing-the- informal-sector.pdf

UNCTAD. (2018). *How to formalize the informal sector: Make formalization easy and desirable*. Retrieved from https://businessfacilitation.org/assets/documents/pdf/formalizing-the-informal- sector.pdf

UN-DESA. (2014). *World Urbanization Prospects –Revision*. Retrieved from https://esa.un.org/unpd/wup/publications/files/wup2014-report.pdf

UNDESA. (2014). *World Urbanization Prospects, 2014*. Author.

UNDESA. (2018). *Revision of World Urbanization Prospects*. Retrieved from https://www.un.org/development/desa/publications/2018-revision-of-world-urbanization- prospects.html

UNEP. (2012). *Global Environment Outlook 3*. Retrieved from https://wedocs.unep.org/bitstream/handle/20.500.11822/8609/GEO-3%20REPORT_English.pdf?sequence=7&isAllowed=y

UNESCAP. (2011). *Economic and Social Survey of Asia and the Pacific 2011*. Retrieved from https://www.unescap.org/resources/economic-and-social-survey-asia-and-pacific-2011

UN-Habitat. (2008). *The state of Africa's Cities. A framework for addressing urban challenges in Africa*. Nairobi: UN-Habitat.

UN-Habitat. (2009). *Global Report on Human Settlements 2009: Planning Sustainable Cities*. Retrieved from https://unhabitat.org/books/global-report-on-human-settlements-2009-planning- sustainable-cities/

UN-Habitat. (2009). *Planning Sustainable Cities: Policy Directions. Global Report on Human Settlements*. Nairobi: UN-Habitat.

UN-Habitat. (2010). *State of the World's Cities 2010/2011- Cities for All*. Retrieved from https://unhabitat.org/books/state-of-the-worlds-cities-20102011-cities-for-all-bridging-the-urban-divide/

UN-Habitat. (2011). *Cities and Climate Change: Global Report on Human Settlements 2011*. Retrieved from https://unhabitat.org/books/cities-and-climate-change-global-report-on-human- settlements-2011/

UN-Habitat. (2014). The Evolution of National Urban Policies: A Global Overview. Nairobi: United Nations of Human Settlements Programme (UN-Habitat).

UN-Habitat. (2016). *Draft outcome document of the United Nations Conference on Housing and Sustainable Urban Development (Habitat II)*. Available: http://nua.unhabitat.org/uploads/DraftOutcomeDocumentofHabitatIII_en.pdf

UN-Habitat. (2016). *From Habitat II to Habitat III: Twenty Years of Urban Development*. UN-Habitat.

UN-Habitat. (2018). *At a Glance*. Retrieved from https://unhabitat.org/un-habitat-at-a-glance/

UN-Habitat. (2018). *Country Profile: Egypt*. Available at https://unhabitat.org/egypt/

UNHCR. (2007). *Internally Displaced Persons: Questions and Answers*. UNHCR. Retrieved from http://www.unhcr.org/basics/BASICS/405ef8c64

United Cities & Local Governments. (2017). *Subnational governments around the world Structure and finance*. Retrieved from https://www.oecd.org/regional/regional-policy/Subnational-Governments-Around- the-World-%20Part-I.pdf

United Nations Department of Economic and Social Affairs. (2014). *World Urbanization Prospects: The 2014 Revision.* United Nations, Department of Economic and Social Affairs/Population Division. UN-DESA.

United Nations Human Settlements Programme (UN-Habitat). (2016). *Urbanization and Development: Emerging Futures*. Nairobi, Kenya: UN-Habitat.

UN-Regional Commissions. (2018). Retrieved from http://www.regionalcommissions.org/

Urbano, D. Y., & Díaz, J. C. (2009). Creación De Empresas E Instituciones: Un Modelo Teórico. In M. F. R. Hernández (Ed.), Creación De Empresas. Aproximación Al Estado Del Arte. Lisboa: Juruá.

Urry, J. (2016). *Mobilities: new perspectives on transport and society*. Routledge.

Urteaga, E. (2013). *La teoría del capital social de Robert Putnam: Originalidad y carencias. Reflexión Política*. Recuperado de http://www.redalyc.org/articulo.oa?id=11028415005

Usoltseva, A.V. (2017). Re-industrialization of industry as a state's priority objective. *NovaInfo*, *3*(62), 198-202.

Van Leeuwen, K., & Sjerps, R. M. A. (2015). The City Blueprint of Amsterdam: An assessment of integrated water resources management in the capital of the Netherlands. *Water Science and Technology: Water Supply*, *15*(2), 404–410. doi:10.2166/ws.2014.127

Vargas, J., Guerra, E., Bojórquez, A. Y., & Bojorquez, F. (2014). Gestión Estratégica De Organizaciones. Elaleph, 134.

Vargas-Hernández, J. G. (2006). *Trapped development: the shrinkage of mining town Mexico. The Cerro de San Pedro Case.* Working Paper. Instituto Tecnológico de Cd. Guzmán.

Vargas-Hernández, J. G. (n.d.). Economic and environmental shrinkage of Atenquique. Instituto tecnológico de Cd. Guzmán, Jalisco.

Vasin, S. M., & Gamidullaeva, L. A. (2015). Methodical Approach and Tools to Improve the Efficiency of Managing of the Innovation Potential in the Context of Economic Globalization. *Review of European Studies*, *3*, 124–139.

Vasin, S., & Gamidullaeva, L. (2017). About Russian Regional Users' Innovation Based on Digital Information. In P. Isaias & L. Carvalho (Eds.), *User Innovation and the Entrepreneurship Phenomenon in the Digital Economy* (pp. 304–319). Hershey, PA: IGI Global. doi:10.4018/978-1-5225-2826-5.ch015

Vavrek, R., & Chovancova, J. (2016). *Decoupling of Greenhouse Gas Emissions from Economic Growth in V4 Countries.* Retrieved from https://www.sciencedirect.com/science/article/pii/S2212567116302957

Venkatesh, G. (2014). A critique of the European Green City Index. *Journal of Environmental Planning and Management*, *57*(3), 317–328. doi:10.1080/09640568.2012.741520

Victorian Competition and Efficiency Commission. (2008). *A state of liveability: An enquiry into enhancing Victoria's liveability*. Melbourne, Victoria: Victorian Competition and Efficiency Commission.

Vidican, G. (2012). *Building Domestic Capabilities in Renewable Energy. A case study of Egypt. German Development Institute / Deutsches Institut für Entwicklungspolitik*. DIE.

Villa, M., & Rodríguez, J. (1997). *Dinámica sociodemográfica de las metrópolis Latinoamericanas durante la segunda mitad del siglo XX. Notas de Población, Año XXV, n° 65*. Santiago: Centro Latinoamericano de Demografía, Celade.

Vuchic, V. R. (1999). *Transportation for Livable Cities*. Center for Urban Policy Research.

Wallis, A. (1998). Social capital and community building. Building Healthier Communities: Ten Years of Learning. *National Civic Review*, *87*, 317–319. doi:10.1002/ncr.87404

Watson, V. (2009). *Seeing from the South: Refocusing Urban Planning on the Globe's Central Urban Issues*. Retrieved from https://www.jstor.org/stable/43198476?seq=1#page_scan_tab_contents

Watson, V. (2009). 'The planned city sweeps the poor away…' Urban planning and 21st-century urbanization. *Progress in Planning*, *72*(3), 151–193. doi:10.1016/j.progress.2009.06.002

Wenger, E., White, N., & Smith, J. (2009). Digital habitats: Stewarding technology for communities. Portland, OR: CPSquare.

White, J. T. (2015). Measuring Urban Design: Metrics for Livable Places, by Ewing, R. and Clemente, O. *Journal of Urban Design*, *20*(2), 291–292. doi:10.1080/13574809.2015.1008881

Wikipedia. (2018a). *List of IT Consulting Firms*. Retrieved from https://en.wikipedia.org/wiki/List_of_IT_consulting_firms

Wikipedia. (2018b). *Grey market goods are legal, non-counterfeit goods sold outside normal distribution channels*. Author.

Wilde, R. (2018). *Steam in the Industrial Revolution*. Available from: https://www.thoughtco.com/steam-in-the-industrial-revolution-1221643

World Bank Group. (2016). *From Oil to Cities - Nigeria's Next Transformation.* WBG Publishing.

World Bank Group. (2017). *Doing Business in 2018*. Retrieved from http://www.doingbusiness.org/reports/global-reports/doing-business-2018

World Bank Group. (2017). *End Extreme Poverty Boost Shared Prosperity.* World Bank Group.

World Bank. (2000). *Attacking Poverty*. Retrieved from https://openknowledge.worldbank.org/handle/10986/11856

World Bank. (2010). *Development and Climate Change*. Retrieved from https://siteresources.worldbank.org/INTWDR2010/Resources/5287678- 1226014527953/WDR10-

World Bank. (2015). *Ending Poverty and Sharing Prosperity*. Retrieved from http://www.worldbank.org/content/dam/Worldbank/gmr/gmr2014/GMR_2014_Full_Report.pdf

World Bank. (2015). *Rising through cities in Ghana: urbanization review - overview report.* Washington, DC: World Bank Group.

World Bank. (2016). *Doing Business: Measuring Regulatory Quality and Efficiency.* Washington, DC: World Bank.

World Bank. (2016). *From Oil to Cities: Nigeria's Next Transformation.* Available at http://documents.worldbank.org/curated/en/711661468010811972/pdf/106150-PUB-ADD-DOI-ISBN-SERIES-OUO-9.pdf

World Bank. (2016). *From Oil to Cities: Nigeria's Next Transformation. Directions in Development.* Retrieved from http://documents.worldbank.org/curated/en/711661468081l972/pdf/106150/PUB-ADD-DOI-ISBN-SERIES-OUO-9.pdf

World Bank. (2018). *The Changing Wealth of Nations*. Author.

World Economic Forum. (2017). *The African Union is on a mission to transform the continent by 2063. This is what you need to know.* Africa Union.

World Resources Institute. (2018). *What We Do*. Retrieved from http://www.wri.org/

World Steel Association. (2010). *Steel Statistical Yearbook 2010.* Retrieved from https://www.worldsteel.org/en/dam/jcr:1ef195b3-1a46-41c2-b88b-6072c2687850/Steel+statistical+yearbook+2010.pdf

World Wide Fund (WWF). (2010). *Biodiversity Loss And The Human Footprint.* Retrieved from https://www.footprintnetwork.org/content/images/uploads/CBD_2010_and_Beyond.pdf

Worldometer.info. (2018). *Geography: Continents.* Retrieved from http://www.worldometers.info/geography/7-continents/

Wright, P. M., & Snell, S. A. (1991). Toward an integrative view of strategic human resource management. *Human Resource Management Review, 1*(3), 203–335. doi:10.1016/1053-4822(91)90015-5

Wu, W. (2005). *Dynamic Cities and Creative Clusters.* Retrieved from http://documents.worldbank.org/curated/en/441151468762563308/pdf/WPS3509.pdf

Yermakova, Zh. A. (2013). Scientific and technical progress as a basis of social and economic development of the region. *Bulletin of the OSU, 3*(152), 202–208.

Yigitcanlar, T., & Bulu, M. (2016). *Urban Knowledge and Innovation Spaces.* Retrieved from https://www.tandfonline.com/doi/full/10.1080/10630732.2016.1164443

Zanella, A., Bui, N., Castellani, A., Vangelista, L., & Zorzi, M. (2014). Internet of things for smart cities. *IEEE Internet of Things Journal, 1*(1), 22-32.

Zelinsky, W. (1971). The Hypothesis of the Mobility Transition. Geographical Review, 61(2), 219-249.

Zeng, D. Z. (2015). *Global Experiences with Special Economic Zones: Focus on China and Africa.* Policy Research Working Paper. World Bank Group.

Zeng, D.Z. (2012). *Special Economic Zones: Lessons from the Global Experience.* PEDL Synthesis Series No. 1.

Zhou, G., & Zvoushe, H. (2012). Public Policy Making in Zimbabwe: A Three-Decade Perspective. *International Journal of Humanities and Social Science, 2*(8), 212–222.

ZIMSTAT. (2013). *Census 2012. Zimbabwe National Report.* Harare: ZIMSTAT.

About the Contributors

Umar G. Benna holds Master of Regional Planning (1973) and a Ph.D. from the University of North Carolina at Chapel Hill (1975) and is the Distinguished Professor of the Nigerian Universities Commission and is a SPURS Fellow at MIT, USA. He has a multidisciplinary background in architecture and city and regional planning. He has integrated academic and research pursuits with intense professional and administrative experience locally and internationally. Dr. Benna has over 45 years of teaching experience in universities in Nigeria, Saudi Arabia, Germany and USA. His research interests include urbanization issues in developing countries, urban activity systems, the role of large-scale projects on cities and regions, and the impact of new technologies on cities and regions. His professional activities – with Benna Associates – include architecture and urban design as well as the planning of new university campuses, master planning of many cities in Nigeria and Saudi Arabia. Urban administration experience came in the form of membership of the board of directors of the development authorities of Nigerian cities, Federal Housing Authority and similar agencies. He has hundreds of publications in the form of scientific papers, book chapters and books, as well as professional reports. Prof Benna is principal partner in Benna Associates, Nigeria, specializing in Urban Design, campus planning and design, and new towns development.

* * *

Hisham G. Abusaada is an Egyptian architect, educator, theoretician, critic and academic scholar. He concerns himself with the socio-cultural aspects and special problems of urban community and development projects. Abusaada is known for his many books on architecture and urban design including Efficiency and Urban Form Generation: Approach to Site Planning and Design (1992), Post Occupancy Evaluation (translated book, 2004), Topics in Landscape Architecture Profession (Arabic 2007), The Art of the City, Refutation of Intellectual Discourse towards knowledge, Enlightenment (in Arabic and English, 2015), The Unknown Cities, From Loss of Hope to well-being (2016), What is Urban Design? Teaching and Learning (English (2015) and Arabic, (2016)), and Back to the Order: The Chaos in the Cities of Hardship (2017), and Language of Urban Design (Arabic, 2017). Abusaada attended Al Azhar University, Egypt. He obtained a Bachelor's and a Master's degree in Architecture (1980, and 1987). His doctorate is in the urban design discipline attained from Cairo University (1992). He is currently an emeritus professor at the Housing and Building National Research Center (HBRC), Cairo, Egypt. He was a faculty member in the Urban Design program in the Department of Landscape Architecture at King Faisal University (now Dammam University), Saudi Arabia (1995 to 2004). He also works in some Egyptian Universities and other higher institutions in Egypt.

Adeyemi Oluwaseun Adepoju (PhD) currently lectures in the Department of Project Management Technology, School of Management Technology, Federal University of Technology, Akure. He was formerly a Researcher in Science Policy Research and Innovation Studies Department at National Centre for Technology Management, Obafemi Awolowo University Nigeria. He possesses Bachelor and Master in Chemical Engineering. He also possesses a PhD in Technology Management at the African Institute for Science, Policy and Innovation (AISPI), OAU Ile-Ife. He has participated in many international conferences/workshops/seminars and published articles in several international journals. His research interest is in the area of Energy policy and management, separation techniques in distillation column, technological capabilities, and project management.

John-Felix K. Akinbami is a Research Professor and Head, Energy Management and Technology Division at the Centre for Energy Research and Development, Obafemi Awolowo University, Ile-Ife, Osun State, Nigeria. His research focus includes Energy and Environmental Management; Energy Systems Modeling, Energy Policy and Analysis, Energy Efficiency and Conservation, Energy and Building, Electricity Sector Reform, Restructuring and Regulation, Renewable and Alternative Energy Resources, Sustainable Development and Climate Change (Adaptation & Mitigation). He has published extensively in reputable local and international journals including International Journal of Global Energy Issues, Mitigation and Adaptation Strategies for Global Change, Renewable and Sustainable Energy Reviews, Applied Energy, Nigerian Journal of Renewable Energy, etc. He was also a resource person/consultant on various study projects for both national and international organizations including European Commission, African Development Bank, World Bank. He was actively involved in policy development such as Renewable Energy Master Plan and the National Energy Master Plan for Nigerian government and its agencies. He is a member of various professional bodies nationally and internationally.

Yusuf Opeyemi Akinwale is a first class economics graduate of Obafemi Awolowo University, Nigeria. He is currently an Assistant Professor of Economics at College of Business Administration, Imam Abdulrahman Bin Faisal University (Formerly University of Dammam) Saudi Arabia. He was a postdoctoral fellow and extraordinary research fellow at Faculty of Economic Sciences, North West University, South Africa. Dr Yusuf was formerly Head of Department and Senior Research Officer at Technology Management Education Department, National Centre for Technology Management, Obafemi Awolowo University Nigeria. His specialization includes economics of innovation and developmental studies, energy and petroleum. He has published in reputable journals in areas including technology innovation, entrepreneurship, science policies, small and medium enterprises, renewable energy, oil and gas, energy management, and economic growth & development. He bagged his MBA and PhD from Obafemi Awolowo University and his MSc from University of Aberdeen, Scotland, UK. He is a member of some professional bodies.

Lubov Belyanina is a candidate of pedagogical Sciences, associate Professor Astrakhan state University, leading researcher of the Institute of education development. Author of a comprehensive program of continuous environmental education "Waterfall of knowledge" (2003) and "Neskuchny Academy of Sciences" (2007); master's program "Theory and methods of teaching biology" (2015). In 2008 he defended his thesis on the methodology of biology "Methods of personality-oriented teaching of biology on excursions in 6-9 classes." The author of methodical recommendations "the Project is simple. A practical guide to the organization of project activities in the educational institution", "Organization of research activity of students in the field", co-author of the collective monograph "the Implementation of the competence approach in the higher school", "New educational technologies and pedagogical practices." 54 scientific publications, including the Handbook of Research on Estimation and Control Techniques in E-Learning Systems Chapter 6 "The Pedagogical and Engineering Features of Eand Blended-Learning of Adults Using Triple H-Avatar in Russian Federation", Optimizing an Online Learning Course Using Automatic Curating in Sliding Mode, Handbook of Research on Students' Research Competence in Modern Educational Contexts.Lubov. Belyanina is Dr.Sc. (Education) from HHH Technology Incorporation Australia, Sydney.

Rabiu Abdullahi Bena graduated with MSc Degree in Urban and Regional Planning from famous Ahmadu Bello University, Zaria Nigeria in the year 1995.He gained practical experience in urban and regional planning while working with Benna Associates, Zaria, and is currently a lecturer in the Department of Urban and Regional Planning at Waziri Umaru Federal Polytechnic, Birnin Kebbi, Nigeria. He is a registered Town Planner and Registered Teacher (Tpl, TRC), with dozens of publications in local journals, international scientific journals, conference proceedings and book chapters.

Serge V. Chernyshenko graduated from the Dnipropetrovsk State University, Ukraine in 1978 as MS in applied mathematics. After obtaining PhD degree on computing in 1986, was, successively, Head of Laboratory of Mathematical Modeling in Biology, Head of Computer Science Department, Dean of Applied Mathematics Faculty at Dnipropetrovsk National University, Visiting Professor of Faculty of informatics of Koblenz-Landau University, Germany, He is author of more than 250 publications, including three articles to the Encyclopedia of Ecology (2008, Oxford) and the monograph 'Nonlinear analysis of forest ecosystems dynamics (2005, Dnipropetrovsk).

Innocent Chirisa, DPhil, MSc, BSc Hons. Rural & Urban Planning, (University of Zimbabwe), DipLMISR (IHS, Erasmus University), MZIRUP (Zimbabwe), Full Professor teaching Urban and Environmental Planning courses in the Department of Rural & Urban Planning, University of Zimbabwe. Currently is serving as the Deputy Dean of the Faculty of Social Studies, University of Zimbabwe. Also he is currently serving as the Acting Chairman of the Department of Rural & Urban Planning, University of Zimbabwe Prof Chirisa was recently appointed as a Research Fellow, Department of Urban and Regional Planning, University of Free State, Bloemfontein, South Africa for the period 2016 to 2020.

Yulia A. Efimova is an assistant professor in the Financial University under the Government of the Russian Federation, Kursk branch. She has a degree in pedagogics. A thesis on problem-activity approach was successfully defended in 2007. She has numerous research, articles and monographs in the sphere of higher education.

Abeer Elshater is an associate professor at Ain Shams University. She obtained her BSc in urban design and spatial planning in 1999 from Ain Shams University, Cairo, Egypt. In 2009, she received her Ph.D. in urban design from the same university. Since then, she has acted as an assistant professor then an associate professor, teaching and supervising multidisciplinary topics in the ideology of urban design. She has worked on some international research projects with international universities. In 2011, she joined the program Integrated Urbanism & Sustainable Design—IUSD as a teaching staff and academic adviser of post-graduate students. She is the author and co-author of four books entitled "Urban

Design Paradigm" (2015), "The Unknown Cities" (2016), What is Urban Design?" (2016) and "Back to the Order" (2017) as well as twenty –one scientific manuscripts in international journals and conference proceedings. She is a vice-director of Contagious Improvement of Quality Assurance Unit—CIQAU at Faculty of Engineering, Ain Shams University—ASU. Recently, she acts as an ambassador of Regional Studies Association, the United Kingdom (UK) to Egypt.

Juan José Esparza-López is a Research Assistant.at the University Center for Economic and Managerial Sciences, University of Guadalajara, from which he holds a Master of Business and Economic Studies. He has contributed to many papers published in local and international scientific journals and in book chapters.

Alexey Finogeev, Doctor of Science (Engineering), Professor, Honored Worker of Higher Professional Education of the Russian Federation received his Doctorate of Sciences from Penza State University (Penza, Russia). During his research career worked as an engineer (Penza Politechnical Institute), researcher (Ottawa University), assistant professor, associate professor, professor (Penza State University). Since 2004, he is the fulltime professor at the Department of Computer Aided Design of Penza State University. The area of the scientific research is connected with information technologies, network technologies, wireless technologies, technologies for digital economy, BigData, sensor networks, SCADA system, 3D modeling and virtual reality, computer aided design. Main science activities are related with design of intellectual and analytical systems, wirless sensor networks, fog and grid computing, SCADA systems, adaptive decision-making systems, Geo-information systems. Member of The Russian Academy of Natural History.

Natalya Firsova works in Voronezh State Technical University Author of more than 400 papers.. Spheres of interests: economic policy, regional economy, economic and national security, sectoral structure of economy, technological development, management of innovations, socio-economic development, industrial policy and other.

Leyla Gamidullaeva holds a PhD in Economics. In 2014 she was hired as the Penza State University and is currently a doctoral candidate and an associate professor at the Department of management and economic security. She has authored over 200 refereed publications and over ten books on issues of innovation management, regional innovation growth, networking and collaboration.

Olga Gavrilova graduated from Petrozavodsk State University in 1979 with a degree in Forestry. She worked in scientific institutions and at work, since 1993 she has been teaching at PetrSU. After receiving his doctorate in 2012, she headed the Department of Forestry and Landscape Architecture. His area of interest is reforestation in the taiga zone, artificial plantings in cities. He has published over 120 publications, including the monograph "Artificial reforestation in Karelia" (2007, Moscow), "Introduction to the Ecology of Coniferous Artificial Plantations", (2018, Arkhangelsk).

Blanca C. Garcia is an Associate Professor at El Colegio de la Frontera Norte (COLEF). Blanca earned her MSc (2002) and her PhD (2007) in Development Policy Administration and Management at the University of Manchester, United Kingdom, with a Federal Government grant from her home country. Blanca has embraced learning as a process that triggers collective development. She is a developer dedicated to the facilitation, creation and research of knowledge-generative networks that engage people at the city-region level. Since 2009, she works as a Researcher (Tenure track) in the Public Policy Department of the Northern Borderlands Research College (COLEF) based in Monterrey, Mexico. She works under the flag of Knowledge City schemes, particularly interested in exploring the human systems of learning and knowing in city-regions, and their impact on their development. She explores knowledge-based learning environments, repositories, networks and systems, and the social learning and management aspects as some of the key processes of Knowledge-based Development (KBD) in the urban context. She also manages the knowledge-based development international consultation exercise for cities known as MAKCi Awards for the World Capital Institute (WCI). Blanca has contributed to the growing KBD literature with publications on knowledge city case studies and KBD models in spaces such as Elsevier-Heinemann and Interscience brands.

Anastasiia Ioffe is Ph.D student of Petrozavodsk State Universityshe of the Department of Forestry and Landscape Architecture. His area of interest is reforestation in the taiga zone, artificial plantings in cities. He has published over 12 publications, including the monograph "Artificial reforestation in Karelia" (2007, Moscow), "Introduction to the Ecology of Coniferous Artificial Plantations", (2018, Arkhangelsk).

Sergey Kanarev is now student at the CAD Department of Penza State University and has contributed to a number research projects and some published research papers.

Dina Kharicheva is head the department of technological and information systems in MPSU. Her research interests include sociology, management, economics, world economy and international relations.

Zoya Kondrateva is an assistant professor in the Financial University under the Government of the Russian Federation, Kursk branch. She has a degree in economics. A thesis on strategies of individual investing was successfully defended in 2001. She has numerous research, articles and monographs on different topics of financial management.

Lyudmila Kryachkova is a Professor of Finance University under the Government of the Russian Federation, Kursk branch. She has received the Doctorate degree in Economics in 2002. She is a specialist in the field of bank management and is the author of numerous articles and monographs on issues of financial management and implementation of banking technologies.

Adam Konto Kyari received his Ph.D. degree in Accounting from the Robert Gordon University, Aberdeen. He is a Fellow of the Institute of Chartered Accountants of Nigeria (ICAN) and a Member of the Association of Chartered Certified Accountants (ACCA), UK. He started his teaching career in 1995 at the Ramat Polytechnic Maiduguri. In 2000, he was employed by the University of Maiduguri and has been there until 2014 when he joined the Yobe State University, Damaturu. He has taught at various other Universities including the Federal University of Technology Yola, Adamawa State University Mubi and the Imam Abdulrahman Bin Faisal University Dammam at different times on contract or visiting appointments. He has a good number of publications in books and journals on financial, management and petroleum accounting issues and is a co-author of Sustainable Energy Policy Option: Strategies for the Utilisation of Renewable Energy for Nigeria (Journal of Management Studies, 2017). His current research interest is on issues relating to information disclosure in financial statements.

Wendy W. Mandaza-Tsoriyo is a Lecturer in Urban Planning and Development at Great Zimbabwe University. She has lecturing experience in Zimbabwe as well as well as training experience in community capacity building and development in Zimbabwean marginalized communities. Wendy is currently studying for a PhD in Urban and Regional Planning. Her research interests are in areas of spatial transformation of urban areas, participatory planning and urban design and management. Wendy enjoys volunteering her services for the betterment of her community and spending time with her children who are also her source of inspiration.

Svetlana Markosyan is a student of UTS and works in HHH University as secretary, while participating in research projects and contributing to in a number of publications.

Abraham R. Matamanda is a registered full time PhD student in the department of Urban and Regional Planning, University of Free State in South Africa. He holds Master's degree in Social Ecology from the Graduate, Centre for Applied Social Studies and a BSc Honours degree holder in Rural and Urban Planning. Both degrees were obtained from the University of Zimbabwe. Currently, Abraham's PhD study focuses on emerging human settlement forms and urban dilemmas nexus focusing on water, sanitation, public transport and security issues. He is a keen researcher and emerging academic who has shown his interest in research work through publications in peer reviewed local and international journals such as City, Territory and Architecture, Regional Development Dialogue and Zambezia among others. Specifically Abraham's researches focus on urbanisation, sustainability, environmental planning, rural development and the planning of cities and towns.

Sergey Matukin holds a PhD in Economics. In 2017 she was hired as the Penza, University and is currently an associate professor at the Department of management and economic security. He is widely published on the topic of regional innovation cluster development.

Brilliant Mavhima is a 26 years old man. He holds a Bachelors degree in rural and urban planning and is currently a Master student at the University of Zimbabwe studying rural and urban planning. He is currently a graduate teaching assistant at the same institution. His focus is in urban design. He spends most of his time researching on urban design as well as designing building plans for different clients. Brilliant has one publication, 8 paper in press and two book chapters in press.

Natalia Merkulova received the degree in economics in the Oryol state technical university in 2010. In 2013, she was adopted in Kursk state university and is currently associate professor in the department of finance, credit and accounting. She is widely published on the topic of banking sector and is the author of monographs on the capitalization of commercial bank.

Vardan Mkrttchian received his Doctorate of Sciences (Engineering) in Control Systems from Lomonosov Moscow State University (former USSR). Dr. Vardan Mkrttchian taught for undergraduate and graduate student's courses of control system, information sciences and technology, at the Astrakhan State University (Russian Federation), where he was is the Professor of the Information Systems (www.

aspu.ru) six years. Now he is full professor in CAD department of Penza State University (www.pnzgu.ru). He is currently chief executive of HHH University, Australia and team leader of the international academics (www.hhhuniversity.com). He also serves as executive director of the HHH Technology Incorporation. Professor Vardan Mkrttchian has authored over 400 refereed publications. He is the author of over twenty books published of IGI Global, included ten books indexed of SCOPUS in IT, Control System, Digital Economy, and Education Technology. He is also has authored more than 200 articles published in various conference proceedings and journals.

Tariro Nyevera is a 27 years old man. He holds a Bachelor's degree in Rural and Urban planning and is currently a Master student at the University of Zimbabwe studying Rural and Urban Planning. He is currently a graduate teaching assistant at the same institution. His focus is in housing development and management. His research interests are, among others housing development and management, peri-urban transformation, land rights and conflicts, and inclusive cities. Tariro has six papers two book chapters in press.

Ibikunle Olalekan Ogundari is a Research Fellow at the African Institute for Science Policy and Innovation (AISPI), Obafemi Awolowo University, Ile-Ife, Nigeria. He studied Chemical Engineering, Financial Management, and Technology Management at the Obafemi University, Ile-Ife where he earned his PhD in Technology Management. A Certified Safety Professional, he is also a Science Policy and Development Planning Specialist with expertise in Energy, Environment &Natural Resources Policy and Management, Critical Infrastructure Planning, and Industrial Projects Assessment.

Svetlana Viktorovna Panasenko received higher economic education in 1992 at the Stavropol Polytechnic Institute with a degree in Economics and management, from 1992 to 1996 she worked as a chief economist in business organizations, in 2007 she received a degree of doctor of economic Sciences at the North Caucasus state technical University, where from 2007 to 2010 she worked as a Professor at the faculty of Economics and Finance. In 2015, she received a master's degree in practical psychology from Moscow state University of psychology and education. Since 2010 she has been accepted to the position of Professor at the Plekhanov Russian state University in Moscow and currently holds the position of head of the Department of trade policy at this University. She writes and widely represents the issues of e-Commerce, Neurotechnology, marketing and management in the digital economy. She is the author of works on the analysis of export-import relations between Russia and other countries, innovative approaches to the development of various sectors of the economy (Espacios, 2018).

Vladimir Plotnikov work in St. Petersburg State University of Economics. Doctor of Sciences (Economics). He is a professor and the author of more then 300 papers. Editor of some Russian scientific journals. Prof. Plotnikov have established the scientific school: he have more then 50 science purples with PhD degree. Spheres of interests: economic policy, regional economy, economic and national security, sectoral structure of economy, technological development, management of innovations, socio-economic development, industrial policy and other.

Liliya Valerievna Rozhkova received her doctorate in sociological sciences at the Institute of Socio-Political Research of the Russian Academy of Sciences in 2014 and candidate degree in sociology at the Penza State University in 2004. She was hired as the associate professor at the Department of Sociology and Personnel Management at the Penza State University in 2005, she became the professor in the Department of Economic Theory and International Relations in 2014 and she became the head of the Department of Economic Theory and International Relations in 2018. Her research interests include sociology, management, economics, world economy and international relations.

Elena Shkarupeta received her PhD in Economic Science from the Voronezh State Technical University (VORSTU, Russia) in 2008. In 2005 she was hired at the VORSTU and is currently the associate professor. She writes and presents widely on issues of global innovation breakthrough development.

Muhammad A. Suleiman obtained his MS in Computer Science from King Fahd University of Petroleum & Minerals, Saudi Arabia, and his Ph.D. in Computer Science from the University of Malaysia Sarawak (UNIMAS). He works as both Graduate Academic and IT Technical Specialist in the Deanship of Graduate Studies, KFUPM. Dr. Suleiman's research interest among other things includes the role of digital technology analysis of social equity and inclusiveness of development issues.

Galina Surovitskaya is Doctor of Economic Sciences and Professor at K.G. Razumovsky Moscow State University of technologies and management (the First Cossack University), Russia. She received the degree of doctor of Economic Sciences in Ogarev Mordovia State University in 2012. In 2014, she became a Professor at Razumovsky MSUTM (FSU) and is currently involved in the implementation of master's and bachelor's degree programs on innovation management. She writes and presents widely on issues of quality management and educational management theory.

Tatiana Olegovna Tolstykh graduated from the Voronezh State University. Lenin Komsomol specialty "Applied Mathematics" in the department "Mathematical methods of operations research". After graduating from the university in 1985, she entered full-time postgraduate study in the specialty "Computer-aided design systems and in 1990 successfully defended her thesis. n 2005, she successfully defended her doctoral thesis on "Theory and methodology of managing the development of regional educational complexes," and in 2006 she received the title of professor. From 2001 to 2003 she worked as the director of the regional center for distance education of the Voronezh Institute of Management, Marketing and Finance. In 2003, she moved to Voronezh branch of the Russian State University of Trade and Economics for the position of first deputy director, concurrently managing the department of management and the world economy. From 2013 to 2017 she worked as a professor at VSTU. Since 2017 he has been working as a professor at the Department of Industrial Management of MISIS.

Dmitry Treshchevsky works in Voronezh State University. Author of more then 100 papers.. Spheres of interests: economic policy, regional economy, economic and national security, sectoral structure of economy, technological development, management of innovations, socio-economic development, industrial policy and other.

Yuri Treshchevsky,, D.Sc.(Economy) is Head of Department of economics of Voronezh State University, Russian Federation. His is the leading scientist of Smart City, strategic management, socio-economic systems, indicative planning, regional economics, socio-economic forecasting, proactive management, reengineering of business processes.

Svetlana Valerievna graduated from the Radio Engineering Institute, Taganrog, 1989, with a degree in radio engineering. Candidate of Economic Sciences on 08.00.05 - Management of the national economy and 08.0013 Instrumental and mathematical methods of economics. He is the author of more teaching aids on the IT toolkit, designing a database of technical documentation, outsourcing, digital economics, digital data ecosystem, author of 3 monographs, 150 papers, incl. Germany, Czech Republic, Australia, Indonesia, Iran, Spain. Deputy Dean for Research, Russian State Social University, Moscow.

José G Vargas-Hernández is a Research Professor Professor José G. Vargas-Hernández, M.B.A.; Ph.D. Member of the National System of Researchers of Mexico and a research professor at University Center for Economic and Managerial Sciences, University of Guadalajara. Professor Vargas-Hernández has a Ph. D. in Public Administration and a Ph.D. in Organizational Economics. He has undertaken studies in Organisational Behaviour and has a Master of Business Administration, published four books and more than 200 papers in international journals and reviews (some translated to English, French, German, Portuguese, Farsi, Chinese, etc.) and more than 300 essays in national journals and reviews. He has obtained several international Awards and recognition.

Sergey Vasin from 2003 to 2006 pursued doctoral studies in St. Petersburg State University. In 2007, he defended the thesis on "Transformation of regional social and economic system" and is currently a Doctor of Economic Sciences, a Professor and Vice-President for International Affairs at the Penza State University. He has authored more than 250 publications in social and economic system transformation and regional economic development.

Yulia Vertakova is Professor, D.Sc.(Economy) is Head of Department of regional economics and management of Southwest State University, Russian Federation. She is the leading scientist of digital economy, industry development 4.0, indicative governance of sustainable development of regional economy, cluster initiatives in the region, structural transformation industrial complex regulation in terms of digitalization of economy, green economy, scaling business models, business planning, innovative management, strategic management, socio-economic systems, indicative planning, regional economics, socio-economic forecasting, proactive management, reengineering of business processes.

Justyna Zdunek-Wielgołaska is currently an assistant professor at Department of Polish Architecture, History of City Planning Lab at Warsaw University of Technology (WUT), Poland. He graduated from WUT, Faculty of Architecture in 2002, graduated from the Post-graduate Estate Appraisal Studies and obtained a Ph. D (with honors) in 2010. Dr. Justyna Zdunek-Wielgołaska was awarded scholarships and research grants including Dean's grants and Research Project for doctoral dissertation by the Ministry of Science and Higher Education in 2006. He was also a beneficiary of Fulbright scholarship (visiting scholar at UC, Berkeley, USA, 2004-2005; the Institut Für Stadt- und Regional planung Technische Universität scholarship, Berlin, Germany and a laureate of the Start for Young Academics Programme of the Foundation for Polish Science in 2007. His research experience include: 1. Future of the large city suburbs. Smart suburbs – analysis for the Warsaw agglomeration (2017), 2. N-S artery and its role in functional and spatial shaping of interwar Warsaw. Idea and completion (2012), 3. Legal aspects of Warsaw public spaces shaping; premise and completion (2011), 4. Modernization of public spaces in the sense of city revitalization. Comparative study of the large American and Polish cities (2005).

Index

R

S

T

U

W

www.ingramcontent.com/pod-product-compliance
Lightning Source LLC
LaVergne TN
LVHW062111300926
849161LV00010B/2426